ARCHAEOLOGICAL STUDIES LEIDEN UNIVERSITY

Archaeological Studies Leiden University is published by the
Faculty of Archaeology, Leiden University, The Netherlands.

Editors: M. van Kolfschoten, L.B. van der Meer

ISBN: 90-76368-04-X

All correspondence should be addressed to:

M. Wanders
ASLU, Faculty of Archaeology
P.O. Box 9515
NL 2300 RA Leiden

Archaeological Studies Leiden University

Archaeological investigations on St. Martin (Lesser Antilles)

The sites of Norman Estate, Anse des Pères and Hope Estate
with a contribution to the 'La Hueca problem'

Edited by
Corinne L. Hofman
and
Menno L.P. Hoogland

Faculty of Archaeology, Leiden University, 1999

contents

Préface

La publication des fouilles archéologiques menées à Saint-Martin sous la direction des Dr Corinne Hofman et Menno Hoogland de l'Université de Leiden inaugure une série de recherches scientifiques développées par la Faculté d'Archéologie de l'Université de Leiden (Pays-Bas) et le Service Régional de l'Archéologie de la Direction Régionale des Affaires Culturelles de Guadeloupe (France).

Cette initiative entre dans le cadre d'un accord de coopération scientifique établi entre nos deux organismes depuis 1993 et qui porte sur l'étude des sociétés amérindiennes dans la Caraïbe. Cette collaboration consiste dans des prospections et des fouilles archéologiques menées en Guadeloupe sur les sites de Morel (1993-95), des roches gravées de Trois-Rivières (1994), de l'Anse à la Gourde (1995-98) et de nombreux autres sites, auxquelles participent, sous la direction conjointe des Dr Corinne Hofman et Menno Hoogland et de moi-même, de nombreux chercheurs et étudiants hollandais et français. Ces recherches incluent les études de laboratoire et toutes les formes de diffusion (publications, expositions et conférences).

La publication monographique détaillée des fouilles menées, en 1993, sur trois sites précolombiens de la partie française de Saint Martin, dans la région Guadeloupe, entre pleinement dans cette dynamique de coopération internationale. Il est d'ailleurs singulier de noter que celle-ci se traduit par un premier ouvrage scientifique portant sur l'île franco-hollandaise de Saint-Martin.

Grâce à cette édition présentant de la manière la plus exhaustive les résultats de ces trois fouilles dans le nord des Petites Antilles, nous entendons combler un certain manque concernant ce type de publication dans la Caraïbe. Il est, en effet, souvent difficile de consulter le détail des résultats des différentes fouilles réalisées dans la région. Le chercheur doit se contenter d'articles synthétiques donnant seulement les grandes lignes des découvertes et présentant des synthèses interprétatives avec, en illustrations, les seuls éléments caractéristiques.

Ces publications monographiques détaillées, dont la présentation des sites de Saint-Martin dans ce volume est un bon exemple, constituent des bases et des outils de recherche indispensables afin que d'autres chercheurs puissent comparer avec leurs propres données et, à leur tour, valider ou infirmer leurs interprétations sur l'histoire des Antilles. Avec la publication des fouilles sur les sites de Norman Estate, de l'Anse des Pères et de Hope Estate à Saint-Martin, notre coopération franco-hollandaise ne pouvait mieux commencer en couvrant la plus large partie de l'histoire amérindienne des Antilles, des premiers peuplements précéramiques, deux millénaires avant notre ère, aux groupes horticulteurs de la phase Cedrosan Saladoïde tardive, vers les VIII-Xème siècles de notre ère.

André Delpuech
Conservateur régional de l'archéologie de Guadeloupe
Avril 1999

Foreword

The Leeward Islands constitute one of the last remaining gaps in our knowledge of the prehistory of the West Indies. There are two ways of filling such a gap. One is to project our knowledge of the archaeology of the neighbouring regions into it and the other is to acquire information about the situation in the gap, as previously done in the neighbouring regions.

The island of St. Martin invites the first of these alternatives because it is the closest to the centre of archaeological knowledge in the Greater Antilles. Some researchers have simply applied conclusions reached in the Greater Antilles to St. Martin on the assumption that the inhabitants of the two places must have developed similarly.

The authors of the present volume have chosen instead to study the developments on St. Martin per se in an effort to determine to what extent they parallelled or diverged from the developments in the Greater Antilles. The authors are to be commended for taking both of these possibilities into consideration and for bringing an exceptionally broad range of evidence to bear upon them.

The information reported contributes to the solution of a number of culture-historical problems, such as the question of the introduction of the Ceramic age into the Greater Antilles and the concomitant spread of agriculture. In the 1950's and 1960's archaeologists excavating at the site of Hacienda Grande on the northeastern coast of Puerto Rico concluded that the kind of people who settled there had introduced the Ceramic age to that island. Subsequent research confirmed their conclusion; similar sites, also dating from the beginning of the Ceramic age, were found all along the north, west, and south coasts of the island (Rouse and Alegría 1990).

Later excavations by Luis A. Chanlatte Baik (1979) at the Sorcé site on Vieques Island, off the east coast of Puerto Rico, and by Miguel Rodríguez (1991a) at Punta Candelero on that coast itself, showed that a different, La Hueca people had brought the Ceramic age to those places. To be sure, Hacienda Grande people from the rest of Puerto Rico did live at the La Hueca site, but only later, and they never settled at Punta Candelero.

It is now clear, therefore, that two cultural groups introduced the Ceramic age into Puerto Rico, the Hacienda Grande people to all of Puerto Rico except the east coast and the La Hueca people to Vieques Island and the east coast.

Both movements apparently took place around the time of Christ; the radiocarbon dates for the Hacienda Grande people begin several centuries prior to those for the La Huecans (Narganes Storde 1991).

The Hacienda Grande and La Hueca cultures diverged from a common ancestor. Chanlatte has assumed that the divergence took place in South America. Alternatively, it may have happened in the Lesser Antilles, possibly as far north as Guadeloupe or St. Martin.

The ancestry of Hacienda Grande people has been studied in some detail. That people has been assigned to a subseries of peoples and cultures known as Cedrosan Saladoid, which arose along the Guianan coast of South America and expanded northward through the Lesser Antilles and Puerto Rico to the eastern tip of Hispaniola (Rouse 1992, 77-90). Cedrosan Saladoid remains have been found on almost all of the islands along this route. The Cedrosan Saladoids are known to have reached the Trants site on Montserrat Island by 500 BC (Petersen and Watters 1995) and to have arrived in Puerto Rico a few centuries later, as noted above.

The La Hueca people has been assigned to a Huecan Saladoid subseries. It has been traced back only to the Hope Estate site on the island of St. Martin and possibly also the Morel site on Guadeloupe. The earliest radiocarbon dates for these two sites are ca. 300 and 1 BC, respectively, appreciably later than the earliest dates of the Cedrosan Saladoid site on Montserrat Island. These facts suggest that the Huecan Saladoid subseries may have diverged from Cedrosan Saladoid in the vicinity of St. Martin or Guadeloupe during the first centuries BC.

Hope Estate is the only place where we can presently test the hypothesis of divergence. Too little is left of the Morel site to determine what happened there.

The excavations at Hope Estate reported in the present volume were not sufficient to make the test, but they illustrate how it should be done. More extensive fieldwork is needed, paying that meticulous attention to the details of the site's stratigraphy and taking the same care to segregate the artefacts and ecofacts into assemblages and to organize the assemblages into components. Then it will be possible to

compare the assemblages from the different components, to
identify the cultural or social group that lived in each one,
and to determine the relationships among those groups.

Irving Rouse
Department of Anthropology
Yale University
August 1995

Acknowledgements

The present research project formed a cooperative effort between Leiden University (The Netherlands), the Archaeological-Anthropological Institute of the Netherlands Antilles AAINA, Curaçao) and the Association Archéologique Hope Estate (St. Martin) under the responsibility of André Delpuech, Conservateur Régional de l'Archéologie, Service de l'Archéologie of the Direction Régionale des Affaires Culturelles (DRAC, Guadeloupe). Many people contributed to the successful conclusion of the project and we would like to express our gratitude to François Petit, Christophe Henocq and Barbara Oberlé for making this project possible and for their hospitality on St. Martin.

The prospective investigations of the preceramic site of Norman Estate and the Cedrosan Saladoid site of Anse des Pères were executed by a team of Leiden University under the responsibility of Dr. C.L. Hofman and Dr. M.L.P. Hoogland. The team consisted of Alex Brokke, Sebastiaan Knippenberg, Tom Hamburg and Mark Nokkert, all M.A. students.

The 1993 excavations at the multi-component Saladoid site of Hope Estate were executed by Dr. C.L. Hofman, Dr. M.L.P. Hoogland and Dr. J.B. Haviser under the auspices of the Association Archéologique Hope Estate.

Many people contributed to the 1993 field season and we specifically would like to acknowledge the students of Leiden University for their enthusiasm during the fieldwork and research in the laboratories. Some of them participated in this publication. The following students took part in the fieldwork: Steffen Baetsen, Martijn van den Bel, Laura van Broekhoven, Richard Jansen, Michiel Kappers, Jantien Molengraaff, Willy Minkes and Maaike de Waal. In addition, Céline van Aalst, Simone Bloo, Olivier van Buren, Arjan Luyten, Martijn Valk and Freek Ypey were very helpful in the laboratories. Special thanks to Pascale and Céline, two St. Martin volunteers.

The present volume is a joint effort of many of the above mentioned people. Many thanks go out to Elisabeth S. Wing for her guidance in the analysis of the faunal remains. She also provided unpublished data of the Jolly Beach site (National Science Foundation grant BNS-8903377, granted to Dr. E.S. Wing). The data on analysis of the fauna materials from Saba was supported by National Science Foundation grant BNS-8903377 (granted to Dr. Elisabeth S. Wing). She also gave some useful comments on chapters 5 and 10. Thanks are due also to Prof. Dr. C.C. Bakels, Faculty of Archaeology, Leiden University, The Netherlands, who placed the zoological reference collection at the disposal of the project. Dr. A.H. Versteeg gave permission to publish a drawing of the worked turtle bone from the Golden Rock site.

Regarding the paleoethnobotanical research many thanks go out to the Florida Museum of Natural History, and the Centre for Archaeological Investigations, Southern Illinois University at Carbondale for providing laboratory space and necessary equipment. Partial support for this research was provided by the National Science Foundation, grant number BNS 8903377, awarded to Dr. E.S. Wing and Dr. L.A. Newsom. In this respect we are indebted also to Dr. P.J.M. Maas (Univ. of Utrecht) and Dr. F. Bouman (Univ. of Amsterdam) for the time they spent on trying to identify one of the seed specimens recovered.

As regards to the study of shells we are much indebted to Dennis Nieweg who was so kind to share his knowledge on Caribbean shells and to provide comments on chapters 4 and 9. Joep Arts performed the ceramic analysis presented in chapter 21 and also made the drawings of the pottery in this chapter.

Acknowledgements go out to Renzo Duin and Dennis Nieweg who made the drawings of the artefacts in chapters 4, 8 and 9; to Rineke van den Muysenberg who helped with making the drawings of chapters 5 and 10; to Michiel Kappers and Peter Deunhouwer who did the computer editing of the maps and to Jan Pauptit who made the photographs of all the artefacts.

We have extensively benefited from the numerous and pleasant discussions on ceramic chronology with Irving Rouse, Aad Boomert and José Oliver. We would also like to express our gratitude to Aad Boomert, James Petersen and Monique Vilders for the tremendous work and time they put in correcting the English texts. In the same way our gratitude goes out to our dear friends and colleagues Marlena and Andrzej Antczak and our friends Aleid and Gert-Jan Wijers for their editorial and mental assistance in the last stage of preparation of this publication.

Finally, we thank Thijs van Kolfschoten and Bouke van der Meer, series editors, for their helpful comments.

Most of all, however, we would like to thank our son Yann, for his understanding and motivation to follow us during field campaigns and to endure our everlasting talks about Caribbean archaeology.

List of contributors

Steffen Baetsen, c/o Faculty of Archaeology, Leiden University, P.O. Box 9515, 2300 RA Leiden, The Netherlands.

Alex J. Brokke, c/o Faculty of Archaeology, Leiden University, P.O. Box 9515, 2300 RA Leiden, The Netherlands.

André Delpuech, Service de l'Archéologie, Direction des Affaires Culturelles, 14 Rue Maurice Marie-Claire, 97100 Basse-Terre, Guadeloupe. andre.delpuech@wanadoo.fr

Maaike S. de Waal, c/o Faculty of Archaeology, Leiden University, P.O. Box 9515, 2300 RA Leiden, The Netherlands. m.de.waal@arch.LeidenUniv. NL

Tom Hamburg, c/o Faculty of Archaeology, Leiden University, P.O. Box 9515, 2300 RA Leiden, The Netherlands.

Jay B. Haviser, Archaeological-Anthropological Institute of the Netherlands Antilles (AAINA). Johan van Walbeeck-plein 6b, Curaçao. naam_haviser@curacao.com

Corinne L. Hofman, Faculty of Archaeology, Leiden University, P.O. Box 9515, 2300 RA Leiden, The Netherlands. C. Hofman@arch.LeidenUniv. NL

Menno L.P. Hoogland, Faculty of Archaeology, Leiden University, P.O. Box 9515, 2300 RA Leiden, The Netherlands. Hoogland@arch.LeidenUniv. NL

Richard Jansen, c/o Faculty of Archaeology, Leiden University, P.O. Box 9515, 2300 RA Leiden, The Netherlands.

Sebastiaan Knippenberg, c/o Faculty of Archaeology, Leiden University, P.O. Box 9515, 2300 RA Leiden, The Netherlands. s.knippenberg@arch.LeidenUniv.NL

Lee A. Newsom, Center for Archaeological Investigations, Southern Illinois University. 3479 Famer Hall, Carbondale, IL62901-4527, USA. lnewsom@siu.edu

Mark Nokkert, c/o Faculty of Archaeology, Leiden University, P.O. Box 9515, 2300 RA Leiden, The Netherlands.

Jantien Molengraaff, c/o Faculty of Archaeology, Leiden University, P.O. Box 9515, 2300 RA Leiden, The Netherlands.

José R. Oliver, Institute of Archaeology, 31-34 Gordon Square, London WC1H 0PY, England. j.oliver@ucl.ac.uk

James B. Petersen, Anthropology Department, University of Vermont, Williams Hall, Burlington, VTO 5405, USA. jpeterse@zoo.uvm.edu

David R. Watters, Carnegie Museum of Natural History, 5800 Baum Boulevard, Pittsburgh, PA 15206-3706, USA. dwatters+@pitt.edu

1   Introduction

Corinne L. Hofman and Menno L.P. Hoogland

1.1   Introduction

This volume discusses the results of archaeological surveys and test investigations of three pre-Columbian sites on the island of St. Martin early 1993. It is divided into four parts. The first three parts describe the sites of Norman Estate, Hope Estate and Anse des Pères. These sites date from the end of the third millennium BC to the ninth century AD and thus cover an important part of the occupation history of the island, i.e., from the preceramic until the Late Saladoid period. The Early Ceramic occupation of St. Martin, present at the site of Hope Estate, has recently led to much debate in a broader Caribbean context. Several scholars working on islands surrounding St. Martin have made contributions to this debate in the fourth part of this volume.

1.2   St. Martin

St. Martin is one of the islands of the Lesser Antilles (fig. 1.1). It is situated at 63° western longitude and just north of 18° northern latitude in the Western Hemisphere. The island is politically divided into two parts, a northern, French part, and a southern, Dutch part. The French side, with its capital Marigot, is larger, about 52 km², to 32 km² for the Dutch side (Palm 1985). The Dutch part, with its capital Philipsburg, belongs to the Netherlands Antilles. The French side of St. Martin is incorporated in the Department of Guadeloupe which forms part of France.

The eastern side of the island is mountainous with its highest point, Pic du Paradis, at 424 m. The western side is flat. There are several bays lined by sand beaches around the island.

St. Martin is one of the so-called "composite" islands of the Lesser Antilles. It is a partially volcanic island with mostly porphyrite, diorite and limestone geological formations. It consists partially of elevated ocean floors. The island is built up of Eocene to Miocene sedimentary, volcanic and intrusive rocks. It is considered to belong to the calcareous islands of the Antilles (Andreieff et al. 1988, 72). Basically, there are three types of geological formations on St. Martin:

1) Sedimentary and volcanic-sedimentary formations, such as the Pointe Blanche Formation (Upper Eocene Age), which are to be found mainly in the centre and the western part of the island. This formation may be as thick as over 100 m and is made up of layers of crystallized tuffs, alternating with crystallized limestones. It can be considered as an old marine floor which was formed during a period of volcanic activity occurring somewhere at the location of present-day St. Barthélemy.

2) A chain of magmatic rocks that intrudes into the Pointe Blanche Formation. This marine floor was lifted up and folded by magma flows which were pushed up as the result of pressure and temperature differences in the earth's mantle. Most of the magma did not reach the outer surface, but was stopped by the thick Pointe Blanche Formation. At some places it can be seen today that the magma intruded the Pointe Blanche formation. Being stopped, the fluid lava had time to cool down resulting in the formation of diorites. Probably four different intrusions took place. Half of the island consists of intrusive rocks dating from the end of the Eocene and the lower Oligocene. Andesite and diorite are the most frequently occurring intrusives, while basalts and dacites are also present. The tuff layers in the Pointe Blanche Formation made place for well-stratified silicious limestone formations. The silicious tephrite formations are very resistant to weathering and constitute the highest summits of the island.

3) A series of Miocene clayish limestones, in the western and southwestern part of the island forming the Low Lands Formation (Solomiac 1974, 98-100; Andreieff et al. 1988, 71-74). Local subsidence of the island caused the deposition of marine sediments in its western part, resulting in the formation of bedded limestones. Using analysis of fossil foraminifera, the Low Lands Formation could be dated to the Early Miocene (Drooger 1951). Succeeding tectonic movements provided the last step in the geological history of St. Martin by uplifting and folding the island into its present form.

1.3   History of archaeological research

St. Martin is one of those Caribbean islands that lacked any substantial archaeological research until very recently. The amount of archaeological excavations does not exceed five

Fig. 1.1. The islands of the Lesser Antilles.

to date. The first people who made some contribution to the archaeological record, were three local amateur archaeologists, Hyacinth Corner and John and Dorothy Cooper, who identified the archaeological sites of Pic Paradis, Mount William, Billy Folly, Red Pond, and Cupecoy Bay during the 1950's.

Ripley P. Bullen and Adelaide K. Bullen were the first to make test excavations on the island (Bullen and Bullen 1966). They excavated 1.5×3.0 m test units at Cupecoy Bay. This site, situated in the Low Lands area, was the largest known site at that time, having a diameter of about 150 m. Apart from this test excavation the Bullen's collected surface material at the sites of Red Pond and Terres Basses, also situated in the Low Lands area. At Cupecoy Bay they mainly found pottery and a few shell and stone artefacts. They concluded that the pottery of Cupecoy Bay and Terres Basses showed many similarities with that of the Caliviny and Magens Bay sites. Probable dates would be between AD 800 and 1200 which would place the Cupecoy Bay pottery in the Troumassoid series of the Lesser Antilles (Hofman 1993).

The next person to do archaeological research on the island was Menno Sypkens-Smit (Sypkens-Smit and Versteeg 1987). He compiled an inventory of the then known archaeological sites and recorded in all 25 sites. In addition, he made test excavations at Red Bay, Ravine Caréta, and Great Bay (Philipsburg). A small single-component settlement was found at Red Bay, but post-depositional processes considerably had affected the site at Ravine Caréta, while Great Bay yielded finds from pre-Columbian as well as colonial times.

In 1986 and 1987 Jay B. Haviser of the Archaeological-Anthropological Institute of the Netherlands Antilles (AAINA) executed a salvage excavation at Cupecoy Bay and conducted a survey of the entire island. He located 39 sites, of which six sites had been destroyed but were recorded in the past. Seven sites belong to the colonial period, the rest dates back to pre-Columbian times. The latter include caves, petroglyphs, small artefact scatters and large midden areas. Sites belonging to the preceramic period were lacking. In addition to the survey, Haviser made some test excavations at the sites of Cupecoy Bay and Hope Estate (Haviser 1988, 1991c).

Since the late 1980's the Association Archéologique Hope Estate has been very active on the French part of St. Martin. Several sites have been added to the archaeological map of the island and the projects presented in this volume are a good example of this impetus. However, it has to be stated that the archaeology of St. Martin is still in the initial period of investigating its potential. Thusfar, mostly small scale projects have been conducted with the aim of locating sites and small test excavations in order to enhance a chronological context. Larger projects, such as the one described in

Versteeg and Schinkel (1992), Hofman (1993), Petersen and Watters (1995), Hoogland (1996), and Delpuech et al. (1996), are needed to learn more about the ways of life of the various pre-Columbian groups which inhabited St. Martin.

1.4   The 1993 investigations

The three sites discussed in the present volume are located on the French part of the island, i.e., its northern portion (fig. 1.2). These sites can broadly be dated from the end of the third millennium BC to the ninth century AD and, consequently, cover a large part of the early pre-Columbian occupation of the island.

The investigations of the preceramic site of Norman Estate form the first part of this volume. Four chapters are presented including discussions of the methods and research strategies, as well as the analyses of the lithic, shell and faunal materials.

Norman Estate is the first preceramic site which was discovered on the island. On a regional scale few sites are known from this period, e.g., Krum Bay on St. Thomas, Whitehead's Bluff on Anguilla, Core Core Bay on St. Eustatius, Sugar Factory Pier on St. Kitts and Jolly Beach on Antigua. Consequently, the results from the site survey and test excavations, presented here, offer many possibilities for expanding our knowledge on this period.

The Cedrosan Saladoid site of Anse des Pères forms the second part of this volume. The methods and research strategies, the analyses of the pottery, lithic, shell and faunal remains are discussed in five chapters. The survey results revealed a single component, i.e., a settlement site occupied for a short time, and demonstrate the potential for further excavations focussing on the layout of this site, the reconstruction of the residential structures and the compositional study of the pottery assemblage and especially its functional aspects.

The multi-component Saladoid site of Hope Estate is treated in the third part of this volume. Apart from a chapter dealing with the methods and research strategies, seven chapters discuss the pottery, lithics, shells, archaeobotanical and human remains from Hope Estate. The importance of this site lies in its possibilities to contribute to the issue of the Early Ceramic colonisation of the Caribbean islands. Several mechanisms, i.e., migration and divergence, have been hypothesized as being responsible for the occurrence of two distinct ceramic styles or wares in the region several centuries BC. To date insufficient evidence has been found to support either of these hypotheses. As Prof. Dr. Irving Rouse states in his foreword to this volume, "Hope Estate is the only place where we can presently test the hypothesis of divergence".

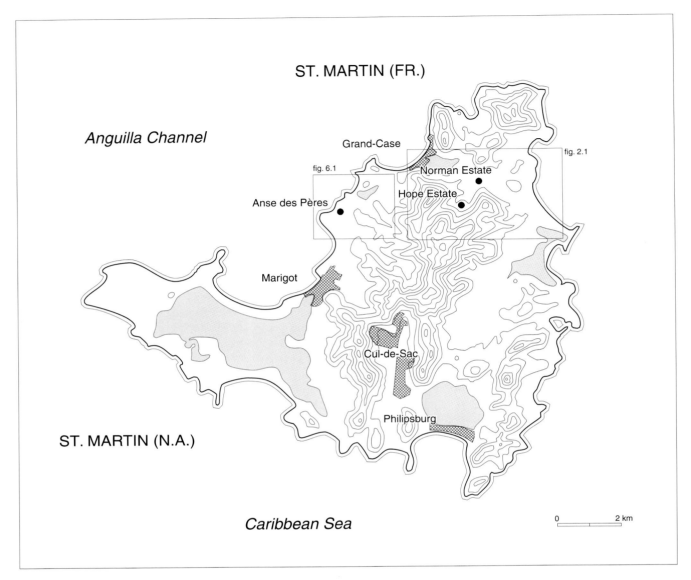

ST. MARTIN (FR.)

Anguilla Channel

Grand-Case

fig. 6.1

fig. 2.1

Norman Estate

Hope Estate

Anse des Pères

Marigot

Cul-de-Sac

ST. MARTIN (N.A.)

Philipsburg

Caribbean Sea

0   2 km

Fig. 1.2. The island of St. Martin.

The results presented in this volume thus only refer to the 1993 campaign. The Hope Estate excavations continued since 1994 by a new team, directed by D. Bonnissent.

In the fourth and last part of this volume, the issue of Early Ceramic occupation, the so-called 'La Hueca problem', is viewed from beyond St. Martin. Contributions by José Oliver on the site of La Hueca on Vieques island, by David Watters and James Petersen on the site of Trants on Montserrat and by Corinne Hofman, Menno Hoogland and André Delpuech and others on the site of Morel on Guade-

loupe reveal new evidence as to the distribution patterns and context of the Early Ceramic period on the northern Lesser Antilles.

PART ONE
NORMAN ESTATE

2 Methods and strategies

Sebastiaan Knippenberg

2.1 Site location

Norman Estate is situated on a level plateau showing smooth slopes on its north and south sides. This plateau runs from Grand-Case across the northern part of the island, rising about 10 metres in the centre in order to descend smoothly to Orient Bay. The Norman Estate area forms an offshoot of one of the slopes of Hope Hill. It descends slightly towards the north-west (fig. 2.1). The base is formed by quartz diorite formations of intrusive volcanic character.

The area is crossed by the N7 highway. Its old trajectory transverses the village of Grand-Case; a new section runs south of the airstrip. The Archaic site, discovered by Henocq and Petit, is to be found close to a farmyard with a little barn and a garden centre with greenhouses, situated to the north of the N7 highway. Fallow land stretches to the south of the N7. A second site was discovered on this land, which belongs to the Petit family. It is bordered by the foot of Hope Hill to the east and the Ravine Caréta, a small stream, to the south and west. This stream originates in the hills of the central part of St. Martin. Due to the construction of a flood-control dam upstream, near a quarry, it does not carry much water any longer. The fallow land south of the N7 is covered with grass varying in height from a few centimetres to more than a metre, a few thorny bushes and some big trees. Two elongated depressions are shown in the contour map (fig. 2.2). They can be considered to represent shallow gullies. These zones are wetter than the surrounding areas, although they contain no standing water. The northwestern and eastern seashores are about 1.5 kilometres from both sides.

2.2 Site discovery

In the late eighties two archaeological sites, Norman Estate 1 (NE1) and 2 (NE2), were discovered by Dr. F. Petit and Ch. Henocq, the director of the local St. Martin museum in the area of Norman Estate on the French side of the island (fig. 2.2). Henocq and Petit made their first discovery during the digging of a trench for the construction of a new road which branches off the N7 highway and runs along the south side of the Grand-Case airport and salt ponds, in order to reach the old trajectory of the N7 again. They noticed that a mechanical shovel had cut straight through a shell deposit

which they recorded by making photographs. In addition, they collected some artefacts, including flint flakes, river pebbles and shell axes. The absence of pottery and a radiocarbon date of 3560 ± 90 BP, i.e., 2234-1742 cal BC, suggest the presence of an Archaic site. No test excavations were made at the time. At present, one can clearly observe patches of this shell deposit in the section made by the ditch running along the road. The second discovery was made some 400 metres to the southeast. On Dr. Petit's land, to the west of the macadam road, giving access to a quarry, shell remains were found during the digging of small holes for the construction of a fence. Most shells appeared to be small and broken. No further investigation was made at this site and no radiocarbon samples were obtained. Neither of these discoveries is mentioned by Haviser (1988) in his report on his St. Martin survey of 1987. It is not certain whether he visited this part of Norman Estate. It is possible that he missed both sites during his surface inspection, as they are covered by a sterile layer of sediment.

2.3 Research objectives

The investigation of Norman Estate had three general research objectives, i.e., firstly, that of determination of the extension of the sites and the potential degree of post-depositional disturbance, secondly, interpretation of the structure of the sites and, if possible, location of functional areas within them, and thirdly, determination of the position of the sites within the cultural context of the Caribbean. The project was considered a pilot study. Its results provide an indication of the archaeological value of the investigated sites. In addition, they can be used to inform possible future excavators as well as the authorities responsible for cultural resource management in decisions concerning objectives of study and excavation strategies or future protection.

To achieve the aims stated above, the research program was divided into three consecutive steps. Each phase of investigation was determined a priori, and differed in some instances from the actual methodology followed. These three phases included, firstly, survey of the site, secondly, excavation of randomly chosen test units within highly concentrated artefact scatters, located and delimited by the survey,

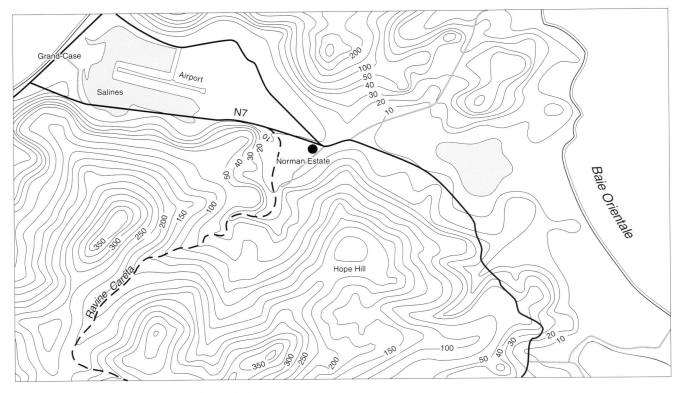

Fig. 2.1. The surroundings of the site of Norman Estate.

and, thirdly, analysis of a sample of cultural remains (artefacts and food remains) obtained during the excavation of the test units.

The survey of the site area was conducted to determine its extension and to locate functional areas within the site. The site area is defined by the spatial distribution of artefacts and ecofacts on the surface of the ground. In some cases the determination of functional areas within a site is hypothetical. A possible distinction can be made between refuse or midden areas, dwelling areas, food-growing areas and burial areas. The test excavations within the high-concentration refuse areas served a number of purposes, i.e., collection of a sample of cultural remains, collection of samples for radiocarbon dating, analysis of the stratigraphy of the site, and finally, obtaining insight into the post-depositional processes which took place in the area.

The location of the test units were chosen at random. The use of randomness offers the possibility of making generalisations about the areas within which sampling took place (Flannery 1976; Cochran 1963), in this case highly concentrated artefact scatters which functioned predominantly as refuse areas. A good characterization of the refuse area

makes the results comparable with other sites within the Caribbean region. Most sites in the Antillean archipelago have been characterized on the basis of test excavations within highly concentrated refuse areas. Whether these samples can be taken to be representative of the cultural remains of the peoples who inhabited the site is unclear. Schinkel (1992) correctly indicates that excavations within dwelling areas provide a great deal of additional cultural information, including plans of house structures and data on the organisation of the village. A number of social, religious and technological conclusions can be drawn from the latter.

On the artefactual level a refuse area can be taken to be representative of the material culture of a group. Caution is necessary, however. Many refuse areas yield a wide variety of food remains, utensils and religious objects. In contrast, some middens have been used also as burial grounds, as is shown at Hope Estate (cf. chapter 17), or as ceremonial areas (Siegel 1989, 1992). These additional functions may have severe implications for the characteristics of the archaeological materials found. Therefore, testing for these possible additional activities should be carried out at every midden area. In addition, samples for radiocarbon dating should be taken from an undisturbed context. [14]C determination of

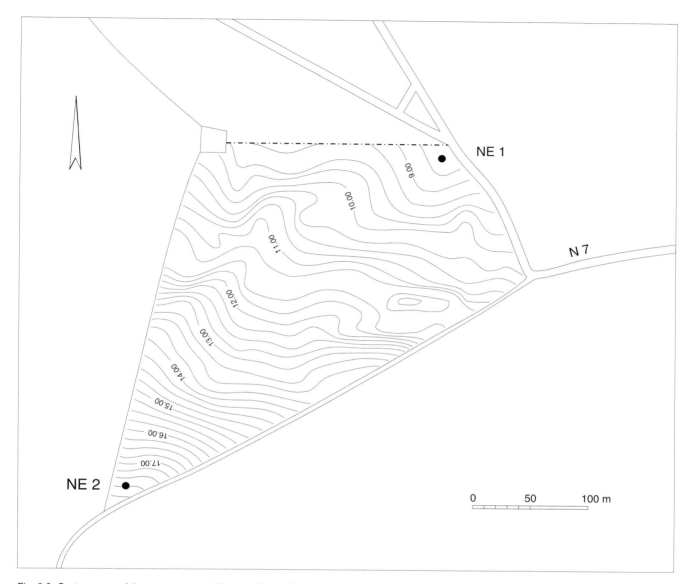

Fig. 2.2. Contour map of the survey area at Norman Estate. The sites Norman Estate 1 and 2 (NE1 and NE2) located by Petit and Henocq are indicated by dots.

these samples, together with conclusions drawn from the stratigraphy of the site, and analysis of the material remains found should provide indications of the duration of occupation of the site and its character as a one- or multi-component site. Stratigraphical data and conclusions drawn from the refitting of the pottery material can be used to arrive at an insight into the post-depositional processes which may have taken place.

The final phase of the research, the study of the archaeological finds, involves an analysis of the four categories of finds

recovered, i.e pottery, lithics, shell and bone remains. Analysis of material remains encountered yield evidence regarding the position of the site within the cultural context of the Caribbean, based on the style of pottery, the stone, shell and bone technology, and finally, the food acquisition strategies and choice of animal and fish species.

2.4 Survey strategy

The area of Norman Estate which had to be surveyed was divided into two parts, firstly, the fallow land to the south of the N7, and, secondly, the partially built-up area to the north of

Fig. 2.3. The location of the auger tests in the survey area.

the road. It was decided to conduct a systematic auger test in the former. The area was divided according to a 15×15 m grid system. An auger test was made at each point of the grid. In the second area only three auger tests were made due to limited access. A surface inspection was executed in the farmyard. In the Garden Centre, only the greenhouses could be checked. Due to gardening activities here the topsoil had been turned recently, as a result of which a good opportunity was offered, to see whether remains of human occupation were present.

The survey area was bordered to the north by a fence, i.e., an arbitrary limit. To the east and south, the area was bordered by a macadam road and to the west by the Ravine Caréta. Both of them are natural boundaries as they mark the onset of various steep slopes, each unsuitable for habitation. A number of considerations were taken into account before deciding on the survey design. Firstly, the occasionally dense vegetation, together with the observation that both sites are covered by a sterile deposit, made it obvious that a surface survey would be highly unproductive. A subsurface method had to be found. Auger testing is a relatively fast method of sub-surface testing compared to the digging of small test units. Considering the size of the area which had to be surveyed (ca. 60,000 m^2) and the limited time (about three weeks), and man power (four men) available, this method was considered to be suited for our purposes. As preceramic refuse areas form highly concentrated man-made deposits they are easily located using only small-volume techniques such as auger testing. Intervals of 15 metres were chosen in order to get a complete coverage of the research area. It was expected that possible refuse areas would be larger than 225 square metres and would not be distributed in a systematic way. This, at least, is suggested by data from other preceramic sites in the Caribbean (Veloz Maggiolo and Ortega 1973; Lundberg 1989).

Augering took place using a riverside auger with a diameter of 10 cm. Moreover, an attempt was made to auger to at least 40 cm depth. The auger samples were water-screened using a 2.7 mm mesh-screen. All artefacts indicating possible human occupation such as shells, faunal remains and charcoal etc. were recorded. Finally, additional auger tests were made close to primary auger tests, which proved to yield finds in order, firstly, to establish whether these finds belonged to a more extended cultural deposit, and secondly to determine the size of the artefact scatter. The results of the auger testing were intended to locate areas where test excavations should produce the best results.

2.5   Survey results

In all, 269 auger tests were made on the fallow land next to three tests in the farmyard (fig. 2.3). The presence of large stones in the soil prevented that all tests reached a depth of 40 cm. However, in most cases, augering was possible to at least 30 cm below the surface. Considering the depth at which the finds in the road trench were made, between 0 and 20 cm below the present surface, the depth of 30 cm appeared to be sufficient to locate any archaeological materials.
A total of 21 out of the 269 auger tests produced archaeological finds, including shells, faunal remains and small flint flakes (fig. 2.4). Twenty-five auger tests contained charcoal, mostly not associated with other finds. Due to the possibility that this charcoal resulted from burning gardens in colonial times, it was not seen as an indicator of pre-Columbian occupation. NE1 and NE3 were expected to yield finds as these formed the sites discovered by Dr. Petit and Christophe Henocq. The auger tests containing flint flakes were of special interest, because they seemed to indicate special activity areas.

None of the 21 auger tests yielding archaeological finds went through a refuse deposit. It was possible to see a very clear deposit of compact shells in the section of the road ditch of NE1. Many shells were found in the two auger tests situated six metres from this trench. However, these shells appeared to be scattered and occurring in lesser concentrations than the major deposit, indicating that it did not extend much in westerly direction. The three auger tests in the farmyard yielded low concentrations of shell fragments as well. No remains were found during the prospecting of the greenhouses. In NE3 the three auger tests contained low concentrations of shell fragments, together with little pieces of a concrete-like substance. The other auger tests yielded one to four finds, which were recovered only after sieving. No exact depths can be given.

Four additional auger tests were made at a distance of 5 metres from all the primary auger tests, which yielded archaeological materials. Another strategy was followed in NE1. Here an attempt was made by augering to determine, firstly, the limits of the dense shell deposit visible along the road, and secondly, the limits of the scatter of finds in southwesterly direction. In all, 29 additional auger tests were made on this spot. This enabled us to construct a map showing the area, yielding shell remains in the auger tests as well as the situation of the compact shell deposit within this area (fig. 2.4). This could be accomplished for the area south of the road. In the farmyard north of it only a small test unit (30 by 30 cm) could be dug near the road. This test confirmed the results of the auger tests indicating that no significant deposits were present. Apparently, a large part of the original shell midden is destroyed due to the construction of the road.

The additional auger tests in NE2 produced similar results. However, close inspection of the surface revealed the remains of a stone house structure dating from colonial times. A blank of a conch celt was found within this structure. In addition to the small size of the shell pieces encountered and the presence of a stucco-like substance, this indicated that the colonial occupation disturbed the shell remains and mixed both deposits. The additional auger tests in the other areas yielded only finds in NE3, where in all 13 additional auger tests were executed. The initial auger test at coordinates 440/2000 produced only one small piece of flint. The additional augers yielded faunal remains as well as shell fragments alongside small flint flakes (fig. 2.4). These finds suggest an ephemeral human occupation on this spot. According to the research strategy followed, actually additional auger tests should have been made since archaeological materials were still present in the outermost auger tests, indicating that the limits of the deposit had not been reached yet. However, no further tests were made as the discovery of an area with a low concentration of finds was not expected. Using this auger tests method for more detailed purposes than prospecting, e.g, for determining site boundaries, would reduce the reliability of the results. In this case the presence of a substantial amount of finds, suggestive of human presence, was attested. Another,

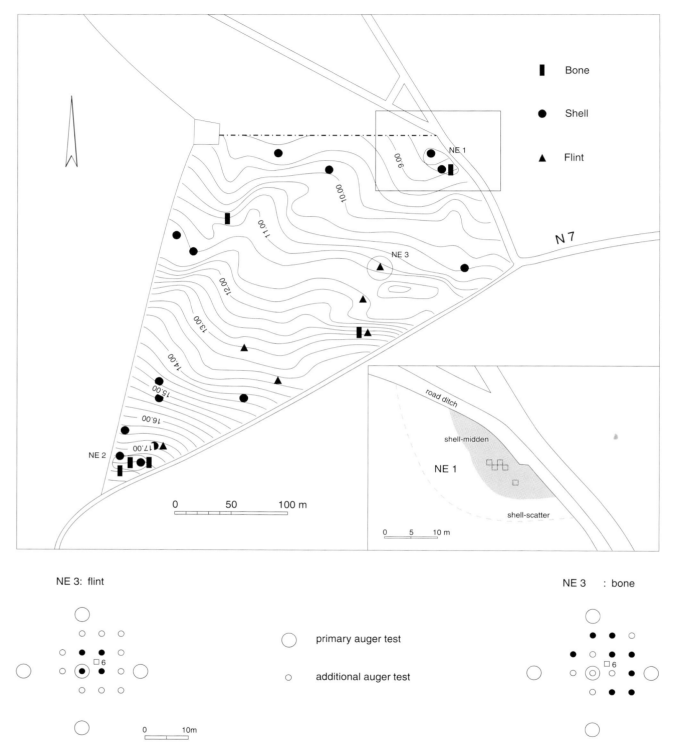

Fig. 2.4. Distribution of the artefacts and ecofacts: flint, shell and faunal bone in the auger tests. Norman Estate 1: the boundary of the shell midden and scatter, and the location of the 1x1 m test units (1-5). Norman Estate 3: the distribution of shell and animal remains in the additional auger tests. The location of the 1x1 test unit 6 is indicated as well.

more in-depth and, therefore, more time-consuming method, such as excavating test units, could have provided more information on the size of the site and its patterning. Unfortunately, it was not possible to adopt such a method within the scope of this project.

The additional auger tests in other areas were inconclusive. They yielded no finds, but as noted above, low-concentration areas can be missed with the research method used. The two areas which yielded flint flakes in the auger tests, are particularly interesting. When these areas are plotted on a contour map, they appear to be situated in relatively elevated areas, just like NE3. This may reflect a preference for high and dry areas for occupation. If so, the question may be asked whether the natural environment of the Norman Estate region in preceramic times was similar to the present situation. The differences in altitude are small and the morphology of the area may have changed over the past 4000 years. Unfortunately, no systematic research has been done on this topic to date.

2.6   An additional discovery
During the field project an archaeological deposit has been discovered at the crossroads of the N7 and the roads which runs to Cul de Sac (cf. fig. 2.1). The site forms the most elevated area of the valley. Shell fragments appeared to be scattered over an area of some ten square metres, just behind a stone fence. One auger test was conducted yielding shell and faunal remains.

2.7   Test excavations
Test excavations were made in two of the three site areas, i.e., NE1 and NE3. NE2, which yielded small fragments of shell and a stucco-like substance together with a colonial structure, was not further investigated due to limited time and manpower. Preference was given to the other two areas as it was expected that they would yield undisturbed archaeological deposits. NE1, the dense shell deposit dating from preceramic times, most likely represents a refuse area of preceramic fishers and shell collectors. The low concentration of food remains in association with flint flakes at NE3, is more likely to form the remnant of a preceramic camp site or residence area. Both these initial interpretations need to be tested by excavation of test units. According to the above-mentioned aims, it had to be tested whether the archaeological remains at the two areas could be ascribed to a contemporary occupation, or whether they belonged to entirely different periods.

2.8   Location of the test units
Five test units of one m² were dug in NE1, i.e., within the limits of the shell midden. The location was not chosen randomly, as the survey showed that probably more than half of

the site had been destroyed due to road construction. It was decided to map only the remaining part of the site. The five test units were excavated at two different locations within the shell midden. Four tests were dug according to a chess-board pattern. This was done to obtain as many sections as possible given the excavated four m². The fifth one was dug some metres apart from the other units in order to see whether the two locations differed in content and structure. Both locations were chosen haphazardly in the part of highest refuse concentration of the undisturbed portion of the shell midden. Only one test unit was dug at the NE3 site. This test was located within the area promising most finds (fig. 2.4).

2.9   Excavation methods
The five units at NE1 were dug in arbitrary levels. The topsoil, recently thrown up during road construction, was first removed. It was not sifted. On reaching brown-coloured soil indicating the original occupation layer, excavating continued using arbitrary levels of 5 cm in thickness. The dirt was water-screened through nested sieves for technical and sampling purposes. A 10 mm mesh sieve was put on top, surmounting 4 mm, and 2.7 mm mesh sieves. In this manner it was possible to separate various residues and analyze them in stages.
All the materials obtained from the 10 mm mesh were analyzed. A 25% weight sample was taken from the residues from the other two sieves. This amount was divided into ten randomly chosen samples of 2.5% each. These samples were used to analyze the faunal remains present. The test unit at NE3 was dug differently. Here the topsoil was not removed and the entire one m² unit was dug in arbitrary levels, the upper one 5 cm in thickness and the following ones 10 cm each. The same mesh screens were used. However, the sample procedures were different. As the amount of material appeared to be small, residues from the 10 and 4 mm sieves were analyzed completely and randomly chosen samples of 10 × 2.5% samples were taken only from the 2.7 mm mesh sieve. The archaeological material was divided into three categories: faunal remains, shells and lithics. These were analyzed separately; the results of which are presented in the following chapter.

2.10   Stratigraphy
A number of sections were obtained at NE1. As access was easy, long sections could be made in the ditch stretching along the road. These were analyzed together with the vertical sections of the test units. Section 4 typifies the stratigraphy of the site (fig. 2.5). A series of strata can be distinguished, from bottom to top, as follows.
(1) Stratum of sandy to gravelly clay, strong brown (7.5YR 5/6) in colour according to the Munsell Color Soil Chart. This stratum appeared to be sterile.

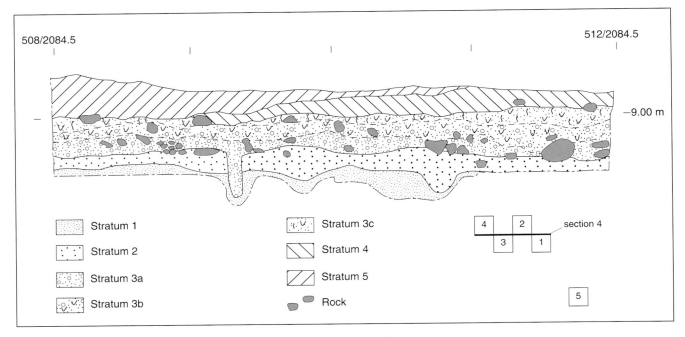

Fig. 2.5. Stratigraphy of Norman Estate 1 (see text for the description of the strata).

(2) Stratum of sandy to gravelly clay, dark brown (7.5YR 4/4) in colour. This stratum, too, appeared to be sterile.
(3) Stratum of sandy clay, dark brown (7.5YR 3/2) in colour. This stratum represents the archaeological deposit. However, the concentration of the remains differed.
(3a) This part of stratum (3) contained between a few to no shell fragments. In contrast a substantial amount of faunal remains was present.
(3b) This stratum forms the core of the refuse deposit. It yielded high concentrations of shells and faunal remain fragments, and to a lesser extent, stone artefacts. It is a distinct and easily recognizable deposit.
(3c) This can be considered as the disturbed portion of the midden deposit. Scattered pieces of shell were found together with recent materials such as glass particles.
(4) Stratum of clay, dark brown (10YR 3/3) in colour. This stratum was formed recently. A part of a shoe was found at the base of this stratum, indicating its recent formation. No shells or other archaeological materials were recovered from this stratum.
(5) Stratum of sandy clay, recently thrown up during road construction. The stratum consisted of multi-coloured soil, which suggests that it forms a mixture of various layers. Soil originating from the destroyed part of the midden containing shells, faunal remain fragments and stone artefacts, could easily be recognized.

Inspection of the sections shows that the shell midden deposit (Stratum 3b) is thickest along the road, close to unit 1, where it reaches a thickness of 25 cm. It decreases gradually in southeastern direction. Besides, at unit 5 the decline is steeper. Analysis of the sections clearly shows that the thickest parts of the original midden have been destroyed by road construction. Evidence of these activities can also be seen in section 3, where clear shovel cuts penetrated and partly disturbed the concentrated shell deposit. On the other side of the road it was possible only to dig a 30 × 30 cm testpit. Although it was not possible to recognize a concentrated shell deposit, shell remains, faunal remains, and stone artefacts were found to be scattered through a 40 cm thick stratum with the similar texture and colour as Stratum (3). It is capped by the sterile clay layer recognized in the other sections.

The vertical sections of NE3 showed two major strata, from bottom to top as follows.
(1) A sterile sub-stratum of sandy to gravelly clay, strong brown in colour, from 35 cm below the present surface to as far down as the base of the deposit.
(2) A 35 cm thick stratum of sandy clay, reddish brown in colour. All four excavated layers belong to this stratum. The archaeological materials recovered from this stratum do not form a distinct deposit. Finds were made in all four layers; the highest concentration was encountered between 15 and 25 cm below the present surface.

Unit	lab. No	material	age BP	calibrated date (95% confidence level)
1	GrN-20157	Strombus	3730 ± 30 BP	2302 cal BC – 2136 cal BC
3	GrN-20158	Strombus	3590 ± 50 BP	2152 cal BC – 1890 cal BC
5	GrN-20159	Strombus	3780 ± 40 BP	2362 cal BC – 2180 cal BC
–		Strombus	3560 ± 90 BP	2234 cal BC – 1742 cal BC

Table 2.1. Radiocarbon dates. In order to allow for the reservoir effect, 400 years have been substracted from the BP values.

2.11 Radiocarbon dates

Three samples of unmodified *Strombus* were collected from Stratum (3b) in the test excavations, i.e., the core layer of the shell midden. They were taken from units 1, 3 and 5 (table 2.1). The amount of shells in area NE3 was insufficient for radiocarbon dating. The samples were analyzed by the Laboratory for Isotopic Research of the University of Groningen, The Netherlands. A fourth shell date was obtained before the project started. However, it is was not known whether the result of this measurement has been corrected for reservoir effect. The BP values have been calibrated using the Groningen calibration program CAL 15.

There is some variation in the dates, even at 95% confidence level the dates do not overlap. Reliable statements about the duration of occupation based on radiocarbon measurements cannot be made due to the possibility that the shells died long before they were taken to the site.

2.12 Post-depositional processes

The various behaviourial processes that lead to the formation of a site and those that can take place after a site has been formed have been studied by Schiffer (1976, 1987). The latter, the post-depositional processes, may cause its deformation. They can be divided broadly into deformations caused by man and by nature.

Three periods can be distinguished in the past of St. Martin during which humans had a potential impact on site formation at Norman Estate, i.e., the Archaic, Ceramic and Historic ages. Questions about possible site deformation in the Archaic period relate to the formation and chronological interpretation of the preceramic midden. It may be asked whether NE1 was occupied sequentially by a single group of hunters, fishers and foodcollectors or whether the site was inhabited by a series of subsequent preceramic peoples of different cultural affiliations. The first question is dealt within the section on dating. Due to the relatively imprecise nature of the radiocarbon measurements and the lack of any other techniques providing answers on the question of periodization, such as for instance, determination of seasonality of collecting shells, this question cannot be answered sufficiently. The second question is easier to answer. The present data do not suggest that preceramic groups of varying cultural affiliations occupied the site sequentially. For instance, the same shells and animal species are recovered throughout the midden, pointing to uniform hunting and collecting habits during its entire occupation (cf. chapters 4 and 5). As no pottery was found the question whether any Ceramic groups occupied the site can be answered negatively.

The remaining period covers the Historic age. Agriculture and house construction during Early Colonial times probably affected the site. The area of Norman Estate was used for sugarcane cultivation. The remains of a small colonial house in the southern part of the surveyed area attests to this use. A distinct 'plough zone' could not be identified. However, at both sites, particularly at NE3, evidence was found that particular objects had moved in a vertical direction, possibly due to agricultural activities. At NE3 stone artefacts and fish bones were found dispersed in a zone 35 cm in thickness. Most finds were made in the third arbitrary level, indicating that the preceramic occupation layer was originally situated somewhere at this depth. Ploughing disturbed only the upper portion of the shell midden at NE1. This part corresponds with Stratum (3a), which yielded tiny shell fragments, mixed with colonial remains such as pieces of glass.

Road construction and other building activities caused most recent disturbances. Road construction took place in two phases. Firstly, the N7 was constructed and afterwards an additional section was joined to it, running along the south side of the Grand-Case airport, which joins the N7 right at the area of the site. The construction activities for both roads damaged NE1. The N7 runs straight through the shell midden, and has destroyed an unquantifiable part of it. The construction of the new section of the N7 reduced the refuse heap a second time, though not as badly as the first time.

The second phase of road construction also damaged the upper layer of the site. As noted above, evidence of cutting by a mechanical shovel can be seen in section 3. Besides, soil from the destroyed part of the midden was thrown on the portion of the site where the test excavations were conducted. This was easily to be seen in section 4 (fig. 2.5).

Here Stratum (5) consists of soil deriving from various, mixed-up strata of the midden. It yielded shells, faunal remains and lithics, as well as soil from the substratum. The disturbance of the site explains the presence of artefacts on the surface of the excavated area.

It is not clear to what extent these recent activities disturbed any preceramic remains on the other side of the road in the farmyard. Auger testing showed that, although shell remains are present, they are not found within a compact midden deposit. It appears that the archaeological remains were below a stratum of clay (Stratum 4), dispersed in a zone of 40 cm thickness. Disposition must have occurred before the second construction phase.

Post-depositional processes of natural character are due to chemical, biotic or geological causes. Chemical processes affect the preservation of certain materials. Extremely wet or dry conditions do not prevail at Norman Estate, as a result perishable materials such as wood and natural fibres have decayed in the soil. Biotic processes, caused by roots and animals moving their way through the ground, may result in the displacement of artefacts and ecofacts. One of the sections revealed the remains of a root hole, indicating that the vegetation may have affected the site. Indications that this occurred frequently have not been found. Hydrological processes certainly affected the locations of the small remains. Analysis of the shells, faunal remains and stone artefacts revealed that significantly more bone fragments than shell remains and stone artefacts have been found in the bottom level of the deposit. This can be related to the appearance of the bone remains which show worn, rounded shapes (cf. chapter 5). This suggests that vertical movements, possibly the result of hydrological processes, caused transportation of the smaller items.

It can be concluded that recent activities severely damaged the midden area of NE1. Estimations of the size of the affected part are difficult to make. However, it is obvious that the thickest portion of the deposit was damaged. The remaining midden to the south of the road was affected as well. Agricultural activities have disturbed its upper levels and hydrological processes caused the vertical disposition of the smaller faunal remains. Finally, to the north of the road, various construction activities damaged the preceramic refuse layer significantly.

Colonial cultivation disturbed the original occupational layer at NE3. As a result, the finds were distributed throughout a stratum of 35 cm thickness. Most likely, the pre-Columbian occupation layer was situated originally somewhere between 15 and 25 cm below the present surface.

2.13   Conclusions

An area of approximately 60.000 m² at Norman Estate was systematically surveyed by auger prospecting. The investigation resulted in the identification of five different areas showing remains of possible human occupation. Two areas contained shells and faunal remains, the other three areas yielded flint material. Additional auger tests, followed by surface inspection of these areas, produced more finds at three of them. Evaluation of the results suggest that the site of Norman Estate 2 in the southern part of the prospected area was disturbed due to occupation in colonial times. Therefore, excavations were conducted only in NE1 and NE3, respectively. At NE1 five test units of 1 m² were excavated and a series of vertical cross sections inspected. These revealed the remains of a 20 cm thick refuse deposit, consisting of high concentrations of shells, faunal remains, and, to a lesser extent, stone artefacts. This deposit was severely damaged due to road construction activities in the recent past. The 125 m² area still left of this deposit probably represents approximately half of the original extension of the site. Apart from the road constructing activities, the vertical movement of little particles caused by still unexplained hydrological phenomena formed a factor of post-depositional disturbance. This movement has resulted in the concentration of most bone remains at significantly lower levels than the shells and stone artefacts.

Three *Strombus gigas* samples were taken from the refuse deposit for radiocarbon measurement. Together with a date obtained by Ch. Henocq, the results indicate that Norman Estate was occupied between 2350 to 1800 cal BC. The dates are inconclusive to decide whether the site lasted for one uninterrupted period of time or was characterized by a series of recurrent short occupations. The latter possibility is more likely, especially when taking into account the small extension of the site. The radiocarbon dates provide additional evidence that NE1 can be interpreted as a campsite with a refuse area where Amerindians from preceramic times deposited their food remains and discarded tools.

A 1×1 m test unit was excavated at NE3. This test unit did not reveal a distinct deposit or occupation layer. Small flint artefacts and faunal remains were found to be dispersed throughout a layer of 35 cm thickness, showing the highest concentration of finds between 15 and 25 cm below the present surface. This indicates that, most likely, the original occupation layer was disturbed by agricultural activities in colonial times. As shells were not encountered, radiocarbon dates could not be obtained. However, the absence of pottery at this location suggests that NE3 was occupied during the preceramic period as well. The finding of a small amount of lithic artefacts in association with faunal remains makes it likely that this location was used as a small campsite in the Archaic age.

3   Lithics

Sebastiaan Knippenberg

3.1   Introduction

The research project at the Norman Estate site yielded 265 prehistoric lithic artefacts. Some 160 artefacts came from the excavation of the test units at Norman Estate 1 (NE1), 60 from test unit 6 at Norman Estate 3 (NE3), 33 were found during the preparation of a long section along the road at NE1, and the remaining 12 were collected on the surface in the area of the test units at Norman Estate 1 and on the surface of the farmyard across the road from Norman Estate. All artefacts from the test units were collected using a 10 mm mesh screen. Some lithics among the residues collected from the 2.7 mm and 4.0 mm screens were not used in the lithic analysis.

All lithic artefacts were analysed according to a predefined scheme. The main aim was to reconstruct activity sets of lithic technology, as defined by Collins (1975; see also Driskell 1986). A secondary aim was to test whether the NE3 area is similar to NE1 by comparing their lithic assemblages (for a comparison of the faunal remains from these two areas see chapter 5). Finally, the lithic assemblages have been compared with contemporary sites across the region.

3.2   Artefact distribution

Only at NE 1 was it possible to do inter-site comparisons. Artefacts were collected at NE1 using three different techniques: excavation and systematic sieving of the test units; collection of material from the surface in a non-systematic manner; and collecting of material during preparation of the sections along the road at the site. No sieving was done during the preparation of these sections, so that the findings are likely biased towards the larger artefacts in this case.

Table 3.1 shows the frequencies of lithic artefacts found in each test unit. Test unit 1 contained most of the lithic sample from the excavations. This high frequency of lithics is correlated with the thickness of the shell-midden there, which was thickest in this unit. Most lithic artefacts were found in the arbitrary levels which correspond with stratum 3b, the densely concentrated shell layer (cf. chapter 2). Little variation in terms of lithic raw material types was found between the different units (table 3.2). Flint and volcanic rock were the two major rock types excavated in all four units. The other types were found in smaller quantities and they differ more between the excavation units.

By comparing the artefacts from the test units with the artefacts collected from the surface and the profile sections, some differences were seen (table 3.1). Among the profile section and surface finds, one type of artefact, a percussion hammerstone, was found which is lacking in the subsurface deposits reflected by the test units. The preparation of the profile sections yielded two artefacts which might have been used as hammerstones or anvils. A similar artefact was also recovered from the test units, but it is smaller and its use-wear is less obvious. Another difference was found among the volcanic flakes, where two flakes from the surface and the profile sections were significantly larger. Differences between samples from the test units and other finds, were also seen among the shell artefacts (cf. chapter 4). The differences suggest that the lithic sample from the test units only includes a portion of the total lithic artefact assemblage presented at the site and that statements about stone working at Norman Estate based on these findings are inconclusive.

At NE3, most of the lithic artefacts were collected from the arbitrary layer of 15-25 cm below the surface. No distinct human occupational levels were noticed in the profile sections, and the artefacts and related food remains probably have been scattered within the Amerindian occupation level.

3.3   Raw materials

Different raw materials were identified among the lithic artefacts. Besides these rock types, both red (10YR 7/8) and yellow (2.5 YR 4/6) haematite in the form of unmodified pieces were recorded. The yellow type was quite abundant. The degree of haematite use, however, could not be specified since both types can be found naturally scattered throughout the Norman Estate area. Frequent association of this material with other preceramic sites in the region makes it probable that haematite was in fact used for some purpose at the site (Lundberg 1989). A clear difference exists between NE1 and NE3 in terms of the amount of volcanic rock in the lithic sample, far less volcanic rock was used at NE3, where flint and, to a lesser degree, red-stone were used.

	Unit 1	Unit 2	Unit 4	Unit 5	Surface	Section	Total NE1	Unit 6 NE3
Flake	31	20	22	24	7	12	116	39
	56.4	52.6	66.7	70.6	58.3	36.4	56.6	65.0
Shatter	6	2	–	–	1	–	9	4
	10.9	5.3	0.0	0.0	8.3	0.0	4.4	6.7
Flake Core	1	4	3	–	1	1	10	1
	1.8	10.5	9.1	0.0	8.3	3.0	4.9	1.7
Hammerstone	–	–	–	–	–	3	3	–
	0.0	0.0	0.0	0.0	0.0	9.1	1.5	0.0
Hammerstone / anvil	1	1	–	–	1	5	8	–
	1.8	2.6	0.0	0.0	8.3	15.2	3.9	0.0
Rubbing/grinding stone	2	1	2	4	1	1	11	–
	3.6	2.6	6.1	11.8	8.3	3.0	5.4	0.0
Unmodified water-worn pebbles	11	8	6	5	–	10	40	5
	20.0	21.1	18.2	14.7	0.0	30.3	19.5	8.3
Other	1	–	–	–	–	–	1	–
	1.8	0.0	0.0	0.0	0.0	0.0	0.5	0.0
Unidentified	2	2	–	1	1	1	7	11
	3.6	5.3	0.0	2.9	0.0	3.0	3.4	18.3
Total	55	38	33	34	12	33	205	60
	100.0	100.0	100.0	100.0	100.0	100.0	100.0	100.0

Table 3.1. Amounts and percentages of artefact types found in the test units, sections, and on the surface at NE1 and NE3.

Flint

The flint artefacts are all small and typically lack their outer, cortical surface. These circumstances make it difficult to classify the flint into different raw material types, keeping in mind the variability of colour and grain size that can exist within one nodule of flint.

One large group of fine-grained flint was recognized, in which macroscopically visible fossils were not present. The only clasts visible in this type of flint are small (less than 1 mm) round, white, unidentifiable clasts. Colour differences were present within this type, ranging from black, dark-light grey, brown, (very) pale brown to yellow. Within this group some specimens are banded. The macroscopic similarity with flint from Long Island, an islet to the north of Antigua, has been further proven by petrological and chemical analyses (Knippenberg 1995; Knippenberg et al. 1995).

Along with this majority type of fine-grained flint other specimens significantly differ from the fine-grained group, having a coarser grain size and containing lithic clasts and diaclases. This coarser flint may represent a second source area, but this remains uncertain.

Red-stone

Numerous pieces of red-coloured rock were recovered; these are (very) dusky red to dark red. This type is generally not isotropic, and is composed of small particles (3 mm in size) having the same colour and fine grain size. Therefore, it does not fracture uniformly with a clear conchoidal form, making flakes difficult to identify. Due to this irregular form, it could not be determined whether many specimens are unequivocal artefacts.

Volcanic and hypabyssal rock

Volcanic and hypabyssal rock artefacts were found in the form of flakes and water-worn pebbles. The second group was difficult to analyze geologically because the water-worn surface has made it difficult to distinguish grain size and grain type, however differences are present among the different types, especially in colour.

Limestone

Fine-grained limestone was found in small quantities, both in the form of water-worn rocks and flaked material. Two different types of limestone were distinguished. The water-worn

	Unit 1	Unit 2	Unit 4	Unit 5	Total NE1	NE3 Unit 6
Flint	19 34.5	14 36.8	12 36.4	10 29.4	55 34.4	38 63.3
Limestone	3 5.5	7 18.4	3 9.1	3 8.8	16 10.0	6 10.0
Volcanic rock	21 38.2	9 23.7	10 30.3	15 44.1	55 34.4	9 15.0
Hypabyssal rock	5 9.1	– 0.0	– 0.0	2 5.9	7 4.4	– 0.0
Red stone	4 7.3	5 13.2	7 21.2	2 5.9	18 11.3	5 8.3
Unidentified	3 5.5	3 7.9	1 3.0	2 5.9	9 5.6	2 3.3
Total	55 100.0	38 100.0	33 100.0	34 100.0	160 100.0	60 100.0

Table 3.2. Amounts and percentages of rock types found in each test unit.

pebbles consist of a fine-grained silicified rock, which is similar to the cherty carbonate found at Anse des Pères (cf. chapter 8). However, these cobbles may or may not be artefacts. The other type, from which flakes were made, is less chert-like in appearance and has a coarser grain size.

3.4 Lithic technology

Part of the lithic technology seemed to have aimed at simply producing flakes of flint and red-stone, no systematically formed flaked tools were being produced. Further, there are volcanic, hypabyssal, and limestone flakes which could not be ascribed to a technology, due to the absence of related core artefacts produced by the lithic reduction. A third group consists of unworked water-worn pebbles which had been modified by use only.

Flint and red-stone material
Flint and red-stone were worked using a technology aimed at production of flakes. The flint artefacts offered the possibility to analyze the characteristics of this technology. Due to the nature of the red-stone, technological traits were difficult to identify, making this material of limited value for investigation of the lithic technology. The small frequencies of the red-stone artefacts hampered reconstruction of the different activity sets related to this material. In the following sections, the activity sets of the flake technology are discussed, where possible.

3.4.1   ACQUISITION AND SELECTION OF RAW MATERIAL
No flint occurrences are known on the island of St. Martin (Christman 1953). Study of the provenance of the flint revealed that the majority of the flint seemingly originated

from the flint source on Long Island near Antigua; the origin of the other flint artefacts is completely unknown (Knippenberg 1995). This exotic, non-local origin is supported by the absence of unworked or only slightly worked nodules in the available lithic sample.

The source of the red-stone is unknown. However the discovery of several unmodified blocks and the minor reduction which most cores had undergone indicate that the red-stone is likely to be locally available on or around St. Martin. As no references are made in the geological literature, the provenance of this material needs to be further investigated in the future.

3.4.2   PRIMARY REDUCTION AND CORE PREPARATION
Primary flint flakes (with 75-100% outer surface) are almost absent in the available samples indicating primary reduction of flint nodules did not take place at either site (fig. 3.1). It probably occurred at or near the source area for practical reasons. Verpoorte (1993) has shown that preceramic flint knappers initially reduced their blade cores at the source on Long Island near Antigua before transport to other areas. In light of the probable non-sedentary life ways of preceramic people in this region, this strategy would reduce the weight of rock, which had to be transported. In any case no signs of any core preparation were found among the flint specimens. The analysis of the red-stone cores revealed that primary reduction of the cores was undertaken at both sites since all of them were still in their initial stage of reduction, exhibiting one or two flake scars. These cores also revealed that core preparation was not undertaken; rather the flakes were struck off wherever possible.

Artefact type	N		Length (cm)	Width (cm)	Thickness (cm)	Weight (gm)
Complete flake	20	Mean	1.5 ± 0.5	1.7 ± 0.8	0.6 ± 0.4	1.5 ± 2.1
		Range	0.5 - 2.4	0.9 - 4.2	0.1 - 1.6	0.1 - 9.1
Modified flake	9	Mean	1.8 ± 0.6	1.6 ± 0.6	0.9 ± 0.4	2.1 ± 1.5
		Range	1.2 - 3.0	1.1 - 2.7	0.3 - 1.5	0.6 - 5.0
Flake fragment	13	Mean	1.4 ± 1.3	1.4 ± 0.7	0.5 ± 0.3	0.5 ± 0.5
		Range	0.6 - 5.7	0.6 - 3.0	0.2 - 1.4	0.1 - 2.0
Shatter	8	Mean	1.0 ± 0.3	0.7 ± 0.2	0.4 ± 0.2	0.3 ± 0.1
		Range	0.8 - 1.6	0.4 - 1.1	0.2 - 0.7	0.1 - 0.45
Flake core	3	Mean	2.6 ± 0.8	1.9 ± 0.3	1.3 ± 0.3	5.7 ± 3.2
		Range	1.7 - 3.2	1.6 - 2.2	1.1 - 1.6	2.0 - 8.0

Table 3.3. NE1: length, width, thickness, and weight of the flint artefacts.

Artefact type	N		Length (cm)	Width (cm)	Thickness (cm)	Weight (gm)
Complete flake	13	Mean	1.1 ± 0.3	1.3 ± 0.6	0.3 ± 0.2	0.4 ± 0.4
		Range	0.8 - 1.6	0.5 - 2.5	0.1 - 0.7	0.1 - 1.6
Modified flake	2	Mean	1.4 ± 0.2	1.8 ± 0.4	1.0 ± 0.5	2.2 ± 2.3
		Range	1.2 - 1.5	1.5 - 2.0	0.6 - 1.3	0.6 - 3.8
Flake fragment	8	Mean	1.2 ± 0.5	1.1 ± 0.6	0.4 ± 0.1	0.5 ± 0.5
		Range	0.8 - 2.2	0.5 - 2.3	0.2 - 0.6	0.1 - 1.7
Shatter	3	Mean	1.4 ± 0.6	0.9 ± 0.4	0.6 ± 0.1	0.6 ± 0.4
		Range	0.9 - 2.1	0.5 - 1.2	0.5 - 0.7	0.2 - 1.0
Flake core	–	Mean	–	–	–	–
		Range	–	–	–	–

Table 3.4. NE3: length, width, thickness, and weight of the flint artefacts.

3.4.3 CORE REDUCTION

The discovery of both flint cores and flint flakes clearly reflects that flint knapping occurred in both areas at Norman Estate. Four flake cores and four flakes, which had been used as cores after flaking were distinguished. One core was found at NE3 and the others were recovered from NE1. Most cores were classified as polyhedral (Hutcheson and Callow 1986) (fig. 3.2a). Flakes were removed in any direction from any platform possible in this case. Two other types of cores include double and single platform specimens (Hutcheson and Callow 1986) (fig. 3.2b). All cores are very small ranging from 16 to 32 mm in maximum length. Along with the small flake scars, remains of larger flake scars from earlier reduction stages are visible on the cores. These cores might have been classified differently, when discarded in an earlier stage of reduction. However, most cores are exhausted, possessing shattered sides which indicate that flaking was unsuccessful during the last stages of reduction. This non-systematic method of flaking produced an amorphous set of small flakes (table 3.3 and 3.4). Complete

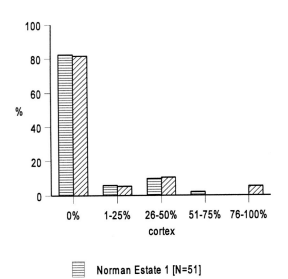

Fig. 3.1. Percentages of cortex on flint flakes.

		N	%
Bulb of force	Pronounced	15	50.0
	Diffuse	14	46.7
Point of percussion	Clear	17	56.7
	Vague	13	43.3
Cone of percussion	Clear	8	26.7
	Vague	22	73.3
Butt	Lipped	27	90.0
	Unlipped	3	10.0
Conchoidal fracture marks on the bulb	Pronounced	11	36.7
	Indistinct	19	63.3

Table 3.5. Characteristics related to the mode of flaking after Ohnuna & Bergman (1982). Sample size = 30.

flakes, flake fragments, and modified flakes are present in the overall sample. Most flakes possess hinged ends which are attributable to this non-systematic method of flaking and the exhaustive use of the cores (fig. 3.3). Most striking platforms were plain (with flake scars) on specimens from both sites (fig. 3.4).

Given the size of the cores which are very small, bipolar flaking may have been used in the last stages of reduction. However, actual evidence that the core rested upon an anvil during the reduction was not discovered.

The results of the analysis of the flakes for the presence of traits relating to flaking techniques are difficult to interpret (table 3.5). The quantitative data do not reflect that hard hammer direct freehand percussion was the only technique used, for diffuse bulbs of force and vague cones of percussion,

traits uncommon for this flaking mode, occur frequently (Ohnuna and Bergman 1982). This difference may be the result of the type of hammer. Soft stone hammers or exhaustively used hard-stone hammers may generate flakes which possess diffuse bulbs and vague cones of percussion (Beuker 1983; Ohnuna and Bergman 1982). The use of a bipolar technique, although not recognized among the flakes, may have blurred the characteristics (Rostain 1994). Whether the small size of the flakes has any consequences for the development of the characteristics analysed, has not been tested and remains uncertain. It can be concluded that at least hard hammer freehand direct percussion was used in the lithic reduction. The quantitative data and the size of the cores, however, have established that this technique may not have been the only technique used; the bipolar technique may have been applied too.

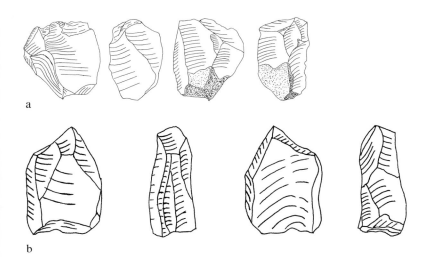

a

b

Fig. 3.2. Flint cores: a. polyhedral flint core, the upper face exhibits a shattered surface, b. double platformed flint core (scale 1:1.).

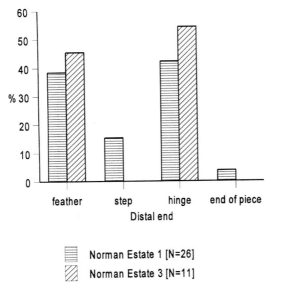

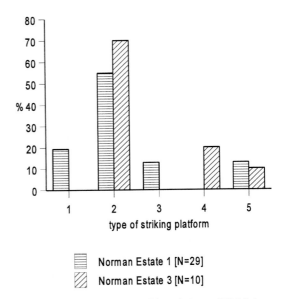

Fig. 3.3. Percentages of type of distal end of flint flakes. Sample size NE1= 26, sample size NE3= 11.

Fig. 3.4. Percentages of type of striking platform of flint flakes. 1= outer surface (cortex), 2= plain (scarnegative), 3= two scarnegatives, 4= scar negative + diaclase, 5= punctiform. Sample size NE1= 29, sample size NE3= 10.

The frequency of red-stone flakes is too small to make any reliable statements about its reduction. The flakes fall within the size range of the flint material. Among the cores, only initially reduced cores were found, as noted above. This shows that the red-stone was only worked to a limited degree and this material may have been tried as an alternative to the flint.

3.4.4 SHAPING OF THE TOOLS
No signs of intentional retouch were found on any of the flint and red-stone flakes. Some flint flakes were produced that may have been useful for certain tasks, but these forms may not have been intentionally shaped. Other flakes, however, were further modified to produce additional flakes.

3.4.5 USE
From the morphological point of view no standardized tool shapes were apparently aimed at. The aim of the flint knappers at Norman Estate, was the production of suitable cutting edges, rather than specific tool forms. None of the artefacts possess clear macroscopic use retouch. The actual use of the artefacts has to be determined using more sophisticated techniques. Several potential tools, possessing sharp edges or sharp points, were found among the overall lithic sample. No research has been done on the actual function of chipped tools from the preceramic period in the Caribbean, although various ideas have been suggested in the past. It is likely that the small sharp flint flakes had been used to

process fish. They would also have been suitable to work fibers, and light woodworking tasks. In the case of heavy woodworking, such as cutting, scraping, and sawing, most edges among the lithic sample were too thin (cf. O'Miller 1979).

The red-stone is problematic in terms of its usage. Its characteristics make recognition of use retouch difficult. Although the flakes sometimes possess sharp edges, they are not as sharp as the flint material in general.

3.4.6 REUSE
No signs of resharpening were found within the lithic sample for Norman Estate.

3.4.7 DISCARD
At NE1, all lithic artefacts were discarded within a distinct refuse deposit. At NE3, the concentration of flint material is significantly higher. The association of the lithic artefacts with fish bones at NE3 may indicate that fish was being processed using the flint flakes.

Although lithic working took place in both areas no refitting was possible. At NE3, this could partly be ascribed to post-depositional processes which have disturbed the original provenance of the artefacts. At NE1, these processes had only affected the horizontal position of the artefacts. In any case, the absence of fits in both areas can only be explained by the fact that lithic working did not take place in the

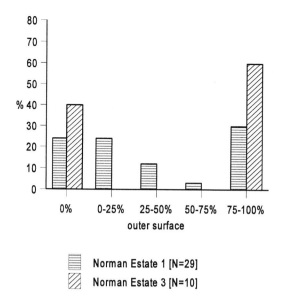

Fig. 3.5. Percentages of water-worn (outer) surface on volcanic and hypabyssal rock flakes. Sample size NE1= 32, sample size NE3= 5.

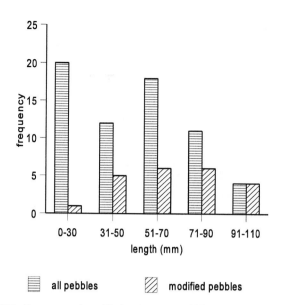

Fig. 3.6. Frequency of modified water-worn pebbles compared with the frequency of total waterworn pebbles by length.

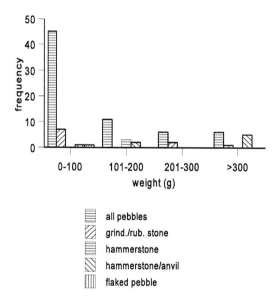

Fig. 3.7. Frequency of type of modification compared to frequency of total water-worn pebbles by weight.

midden area itself. Only individual pieces had been discarded in the midden.

3.4.8   COMPARISON BETWEEN FLINT FROM NE1 AND NE3
The results from the flint analysis show that flakes from both NE1 and NE3 are small in size, generally do not possess any outer cortical surface, frequently possess hinged and stepped distal parts, plain striking platforms, and were not chipped into standardized tool forms. For cores, the comparison is less possible since only one flake used as a core was recovered at NE3. Yet, this single artefact clearly corresponds to these from NE1, where most cores had been flaked from any direction possible. These close similarities point out that both flint assemblages were produced in a similar way. This supports the idea that both assemblages were made by the same group of people. Whether this has occurred simultaneously or over time can not be established on the basis of the available evidence.

Volcanic, hypabyssal, and limestone rock flakes
The absence of any cores or core fragments made out of volcanic, hypabyssal, or limestone rock makes the flake assemblage of these rock types difficult to interpret. The primary hypabyssal and volcanic rock flakes show that water-worn pebbles had been used as core material (fig. 3.5). This is not clear for the limestone flakes. All three rocktypes most likely have originated on St. Martin itself. Volcanic and hypabyssal outcrops occur at different places on the island and different types of limestones can be found within the Pointe Blanche and Low Lands formation

(Christman 1953). The water-worn rocks may have been obtained from the small stream, Ravine Caréta, a few hundred metres to the south, or from the nearby coastal zone, which were exploited by the Amerindians for the gathering of shells and the catching of reef fish (cf. chapters 4 and 5).

It remains unclear whether these different rock types were used to produce core tools, or flake tools. It can be hypothesized that these flakes were generated during the production of core tools such as axes. These tools are most likely to occur less frequently within a refuse dump than would-be flake cores, because they are more carefully curated and are often lost or discarded at places where they are used (in case of axes, the forest). The analysis of the shell artefacts reveals that the Amerindians at NE1 were familiar with the technique of grinding (cf. chapter 4). The use of stone axes, therefore, can not be excluded.

This lack of core tools and cores in general, limits conclusions about the whole lithic assemblage from the two Norman Estate sites. The excavated sample does not seem to be representative of the entire inventory of artefact types which were made and/or used by the Amerindians at Norman Estate.

Water-worn pebbles

A substantial number of water-worn pebbles was found in the test units at NE1 and NE3, as well as on the surface and from the profile sections. These rounded rocks do not occur naturally in either site area, so they must have been brought there by the preceramic Amerindians.

No signs of any deliberate shaping to make tools were found on these pebbles. Some, however, do show signs of possible human alteration due to use. The ascription of these traces to human alteration, instead of post-depositional processes, is in some cases very subjective. Three types of modification were recorded: abrasion, pits, and flake scars. The first type of modification may be the result of two objects touching each other, in which the movement is parallel to the surface of contact, whether intentional or unintentional. The second and the third types of alteration are the result of two objects touching each other, where the movement is perpendicular to the surface of contact. Figures 3.6 and 3.7 show that most modification occurs on the larger and heavier pebbles in the available sample. This, most likely, indicates human modification. Comparison with other preceramic sites suggests that most used water-worn rocks are larger than 30 mm (cf. for example Veloz Maggiolo and Ortega 1973, 25, 38-39; Lundberg 1989, 107-108, 111-112). This agrees with the Norman Estate sample. Another striking fact is the near absence of modified limestone pebbles. Most modified pebbles are volcanic or hypabyssal rocks. Only one limestone pebble possesses a flake scar. This preference towards volcanic and hypabyssal rock can be explained by its higher density and a lesser inclination to break, both of which are preferable properties when using it as a hammerstone or an anvil.

NE1 and NE3 differ in the amount of their used water-worn pebbles. Only one water-worn pebble possessing a flake scar was found at NE3, but NE1 produced a larger number. This difference may be the result of the different activities reflected on these areas, given that NE1 was a refuse area where a wider range of artefacts than at a single activity area may be expected.

Rubbing stones

Abrasion is the most common type of modification in the available sample of water-worn pebbles. It occurs mostly in small areas with a limited degree of abrasion. Some specimens show more significant abrasion (fig. 3.8a-b). These artefacts might have been used for rubbing tasks during the processing of, for example, vegetal foods or some comparable task.

Hammerstones

Small pits are the second most common types of modification among the water-worn lithic artefacts. Only two pebbles with such pits were found in the test units. Most came from the profile sections and the surface. These latter specimens possess more significant modifications. Two morphological types can be distinguished: an elongated type with pits on one or both ends (fig. 3.8c), and a round type with pits on the flat face (fig. 3.8d,e). The first type is likely to have been used as a hammerstone for stone working, and the second type may have been used either as a crushing stone for nuts, haematite, or shells, or it could have been used as an anvil against which objects were crushed (Rostain 1994). Specimen NE Pr3/4 (fig. 3.8e) especially has the size and shape to be a suitable anvil.

Only two pebbles with flake scars were recorded. In one case, it was uncertain whether the flake scar was cultural or natural. In the other case, only one flake scar is present together with pits, both on the end. The co-occurrence of pits and a flake scar, plus the location of both traces on the end, and the elongated shape of the pebble seemingly indicates that this artefact was used as hammerstone for flaking. The flake scar was probably produced accidentally during use of the hammerstone.

3.5   Comparison with contemporary sites

In this section, the lithic sample from Norman Estate is compared with contemporary sites in the region, particularly the local region. The comparisons focus on the distinction between variability which is the result of cultural habits, and variability which is the result of environmental or raw material factors.

In the local region, the Jolly Beach site on Antigua is contemporary with Norman Estate (Davis 1982). Whitehead's Bluff on the neighbouring island of Anguilla is younger (Crock et al. 1995). The lithic assemblages from both sites show differences with that from Norman Estate. The main difference is the absence of ground lithic artefacts at Norman

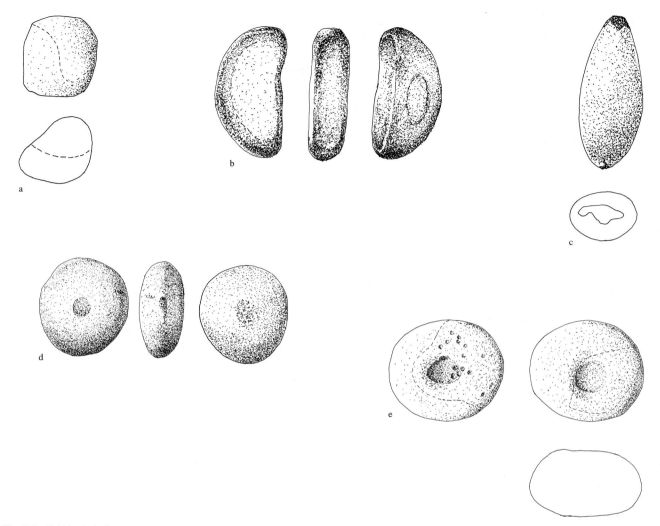

Fig. 3.8. Rubbing/grinding stones, hammerstones and hammer/anvils: a. rubbing/grinding stone, volcanic rock, abraded surface within dotted line (scale 1:2), b. rubbing/grinding stone, limestone (scale 1:2), c. hammerstone, volcanic rock, pits on both ends of the artefact (scale 1:2), d. hammerstone/anvil, volcanic rock, pits on both faces and on one side (scale 1:3), e. hammerstone/anvil, volcanic rock, profound modifications on both faces (scale 1:3).

Estate. At Jolly Beach and Whitehead's Bluff, ground lithic artefacts, such as axes and enigmatic, perhaps symbolic objects, were only found in relatively small quantities (Davis 1982; Crock et al. 1995). Their absence at Norman Estate may be the result of the small size of the available sample, or perhaps it reflects site-specific activities there.

A second difference can be seen in the technology of the flint working. At Jolly Beach and other undated preceramic sites on Antigua, blade production was the main technology used (Davis 1982, 1993; Verpoorte 1993). An abundance of flint at different places on Antigua (Martin-Kaye 1959; Verpoorte 1993) may have made it possible for the

Amerindians to develop a blade technology (Davis 1993; Verpoorte 1993).

At Whitehead's Bluff, only one blade and some cores with traces of blade production were found, together with a substantial amount of flake cores and flakes (Crock et al. 1995). Crock et al. hypothesize on the basis of macroscopic similarities that the flint at the Whitehead's Bluff site originated on Antigua. This exotic origin would explain why the Amerindians made extensive use of the flakes (Crock et al. 1995).

If an Antiguan origin is valid, the Whitehead's Bluff example shows that limited lithic resources influence the technology used with a shift from blade technology towards a focus on flake technology. This again stresses the importance of the points Pantel (1991) made concerning the possible environmental (instead of cultural) cause of technological differences. Looking at the Norman Estate material, it has been determined that the majority of the flint likely originated at Long Island near Antigua. Therefore, the use of a flake technology rather than one based on blades may be at least partially ascribed to the limited availability of flint, an environmental variable, rather than cultural differences alone.

All three lithic samples from the Lesser Antilles are similar in another respect: the absence of secondary working, since none of the samples revealed the use of rechipping on the blades or flakes. This characteristic makes the Antiguan blades different from the blades found at Levisa and similar sites in the Greater Antilles (Koslowski 1974). This lack of secondary working in the Norman Estate samples may reflect a difference in attitude towards tool production. The absence of secondary working indicates that the flakes had an ad-hoc use, and shows that little attention was paid to the durability of the tools. In contrast, rechipping and shaping the tools, where present, show that more time was spent to produce them, time which was repaid by an increased durability. Secondary working may also result in a more economic use of the raw materials with respect to cutting edges, an important trait for non-sedentary people, at least in some cases (Parry and Kelly 1987).

The absence of secondary working in association with scarcity of raw material seems illogical from a functional, adaptive point of view. Therefore, this co-occurrence at Norman Estate seems to reflect cultural practices, at least in part, rather than simply an adaption to environmental conditions. Again, it should be noted that the preceramic flint technologies from Whitehead's Bluff, Jolly Beach, and Norman Estate are somewhat different. These differences, however, are more likely due to environmental rather than cultural differences.

A very small tool assemblage comes from the two preceramic occupational levels at the Sugar factory Pier site on St. Kitts. The older level was contemporary with Norman Estate. The main similarity with Norman Estate is the use of the shell celt and flake lithic technology. No flint was found, however; only basalt was used for the production of flakes. Armstrong (1980) noted that preceramic Amerindians at Sugar Factory Pier only exploited St. Kitts for their lithic resources, which is quite different from the Amerindians at Norman Estate. Considering the limited size of the excavations at Sugar Factory Pier and the small sample of lithic artefacts recovered, the absence of certain artefacts such as core tools may be simply the result of the limited sample size. The absence of flint artefacts, however, can not be merely ascribed to the sample size given that flint was abundant in the samples from Norman Estate and Whitehead's Bluff.

In the Virgin Islands, Vieques, and Puerto Rico, sites with generally similar artefacts to Norman Estate are known. Most of these sites are younger than Norman Estate. However, one date goes back to ca. 3500 BP (Lundberg 1989, 1991). At Krum Bay, a well investigated site, the same flaking technology as Norman Estate is seemingly represented. The main difference between Norman Estate and Krum Bay, is the presence of bifacially worked, celt shaped artefacts at the latter. The small lithic sample from Norman Estate limits sound comparisons in terms of whether or not this is a cultural difference. One clear difference between these sites may be ascribed to different cultural habits, namely, the use of shell celts at Norman Estate. Shell celts are lacking at Krum Bay, which was thoroughly sampled. No environmental restrictions on the use of *Strombus gigas* seem pertinent at Krum Bay, considering the fact they used the *Strombus gigas* to make other artefacts.

Contemporary sites in the Greater Antilles, such as El Porvenir and Damajayabo have yielded a broader range of lithic artefacts (Koslowski 1974). Ground lithic artefacts, such as axes, grinders, mortars, anvil stones and stone balls occur alongside shell artefacts such as axes, vessels, dishes, beads and pendants. Among the flint artefacts, the products of both flake and blade technology have been recognized.

At Hoyo de Toros, the main difference in contrast to Norman Estate is the discovery of stone axes and coral bowls; the remaining tooltypes include manos, mortars, and choppers (Veloz Maggiolo and Ortega 1973). Within the middle strata of Levisa mainly flint artefacts, such as blades and flakes with and without rechipping, were found together with shell beads (Koslowski 1974). The Funche assemblage seems most similar to the Norman Estate assemblage. An expedient flake technology and other lithic artefacts, such as hammers and anvils, were found together with shell vessels and ground shell specimens such as axes and beads (Koslowski 1974).

3.6 Conclusions

The lithic samples from NE1 and NE3 indicate that both were produced using similar technologies. Whether both lithic assemblages were formed simultaneously by the same group of people remains unknown, but it seems they were closely related in any case.

The lithic samples from both areas are obviously limited. This is partly due to the fact that certain artefact types are missing. For example, lithic core tools were made there on the basis of the available evidence, but none have been recovered thus far. The absence of these artefacts and perhaps others, limits final conclusions about the complete lithic assemblage made and used by the preceramic Amerindians at Norman Estate.

Among the recovered lithic artefacts, a distinction can be made between three groups. The first group is associated with an expedient flake technology. Flakes were removed from flake cores, wherever possible, using direct freehand percussion and in the last stages probably the bipolar technique. Little to no core preparation is evident. The aim of this technology was the production of sharp edges, rather than specific tool types. The flakes and debitage produced show no signs of any rechipping. However, modification after flaking did occur.

These artefacts were probably used for scraping, cutting, and drilling tasks. Two rock-types were associated with this technology: flint and red-stone. Flint artefacts form the largest group the red-stone, was probably used as a substitute for the non-local flint, given that its flaking properties seem poor.

The second group includes unworked water-worn pebbles, mainly made of volcanic rock, which could be obtained locally. About 36% of these pebbles possess signs of modifications due to probable use. These include pits and abrasion, resulting from use as hammerstones and rubbing stones, respectively. It would seem that the Amerindians chose certain shapes of pebbles for certain tasks.

Along with these two groups of artefacts, volcanic, hypabyssal, and limestone flakes were also found, which can not be associated with a specific reduction technology yet. Although a large part of the volcanic and hypabyssal flakes possess water-worn outer surfaces, indicating that water-worn pebbles were used as cores, no cores or core tools, of volcanic or hypabyssal rock have been recovered to date. Comparison with contemporary sites in the region reveals that the lithic assemblages from Jolly Beach on Antigua, and Whitehead's Bluff on Anguilla differ from the Norman Estate assemblages on the basis of the available information. These differences, however, seem to be the result of environmental restrictions and sample size, rather than cultural habits perse. At Sugar Factory Pier on St. Kitts, a clear difference from Norman Estate can be seen in lithic exploitation, which was orientated strictly towards local raw material sources. This is clearly different for the lithics recovered from Norman Estate. The small sample from Norman Estate again hampers comparison with sites such as Krum Bay. Nonetheless, differences between Norman Estate and Krum Bay do seem apparent among the shell artefacts. In the greater Antilles, preceramic lithic samples often include a broader range of artefact types such as ground stone tools and other objects. The meanings of these local and regional variations in the lithic (and other) industries remains to be worked out in the future.

4   Shell

Alex J. Brokke

4.1   Introduction

There are two orders of importance among shellfish including the Gastropoda or snails, and Pelecypoda or bivalves. The gastropods have a single spiral shell coiled around its own axis. About 75% of the West Indian marine shells belong to this class (Humfrey 1975). They live in every conceivable environment, but the majority lives in shallow water close to shore. Most of these species do not like sunlight and hide under rocks or are buried in the sand during the day. Many species have dedicated themselves to a particular environment such as in mud, mangrove swamps or on the reef. All gastropod species are mobile and although they typically hide during the day they roam around at night looking for food. Their feeding habits range from carnivorous to vegetarian, the Queen Conch being a famous example of the latter, but most species are omnivorous. Pelecypoda or bivalves have paired valves joined with a hinge so that the animal can open and close its shell. The hinge is very useful for identification of the different species. Bivalves are not only sedentary but they also have the capability to move. Most of them live in muddy or sandy substrates, buried just below the surface, others are attached to more solid objects such as rocks. They feed through filtering water and extracting minute organisms with their gills.

4.2   Methods and strategies

The Norman Estate site can be described as a "blanket midden". These middens are generally homogeneous, have no discernable strata, often cover a large area, and possibly only reflect a single activity or occupation (Waselkov 1982). The last remark is difficult to certify based on the limited investigation at Norman Estate.

In the midden area, six square metre units were excavated. Only the shells from the 10 mm sieve were used for this analysis. The fragments in the smaller sieves were often too small for identification and do not seem useful for the analysis. All complete shells and shell fragments from the 10 mm sieve were counted and weighed. Weighing is the fastest method to estimate the total minimum number of individual shells represented on the basis of the weight of a modern specimen for a given species. This method, however, is somewhat compromised in archaeological sites where leaching has

reduced the weight of the shells (Waselkov 1982, 77). To estimate the weight loss in a midden one can measure the shells, take their weight, and compose them into modern specimens. The time involved is about the same as simply counting and weighing the individual shells, without bothering about the weight loss as compared to modern specimens. Another problem occurs when only weights are used since there are obvious differences between species. *Codakia orbicularis*, for example, is a fairly large bivalve that breaks relatively easy due to the thinness of the shell. As a result almost no complete valves of these species were recovered at Norman Estate. The individual count, only needing the hinge which is the strongest part of the valve, was about two percent to almost 15 percent of the total sample (both complete shells and countable pieces). On the other hand, *Chama sarda*, another bivalve, is thicker and less likely to break than is *Codakia*. For *Chama sarda*, more complete valves were recovered and fewer examples were represented in the individual and fragment categories.

Therefore, counting was considered adequate for analysis of the shells from Norman Estate. As most of the species are bivalves, it was necessary to count the valves separately as left and right valves. Among the bivalves, when the fragments bore a single characteristic such as the hinge, they were assigned to the individual category. Together these represent the amount of individuals brought to the site by the preceramic Amerindians. The percentages of the total count of individuals present in every unit are regarded, meaning complete and individual valves are added because the completeness or size of the fragment is not necessarily important. For the main species, all the counts are summed up and in the column total, the percentage of left/right valves are also calculated compared to the total count. Fragments were weighed and for the main species the percentage of the total weight is given. Time did not allow calculation of the mean weight for every species using the fragment weight to estimate the minimum number of individuals represented.

4.3   Exploited shell species

At Norman Estate, the exploited shell species occur in the following order of importance (cf. tables 4.1-4.4 for shellfish composition in units 1, 2, 4, and 5):

Species	Complete left valves	Complete right valves	Individual left valves	Individual right valves	Total left right	Fragm.
Arca zebra	4.9	6.6	26.4	24.2	62.1	50.4
Chama sarda	4.9	9.1	3.8	2.2	20.0	5.6
Plicatula gibbosa	4.1	1.9	1.1	0.8	7.9	0
Codakia orbicula ris	0	0.3	3.8	4.9	9.0	14.4

Table 4.1. Shell fish composition in Unit 5. Complete count Left and Right valves and Individual count Left and Right valves = 364. All values are percentages of 364 total Individuals. Fragment weight is 3513 g for all shells in Unit 5, percentage is from the total amount of 3513 g fragment weight. The Column Total reflects 99.1 percent of all Individuals present in Unit 5.

Species	Complete left valves	Complete right valves	Individual left valves	Individual right valves	Total left right	Fragm.
Arca zebra	5.9	7.4	24.3	23.5	61.1	43
Chama sarda	1.5	2.2	1.5	2.9	8.1	5.1
Plicatula gibbosa	0	2.2	0	0	2.2	0.2
Codakia orbicularis	0	0	4.4	2.9	7.3	8.1
Anadara notabilis	2.2	1.5	1.5	1.5	6.7	19.4
Pseudochama radians	9.6	0	0	0	9.6	0

Table 4.2. Shell fish composition in Unit 4. Complete count Left and Right valves and individual count Left and Right valves = 136 All values are percentages of 136 total Individuals. Fragment weight is 2883 g for all shells in Unit 4, percentage is from the total amount of 2883 g fragment weight. The Column Total reflects 94.7 percent of all Individuals present in Unit 4 (5.1% is represented by *Cittarium pica* and *Thais deltoida*).

Species	Complete left valves	Complete right valves	Individual left valves	Individual right valves	Total left right	Fragm.
Arca zebra	10	10.8	19.8	20.9	61.5	37.6
Chama sarda	3.4	7.1	2.4	3.4	16.3	3.3
Plicatula gibbosa	1	0.5	0.2	0.8	2.5	0.3
Codakia orbicularis	0.2	0.2	6.9	6.6	13.9	22.5
Anadara notabilis	0.3	0.6	1.1	1.5	3.5	22.5

Table 4.3. Shell fish composition in Unit 2. Complete count Left and Right valves and individual count Left and Right valves = 622 All values are percentages of 622 total Individuals. Fragment weight is 6029 g for all shells in Unit 2, percentage is from the total amount of 6029 g fragment weight. The Column Total reflects 97.6 percent of all Individuals present in Unit 22.

Species	Complete left valves	Complete right valves	Individual left valves	Individual right valves	Total left right	Fragm.
Arca zebra	4.8	5.7	22.2	21.3	54.0	44.3
Chama sarda	1.4	5.3	1.1	2.5	10.3	0.6
Plicatula gibbosa	1.2	1.2	0.5	1.2	4.1	0.5
Codakia orbicularis	0	0	11.9	14.7	26.6	20.3
Anadara notabilis	0.7	1.1	0.7	0.4	2.9	10.4

Table 4.4. Shell fish composition in Unit 1. The complete count of the left and right valves, and the individual count of Left and Right valves = 564. All values are percentages of 564 total Individuals. Fragment weight is 5401 g for all shells in Unit 1, percentage is from the total amount of 5401 g fragment weight. The Column Total reflects 98 percent of all Individuals present in Unit 1.

1) *Arca zebra* (Swainson 1883), popularly known as "Turkey Wing". It lives attached to rocks in one to 20 feet (± 0.30 to ± 7 metres) of water. These represent 59.4% of the total individuals and the fragments represent 43.8% of the total;

2) *Codakia orbicularis* (Linné 1758), popularly known as "Tiger Lucina", It is a common species on St.Martin living in muddy or sandy areas. Live shells are often exposed on the mud flats at low tide (Humfrey 1975) and they live at depths of one to 10 feet (± 0.30 to ± 3 metres) in the water. These represent 14% of the total individuals while the fragments amount to 13.8 %;

3) *Anadara notabilis* (Röding 1798), popularly known as "Eared Ark". It can be found on mud or grass bottoms in one to 6 feet (± 0.30 to ± 2 metres) of water. These represent 3.3% of the total individuals, while the fragments amount to 13.1 %;

4) *Chama sarda* (Reeve 1847), popularly known as "Red Jewel Box". It lives in rocky areas in one to 50 feet (± 0.30 to ± 16.5 metres) of water. These represent 3.7% of the total individuals and fragments constitute 3.7 %;

5) *Plicatula gibbosa* (Lamarck 1801), popularly known as "Kittens Paw". It lives attached to solid objects in at least 1 foot (± 0.30 metre) of water, but it also occurs in deeper water. These represent 4.2 % of the total individuals and fragments amount to 0.3 %; and

6) *Strombus gigas* (Linné 1758), popularly known as "Queen Conch". It lives in eel grass beds at depths of one to 60 feet (± 0.30 to ± 20 metres) below the surface. No complete specimens or individuals were recognized. Fragments amount to 11.5 %.

4.4 Gathering

Most of the shellfish gathering was undertaken in reef environments where *Arca zebra*, *Chama sarda* and *Plicatula gibbosa* were collected. *Codakia orbicularis* and *Anadara notabilis* reside on or in mud/sand substrates, as noted above. At present the western side of St.Martin is where reef species occur, whereas species that live in the sand are found both on the eastern and western sides of the island. Both settings are about the same distance from Norman Estate, and if both environments were exploited simultaneously, than the western side of the island seems to be the better location given both environmental types occur there. Gathering methods probably included, hand picking from the reefs and sifting the sand with the fingers or toes. The shells were then probably carried to the site in baskets where they were cooked or roasted.

4.5 Shell artefacts

A smaller number of shellfish species were used for artefact production than those that were presumably eaten. The total quantity is low as might be expected from a preceramic site. All shell artefacts were made from *Strombus gigas*. All these artefacts have been severely affected by post-depositional processes such as leaching. Their outer surfaces are brittle, much like chalk. Traces of manufacture and/or usewear have been obliterated by the alteration of the surface, making it sometimes difficult to recognize them as artefacts. Thus only four tools are represented, three made from the lip and one from the columella of *Strombus gigas*. These include:

– One celt fragment with a very clear cutting edge which was carefully ground (fig. 4.1a);

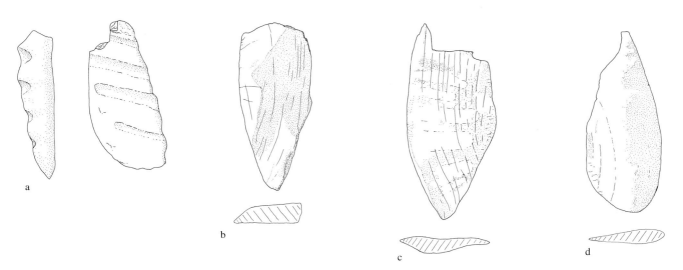

a

b

c

d

Fig. 4.1. Artefacts made of *Strombus gigas*: a. celt fragment (scale 1:3), b-d. three objects with a worked edge on the longest side (scale 1:3).

– Two objects made from the outer lip of *Strombus gigas*, both of which have a worked edge on the longest side. They have a triangular shape of which the diagonal side is the sharp edge (fig. 4.1b, c). A similar object also exhibits a cutting edge on the longest side, but the overall shape is rounded instead of triangular in this case (fig. 4.1d);
– A gouge was recovered, made from the columella of *Strombus gigas*, with a ground edge.

All the shell artefacts from Norman Estate are very badly preserved, making full interpretation difficult. No shell artefacts were recovered from the excavation units, suggesting perhaps that food production was the main activity undertaken there. However, the small sample of shell tools suggests other activities, such as woodcarving, were also undertaken by the Amerindian occupants.

4.6 Conclusions

Norman Estate fits within the pattern of preceramic sites known from elsewhere within the local and more distant region. A high dependency on a single shellfish species has also been reported for the Jolly Beach site and the South Pier site on Antigua (Davis 1982). Generally similar to Norman Estate, Krum Bay on St. Thomas shows this same pattern, with one species of shellfish again dominating the sample. On St. Kitts, the Sugar Factory Pier site produced two main species: *Anadara notabilis* and *Arca zebra* (Goodwin 1978), and although precise figures are not given, it seems much like Norman Estate, in this regard. Shell artefacts are difficult to compare mainly due to the small samples recovered from these sites. Still, Norman Estate seems fairly typical regarding the other preceramic sites in the region. One exception is the Whitehead's Bluff site on Anguilla, where the main shell species found is the *Cittarium pica* and the artefacts include shell vessels, a Casimiroid trait not present at Norman Estate (Crock et al. 1995). However, these authors link the Whitehead's Bluff site to sites in the region by emphasizing the marine oriented subsistence strategy, a feature that is also clearly present at Norman Estate.

5   Faunal exploitation

Mark Nokkert

5.1   Introduction

Research on preceramic resource exploitation in the northern Lesser Antilles has been relatively rare so far. The discovery of the preceramic Norman Estate site, on the island of St. Martin gave a great opportunity for the study of faunal exploitation by this preceramic group, which can be classified into the Ortoiroid series as defined by Rouse (1992). Faunal analyses of preceramic sites have, amongst others, been carried out for the Krum Bay site on St. Thomas (Lundberg 1989), and the Jolly Beach site on Antigua (Wing, pers. comm.). The geographical position of St. Martin, somewhere in the middle of these two islands, makes the Norman Estate site all the more interesting. In this chapter a picture of the basic food economy of the group that lived at the Norman Estate site will be given.

5.2   Sampling and identification methods

The 1993 survey and subsequent test excavations in the area of the Norman Estate site resulted in the discovery of at least two activity areas (cf. chapter 2). Both areas yielded animal bones, though there were clearly more bone and certainly more shell fragments present at NE1, the midden area, than was found at NE3, tentatively interpreted as a residence area.

All the dirt from the 1×1 m test units (6 in NE1 and 1 in NE3) was water-screened through three nested sieves with a 10 mm, a 4 mm and a 2.7 mm mesh screen. Ten samples of each 2.5% of the total weight of the material found in both the 2.7 and 4 mm screens were then taken out for analysis (cf. also chapter 2). Levels 2C and 5E from NE1 and level 6C from NE3 were analyzed.

Identification of the fauna from level 2C was done by comparing the remains to reference skeletons in the collections of the Florida Museum of Natural History in Gainsville. Samples from levels 5E and 6C were identified making use of the smaller reference collection of the Faculty of Pre-and Protohistory of the Leiden University in The Netherlands. This collection was made by Heleen van der Klift, for the identification of the faunal remains from the Golden Rock site at St. Eustatius (van der Klift 1992).

5.2.1   ZOOARCHAEOLOGICAL TECHNIQUES

The faunal analysis was done using standard zooarchaeological techniques (cf. Wing and Brown 1979). Quantification was done using NISP (the Number of Identified SPecimens), MNI (the Minimum Number of Individuals), and the weight of the bone fragments. Comparisons within and between the different levels are based on the MNI%, which is the percentage of the MNI of a certain species in a level in relation to the total MNI of that level. In this way one can start answering questions such as, 'which species were most abundant in the food economy?', 'what habitats did the inhabitants exploit?', and 'how can the overall food-pattern be compared to other sites in the region?'.

5.2.2   BIASES INVOLVED IN THE METHODS

Owing to the sampling procedures used for the site, slight biases might have come into the results of the analyses of the bone material. First of all, the mesh size of 2.7 mm, the smallest of the three screens in use, might not have been small enough. The mesh size of 2.7 mm was used for practical purposes. A smaller mesh size would have made the sieving procedures too time-consuming (it already took a lot of time to get the clayish soil to dissolve while sieving). To test whether the 2.7 mm mesh size would be too small for recovering all the faunal remains, small soil samples (0.5 litres) from different levels in different units were screened through a 1 mm screen. One of these samples (taken from level 2C) was analyzed. In this sample many bone fragments were found. Most of it consisted of unidentifiable pieces. The identifiable parts were mostly very small fish atlases, most of which were identified to Haemulidae (grunts). There also turned out to be a lot of elements belonging to Scaridae (parrotfish), mostly complete dentaries, premaxillaries and lower pharyngeals. Due to the fact that Scaridae comprise almost half of the MNI identified (cf. table 5.5), it is not very surprising to find bones belonging to this fish family in the 1 mm screen as well. However, the discovery of complete elements belonging to very small fish was surprising and has to be kept in mind when interpreting the results for a reconstruction of the fishing methods that have been used. The ratios of the various species were not much different in

TAXA	NISP	MNI	MNI %	WEIGHT (G)
Oryzomyini	1	1	0.8	0.20
TOTAL MAMMAL	1	1	0.8	0.20
Cheloniidae	1	1	0.8	0.76
Ameiva sp.	1	1	0.8	0.02
Unid. Lizard	1	–	–	0.01
TOTAL REPTILE	3	2	1.6	0.79
Belonidae	48	1	0.8	1.75
Sphyraenidae	3	1	0.8	0.08
Serranidae	5	2	1.6	0.95
cf. Serranidae	1	–	–	1.88
Caranx sp.	7	2	1.6	0.27
Carangidae	47	–	–	5.80
Lutjanidae	18	12	9.4	0.69
Haemulidae	30	22	17.3	0.94
Calamus sp.	1	1	0.8	0.01
Sparidae	5	–	–	0.15
cf. Sparidae	5	1	0.8 / [1.6]	0.20
Mullidae	4	4	3.1	0.05
cf. *Holacanthus* sp.	1	1	0.8	0.09
Labridae	7	1	0.8	0.93
Sparisoma sp.	282	56	44.1	23.85
Scarus sp.	19	6	4.7	0.44
Scaridae	100	–	– / [48.8]	3.76
Acanthuridae	36	9	7.1	0.94
Balistidae	7	1	0.8	0.23
Ostraciidae	4	1	0.8	0.03
Diodontidae	1	1	0.8	4.05
Unid. Fish	n.c.	2	1.6	32.93
TOTAL FISH	631	124	97.6	80.02
Unid. Bone	n.c.	–	–	99.74
TOTAL VERTEBRATE	635	127	100.0	180.75

Table 5.1. Faunal remains from Unit 2C (NE1); n.c. = not counted.

the 2.7 mm screen. Again the most abundant species are Scaridae and Haemulidae, but in the 1 mm screen there are slightly more Haemulidae than Scaridae while in the 2.7 mm screen it is the other way around. Searching through the 1 mm-sample yielded no species that were not represented in the analyzed samples. To conclude, one could say that the biases involved in using the 2.7 mm screen are not extreme but for conclusions based on the lists of the analyzed levels these biases do have to be kept in mind. Any future research on the Norman Estate site will have to take these results in account for choosing both the mesh-size of the screens and the sampling procedures.

Other possible biases in the research procedures of the analysis of the bone materials could be in the sampling methods used. For statistical reasons (cf. chapter 2) ten 2.5% samples of the total weight of the materials found in the 4 and 2.7 mm screens were taken. By doing so, several smaller samples of different proveniences could be analyzed instead of only one large sample. To get adequate samples the ten samples of level 5E and level 6C were later combined again into one sample of 25%. If each 2.5% had been analyzed separately, the results would definitively not have been reliable because the samples would have been far from large enough to get a good picture. The procedures for level 2C were slightly different; here the ten 2.5% samples were first combined into two larger samples of each 12.5%, separate lists for these two samples were made, after which these two lists were combined into one list for the total of the level (table 5.1). This was done to check how close the separate lists would look alike (which they did), and to see what would be the effect of sample size on the results. The only

TAXA	NISP	MNI	MNI %	WEIGHT (G)
Cheloniidae	15	1	1.9	4.13
Ameiva sp.	1	1	1.9	0.03
TOTAL REPTILE	16	2	3.8	4.16
Carcharhinidae	3	1	1.9	0.28
Belonidae	10	1	1.9	0.29
Hemiramphidae	1	1	1.9	0.01
Sphyraenidae	4	1	1.9	0.34
Epinephelus sp.	3	2	3.8	0.04
Serranidae	3	–	–	0.24
Caranx sp.	5	3	5.7	0.13
Carangidae	22	–	–	0.70
Lutjanus sp.	9	3	5.7	0.21
Lutjanidae	3	–	–	0.06
Haemulon sp.	9	5	9.6	0.20
Haemulidae	4	–	–	0.06
Calamus sp.	3	2	3.8	0.16
Sparidae	6	–	–	0.13
Mullidae	2	2	3.8	0.03
Sparisoma viride	1	1	1.9	0.11
Sparisoma sp.	145	20	38.5	7.85
Scarus sp.	6	2	3.8	0.33
Scaridae	28	–	– / [44.2]	1.03
Acanthuridae	22	5	9.6	0.87
cf. Ostraciidae	1	1	1.9	0.02
Unid. Fish	n.c.	–	–	8.81
TOTAL FISH	290	50	96.2	21.90
Unid. Bone	n.c.	–	–	35.12
TOTAL VERTEBRATE	306	52	100.0	61.18
Cardisoma guanhumi	1	1	100.0	0.05
Brachyura	89	–	–	1.71
TOTAL INVERTEBRATE	90	1	100.0	1.76
TOTAL VERT. + INVERT.	396	53	–	62.94

Table 5.2. Faunal remains from Unit 5E (NE1); n.c. = not counted.

problem in this whole procedure is that no samples from the 10 mm screen were taken. This was not done because there was already very little bone in this screen. First separate lists were made; one of the combination of the 2.7 and 4 mm samples, and one of the 10 mm material. Then they were combined into one list as presented in this chapter. These final faunal lists are based on 25% of the 2.7 mm screen, 25% of the 4 mm screen, and 100% of the 10 mm screen. The MNI% of the species of the 2.7 + 4 mm lists did not differ much from the final lists where the 10 mm sample was also included. Thus, although the 10 mm mesh screen materials are four times as relative abundant as the smaller materials in the final lists, this resulted only in slight biases. In level 5E there was no bone in the 10 mm screen at all, so for this level there was not such a problem. For level 6C the 10 mm mesh was not used, and the 4 mm material had not been sampled; so for this level 25% of the 2.7 mm screen and 100% of the 4 mm screen was analyzed.

5.3   Results of analysis

Tables 5.1-5.3 present the results of the analysis of each level. In table 5.4 these levels have been combined providing a picture of the whole of the Norman Estate site (NE1 and NE3 combined). In all 1203 elements were identified, representing 220 individuals and weighing 294.33 g. There is a very high percentage of fish in the samples (96.3% for the total of the site). Of the vertebrate almost half of the individuals belonged to Scaridae (42.5% *Sparisoma* sp. and

TAXA	NISP	MNI	MNI %	WEIGHT (G)
Unid. Bird	n.c.	1	2.5	0.04
TOTAL BIRD	n.c.	1	2.5	0.04
Cheloniidae	1	1	2.5	0.16
Unid. Reptile	n.c.	1	2.5	0.30
TOTAL REPTILE	1	2	5.0	0.
Carcharhinidae	1	1	2.5	0.02
Tylosurus sp.	1	1	2.5	0.01
Belonidae	9	–	–	0.46
Hemiramphidae	2	2	5.0	0.04
Serranidae	4	2	5.0	0.48
Carangidae	12	2	5.0	0.94
Lutjanus sp.	2	1	2.5	0.11
Lutjanidae	1	–	–	0.03
cf. Lutjanidae	1	–	–	0.02
Haemulon sp.	2	2	5.0	0.08
Haemulidae	6	–	–	0.15
Archosargus sp.	1	1	2.5	0.03
cf. *Calamus* sp.	1	1	2.5	0.08
cf. Sparidae	1	–	– / [5.0]	0.06
cf. Labridae	1	1	2.5	0.03
Sparisoma sp.	93	16	40.0	8.22
Scarus sp.	6	1	2.5	0.22
Scaridae	14	–	– / [42.5]	0.93
Acanthuridae	9	3	7.5	0.27
cf. Ostraciidae	3	1	2.5	0.06
Unid. Fish	n.c.	2	5.0	8.69
TOTAL FISH	170	37	92.5	20.93
Unid. Bone	n.c.	–	–	29.21
TOTAL VERTEBRATE	171	40	100.0	50.64

Table 5.3. Faunal remains from Unit 6C (NE3); n.c. = not counted.

4.1% *Scarus* sp.). Other important fish species were Haemulidae (grunts), Acanthuridae (surgeonfish) and Lutjanidae (snappers).

The only mammal bone in the whole of the assemblage is a tibia of the extinct West-Indian rice rat (Oryzomyini). This bone is perhaps a more recent intrusion in the site. Firstly, it was found in one of the upper levels of the site (2C). Secondly, the colour and good preservation of this bone clearly distinguishes it from the rest of the bone material. Thirdly, the tibia is the only bone of this species present in the analyzed material. One would expect to find several vertebrae or other well-preservable bones in the assemblage as well.

There were almost no bird remains in the assemblage (only 3 unidentifiable pieces) and not many reptile remains either. Remains of sea turtles (Cheloniidae) were not abundant and

also very small in size. Although there were sea turtle remains in each of the three levels, the total weight of the remains (5.05 g) is almost negligible. Sea turtles were not very important for the inhabitants.

Except for the shellfish remains, which were identified and quantified by Brokke (cf. chapter 4), there were not much other invertebrate remains in the site. Only one small chela (claw) of a *Cardisoma guanhumi* with some little pieces of land crab were found. Crabs were not a favourite source of food for the occupants of Norman Estate. Post-depositional processes have played a mayor role at Norman Estate. This resulted in high fragmentation of the bone remains. Some crab remains may not have survived.

Table 5.5 presents the eight most abundant species in the different levels. As one can see, the percentages of the

TAXA	NISP	MNI	MNI %	WEIGHT (G)
Oryzomyini	1	1	0.5	0.20
TOTAL MAMMAL	1	1	0.5	0.20
Unid. Bird	n.c.	1	0.5	0.04
TOTAL BIRD	n.c.	1	0.5	0.04
Cheloniidae	18	3	1.4	5.05
Ameiva sp.	2	2	0.9	0.05
Unid. Lizard	1	–	–	0.01
Unid. Reptile	n.c.	1	0.5	0.30
TOTAL REPTILE	21	6	2.7	5.41
Carcharhinidae	4	2	0.9	0.30
Tylosurus sp.	1	1	0.5	0.01
Belonidae	67	2	0.9 / [1.4]	2.50
Hemiramphidae	3	3	1.4	0.05
Sphyraenidae	7	2	0.9	0.42
Epinephelus sp.	3	2	0.9	0.04
Serranidae	12	4	1.8 / [2.7]	1.67
cf. Serranidae	1	–	–	1.88
Caranx sp.	12	5	2.3	0.40
Carangidae	81	2	0.9 / [3.2]	7.44
Lutjanus sp.	11	4	1.8	0.32
Lutjanidae	22	12	5.5 / [7.3]	0.7
cf. Lutjanidae	1	–	–	0.02
Haemulon sp.	11	7	3.2	0.28
Haemulidae	40	22	10.0 / [13.2]	1.15
Archosargus sp.	1	1	0.5	0.03
Calamus sp.	4	3	1.4	0.17
cf. *Calamus* sp.	1	1	0.5	0.08
Sparidae	11	–	–	0.28
cf. Sparidae	6	1	0.5 / [2.7]	0.26
Mullidae	6	6	2.7	0.08
cf. *Holacanthus* sp.	1	1	0.5	0.09
Labridae	7	1	0.5	0.93
cf. Labridae	1	1	0.5 / [0.9]	0.03
Sparisoma viride	1	1	0.5	0.11
Sparisoma sp.	520	92	42.0	39.92
Scarus sp.	31	9	4.1	0.99
Scaridae	142	–	– / [46.6]	5.72
Acanthuridae	67	17	7.8	2.08
Balistidae	7	1	0.5	0.23
Ostraciidae	4	1	0.5	0.03
cf. Ostraciidae	4	2	0.9 / [1.4]	0.08
Diodontidae	1	1	0.5	4.05
Unid. Fish	n.c.	4	1.8	50.43
TOTAL FISH	1091	211	96.3	122.85
Unid. Bone	n.c.	–	–	164.07
TOTAL VERTEBRATE	1113	219	100.0	292.57
Cardisoma guanhumi	1	1	100.0	0.05
Brachyura	89	–	–	1.71
			100.0	1.76
TOTAL VETEBRATE	1203	220	–	294.33

Table 5.4. Faunal remains from NE1 and NE2 combined; n.c. = not counted.

	NE 2C 2.7 mm (12.5%) + 4.0 mm (12.5%) (sample 1-5)	NE 2C 2.7mm (12.5%) + 4.0 mm (12.5%) (sample 6-10)	NE 2C 10 mm (100%) + 2.7 mm (25%)	NE 5E 2.7 mm (25%) + 4.0 mm (25%)	NE 6C 2.7 mm (25%) + 4.0 mm (100%)	NE 3C + 5E + 6C = average of the site
SCARIDAE	53.7	39.7	48.8	44.2	42.5	46.6
HAEMULIDAE	16.4	17.5	17.3	9.6	5.0	13.2
ACANTHURIDAE	7.5	6.3	7.1	9.6	7.5	7.8
LUTJANIDAE	7.5	11.1	9.4	5.7	2.5	7.3
CARANGIDAE	3.0	3.2	1.6	5.7	5.0	3.2
SERRANIDAE	1.5	1.6	1.6	3.8	5.0	2.7
SPARIDAE	1.5	3.2	1.6	3.8	5.0	2.7
MULLIDAE	–	6.3	3.1	3.8	–	2.7
percentage of total MNI	61 / 67 = 91.0%	56 / 63 = 88.9%	115 / 127 = 90.6%	45 / 53 = 84.9%	29 / 40 = 72.5%	189 / 220 = 85.9%

Table 5.5. The most abundant species in Units 2C, 5E and 6C, and the average percentage of the site.

various species in this table do not differ much from the average percentages of the site. Thus the total list of the Norman Estate site gives a representative picture of the faunal assemblage of the preceramic inhabitants. This list can be used for comparison with other preceramic faunal assemblages from the Caribbean region. From the species lists it is also clear that the vertebrate remains from NE3 (level 6C) do not differ much from the remains of NE1 (levels 2C and 5E). The remains from the two areas probably have been left by two groups that shared the same cultural tradition. NE1 and NE3 could even have been two different activity areas of one single occupation period. Future research, especially on NE3 which lacks any radiocarbon dates so far, might bring more light on this subject.

All of the 10 mm material (and some of the smaller material) excavated was examined for any additional, relatively rare species missing in the analyzed levels. This resulted in the following species:
– one snake vertebra (Alsophis sp.) was found in level 1F.
– one vertebra of a ray (Rajiformes) was found in level 1D.
– in level 3C, as well as level 6C a shark tooth (Carcharhinidae) was found, as well as two identical shark vertebrae in levels 1C and 3C.
– Besides the sparse crab remains in the NE1 area (found in level 5E), two tiny pieces of Brachyura (probably land crab as well) were also recorded from the NE3 area (in level 6B).

The material of the augers that were made during the survey of the Norman Estate area was analyzed as well. For the location of the different areas see fig. 2.4.
– The augers in and around NE1 and NE3 gave the same picture as was observed from the faunal analyses and did not yield any extra species.
– Four augers made in NE2 (215/1813, 209/1820, 215/1820, 230/1820) gave the impression that this site was also a preceramic site, although it must have been rather disturbed because colonial remains have been found around this area. The distribution of the species in the augers was as follows: Cheloniidae, MNI=1; Unid. Bird, MNI=1; Carangidae, MNI=1; Haemulidae, MNI=1; Sparisoma sp., MNI=2; Scaridae, MNI=1.
– Auger 410/1955 yielded one lower pharyngeal of a parrotfish (Sparisoma sp.).
– Outside of the original area surveyed, some 200 m to the east of NE 1 along the road to the Cul de Sac (cf. fig. 2.1), one test auger was made which yielded the following distribution:Belonidae, MNI=1; Haemulidae, MNI=1; Sparisoma sp., MNI=2.

All the bone found in the different areas had the same general appearance and yielded the same species as NE1 and NE3. Therefore, all of the materials found in the various areas are probably of preceramic origin.

5.4 Habitats

Table 5.6 and fig. 5.1 give a picture of the different habitats exploited by the archaic occupants of the Norman Estate sites. A highly specialized pattern can be observed. Land

	TAXA	MNI	MNI %
TERRESTRIAL	Oryzomyini	1	0.5
	Unid. Bird	1	0.5
	Ameiva sp.	2	0.9
	Unid. Reptile	1	0.5
	TOTAL	5	2.3
BEACH-TURTLE GRASS	Cheloniidae	3	1.4
INSHORE-ESTUARINE	Carcharhinidae	2	0.9
	Sparidae	6	2.7
	Mullidae	6	2.7
	TOTAL	14	6.4
REEF-SHALLOW CORAL REEFS	Pomacanthidae	1	0.5
	Labridae	2	0.9
	Scaridae	102	46.6
	Acanthuridae	17	7.8
	Ostraciidae	3	1.4
	Diodontidae	1	0.5
	TOTAL	126	57.5
REEF-DEEP REEFS / ROCKY BANKS	Serranidae	6	2.7
	Carangidae	7	3.2
	Lutjanidae	16	7.3
	Haemulidae	29	13.2
	Balistidae	1	0.5
	TOTAL	59	26.9
[SHALLOW+DEEP REEFS]	TOTAL	185	84.5
OFFSHORE-PELAGIC	Belonidae	3	1.4
	Hemiramphidae	3	1.4
	Sphyraenidae	2	0.9
	TOTAL	8	3.7
SEA	Unid. Fish	4	1.8
TOTAL OF THE SITE		219	100.0

Table 5.6. Different habitats exploited by the archaic occupants of the Norman Estate site.

species account for only 2.3% of the total MNI, the rice rat bone included, and sea turtles only 1.4%. Most of the identifications of the fish could not be made to the specific level as the bone remains were badly preserved. Hence, the exact nature of the habitats from which the fish were taken is uncertain. Still, most fish families can be assigned to a habitat in which they occur most of the time. Information about the different habitats is obtained from Randall (1968) and Wing and Reitz (1982). Most of the fish caught can be found over coral reefs and rocky banks. Of these, the more important species belong to the Scaridae (parrotfish), Haemulidae (grunts), Acanthuridae (surgeonfish), Lutjanidae (snappers), Carangidae (jacks) and Serranidae (groupers). Of the reef fish caught (84.5% of the total MNI of the assemblage), a majority of 57.5% can be assigned to species that mostly inhabit shallow coral reefs, against 26.9% of species

that mostly inhabit deeper reefs and rocky banks. Haemulidae are usually found in large aggregations over reefs or tidal grass flats. Serranidae and Lutjanidae are carnivores which enter shallow grass flats primarily to feed. Belonidae (needlefish), Hemiramphidae (halfbeaks) and Sphyraenidae (barracudas) can mostly be found in pelagic waters, but sometimes also over reefs and in inshore waters. Sparidae (porgies), Mullidae (goatfish) and Carcharhinidae (sharks) are, generally, inshore species, but they can sometimes also be found over reefs. Ostraciidae (boxfish) and Diodontidae (puffers) were assigned to shallow coral reef habitat, although they can also be found over sand or grass flats.

The location of the Norman Estate site is somewhat peculiar when one notices the clear marine orientation of the inhabitants. The site is situated somewhat inland, approximately

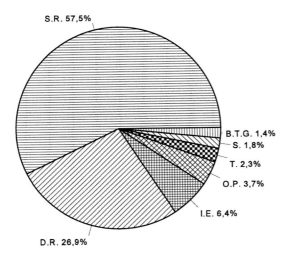

Fig. 5.1. Archaic age habitat exploitation at the Norman Estate sites. Reconstruction has been based on the analysis of vertebrate remains only (total MNI = 219). S.R.= Shallow reef, D.R.= Deep reef, I.E.= Inshore-estuarine, O.P.= Offshore pelagic, T.= Terrestrial, S.= Sea, B.T.G. =Beach-turtle grass.

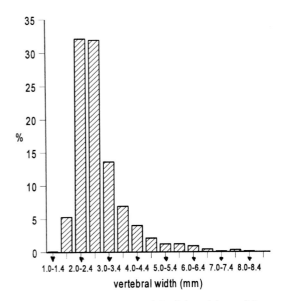

Fig. 5.2. Frequency in percentage of the fish vertebrae of the combined 2.7 and 4 mm mesh samples from NE2C (N = 780).

1.5 km from both the east and north coasts. On the other hand, this might have been a well-chosen spot because of equal-access possibilities to both coasts, each with its own potentials for marine resources (both fish and shellfish). Along the beach of Baie Orientale, to the south-east of Norman Estate, shallow reefs and large shallow grass flats can be found.

An extreme example of dependence on the resources of a barrier reef is seen at the Palmetto Grove Site on San Salvador Island in the Bahamas. Here 96% of the vertebrate remains are fish and of these 63% are parrotfish (Wing 1969). Although this is not a preceramic site, the results are comparable to the Norman Estate materials. Both sites are in the vicinity of shallow waters and a barrier reef. Most likely, this location is reflected in the faunal remains of these sites.

5.5 Fishing methods

Because most of the fish caught belong to reef species, one can assume that these species were caught with traps or by hook and line. Nets and weirs would have been impractical over reefs. Herbivorous reef species, such as parrotfish and surgeonfish are typically caught in traps nowadays (Wing 1991, 363). Parrotfish and surgeonfish will not take a hook and could not easily be speared (Wing and Reitz 1982, 25). Groupers, jacks, snappers and grunts can be caught in traps but they can also be taken with hook and line. There is no

conclusive evidence that the inhabitants fished off-shore as well. Needlefish, halfbeaks, and barracudas can sometimes also be found on reefs and inshore waters.

According to Randall (1968) parrotfish are often the dominant fish on West Indian reefs on a weight basis. So the dominance of parrotfish in the Norman Estate assemblage could be explained if the inhabitants used mostly traps in reef areas.

Experimental studies of basketry trap yields indicated that the highest returns were in traps set near the interface of the tidal flat with the reef flats (Keegan 1985, 1986). This way the shallow reef herbivores can be caught, as well as the deeper reef carnivores that come to the grass flats to feed during the night. Schools of parrotfish, surgeonfish, snappers and grunts can be caught in traps set along their crepuscular migration routes (Keegan 1985, 155-158). These four fish families are most abundantly represented in the samples from the Norman Estate sites; when all samples are combined, these four fish families account for 74.9% of the individuals identified.

Measurements of the atlases and vertebrae of the fish species caught can bring more light on the fishing methods employed. The use of basketry traps might be inferred when a limited range is found in the measurements. The size of the entrance to the traps excludes individuals too big to enter; and through the gauge mesh of the basketry weave of the traps the smaller individuals can escape

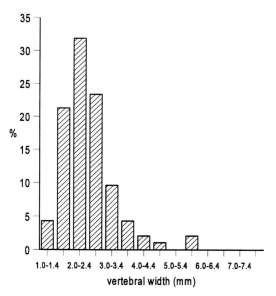

Fig. 5.3. Frequency in percentage of the fish atlasses of the combined Norman Estate 1 and 3 faunal assemblages (N = 94).

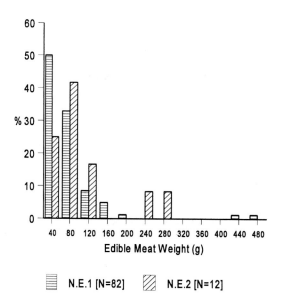

N.E.1 [N=82]   N.E.2 [N=12]

Fig. 5.4. Frequency in percentage of the estimated fish weight of the combined Norman Estate 1 and 3 faunal assemblages (N = 94).

(Wing and Reitz 1982, 26). The measurement obtained from the fish vertebrae is the greatest medial-lateral breadth of the centrum, taken at the anterior surface of the vertebrae (Morales and Roselund 1979, 44-45). Figure 5.2 presents the results of these measurements for the vertebrae found in level 2C. All the vertebrae present in the analyzed 25% of both the 4 and 2.7 mm mesh screens have been measured. In the 10 mm mesh screen of level 2C only three vertebrae were found; therefore these measurements have not been taken in the calculations. 64% (N=499) of the vertebrae measured have a breadth that falls between 2.0 and 2.9 mm. The results clearly show that the majority of the fishes caught by the Norman Estate inhabitants are within a restricted size range. Therefore, the use of traps can be postulated. The small size of the vertebrae indicate that the mesh size of the traps would have been small.

All atlases found in the analyzed faunal material were also measured (fig. 5.3). The small size of most of the atlases found in the Norman Estate sites is remarkable.
The occurrence of many very small atlases and vertebrae in the 1 mm-sample analyzed (see above) might indicate that schools of young individuals (especially grunts) were caught close to shore, with the use of small-sized nets.
The measurements of the atlases were used to calculate the weight of the edible meat each fish could have provided. The allometric formula to calculate the edible meat weight is the following (from Quitmyer 1985):

Log Y = 0.70 + 2.57 (Log X) (r^2 =.98), whereby:

X = Anterior width of the atlas (mm)
Y = Maximum edible meat weight (g)

The results are presented in fig. 5.4 for both of the Norman Estate sites. Mainly small individuals were caught; the average fish caught at Norman Estate 1 could provide 59 g of meat; at Norman Estate 2 this was somewhat more, 91 g. Almost all fishes eaten provided less than 100 g of meat. The average parrotfish (*Sparisoma* sp.) eaten at Norman Estate 1 provided only 49 g of meat, and the average grunt (Haemulidae) eaten at Norman Estate 1 provided even less, 44 g of meat.

5.6 Comparison with other sites in the region
For Lesser Antillean Archaic sites, a pattern in the location of the sites can be observed. These are usually coastal sites and are often near mangrove stands (Davis 1982).

The Norman Estate faunal assemblage can best be compared to the Krum Bay site at St. Thomas, US Virgin Islands. This site was dated to 1680-1530 BC. Elizabeth Reitz examined a sample of vertebrate material from which she identified 131 individuals, of which 45.8% were *Sparisoma* sp. and 4.6% were *Scarus* sp. (Reitz 1989). The majority of the individuals were marine fish from a reef habitat (80.3%). Fish made up 93.4% of the vertebrates. No pelagic fish was found. Mammalian, reptilian, and avian fauna was very rare in the collection (MNI=8, of which Cheloniidae=4). A total absence of small terrestrial species in the Krum Bay sample (such as Oryzomyini rice rats) is remarkable. Reitz had no clue why this was the case (Reitz 1989, 288). At the Krum Bay site a 6.3 mm mesh screen was used. This could be the cause for the absence of, for instance, Belonidae, Hemiramphidae, Mullidae and Acanthuridae remains in the Krum Bay sample, as well as an over-representation of Serranidae (12.3%) and Lutjanidae (12.3%), and a strong under-representation of Haemulidae (1.5%) (compare with table 5.4). Despite these differences, the general resource exploitation patterns are very similar.

A recent discovery and partial excavation of a preceramic site, Whitehead's Bluff, at Anguilla yielded rocky shore shellfish species and some land crab, but no vertebrate remains. This could be the result of bad preservation because of strong erosive forces during recent historic times (Crock et al. 1995, 286) and the use of only 6.3 mm mesh screen. Alternatively, the inhabitants might have made use of only a limited set of readily-accessible food resources. A total of four dates between 1655 BC and 1290 BC have been provided for this site.

At the island of Antigua, more than 50 a-ceramic sites have been identified so far (Nodine 1990, 2). The Jolly Beach site, one of the sites with the deepest deposits, has got two dates: a corrected date of 2100 ± 180 BC, and a corrected date of 1580 ± 180 BC (Nodine 1990, 9-10). Some of the Jolly Beach vertebrate material from the 1985 excavations was analyzed by Dr. E.S. Wing (Wing, pers. comm.). The fish species used do not differ much from the Norman Estate material, and again the Scaridae are the most represented of the vertebrates (32.9% of a total MNI of 79). At this site the terrestrial component was better represented. Mammals and reptiles account for 20.3% of the MNI, of which 10.1% is from the rice rats (Oryzomyini).

A preliminary analysis of faunal material from Hichman's Shell Heap (GE-6), one of the two known preceramic sites on Nevis, was conducted by Dr. E.S. Wing. The vertebrate faunal data are unpublished, but some preliminary results were published by Wilson (1989, 435; 1991, 270). Like Norman Estate and Krum Bay here also an abundance of parrotfish (*Scarus* sp. and *Sparisoma* sp.) was reported. Groupers (Serranidae), surgeonfish (*Acanthurus* sp.) and barracudas (Sphyraenidae) were common species. Muraenidae, Belonidae, Labridae and Diodontidae were also reported, as well as sea turtle. Land crab was also found. The molluscan fauna was dominated by *Cittarium pica* and *Arca zebra*. This site was radiocarbon dated to 2490 ± 60 BP (605 ± 190 BC), much later than the Norman Estate site.

5.7   Conclusions

During the Norman Estate survey several small areas could be identified which are probably all of a preceramic origin. Analyzed faunal material from NE1 and NE3 indicated that these areas could have been formed during the same period. The inhabitants relied heavily on marine vertebrates. Of these, especially the shallow reef species were a favourite source of food.

Based on the composition of the fish species, and on measurements taken of vertebrae and atlases of the fish caught, it could be postulated that most fish had been caught with the use of traps. Most fish caught were small-sized individuals, providing less than 100 g of meat.

The faunal remains from the Norman Estate site very much resemble those from the Krum Bay site on St. Thomas. Both sites yield extreme high percentages of (mostly reef) fish remains, of which the special preference for parrotfish is remarkable. This preference for parrotfish could also be seen in Jolly Beach on Antigua and Hichman's Shell Heap on Nevis. The use of the same fishing technique, i.e., traps set near shallow coral reefs, might be responsible for this resemblance.

There seem to be some substantial differences in the exploitation of other habitats besides the shallow coral reefs. A strong terrestrial component as found at the Jolly Beach site, was not found at Norman Estate. More research on faunal remains from Archaic sites may bring more clarity in this diffuse pattern in the northern Lesser Antilles.

PART TWO
ANSE DES PERES

6 Methods and strategies

Sebastiaan Knippenberg

6.1 Site location

The Anse des Pères site is located in a level area, close to the bay of Anse des Pères (fig. 6.1). A permanent stream known as Ravine du Colombier, which originates in the small village of Colombier debouches into this bay. The site rests upon a remaining part of the Pointe Blanche Formation, an old marine floor dating from the Late Eocene times, consisting of recrystallised tuffs, cherty and calcareous tuffs, and cherts. Much of the Anse des Pères region is built-up. Only a stretch of 150-200 m along the seashore is still covered with the natural vegetation of the area, mainly formed by dense thorny bush and small-sized trees. Pedologically, the site consists of medium to fine-grained sand, intersected with rocks. The area of the site is covered with dense thorny bush and a few trees. Towards the east it is bounded by some small gardens, towards the south by the Ravine du Colombier. This stream has made a deeply entrenched, occasionally more than three metres deep gully. At the time of the research, only 10 to 20 cm water was standing in the gully. The coastline to the south of the Ravine du Colombier was used as a garbage dump in the recent past.

6.2 Site discovery

In the late eighties the presence of Amerindian artefacts was noted by a local inhabitant at Anse des Pères. The site is found some 30 metres inland from the seashore, just to the north of the Ravine du Colombier. Christophe Henocq did some prospecting, collected surface finds, and, dug a test unit. He found pottery, shells, animal bones, stone artefacts and, at the bottom of the deposit, numerous crab remains. The ceramics exhibited Saladoid traits. However, the crab layer suggested to Henocq, the possibility that occupational remains from an earlier period might be present, although pottery with 'La Hueca' traits was not encountered. These ideas were not further tested by any new excavations or the obtaining of any radiocarbon dates. Jay Haviser visited the Anse des Pères area during his St. Martin survey. He succeeded in locating a small scatter of shell and lithic flakes along the shore, just to the north of Ravine du Colombier (Haviser 1988). The location of this site, called Friar's Bay (SM-015) by Haviser, does not fully coincide with the more inland situation of the site described by Henocq. Apart from this surface deposit, Haviser

mentions a larger scatter of shells in the northeasternmost portion of Anse des Pères, although he doubts whether the latter represents a human deposit. Finally, he discovered another small surface scatter of shells and chert artefacts found at a distance of 250 m from the shore, amidst construction activities (Haviser 1988). It is unknown where exactly the latter deposit is situated. However, it is certain that it represents a site, different from the one noticed by Henocq. This is confirmed by Haviser (pers. comm., 1993).

6.3 Survey

It was decided to determine the overall size of the Anse des Pères site and to locate areas of high artefact concentration (cf. chapter 2 for aims of survey and test excavations). Due to the presence of poisonous vegetation, it was not possible to survey close to the seashore. As a result the survey area was limited to the east side of the macadam road which runs along the bay. A grid with units of 10×10 m was plotted on the area. As the dense vegetation of thorny bush and small trees would make a surface-survey testing very time-consuming, systematic sub-surface testing, with small shovel pits excavated on every corner of the grid units, was accomplished. Although a relatively small part (a test pit every 10 m) of the site was surveyed, this strategy of sub-surface testing provided a good insight into the distribution of the archaeological deposits present.

Shovel testing rather than auger testing was chosen to detect areas with high artefact concentrations. Use of shovel pits of 20 to 20 cm size was thought to form a good compromise between the time-consuming digging of 1×1 m test units and the augering of small-volume tests. An arbitrary interval of 10 m was chosen, especially taking into account the limited time and manpower available, still hoping that it would be enough to discern artefact distribution and other patterns within the site. Measuring the various structures and the midden area at the site of Golden Rock on St. Eustatius showed, that their overall size exceeded 10 m (Versteeg and Schinkel 1992). Consequently, similar site patterns at Anse des Pères would not be missed by the shovel tests.

Shovel testing was executed as follows. A pit of 20 to 20 cm was excavated until a depth of 20 cm below the deepest

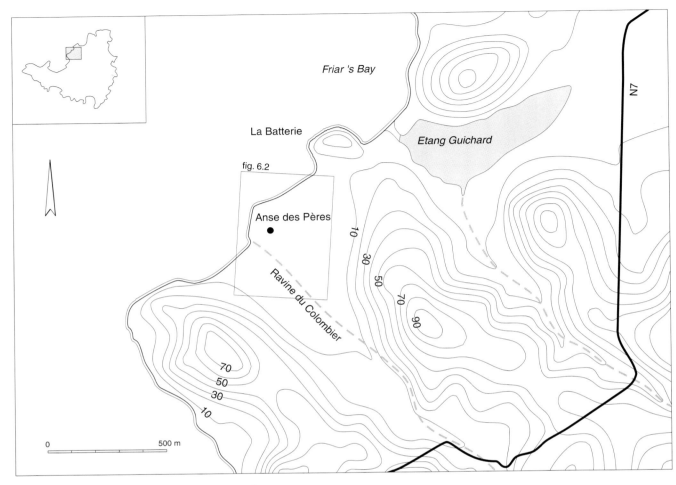

Fig. 6.1. The surroundings of the site of Anse des Pères.

finds or until the hardness of the soil did not allow any further digging. The excavated material was sifted using a 4 mm sieve. All finds, e.g., shells, coral fragments, animal bones, charcoal and artefacts, were collected and recorded. The depth of deepest finds was measured. The survey was terminated when two subsequent shovel tests did not yield any archaeological finds. The results of the survey led to the identification decisions of locations where test excavations could be supposed to yield the best results.

6.4   Survey results

In all 127 shovel tests were excavated (fig. 6.2). One shovel-test was not finished because of the presence of a human burial. Continuation of digging would have destroyed part of it. Due to time constraints, the proposed strategy could not be followed for the entire area. The western and northern parts of the site contained little archaeological materials and, therefore, here larger intervals were taken to determine the distribution

of it. The accurately surveyed part contains high concentrations of archaeological material. The material consisted of pre-Columbian and colonial pottery, crab, shell, coral, animal and human bone, lithics, charcoal, iron, and glass fragments.

Pre-Columbian finds are scattered over an area of approximately 15,000 m². Within this area the concentration of archaeological material varies significantly.
An area with a length of 110 m and maximum width of 30 m yielded a substantial amount of shell, crab, animal bone, pottery and lithic material. This deposit of archaeological material had a thickness ranging from 30 to 90 cm. The occurrence of a high concentration of food remains, together with pottery and lithic artefacts provided evidence of an area where refuse had been discarded (fig. 6.3a-e). The presence of crab and animal bone by comparison with the other finds, is less dispersed and is more tied to areas where the remains are found in higher concentrations and thicker deposits. In

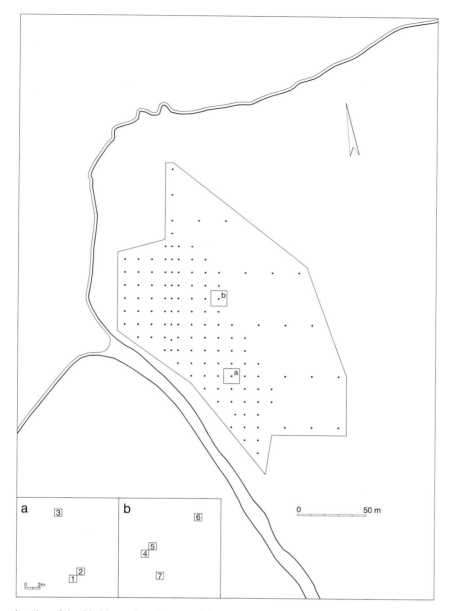

Fig. 6.2. Anse des Pères, location of the 20×20 cm shovel tests and the 1×1 test units.

this case, the presence of these two categories can be used broadly to limit the refuse area.

Within the refuse area, at the northeast part, a tibia was recognized in one of the shovels at a depth of 30 cm below surface. This burial was not excavated, so its state of preservation, position and orientation remain uncertain. Considering this depth, there is the possibility of either a colonial or Amerindian burial.

The shovel test survey resulted in the discovery of the remains of a village belonging to the ceramic period, and in

the determination of an approximate size for it. Within this site, an elongated area, with high concentrations of archaeological material was recognized, and interpreted as the refuse area. Within that area two small areas, each with a relatively high concentration of finds, were distinguished.

It is likely that house-structures had been located in the near vicinity of these core areas. This, however, has to be tested by future excavations.

Close inspection of the distribution maps has indicated that two places within this elongated refuse area can be considered

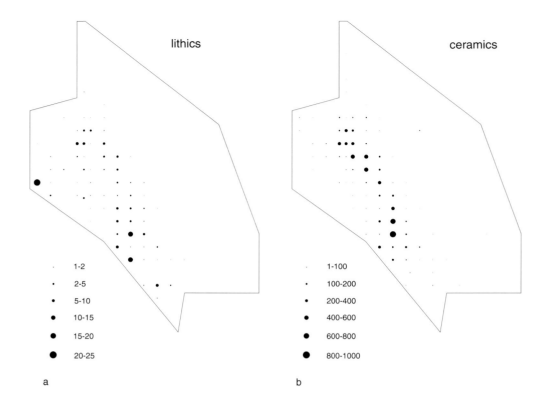

lithics

1-2
2-5
5-10
10-15
15-20
20-25

a

ceramics

1-100
100-200
200-400
400-600
600-800
800-1000

b

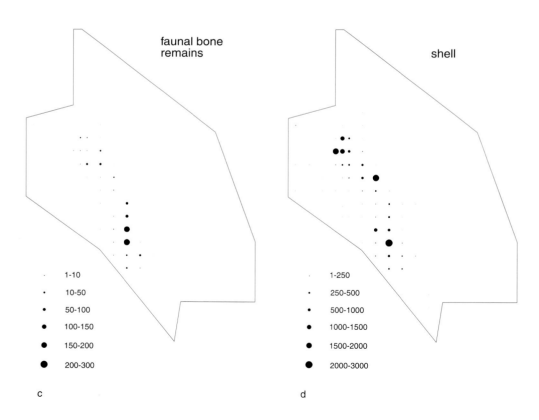

faunal bone
remains

1-10
10-50
50-100
100-150
150-200
200-300

c

shell

1-250
250-500
500-1000
1000-1500
1500-2000
2000-3000

d

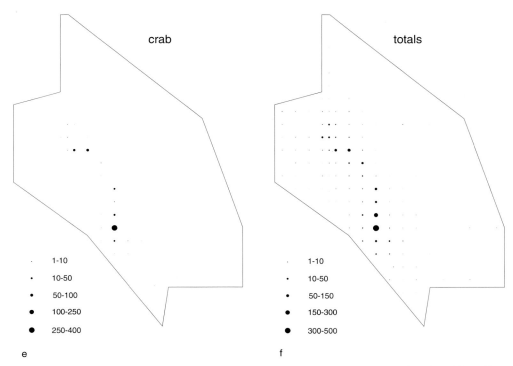

Fig. 6.3. Distribution of five artefact categories in the shovel tests and the weighted sum of ceramics, shell, crab and faunal bone remains: a. number of lithics, b. weight of ceramics, c. weight of faunal bone remains, d. weight of shell, e. weight of crab remains, f. total, i.e. the weighted sum of ceramics, shell, crab and faunal bone remains.

as core areas. These areas are separated by an area with a deposition which is less thick and which is less concentrated in finds. It is not clear whether these two cores must be considered as two distinctive refuse areas, belonging to different periods of deposition, or whether they can be associated with different houses or clusters of houses within one period. The Golden Rock site shows that distinct refuse areas with a size comparable to the one of Anse des Pères, are associated with distinct house structures (Versteeg and Schinkel 1992). The excavations at Golden Rock have shown that several houses from different phases are associated with the same midden. Determination of these phases, however, has been based on the dating and stratigraphy of the postholes. This periodization has not been distinguished within the refuse area itself on the basis of differences between the nature of depositional layers or on the basis of variation within pottery style, shell, or animal bone species. This indicates that the information that has been collected from the shovels and test units at Anse des Pères is of limited use in determining any possible periodization of the refuse area.

The discovery of a midden, being part of a settlement from Ceramic times, poses the question as to whether indications can be given for the location of the habitation. Studies

within present day agriculture in Amerindian societies show that activity areas, such as the inside of houses and surrounding areas, are kept clean and that refuse is dumped or swept somewhere else (DeBoer and Lathrap 1979; Kloos 1975; Kozák et al. 1979; Murray 1980; Seiler-Baldinger 1987). The exact location of the refuse area is only mentioned in a few cases and shows some variation. The Xingu Indians of the Mato Grosso bring their refuse, which is often very little, into the forest, some distance away from the village (Seiler-Baldinger 1987), whereas the Shipibo-Conibo of eastern Peru, keep the plaza in front of their house clean and the refuse is swept "centrifugally away from the household and accumulates immediately beyond the perimeter of clearing. In isolated households, the effect over time is a doughnut-shaped midden" (DeBoer and Lathrap 1979,128). When one looks to the archaeological example of Golden Rock, which is similar to the Anse des Pères site in natural setting and nature and amount of the refuse, the midden area is situated just behind the house(s) (Versteeg and Schinkel 1992). Being close to the house, wind directions can play a role in distributing the refuse (Murray 1980).
At Anse des Pères, the elongated shape of the refuse area, makes it most probable that the houses have stood either on the east or west side of it. The latter location would be

preferable considering wind directions, the former would be preferable, considering the distance to the sea, which had been exploited by the Amerindian people of Anse des Pères.

6.5 Test units

To locate the test units, a map of the spatial distribution was reconstructed. The reconstruction was executed using weighted sums of findings of pre-Columbian pottery, crab, shell and animal bone (fig. 6.3f). Lithic material was put aside, because in many cases it could not be tested as to whether they represent artefacts or not. This uncertainty could give erroneous indications of the presence of human activity.

The weighted sum has been calculated as follows:

- The mass (in g) was used as the measure.
- It was decided that no preference would be given to any of the material categories, so the total weights of all the shovel tests for each category was taken as the same. This meant that 1 g of crab was comparable with, and given the same weight as, 17 g of shell. The total mass of shell from all shovels being 17 times heavier than the total mass of crab.

The formula can be written as follows:

$$C_{wi} = Q_p \cdot P_i + Q_c \cdot C_i + Q_s \cdot S_i + Q_b \cdot B_i$$
$$= 0.053 \cdot P_i + 0.515 \cdot C_i + 0.030 \cdot S_i + 0.401 \cdot B_i$$

with:

C_{wi} = the weighted concentration (in g) of shovel test i.

Q_x = weighting coefficient for category x.

= $1/(W_x(1/W_s+1/W_c+1/W_p+1/W_b))$

W_x = the sum of weights from each shovel test (in g) of category x (with W_s= 24715g, W_c = 1433g, W_p=13769g, W_b=1838g).

P_i = weight (in g) of pottery in shovel test i.

C_i = weight (in g) of crab in shovel test i.

S_i = weight (in g) of shell in shovel test i.

B_i = weight (in g) of animal bone in shovel test i.

For each shovel test the C_w was calculated. The value 105 marked a gap within the frequency distribution. This value was therefore taken to limit the areas within which the test units should be located. The two constituted areas assume separate refuse dumps and therefore were treated as two distinct population units from which two samples were taken. It was tested, whether these two areas can be considered as separate from each other in contents and time, or whether they should be considered as refuse dumps belonging to a single occupation.

Sampling only within a refuse area could give biased results, when using such a sample as representative for the site. Due to time constraints it was not possible to get an adequate sample of the whole site. This would have required the excavation of large areas within the low concentrated parts, to know which area within the site one is dealing with, and to obtain a good amount of material to characterize that area. The fact that most test excavations in the Caribbean had been done in the highest concentration areas, in most cases interpreted as refuse dumps or middens, made the decision as to where to dig easy. Following that strategy would make the material from Anse des Pères comparable to other sites in the Caribbean.

The two high concentration areas were treated as two different units. Within each of these units two test units were chosen using random numbers. A third test unit was attached to the first one within each unit. This was done to obtain a larger section, which would make the interpretation of the stratigraphy easier. In total six units of 1 m² were excavated. However during the excavation of unit 4 human remains were discovered. Excavating and drawing this burial would have been too time consuming. So it was decided to stop excavating in unit 4 and to refill it. Another unit was chosen randomly, unit 7. For location of the test units see fig. 6.2.

All units were excavated in arbitrary levels of 10 cm. The dirt from these units was waterscreened through nested sieves with 2.7, 6.0 and 10.0 mm meshes, for the same reasons as at Norman Estate (cf. chapter 2). The dirt coming from the disturbed upper ploughzone was sieved through a 6 mm mesh, and only pottery, lithic artefacts and colonial artefacts were kept. From the other levels, all archaeological material was collected.

The material sorted from the 10 mm residue was analyzed completely. The residues from the 2.7 and 6.0 mm were sampled. Five weight samples, each consisting of 2.5% of the total, were taken randomly from the residue of each level. These samples were analyzed on their animal bone material.

All sections within the units were drawn and photographed.

6.6 Stratigraphy

The first aim was to test whether the site is a one-component site. This could be done with the aid of the profile sections, the artefacts and the dates. Due to the strategy followed concerning the choice of the test units, only small profile sections were obtained. This limits a good understanding of the stratigraphy, especially when deposition took place in a horizontal direction.

In total, 24 m of profile section were obtained, subdivided into 20 sections of 1 m, and 2 sections of 2 m. The main distinctions that could be made, were colour differences; sometimes a difference in texture could be appreciated. All the arbitrary levels contained the same kind of material, pottery, lithic and subsistence debris. Concentration differences existed between

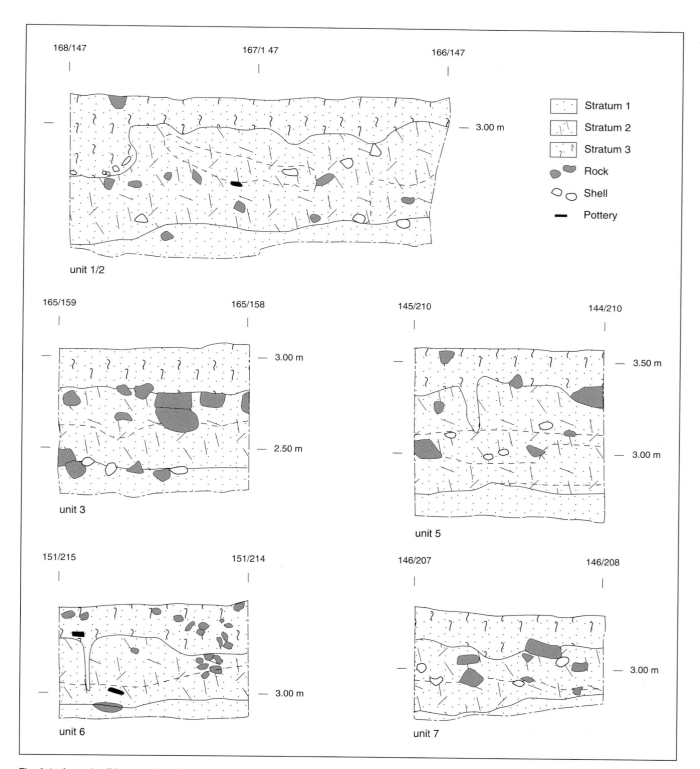

Fig. 6.4. Anse des Pères, stratigraphic sections of the 1×1 m test units.

Unit	lab. No	material	age BP	calibrated date (95% confidence level)
2	GrN-20160	land crab	1180 ± 30 BP	cal AD 790 – cal AD 950
3	GrN-20162	land crab	1170 ± 30 BP	cal AD 802 – cal AD 959
5	GrN-20161	land crab	1225 ± 30 BP	cal AD 730 – cal AD 888

Table 6.1. Radiocarbon dates (GrN = Groningen). The dates are calibrated with 'Groningen Radiocarbon Calibration Program Cal15', version april 1993 (Center for Isotopes Research, Groningen University). The results of the datings of the terrestrial crab samples are calibrated with the calibration curve by Stuiver et al. (1993).

them, although these were hard to recognize in the field. The following general picture emerges from the different sections (fig. 6.4):

1. Sub-stratum of sand, yellowish brown colour (10YR 5/4). In the upper part there are some cultural remains. In the lower parts the soil was very compact.
2. Stratum of (fine) sand, a range of colours differing from (light/dark) greyish brown in the upper zones to brownish grey – (light) grey in the lower zones. Within this deposit minor colour differences were seen. It is not certain whether they reflect different depositions in time or whether they can be ascribed to soil processes. As already stated this deposit contained high concentrations of shell, animal bone, crab remains, pottery and natural stone together with lithic artefacts, charcoal and seeds. This can be considered the refuse deposit.
3. Stratum of sand, dark (greyish) brown colour (10YR 4/2, 3/3). This stratum can be considered as a colonial ploughzone. Material was mixed up with colonial material and pottery is fragmented.

Some small variation exists between the units. The most remarkable are the differences in thickness of the Amerindian refuse deposit; in unit 5 the deposit is the thickest, in unit 7 the thickness is reduced significantly. In unit 5, some clear differences in find concentrations were distinguished in the field. Around 30 to 40 cm below the surface the concentration dropped significantly, rising again in the lower levels of the unit. Near unit 1, a pig had been buried during colonial times. On the profile section the colonial pit penetrates the Amerindian deposit to a depth of 50 cm below the surface.

6.7 Radiocarbon dates

Three samples, consisting of fragments of exoskeletons of land crabs, were obtained from three different test units, namely units 2, 3 and 5 (table 6.1). They were all taken from the Amerindian refuse deposit (stratum 2), however depths below the surface were different. The BP ages were calibrated, using the Stuiver et al. (1993) curve of the Groningen calibration programme CAL 15. It was smoothed over

100 years (N=5), because the crab fragments came from different crab individuals.

Even when 68% intervals (1 sigma) are used, the dates overlap. These dates show that the site had not been occupied over a long period, either continually or within several distinct occupations. Although no statistical statements can be made about the differences between the dates, they are consistent, with the youngest date coming from the highest levels, and the oldest from the lowest. Also both dates from one core area (GrN-20160 [unit 2], GrN-20162 [unit 3]) lie closer to each other than to the third one coming from unit 5. This might mean that both core areas are indeed distinct refuse areas, belonging to different phases of occupation.

6.8 Post-depositional processes

This section describes the processes that had taken place after the deposition of the refuse by the Amerindian inhabitants of the site. In general it can be stated that for the most part the refuse area was well preserved, and that post-depositional processes had not affected the artefacts' original places of deposition. The main fact for arguing this, has been the discovery of almost complete pots within the test units. Additional refitting proved to be very successful and resulted into the construction of several large pot parts. Although most parts of the refuse area have been preserved well, there are indications that human activities disturbed the site to some extent during colonial times. Throughout the whole site area, remains of these activities were found. The whole area is covered by a 20 cm thick ploughzone, where colonial pottery and glass has been mixed-up with Amerindian material, indicating the area had been used as agricultural land. Some local inhabitants confirmed this use up until recently. In some shovels colonial artefacts occur until around 40 cm below the surface. The excavation of unit 1 revealed a colonial pit, filled with the bones of a pig, disturbing more than 50 cm of the Amerindian refuse deposit. Inspection of the surface of the area revealed a stone wall, probably serving as a limit marker of agricultural land. It is for most part situated in the low concentration area to the west side of the refuse area.

Recently some disturbing activities occurred, namely the small macadam road which runs parallel to the sea, together with the digging of a large rounded pit, clearly visible on the contour map. On the east side of the site house building occurred. Although the houses are situated on the border area, where the concentration of finds is almost zero, they might still be situated in areas that the Amerindians had used, as gardening fields.

No signs were found that the site had been reoccupied during Amerindian times by other groups. All pottery characteristics could be ascribed to the Cedrosan Saladoid subseries (cf. Hamburg 1994 and chapter 7). Also based on the dates, it can be concluded that this site has been occupied during a single period.

No systematic research was done on the disturbing effects of natural processes. Considering the nature of the archaeological material found, it is likely that part of the material has perished. The conditions on the site were not extremely wet or dry and the soil mainly consisted of compact (fine) sand. Wood and other vegetal remains are likely to have perished under these circumstances.

No signs indicate that geological processes have disturbed the site significantly. Biotic processes might have played a role; the frequent appearance of crab holes and the dense vegetation nowadays, will certainly have caused small volumes within the midden to be mixed-up.

It can be concluded that the refuse area is well preserved for the most part. On this part only small biotic disturbances have played a role. Historic and recent activities were among the most disturbing agents. Only agricultural activities had affected the entire site. Other disturbances are only present locally.

6.9 Conclusions

At Anse des Pères an area of approximately 15,000 m^2 was systematically prospected by means of shovel tests. The prospection revealed an area with a length of 110 m and a width of maximum 30 m containing a deposit on average 60 cm thick, with a high concentration of pottery, lithic artefacts, shell, crab, and animal bone remains. Around this area the concentration of finds was considerably smaller and no distinct deposits were recognized. Close inspection of the concentration maps pointed to two areas with significant higher concentrations. Within each of both areas three 1×1 m test units were excavated.

The stratigraphy within both areas was the same: an impenetrable substratum, overlain by a mutual indistinguishable deposit, of which the upper 20 cm had been mixed up by agricultural activities during colonial times. The high concentrated refuse deposit has been preserved well. Post-depositional human activities have disturbed only the upper 20 cm. At some locations these activities, however, have resulted in deeper intrusions. From the undisturbed part it was possible to refit many pottery fragments coming from the same levels within the units, indicating an in-situ preservation.

Three crab samples were taken for radiocarbon dating. All dates overlap and span a period from cal AD 750 to 950. The dates and the stratigraphy strongly suggest that the site is a single-component one occupied during the late period of the Cedrosan Saladoid subseries.

The deposits with the high concentrations of finds can be interpreted as a refuse area belonging to a small village. Both areas are comparable in size to the refuse area found at the contemporary Golden Rock site on St. Eustatius. Considering the settlement lay-out at Golden Rock it is likely that the house structures had been closely situated to these spots, either at the west or east of it. Two hypotheses come to mind; either each distinct refuse area represents a distinct subsequent period of occupation, or both areas belonged to different house structures/clusters within the same period of occupation. This problem cannot be solved with the present data. These dates, however, suggest that both areas belonged to different occupational periods. Future research should provide additional information with respect to this topic.

7   Pottery

Tom Hamburg

7.1   Stylistic and morphological analysis

The Anse des Pères pottery was recovered from seven 1×1 m excavation units. Unit 4 was not fully excavated due to the discovery of human skeletal remains at 20 cm below the present surface. However, the pottery of the first two levels of this unit is used in the following discussion of the pottery assemblage. The description gives a quantitative and qualitative account of the various aspects shown by the pottery of the Anse des Pères assemblage.

In all 6,654 pottery sherds were found at the Anse des Pères site. They can be divided into five categories (table7.1), i.e., body sherds (79.3%), rim sherds (11.9%), base sherds (3.0%), griddle (4.2%), and appendages/other sherds (1.6%). The total weight of the pottery is 63.696 kg; the average sherd weight is 9.6 grams. The weight per category shows a slightly different distribution as that of the potsherd numbers for all categories (table 7.2): body sherds (55.9%), rim sherds (21.9%), base sherds (7.8%), griddle sherds (9.7%), and appendages/other sherds (4.6%).

	body	rim	base	griddle	app / oth	total
Unit 1	998	104	20	31	11	1164
	83	41	21	14	5	164
	1081	145	41	45	16	1328
Unit 2	555	72	27	40	11	205
	106	43	21	10	11	191
	661	115	48	50	22	896
Unit 3	601	82	31	28	9	751
	68	22	12	5	5	112
	669	104	43	33	14	863
Unit 4	754	65	9	19	12	859
	14	4	0	2	3	23
	768	69	9	21	15	882
Unit 5	594	95	17	53	9	768
	49	19	8	9	6	91
	643	114	25	62	15	859
Unit 6	694	95	6	23	8	823
	72	57	10	8	4	151
	766	152	16	31	9	974
Unit 7	645	79	9	32	7	772
	43	13	10	8	6	80
	688	92	19	40	13	852
Total <5	4841	592	119	226	64	5841
Total >5	435	199	82	56	40	812
Total all	5276	791	201	282	104	6654
Perc.	79.3%	11.9%	3.0%	4.2%	1.6%	100.0%

Table 7.1. The pottery number smaller than 5 cm, larger than 5 cm and the total amount of pottery in each unit.

	body	rim	base	griddle	app / oth	total
Unit 1	6959	2712	1116	1351	372	12510 19.6%
Unit 2	6380	3030	1117	1280	529	12336 19.4%
Unit 3	4682	1826	860	468	391	8227 12.9%
Unit 4	2985	438	66	276	238	4003 6.3%
Unit 5	4048	1242	670	1125	444	7529 11.8%
Unit 6	5949	3596	562	1034	491	11632 18.3%
Unit 7	4594	1136	609	647	473	7459 11.7%
Total	35597	13980	5000	6181	2938	63696
Perc.	55.9%	21.9%	7.8%	9.7%	4.6%	100.0%

Table 7.2. The total weight of the various pottery categories in each unit.

7.1.1 DECORATIVE MOTIFS

The decorative motifs on all of the sherds in the assemblage have been analysed. All modes were counted including cases in which more than one mode of decoration was present on one and the same sherd. This enables us to present a complete view of the different design motifs used. The total number of decorated sherds was recorded as a separate category. In all 590 of the 6654 sherds of the assemblage are decorated. A total number of 637 individual designs has been recorded. Figure 7.1 shows the distribution of decoration modes. Incision (48.8%) and white-on-red painting (31.6%) are the predominant decoration modes in the Anse des Pères pottery assemblage.

Other types of decoration occur in small numbers, i.e., zoned-incised crosshatching (ZIC; 3.3%), nubbins (2.8%), polychrome painting (1.1%), zoomorphic modelling (0.5%), and anthropomorphic modelling (0.2%) (fig. 7.2).
The category 'other decorative modes' (11.8%) consists of a number of designs which have not been recorded individually. These motifs include: white slip (52.0%), black paint (21.3%), orange slip (6.7%), red slip applied as a design (5.3%), white on beige slip (2.7%), white on orange slip (2.7%), beige on white slip (2.7%), white and red slip (2.7%), beige slip (1.3%), brown slip (1.3%), and red on orange slip (1.3%).

The combinations of decoration modes, most frequently occurring in the pottery assemblage, comprise white-on-red painting and incision. White slip occurs in combination with incisions on 13 sherds while 11 pieces show white paint filled incisions. Other combinations are less frequent. Three sherds are decorated with white-on-red painted motifs while showing black painted interiors, one sherd has polychrome painting and incisions, and another white and orange painted designs next to incisions.

Red slip has been recorded separately as it serves not only as a decorative technique but has also been used functionally, for example, in order to make a vessel suitable for the storage

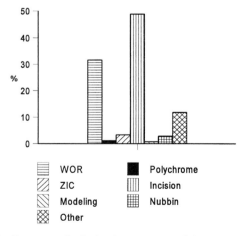

Fig. 7.1. Frequency distribution in percentage of decoration modes in all units.

74

Fig. 7.2. Decorative modes: a. incision (scale 1:3), b. incision, red slip on plain (scale 1:3), c-d. incision (scale 1:3), e. incision (scale 1:2), f. incision and red slip (scale 1:2), g. incision (scale 1:2), h. incision, ZIC and red slip (scale 1:3), i-k. incision and ZIC (scale 1:3), l. incision, ZIC and red slip (scale 1:2), m. incision and ZIC (scale 1:2), n-p. modelling (scale 1:2), q. modelling, incision and ZIC (scale 1:2), r. modelling (scale 1:2).

of liquids. In all 504 sherds showing red slipped surfaces have been recorded, accounting to 7.6% of the total number of potsherds of the assemblage.

7.1.2   VESSEL SHAPES

The rim sherds longer than 5 cm have been used for a more elaborate analysis of the Anse des Pères pottery (after Hofman 1993). The vessel shape could be identified for 152 sherds.

Nine vessel contour/orifice combinations have been recognized in the Anse des Pères assemblage (fig. 7.3), i.e.,

1. Dish with unrestricted simple contour.
2. Bowl with unrestricted simple contour.
3. Jar with unrestricted simple contour.
4. Dish or bowl with unrestricted composite contour, either
   A. showing a concave profile above the corner point, or
   B. showing a straight profile above the corner point.

Unrestricted orifice

Restricted orifice

Independent restricted orifice

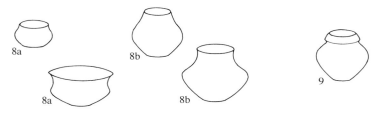

Fig. 7.3. Nine combinations of vessel shapes (Hofman 1993, 65).
 1. Dish with an unrestricted simple contour,
 2. Bowl with an unrestricted simple contour,
 3. Jar with an unrestricted simple contour,
 4. Dish or bowl with an unrestricted composite contour (with two variants a and b; variant a has a concave wallprofile above the carination point and variant b has a straight wallprofile above the carination point,
 5. Jar with an unrestricted composite contour,
 6. Bowl with an unrestricted, inflected contour,
 7. Bowl with a restricted simple contour (with two variants a and b; variant a has the largest diameter above the half of the height and variant b below the half of the height),
 8. Bowl or jar with a restricted composite contour (variant a is a bowl and b is a jar),
 9. Bowl with a restricted, complex contour,
 10. Bowl or jar with an independent restricted, inflected contour (with four variants a-d; these vessels are either bowls or jars, they have a globular body and the collar or neck can be either straight (a, c) or outflaring (b, d),
 11. Bowl or jar with an independent restricted, complex contour.

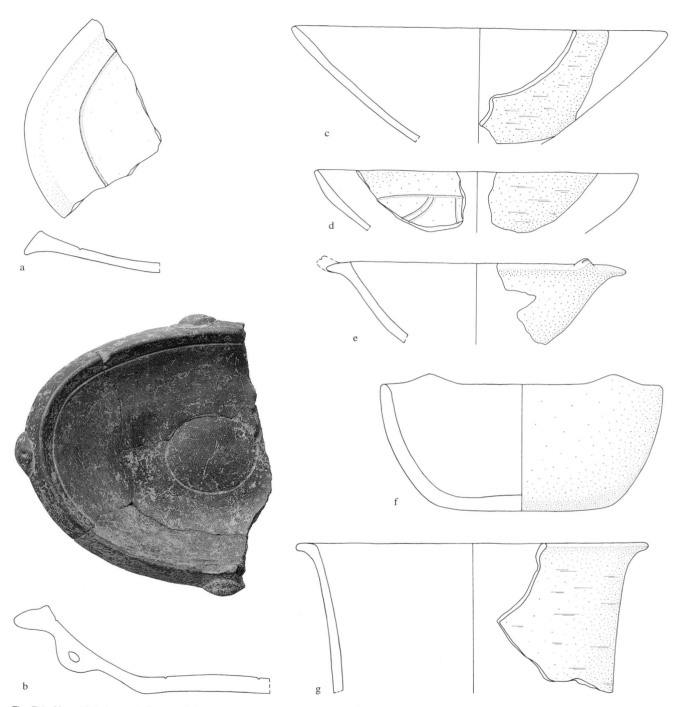

Fig. 7.4. Unrestricted vessel shapes; dish-, bowl- and jar-shaped vessels with simple contours: a-b. oval dish-shaped vessels (scale 1:2), c-e. bowl-shaped vessels (scale 1:2), f. bowl-shaped vessel (scale 1:3), g. jar-shaped vessel (scale 1:3).

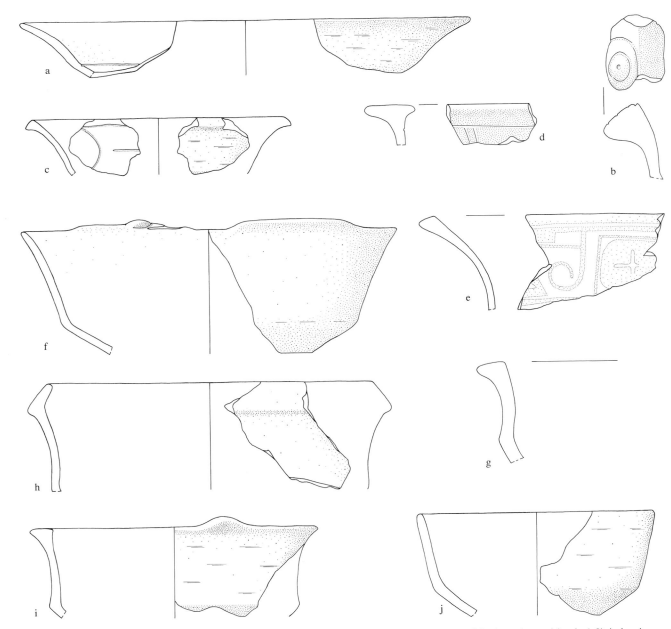

Fig. 7.5. Unrestricted vessel shapes; dish-, bowl- and jar-shaped vessels with composite contours: a. dish-shaped vessel (scale 1:3), b. bowl-shaped vessel with decoration on rim (scale 1:2), c. bowl-shaped vessel with incision (scale 1:3), d. bowl-shaped vessel with decoration inside (scale 1:2), e. bowl-shaped vessel with WOR (scale 1:3), f. bowl-shaped vessel with decoration on rim (scale 1:3), g. bowl-shaped vessel (scale 1:2), h-j. bowl-shaped vessels (scale 1:3).

Fig. 7.6. Vessel shapes (scale 1:4): a. oval bowl-shaped vessel with an unrestricted simple contour, b. bowl-shaped vessel with an unrestricted composite contour, c. jar-shaped vessel with a complex contour.

5. Bowl with unrestricted inflected contour.
6. Bowl with restricted simple contour, showing its largest diameter in the top half of the vessel.
7. Bowl or jar with restricted composite contour.
8. Bowl or jar with independent restricted inflected contour, showing a straight or outflaring neck. This category can be subdivided into:
   A. bowl with straight/outflaring neck.
   B. jar with straight/outflaring neck.
9. Bowl or jar with independent restricted complex contour.

Unrestricted vessel shapes
Unrestricted vessels form the most frequent pottery shape in the Anse des Pères assemblage (128 sherds, 84.2%). Unrestricted vessel shapes can be subdivided into five sub-groups. Sub-group (1) consists of dish-shaped vessels showing simple contours. This vessel shape is common in the assemblage (9.2%)(fig. 7.4a-e). Sub-group (2) includes bowl-shaped vessels showing simple contours (14.5%). Sub-group (3) is made up of jar-shaped vessels with simple contours (10.5%) (fig. 7.4f-g). Sub-group (4) can be further subdivided into two groups: (4A) and (4B). Both of these sub-groups comprise dish- or bowl-shaped vessels with composite contours. Sub-group (4A) shows a concave profile above the corner point. This group predominates in the assemblage (21.7%)(fig. 7.5a-i and 7.6b). Sub-group (4B)

shows a straight profile rather than a concave profile above the corner point (7.9%)(fig. 7.5j). Sub-group (5), finally, consists of bowl-shaped vessels with inflected contours. This group ranges second in the assemblage (20.4%). One vessel shape, ascribed to sub-groups (1) and (2) should be mentioned separately. This form involves dishes and bowls with simple contours showing, oval- or boat-shaped orifices. This vessel shape occurs seven times (4.6%) in the assemblage (figs 7.4a-b and 7.6a).

Restricted vessel shapes
Restricted vessel shapes occur less frequently than unrestricted forms (8.6%). Two sub-groups can be distinguished. The first sub-group (6) consists of bowl-shaped vessels with simple contours showing the largest diameter in the top half of the vessel. It is represented by 7.9% of the sherds in the assemblage (fig. 7.7a-c). The second sub-group (7) consists of bowl- or jar-shaped vessels showing composite contours. It is represented by 0.7% (fig. 7.7d).

Independent restricted vessel shapes
Independent restricted forms are rare in the Anse des Pères assemblage (7.2%). Two sub-groups can be distinguished, of which the first sub-group (8) has been further subdivided into two sub-groups: (8A) and (8B). Both these sub-groups belong to the category of bowl- or jar-shaped vessels with

Fig. 7.7. Restricted vessel shapes; bowl-shaped vessels with simple contours and bowl-and jar-shaped vessels with composite contours: a-b. bowl-shaped vessels with simple contour (scale 1:3), c-d. bowl-shaped vessels with restricted composite contour (scale 1:3), e-f. jar-shaped vessels with independent restricted complex contour (scale 1:2), g. jar-shaped vessel with independent restricted complex contour (scale 1:3).

inflected contours. Sub-group (8A) consists of bowl-shaped vessels with straight/outflaring necks. It is represented by 2.0% of the sherds. Sub-group (8B) is composed of jar-shaped vessels with straight/outflaring necks. It is represented by 2.6% of the sherds. The second major sub-group (9) consists of bowl- or jar-shaped vessels with complex contours. It is represented by 2.6% of the sherds (fig. 7.6c).

7.1.3 RIM SHAPES
The shape of four rim sherds could not be determined. Rounded (45.9%) and outward thickened rims (39.2%) form the two most predominant shapes in the Anse des Pères assemblage. Flat (4.7%), inwardly-thickened (2.7%), double-thickened (2.7%), and bevelled (4.7%) are rare.

The profile of two rim sherds could not be determined. The straight/vertical profiles predominate (93.3%). All other rim profiles are rare: bevelled/inverted, flaring, and incurved profiles amounting to 0.7%, 4.7% and 1.3% of the sherds, respectively.

7.1.4 WALL THICKNESS
Vessel walls range in thickness from 1 to 10 mm. Three groups can be distinguished, showing walls of: 1-5 mm, 6-8 mm, and 9-10 mm in thickness, respectively. Most rim sherds (71.1%) are 6 to 8 mm thick. The 1-5 mm group contains 8.6% and the 9-10 mm group 20.4% of the total amount of rim sherds.

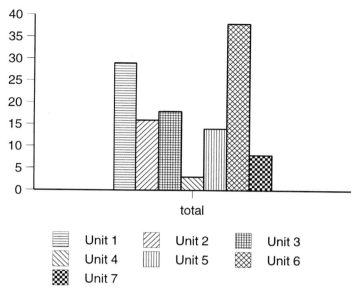

Fig. 7.8. Frequency distribution in number of orifice diameter on rim sherds in each unit.

7.1.5 ORIFICE DIAMETERS

The diameter of 26 rim sherds could not be determined. The others are grouped in one of the five groups. The highest percentage is found in the third group (21-30 cm) 42.1%. The second (11-20 cm) and third (31-40 cm) group are as follows with 36.5% and 19.0% respectively. The two most extreme groups are small, the fifth (41-50 cm) group with 1.6% and the first (1-10 cm) group with 0.8% (fig. 7.8).

Figure 16.11. Average orifice diameters of vessels in all units.

7.1.6 SURFACE COLOURS

The Anse des Pères rim sherds show surface colours ranging from light-grey and light-brown to dark-grey/black, dark brown/very dark brown, reddish brown, and red[1].
The exterior surface colours of 150 rims could be determined. Most sherds are dark brown/very dark brown in colour (33.3%). Other colours, i.e., reddish brown (24.0%), red (18.7%), light brown/brown (10.0%), dark grey/black (10.0%), light grey (2.7%), dark greyish brown (0.7%), and reddish grey/dark reddish grey (0.7%) are less well represented (table 7.11). The interior surface colours of 148 sherds could be determined and show a more or less similar pattern. Dark brown/very dark brown is predominant (45.9%). Reddish brown (31.8%), light brown/brown (9.5%), dark grey/black (6.1%), red (4.7%), grey (0.7%), dark greyish brown (0.7%), and reddish grey/dark reddish grey (0.7%) form minorities. Forty of the coded rim sherds show a red slip applied to various areas of the vessel. Most of these sherds have red-slipped rims (52.5%). Rim sherds showing both red-slipped exterior surfaces and rims range second (17.5%), red-slipped rims and interior and exterior surfaces, slipped red all over range third (15.0%), and interiorly red-slipped surfaces and red-slipped rims range fourth (12.5%). Exclusively interiorly red-slipped surfaces are rare (2.5%).

7.1.7 FIRING ATMOSPHERE

The firing atmosphere determines the colour of the sherd core. According to Rice (1987, 345) the following relationship exists between firing colour and firing atmosphere.

– Incomplete relatively high oxidation: grey or brown core and brown to reddish-brown outer zones;
– Complete reduction: dark grey or black core and outer zones;
– Incomplete oxidation or reduction: light grey core and outer zones;
– Complete oxidation: red core and outer zones.

Most sherds are incompletely, relatively well oxidized (74.8%). Complete reduction (13.2%), incomplete oxidation or reduction (9.9%), and complete oxidation (2.0%) are less well represented.

7.1.8 SURFACE FINISHING

Exterior surface finish of 13 rim sherds could not be determined. Most sherds are highly burnished (64.7%). Polished

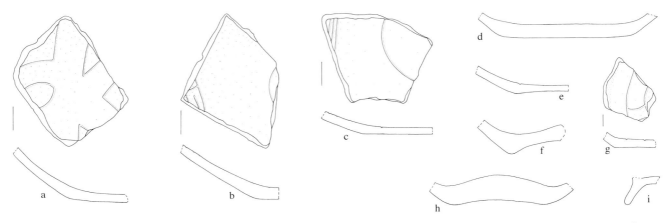

Fig. 7.9. Base shapes (scale 1:3): a. flat base with red slip and incision on the inside, b-c. flat bases incision on the inside, d. flat base, e-f. concave bases, g. flat base, h. concave base, i. pedestal base.

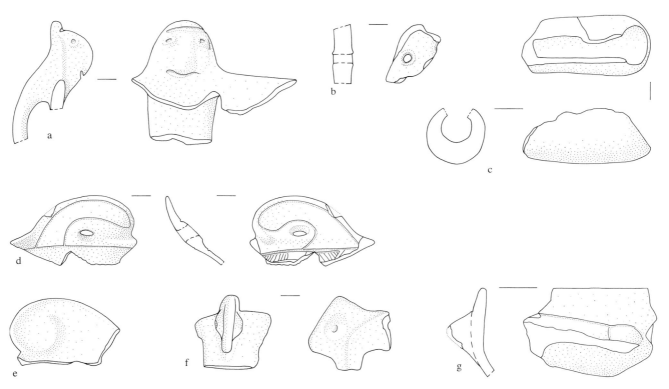

Fig. 7.10. Appendages and sieve: a. handle with modelling (scale 1:2), b. fragment of a sieve (scale 1:2), c. spout (scale 1:2), d. ear-shaped lug (scale 1:2), e. lug (scale 1:2), f. modelled lug (scale 1:2), g. oval-shaped lug with incision.

(20.9%) and lightly burnished (14.4%) are less well represented.

Interior surface finish of 14 rim sherds could not be determined. Most sherds show highly burnished interiors (55.8%). Lightly burnished (23.2%), polished (19.6%), and smoothed (1.4%) are less well represented.

7.1.9 BASES

The shapes of 80 of the in all 201 base sherds could be determined. Flat bases form the majority (73.8%). Concave bases (13.8%), convex bases (7.5%), and pedestal bases (5.0%) are less common (fig. 7.9).

7.1.10 APPENDAGES

The 'appendage/other' category consists of 104 sherds. The various features found in the assemblage comprise handles (48.1%), lugs, including the ear-shaped ones (16.3%), spouts (5.8%), pieces of locally worn pottery (3.8%), a fragment of a sieve (1.0%), a leg in the shape of a human leg (1.0%), a piece of a square pot or lid (1.0%), and a series with unidentified sherds (23.1%) (fig. 7.10).

7.1.11 GRIDDLES

Griddle sherds can be subdivided according to rim shape. The shapes of 23 of the in all 282 griddle pieces could be determined (fig. 7.11). They are straight (52.2%), rounded (34.8%), triangular (8.7%), and overhanging (4.3%).

7.2 Synthesis and conclusions

7.2.1 STYLE AND MORPHOLOGY

The results of the Anse des Pères pottery analysis can be combined with the data obtained from the stratigraphical observations and the radiocarbon measurements in order to date the site as accurately as possible and to establish its regional cultural and chronological affiliations.

Summarizing, the pottery from Anse des Pères can be characterized as follows:

Unrestricted vessels form the predominant vessel shape, showing a predominance of dishes or bowls with unrestricted composite contours, next to bowls with unrestricted inflected contours. The two most frequently represented shapes comprise unmodified rims with rounded lips and outwardly thickened rims. Wall thickness ranges from 6 to 8 mm. Surface colours on the exterior and interior surfaces of the vessel vary from reddish brown and very dark brown to red. The majority of the analysed rim sherds have been fired under incompletely oxidizing conditions. Most exterior and interior vessel surfaces are highly burnished. In all 8.9% of the total number of pottery sherds is decorated. Incision and white-on-red painting represent the predominant decorative modes in the assemblage. Polychrome painting, zoned-incised crosshatching (ZIC), modelling, and slipping

in various colours are less well represented. Red slip is most frequent. The slip covers the body of the vessel on the exterior and/or interior surfaces. Red slip on the coded rim sherds occurs predominantly on the lip of the vessel. The predominant rim shapes of griddles are straight and rounded. Bases are predominantly flat. The category of appendages and other designs comprises mostly D-shaped handles and lugs.

7.2.2 DATING AND REGIONAL ASSOCIATIONS

According to the Anse des Pères radiocarbon dates ranging from cal AD 730 to 959 the site should correspond to the IIIA period in Rouse's chronology of Caribbean archaeology placing it outside the Cedrosan Saladoid subseries. However, the style and decoration of the pottery assemblage at Anse des Pères clearly show that it belongs to this subseries. Rouse's dates for this subseries range from AD 400 to 600 but the Anse des Pères dates show that the upper date range can be extended to AD 950. The final period of the Cedrosan Saladoid is defined by the Cuevas style on Puerto Rico and the Coral Bay Longford style in the Virgin Islands. The pottery of these areas shows a general decline in technology and a gradual disappearance of the elaborately painted modelled-incised designs which can be observed in the Cedrosan Saladoid subseries.

In contrast to this the pottery of the Anse des Pères site does not correspond to this general description. The ceramic assemblage shows much more similarities with the Saladoid pottery complexes found on the Lesser Antilles.

In this island chain the latter portion of the Cedrosan Saladoid subseries witnesses an increase in the complexity of the white-on-red painted designs, next to a predominance of

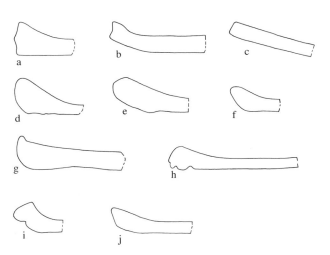

Fig. 7.11. Griddles rim shapes (scale 1:3): a-c. straight, d-g. rounded, h-i. triangular, j. overhanging rim.

polychrome painting, and the development of flanged-rim bowls and incense burners. The unrestricted vessel form, the so-called inverted-bell shape predominates in this period. Sites associated with this period have been found, amongst others, on St. Eustatius, the Golden Rock site and Antigua, the Indian Creek II site (Versteeg and Schinkel 1992; Rouse 1976).

The pottery assemblage of the Anse des Pères site shows close cultural affiliations with the materials of Golden Rock and Indian Creek. A more elaborate description will be given of the pottery assemblages of these two sites in order to show the similarities and the differences with Anse des Pères. Furthermore, a short description will be given of the Sugar Factory Pier, St. Kitts (Goodwin 1979; based on the chronology of Rouse 1992, 52-53), another site dating from Late Cedrosan Saladoid times. A number of sites in the Lesser Antilles which, according to Rouse's chronology (1992) are associated with the Cedrosan Saladoid with Barrancoid influences, are described in order to compare them to the Anse des Pères site. These sites include Le Diamant, Martinique (Petitjean Roget 1968; Vidal 1992), Morel II, Guadeloupe (Clerc 1968; Barbotin 1970), and Chancery Lane, Barbados (Drewett 1991). The following radiocarbon dates have been obtained for these sites:

Golden Rock	1755 ± 20-1205 ± 30 BP
Indian Creek	1765 ± 80-1440 ± 85 BP
Morel II	1400 ± 80-1380 ± 100 BP
Chancery Lane	1570 ± 95 BP
Le Diamant	–
Sugar Factory Pier	–

Golden Rock, St. Eustatius

The excavations at the Golden Rock site on St. Eustatius have yielded much additional information on the pottery of the Late Cedrosan Saladoid subseries. The most common vessel shape of this assemblage is the unrestricted shape like the one encountered in Anse des Pères. Firing conditions of the Golden Rock pottery ranged from oxidizing to reducing. The firing took place in open fires with temperatures of 850 to 900° C. A high percentage (± 20%, red slip included) of the pottery excavated in 1984 at the Golden Rock site, is decorated (Versteeg and Schinkel 1992). White-on-red and incised designs occur frequently. The same applies polychrome painting. The Golden Rock assemblage contains a large number of *adornos* both anthropomorphic and zoomorphic. Vessel bases are predominantly flat like those at Anse des Pères. Another minor pottery feature that deserves attention is the presence of a similar type of leg, in the shape of a human foot, in both Golden Rock and Anse des Pères assemblage. Other resemblances between Golden Rock and

Anse des Pères pottery include the D-shaped handles and lugs, the many nubbins and pieces of secondarily worn sherds. The occurrence of part of a pottery sieve in Golden Rock forms a final similarity with the Anse des Pères assemblage (Steenvoorden 1987). Incense burners have been reported from the Golden Rock site but are unknown from Anse des Pères. The Golden Rock griddle rims show a great diversity of shapes.

Indian Creek, Antigua

The Indian Creek excavations yielded pottery of both the Early Cedrosan Saladoid and Late Cedrosan Saladoid periods. The predominant vessel shape in this assemblage is the unrestricted (inverted bell-shaped form). Flanged rim bowls make their first appearance. Pottery decoration in Late Cedrosan Saladoid at Indian Creek differs in complexity from that of Early Cedrosan: white-on-red painting improves in quality and polychrome painting is introduced for the first time. These decorative motifs are found at Anse des Pères as well. However, a number of the designs typical of Early Cedrosan ceramics persist in the late phase of this subseries, e.g., zoned-incised crosshatching, various incised motifs and the anthropomorphic and zoomorphic *adornos*.
Griddles are present in the Indian Creek assemblage but no specifications are given concerning rim shape or thickness. D-shaped handles and lugs, similar to those at Anse des Pères are to be found at the Indian Creek site. Incense burners make their first appearance in the Late Indian Creek (Faber Morse and Rouse 1995; Rouse 1974, 1976).

Sugar Factory Pier, St. Kitts

Sugar Factory Pier is the largest late Cedrosan Saladoid site on St. Kitts. Unfortunately, the elaborate descriptions of the pottery of this site are not available for study. Using the dissertation of Goodwin (1979), only a very general description of the decorative motifs found in the Sugar Factory Pier assemblage can be given. Polychrome painting, elaborate white-on-red painted designs, flanged rims, and incense burners form characteristic ceramic elements at this site. According to Veloz Maggiolo (1991, 237) an *adorno* found at Sugar Factory Pier shows influence from the Barrancoid series. This is confirmed by Rouse who recently identified Barrancoid influences on Antigua pottery (Rouse 1995).

Chancery Lane, Barbados

Chancery Lane, Barbados, is the major Cedrosan Saladoid site of the island. According to Drewett (1991, 59), it has yielded Cedrosan Saladoid pottery with Barrancoid influences. The most common vessel shapes found at Chancery Lane include unrestricted inverted-bell shaped forms showing composite contours and outwardly thickened or flanged rims next to restricted vessels with concave necks. Vessels are thin to medium thick, wall thickness of the ranges from below 5 mm to 5-7 mm. They are predominantly relatively well finished. Pottery decorations include polychrome painting in red, white and black, incision on top of flanged rims and modelling combined with incision, elaborately white-on-red painted designs, and red slip applied to the body or rim. Zoned-incised crosshatching is rare but fine-incised parallel-lined designs connecting semi-circles are common. A small number of *adornos* have been found, showing pronounced snouts and modelled-incised nostrils, eyes, ears and mouths. Most vessel surfaces are polished. Bases are predominantly flat and concave. Incense burners and possible pot-stands are also known from Chancery Lane (Boomert 1987b; Drewett 1991). According to Drewett and Boomert Chancery Lane pottery shows ceramic influences originating in the Barrancoid series. However, in view of the fact that the Chancery Lane assemblage does not contain any direct Barrancoid imitations, both authors think that this influence was weak. In the Windward islands Barrancoid influence on the Cedrosan Saladoid series was much more profound.

Le Diamant, Martinique

The most common vessel shape at the site of Le Diamant is the unrestricted inverted-bell shaped form with composite contours. Oval vessels are also present in this assemblage, although, they remain rare. Predominant rim shapes include outwardly thickened and flanged, often red-slipped, rims. Decoration include elaborately white-on-red and polychrome (white, red, black and orange) painted designs, incision, red-painted rims and hollow-backed zoomorphic and anthropomorphic, modelled-incised *adornos*. Base shape are predominantly flat. Handles are attached to the rim, showing D-shaped forms. Pottery is much more complex than that of the Early Cedrosan Saladoid times, while it shows an emphasis on modelled-incised motifs (Petitjean Roget 1968; Vidal 1992).

Morel II, Guadeloupe

The Morel II site of Guadeloupe yielded Barrancoid influenced Cedrosan Saladoid pottery. A great variety of vessel shapes is present in the assemblage. The predominant forms include unrestricted inverted-bell shaped vessels with composite contours, unrestricted bowl and dishes and boat- and animal-shaped vessels, the latter showing heads and feet attached to the vessel rims. Outwardly thickened and flanged rims are predominant. Decoration includes white-on-red and polychrome (red, white, black, orange and yellow) painted designs, red-slipped surfaces (on the interior, the rim and the top of the body exterior), zoned-incised crosshatching, incised lines (occasionally surrounding painted areas), spirals and circles and, finally hollow-backed zoomorphic and anthropomorphic, modelled-incised *adornos*.

Handles, attached to the vessel rims, are D-shaped or ear-like (Clerc 1968; Barbotin 1970).

7.3   Conclusions

The main aim of this chapter was to describe the Anse des Pères pottery assemblage and to place it in the regional cultural chronology. According to Rouse, the Cedrosan Saladoid subseries can be subdivided into two phases (Rouse 1992; Hofman 1993): Early and Late Cedrosan Saladoid of which the latter phase may or may not show Barrancoid influence. In the Lesser Antilles the ceramic developments of Late Cedrosan Saladoid phase were quite distinct from those on the Greater Antilles. In the latter islands the pottery of this period is characterized by an overall decline in complexity of decoration and pottery technology, compared to the Early Cedrosan Saladoid phase in the area. In contrast, the pottery of the Lesser Antilles displays an increase in complexity in, for example, the white-on-red and other polychrome painted designs and new forms such as flanged rim bowls. Also, incense burners appear for the first time.

The Anse des Pères material shows great similarity with the Cedrosan Saladoid pottery of the Leeward Islands including St. Eustatius, St. Kitts and Antigua. The predominant vessel shape is the unrestricted form while the decorative motifs are similar in their use of white-on-red and polychrome painting and incision. Moreover, D-shaped handles are frequently encountered. The pottery assemblages of the Windward Islands show similarities with the Leeward Island assemblages. However, the Barrancoid influenced Cedrosan Saladoid pottery of the Windwards is heavier, thicker and softer. The most significant difference between the Cedrosan Saladoid pottery of the Leeward and Windward Islands can be detected in the *adornos*. A large variety of hollow-backed zoomorphic and anthropomorphic, modelled-incised *adornos* is to be found on the Windward Islands, showing Barrancoid influence. This is obvious from the frequent use of modelled-incised motifs. Another difference between the Late Cedrosan Saladoid pottery of the Windward and Leeward Islands is the frequent occurrence of thickened and flanged rims on Windward ceramics. The identification of Barrancoid influence on Cedrosan Saladoid pottery is based on a combination of various ceramic modes which find their origin in the Barrancoid series. Some of these characteristics have been documented for the pottery of the Leewards and attest for minor Barrancoid influence on these islands. Barrancoid influences are absent in the Anse des Pères assemblage, but this may be due to the small sample size. The Anse des Pères pottery has been recovered from seven 1×1 m test units, which represents only a small percentage of the total Anse des Pères site area. The predominant vessel shape in the Anse des Pères assemblage is the unrestricted form, typically showing unmodified rims with rounded lips. The pottery is frequently decorated with incised and white-on-red painted designs. Polychrome painting, zoned-incised crosshatching, and modelling are also present in the pottery assemblage. Decorated potsherds comprise 8.9% of the total number of pieces. Appendages such as D-shaped handles and eared lugs are frequently found.

If calibrated, radiocarbon dates of Anse des Pères range from the 8th to halfway through the 10th century AD. This indicates that the site belongs to the Late Cedrosan Saladoid phase in the Lesser Antilles, which can be taken to have lasted from ± AD 400 to 600/850. This dating is supported by the diagnostic ceramic traits shown by the Anse des Pères pottery. Other Late Cedrosan Saladoid sites in the area, i.e., Golden Rock, (St. Eustatius), Indian Creek, (Antigua), and Sugar Factory Pier, (St. Kitts), provide further confirmation of this chronological placement by showing great similarity to the Anse des Pères assemblage. Anse des Pères can be considered a single component site, showing no variation in pottery across the site or in the stratigraphy.

The Anse des Pères site yielded some extraordinary archaeo-logical finds. The presence of a large number of almost complete vessels in the 1×1 m excavation units is an indica-tion of the great potential for further examination of the site.

The site is largely undisturbed at present, however, as con-struction activities are going on in the area, this may change rapidly. It is obvious that more extensive excavations are necessary to deepen our knowledge regarding the material culture in the Late Cedrosan Saladoid phase in St. Martin.

notes

1 These colours are defined as follows using a Munsell Color Soil Chart:
- light grey: Hue 10 YR 7/1, 7/2, 6/1; Hue 7.5 YR N7/;
- grey: Hue 10 YR 5/1, 4.1; Hue 7.5 YR N6/, N5/;
- very dark grey/black: Hue 10 YR 3/1, 2/1, 2/2; Hue 7.5 YR N4/, N3/; Hue 5 YR 4/1, 3/1;
- light brownish-grey/greyish brown: (Hue 10 YR 6/2, 5/2; Hue 5 YR 7/1, 6/1, 5/1);
- dark greyish-brown: Hue 10 YR 4/2, 3/2, 3/3;
- light brown/brown: Hue 10 YR 6/3, 5/3, 5/4, 5/6, 5/8, 4/3, 4/4, 4/6; Hue 7.5 YR 6/4, 6/6, 5/6;
- dark brown/very dark brown: Hue 7.5 YR 5/2, 5/3, 5/4, 4/2, 4/3, 4/4, 3/2;
- reddish/dark reddish: Hue 5 YR 5/2, 4/2;
- light reddish-brown/reddish-brown: Hue 5 YR 6/3, 6/4, 6/6, 5/3, 5/4, 5/6, 4/3, 4/4, 3/2, 3/3, 3/4, 2/2; Hue 2.5 YR 5/4, 4/4;
- red: Hue 2.5 YR 5/2, 4/2; Hue 10 R 5/2, 5/3, 5/4, 4/2, 4/3, 4/4, 4/6, 4/8, 5/6, 5/8.

8 Lithics

Sebastiaan Knippenberg

8.1 Introduction

This chapter deals with the lithic artefacts recovered from the test units at Anse des Pères. These were randomly sampled and therefore, provide an opportunity to draw general conclusions about the whole lithic assemblage at the site. The lithic artefacts recovered from the shovel tests and the surface are only described here where they differ from the test units. These differences enable evaluation of the test units sample in terms of its representativeness. The fieldwork produced a total of 1227 lithic artefacts. Of these, 21 were found on the surface,[1] 300 were collected in the shovel tests and 906 were recovered from the test units (tables 8.1 and 8.2).[2] All were analysed according to a predefined scheme, as done for Norman Estate. The main aim was to reconstruct the different activity sets of lithic technology, as defined by Collins (1975; see also Driskell 1986).

8.2 Variation within the site

Potential differences between the test units were explored in terms of rock types and artefact types. In addition, the lithic artefacts from the test units and the shovels were compared. Analysis of the frequency of lithic artefacts within each test unit suggests that the lithic artefacts were evenly spread among the separate arbitrary levels. Large differences occurred only incidentally, and no meaningful pattern of distribution could be recognized within the variable concentrations of lithics.

When looking at the raw material of the artefacts found within each level, differences do occur (table 8.3). For example, most of the flint artefacts were found in the uppermost level (35%), in contrast to the cherty carbonate which was mostly concentrated (20%) within a level ca. 50 to 60 cm below the surface.

The comparison of test units excavated in both core areas of the site reveals differences in rock types (table 8.4). Test units 1, 2, and 3 contained significantly more flint and less cherty carbonate than did units 5, 6, and 7. Looking at the artefact types, the only difference exists in the number of axes, which came almost solely from test unit 6.

Comparison of the test unit finds with the shovel test finds and the surface finds reveals that the larger sample from the test units contains all of the artefact types, also recovered from the shovel tests and on the surface (tables 8.1-8.2). The shovel and surface finds, however, yielded preforms and core tools, which possess technological traits not found among the core tools recovered from the test units. This difference is the result of the small sample size from the test units and it only concerns relatively rare artefact types. Comparison of the lithic rock materials between the test units and the shovel tests reveals that the percentage of cherty carbonate and volcanic rock differ significantly across these samples. Part of this difference may have been caused by the different manner of sieving used during the excavation of the shovel tests. Due to dry sieving and less accurate sorting of the material during the shovel excavation, it is likely that the amount of cherty carbonate was biased towards lower values, cherty carbonate being more difficult to recognize in comparison with flint and volcanic rock. Differences in volcanic rock can be partly explained by the recovery of a large amount of this rock type from some of the shovel tests outside the refuse area.

8.3 Raw materials

Four main rock types were distinguished: flint, cherty carbonate, volcanic rock and hypabyssal rock. Beside these other types, such as quartz, plutonic rock, haematite, red stone, and sandstone, occur in small quantities. Most of the unidentified rock specimens are water-worn pebbles. These pebbles are often difficult to identify, given that only the polished outer surface is visible, obscuring the internal structure of the rock.

Flint

The flint, or nodular chert,[3] sample consists of a multi-coloured collection of artefacts. Given that few flint artefacts have preserved cortex, they were examined in terms of their grain size, colour and clast contents. Three types were distinguished. The first type is fine-grained, dull flint with almost no clasts. Colour differences are significant within this category, ranging from very dark (greyish) brown, dark (greyish) brown, pale brown to light yellowish brown. Even within a single piece, colour differences occur. Macroscopically, this type of flint is very similar to the flint found on Long Island near Antigua.

	Unit 1	Unit 2	Unit 3	Unit 4	Unit 5	Unit 6	Unit 7	Total
Flake	113	67	67	53	107	87	39	533
	58.2	60.4	50.0	61.6	64.5	62.6	51.3	58.8
Blade	–	–	–	–	1	–	1	2
	0.0	0.0	0.0	0.0	0.0	0.0	1.3	0.2
Shatter	18	12	10	8	4	3	2	57
	9.3	10.8	7.5	9.3	2.4	2.2	2.6	5.7
Flake Core	7	–	3	1	2	1	2	16
	3.6	0.0	2.2	1.2	1.2	0.7	2.6	1.8
Preform	4	2	3	–	4	5	3	21
	2.1	1.8	2.2	0.0	2.4	3.6	3.9	2.3
Axe/adze	1	–	1	–	–	6	2	10
	0.5	0.0	0.8	0.0	0.0	4.3	2.6	1.1
Butt-end	1	–	2	–	3	–	3	9
	0.5	0.0	1.5	0.0	1.8	0.0	3.9	1.0
Rubbing / grinding Stone	2	–	2	2	2	2	2	12
	1.0	0.0	1.5	2.3	1.2	1.4	2.6	1.3
Hammerstone / butt-end	–	–	–	1	1	1	1	4
	0.0	0.0	0.0	1.2	0.6	0.7	1.3	0.4
Hammerstone	3	–	2	–	1	1	1	8
	1.6	0.0	1.5	0.0	0.6	0.7	1.3	0.9
Pestle	–	–	1	–	–	–	–	1
	0.0	0.0	0.0	0.0	0.0	0.0	0.0	0.1
Unmodified waterw. pebble	18	21	26	12	26	20	11	134
	9.3	18.9	19.4	14.0	15.7	14.4	14.5	14.8
Natural stone	–	1	–	–	–	–	–	1
	0.0	0.9	0.0	0.0	0.0	0.0	0.0	0.1
Unidentified	26	8	17	9	15	13	9	97
	13.4	7.2	12.7	10.5	9.0	9.4	11.8	10.7
Total	194	111	134	86	166	139	76	906
	100.0	100.0	100.0	100.0	100.0	100.0	100.0	100.0

Table 8.1. The lithic artefact types found within the test units. Note that Unit 4 was not completely excavated.

The second type is a fine-grained, translucent flint containing white bioclasts, which are macroscopically difficult to identify. Besides these bioclasts, remaining parts of the cortex are present as inclusions due to the irregular form of the original cobbles. Little variability in terms of colour is present in this material ranging from light grey to pale brown.

The third type consists of fine-grained, dull flint. However, its grain size is coarser than the other two. This flint contains small white inclusions which are macroscopically difficult to identify. Its colour differs little, ranging from light grey to very pale brown.

Besides these three types of flint, other individual specimens occur, which are significantly different than the three defined types relative to grain size, colour, and clast contents.

As said before (cf. chapter 3), no flint occurrences are mentioned in the geological literature for St. Martin (Christman 1953; Westermann 1957). Likewise, modern day residents of the island have never seen flint sources there. Geochemical study of the flint has revealed that the majority originated from the natural flint occurrence on Long Island, a small island to the north of Antigua. Some flint may have come from St. Kitts, while the remainder of the flint has unknown origins (Knippenberg 1995).

	Shovel tests	Surface
Flake	169	1
	56.3	4.8
Blade	1	–
	0.3	0.0
Shatter	19	–
	6.3	0.0
Flake core	2	–
	0.7	0.0
Preform	8	8
	2.7	38.1
Axe / Adze	1	–
	0.3	0.0
Butt-end	–	–
	0.0	0.0
Rubbing / Grind-ing stone	5	–
	1.7	0.0
Hammerstone / Butt-end	–	–
	0.0	0.0
Hammerstone	3	–
	1.0	0.0
Pestle	–	–
	0.0	0.0
Unmodified Water-worn pebble	73	2
	24.3	9.5
Natural stone	1	–
	0.3	0.0
Unidentified	18	10
	6.0	47.6
Total	300	21
	100.0	100.0

Table 8.2. The artefact types found within the shovel units and on the surface. The surface finds were done unsystematically. Not much value should therefore be given to the percentages.

Cherty carbonate

This rock type was initially classified as radiolarian lime-stone (Haviser 1989). Recent analysis of thin-sections, how-ever, has pointed out that the amount of radiolarian in it is very small (Knippenberg 1995). Thus, the term "radiolar-ian" is misleading. Carbonate in the form of micrite is the main component of this rock type, along with cryptocristalline quartz. Therefore, this type is classified as cherty carbonate[4]. Macroscopically, the rock is chert/flint-like in appearance. It is a fine-grained rock with a greenish grey to greyish green colour. Notably, it produces the same conchoidal fracture as flint. The main difference between it and flint is its mode of formation. Unlike flint which is found in the form of nodules, this stone occurs in the form of bedded layers. This layering affects its suitability for stone working.

Provenance research has shown that the cherty carbonate from this archaeological site is similar to rock samples taken from an outcrop of the Point Blanche Formation at Hope Hill (Knippenberg 1995). This old marine floor, consisting of alternating layers of recrystallised tuffs, cherty and cal-careous tuffs, and cherts, can be found at different places on St. Martin (Christman 1953). Although the exact source location was not searched for, it may well have been in the vicinity of the site where parts of this formation are still preserved.

Cherty carbonate often has a completely different appear-ance in the archaeological record than it does in its original formation. Almost all of the lithic artefacts of this rock type are covered with a corrosive cortex layer which is chalk-like in appearance. This layer is the result of a weathering process during which the outer surface silica (cryptocrys-talline quartz) disappears and the carbonate (micrite) remains (Knippenberg 1995). The causes for this severe weathering are unclear. In any case, the results of this weathering is unfortunate for archaeologists, given that a lot of technologi-cal traits such as flake scars, bulbs of force, undulations and, polished surfaces have been obscured by the weathering. Different degrees of weathering can be seen among the cherty carbonate artefacts, ranging from specimens where the weathering is totally absent, and others with a thin, weathered chalk-like layer, to these where the original tex-ture has completely disappeared. In the latter case, a cor-roded stone survives, for which no technological traits are visible at all, only the crude shape of the stone may provide some clues on the type of the artefact it was originally. Almost all of these heavily weathered cherty carbonate artefacts were found within the excavation levels corre-sponding to the modern ploughzone. It is possible that the greater wetness of this stratum caused the carbonate to dissolve, but this was not tested.

Thin-sections analysis revealed that no differences in rock type occur between specimens which have been weathered differently. The unweathered artefacts were recovered throughout the test units along with the weathered pieces. Thus, it remains unclear what causes this differential weath-ering, although it is likely attributable to variability within the rock type itself.

Other raw materials

Besides the above mentioned rock types other types of rock were used by the Amerindians at Anse des Pères. Some could be obtained near the site in the form of water-worn

	1	2	3	4	5
Level 1	51 35.4	35 8.7	33 30.3	22 28.6	16 59.3
Level 2	21 15.6	49 12.2	18 16.5	13 16.9	3 11.1
Level 3	14 9.7	45 11.2	9 8.3	8 10.4	2 7.4
Level 4	16 11.1	58 14.4	9 8.3	9 11.7	1 3.7
Level 5	11 7.6	72 17.9	10 9.2	8 10.4	3 11.1
Level 6	16 11.1	81 20.1	15 13.8	8 10.4	2 7.4
Level 7	11 7.6	31 7.7	8 7.3	7 9.1	– 0.0
Level 8	3 2.1	26 6.5	7 6.4	1 1.3	– 0.0
Level 9	2 1.4	5 1.2	1 0.9	1 1.3	– 0.0
Level 10	– 0.0	– 0.0	– 0.0	– 0.0	– 0.0
Total	144 100.0	402 100.0	109 100.0	77 100.0	27 100.0

Table 8.3. Amount of most abundant rock types within the different arbitrary levels. Unit 4 is not included. 1 = Flint, 2 = Cherty carbonate, 3 = Volcanic rock, 4 = Hypabyssal rock, 5 = Quartz.

pebbles. Volcanic rock and hypabyssal rock dominate. Further characterisation of the different rock types was abandoned because of the difficulty of differentiating types where they occur as water-worn pebbles. Rocks with different colour types were obviously used. Most of these rocks probably were collected locally along the beach or from the small stream, both near the site.

Quartz is still another rock-type found in small quantities at Anse des Pères. Its properties are generally similar to flint. Quartz is less suitable for making tools, however, due to inclusions within the rock. All the quartz specimens are fine to medium-grained, and white in colour. The geological literature does not specifically mention any quartz outcrops on St. Martin. However, a lot of small, detrital quartz pieces, are found at and around the Norman Estate region, probably originating from the neighbouring hills. Thus, quartz sources are very likely to be found on St. Martin.

Haematite, red in colour, was only found at Anse des Pères in the form of raw material. It also probably originated on St. Martin (cf. chapter 13).

8.4 Lithic technologies

8.4.1 INTRODUCTION

Among the artefacts, both the products and the waste resulting from the application of two lithic technologies were distinguished. A minor portion of the lithic sample was produced using a flake technology while the majority of the lithics were produced as the result of a core tool technology. Along with the products and waste of these technologies, a third group was recognized in the lithic sample, consisting of water-worn pebbles. These pebbles were not worked, but had been only altered through use.

Flake technology is associated with the flint and quartz artefacts. The cherty carbonate, the volcanic rock, and to a small degree the hypabyssal rock were used for the production of core tools. The used, water-worn pebbles were made of volcanic rock, hypabyssal rock and cherty carbonate.

In the following sections, the activity sets, as defined by Collins (1975; see also Driskell 1986) are discussed for each technology separately. The used, water-worn pebbles, are considered to be unworked core tools, and are described in the section dealing with core tool production.

	Unit 1	Unit 2	Unit 3	Unit 5	Unit 6	Unit 7	Total Units	Total Shovels
Flint	60	22	26	13	16	8	145	62
	30.9	19.8	19.4	7.8	11.5	10.5	17.7	20.7
Cherty carbonate	60	40	75	98	82	47	402	91
	30.9	36.0	56.0	59.0	59.0	61.8	49.0	30.3
Volcanic rock	19	24	8	25	21	12	109	88
	9.8	21.6	6.0	15.1	15.1	15.8	13.3	29.3
Hypabyssal rock	16	13	13	16	11	6	75	26
	8.2	11.7	9.7	9.6	7.9	7.9	9.1	8.7
Plutonic rock	7	2	2	2	1	–	14	–
	3.6	1.8	1.5	1.2	0.7	0.0	1.7	0.0
Haematite	–	1	–	–	–	–	1	1
	0.0	0.9	0.0	0.0	0.0	0.0	0.1	0.3
Quartz	11	2	4	5	3	1	26	15
	5.7	1.8	3.0	3.0	2.2	1.3	3.2	5.0
Red stone	1	–	1	–	–	1	3	–
	0.5	0.0	0.7	0.0	0.0	1.3	0.4	0.0
Sandstone	–	–	–	1	–	–	1	1
	0.0	0.0	0.0	0.6	0.0	0.0	0.1	0.3
Unidentified	20	7	5	6	5	1	44	16
	10.3	6.3	3.7	3.6	3.6	1.3	5.4	5.3
Total	194	111	134	166	139	76	820	300
	100.0	100.0	100.0	100.0	100.0	100.0	100.0	100.0

Table 8.4. Amounts and percentages of each rock type found within the test units and the shovel units. Unit 4 has been left aside because of incompleteness.

8.4.2 THE FLAKE TECHNOLOGY

A total of 167 flint and 40 quartz artefacts were associated with the flake production technology (table 8.5). Among the cherty carbonate artefacts, two flake cores were recognized along with a substantial amount of core preforms and core tools. These two flake cores point out that the cherty carbonate was used to produce flakes. Their small numbers in comparison with the core preforms and core tools, however, indicate that this flake technology only played a minor role. A distinction between flakes generated by the flake technology and these generated by core tool production could not be made. The cherty carbonate flakes are, therefore, dealt within the section which discusses the core tool technology.

(1) Acquisition and selection of raw material: the majority, i.e., 70% of the flint originated from Long Island, Antigua, while small numbers, around 12%, came from St. Kitts. For 19% is is still unknown from where it had be obtained (Knippenberg 1995 and Knippenberg et al. 1995). This exotic origin is supported by the absence of any unworked or slightly reduced flint nodules at Anse des Pères. The provenance of the quartz material remains unknown. A local origin is possible because detrital quartz specimens were found during the auger test prospection at Norman Estate.

(2) Primary reduction and core-preparation: the number of flakes with dorsal surfaces completely covered by "cortex" is very small, indicating that primary reduction only played a minor role in lithic reduction at the site (fig. 8.1). A mayor part of the raw material had already been worked at some other place, probably the source area. No signs of systematic core preparation were recognized. An attempt was made to systematize the flake scar pattern on the dorsal surfaces of the flakes, but their small size made it difficult to interpret the flake scars. The larger flakes, large enough to reflect this do not show any systematic patterning, however.

(3) Core-reduction: ten flake cores were identified. The flint cores are very small in size and often have been exhausted. Due to their small size and exhausted condition,

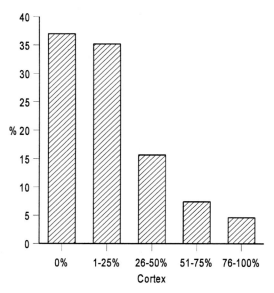

Fig. 8.1. Percentages of cortex on flint flakes.

this classification may be misleading because cores likely had different shapes during the reduction process. In any case, most cores were classified as polyhedral (3) or shapeless (3); flakes had been removed from any direction possible in other words (fig. 8.2a). Two discoidal cores with a radial pattern (fig. 8.2b), and one bifacial core with a single platform were identified. It is clear that no standardized core reduction was used by the Amerindians. Flakes were removed from any side possible. Even in case of one of the discoidal cores, its initial shape as a flake forced the knapper to reduce it along the edges.

This unstandardized reduction is also reflected by the debitage. The flakes are heterogeneous in shape. Blades are absent. The amount of "shatter", or angular blocks is relatively high (22%). Among the flakes, complete specimens, flake fragments, and modified flakes were identified. A substantial amount of the flakes possess hinged ends (40%). Stepped ends also occur (12%) (fig. 8.3). Both of these reflect knapping error, either the result of the expertise of the knapper, or the quality of the material. The exhaustive use of these cores, flaked using a non-standardized core approach, certainly explains most of these knapping errors. Striking platforms are mostly plain or pointed (fig. 8.4). Facetted striking platforms, often associated with standardized tool

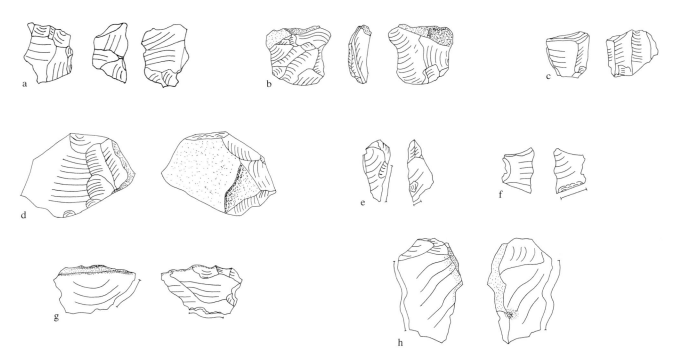

Fig. 8.2. Flint cores and flakes (scale 1:2): a. polyhedral flint core, b. discoidal flint core, c. single platformed flint core, d. modified flint flake, e. modified flint flake with unifacial use-retouch on two sides, f. modified flint flake with profound unifacial use-retouch, g. complete flint flake with two unifacial chipped edges, which possess use-retouch, h. modified flint flake with one edge exhibiting use-retouch.

Artefact type	N		Length (cm)	Width (cm)	Thickness (cm)	Weigth (g)
Complete flake	60	Mean	2.1 ± 1.2	2.0 ± 1.0	0.6 ± 0.4	3.4 ± 4.5
		Range	0.6 - 5.1	0.7 - 4.7	0.1 - 1.7	0.1 - 20.9
Modified flake	19	Mean	2.7 ± 1.0	2.7 ± 1.4	1.0 ± 0.5	7.8 ± 10.3
		Range	1.3 - 5.7	0.8 - 6.0	0.3 - 1.9	0.3 - 37.0
Flake fragment	34	Mean	1.6 ± 0.6	1.5 ± 0.6	0.5 ± 0.3	1.2 ± 1.2
		Range	0.6 - 4.1	0.6 - 2.9	0.2 - 1.3	0.2 - 5.3
Shatter	37	Mean	1.7 ± 0.8	1.2 ± 0.5	0.8 ± 0.4	1.7 ± 2.6
		Range	0.7 - 4.4	0.5 - 2.6	0.1 - 1.8	0.1 - 14.0
Flake core	10	Mean	2.5 ± 0.6	2.0 ± 0.7	1.1 ± 0.5	5.2 ± 4.7
		Range	1.6 - 3.7	1.2 - 3.6	0.7 - 2.1	1.0 - 13.1

Table 8.5. Length, width, thickness, and weight of the flint artefacts.

producing technologies (Sullivan and Rozen 1985), are notably absent.

Investigation of the percussion technique used in stone making was attempted, the bipolar technique or the direct freehand percussion could be recognized. Among the cores, one, the bifacial specimen with a single platform, clearly indicates that it was rested upon an anvil during reduction (fig. 8.2c). The side opposite the platform was shattered as a result. Also the small size of most of the cores indicates that they were likely reduced with the bipolar technique during the later stages of their reduction.

True intentional flakes (29 artefacts) were analyzed for additional traits such as bulb of force, point of percussion, cone of percussion, and conchoidal fracture marks after Ohnuma and Bergman (1982) (table 8.6). Five flakes were classified as true hard hammer, direct percussion flakes, possessing a pronounced bulb of force, a clear point of percussion, a clear cone of percussion, and clear conchoidal fracture marks. Only one of them could be directly classified as a bipolar flake with a diffuse bulb of force, and a cone of percussion on both proximal and distal ends. The quantitative data show that both techniques were used making the results difficult to interpret. Experiments in direct hard hammer, freehand percussion showed that more than 90% of the resultant flakes possess a pronounced bulb, a clear point of percussion, a clear cone of percussion, and distinct conchoidal fracture marks (Ohnuma and Bergman 1982). The bipolar technique would blur these figures since such flakes often have no pronounced bulb of force and a less clear cone. This becomes even more difficult when unsophisticated bipolar flaking techniques, such as these described by O'Miller (1979), were used. In this technique, one strong percussion blow often produces a lot of uncontrolled debitage, consisting of flakes, chips, and angular blocks or shatter. The common occurrence of shatter (22%) indicates this uncontrolled bipolar technique may have been employed.

(4) Tool finishing: the debitage was the expected outcome in this case. This unstandardized technology produced a heterogeneous set of flakes and a substantial amount of shatter (22%). Among the flakes, flake fragments and modified flakes were identified. Further modification by flaking, not chipping, was done to obtain additional flakes (fig. 8.2d). Tool finishing by chipping played a minor role. Only two flakes were modified to obtain a recognizable tool shape (fig. 8.2e,f). Another two possess edges which were chipped to (re)sharpen the edge (fig. 8.2g). This clearly shows that the aim was to produce suitable edges, rather than pre-defined tool shapes.

		N	%
Bulb of force	Pronounced	16	55.2
	Diffuse	12	41.4
Point of percussion	Clear	26	89.7
	Vague	2	6.9
Cone of percussion	Clear	9	31.0
	Vague	18	62.1
Butt	Unlipped	27	93.1
	Lipped	1	3.4
Conchoidal fracture marks on bulb	Pronounced	14	48.3
	Indistinct	13	44.8

Table 8.6. Characteristics relating to flaking mode after Ohnuna and Bergman (1982). Sample size = 30.

93

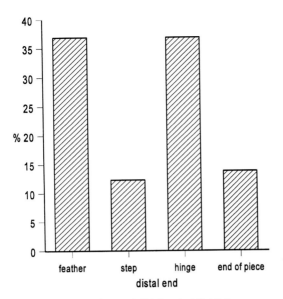

Fig. 8.3. Percentages of type of distal end of flint flakes.

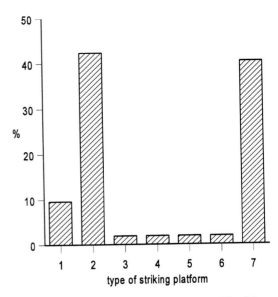

Fig. 8.4. Percentages of type of striking platform of flint flakes.

(5) Use: macroscopical analysis has shown that some of the flakes possess clear signs of use-retouch. Probably more flakes had been used; this, however, can only be determined by analyzing use-wear using high-magnification. Among the identified used specimens the following could be recognized:

a) a pointed artefact, with unifacial use-retouch on several edges, probably used as drill (fig. 8.2e);

b) flakes with long sharp edges, probably used as cutting tools (fig. 8.2h); and

c) modified flakes with clear unifacial use-retouch on one edge, probably used as scrapers (fig. 8.2f).

Syllacio, a companion of Columbus during his second voyage, was one of the first to notice the use of sharp stones as knives among the Amerindians of Guadeloupe (Morrison 1963). Walker (1981) analysed use-retouch and use-wear on the chipped lithic artefacts from the Saladoid portion of the Sugar Factory Pier site, St. Kitts which also has preceramic deposits, and found that the chipped lithic industry had been used for several tasks. These included activities such as cutting, sawing, planing, drilling and grating various materials, among which were suggested wood, animal skin, bone, and manioc. These findings agree with the description O'Miller (1979) presents about the use of lithic flakes among the Xeta Indians of Brazil, who used different flakes for the construction of wooden arrows. Other flakes were used to cut meat, hide, and vegetables.

(6) Re-use: two flakes were found with modified edges, as noted above. It remains unclear whether this edge modification should be classified as resharpening or sharpening. However, it is obvious that (re)sharpening had not been employed systematically.

(7) Discard: the excavation within the refuse area yielded an almost complete sequence from raw material to flakes, the final products which were then used. Only unmodified raw material was missing. This sequence shows that flintknapping and the use of flint artefacts both occurred at the site. An attempt was made to refit flint artefacts to see whether flintkapping occurred in the refuse area itself. No fits could be established, however, indicating that flintknapping did not occur specifically in the refuse area on the basis of the available evidence. It probably occurred elsewhere within the village and specimens derived from other places were thrown on the refuse pile.

It can be concluded that this flaking technology is classifiable as an expedient technology, as defined by Parry and Kelly (1987). Flakes were produced and used in a unsystematic manner.

8.4.3   CORE TOOL TECHNOLOGY

Three rock types were associated with the production and use of core tools, cherty carbonate, volcanic rock, and hypabyssal rock. The cherty carbonate was found in especially large quantities (420) and different types of artefacts belonging to different steps of the production process were identified. For the volcanic and hypabyssal material the range of artefacts is more limited. Table 8.7 shows the

	1	2	3	Total
Flake	244	87	34	365
	58.1	70.7	37.8	57.7
Blade	–	2	–	2
	0.0	1.6	0.0	0.3
Shatter	5	4	2	11
	1.2	3.2	2.2	1.7
Flake core	2	–	–	2
	0.5	0.0	0.0	0.3
Preform	11	5	4	20
	2.6	4.1	4.4	3.2
Axe / adze	10	–	–	10
	2.4	0.0	0.0	1.6
Butt-end	9	–	–	9
	2.1	0.0	0.0	1.4
Rubbing / grinding stone	6	2	2	10
	1.4	1.6	2.2	1.6
Hammerstone / butt-end	4	–	–	4
	1.0	0.0	0.0	0.6
Hammerstone	2	2	2	6
	0.5	1.6	2.2	0.9
Pestle	1	–	–	1
	0.2	0.0	0.0	0.2
Unmodified water-worn pebble	38	20	44	102
	9.0	16.3	48.9	16.1
Unidentified	88	1	1	90
	21.0	0.8	1.1	14.2
Total	420	123	90	633
	100.0	100.0	100.0	100.0

Table 8.7. Artefact types made of the rock types that have been associated with the core tool technology. 1 = Cherty carbonate, 2 = Volcanic rock, 3 = Hypabyssal rock.

amounts of the different artefact types for the different rock types. The relative small amount of preforms and core tools in the available sample may imply that the description of the activity sets does not cover all the characteristics of the Anse des Pères core tool production. Information about characteristics such as hafting, grinding, and polishing was only scarcely found.

(1) Acquisition and selection of raw material: the volcanic and hypabyssal rocks were obtained in the form of water-worn pebbles near the site, along the stream and the beach. This also accounts for the cherty carbonate water-worn pebbles. These pebbles, however, do not exhibit any signs of weathering, as is characteristic for most of the cherty carbonate artefacts. The weathered cherty carbonate artefacts do not possess any traces indicating that water-worn pebbles were used as the source of this raw material (e.g., the flakes and preforms do not exhibit any water-worn surface on either side). Probably, the artefact specimens of cherty carbonate were obtained locally from outcrops of the Pointe Blanche Formation, which is the underlying geological formation in the site area. The exact mining location was not systematically searched for and it remains unknown.

(2) Primary reduction and core-shaping: primary reduction and core shaping took place at the site. The test unit excavations yielded 20 preforms (table 8.2). They were analysed together with 7 preforms from the shovel tests and the surface

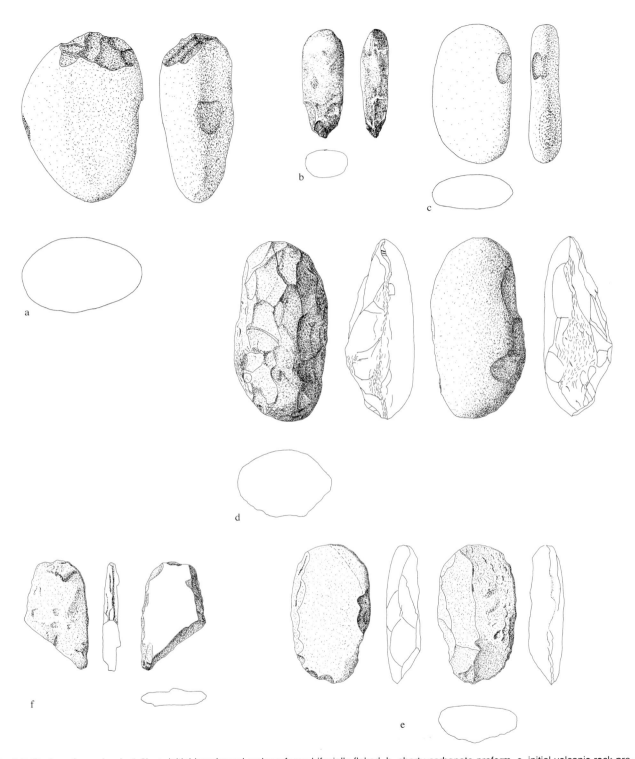

Fig. 8.5. Rock preforms (scale 1:3): a. initial hypabyssal rock preform; bifacially flaked, b. cherty carbonate preform, c. initial volcanic rock preform, d.volcanic rock preform; mainly unifacially flaked, e. volcanic rock preform; mainly unifacially flaked. The edge sides are bifacially chipped. The flaked face is pecked for 50%. The other face has been ground slightly (dotted line), f. cherty carbonate preform; the edges are chipped and left face is completely pecked.

which added information about the method of reduction. These preforms represent the different steps in making an axe, spanning a range from slightly modified water-worn pebbles with only a few flake removals (fig. 8.5a) to almost finished axes lacking a sharply ground edge (fig. 8.5b). Analysis of the volcanic and hypabyssal flakes has shown that a substantial number of these are primary flakes, providing clear evidence that primary reduction took place at the site (fig. 8.6). This could not be investigated for the cherty carbonate because of its possible derivation from local outcrops where it occurs in a bedded form, making analysis of a distinct outer surface impossible.

The various preform stages make it possible to reconstruct the different steps used in axe production. The water-worn pebbles were obtained from the beach or a stream. Several of these pebbles possess pits on the unflaked surface around the first flake removals (fig. 8.5c). These pits might have been generated to roughen the surface, which would facilitate the initial flaking. Another explanation for the presence of these pits might be related to the possible use as hammerstone before the pebbles were intended to serve as core artefact for the production of axes.

Flakes were struck off bifacially along the edges to reduce the thickness of the preform. If the original surface of one face was smooth enough, the preform was only flaked unifacially on the opposite face, with some minor flaking on the smooth face (fig. 8.5d, e). The example from figure 8.5d shows that this preform never passed this stage due to the failure to remove the middle part of the flaked face despite the knapper's subsequent efforts to do so, as is indicated by the clear shattered areas on the left and right edges of the artefact.

(3) Secondary reduction: after initially shaping the preform, the edges were chipped into sharper ones and the flaked surface was pecked to thin the preform and to facilitate grinding (fig. 8.5e, f).

(4) Grinding and polishing: several finished axes, although incomplete, were found. They all had been ground. Due to the absence any finished volcanic axes and the poor preservation of the finished cherty carbonate specimens, it remains uncertain whether polishing was applied after grinding. Kozák et al. (1979) describe the manner of grinding among the Héta Indians. They report that the Héta used wetted fine sand and white clay for grinding. This combination actually ground and polished the stone at the same time. It could not be determined whether axes were completely ground or not, obviously the absence of complete tools made this assessment difficult. Some ground blunted ends were found, however, and these might have been the butt ends of core tools. On the other hand, a single butt end with two inflections, probably made for hafting, was not ground.

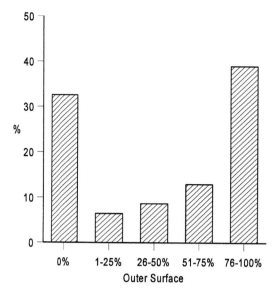

Fig. 8.6. Percentages of outer surface on volcanic and hypabyssal rock flakes.

(5) Finished core tool and use: among the lithic artefacts from Anse des Pères, two groups of core tools were recognized: finished products of the core tool technology, and unworked water-worn pebbles which possess traces of use. Among the former groups mostly incomplete cherty carbonate tools were identified. Traces of use could not be analysed for these tools due to the weathering of the rock. The following types of core tools or fragmentary core tools were identified:

Axes[5]: ten axes were recovered in the test units. Differences in shape and size occur. Specimen FB 6A4/7 is from a morphological point of view an axe (fig. 8.7a). Its small size, however, makes it highly unlikely that it had been used for heavy wood splitting tasks.[6] One petaloid axe was recognized (fig. 8.7b). One axe is slightly asymmetrical (plano-convex) in shape (fig. 8.7c). The others are all symmetrical (fig. 8.7a, b, d-f). The shape of the edge varies from straight (fig. 8.7c, e), round (fig. 8.7b, d, f) to pointed (fig. 8.7g).

The absence of finished axes of volcanic rock may have implications for our understanding of the axes, for there are indications that these axes were heavier than the axes made from cherty carbonate. This difference may reflect a difference in their use; the heavier axes may have been taken to the forest to cut down trees and are more likely to have been lost or discarded there, in contrast with the smaller axes/adzes, which might have been used to perform lighter woodworking tasks at the settlement, such as hollowing out a dugout canoe.

Fig. 8.7. Cherty carbonate axes (scale 1:2): a. broken and heavily weathered, b. petaloid axe; broken and weathered, c. assymetrical axe; broken and weathered, d. complete and weathered, e. broken and weathered, the edge had been resharpened, f-g. broken and heavily weathered.

– Blunted-end artefacts: 13 parts of core tools were found, all possessing a blunted end. Interpreting them as butt ends of core tools is very plausible. Whether these butt ends belong to finished core tools remains uncertain, however. Two artefacts exhibit clear shallow indentations on both sides; these may indicate hafting (fig. 8.8a). Three artefacts were ground (fig. 8.8b,c), while others were only pecked. One of the artefacts exhibits characteristic breakage often seen on broken axes (fig. 8.8d). The breakage results from use of an improper angle used when felling a tree (Brounen, pers. comm. 1994). Four artefacts may have served as several hammerstones

(fig. 8.8e, f). The weathering of the cherty carbonate rock makes it impossible to see any traces of usage on them. Specimens FB7A4/2 and FB4A1/46 (fig. 8.8e,f) were portions of large, heavy tools. They may have served as hammerstones. Specimen FB5A4/1 (fig. 8.8g) exhibits two visible flake scars, indicating either two blows had been struck on the butt end of the tool, or it was used as a chopper or hammerstone.

– Pestle: one artefact has the shape likely necessary for use as a pestle (fig. 8.7h). It has been pecked, elongated with a

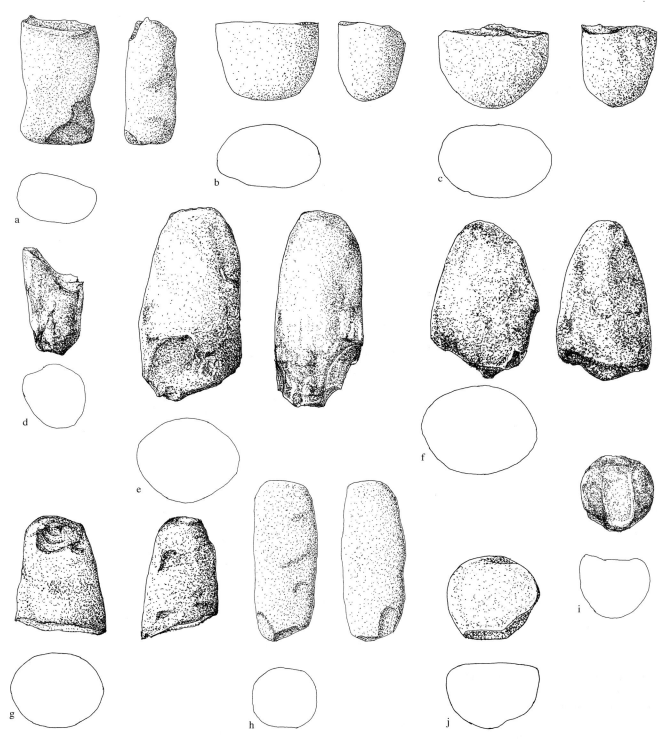

Fig. 8.8. Cherty carbonate butt-ends, hammerstone/butt-ends, pestle, rubbing/grinding stones (scale 1:2): a. butt-end broken and weathered, with undeep indentations, b-c. grounded butt-end broken and weathered, d. butt-end with characteristic breakage, weathered, e-f. hammerstone/butt-end; broken and weathered, g. hammerstone/butt-end with scarnegatives; broken and weathered, h. pestle; broken (?) and weathered, i. rubbing/grinding stone; with a 1.7 cm wide elongated abraded strip on one face; weathered, j. rubbing/grinding stone; one face is completely abraded; weathered.

	1	2	3	Total
Flake	244	87	34	365
	58.1	70.7	37.8	57.7
Blade	–	2	–	2
	0.0	1.6	0.0	0.3
Shatter	5	4	2	11
	1.2	3.2	2.2	1.7
Flake core	2	–	–	2
	0.5	0.0	0.0	0.3
Preform	11	5	4	20
	2.6	4.1	4.4	3.2
Axe / adze	10	–	–	10
	2.4	0.0	0.0	1.6
Butt-end	9	–	–	9
	2.1	0.0	0.0	1.4
Rubbing / grinding stone	6	2	2	10
	1.4	1.6	2.2	1.6
Hammerstone / butt-end	4	–	–	4
	1.0	0.0	0.0	0.6
Hammerstone	2	2	2	6
	0.5	1.6	2.2	0.9
Pestle	1	–	–	1
	0.2	0.0	0.0	0.2
Unmodified water-worn pebble	38	20	44	102
	9.0	16.3	48.9	16.1
Unidentified	88	1	1	90
	21.0	0.8	1.1	14.2
Total	420	123	90	633
	100.0	100.0	100.0	100.0

Table 8.7. Artefact types made of the rock types that have been associated with the core tool technology. 1 = Cherty carbonate, 2 = Volcanic rock, 3 = Hypabyssal rock.

round section and a flat end. Although nowadays most pestles are considerably larger and made of wood in the Amazon, Rostain (1994) mentions a few stone pestles recovered from archaeological contexts in French Guyana.

– Rubbing/grinding stones: four artificially rounded balls were found. These balls were not completely round, one side having flattened by abrasive motion. Specimen FB 5-A-4/2 (fig. 8.7i) is the best preserved of these; it exhibits one side on which a 1.7 cm wide, elongated strip can be recognized which had been completely flattened. The other balls all had one completely flattened side as well (fig. 8.7j).
The function of specimen FB 5-A-4/2 is difficult to interpret. The elongated flattened strip indicates that a rectangular object about 1.7 cm wide had been abraded or polished

using this specimen. This object might have been something like the rim of a ceramic vessel, but it remains unclear whether polishing of ceramic vessels would cause such significant use wear. The other artefacts may have been used as a small manos.

In addition to these core tools, the debitage generated during the production of these tools may have been also used. The cherty carbonate rock is especially suitable for the production of sharp-edged flakes.
Weathering made it impossible to determine if these numerous flakes had been used.

Among the group of unworked water-worn pebbles, two types of use wear were found: pits resulting from contact

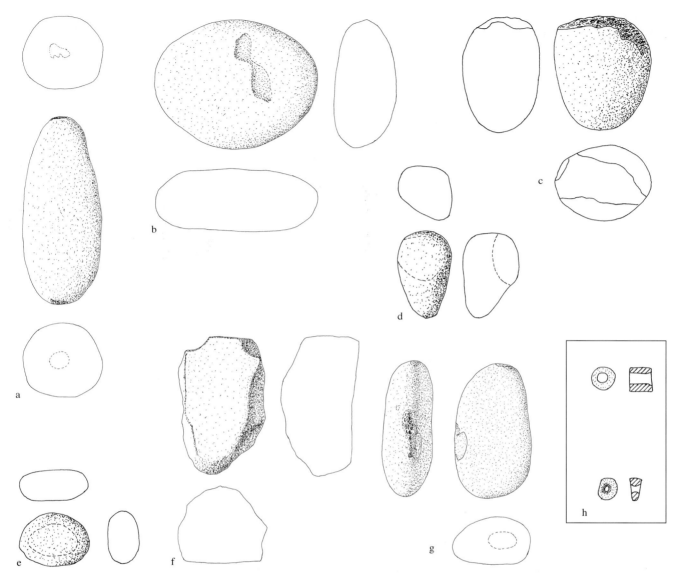

Fig. 8.9. Hammerstones, hammerstones/anvil and rubbing/grinding stone: a. volcanic rock hammerstone for percussion flaking; used areas within dotted lines; weight = 890 g (scale 1:3), b. volcanic rock hammerstone/anvil; weight = 1020 g (scale 1:3), c. volcanic rock hammerstone; profoundly used; weight = 190 g (scale 1:2), d. cherty carbonate rubbing/grinding stone; polished surface between dotted line (scale 1:2), e. volcanic rock rubbing/grinding stone; abrasion on one face (between dotted line) (scale 1:2), f. volcanic rock rubbing/grinding stone (mano); one face is completely abraded (scale 1:3), g. initial volcanic rock preform, which had also been used as hammerstone (scale 1:3), h. two beads made of exotic stone (scale 1:1).

between objects in which the direction of movement is perpendicular to the surface of the contact, and abrasion in which the direction of movement is parallel to the surface of contact.

– Hammerstones: eight water-worn pebbles with small pits on either side were recovered from the test units. Most of them are elongated in shape and possess pits on one or both ends (fig. 8.9a). Two artefacts, however, are flat and more rounded in shape and have pits on one face each (fig. 8.9b). The elongated types are likely to have been used as percussion stones in stone working, and the others may have been used as hammerstones for crushing nuts or other materials (Rostain 1994).

Within the shovel tests a heavily battered hammerstone was recovered. It has significant battering on a large part of its surface, indicating long-term and/or intensive use (fig. 8.9c).

– Abraders/grinding stones: seven water-worn pebbles with abraded areas were recognized. In most cases, this abrasion is located on one restricted surface (fig. 8.9d, e). In all cases, only small abrasions are present, indicating limited usage. In general, the rubbing stones are smaller than the hammerstones. Pebbles often recognized as polishing stones for pottery are included (Walker 1985; Rostain 1994).
The shovel tests yielded yet another type of artefact which is classified on the basis of size as a mano (fig. 8.9f). It is an unmodified volcanic block which is not water-worn. One side of the stone has a flat and abraded face, however.

The analysis of both the abraders and hammerstones have established that these tools were only used in a limited fashion and discarded without being broken or used exhaustively. This may be explained by the common, easily accessible nature of the water-worn rock.

– Pebbles without use wear: the excavations yielded a large amount of water-worn pebbles without any traces of use wear. The beach and the stream make it likely that many of these pebbles naturally occurred in the site area. Small cherty carbonate pebbles with a polished surface, however, made up 20% of the total. Excavations at Kelbey's Ridge on Saba produced the same kind of polished stone in archaeological contexts (Hoogland 1996). This site naturally lacks water-worn materials, meaning that Amerindians brought it there. The reasons for doing so remain unclear. It is not clear whether the polish has been caused by natural processes or whether it is the result of use. These stone might have been used as pottery polishing stones. This, however, has to be studied microscopically.

(6) Reuse: only one axe had been resharpened (fig. 8.7e). Some initial preforms also exhibit clear pits on one small portion of the end of the artefact (fig. 8.9g). They had been apparently used as hammerstones before flaking was attempted.

(7) Discard and loss: the fact that excavations were done in the refuse area is clearly reflected within the lithic artefact sample related to core tool production. This sample consists of flakes (the debitage), failed preforms, and broken tools. All are artefacts, likely to have been discarded within the village. Complete tools are almost completely absent. This does not account for the unmodified but used water-worn pebbles which are not broken.
Besides the technological analysis, refitting was attempted for the cherty carbonate material. If possible, it would provide

more insight into the lithic technology and the location of the stone working. Within each unit and among the two pairs of neighbouring units, an attempt was made to refit the flakes to one another and to the preforms.
No fits could be established, however. Bearing in mind the good preservation conditions of the characteristic midden area where post-depositional processes had little affected the original provenience, it is obvious that stone working did not occur in the refuse area, but instead was done at some other location within the village. Individual pieces were later incorporated into the refuse pile.

8.5   Ornamental artefacts
Only three beads were found during the test excavations (fig. 8.9a). All three were made of exotic stone. No by-products or other traces of bead production were identified at the site, suggesting that the finished beads had been traded.

8.6   Lithics in the Ceramic period
This section compares the lithic assemblages from other Ceramic period sites with the sample from Anse des Pères. Studies dealing with lithic material are very rare for the Ceramic period in the Caribbean. The few publications about lithic material from ceramic sites show that the samples are quite similar overall. Only incidental differences are recognizable (Bullbrook and Rouse 1953; Walker 1980, 1981, 1985; Allaire 1983; Roe et al. 1990; Bartone and Crock 1991, 1998; cf. also chapters 13 and 14). Most such publications deal with Saladoid sites such as Palo Seco on Trinidad (Bullbrook and Rouse 1953), Sugar Factory Pier on St. Kitts (Walker 1980, 1985), Hacienda Grande on Puerto Rico (Walker 1985), Séguineau and Macabou on Martinique (Allaire 1983) and, Trants on Montserrat (Bartone and Crock 1991, 1998). A problem noted by most scholars studying lithic artefacts is the small number of specimens found during excavation (Bullbrook and Rouse 1953; Roe et al. 1990; Allaire 1983). This relative poverty of lithic artefacts may hamper comparisons between lithic samples, especially where rare artefacts are concerned. An analysis by Bartone and Crock (1991, 1998) is a fortunate exception. They were able to collect a large sample belonging to the flaked-stone production at the Saladoid Trants Site on Montserrat, making statements about technology possible.
A second problem when comparing lithic samples is that many publications are brief and deal only with a part of the entire lithic assemblage (Walker 1980, 1985; Bartone and Crock 1991, 1998), lack essential drawings of the material (Allaire 1983), or describe certain approaches which were attempted only once (use-wear analysis: Walker 1981). Lithic assemblages from Ceramic period sites may be summarized as follows:

– One portion of the lithic assemblage belongs to a technology aimed at production of flakes. This portion consists of flakes, cores, and detritus mostly made of flint; other fine-grained rocks, however, were also used. The techniques that were applied to produce these flakes are freehand direct percussion and bipolar percussion (Allaire 1983; Roe et al. 1990; Walker 1985; Bartone and Crock 1991, 1998). At most sites, both techniques were used together, with a focus on either one of them. The aim was to produce flakes, which could be "randomly" used "as tools in a non-systematic, non-preferential manner" (Bartone and Crock 1991, 1998). Only the Sugar Factory Pier lithics, and to a lesser extent the Trants sample, were analysed in terms of their function. These tools were used for different tasks such as scraping, cutting, sawing, and drilling (Walker 1981). Some tools were used for more than one task (Walker 1981; Bartone and Crock 1991, 1998).

– A second portion of the overall assemblage consists of artefacts that belong to the different technological steps for production of core tools. These occur mainly in the form of ground stone axes or adzes (Bullbrook and Rouse 1953; Allaire 1983; Roe et al. 1990; Walker 1985 and cf. also chapter 14). Most often axes occur only in small quantities.

– A third portion of the overall lithic assemblage consists of ornamental and/or ceremonial artefacts such as beads, zoomorphic pendants, and zemis. These artefacts are often rare (Walker 1985). At the Early Ceramic sites of Vieques and Hope Estate and the Late Ceramic sites on Puerto Rico, however, zoomorphic pendants and beads were found in relative large quantities (Chanlatte Baik 1984; Haviser 1991a; Narganes 1995). They were typically made of exotic (semi-)precious stones not locally available on the islands in the Caribbean, and which probably had been obtained from the South American mainland (cf. chapter 13). At the Saladoid Trants site on Montserrat the production of beads, made out of imported stone, had taken place (Bartone and Crock 1991, 1998).

– The remaining lithic artefacts are unmodified water-worn pebbles, used for different tasks such as hammering (Allaire 1983; Walker 1985; Roe et al. 1990 and cf. also chapter 14), abrading (Allaire 1983; Walker 1985 and cf. also chapter 14) and for milling stones (Allaire 1983).

The pebble or edge grinder must be noted here. This type of artefact has been found at Hacienda Grande on Puerto Rico (Walker 1985). A similar type of artefact is known from preceramic contexts. However, it is absent at the later site of Monserrate on Puerto Rico (Roe et al. 1990) and at other Saladoid sites (Allaire 1983). Therefore, it is considered to be a regional and short-lived artefact, largely related to the preceramic period.

Looking at the Anse des Pères material, the lithic sample fits well within this composite picture. Flaked stone production can be considered the same. Detailed similarities are present between Anse des Pères and the Montserrat material when looking at the cores, size of flakes, absence of intentional retouch, and the flaking techniques (Bartone and Crock 1991, 1998).

The production of axes/adzes is also fully represented at Anse des Pères, as at Hacienda Grande (Walker 1985), Monserrate (Roe et al. 1990), and Hope Estate (cf. chapters 13 and 14). It is interesting to note that the production of axes/adzes did not occur or was not recognized at Séguineau and Macabou, two Saladoid sites on Martinique (Allaire 1983).

Ornamental and ceremonial artefacts are poorly represented at Anse des Pères. Only three stone beads were found and no signs of any bead production such as that known from the Trants site. Zoomorphic stone pendants are absent just like at most Saladoid sites. Among the shell artefacts, carved pendants do occur, however (cf. chapter 9).

Among the unmodified lithic artefacts, hammerstones and abraders occur. Missing, however, are milling stones and edge grinders. The absence of the former may be the result of the small sample size available from Anse des Pères. The latter was only found at one site, Hacienda Grande, and may be limited to that region.

8.7   Conclusions

Analysis of the lithic artefacts recovered from Anse des Pères reveals that two technologies were used in lithic production. These include unstandardized technology aimed at the production of flakes for use as tools, and another technology related to the production of core tools, mainly in the form of axes. It is uncertain whether the flakes and shatter generated during the shaping of the core tools, were also used in some fashion. Considering the use of unstandardized flint tools and the suitability of the cherty carbonate, it is likely this would have been the case. However, the weathering of this rock type makes it impossible to test this hypothesis.

Along with the products of these two technologies, a third type of artefact was recovered but these have been only altered by use and not through intentional reduction. These are the water-worn pebbles and other natural rocks used as hammerstones or abraders.

The flake tool technology is associated with flint and quartz artefacts. During the process of flaking, the freehand direct percussion and bipolar techniques were used to reduce the core following an expedient strategy. The aim was the production of unstandardized flakes with edges suitable for tasks such as scraping, cutting, and drilling.

The core tool technology is mainly associated with the cherty carbonate and the volcanic rocks. Along with pestles and abraders, the main products of this production were axes. Volcanic water-worn pebbles and cherty carbonate rocks were flaked into a desired shape, then pecked to thin the object and facilitate its grinding. Grinding was done last. It could not be determined whether polishing had been applied as well. The third group of artefacts, the unworked water-worn pebbles, is mainly associated with the volcanic and hypabyssal rock.

All raw materials except flint, may have been obtained near the site or somewhere else on the island of St. Martin. The flint had an exotic origin, the major part coming from Long Island near Antigua.

The lithic assemblage from Anse des Pères does not differ much from lithic samples from other Saladoid sites. Differences occur only incidentally. The main difference with Early Ceramic sites seems to be the absence of lithic (zoomorphic) pendants at Anse des Pères.

notes

1 No systematic surface collecting was executed, only incidentally artefacts were collected.

2 Three beads, recovered from the residues of the small mesh screens, are not included in these numbers. They, however, are dealt with at the end of this chapter.

3 In this study a distinction is made between flint and chert. Flint can be considered as a type of chert which is found in the form of nodules within chalk formations. It mainly consists of micro- to crysptocristaliline quartz (Bush and Stieveking 1986). It is comparable with the well known flint sources within the Upper Ctretáceous Chalk formations of northwestern Europe. Chert, or cherty carbonate, is a type of chert which occurs in bedded form. These bedded layers are mostly associated or interlayered with pyroclastic rock. It consists mainly of micro- to cryptocristalline quartz, or other forms of silica, together with carbonates. Often these cherts contain high amounts of tests of radiolaria (Grunau 1963; Garrison 1974).

4 Van Tooren analysed two lithic samples from Hope Estate (cf. Haviser 1993). Both samples belonged to a large group of limestone artefacts, classified as tephrite A and B. The tephrite was identified within an altered tuff, that was attached to the limestone rock. The constituent rock types of the Pointe Blanche Formation make it likely that altered tuffs were collected in co-occurence with the fine-grained chert rock by the Amerindians. These altered tuffs were not recognized among the lithic artefacts from Anse des Pères. Macroscopic comparison to the chert atrefacts from Hope Estate and the cherty carbonate artefacts from Anse des Pères, reveals that all are very similar in appearance and exhibit the same kind of weathering. Some of the chert rock found at Hope Estate possessed this tephrite rock still attached to it. The majority part consisted of pure chert rock, however.

5 No distinction was made between axes and adzes in this study. Although differences in shape can exist between both tools, Chappell (1987) argues on basis of ethnographical research in New Guinea that the only valid base for distinction is the manner of hafting. Having only incomplete axes, this distinction was beyond dertermination.

6 Miron (1992) states that the general function of an axe/adze is to chop, peel, pound or scrape wood. An axe penetrates the wood when chopping with its blade perpendicular to the surface, and an adze peels, or shaves the wood with its edge in an oblique angle to the surface.

9 Shell

Alex J. Brokke

9.1 Introduction

The site of Anse des Pères is not a real shell midden. Shell is present at the site but it is not a major component. The objective of this analysis is to reconstruct shellfish usage by the Cedrosan Saladoid occupants of the site. For the methods of analysis see chapter 4. The analysis differs from that conducted for the Norman Estate site only in the detection of individuals. Because gastropods are the main family of molluscs present at Anse des Pères, it was possible to use the apex for recognition of an individual.

9.2 Exploited shell species

Shells recovered from the 10-mm mesh sieve in the six test units were analysed. Actual frequencies are represented in the tables along with percentages. Left and right valves are counted together to achieve MNI count. Total percentages are regarded as more important than those of the fragments, the fragment percentages are regarded as less important when looking at the overall composition of the shellfish exploited because MNI is not valid for fragments.

The shellfish species recovered from Anse des Pères are all from rocky shore environments. The coast near the site is suitable for these species. The diversity in species is not reflected when the individual amounts are considered. These species include *Cittarium pica* popularly known as 'West Indian Top Shell'. It is found on and under rocks and in coral cavities in intertidal zones. Of the total amount of individuals found at Anse de Pères, 65% are *Cittarium pica*. Counting the fragments, the amount of *Cittarium pica* is even higher, namely 90.4%. Next in importance is the *Arca zebra* popularly known as 'Turkey Wing'. It lives attached to rocks in water one to 20 feet (± 0.30 to ± 7 metres) deep. The individual percentage is 9.7% and fragments constitute 0.4%. Also important is the *Astraea tuber* popularly known as 'Green Star Shell'. It is found in one to 8 feet (± 0.30 to 2.5 metres) of water on and under rocks. The individual percentage is 8.4%, while the fragments represent only 0.1%.

Other shellfish include regular species in small quantities or are species of such irregular appearance that they are not mentioned separately when the composition of the diet is discussed[1]. For the identification of the shellfish composition in the different units a sample was taken from units 1-3 and 5-7 (tables 9.1-9.7). One outstanding feature of the complete sample is the preference for the *Cittarium pica*. In the first

Species	Indiv. count	Compl. count	Total count MNI	Indiv. %	Compl. %	Total %	Indiv.+ Compl. Weight (g)	Total weight %
Cittarium pica	64	25	89	35.8	14.0	49.8	7387	48.0
Arca zebra	1	37	38	0.6	20.7	21.3	414	2.7
Tectarius muricatus	2	6	8	1.1	3.4	4.5	14	0.1
Strombus gigas	–	2	2	–	1.1	1.1	2388	15.5
Astraea tuber	9	9	18	5	5	10.1	71	0.5
Others	5	19	24	2.8	10.6	13.4	97	0.6
Total	81	98	179	45.3	54.8	100.0	10371	67.4

Table 9.1. Shellfish distribution Unit 1, layer 5 to 9. Fragment weight = 5011 g, total weight = 15382 g. Individual and complete percentage are using total individual and complete count that is 100%. Percentage complete and individual of total weight is taken from the total weight = 15382 g (complete weight = 7362 g, individual weight = 3009 g and fragment weight = 5011 g). With Indiv.count = Individual count; Compl.count = Complete count; Total count (MNI) = individual and complete added together; Indiv. % = Individual % (taken from the total amount of all species in the unit); Compl. % = Complete % (taken from the total amount of individuals of all species in the unit); Total % = Individual and Complete % combined; Indiv. + Compl. weight = Total weight without fragments; Total weight % = Complete and Individual weight as percentage of the total weight figure.

Species	Indiv. count	Compl. count	Total count MNI	Indiv. %	Compl. %	Total %	Indiv.+ Compl. Weight (g)	Total weight %
Cittarium pica	64	70	134	24.1	26.3	50.4	16853	63.9
Nerita tesselata	–	8	8	–	3.0	3.0	9	0.03
Arca zebra	–	64	64	–	24.1	24.1	716	2.7
Others	19	41	60	7.1	15.4	22.5	346	1.3
Total	83	183	266	31.2	68.8	100.0	17924	67.9

Table 9.2. Shellfish distribution in Unit 2, layer 3 to 8. Fragment weight = 8436 g, total weight = 26360 g. Individual and complete percentage are using total individual and complete count that is 100%. Percentage complete and individual of total weight is taken from the total weight = 26360 g (complete weight = 14565 g, individual weight = 3359 g and fragment weight = 8436 g).

Species	Indiv. count	Compl. count	Total count MNI	Indiv. %	Compl. %	Total %	Indiv.+ Compl. Weight (g)	Total weight %
Cittarium pica	80	46	126	44.4	25.6	70	1310	66.1
Astarea tuber	8	4	12	4.4	2.2	6.6	50	0.3
Arca zebra	–	19	19	–	10.6	10.6	289	1.5
Others	4	19	23	2.2	10.6	12.8	418	2.1
Total	92	88	180	51.0	49.0	100.0	2067	70.0

Table 9.3. Shellfish distribution in Unit 3, layer 3 to 8, Fragment weight = 5971 g, total weight = 19834 g. Individual and complete percentage are using total individual and complete count that is 100%. Percentage complete and individual of total weight is taken from the total weight = 19834 g (complete weight = 10102 g, individual weight = 3761 g and fragment weight = 5971 g).

two test units, the representation of *Cittarium pica* is slightly less than elsewhere on the site. The reason behind this is that a concentration of *Arca zebra* was located in both units. Interestingly, all the *Arca zebra* shells have a hole in them, just below the hinge, clearly made by humans. This modification was not noted among *Arca zebra* shells from the preceramic site of Norman Estate. It is possible that the high frequency of *Arca zebra* as fragments reflects a different means of preparation than that represented among the complete ones. Surprisingly the fragment percentage is higher than the individual percentage, for *Cittarium pica*, which is opposite the situation at Norman Estate.

9.3 Shell artefacts

Prehistoric artefacts of shell are relatively common in the Caribbean and they apparently had various decorative or tool functions.

9.3.1 ORNAMENTS

Shells are often attractive in colour and form and the prehistoric Amerindians used them as decoration, either worn on the body or used as inlay in woodwork (Rouse 1992, 117,

160). The latter use is usually not found, except among recent evidence. At Norman Estate and Anse des Pères the circumstances are not favourable for wood preservation and it can only be guessed whether shell artefacts were used alone or in combination with other material.

9.3.2 BEADS

Various definitions have been given for beads. According to Webster's (1990) dictionary "a bead is a small ball pierced for threading and used with others for ornament, e.g., in a necklace..". This is not the best definition for shell beads, however, and as a result, many investigators give their own definition for shell beads, for example:
- a bead is a discoidal or cylindrical object, with a hole in the middle, meant to be threaded on a string, together with other beads or pendants (van der Steen 1992), or
- a shell with a truncated spire forming a hole through which a cord can be threaded the length of the shell (Robinson 1978).

At the site of Anse des Pères the following bead types were recovered:

Species	Indiv. count	Compl. count	Total count MNI	Indiv. %	Compl. %	Total %	Indiv.+ Compl. Weight (g)	Total weight %
Cittarium pica	84	73	157	38.9	33.8	72.7	15419	69.6
Astraea tuber	9	11	20	4.2	5.1	9.3	72	0.3
Arca zebra	–	14	14	–	6.5	6.5	169	0.8
Others	9	16	25	4.2	7.4	11.6	366	1.7
Total	102	114	216	47.3	52.8	100.0	16026	72.4

Table 9.4. Shellfish distribution in Unit 5, layer 3 to 10, Fragment weight = 6131 g, total weight = 22157 g. Individual and complete percentage are using total individual and complete count that is 100%. Percentage complete and individual of total weight is taken from the total weight = 22157 g (complete weight = 11398 g, individual weight = 4628 g and fragment weight = 6131 g).

Species	Indiv. count	Compl. count	Total count MNI	Indiv. %	Compl. %	Total %	Indiv.+ Compl. Weight (g)	Total weight %
Cittarium pica	69	38	107	43.1	23.8	66.9	7882	59.6
Astraea tuber	10	13	23	6.3	8.1	14.4	114	0.9
Tectarius muricatus	4	2	6	2.5	1.3	3.8	10	0.1
Others	10	14	24	6.3	8.8	15.1	187	1.4
Total	93	67	160	58.2	42.1	100.0	8193	62.0

Table 9.5. Shellfish distribution in Unit 6, layer 3 to 6. Fragment weight = 5029 g, total weight = 13222 g. Individual and complete percentage are using total individual and complete count that is 100%. Percentage complete and individual of total weight is taken from the total weight = 13222 g (complete weight = 5409 g, individual weight = 2784 g and fragment weight = 5029 g).

– the first type is a shell (*Oliva* sp.) with the apex removed, creating a small hole that is present on three specimens from Anse des Pères. These shells appear worn; the sutures of the spire are only just discernible and the edge of the hole is smoothed, possibly because of constant movement and contact with other beads (fig. 9.1a),

– two *Oliva* sp. have their spire almost completely struck off. The edges are rough and most of the inner whorls are still in place. This is also a naturally occurring phenomenon and it could have been gathered as raw material for further bead manufacture,

– shells of *Olivella* sp. have the same general appearances as *Oliva,* only they are a lot smaller. Two specimens are both clearly modified, one with the top of the spire removed and subsequently ground to produce a flat smooth hole and edges. The other one also had the siphonal canal grinded and smoothed. Both clearly are beads (fig. 9.1b-c),

– *Conus* sp. including two specimens with the top of the spire (apex) removed. These specimens look like they were collected from the beach in that they are all rounded off and the holes may be the result of natural phenomena. However, they may have been used as beads with no further modification necessary; and,

– *Conus regius* as represented by a few specimens has the spire completely removed and does not show beach wear. No traces of smoothing are evident but like the previous ones it is possible to thread it on a string.

9.3.3 PENDANTS

Pendants are defined as -"something suspended"-"a piece of jewellery hanging from a brooch, necklace, chain etc." (Webster 1990). If "jewellery" is replaced with "shell" this definition is useful regarding the function of a pendant. A pendant is an object with a hole at its end or edge, which is also threaded on a string, either alone or with other pendants or beads (van der Steen 1992, 96), or a shell with a single perforation on the body whorl through which a cord can be threaded (Robinson 1978, 171).

At Anse des Pères, pendants are of a high quality. Analysis variable F5 (Robinson 1978, 175) is described as removal of the entire spire along with a part of the

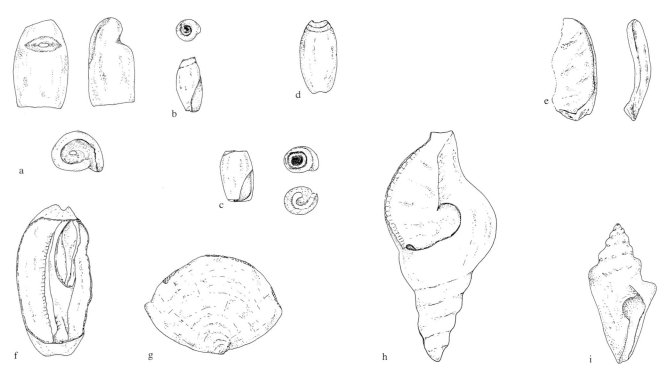

Fig. 9.1. Shell artefacts: a. *Oliva* pendant (scale 1:1), b. *Olivella* sp. Bead (scale 1:1), c. *Olivella* bead (scale 1:1), d. *Olivella* artefact, apex removed (scale 1:1), e. *Cypraea zebra*, part of a spoon (scale 1:1), f. *Cypraea zebra*, waste product of spoon fabrication (scale 1:2), g. *Codakia orbicularis*, scaper (scale 1:2), h. *Charonia variegata*, party processed vessel (scale 1:2), i. *Strombus gigas* (juv.), partly processed (scale 1:1).

Species	Indiv. count	Compl. count	Total count MNI	Indiv. %	Compl. %	Total %	Indiv.+ Compl. Weight (g)	Total weight %
Cittarium pica	39	28	67	47.0	33.7	80.7	6502	57.6
Astraea tuber	3	2	5	3.6	2.4	6.0	34	0.3
Others	2	9	11	2.4	10.8	13.2	210	1.9
Total	44	39	83	53.0	46.9	100.0	6746	59.8

Table 9.6. Shellfish distribution in Unit 7, layer 3 to 6. Fragment weight = 4533 g, total weight = 11279 g. Individual and complete percentage are using total individual and complete count that is 100%. Percentage complete and individual of total weight is taken from the total weight = 11279 g (complete weight = 4769 g, individual weight = 1977 g and fragment weight = 4533 g).

body whorl, with the upper edges from very crude to a ground smooth and very straight. These are combined with a hole in the body whorl opposite the aperture. All the holes are ground 90 degrees to the longitudinal axis of the shell. They were ground until a hole was created in the body whorl. The modified area is elliptical, or slit-like, as is the hole resulting from this type of manufacture.

One of the pendants has a hole centred above the siphonal canal (fig. 9.1d), while others exhibit holes to the left of the siphonal canal, suggesting a different position during manufacture. All these specimens have their upper edges ground smooth and straight.

In one shovel test (shovel test 170/140) a *Conus* sp. pendant was recovered. Its apex was removed and ground smooth, further modification was a hole ground in the body-whorl opposite the siphonal canal.

Species	Unit 1	Unit 2	Unit 3	Unit 5	Unit 6	Unit 7
Acmaea leucopleura						•
Tegula excavata		•		•		•
Astraea caelata		•	•	•		
Astraea tuber		•				
Nerita peleronta				•		
Nerita versicolor	•	•				
Nerita tesselata	•		•		•	
Nerita fulgurans		•				
Nodilittorina tuberculata		•			•	
Tectarius muricatus		•	•	•		•
Planaxis nucleus		•				
Cerithium litteratum			•		•	
Cypraea zebra			•			
Natica canrena	•	•	•			
Murex donmoorei		•				
Phyllonotus pomum	•					
Thais deltoida				•		
Purpura patula	•					
Coralliophyla abbreviata						•
Leucozonia nassa			•			
Leucozonia ocellata	•					
Oliva reticularis	•				•	
Bulla striata/umbilicata		•			•	
Arca zebra				•		
Codakia orbicularis				•	•	•
Chama sarda	•	•	•	•	•	
Pitar albida		•		•		
Cyphoma gibbosum				•		
Mactra fragilus			•			

Table 9.7. Distribution of 'other' shell species in Unit 1 to 7. Anse des pères total weight = 108,234 g. The Queen Conch is only found complete in Unit 1, but if compared with the total shell weight of all the units it is 3.9 %. This with the fragment weight included.

9.3.4 OTHER SHELL OBJECTS

This category includes shell artefacts whose condition is not clear, that is wether or not they were finished.

There are *Oliva* sp. beads recovered that appear like a pendant except that they are missing the hole in the body whorl. Of these, the spire and part of the body whorl are missing, but the remaining edges are ground smooth and straight. There is no hole in the body whorl opposite the siphonal canal and no traces of making a hole are present.

One shell artefact made from *Cypraeacassis testiculus* has had its spire broken off and the edges were left unmodified, no hole is present in the body whorl. This specimen could be classified as a bead, however. Other examples exhibit holes in the body whorl and can be classified as pendants (Drewett 1991, 118; van der Steen 1992, 99). This seems to be the finished product and at least one must be seen as an unfinished pendant. One *Cittarium pica* fragment has a perforation, possibly of human origin. This specimen could be a crude form of a bead, but this is not certain.

9.3.5 PLAQUES

This category consists of shell objects with an intentionally made square or rectangular shape. The same definition as applied to a bead applies here, but the shape and often the finish makes them more special. Two rectangular plaques were recovered. One complete specimen was found, it is only 1.5 cm in size and has been incised with two parallel lines on either side of the hole and one broken specimen was found, its edges are well rounded and hollowed towards the broken off end. The two short sides have been adorned with short incised lines. A similar object was found at the Golden Rock site on St. Eustatius (van der Steen 1992, 117, fig. 82).

9.3.6 UNKNOWN SHELL SPECIES

– One circular bead was recovered, measuring 0.5 cm × 0.3 cm, and with a hole of 1 mm drilled.
– One semi-circular disc, highly polished and with a hole in the centre of it.
– Three discs, all of mother of pearl, two with perforations in the middle and one without perforation. The size of

this specimen is very similar to the other ones and it can be concluded that it represents the same artefact category.

9.3.7 UNFINISHED ARTEFACTS

A circular disc possibly of *Strombus gigas* shell was recovered. It has carefully polished edges, and there is no indication of a hole on it. At Golden Rock, St. Eustatius (van der Steen 1992, 108), five similar discs were found and interpreted as being most likely unfinished artefacts.

9.3.8 SCRAPERS (SPOONS)

The recognition of what are commonly called "spoons" is germane here and their possible use as scrapers is considered a plausible function for this with difficulty to interpret artefact group. Their use for scraping plants like cassava seems plausible and another possibility includes scaling fish for such "spoons" (van der Steen 1992, 96). Bivalve scrapers might be more logical for scaling fish, however, because they are readily available and do not require much modification. The fairly common "measled cowrie" or *Cypraea zebra* was used for the manufacture of these scrapers/spoons at Anse des Pères.

Eight fragmentary and complete specimens are found of which three have blunt edges (fig. 9.1e). One has rough edges all around and the surface looks chipped, it may represent an unfinished specimen. A second specimen has one regularly sharpened edge over the width of the shell; this is perpendicular to the aperture of the complete shell. Only one side was ground round and smooth and the others are broken off. Three fragments were recovered, of which one has a very sharp edge much like the one previously mentioned, while the two others have clearly used edges that are more blunt, and perhaps less used.

Other *Cypraea zebra* artefacts seem to represent the production waste of the spoon/scraper form. They consist of the aperture, sometimes with the body whorl still attached to it (fig. 9.1f) *Codakia orbicularis* is a bivalve that lives in muddy or sandy substrates. Four of these valves show use wear on the edge of the shell. The exterior shows use wear on the edge and the exterior structure of the shell has disappeared, while the interior shows irregular spaced chipping or notching (fig. 9.1g). The valves were not modified because in their original condition they are suited for scraping. The use of bivalves for fish scrapers in Barbados may be a good explanation for these specimens too (Boomert 1987b).

9.3.9 VESSELS

Vessels are made by the extraction of the columella from the shell combined with enlargement of its aperture, leaving it very useful as a cup. Species modified in this fashion from archaeological contexts include *Cassis* sp., *Strombus gigas* and *Charonia variegata* (fig. 9.1h-i).

One vessel was recovered that had been made from *Charonia variegata*; the inner whorls were cut out and the aperture was partly enlarged. The cut edges were not smoothed, but this is more often the case for vessels from elsewhere in the Caribbean.

9.3.10 MISCELLANEOUS SHELL OBJECTS

One example of a *Cypraeacassis testiculus* object was recovered from test unit seven, this specimen had its spire struck off and its body whorl was totally removed, leaving only the outer whorl; the shell looks 'cross sectioned' in other words. It may have been used as a rough spoon, but nothing was done to smooth its cut edges.

9.4 Concluding remarks

The shellfish recovered from Anse des Pères seems much like these known from Golden Rock on St. Eustatius. The shellfish component of the Amerindian diet was clearly focused on *Cittarium pica*. The artefact assemblage is also generally similar, although *Strombus gigas* celts that are present at Golden Rock seem to be absent at Anse des Pères.

notes

1 The small quantity of *Strombus gigas* shells may be caused by dumping the shells on the beach after collection.

10 Faunal exploitation

Mark Nokkert

10.1 Introduction

In this chapter the results of the analysis of vertebrate and invertebrate remains other than shell found during the 1993 test excavations at the site of Anse des Pères will be given. Research on resource exploitation by Amerindians from St. Martin has been done by Dr. Elisabeth Wing for the Early Saladoid site of Hope Estate (Haviser 1991a; Wing 1995a). These data are compared with the results of the analysis of the faunal remains of the later Saladoid site of Anse des Pères to see whether any changes in resource exploitation had occurred.

10.2 Sampling and identification methods

Two areas with deeper and more compact deposits could be identified from the shovel test survey done at the site (cf. chapter 6). In both areas a number of 1 1 1 m test units were dug, which yielded an enormous amount of food remains (both vertebrate and invertebrate). Faunal material from both areas was analysed to see whether any differences or resemblances could be found between them.

All the dirt from the test units was water-screened through a 2.7 mm, a 6 mm and a 10 mm mesh screen. All of the 10 mm material was sorted out into the different categories (pottery, stone, shell, bone, crab, other). From the smaller sieves ten samples of each 2.5% of the total weight of the material found in these sieves were taken.

One level (3-A-6) of one of the dense refuse areas and two levels (6-A-3 and 6-A-4) of the other dense area were analyzed (for the exact location of units 3 and 6, cf. fig. 6.2). The bone material was very well preserved, probably the effect of leaching of calcium of the molluscs present in the midden. This probably is also the cause for the calcium residue attached to some of the bone material in the deeper levels (such as level 3-A-6), which sometimes made identification more difficult.

Identification of the fauna from levels 6-A-3 and 6-A-4 was done by comparing the material to the reference skeletons in the collections of the Florida Museum of Natural History in Gainesville, with help from Dr. Wing. Level 3-A-6 was identified making use of the reference collection of the Faculty of Archaeology of Leiden University in The Netherlands. Quantification was done using standard zooarchaeological methods (Wing and Brown 1979). The NISP (Number of Identified SPecimens), the MNI (Minimum Number of Individuals), as well as the weight of the bone fragments were recorded.

10.2.1 BIASES INVOLVED IN THE METHODS

One 1 mm sample (1 litre) of level 7-A-5 was studied. This sample yielded very little more bone material than the 2.7 mm fraction and no species were recovered that were not recorded in the analysed levels. So, the 2.7 mm mesh screen provided an approximately complete recovery of the vertebrate remains of the site of Anse des Pères. For the Golden Rock site at St. Eustatius a similar sieve mesh was used and by studying smaller fractions the same conclusions could be drawn (van der Klift 1992,76). For Saladoid sites a 2.7 mm mesh screen seems to be a very useful screen for obtaining samples for faunal analysis (in contrast with Archaic sites, cf. chapter 5 on the faunal material from the Norman Estate site).

The same kind of biases involved in the Norman Estate sampling procedures also count for this site. Level 3-A-6 has been analysed as follows: the ten samples of each 2.5% from the 2.7 and 6 mm sieves were combined to get an adequate sample. For this level, then, 25% of the 2.7 mm, 25% of the 6 mm and 100% of the 10 mm sieves has been analysed. From the levels 6-A-3 and 6-A-4 the first five 2.5%-samples from the 2.7 and 6 mm sieves were combined. Thus, for this level 12.5% of the 2.7 mm, 12.5% of the 6 mm and 100% of the 10 mm sieves has been analysed. Although not all of the material of the levels has been analysed this way, more material from different proveniences could be analysed than would have been possible otherwise. To check what would be the effects of these procedures first separate lists were made, one of the 10 mm mesh material and one of the smaller sieves combined. Then it was checked what the effect on the MNI and MNI% for every species would be if these two lists were combined. It turned out that the material of the 10 mm mesh screen did

TAXON	NISP	MNI	MNI %	WEIGHT (G)
Oryzomyini	358	15	20.5	28.25
Dasyprocta sp.	1	1	1.4	3.24
Unid. Mammal	n.c.	–	–	0.59
TOTAL MAMMAL	359	16	21.9	32.08
Columbidae	12	2	2.7	2.34
cf. Columbidae	1	–	–	0.02
Mimidae	3	1	1.4	0.11
Passeriformes	1	–	–	0.04
Unid. Bird	n.c.	1	1.4	2.12
TOTAL BIRD	17	4	5.5	4.63
Cheloniidae	62	2	2.7	216.08
Iguana sp.	3	1	1.4	0.13
Anolis sp.	3	2	2.7	0.05
Ameiva sp.	4	1	1.4	0.17
Unid. Lizard	23	1	1.4	0.74
Alsophis sp.	2	1	1.4	0.02
Unid. Reptile	n.c.	–	–	0.08
TOTAL REPTILE	97	8	11.0	217.27
Clupeidae	1	1	1.4	0.02
Tylosurus sp.	8	1	1.4	1.06
Belonidae	53	2	2.7 / [4.1]	6.23
Holocentridae	3	1	1.4	0.21
Epinephelus sp.	6	2	2.7	4.09
Serranidae	42	2	2.7 / [5.5]	13.76
Caranx sp.	24	6	8.2	1.39
Carangidae	367	1	1.4 / [9.6]	46.98
Lutjanus sp.	4	1	1.4	3.92
Lutjanidae	22	3	4.1 / [5.5]	2.49
Haemulon sp.	24	5	6.8	2.27
Anisotremus sp.	1	1	1.4	2.10
Haemulidae	93	9	12.3 / [20.5]	3.55
Calamus sp.	4	1	1.4	7.13
Mullidae	2	1	1.4	0.12
Halichoeres sp.	1	1	1.4	0.78
Labridae	1	–	–	0.41
Sparisoma viride	2	1	1.4	1.06
Sparisoma sp.	11	1	1.4	1.16
Scarus sp.	1	1	1.4	0.23
Scaridae	3	–	– / [4.1]	0.51
Scombridae	35	2	2.7	30.15
Balistidae	21	1	1.4	4.32
Unid. Fish	n.c.	1	1.4	39.79
TOTAL FISH	729	45	61.6	173.73
Unid. Bone	n.c.	–	–	123.94
TOTAL VERTEBRATE	1202	73	100.0	551.65
Coenobita clypeatus	2	1	1.3	0.95
Cardisoma guanhumi	48	13	16.5	110.99
Gecarcinus sp.	293	65	82.3	598.88
Gecarcinidae	81	–	–	32.61
Brachyura	n.c.	–	–	913.22
TOTAL INVERTEBRATE	424	79	100.0	1656.65
TOTAL VERT. + INVERT.	1626	152	–	2208.30

Table 10.1. Faunal remains from level 3-A-6.

TAXON	NISP	MNI	MNI %	WEIGHT (G)
Oryzomyini	509	15	18.8	29.14
TOTAL MAMMAL	509	15	18.8	29.14
Columbidae	18	3	3.8	3.37
Mimidae	5	1	1.3	0.43
Unid. Bird	n.c.	–	–	2.26
TOTAL BIRD	23	4	5.0	6.06
Cheloniidae	231	3	3.8	936.00
Ameiva sp.	6	1	1.3	0.13
Unid. Lizard	6	–	–	0.06
Alsophis sp.	1	1	1.3	0.09
TOTAL REPTILE	244	5	6.3	936.28
Clupeidae	4	2	2.5	0.07
Tylosurus sp.	8	1	1.3	0.13
Belonidae	72	2	2.5 / [3.8]	4.20
Holocentridae	1	1	1.3	0.02
Serranidae	19	3	3.8	20.95
Caranx crysos	9	4	5.0	1.43
Caranx ruber	3	3	3.8	0.09
Caranx, cf. *ruber*	2	–	–	1.34
Caranx sp.	43	5	6.3	1.98
Carangidae	475	–	- / [15.0]	25.60
cf. Carangidae	1	–	–	0.04
Lutjanidae	10	2	2.5	1.58
cf. Lutjanidae	1	–	–	0.02
Haemulon sp.	20	8	10.0	1.74
Anisotremus sp.	4	1	1.3	5.30
Haemulidae	133	8	10.0 / [21.3]	8.11
Calamus sp.	1	1	1.3	1.62
Sparidae	4	–	–	0.13
Bodianus rufus	2	1	1.3	1.87
Halichoeres sp.	1	1	1.3	0.02
Labridae	7	–	– / [2.5]	1.23
Sparisoma viride	8	3	3.8	5.96
Sparisoma sp.	15	1	1.3	2.76
Scarus sp.	3	1	1.3	0.99
Scaridae	11	–	– / [6.3]	2.20
Euthynnus sp.	60	5	6.3	62.18
Scombridae	40	1	1.3 / [7.5]	32.08
Balistidae	24	1	1.3	0.41
Unid. Fish	n.c.	1	1.3	131.32
TOTAL FISH	981	56	70.0	315.37
Unid. Bone	n.c.	–	–	122.59
TOTAL VERTEBRATE	1757	80	100.0	1409.44
Coenobita clypeatus	11	5	4.3	2.93
Cardisoma guanhumi	81	18	15.4	118.57
Gecarcinus sp.	386	93	79.5	661.10
Gecarcinidae	87	–	–	10.66
Brachyura	n.c.	–	–	715.89
Echinoid	2	1	0.9	0.07
TOTAL INVERTEBRATE	567	117	100.0	1509.22
TOTAL VERT. + INVERT.	2324	197	–	2918.66

Table 10.2. Faunal remains from levels 6-A-3 and 4.

TAXON	NISP	MNI	MNI %	WEIGHT (G)
Oryzomyini	867	30	19.6	57.39
Dasyprocta sp.	1	1	0.7	3.24
Unid. Mammal	n.c.	–	–	0.59
TOTAL MAMMAL	868	31	20.3	61.22
Columbidae	30	5	3.3	5.71
cf. Columbidae	1	–	–	0.02
Mimidae	8	2	1.3	0.54
Passeriformes	1	–	–	0.04
Unid. Bird	n.c.	1	0.7	4.38
TOTAL BIRD	40	8	5.2	10.69
Cheloniidae	293	5	3.3	1152.08
Iguana sp.	3	1	0.7	0.13
Anolis sp.	3	2	1.3	0.05
Ameiva sp.	10	2	1.3	0.30
Unid. Lizard	29	1	0.7	0.80
Alsophis sp.	3	2	1.3	0.11
Unid. Reptile	n.c.	–	–	0.08
TOTAL REPTILE	341	13	8.5	1153.55
Clupeidae	5	3	2.0	0.09
Tylosurus sp.	16	2	1.3	1.19
Belonidae	125	4	2.6 / [3.9]	10.43
Holocentridae	4	2	1.3	0.23
Epinephelus sp.	6	2	1.3	4.09
Serranidae	61	5	3.3 / [4.6]	34.71
Caranx crysos	9	4	2.6	1.43
Caranx ruber	3	3	2.0	0.09
Caranx, cf. *ruber*	2	–	–	1.34
Caranx sp.	67	11	7.2	3.37
Carangidae	842	1	0.7 / [12.4]	72.58
cf. Carangidae	1	–	–	0.04
Lutjanus sp.	4	1	0.7	3.92
Lutjanidae	32	5	3.3 / [3.9]	4.07
cf. Lutjanidae	1	–	–	0.02
Haemulon sp.	44	13	8.5	4.01
Anisotremus sp.	5	2	1.3	7.40
Haemulidae	226	17	11.1 / [20.9]	11.66
Calamus sp.	5	2	1.3	8.75
Sparidae	4	–	–	0.13
Mullidae	2	1	0.7	0.12
Bodianus rufus	2	1	0.7	1.87
Halichoeres sp.	2	2	1.3	0.80
Labridae	8	–	– / [2.0]	1.64
Sparisoma viride	10	4	2.6	7.02
Sparisoma sp.	26	2	1.3	3.92
Scarus sp.	4	2	1.3	1.22
Scaridae	14	–	– / [5.2]	2.71
Euthynnus sp.	60	5	3.3	62.18
Scombridae	75	3	2.0 / [5.2]	62.23
Balistidae	45	2	1.3	4.73
Unid. Fish	n.c.	2	1.3	171.11
TOTAL FISH	1710	101	66.0	489.10
Unid. Bone	n.c.	–	–	246.53
TOTAL VERTEBRATE	2959	153	100.0	1961.09

Table 10.2. continued.

TAXON	NISP	MNI	MNI %	WEIGHT (G)
Coenobita clypeatus	13	6	3.1	3.88
Cardisoma guanhumi	129	31	15.8	229.56
Gecarcinus sp.	679	158	80.6	1259.98
Gecarcinidae	168	–	–	43.27
Brachyura	n.c.	–	–	1629.11
Echinoid	2	1	0.5	0.07
TOTAL INVERTEBRATE	991	196	100.0	3165.87
TOTAL VERT. + INVERT.	3950	349	–	5126.96

Table 10.3. Faunal remains from all analyzed levels combined.

almost add no MNI to the list of the smaller sieves. Of course the NISP and weight of the bone do change somewhat, but for conclusions about habitat exploitation MNI and MNI% is used. The only species that did change in MNI, though, are tunas/mackerels, sea turtles and land crabs, which is not very surprising because these are large animals whose remains are mostly found in the largest screen.

10.3   Results of analysis

Tables 10.1-10.3 present the results of the analyses of the different levels. First levels 6-A-3 and 6-A-4 were combined — further referred to as level 6-A-[3+4] — into one table (table 10.2), taking into account that elements from one species found in both levels might have come from the same individuals. The total MNI of the combined list (197) is smaller than if the MNI of the separate lists had been added, but is probably more reliable because the limit between these two levels is an arbitrary line. This combined list is also better for comparison with the list of level 3-A-6 which has a total MNI (152) that is pretty close to the total MNI of 197 of the combined list. Table 10.3 combines all of the levels analyzed. A total of 3950 bone and crab remains were identified, giving a total MNI of 349 (vertebrates = 153; invertebrates = 196), and weighing 5126.96 g.

The separate lists of the levels 3-A-6 and 6-A-[3+4] show no substantial differences and they do not differ much from the total list of the site. This means that the total list is representative for the site as a whole and can thus be used for comparison with other sites in the region. This also means that the two areas identified on the basis of the shovel test survey as the most dense refuse areas could very well have been formed simultaneously. From the radiocarbon dates obtained for the two areas the same conclusions could be drawn (cf. chapter 6).

Of the vertebrates, most of the MNI belongs to fish (66.0%). Furthermore, 20.3% of the MNI is mammal, 8.5% is reptile and 5.2% is bird. Of the fish, Haemulidae (20.9%) and

Carangidae (12.4%) are the most representative species. Scaridae (5.2%), Scombridae (5.2%), Serranidae (4.6%), Belonidae (3.9%) and Lutjanidae (3.9%) are also well represented in the total food pattern. This pattern is the same for the individual lists of levels 3-A-6 and 6-A-[3 and 4].

Almost all of the mammal bones that were found belong to the Orizomyini rodents, the extinct West-Indian rice rats. From the data of faunal assemblages of Lesser Antillean sites studied so far, Wing (1993) calculated an average relative abundance of rice rats of 14.8% of the MNI. There is a relatively high percentage (19.6%) of Oryzomyini rodents in the Anse des Pères sample, especially when one considers the coastal setting of the site. It seems that only one species of Oryzomyini was present on St. Martin (Wing 1995a), while on other islands in the Lesser Antilles at least two different-sized species were found, e.g., Montserrat (Reitz 1994, 305, fig. 3; Steadman et al. 1984) and Grenada (Lippold 1991, 264). The bones of Oryzomyini found at Anse des Pères have the size of the small Oryzomyini, Undescribed Species A, as first classified by Steadman (Steadman et al. 1984).

Measurements were taken from several different skeletal elements of the rice rats found in the analyzed contexts of the Anse des Pères site (cf. Nokkert 1995). These measurements indicated that indeed there was only one species of Oryzomyini present on St. Martin. Table 10.4 compares the average sizes of the measured Oryzomyini bones with the average of these bones obtained from other archaeological sites in the Leeward Islands. These data have been published before by Wing (1995a) and Reitz (1994). Not surprisingly, the data from the two St. Martin sites (Anse des Pères and Hope Estate) are very similar. The data from the sites on Anguilla, Saba, St. Eustatius, St. Kitts and Montserrat (Oryzomyini-A) are also in the same size range, although they are all slightly larger than the St. Martin examples. The measurements obtained from the skeletal elements of the

	Upper cheek		Lower cheek		Humerus length		Femur length		Femur head		Tibia length		Astragalus length		Calcaneus length	
	N	X	N	X	N	X	N	X	N	X	N	X	N	X	N	X
AP	44	6.4	170	6.7	10	22.4	14	31.2	49	3.2	8	35.5	18	4.4	16	7.5
HE	12	6.5	35	6.7	10	20.6	8	30.9	23	3.2	9	34.6		–		–
RB	1	6.9		–		–		–		–		–		–		–
KR	2	7.4	25	7.0	1	21.6		–	1	3.5		–		–		–
GR	5	6.8	19	7.0	4	21.5	3	31.7	4	3.6	5	35.1		–		–
SFP	2	7.7	16	6.9	6	22.3	13	34.6	22	3.4	5	36.7		–		–
TR-A	1	6.8	3	7.1	1	21.7		–	1	3.2		–	6	4.7	1	6.4
TR-B		–	4	10.1		–	2	46.7	2	5.4	2	45.9	3	6.5	2	9.8
BS		–	8	9.5	2	27.6	3	42.0	12	4.8	2	45.7		–		–

Table 10.4. Summary of measurements (in mm) of Oryzomyini remains from several sites in the northern Lesser Antilles. AP = Anse des Pères, St. Martin; HE = Hope Estate, St. Martin; RB = Rendezvous Bay, Anguilla; KR = Kelbey's Ridge, Saba; GR = Golden Rock, St. Eustatius; SFP = Sugar Factory Pier, St. Kitts; TR = Trants, Montserrat (TR-A = Oryzomyini A; TR-B= Oryzomyini B); BS = Brook Site, Antigua. Data of HE, RB, KR, GR, SFP, and BS are from Wing (1995, table 7); data of TR are from Reitz (1994, table 7).

N.B.: The following measurements have been taken:
- the alveolar length of the upper cheek tooth row.
- the alveolar length of the lower cheek tooth row.
- the length of the humerus without proximal epiphysis.
- the length of the femur without distal epiphysis.
- the greatest width of the femur head with fused femur head epiphysis.
- the length of the tibia without proximal epiphysis.

larger Oryzomyini species found on Montserrat (Oryzomyini-B) and Antigua indicate that this must have been a much larger species, close in size to the genus *Megalomys*.

Predictions of the live weight of the rice rats are based on the allometric correlation that exits for terrestrial mammals between the width of the femur head and original body weight (Wing and Brown 1979, 127-129). This relationship can be described by the following formula:

$$\underline{\text{Log } Y = 2.5569 \text{ (Log } X) + 0.8671} \text{ (r = 0.98)},$$

whereby:
X = Greatest Diameter of the Femur Head (mm)
Y = Body Weight (g)

The average width of the femur head in the Anse des Pères faunal assemblage is 3.2 mm. This size corresponds to a weight of 144 g. For the Hope Estate site the same figures were found (Wing 1995a). Wing (1993) predicted an average weight of 181 g for the smaller West Indian rice rats and up to 300 g for the larger ones. The live weight of the Oryzomyini species that lived on St. Martin was somewhat smaller than the small Oryzomyini species that lived on several of the neighbouring islands. Figure 10.1 presents the size classes of the Oryzomyini from the Anse des Pères assemblage, based on the predicted live weight.

With the data of tooth wear stages relative age estimations of the rice rat population can be established. The mandibles and maxillas of the rice rats found in the Anse des Pères faunal assemblage have been classified in one of four different wear stages of the cheek dentition (Wing 1995a):

1. Pointed cones, unworn
2. Pointed cones with little wear
3. Substantial wear
4. Surface flat, dentine exposed

Individuals with tooth wear stages 1 or 2 are categorized as juveniles, while individuals with wear stages 3 or 4 are assumed to be adults. Despite some dentitions showing extreme wear, the degree of fusion of the limb elements showed that none of the individuals caught by the inhabitants had attained full growth (cf. Nokkert 1995).

Table 10.5 and figure 10.2 show a demographic profile of the rice rats based on the tooth wear stages as observed in the mandibles of the various levels of unit 3-A. The percentages between the young and adult rice rats do change

Level Tooth Wear Stage	Young		% Young	Adult		% Adult	N Total
	1	2	[1+2]	3	4	[3+4]	
3-A-8-FI + 3-A-8 + 3-A-7	–	3	25	6	3	75	12
3-A-6	9	16	48	16	11	52	52
3-A-5	3	17	69	7	2	31	29
3-A-4-FI + 3-A-4	1	17	58	10	3	42	31
3-A-3-FI + 3-A-3	–	3	33	4	2	67	9
Total of Unit 3-A	13	56	52	43	21	48	133

Table 10.5. Demographic profile of rice rats (Oryzomyini), based on Tooth Wear Stages of the lower cheek teeth found in unit 3-A. 3-A-8-FI is the deepest level, and 3-A-3 is the uppermost level of this unit.

through the various levels of the unit. In the lowest levels the ratio of young individuals to adult ones is one to four, in level 3-A-6 this changes to an almost equal distribution, while in level 3-A-5 the younger individuals are even better represented (69%). Then, in the following levels this ratio drops again to a ratio of one young individual to three adult ones in the uppermost levels. The preponderance of juvenile individuals in levels 3-A-5, 3-A-4-F1, and 3-A-4 may represent the response of the rice rats to a lower population density of the rice rats caused by heavy human predation. This response would come in the form of large litters and relatively more young animals in the population (Wing 1995a).

A decreased rate in the intensity of exploitation of rice rats would have been the cause for the preponderance of adult individuals in the uppermost levels again.

Table 10.6 presents the averages of the measurements of the alveolar lengths of the mandibles found in unit 3-A. A change in the size of the alveolar lengths of the mandibles can be noticed. In the lower levels the average of the measurements of the alveolar lengths is 6.9 mm, while in the middle levels this size decreases to 6.7 mm; in the uppermost levels the size increases again to 6.8 mm. Although these differences are not shocking, they can still be noticed

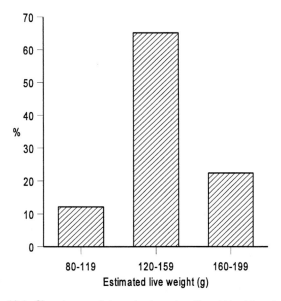

Fig. 10.1. Size classes of rice rats; based on the width of fused femur heads.

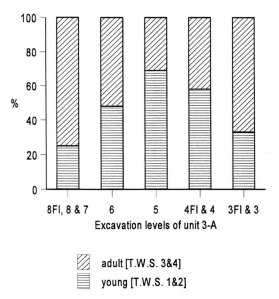

Fig. 10.2. Demographic profile of rice rats, based on tooth wear stages (T.W.S.).

Level	N	Mean	Range	Standard deviation
3-A-8-FI + 3-A-8 + 3-A-7	13	6.9	6.6 – 7.7	0.315
3-A-6	47	6.7	6.2 – 7.3	0.256
3-A-5	29	6.7	6.3 – 7.0	0.201
3-A-4-FI + 3-A-4	35	6.7	6.1 – 7.2	0.311
3-A-3-FI + 3-A-3	11	6.8	6.5 – 7.1	0.174

Table 10.6. Measurements of the lower cheek tooth row = alveolar length (in mm) of rice rats (Oryzomyini) found in unit 3-A. 3-A-8-FI is the deepest level, and 3-A-3 is the uppermost level of this unit.

in the material. Moreover, the levels with the smallest average alveolar length (levels 3-A-6 through 3-A-4) are the same levels that showed more younger individuals than adult ones.

The reduction in size of the rice rats as evidenced by the results presented in tables 10.5 and 10.6, is clear evidence that indeed the inhabitants of the Anse des Pères site are responsible for an overexploitation of this species. The inhabitants cannot have been responsible for a complete extermination of the animals, because the upper levels of unit 3-A showed a recovery of the Oryzomyini population.[1]

The agouti (*Dasyprocta* sp.) was also eaten. This species is represented by one mandible in the site. This is the first discovery of agouti bones on St. Martin. This species has been found in a number of archaeological deposits throughout the Lesser Antilles (cf. Wing 1993, table 2 and Pregill et al. 1994, appendix 1 for a list of the islands where agouti material was found; also St. Lucia (Steininger 1986, 74), Saba (Wing 1996), Les Saintes (Hofman 1995,1997) and La Désirade (De Waal 1996). Agoutis still live — or lived until recently — on some islands e.g., St. Vincent, St. Lucia, Dominica, Guadeloupe, St. Kitts (Westermann 1953), Montserrat (Steadman et al. 1984, 24) and La Désirade (pers. obs. 1993). In this century agoutis have also been introduced on St. Thomas and the Cayman Islands (Westermann 1953, 20-21). The Amerindians brought them from the South American mainland into the Lesser Antilles where they were taken from one island to the other while travelling up the island chain. These mammals were probably kept in captivity (Wing 1993). The mandible found at Anse des Pères shows some abnormalities. These might have come about by inbreeding (Wing, pers. comm. 1993). Agouti material found at St. Kitts and Nevis show comparable

abnormalities.[2] St. Martin is one of the northernmost islands in the Caribbean chain where agouti remains have been found. One could imagine that these animals were never brought to the Greater Antilles because of the existence of a much wider range of exploitable food resources (also relatively large mammals) on these large islands. Amerindians brought the now extinct hutía, *Isolobodon portoricensis*, from Hispaniola (where it was an endemic species) to Puerto Rico, Vieques and the Virgin Islands, where it was found on St. Thomas and St. Croix (Morgan and Woods 1986, 180).

No dog remains have been found at Anse des Pères so far. Dogs were present on St. Martin as the find of a mandible in the 1987 test excavation at the Hope Estate site (Haviser 1991a, 649) attested. Most dog remains in the Caribbean have been recovered from burials (Wing 1989); therefore, more extensive excavations at the site of Anse des Pères will probably result in the discovery of dog remains as well.

Of the birds, most of the bones belong to the family of Columbidae, the pigeons and doves. Remains of these birds are found in most of the sites in the Caribbean (Wing 1989). Thrashers (Mimidae, Passeriformes) are also fairly common in Caribbean sites.

Of the reptiles found in this assemblage, the sea turtles are a well-represented species. They make a substantial contribution to the biomass consumed, although most of the turtles that were eaten must have been relatively young individuals when compared to the specimens in the reference collections of the Florida Natural Museum of History. Only three vertebrae of iguana were found, all in level 3-A-6. It is a question why the inhabitants did not make more use of this nowadays well-appreciated source of food. Iguanas may have been transported between islands by humans to ensure their availability for future consumption (Pregill et al. 1994, 32), but were probably endemic to the region (in contrast with agouties). Furthermore, several small lizards (*Ameiva* sp., *Anolis* sp.) and snakes (*Alsophis* sp.) were found, which were all probably not regular food items and were not very important for biomass consumption.

Most of the invertebrate material consisted of crab remains. Only a few pieces of sea-urchins (Echinoid) were found. The exoskeletons of sea-urchins are very fragile; therefore these animals might be underestimated in this faunal assemblage. Two different species (*Coenobita clypeatus* and *Cardisoma guanhumi*) and one genus (*Gecarcinus* sp., represented by two different species in the Caribbean) of land crabs were found in the assemblage. *Coenobita clypeatus* is a land hermit crab. Its little meat may have been eaten, but it could also have been used as bait for fishing as is done on the islands nowadays. Hermit crabs must have been attracted to middens, to feed themselves and/or for finding them a new 'home' (mostly the *Cittarium pica* shell). Studying all the crab remains in the 10 mm mesh samples — the smaller mesh samples contributed only very little to the MNI of crab — of all the excavated units made clear that the ratio between the *Gecarcinus* sp. and *Cardisoma guanhumi* is just about the same throughout the site, being about 80% *Gecarcinus* sp. and 20% *Cardisoma guanhumi* (Nokkert 1995). Whether this pattern reflects the natural distribution of these species in the vicinity of the site during the period of occupation, or a preference of the inhabitants for one species above the other, is unclear. On present-day rural Dominica both *Gecarcinus lateralis* and *Gecarcinus ruricola* seem definitively to be preferred to *Cardisoma guanhumi* and are apparently more widely available than the latter (Chace and Hobbs 1969, 45). That there is an equal ratio between *Gecarcinus* sp. and *Cardisoma guanhumi* throughout the site is an extra clue to the idea of this site as being a one-component site with a relatively short occupation. A strong decrease in crab throughout the occupation, as reported for other Saladoid sites, could not be observed for Anse des Pères. The abundance of land crab remains is remarkable when one considers the late radiocarbon dates obtained for this site.

Measurements were obtained from crab mandibles found in the Anse des Pères site. The mandible has proven to be amenable to dimensional scaling for predicting total carapace width and average live weight (deFrance 1988, 52-59). Overexploitation of land crabs can eventually result in a reduction in the average size of the crabs (Wing 1995b). At the other hand, crabs recover rather rapidly from exploitation either through the surviving crabs or through the recolonization of an area (deFrance 1988, 83). If any

change in the size of the mandibles could be noticed — as an indication for overexploitation — it should probably have been found in unit 3-A. Unit 3-A was chosen for the measuring of the mandibles, because the youngest radiocarbon date of the site was obtained from this unit. Crab mandibles from unit 6-A have also been measured for the same purposes (Nokkert 1995). No clear change in the sizes of crabs could be noticed between the various levels of unit 6-A. Only a slight decline in the size of the mandibles of the 2.7 mm samples could be noticed: from an average of 9.22 mm in level 6-A-6 to an average of 8.27 mm in level 6-A-3. This decrease in size, however, was not reflected in the material of the 6 mm samples, and could also not be seen when the results of the 2.7 and 6 mm mesh samples were combined.

The dimensional allometric formula for predicting the average live weight from the crab mandibles is the following (taken form deFrance 1988, 55):

$$\underline{Log\ Y = .508 + 1.842\ (Log\ X)\ (r = .90),}$$

whereby:
X = Merus Height (MH) of the maxilaped (mm).
Y = Estimated Average Live Weight (g).

In figure 10.3 the estimated live weights of the crabs have been plotted for both the units 3-A and 6-A. The graph shows the results for the different mesh screens analyzed.

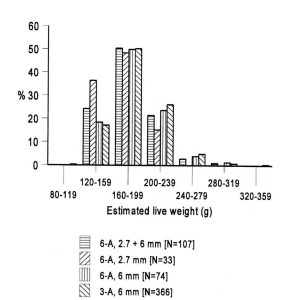

Fig. 10.3. Size classes of land crabs; Units 3-A and 6-A.

119

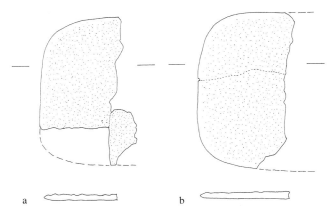

Fig. 10.4. Modified turtle bones: a. Anse des Pères, b. Golden Rock, St. Eustatius (scale 1:2).

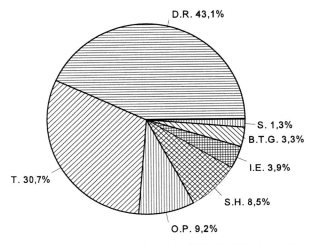

Fig. 10.5. Habitat exploitation; based on MNI of vertebrate remains.

There clearly is a restricted range in the size classes of the crabs. About half of all crabs harvested fall in the size class of 160-199 grams. This is the same for the 2.7 mm and the 6 mm mesh samples of unit 6-A, and is also true for the 6 mm mesh sample of unit 3-A. Furthermore it can be noticed that the distribution of the crabs over the various size classes is almost equal for the 6 mm mesh samples of units 3-A and 6-A. The distribution of the 2.7 mm mesh sample over the various size classes is slightly different. As could be expected, the 2.7 mm mesh sample shows a higher amount of individuals in the smaller size class of 120-159 grams compared to the 6 mm mesh samples. The estimated average live weight of the crabs found in unit 6-A is 181 g (2.7 + 6 mm mesh samples), while the estimated average live weight of the crabs found in unit 3-A (6 mm mesh sample

only) is 188 g. These weights are considerably smaller than the weights Wing (1995a) obtained for the crabs of the Hope Estate site, where she found an average of 214 g. A decline in the size of crabs in later deposits has also been observed on other islands (Wing 1995b).

All of the 10 mm material excavated was examined for any additional, relatively rare species missing in the analyzed levels. This resulted in the following species:
– Several large bird bones belonging to *Phoenicopterus ruber*, the Greater Flamingo, were found in the following levels: 1-A-8; 2-A-3, 2-A-4, 2-A-5, 2-A-6, 2-A-8; 3-A-4, 2 a shark tooth (Carcharhinidae); in 7-A-6 one vertebra, probably from a small Lemonshark, *Negaprion breviostris* (tentatively identified as such by Laura Kozuch, Florida Museum of Natural History).
– Barracuda remains (Sphyraenidae) were found in three different units. In each of the levels 2-A-3, 5-A-7 and 6-A-4-F.I, one vertebra was present.
– Two spines of *Diodon* sp. were found, one in level 2-A-3 and one in level 2-A-4, probably belonging to the same individual.
– One chela of the Coral crab (*Carpilius corallinus*) was also found. This is a large West-Indian sea crab (upto 12.5 cm.). On St. Eustatius this crab is caught in fishpots during the lobsterseason (throughout the winter until April) (van der Klift 1985, 18).
– An additional iguana vertebra was found in level 1-A-2.
– A piece of bone, found in 3-A-3, is probably of human origin. It is a small cranial part of an approximately one year old child (Hoogland, pers. comm. 1995). The bone was burned.

– A colonial intrusion was found in excavation unit 1. A complete pig (ca. 14-16 months old female) was dug into level 1-A-4 and 1-A-5. In the east-profile of the unit the intrusion is clearly visible. Also in unit 1 a tooth of a sheep or goat was found. This tooth was identified by Dr. Th. van Kolfschoten (Faculty of Archaeology, Leiden University) as a left second premolar. It was found in level 1-A-2, a disturbed level in the plowzone, so its find is not very surprising.

10.4   Bone modification
In contrast to the use of shell as basic material for the preparation of artefacts (cf. chapter 9), bone was not a favourite material at the site of Anse des Pères. Only one piece of modified bone was found (fig. 10.4a). This is a part of one of the costal plates (=pleurals) of the carapace of a sea turtle. It has been smoothed at the edges and has been bisected, so that the rough interior of the plate is exposed at the bottom side. Interestingly, an almost

	TAXA		MNI	MNI %
TERRESTRIAL	Oryzomyini		30	19.6
	Dasyprocta sp.		1	0.7
		MAMMAL	31	20.3
	Columbidae		5	3.3
	Mimidae		2	1.3
	Unid. Bird		1	0.7
		BIRD	8	5.2
	Iguana sp.		1	0.7
	Anolis sp.		2	1.3
	Ameiva sp.		2	1.3
	Unid. Lizard		1	0.7
		REPTILE	8	5.2
		TOTAL	47	30.7
BEACH-TURTLE GRASS	Cheloniidae		5	3.3
INSHORE-ESTUARINE	Clupeidae		3	2.0
	Sparidae		2	1.3
	Mullidae		1	0.7
		TOTAL	6	3.9
REEF- SHALLOW CORAL REEFS	Holocentridae		2	1.3
	Labridae		3	2.0
	Scaridae		8	5.2
		TOTAL	13	8.5
REEF- DEEP REEFS/ROCKY BANKS	Serranidae		7	4.6
	Carangidae		19	12.4
	Lutjanidae		6	3.9
	Haemulidae		32	20.9
	Balistidae		2	1.3
		TOTAL	66	43.1
[SHALLOW+DEEP REEFS]		TOTAL	79	51.6
OFFSHORE-PELAGIC	Belonidae		6	3.9
	Scombridae		8	5.2
		TOTAL	14	9.2
SEA	Unid. Fish		2	1.3
TOTAL OF THE SITE			153	100.0

Table 10.7. Habitats exploited

identical example was found in the Golden Rock site on the nearby island of St. Eustatius (fig. 10.4b). This piece had not been described or published before. Both of these modified turtle bones were made from the first costal plate of the carapace. Modified sea turtle shell has also been reported from Barbados and Martinique (Wing 1991a, 362). Descriptions of 16 modified sea turtle shell fragments from Barbados probably point to the same kind of pieces as the ones from St. Martin and St. Eustatius. Their function is not known.

10.5   Habitats exploited

Table 10.7 and figure 10.5 give an overview of the habitats exploited by the Amerindians of this site. The species identified are classified in one of five categories based on habitat preferences: Terrestrial, Beach-Turtle Grass, Inshore-Estuarine, Reef, and Offshore-Pelagic. Information for this classification is obtained from Randall (1968) and Wing and Reitz (1982). All mammals, birds and reptiles (except sea turtles) were classified as terrestrial. Sea turtles might have been caught on beaches while laying their eggs. Because most of

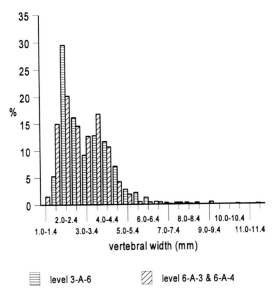

Fig. 10.6. Fish vertebrae of various levels.

▤ level 3-A-6   ▨ level 6-A-3 & 6-A-4

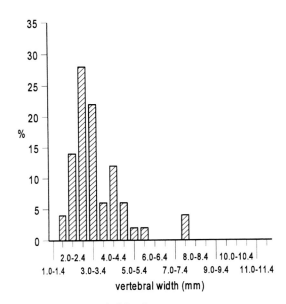

Fig. 10.7. Fish atlases of all levels.

the sea turtles found in the site were relatively young individuals (cf. above), they could have been taken from the seagrass beds as well. The only inshore taxa were Sparidae (porgies), Clupeidae (sardines/herrings) and Mullidae (goatfish). The only pelagic fish were Scombridae (tunas/mackerels) and Belonidae (needlefish). All other fish were classified as reef inhabitants. The reef species found at Anse des Pères can be divided into two groups, species that can mostly be found in shallow coral reefs, such as Scaridae (parrotfish) and Labridae (wrasses), and species that inhabit deeper rocky banks, such as the carnivorous Serranidae (groupers), Lutjanidae (snappers), Carangidae (jacks) and Haemulidae (grunts). The latter group is clearly better represented at the site of Anse des Pères (43.1%, against 8.5% for shallow coral reef species). Most fish species can be found in different habitats. This classification only reflects the location most members of each family commonly frequent and hence the most likely habitat in which they would have been captured.

10.6   Fishing methods

The fish species considered deep reef/bank species are usually caught with nets or hooks (Wing and Scudder 1980, 237). Species inhabiting reefs in shallow waters are mostly caught with fish traps. These traps can also capture the carnivorous deep reef species that come to shallow grass flats to feed. Pelagic species such as Scombridae are usually caught with hook and line. Small inshore schooling species such as Clupeidae could be captured using seine nets close

to the beach. The impression is that a variety of fishing methods were employed by the inhabitants from Anse des Pères. All of the sea water between NW St. Martin and western Anguilla falls within a 20 m isobath (Watters and Rouse 1989) and contains large reef areas (Haviser 1992a, 5, fig. 3). Most likely all of the fish found at Anse des Pères was caught in this part of the sea around the island, directly accessible from the site.

Measurements were taken on the fish atlases and fish vertebrae found in the faunal material. This was done in order to determine the size ranges of the fishes caught by the inhabitants. In figure 10.6 the measurements of the vertebrae from levels 3-A-6 and 6-A-5 (3 and 4) are combined in one graph. A much broader range can be observed than was found in the measurements obtained from the vertebrae of the Norman Estate site. Unlike the Norman Estate sites, the use of traps cannot be postulated for the Anse des Pères site as the main fishing method used. A more diverse range in the employment of fishing methods is more likely (e.g., hook-and-line fishing, spearing, trapping and netting).

Figure 10.7 presents the results of the measurements of the fish atlases found in the analyzed faunal material. As was done for the Norman Estate sites, the measurements of the atlases were used to calculate the weight of the edible meat each fish could have provided. The results are presented in

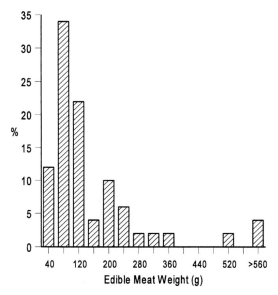

Fig. 10.8. Estimated fish weight; based on atlas width.

figure 10.8. Most fish caught must have been moderately sized; the average fish caught at Anse des Pères could provide 149 g of edible meat. This figure is substantial higher than was obtained for the fish eaten at the Norman Estate sites. The average meat weight of the fishes eaten differs considerably between the Hope Estate and Anse des Pères sites. The average sized fish at the Hope Estate site could have provided approximately 500 g of meat; groupers could provide 531 g, grunts 775 g, and parrotfishes 473 g (Wing 1995a). for the Anse des Pères site the smaller size of the fishes caught is remarkable: groupers provided 218 g, jacks provided 106 g, and grunts 82 g of usable meat on the average.

10.7   Comparison with other sites in the region

10.7.1   HOPE ESTATE, ST. MARTIN

If one looks at the faunal assemblages of the two Saladoid sites of Anse des Pères and Hope Estate one can see some differences and similarities in the composition of the animal component. Vertebrate faunal and crab remains from the 1988 excavations on Hope Estate were identified by Dr. E.S. Wing. She studied 2.8 mm mesh screen material (therefore comparison with the faunal materials from Anse des Pères is possible) from one of the 10 cm arbitrary levels in the primary midden of the site. She points out the distinctiveness of this site in the Lesser Antilles because of its great abundance of terrestrial vertebrates — a lot of birds (Columbidae and Passeriformes) and a very high percentage of Oryzomyini —, as well as a unique emphasis placed by the inhabitants on

hermit crabs as almost equal to land crabs (Haviser 1991a, 649; Wing, pers. comm. 1993). At Hope Estate the fish component in the food pattern is relatively small, but comprises reef, inshore and pelagic species. Turtle remains were also sparse. Remarkably the proportions between the shallow reef fish species and deep reef/rocky bank species is almost the same as in the Anse des Pères site. The emphasis on land species in the Hope Estate food pattern can very well be a result of the location of the site, atop a flat plateau at 50 m elevation in the interior of the island surrounded by steep hills and some 2 km from the coast (Haviser 1991a, 647). A location-dependent food exploitation pattern can also be postulated for the site of Anse des Pères. Its location on a flat plain at the coast, quite some distance from the hilly interior can account for a lower percentage of mammal and bird remains, as well as a higher percentage of fish and turtle remains in the site. The shift from an interior to a coastal setting during the Saladoid period has been noticed on other Lesser Antillean islands as well (such as St. Kitts, cf. below). A possible over-exploitation and therefore depletion of terrestrial resources may have been a cause for the shift in site location.

10.7.2   OTHER ISLANDS

Recent investigations brought about quite some information concerning Saladoid subsistence patterns in the Lesser Antilles, e.g., Golden Rock, St. Eustatius (van der Klift, 1985,1992); Kelbey's Ridge 1 and Spring Bay 1a, Saba (Wing 1996); Cayon and Sugar Factory Pier, St. Kitts (Wing 1989; Wing and Scudder 1980); Trants, Montserrat (Reitz 1994; Reitz and Dukes 1995; Steadman et al. 1984); Indian Creek, Antigua (Jones 1985); Folle Anse, Marie Galante (Wing and Reitz 1982); Pearls, Grenada (Fandrich 1990; Lippold 1991; Stokes 1993), as well as Puerto Rico and the Virgin Islands, e.g., Sorcé, Vieques (Narganes Storde 1982); Maisabel and Hacienda Grande, Puerto Rico (deFrance 1988, 1989; Wing 1990). Saladoid groups used both terrestrial and marine resources. Extensive use of terrestrial resources was a consistent Saladoid feature. Wing (1989) found that an average of 38% of the individuals in early Lesser Antilles faunal assemblages were terrestrial animals, and 19% of the individuals in late sites in the Lesser Antilles. For the Greater Antilles she found an average of 34% for the terrestrial component of the faunal assemblages.

Besides the consistent pattern in the use of terrestrial resources, there is much variation in the subsistence strategies during the Saladoid period in the Lesser Antilles. But there seems to be a correlation between site-location and the habitats exploited. In Saladoid sites the habitats that were most preferred for exploitation were the ones most accessible and close to the sites. Early Saladoid sites can be found more inland (e.g., Hope Estate on St. Martin and Cayon on St. Kitts). These sites yielded substantial more terrestrial vertebrates than coastal sites. Late Saladoid sites (e.g., Sugar Factory Pier, St. Kitts, and Golden Rock, St. Eustatius) were located in coastal settings and/or on lower elevation plains. The marine component is relatively more important in these sites. Coastal sites on islands surrounded by very narrow shelves (and therefore restricted reef areas) show a preference for deeper reef and pelagic fish species. Examples of this kind of settlement can be found on St. Kitts (Sugar Factory Pier), Montserrat (Trants) and Marie Galante (Folle Anse). In contrast, on islands with large shelves (with shallow waters and extensive reefs) surrounding it, coastal sites show a preference for species that live predominantly in these habitats. This could be seen at the (post-Saladoid) Mill Reef site, Antigua (Wing et al. 1968) and the (post-Saladoid) Indian Town Trail site, Barbuda (Watters et al. 1984). Reitz, who compared the vertebrates from the Cayon, Pearls and Trants site concluded that the ratios between the inshore, reef and pelagic fish species exploited at these sites reflected the types of marine habitats associated with each island (Reitz 1994, 315).

Whether Saladoid groups located their settlement at certain specific locations because of the possibilities the habitats in the vicinity had for them (and which they preferred above others), or whether the location of the settlement determined the food exploitation patterns of the inhabitants (so other motives besides food possibilities were more important for them in their choice of site location), is not clear but is nonetheless an interesting subject for future research in the Antilles.

From Trants, an Early Saladoid site on Montserrat, vertebrate materials have been analyzed from excavations done in 1979 (Steadman et al. 1984) and 1990 (Reitz 1994). Land crabs were not included in the calculations, although they were very common in the collection (Reitz 1994,314). The analyses indicated a relatively high percentage of terrestrial resources, compared to the figures as calculated by Wing (cf. Reitz 1994, table 1). Columbidae (8%) and Passeriformes (9%) were very common (Reitz 1994, 305), and there was 9% of Oryzomyini rodents present in the 1/8"samples (Reitz 1994, table 6). Groupers were the most abundant fish family in the Trants collection, constituting 28% of the individuals in the 1/8" component, and only few inshore species were found. This pattern reflects the natural distribution of the different habitats most accessible from the site. Shallow water areas are limited around Montserrat, which has more patch reefs than fringe reefs compared to islands such as Grenada and Barbuda (cf. Watters and Rouse 1989, fig. 1).

Pearls, an Early Saladoid site on Grenada, contained a high percentage of Oryzomyini rodents (17%), comparable to the Anse des Pères collection. Terrestrial species contributed to 32.8% of the total MNI. Of the fish species, mostly reef and inshore species were caught (Reitz 1994,315, table 9), reflecting the distribution of the different marine habitats around the island.

Wing and Scudder (1980) compared two Saladoid sites on St. Kitts, the Cayon and Sugar Factory Pier site. The first showed a greater dependence on terrestrial species (mostly rice rats and doves) than the latter site, which had a predominance of pelagic fish species. Wing and Scudder hypothesized that the location of the sites might be responsible for this pattern, the Cayon site located inland and the Sugar Factory Pier site on the coast. This pattern corresponds to the pattern seen at St. Martin (Hope Estate and Anse des Pères). Habitation of the Cayon site (Early Saladoid) was contemporary with the earlier occupation of the Sugar Factory Pier site. When the invertebrate (crab and shell) remains were included in the calculations, a shift in emphasis from predominantly terrestrial species towards a more marine orientation could be seen at the Sugar Factory Pier site (cf. also Wing 1989).

Large investigations on the Golden Rock site, St. Eustatius yielded enormous amounts of vertebrate and invertebrate remains (van der Klift 1992). The fauna is characterized by an overwhelming abundance of fish remains (80% of the total MNI). Rice rats contributed to 13% of the total MNI. The grouper, the small schooling scad and tuna were the major contributors to the prehistoric diet, if one looks at the Maximum Biomass Estimates (van der Klift 1992, fig. 52). Groupers are very abundant around the island, which lacks a developed coral reef (Nagelkerken 1981). The distribution of the species at the Golden Rock site may, therefore, very well be a result of the distribution of the species around the island.

Recently, Dr.Wing analysed faunal material from five Saladoid and post-Saladoid sites on the small island of Saba, approximately 50 km south of St. Martin (Wing 1996). The oldest Ceramic sites known on the island are Kelbey's Ridge 1 and Spring Bay 1a (Period I; ca. AD 400-850). Samples from Spring Bay 1b and 3 (Period II) date from ca. AD 850-1300. Kelbey's Ridge 2 samples (Period III) come from deposits that date from ca. AD 1300-1400 (Hofman 1993, Hoogland 1996). All sites are very close to each other. The small, Late Saladoid site of Kelbey's Ridge 1 is distinguished by a relatively great abundance of land crabs. The Spring Bay 1 site has a Saladoid and a post-Saladoid component. In the lower levels of one of the trenches at this site, moderately amounts of landcrab chelae (claws) were found, while in upper levels no more land crab was found (Hofman 1993, Hoogland 1996). Both the Kelbey's Ridge 1 and the Spring Bay 1 and 3 sites have an overlap with the dates provided for Anse des Pères. Wing (1996) remarks the abundance of crab remains for a site with such late dates as Kelbey's Ridge 1. Furthermore, a shift from predominantly reef carnivores in the earlier sites to predominantly reef omnivores/herbivores in Kelbey's Ridge 2 could be observed. A relative increase of rice rats, and a concomitant increase in terrestrial vertebrates could also be observed. Rice rats constitute 5% of the MNI of the vertebrate fauna in Kelbey's Ridge 1, 9% in Spring Bay 1/3, 19% in Kelbey's Ridge 2, and even 33% in material from a hearth at Kelbey's Ridge 2 (Wing 1996).

A general dietary change from land crabs to shellfish during the Saladoid period (the so-called land crab-marine shell dichotomy) has been documented in many sites on the Greater and Lesser Antilles (see for instance Keegan 1989; deFrance 1988,1989; Jones 1985; Goodwin 1980 for discussions on this subject). At the Sugar Factory Pier site on St. Kitts, the contribution of land crabs to the diet between the early occupation and late occupation levels diminished from 73.0% to 6.6% of the biomass consumption (Wing and Scudder 1980, table 3). No crab at all was recovered from samples from the Late Saladoid/Ostionoid transitional and Ostionoid periods on Maisabel, northern Puerto Rico (deFrance 1989, 60), while older levels contained many crab remains. Based on radiocarbon dates, the crab/bivalve transition at the Indian Creek site, Antigua could be dated from the middle to the later half of the ninth century AD (Jones 1985). In the northern Lesser Antilles there seems to be a long history in the use of land crabs as an important source of protein. This could be attested in four Late Saladoid sites, the Golden Rock site on St. Eustatius, the Kelbey's Ridge 1 and Spring Bay 1a sites on Saba, and now also the Anse des Pères site on St. Martin.

Interestingly, a substantial use of land crabs during the post-Saladoid period was testified by excavations at the post-Saladoid site of Cupecoy Bay (SM-001) on the southwest coast of St. Martin. Here, 671 land crab fragments, almost as much as vertebrate remains (790 fragments, mostly fish) were reported (Haviser 1987). Radiocarbon dates obtained for this site gave three very different dates of 1715 ± 45 BP (± AD 235), 1045 ± 25 BP (± AD 905) and 790 ± 35 BP

(± AD 1160) (Haviser 1988, 23). There were no Saladoid ceramics found at the site. The overlap with the dates of Anse des Pères is noteworthy.

10.8   Conclusions

The faunal exploitation pattern of Anse des Pères could be called typically Saladoid. The late radiocarbon dates obtained for this site make it contemporary to the Golden Rock site on St. Eustatius (Versteeg and Schinkel 1992) and confirm the continuation of the Saladoid into the 9th and 10th century AD.

In the northern Lesser Antilles, the site of Anse des Pères stands out between other Late Saladoid sites because of its relatively high percentage of terrestrial vertebrates (almost as much as Early Saladoid sites) and the abundance of land crab remains. Of the fish species caught most come from deeper reefs and banks.

When compared to the other faunal assemblages on St. Martin, Norman Estate and Hope Estate, one notices three very different resource exploitation patterns. The Archaic inhabitants of Norman Estate were almost entirely marine-orientated, with a preponderance of shallow reef fish exploited; the Saladoid inhabitants of Hope Estate had a clear preference for terrestrial animals, while the later Saladoid inhabitants from Anse des Pères returned to a somewhat more marine orientation. Complete faunal information from a post-Saladoid site is missing for getting a complete picture of the resource-exploitation history of St. Martin. But information obtained from the nearby island of Saba gives some clues to the post-Saladoid pattern.

notes

1 The observed changes in demographic profile may have also been caused by an attempt of the occupants to exterminate the animals. Not necessarily these animals have all been hunted for food. Perhaps they were perceived as a nuisance (J. Oliver, pers. comm. 1999).

2 Dr. E.S. Wing pointed out some extraordinary traits on the mandible found at Anse des Pères. *Dasyprocta* sp. mandibles with abnormalities were also found in samples of analyzed faunal material of Cayon, St. Kitts and Hichman's, Nevis. These remains are stored in the Zooarchaeological Range of the Florida Museum of Natural History, Gainesville.

PART THREE
HOPE ESTATE

11 Methods and strategies

Menno L.P. Hoogland

11.1   Site location

The site of Hope Estate is to be found in the northeastern part of St. Martin. It is situated among "intrusive rocks" consisting of diorite, microdiorite, and tonalite dating from the Oligocene period. The mountains surrounding the Hope Estate site belong to the Pointe Blanche Formation and consist of tuff and silicious limestones.

The site occupies a plateau with an elevation of 85 m asl which dominates the alluvial plain of Grand-Case and Etang Chévrise. This plateau measures approximately one hectare in area and is cut off in the west by the Ravine Caréta. It is bounded by the Mont Caréta (401 m) in the southwest, by the Montagne France (360 m) in the south and by Hope Hill (292 m) in the east (fig. 11.1).

Hope Estate is the property of the Petit family. The archaeological site was discovered in 1987 by Dr. Michel Petit and has been the subject of test investigations by Dr. Jay B. Haviser of the Archaeological-Anthropological Institute of the Netherlands Antilles (AAINA), Curaçao, and the Direction des Antiquités de Guadeloupe in 1987 and 1988. In 1993 excavations were conducted by the Association Archéologique Hope Estate under the direction of Christophe Henocq in collaboration with Dr. Jay B. Haviser of the AAINA and a team of Leiden University under the direction of Dr. Corinne L. Hofman and Dr. Menno L. Hoogland. This volume analyses the results of the 1993 campaign.

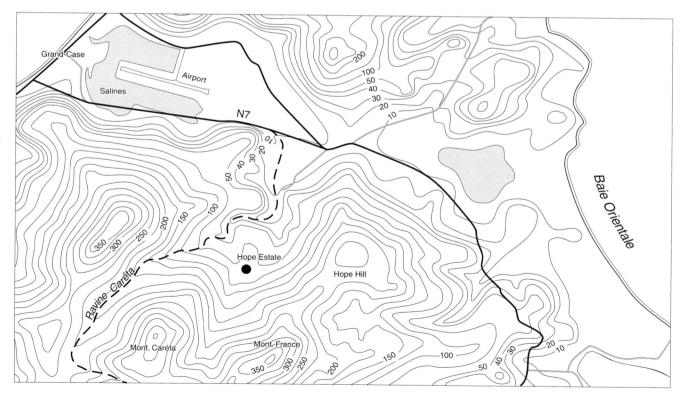

Fig. 11.1. The surroundings of the site of Hope Estate.

Unit	lab. No	material	age BP	calibrated date (95% confidence level)
Test 1-5	PITT-0219	charcoal	2275 ± 60 BP	410-180 cal BC
Test 1-6	PITT-0220	charcoal	2250 ± 45 BP	390-200 cal BC
A3-2	PITT-0445	charcoal	1490 ± 35 BP	cal AD 535-650
A3-3	PITT-0446	charcoal	2225 ± 40 BP	380-190 cal BC
A5-8	PITT-0448	charoal	2050 ± 45 BP	165 cal BC-cal AD 60
T20-3	PITT-0449	charcoal	2300 ± 55 BP	480-450, 415-190 cal BC
T20-3	PITT-0450	charcoal	2510 ± 40 BP	795-510, 495-490, 445-420 cal BC
A25-3	PITT-0451	shell	1515 ± 35 BP	unknown
A3-7	PITT-0452	charcoal	1660 ± 55 BP	cal AD 225-295, 320-540
coord. 1	GrN-20168	land crab	1530 ± 30 BP	cal AD 445-610
coord. 2	GrN-20169	land crab	1520 ± 35 BP	cal AD 445-625
coord. 3	GrN-20170	land crab	1535 ± 30 BP	cal AD 445-605

Table 11.1. Radiocarbon dates (GrN=Groningen and PITT = Pittsburgh). The dates are calibrated using the 'Groningen Radiocarbon Calibration Program Cal15', version april 1993 (Center for Isotopes Research, Groningen University). The results of the datings of the charcoal and terrestrial crab samples are calibrated using the calibration curve by Stuiver et al. (1993). The shell sample has not been calibrated, because it is unknown whether the sample has been corrected for δ ^{13}C. Coord. 1 = 226,80/699,75/8,34; coord. 2 = 224,00/632,30/8,99; coord. 3 = 225,80/671,90/8,36.

11.2   Previous research

The 1987 test pit revealed an archaeological deposit with a thickness of 75 cm (cf. Haviser 1988). At a depth of 25 cm the upper part of a human skeleton was encountered. Dense deposits of subsistence remains were noted at a depth of 50 -65 cm below the present surface, below which artefacts rapidly decreased (Haviser 1988). Two charcoal samples were collected for radiocarbon dating from a dense deposit, providing dates of 2275 ± 60 and 2250 ± 45 BP (table 11.1). Haviser (1988, 18) attributed the pottery to the Huecan Saladoid and Cedrosan Saladoid subseries.

The vertical distribution of the ceramic and lithic artefacts displays a gradual increase in overall weight from level 1 (0-10 cm) to level 4 (30-40 cm), a slightly lower weight in level 5 (40-50 cm), and again an increase in level 6 (50-60 cm). In level 7 (60-70 cm) the weight of the ceramic and lithic artefacts decreased and only a single artefact was recovered from level 8 (70-80 cm). The vertical distribution of decorated pottery remains shows that Cedrosan Saladoid decorative modes, such as white-on-red painting, are to be found throughout the deposit, from level 1 to level 6. This means that there is a discrepancy between the results of the radiocarbon dating and the relative dating of the pottery.

The test excavations were continued by Haviser in 1988. It provided evidence of the existence of three archaeological strata in the northeastern sector of the site (Barret and Léton 1989, Haviser 1991a). The two deepest strata (II and III) represent deposits of crab claws and other faunal remains as well as cultural materials. The layers were juxtaposed and could be differentiated only by the texture and compactness of the crab deposits. The bottommost layer was characterized by relatively decomposed, compact crab deposits, whereas the upper layer was typified by somewhat loose crab remains. These strata were covered by a sterile deposit of 20 to 30 cm in thickness. A third, badly delimited Stratum (I) was situated just below the surface of the ground. It consisted of a deposit of pottery sherds, shells and animal bones. The stratigraphy of the test units in the southeastern sector of the site was less complex. Six charcoal and one shell sample were submitted for radiocarbon dating (table 11.1).

The radiocarbon dates and the artefact analysis of the 1988 excavations led to the foundation of the hypothesis that three subsequent cultural groups occupied the Hope Estate site. Early Ceramic Amerindians produced a separate midden in the southeastern sector of the site (XXII T20 and T21) as well the earliest layers at XVII A1-A5 (Stratum III) probably about 560-350 cal BC.

Fig. 11.2. View of the site of Hope Estate seen from Hope Hill.

A second cultural group belonging to the Cedrosan Saladoid occupied the site about 325-290 cal BC. It appears to be responsible for Stratum II. A third cultural group can be dated to about cal AD 435-460. These Amerindians are characterized by the Barrancoid-influenced or Modified Saladoid pottery, typical of Stratum I (Haviser 1991a, 635-654).

11.3   Research objectives

Four main objectives were defined for the excavations of 1993; firstly, testing of the conclusions arrived at after the 1988 tests, secondly, collecting a sample of Huecan Saladoid ceramics, preferably from an isolated context, thirdly, testing the presence of structural features in the central sector of the site, and finally, understanding the post-depositional processes which took place in the midden area.

The research program consisted of a continuation of the excavations in the northeastern and southeastern parts of the midden area, and, in addition, excavations in the habitation area in order to identify possible structural features such as postholes.

In 1988 the area of the site was divided according to a grid system, oriented to the magnetic North. This grid system was renewed in 1993 while retaining the reference datum and the north-south axis. Eight reference points were established in the core area of the site. Within the grid system the west-east coordinate runs from 160 to 240 and the south-north coordinate from 610 to 700. Initially, the elevation of the reference point 200/650 was arbitrarily fixed at 10.00 m; its actual elevation was measured afterwards. At the end of the campaign the site grid system was linked with the topographic grid of the island. The orientation of the north-south axis of the site grid is 12.63° west of the true North.

Reference point 200/500 is situated at 83.90 m asl (reference general level of Guadeloupe).

11.4   Prospective investigation

A preliminary prospective investigaiton was conducted in order to get an idea of the boundaries of the site. The presence of archaeological materials was mapped and the artefact densities on the surface were estimated. It should be noted that the investigation was not meant to form a systematic survey and that site-specific subsurface testing of the site is imperative as a next step.

The results of the preliminary prospective investigation indicate that most of the archaeological materials are deposited on the eastern slope of the site area (fig. 11.2). On its southern and western edges some small surface scatters of artefacts are to be found. It is possible that this picture is influenced by the geographically differential acting of geological processes at the site. Erosion seems to have prevailed on the eastern slope. This resulted in the transport of fine soil particles down the slope and the gradual exposure of coarser, archaeological, materials on the surface. In the southern sector sedimentation apparently prevailed, since this part of the site adjoins the northeastern slope of Montagne France. To a lesser extent the same is true for the western sector of the site. Here it is likely that the archaeological materials are partly covered with sediment. This may imply that the archaeological deposits are better preserved in this part of the site.

The surface distribution of artefacts shows a horseshoe-like shape. This artefact scatter represents a midden area. In contrast, the central part of the site, which is nearly free of archaeological finds, can be interpreted as a *plaza*.

11.5   Excavation methods

The midden area was excavated in units measuring 2×2 m, each subdivided into squares of 1×1 m. The original situation of the finds was registered with reference to the 1×1 m units and arbitrary levels of 10 cm thickness. Reference numbers of arte- and ecofacts combine the number of the 2×2 m excavation unit (numbered 1 to 99), the 1×1 m square (labeled A-D) and the levels (numbered 1 to 9). Features have been labeled F001 to F999. During the campaign it became obvious that digging in arbitrary levels obscured the context of the artefacts to a certain extent. Because of the complexity of the stratigraphy and the apparent mixture of artefacts from various occupation phases in one and the same layer, the excavation method by arbitrary levels of 10 cm thickness was combined with one of excavating in natural layers and features in units 9 and 14.

Initially the material was dry screened through 4 and 6 mm mesh sieves. This way of artefact processing appeared to be both time consuming and inaccurate as the soil was either too dry and hard or too wet and soft to be dry sifted. Besides, the finer constituents of the refuse deposit were not easily recognized in the sieve. Therefore, a more appropriate and efficient method of artefact collecting, i.e., water-screening through nested sieves of 10, 4 and 2.7 mm meshes, respectively, was adopted.

The microfauna and other food remains such as shells were collected from 25% of the total sample, i.e., from all of the A units. Ten-litre soil samples were selected from special contexts, e.g., distinct refuse layers or special features, for flotation of macroremains (cf. chapter 16).

A different excavation method was employed in the central sector of the site, where structural features could be expected. The absence of a refuse layer and the low density of artefacts in the layer of topsoil justified mechanical stripping of the surface zone in this area. After the topsoil had been scraped off, the surface was shovel skimmed and the soil features appearing were drawn to scale. All features were sectioned. Photographs were taken of special features; sections were drawn to scale. The earth filling of these features was water-screened and sampled for flotation.

11.6   Location of the excavation units

The test units of 1987 and 1988 enabled two parts of the midden area in the northeastern and southeastern sectors of the site to be identified. In 1993 nine Units (3-9, 11 and 14) were dug in these sectors (fig. 11.3). An area of 8×13 m (Unit 12) was excavated in the southeastern sector of the site for the identification and study of soil features. In 1993 a

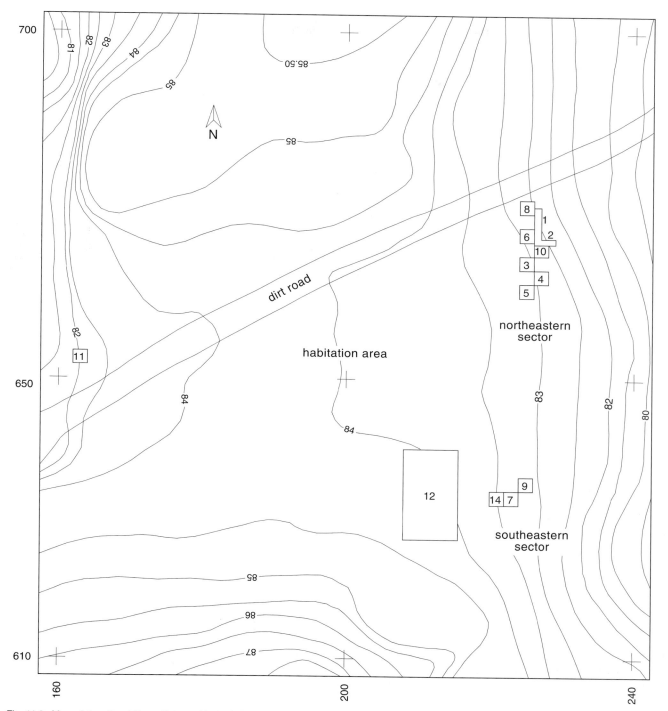

Fig. 11.3. Map of the site of Hope Estate with the location of the excavation units.

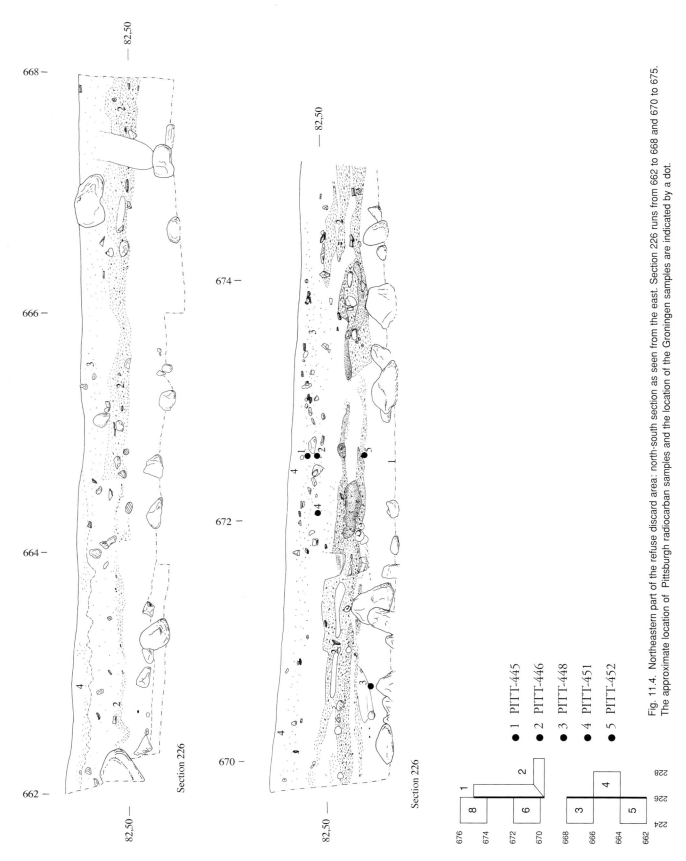

Fig. 11.4. Northeastern part of the refuse discard area: north-south section as seen from the east. Section 226 runs from 662 to 668 and 670 to 675. The approximate location of Pittsburgh radiocarban samples and the location of the Groningen samples are indicated by a dot.

● 1 PITT-445
● 2 PITT-446
● 3 PITT-448
● 4 PITT-451
● 5 PITT-452

Section 226

Section 226

134

total area of 144 m² was excavated. Excavation units 1 and 2 were meant to expose the 1988 section of squares XVII A1, A2, A3, A4 and A5 (Barret and Léton 1989; Haviser 1991a). These units measured 5 × 0.5 m and 3 × 0.5 m respectively. The material was not collected according to depth as the topmost part of the sections collapsed during the work.

A number of excavation units organized in chessboard pattern, were excavated to expand the 1988 section, i.e., one of the research objectives. Units 3, 4, 5, 6 and 8 were dug in order to reveal a 12 m long, north-south bearing, vertical cross-section of the site. As a result, a substantial sample of pottery could be collected, i.e., another one of the research objectives. Units 7, 9 and 14 are located near the 1988 T20 unit, as in this sector of the site the refuse layer seemed to consist of mainly Early Ceramic or La Hueca style pottery (Haviser 1991a). Unit 11 is located in the northeastern sector of the site. The objective of digging this unit was to explore the archaeological deposit in a sector of the site yielding a low surface density of material. Unit 12 is to be found in the central part of the site, i.e., the potential area of Amerindian residential structures. As a test the zone of the topsoil, was initially hand-shovelled in a 4 × 3 m area. The remaining part of the unit was stripped mechanically. The final dimensions of unit 12 became 8 × 13 m.

11.7   Stratigraphy

In order to test the conclusions arrived at after the 1988 investigations, first a section of the 1988 trench in the north-eastern sector of the site was cleared. It showed deposits of refuse mainly characterized by crab remains. A clearly outlined stratigraphic sequence, characterized by distinct properties, i.e., compact (level III) and loose (level II) crab layers, as noticed in 1988, was not encountered. The absence of this differentiation in crab layers may have been caused by changes in soil humidity.

Four main stratigraphic units could be distinguished, from bottom to top, as follows (fig. 11.4).
Stratum 1, a layer of sandy to loamy subsoil, very rocky at the base. In some sectors of the site it contains ceramics in a dispersed to a more concentrated pattern. Stratum 2 consists of various deposits of subsistence remains and artefacts with a simple to more complex stratification in a layer of sandy to loamy earth; Stratum 3 consists of a disturbed sandy to loamy soil including a layer of relatively large artefacts and ecofacts; Stratum 4 is a layer of topsoil.
These four strata can be distinguished throughout the midden area. The stratigraphy will be discussed in detail in four sections, i.e., section 226 from 664 to 675, running north-south, next to section 670 from 224 to 229 running east-west

in the northeastern part of the midden area and section 634 from 220 to 226 running east-west of the stratigraphy of the site, as well as section 224 from 632 to 636 running north-south in its southeastern portion.

Section 226 in the northeastern part of the midden area provides a fairly good picture (fig. 11.3). Generally speaking, the section shows a substratum consisting of weathered saddle of bedrock made up of rounded and angular blocks in a sandy to loamy matrix. The sediment deposits on top of it are 55 to 95 cm thickness. They show several embedded layers of refuse providing evidence of distinct episodes of midden formation.
In section stratum 1 seems to be scarce in artefacts. However, the vertical distribution of pottery reveals that the arbitrary levels below the crab deposits contain a considerable amount of material. The amounts of pottery vary from about 50 to 750 g/m² (cf. chapter 12, table 12.1). The ceramics embedded in this stratum can be attributed exclusively to the Huecan Saladoid subseries (cf. chapter 12).
Stratum 2 provides evidence of a period of intensive discard of refuse, mainly consisting of subsistence debris. The lowest midden deposits are very thin, rather dispersed, and intermittently resting on the sterile or artefacts-containing subsoil. This layer is clearly present in the east-west sections of unit 6. The subsequent refuse deposits are generally denser, thicker and more diverse. In the centre the layers are quite varied in constitution, as lenses of charcoal and ash, shells and pottery alternate with layers of mainly crab remains. At the margins of the midden area, as revealed by the sections of unit 4 and 5, the refuse layers show a simple structure. Apparently, the sequence of refuse deposition is more complex in the eastern part of the section. Probably it constitutes a core of a separate midden in the larger midden area. The structure is clearly outlined in the east-west sections of units 3, 6 and.

The north-south sections provide an indication of the formation process of the refuse midden, as it seems that the layer is constituted of individual discard patches. The discrimination between these patches is mostly obscured in the sense that, for instance, trampling has transformed them into a homogeneous midden. In some parts of the sections, however, the sequence of layers, occasionally interrupted by a sterile layer of sediment, is better preserved. The sections show to which extent the midden has been modified by natural as well as cultural post-depositional processes. The abrupt ruptures of the deposits may be explained by partial erosion or the deposition of refuse in erosion gullies. On the other hand, cultural processes, e.g., penetrating postholes, may have played a role.

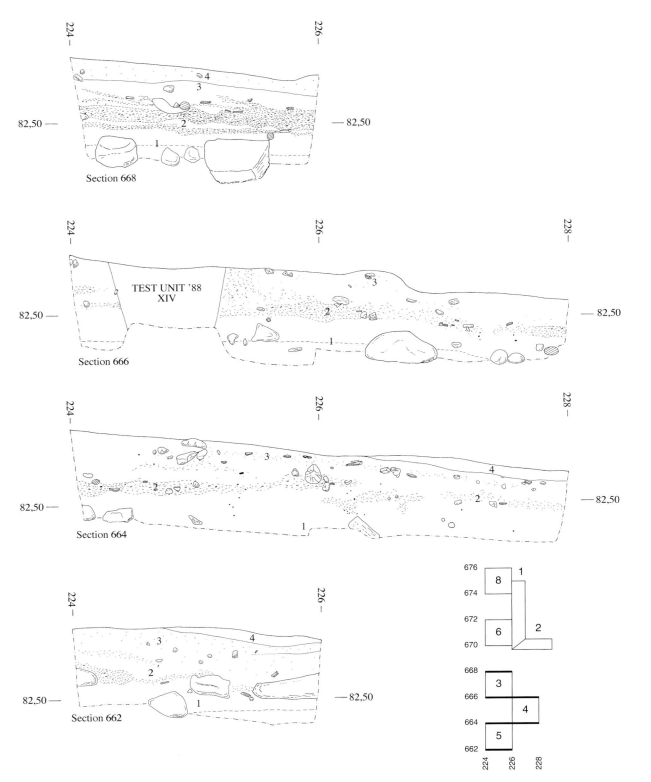

Fig. 11.5. Northeastern part of the refuse discard area: east-west sections as seen from the south. Section 662 runs from 224 to 226, section 664 from 224 to 288, section 666 from 244 to 228 and section 668 from 224 to 226.

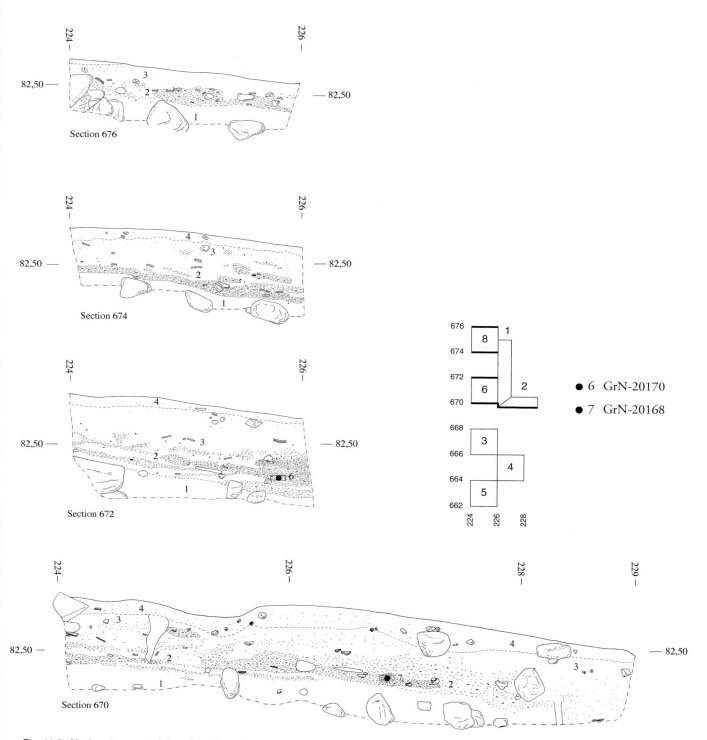

Fig. 11.6. Northeastern part of the refuse discard area: east-west sections as seen from the south. Section 760 runs from 224 to 229, sections 672, 674 and 676 from 224 to 226.

137

a

b

Fig. 11.7. Views of the north-south section in the northeastern part of the refuse discard area: a. section 226 from 670 to 672, b. section 226 from 672 to 674 seen from the east (see fig. 11.4).

The deposits of crab remains are covered by a third stratum, consisting of an earth deposit, containing a low amount of subsistence debris. Throughout this episode of site formation sedimentation processes seem to have prevailed. However, it is remarkable that this stratum appears to contain many pottery sherds. The sections revealed that one layer in this stratum is characterized by a deposit of large ecofacts and artefacts, including complete shells of *Cittarium pica*, pottery sherds and stone artefacts. This feature is not recorded in the vertical distribution of the pottery (cf. table 12.1). Perhaps, the precise distribution of pottery in this stratum is obscured due to the excavation method using arbitrary levels. This stratum is covered by a layer of topsoil.

The east-west sections of this part of the midden area reveal that the bottommost crab layers were deposited on a sloping surface and, consequently, are probably affected by slope wash (fig. 11.5, 11.6). The rather thin and dispersed crab deposits increase in thickness and complexity towards the north. Furthermore, the surface distribution suggests that the core of the midden seems to extend further to the north and the west.

The four stratigraphic units mentioned above can be distinguished in the southeastern part of the midden area (figs 11.7, 11.8). The first stratum consists of angular blocks of weathered diorite in a matrix of sandy loam on diorite bedrock. In units 7 and 14 this stratum showed many rounded boulders (fig. 11.9). Moreover, it included many horizontally orientated pottery sherds. They occurred in quantities ranging from 130 g/m² in unit 7 to 515 g/m² in unit 14. The ceramics from this stratum belong exclusively to the Huecan Saladoid subseries (cf. chapter 12).

The second stratum consists of a 10 to 25 cm thick layer of heterogeneous crab refuse, rich in archaeological materials. The food debris was deposited on a slightly sloping surface. The east-west sections of units 7, 9 and 14 show that the refuse layer increases in thickness and density from west to east. The sections of unit 14 reveal that the boundary of this stratum is to be found in the easternmost part of this unit. The remainder of the unit consists of a deposit of dispersed faunal remains and artefacts. In unit 7 the crab layer reaches its highest density; it decreases in thickness and density in unit 9. It may extend further to the west. The north-south sections of units 7 and 9 suggest that the refuse deposits continue into both directions. Generally speaking, the refuse layers are composed of patches of food debris, which were homogenized by post-depositional processes. In units 7 and 9 the second stratum shows similar properties. It appears to be contemporaneous with the deposits in the northeastern part of the midden area, containing Huecan Saladoid as well

as Cedrosan Saladoid ceramics. The fact that this layer is intersected with soil traces dating to various occupations, including postholes, provides evidence for a change of function of this zone of the site.

A stratum of loamy sand, containing a large amount of pottery sherds is to be found on top of the refuse layers. A layer of predominantly horizontally orientated sherds has been noted within this stratum. Posthole F016 is probably associated with this layer. It is covered with topsoil. Besides, on a few spots a recent layer of sterile sediment was noticed.

The sections of unit 11 in the northwestern part of the midden area show a sediment deposit with dispersed artefacts, but no refuse layer was discovered. Here, the surface prospection pointed to a pattern of midden deposition on more widely separated spots and settlement debris seems have been deposited in depressions such as gullies. However, unit 11 shows evidence of an occupation layer as a nearly complete vessel was found as a primary deposit here.

11.8 Features

Human skeletal remains were encountered in units 3, 4 and 10. They are discussed in chapter 17. The objective of excavating unit 12 was to expose possible features. In all 45 features of different character were recorded in this unit, including geological features, a majority of biotic ones such as tree roots, and 15 postholes (fig. 11.10). The dimensions of the postholes are restricted by the presence of diorite bedrock at a depth of 30 to 60 cm below the original surface (fig. 11.11). The upper layer of the diorite is weathered and soft but its hardness gradually increases with depth. The area of unit 12 is too limited to allow recognition of a pattern in the configuration of the postholes. Feature F016 in the southeastern part of the midden area represents a posthole intersecting the layer of refuse (fig. 11.8). This posthole was dug after the deposition of the refuse on this spot. It belongs to the later part of the Saladoid occupation of the site.

11.9 Radiocarbon samples

In 1993 three samples were submitted for radiocarbon dating to the Groningen Isotopes Laboratory in order to supplement the 1987-1988 Pittsburgh dates. The objective was to obtain dates for the lower 'compact' crab deposits, and hence fragments of exo-skeletons of land crabs were collected as sample materials. In this way an optimal association between samples and features to be dated was guaranteed. Land crab samples have been used for the radiocarbon dating of several sites on Saba, yielding reliable measurements (Hoogland 1996)[1]. Sample provenances are indicated by coordinates. The location of two samples is marked on the vertical cross-sections (cf. figs 11.6b, 11.7). Although much older dates were expected, the radiocarbon age of the three samples (GrN-20168, GrN-20169 and

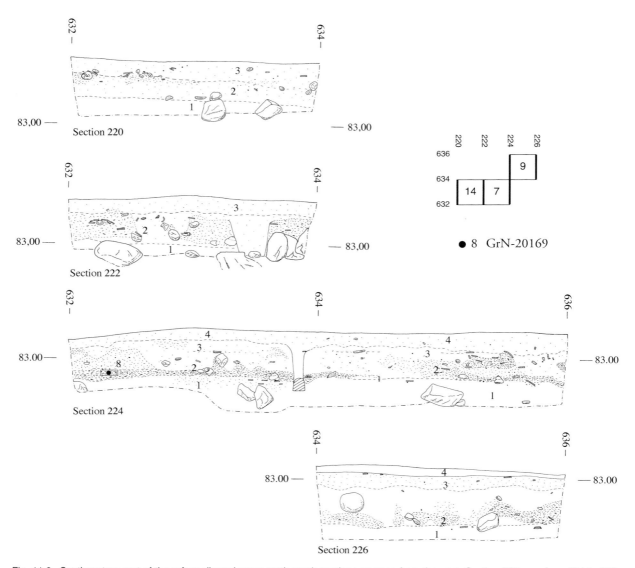

Fig. 11.8. Southeastern part of the refuse discard area: north-south sections as seen from the east. Section 226 runs from 634 to 636, section 224 from 632 to 636, sections 222 and 220 from 632 to 634.

GrN-20170) centres around 1530 ± 35 BP, pointing to an association of the lower crab layers with the Cedrosan Saladoid occupation of the site. The calibrated dates cover the range between cal AD 445 to 625 (cf. table 11.1).

The results of these new dates are difficult to explain if the other radiocarbon dates, the stratigraphy of the site and the vertical distribution of the pottery are taken into account. The 1987 and 1988 radiocarbon dates cover two periods: an older one around 2300 BP and a younger episode around 1550 BP. The oldest dates range between 2510 and 2050 ± 60 BP. Four dates cluster around 2300-2225 BP, one is

much older and the sixth centres around 2050 BP. After calibration this series of dates covers a long timespan from 795 cal BC to cal AD 60. The radiocarbon calibration curve shows two wiggles during this period, i.e., one around 2500 BP and another one around 2250 BP, causing a considerable spread of calibrated dates. The date of 795 cal BC is certainly too early for the beginning of the habitation at the site. A date of ca. 400-300 cal BC seems to be more likely. This first occupation may end around 50 cal BC.

A second series of dates covers the range between 1490 and 1660 ± 55 BP. This series matches the results of the land crab

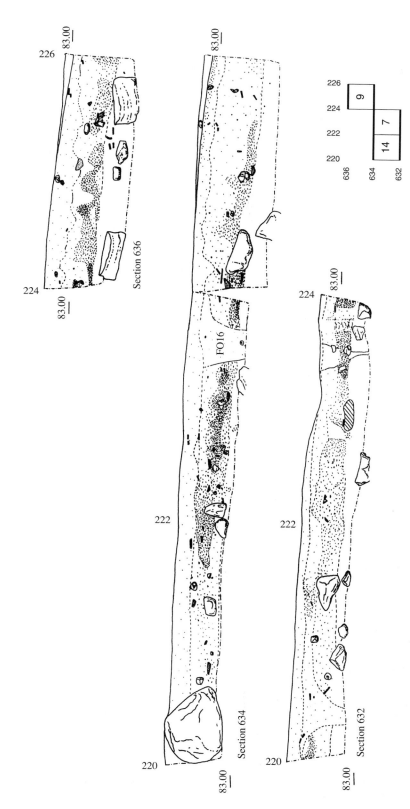

Fig. 11.9. Southeastern part of the refuse discard area: east-west sections as seen from the south. Section 632 runs from 220 to 224, section 634 from 220 to 226 and section 636 from 224 to 226.

a

b

Fig. 11.10. Views of the section in the the southeastern part of the refuse discard area: a. east-west section 634 from 222 to 224, b. section 634 from 224 to 226 seen from the south (see fig. 11.9).

142

dates. If calibrated, they suggest a timespan from cal AD 255 to 650. The latter date seems to be quite acceptable for the end of the Cedrosan Saladoid occupation of the site. However, when the radiocarbon dates are considered in their stratigraphic context, a more complicated picture emerges (cf. below).

11.10   Site formation

Dispersed pottery sherds without proper context in the first stratum at Hope Estate may be explained as the remains of a refuse deposit, which was eroded by slope wash during the later part of the site occupation. The layer of dispersed arte-facts in unit 14 is possibly associated with this stratum. This layer was perhaps situated at the outer edge of a midden, which was largely eroded. Down the slope this deposit was severely eroded and only dispersed pottery sherds remained. The core of the Huecan Saladoid component of the midden area was probably situated to the west of unit 14. The many boulders in the lowest stratum of units 7 and 14 may be the result of the artificial concentration of stones removed from the centre of the site in order to clean the *plaza* and to make its surroundings suitable for the construction of houses. Since unit 14 borders units T20-21 of the 1988 excavations, the radiocarbon samples of T20 might point to a date of 400-300 cal BC for the formation of this stratum.

The 1987 test unit 1 is located between units 2 and 4 in the northeastern part of the midden area. The 1987 radiocarbon samples (PITT-0219 and PITT-0220) were collected from levels 5 (40-50 cm) and 6 (50-60 cm) of a layer of loose crab remains (Haviser 1991a, 653). In unit 4 Huecan Sal-adoid pottery occurred in unmixed context in levels 5 and 6. However, no crab remains were noticed in these levels of unit 4. They may have been disturbed by the Late Saladoid activities at the site and are probably eroded. The deepest, rather thin and isolated crab layers are possibly related to the earliest occupation period of the site, datable to about 400-300 cal BC.

The second stratum represents a series of refuse layers con-sisting of artefacts and food debris, mostly crab remains. These layers are composed of small patches deposited in an arbitrary way and, as a result, the trash does not form a continuous layer. Moreover, the patches of refuse have been transformed by natural and cultural processes in such a way that the interpretation of the stratigraphy becomes difficult. The stratum has been dated by radiocarbon measurements GrN-20168 to GrN-20170, sampled from the lowest dense deposits in units 2, 6 and 7. Although the samples derive from two parts of the midden area, the ages are comparable, dating the beginning of the deposition of the crab remains to the sixth century AD. This date is confirmed by the age of radiocarbon samples PITT-0448 and PITT-0452, which were obtained from the deposits underneath the crab layer. It should be remembered that these samples consisted of char-coal collected from a stratum of sediment including some pottery sherds and charcoal fragments. Such a situation provides a rather weak association between sample and context. The process of crab deposition seems to have pro-ceeded quickly as the radiocarbon measurements PITT-0445 and PITT-0451 date the third stratum to about cal AD 600. Site occupation and the deposition of refuse probably speeded up the sedimentation rate.

The occurrence of Huecan Saladoid artefacts in the stratum is one of the major problems of the site's stratigraphy. At the sites of La Hueca and Punta Candelero, Huecan Sal-adoid pottery has been found in rather islotated contexts. At Hope Estate the presence of Huecan Saladoid artefacts in the refuse layers characterized by Cedrosan Saladoid pottery can be explained by assuming maintenance processes. Apparently, the earliest refuse deposits at the site were swept and cleaned when the habitation area expand towards the perimeter of the settlement. The pres-ence of a posthole bisecting the refuse layer in unit 7, implies that the midden area took the function of a habita-tion area at a developed stage in Saladoid times. It is believed that the Huecan Saladoid potsherds were rede-posited in the Saladoid midden area, together with the actual refuse of this period.

The third stratum seems to have been interfered with after its original formation as it contains artefacts showing vari-ous orientations. This stratum also includes Huecan Sal-adoid pottery, although in much lower amounts than those found in Stratum 2. It is associated with the later occupa-tion of the site and during this phase of habitation refuse was probably discarded further down the slope. Simultane-ously, the area apparently functioned as a burial ground. This is suggested by the many human burials unearthed in the disturbed area east of unit 1 and those unearthed in units 3, 4 and 10. Stratum 3 seems to represent a deposit of mainly dirt probably resulting from a further restructuring of the habitation area. It is possible that the latter was enlarged by levelling the central part of the site. The layer of large artefacts forms part of this stratum. This seems to represent the latest occupation zone of the site.

These site formation processes can be discussed with refer-ence to ethnographic examples from the tropical lowlands of South America. Settlement layout, maintenance and cleaning activities of the functional areas, the refuse disposal behav-iour and site formation among the Amerindians of lowland South America have a special relevance to the investigation of pre-Columbian settlement sites in the Caribbean (Versteeg

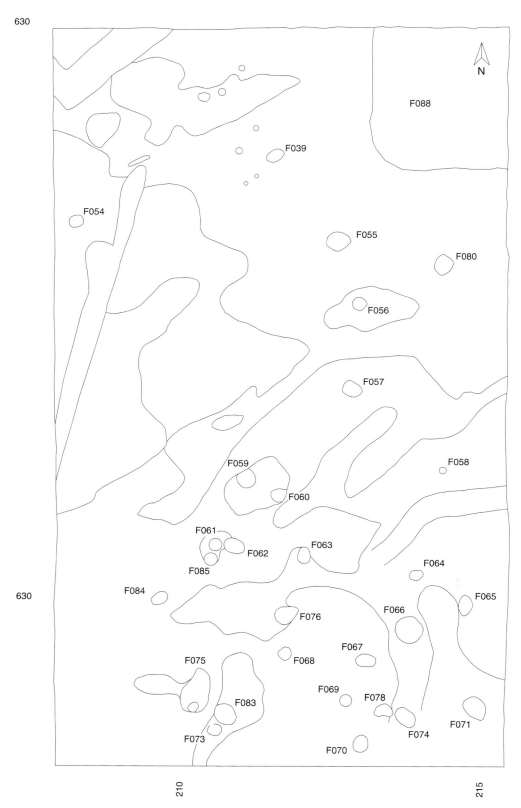

Fig. 11.11. Plan of excavation unit 12; the amerindian features are shallow pits or postholes.

Fig. 11.12. Photographs of two of the postholes in unit 12: a. feature 073, b. feature 076.

and Schinkel 1992, Siegel 1992, Petersen and Watters 1991, 1995; Hoogland 1996).

The Amerindians of Amazonia often live in settlements which, generally speaking, are arranged in a circular fashion. Such villages consist of several components, i.e., a central *plaza* surrounded by a number of residential structures, their domestic areas, paths to the gardens, etc., as well as midden areas. Cleaning and sweeping of house floors and domestic areas are regular activities amongst the Amerindian groups. In this way invasions of pestiferous insects can be avoided which prolongs the effective life of the house involved. The house area, including structures such as cooking sheds, is

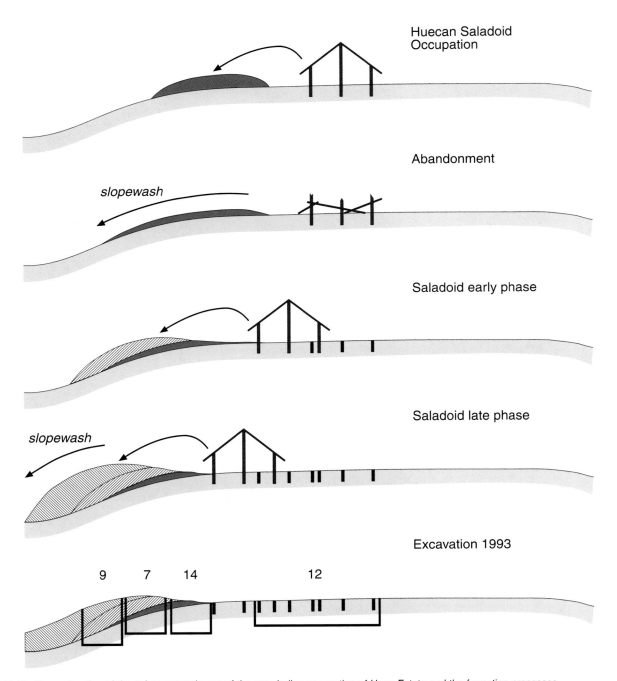

Fig. 11.13. Reconstruction of the subsequent phases of the amerindian occupation of Hope Estate and the formation processes.

maintained in order to keep the surroundings of the residences free of refuse with a hindrance potential and also to provide a barrier between the residential, i.e., cultural area and the natural environment. The maintenance of the *plaza* is a task of the entire community. The frequency of cleaning largely depends on the occasional use of the *plaza* for ceremonies and feasts.

Refuse ends upon a discard location via various waste streams. These different trajectories have been studied in a number of cultural settings (for a review cf. Schiffer 1987). The midden area is usually to be found at the periphery of the settlement. DeBoer and Lathrap (1979) have observed that in the Shipibo-Conibo villages of East Peru kitchen refuse, broken pottery and other debris are cleared away centrifugally from the household. This leads to an accumulation of refuse at the perimeter of the household area. Isolated households are associated typically with doughnut-shaped middens. In contrast, in the case that a number of households share a common *plaza*, the midden takes a scalloped form surrounding the entire *plaza* (DeBoer and Lathrap 1979, 128). This pattern is modified by the topography of the area of the site such as ravines, gullies and local depressions which attract refuse and cause variations on the centrifugal model.

11.11   Conclusions

The Hope Estate stratigraphy and radiocarbon dates show that the site went through several occupation phases. However, the correlation between both sets of data in combination with the ceramic analysis complicates interpretation of the site's habitation. Especially the occurrence of Huecan Saladoid pottery in Cedrosan Saladoid deposits dated by radiocarbon to an early stage of the site occupation, points to the significance of the formative and post-depositional processes determining the structure of the site.

The Huecan Saladoid component was severely affected by apparently post-depositional processes during the later phases of occupation at the site. Initially, the deposits seem to have been altered by slope wash, probably induced by the Saladoid people of this habitation phase. The effects of this process probably prevailed at the edges of the midden area.

Afterwards, the deposits were rearranged and mixed with the Cedrosan Saladoid refuse. This probably resulted from maintenance and cleaning activities of the habitation area in Cedrosan Saladoid times. This process was attested for in nearly all parts of the midden area. Finally, there seems to have been a major reorganization of the site including the levelling of former refuse deposits (fig. 11.11). The character of the redeposition process has still to be determined in detail.

Future research at Hope Estate should focus on the question of the formation processes of the archaeological deposits at the site, especially regarding the soil layers showing a mixed assemblage containing Huecan Saladoid and Cedrosan Saladoid artefacts. The character of these layers should be examined in much more detail. Microscopic analysis of the sediments could provide clues for the interpretation of the processes which affected the formation of the various archaeological deposits.

Furthermore, the possibly individual occurrence of the Huecan Saladoid pottery component should be further explored. A comparable deposit may be discovered in the southwestern part of the midden area. In this sector of the site sedimentation seems to have prevailed. The radiocarbon dates point to an occupation of the Hope Estate site prior to La Hueca and Punta Candelero. The set of radiocarbon dates should be enlarged in order to facilitate detailed reconstruction of the chronology of the site. The contextual situation of the samples should be optimal and the measurements should be of the highest possible quality showing low error ranges.

notes

1 Radiocarbon dating of marine shells yields dates that are too old due to the reservoir effect of the ocean water. In the Caribbean, the dates of marine shells are about 400 years too old. In contrast, land crabs are not effected by the reservoir effect because they spend only their initial stage in the ocean. Once they reached their final stage they are fully terrestrial animals feeding on leaves and fruits. Since the carbonates of the exoskeleton are derived from atmospheric carbon dioxide it is sufficient to calibrate the dates of land crab samples as is usually done for charcoal samples.

12 Pottery

Corinne L. Hofman

12.1 Introduction

This chapter is concerned with the description and analysis of the pottery found during the 1993 excavations at Hope Estate. The analysis includes a detailed study of the stylistic and morphological attributes of the pottery next to a technological analysis encompassing an investigation of the manufacturing techniques and macroscopic and microscopic analyses of the fabrics. The stylistic and morphological study comprises the total amount of pottery collected during the excavations. This collection consists of pottery of both the Huecan and Cedrosan Saladoid subseries. The technological analysis is concerned with only a sample of the Huecan-Saladoid pottery, including the results of a test on two raw clay samples from Hope Estate.

12.2 Sampling methods

12.2.1 FIELD SAMPLING

The pottery was collected from 4 m² units, subdivided in squares of 1 × 1 m controlled in artificial levels of 10 cm. In units 9 and 14 artefacts were collected per feature within these levels. Initially, the pottery was dry-screened through a 2.5 or 5 cm mesh; at a later stage it was water-screened over nested sieves with 10, 4 and 2.7 mm screens.

All of the ceramics collected from the units were cleaned and subsequently bagged and washed. The pottery from units 3 and 4 next to 25% (all A squares) of that found in the other units was analysed on St. Martin. The remaining 75% (the B, C and D squares) was studied in the laboratories at Leiden University.

12.2.2 LABORATORY ANALYSIS, SUBSAMPLE SELECTION

As became clear from out field observations and also from previous excavations (Barret and Léton 1989; Haviser 1988, 1991a), the Hope Estate material consists of ceramics belonging to the Huecan and Cedrosan Saladoid subseries. Unfortunately, ceramics of both subseries were difficult to discern stratigraphically in some parts of the site and the material from the various strata appeared to be mixed (cf. also chapter 11). Post-depositional processes such as erosion, trampling, and agricultural disturbance in colonial and recent times seem to be responsible for the mixing and high fragmentation rate of the potsherds.

A first quantitative analysis was performed of the total amount of pottery collected. It is felt that the first requirement of any pottery analysis is to get a grip on the sample quality, i.e., the sherd quantities and dimensions as well as the individual percentages of diagnostic elements. Therefore, quantitative data have been obtained by simply counting and weighing the sherds in each major category, i.e., body, rim and base pieces, appendages and griddles.

Subsampling was performed to allow further morphological analysis. Only sherds longer than 5 cm were included of a number of major categories, i.e., rim, base and griddle sherds. The degree of fragmentation due to breakage is an important factor which has to be taken into account when selecting a sample based on size. Thin-walled vessels (especially diagnostic of the pottery of the Huecan and Early Cedrosan subseries) tend to break more easily than thick-walled vessels and thus fall apart into smaller fragments. Consequently, the possibility that thin-walled vessels are underrepresented in the sample has to be taken into account. Therefore, diagnostic pieces smaller than 5 cm have been included as well. Another important factor which might have influenced the breakage ratio is the kind of temper included.

The stylistic and morphological analysis consisted of an extensive coding procedure following the Saban model (Hofman 1993; Hofman and Hoogland 1992, 1993), based on vessel contour and orifice (Shepard 1963) as well as and height/diameter ratios. In all eleven vessel shape combinations appear to be possible (fig. 12.1).

The rim sherd analysis has been restricted to vessel shape and to particular stylistic or technological aspects relating to specific shapes. Quantitative and qualitative data on particular vessel or rim shapes or the combination of specific decorative elements may be of chronological and/or functional significance. Moreover, these data are complementary to those acquired during the first part of the analysis, the quantitative study, and provide a more detailed description of the composition of the assemblages.

Computer- based data processing was performed using DBase V and the statistical program SPSS 4.1.

Unrestricted orifice

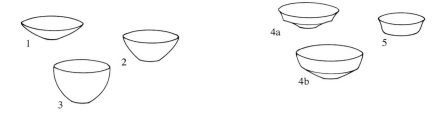

Restricted orifice

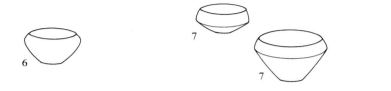

Independent restricted orifice

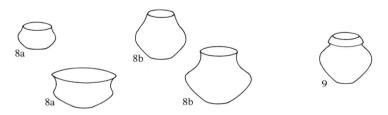

Fig. 12.1. Nine combinations of vessel shapes (Hofman 1993, 65).
1. Dish with an unrestricted simple contour, 2. Bowl with an unrestricted simple contour, 3. Jar with an unrestricted simple contour, 4. Dish or bowl with an unrestricted composite contour (with two variants a and b; variant a has a concave wallprofile above the carination point and variant b has a straight wallprofile above the carination point, 5. Jar with an unrestricted composite contour, 6. Bowl with an unrestricted, inflected contour, 7. Bowl with a restricted simple contour (with two variants a and b; variant a has the largest diameter above the half of the height and variant below the half of the height), 8. Bowl or jar with a restricted composite contour (variant a is a bowl and b is a jar), 9. Bowl with a restricted, complex contour, 10.Bowl or jar with an independent restricted, inflected contour (with four variants a-d; these vessels are either bowls or jars, they have a globular body and the collar or neck can be either straight (a, c) or outflaring (b, d), 11.Bowl or jar with an independent restricted, complex contour.

12.3   Stylistic and morphological analysis

In all 29,527 potsherds with a total weight of 215,4 kg have been collected. Table 12.1 shows the quantitative distribution of the pottery in the various excavation units. Major sherd categories include body, rim, base and griddle pieces next to appendages. Table 12.2 shows the distribution of the pottery according to weight per level in all units as well as the mean sherd weight. The latter is 8.5 grams in the north-eastern part of the midden area (units 3-6 and 8) and in the northwestern part of the midden (unit 11). The mean sherd weight in the southeastern part of the midden area (units 7, 9 and 14) is only 6.0 grams. Here the potsherds are thinner and, perhaps more friable.

Decorated sherds account for 3.9% of the total amount of pottery, with the highest quantity in the northeastern part of

Unit	1	2	3	6	7	8	9	11	14
1	1988	1808	1902	3171	5268	2721	3906	1252	3185
	13790	14047	10811	21251	23146	17945	20289	9881	16325
	1773	1584	1741	2831	4975	2446	3663	1164	2962
	215	228	161	419	293	283	243	88	224
	86.0	85.0	83.0	82.0	88.0	83.0	87.0	87.0	85.0
2	221	96	225	449	500	351	375	142	359
	3061	3323	2447	7213	5636	4763	3476	1559	3388
	162	151	178	308	390	240	308	111	296
	60	46	47	142	109	109	65	31	63
	9.6	9.2	9.8	12.0	8.4	11.0	8.4	9.9	9.5
3	42	57	92	116	89	78	49	11	139
	917	1413	1999	2903	2036	1762	775	226	1734
	25	23	57	61	51	38	32	6	104
	16	32	35	55	38	40	17	5	35
	1.8	2.7	4.0	3.0	1.5	2.4	1.1	0.8	3.7
4	44	39	59	80	102	92	99	22	66
	1822	952	1698	2088	2275	2022	3437	451	1899
	28	27	41	52	72	61	69	15	43
	16	12	18	28	30	31	30	7	24
	1.9	1.8	2.6	2.1	1.7	2.8	1.7	1.5	1.8
5	9	35	12	48	26	26	30	4	12
	131	1092	450	915	467	993	467	55	317
	6	16	7	29	18	15	22	4	7
	2	17	5	19	8	14	8	–	5
	0.4	1.6	0.5	1.2	0.4	0.8	0.7	0.3	0.3
total	2304	2131	2289	3874	5985	3268	4475	1441	3760
	19798	19987	17488	34352	33342	26415	28442	12172	23441

Table 12.1. Distribution of sherd numbers per unit. 1 = body, 2 = rim, 3 = base, 4 = griddle and 5 = appendage/other.

Unit	1	2	3	6	7	8	9	11	14
level 1	4666	5058	6462	6304	6304	3937	4861	2100	3622
level 2	4118	4954	3506	3425	8150	7862	4277	2361	11798
level 3	4050	7465	2862	4458	10766	7998	5990	1569	5935
level 4	3934	1928	2142	9018	7603	5778	9385	5617	2060
level 5	2104	528	2164	7145	519	840	3779	524	26
level 6	853	54	352	2961			150	1	
level 7	73			850					
level 8				191					
mean	8.6	9.4	7.6	8.9	5.6	8.1	6.4	8.4	6.2

Table 12.2. Distribution of total weight per unit and level, and mean sherd weights per unit.

Unit	1	2	3	6	7	8	9	11	14
white-on-red	10	4	9	37	22	28	15	1	–
	10.4	6.1	8.2	15.9	9.3	20.0	13.9	4.2	0.0
polychrome	5	1	1	19	3	12	–	–	1
	5.2	1.5	0.9	8.2	1.3	8.6	0.0	0.0	0.7
zoned-punctate	2	1	4	2	11	3	6	–	12
	2.1	1.5	3.6	0.9	4.7	2.1	5.6	0.0	7.8
zoned-incised crosshatch	14	12	6	25	9	6	14	–	8
	14.6	18.2	5.5	10.7	3.8	4.3	13.0	0.0	5.2
incision	50	37	72	118	146	72	49	15	103
	5.2	56.1	65.5	50.6	61.9	51.4	45.4	62.4	67.3
modelling geometric	–	–	1	–	2	–	3	–	–
	0.0	0.0	0.9	0.0	0.8	0.0	2.8	0.0	0.0
modelling zoomorphic	2	1	4	3	9	5	5	–	4
	2.1	1.5	3.6	1.3	3.8	3.6	4.6	0.0	2.6
modelling anthropomorphic	–	–	1	–	–	–	1	–	1
	0.0	0.0	0.9	0.0	0.0	0.0	0.9	0.0	0.7
punctation	3	2	1	1	2	–	–	–	2
	3.1	3.0	0.9	0.4	0.8	0.0	0.0	0.0	1.3
finger indentation	1	–	–	1	1	–	–	–	–
	1.0	0.0	0.0	0.4	0.4	0.0	0.0	0.0	0.0
nubbin	9	7	9	20	27	13	12	7	22
	9.4	10.6	8.2	8.6	11.4	9.3	11.1	29.2	14.4
other	–	1	2	5	3	–	3	1	–
	0.0	1.5	1.8	2.1	1.3	0.0	2.8	2.8	0.0
total decorated sherds	96	66	110	233	236	140	108	24	153
	4.2	3.1	4.8	6.0	3.9	4.3	2.4	1.7	4.1
total red-slipped sherds	92	87	80	148	51	202	85	31	12
	4.0	4.1	3.5	3.8	0.9	6.2	1.9	2.2	0.3

Table 12.3. Frequency distribution of decorated and red-slipped sherds in all units.

Unit	1	2	3	6	7	8	9	11	14
level 1	–	3	2	7	2	2	–	1	–
level 2	7	2	–	6	5	5	1	–	1
level 3	1	–	2	10	10	16	10	–	–
level 4	2	–	2	15	8	16	4	–	–
level 5	5	–	4	6	–	1	–	–	–
level 6	–	–	–	7			–	–	
level 7	–		–	5					
level 8				–					
total	15	5	10	56	25	40	15	1	1

Table 12.4. Distribution in sherd numbers of the total amount of white-on-red and polychrome painting per unit and level.

152

Unit	1	2	3	6	7	8	9	11	14
level 1	1	–	–	–	5	–	1	–	1
level 2	–	–	2	–	1	2	1	–	3
level 3	–	–	–	–	5	–	1	–	7
level 4	1	–	–	–	–	–	1	–	1
level 5	–	1	1	–	–	1	1	–	–
level 6	–	–	1	–			1	–	
level 7	–		–	–					
level 8				–					
total	1	1	4	–	6	3	5	–	11

Table 12.5. Distribution in sherd numbers of the total amount of zoned-punctated decoration per unit and level.

Unit	1	2	3	6	7	8	9	11	14
level 1	1	2	–	–	1	1	1	–	–
level 2	3	4	3	–	1	1	1	–	3
level 3	4	3	1	4	2	3	6	–	3
level 4	4	3	–	10	5	1	1	–	2
level 5	2	–	2	11	–	–	5	–	–
level 6	–	–	–	–			–	–	
level 7	–		–	–					
level 8				–					
total	14	12	6	25	9	6	14	–	8

Table 12.6. Distribution in sherd numbers of the total amount of zoned-incised crosshatched decoration per unit and level.

Unit	1	2	3	6	7	8	9	11	14
level 1	11	8	32	25	33	11	5	–	12
level 2	9	13	11	17	23	30	9	2	55
level 3	8	9	6	8	36	18	5	8	29
level 4	9	6	8	22	51	11	13	4	7
level 5	11	1	15	14	3	2	14	1	–
level 6	2	–	–	17			3	–	
level 7	–		–	13					
level 8				2					
total	50	37	71	118	146	73	49	15	103

Table 12.7. Distribution in sherd numbers of the total amount of linear and curvilinear incised decoration per unit and level.

Unit	1	2	3	6	7	8	9	11	14
level 1	2	–	–	–	5	3	–	–	2
level 2	1	3	3	1	4	2	2	–	13
level 3	2	1	1	5	11	2	2	4	6
level 4	1	3	1	9	4	5	4	2	1
level 5	3	–	4	1	3	1	3	1	–
level 6	–	–	–	1			1	–	
level 7	–		–	3					
level 8				–					
total	9	7	9	20	27	13	12	7	22

Table 12.8. Distribution in sherd numbers of the total amount of nubbins per unit and level.

Unit	1	2	3	6	7	8	9	11	14
1	17 35.4	18 48.6	14 42.4	17 16.8	11 15.7	31 34.1	11 20.8	2 14.3	11 20.4
2	9 18.8	4 10.8	7 21.2	26 25.7	11 15.7	11 12.1	18 34.0	45 28.6	3 5.6
3	5 10.4	2 5.4	1 3.0	4 4.0	2 2.9	12 13.2	4 7.5	– 0.0	4 7.4
4	5 10.5	4 10.8	3 9.1	19 18.8	8 11.4	10 11.0	6 11.3	2 14.3	7 9.3
5	– 0.0	– 0.0	– 0.0	– 0.0	– 0.0	– 0.0	– 0.0	– 0.0	– 0.0
6	5 10.4	1 2.7	2 6.1	21 20.8	11 15.7	6 6.6	3 5.7	3 14.3	7 13.0
7	2 4.2	1 2.7	3 9.1	5 5.0	13 18.6	15 16.5	4 7.8	3 14.3	12 22.2
8	– 0.0	2 5.4	1 3.0	1 1.0	2 2.9	1 1.1	13 5.7	– 0.0	2 3.7
9	2 4.2	2 5.4	1 3.0	1 1.0	3 4.3	1 1.1	– 0.0	– 0.0	1 1.8
10	2 4.2	1 2.7	1 3.0	7 6.9	9 12.8	2 2.2	24 7.8	– 0.0	6 11.2
11	1 2.1	2 5.4	1 3.0	– 0.0	– 0.0	2 2.2	– 0.0	– 0.0	1 1.9
total	48 100.0	37 100.0	33 100.0	101 100.0	70 100.0	91 100.0	53 100.0	14 100.0	54 100.0

Table 12.9 Frequency distribution of sherd numbers and percentages of vessel shapes in all units. 1 = dishes with unrestricted simple contours, 2 = bowls with unrestricted simple contours, 3= jars with unrestricted simple contours, 4= dishes and bowls with unrestricted composite contours, 5 = jars with unrestricted simple contours, 6 = bowls with unrestricted, inflected contours, 7 = bowls with restricted, simple contours, 8 = bowls and jars with restricted, composite contours, 9 = bowls with restricted complex contours, 10 = bowls and jars with independent restricted contours and 11 = bowls and jars with independent restricted, complex contours.

Unit	1	2	3	6	7	8	9	11	14
1	18	26	19	46	40	42	33	10	26
	37.5	66.7	48.7	41.4	49.4	45.2	50.8	52.6	48.1
2	13	3	11	30	23	17	15	6	21
	27.1	7.7	28.2	27.0	28.4	18.3	23.1	31.6	38.9
3	2	–	2	4	–	13	–	1	1
	4.2	0.0	5.1	3.6	0.0	14.0	0.0	5.3	1.9
4	9	8	5	18	11	12	6	–	5
	18.8	20.5	12.8	16.2	13.6	12.9	9.2	0.0	9.3
5	3	1	1	4	1	2	–	1	–
	6.3	2.6	2.6	3.6	1.2	2.2	0.0	5.3	0.0
6	–	–	–	1	1	1	–	–	–
	0.0	0.0	0.0	0.9	1.2	1.1	0.0	0.0	0.0
7	–	–	–	1	1	–	3	–	2
	0.0	0.0	0.0	0.9	1.2	0.0	4.6	0.0	1.9
8	3	1	1	7	4	6	8	1	–
	6.3	2.6	2.5	6.3	4.9	6.5	12.3	5.3	0.0
total	48	39	39	111	81	93	65	19	54
	100.0	100.0	100.0	100.0	100.0	100.0	100.0	100.0	

Table 12.10. Frequency distribution of sherd numbers and percentages of rim shapes in all units. 1 = rounded, 2 = flattened, 3 = inward thickened, 4 = outward thickened, 5 = double thickened, 6 = inwardly bevelled, 7 = outwardly bevelled and 8 = flanged.

the midden area i.e., units 3, 5, 6 and 8 (table 12.3). For example, 6.0% of the pottery in unit 6 is decorated. The distribution of red-slipped pottery shows a similar pattern, but includes unit 4 as well. The total amount of red-slipped pieces is 2.7%. The highest percentage of red-slipped pottery, i.e., 6.2% was found in unit 8.

Tables 12.4 to 12.8 show the distribution of the characteristic decorative modes (white-on-red and polychrome painting, zoned punctation, zoned-incised crosshatching (ZIC), and incision) per level in the different units. Incision (curvilinear or linear) forms the most-represented decorative mode in all units. White-on-red and polychrome painting are most frequent in units 6 and 8 in the northeastern part of the midden area, but occur also in relatively small sherd quantities in units 7 and 9 in its southeastern part. In units 11 and 14 white-on-red or polychrome painting is to be found very sparsely in the upper levels. On the other hand, zoned punctation is most frequent in the southeastern part of the midden area (units 7, 9 and 14). Zoned-incised crosshatching is present in all units, but prevails in units 3, 4, 6 and 9. Nubbins occur in all units but dominate in units 7, 9, 11 and 14. The data show that white-on-red and polychrome painting occur down to a depth of 40 to 50 cm in the northeastern part of the midden area, except for unit 6 which yielded these modes down to 70 cm below the present surface.

In all 621 rim sherds have been analysed. Tables 12.9 to 12.18 present the analysis of the sherds longer than 5 cm per unit and level. Apart from vessel shapes, base and griddle shapes are presented per unit.

The pottery analysis establishes a relative chronology for the Hope Estate site on the basis of a combination of quantitative and qualitative datasets. The ceramic analysis confirmed the presence of both Huecan and Cedrosan Saladoid pottery at the Hope Estate site (cf. also Haviser 1991a; Rouse 1992). On the basis of the analysis of the pottery, combined with stratigraphic data and radiocarbon dates, a series of observations can be made.

1. The vertical stratigraphy at Hope Estate showed that the site forms a multi-component deposit (cf. chapter 11). Units 3-6 and 8 yielded very low amounts of crab remains in the bottommost levels, below a layer of dense crab remains, followed by a layer containing somewhat more dispersed crab fragments. The top levels in these units contained mixed crab and shellfish refuse. In addition, two distinct layers were identified in units 7, 9 and 14, an occupation layer and a refuse layer. No distinct refuse layer was noticed in unit 11. When considering the pottery data, it becomes evident that in the northeastern part of the midden area Huecan pottery occurs isolated in the lowest levels, i.e., in units 3 and 4 (levels 6

Unit	1	2	3	6	7	8	9	11	14
1-5 mm	10	5	1	10	21	11	17	2	21
	20.8	12.8	2.5	9.0	25.9	11.7	25.8	10.5	38.2
6-8 mm	30	21	29	87	37	67	39	16	31
	62.5	53.8	72.5	78.4	45.7	71.3	59.1	84.2	56.4
9-11 mm	8	13	9	12	20	16	10	1	3
	16.7	33.3	22.5	10.8	24.7	17.0	15.2	5.3	5.5
12-15 mm	–	–	1	2	3	–	–	–	–
	0.0	0.0	2.5	1.8	3.7	0.0	0.0	0.0	0.0
total	48	39	40	111	81	94	66	19	55
	100.0	100.0	100.0	100.0	100.0	100.0	100.0	100.0	100.0

Table 12.11. Frequency distribution of sherd numbers and percentages of average wall thickness of rims in all units.

Unit	1	2	3	6	7	8	9	11	14
1-10 cm	1	–	–	3	4	–	2	–	1
	2.3	0.0	0.0	3.2	5.8	0.0	3.6	0.0	2.0
11-20 cm	6	14	4	11	12	11	22	2	13
	13.6	38.9	12.1	11.8	17.4	13.1	39.3	18.2	26.5
21-30 cm	18	13	17	35	30	41	19	5	17
	40.9	36.1	51.5	37.6	43.5	48.8	33.9	45.5	34.7
31-40 cm	10	7	7	35	16	25	11	4	15
	22.7	19.4	21.2	37.6	23.2	29.8	19.6	36.4	30.6
41-60 cm	9	2	5	9	7	7	2	–	3
	20.5	5.1	15.2	9.7	10.1	8.3	3.6	0.0	6.1
total	90	36	33	93	69	84	56	11	49
	100.0	100.0	100.0	100.0	100.0	100.0	100.0	100.0	100.0

Table 12.12. Frequency distribution of sherd numbers and percentages of average orifice diameter of rim sherds in all units.

and 7), in unit 5 (levels 5-7), in unit 6 (levels 5-8) and in unit 8 (level 5). These levels are to be found below of dense crab remains. Cedrosan pottery is present in large quantities in the upper levels of these units, though mixed with minor amounts of Huecan ceramics. Units 6 and 8 show a mixture of the two subseries in all levels. In the southeastern part of the midden area Huecan pottery is dominant in the lowermost levels (5 and 6) of unit 9 which are characterized by a layer of dispersed crab remains whereas Huecan ceramics are mixed with sherds of the Cedrosan subseries in the upper levels of this unit. The same holds true for units 7 and 14. Unit 7 shows a minority of Cedrosan sherds among a majority of Huecan pottery in its upper four levels (down to a depth of 35 cm below the present surface) with a major concentration (84%) in squares A and B. Level 4 (30-40 cm), representing the layer of dense crab remains, revealed the highest number of artefacts. Huecan pottery occurs as a separate cultural unit in the lowest part of this crab layer and sparsely distributed below this zone (40-50 cm). A few Cedrosan sherds have been recognized in the upper two levels (down to 20 cm below the present surface) in unit 14. Unit 11, in the northwestern part of the site, yielded relatively low amounts of pottery. Cedrosan sherds are present in minor quantities, mixed with Huecan pottery. The percentages of pieces showing zoned punctations, i.e., one of the diagnostic modes of the Huecan subseries, amounts to in all 127 potsherds or 3.2% of the total number of decorated ceramics.

2. The horizontal distribution of pottery and other remains, shown by the different units, confirms the assumed

Unit	1	2	3	6	7	8	9	11	14
1	–	1	1	–	3	–	2	2	–
	0.0	2.6	2.8	0.0	5.1	0.0	3.7	11.8	0.0
2	–	–	–	–	–	–	–	–	–
	0.0	0.0	0.0	0.0	0.0	0.0	0.0	0.0	0.0
3	9	3	3	4	8	3	5	6	10
	19.1	7.9	8.3	4.0	13.6	4.2	9.3	35.3	19.2
4	10	9	10	30	20	17	27	7	27
	21.3	23.7	27.8	30.3	33.9	23.9	50.0	41.2	51.9
5	27	18	21	60	28	39	17	2	15
	57.4	47.4	58.3	60.6	47.5	54.9	31.5	11.8	28.8
6	1	7	1	5	–	12	3	–	–
	2.1	18.4	2.8	5.1	0.0	16.9	5.6	0.0	0.0
total	47	38	36	99	59	71	54	17	52
	100.0	100.0	100.0	100.0	100.0	100.0	100.0	100.0	100.0

Table 12.13. Frequency distribution of sherd numbers and percentages of categories of exterior finishing on rim sherds in all units. 1 = crude, 2 = scratched, 3 = smoothed, 4 = lightly burnished, 5 = highly burnished and 6 = polished.

Unit	1	2	3	6	7	8	9	11	14
1	1	1	1	3	3	3	2	–	6
	2.0	2.6	5.0	2.7	4.1	3.3	3.3	0.0	10.9
2	–	–	–	–	–	–	–	–	–
	0.0	0.0	0.0	0.0	0.0	0.0	0.0	0.0	0.0
3	19	11	16	55	22	38	22	6	22
	41.3	28.9	40.0	50.0	29.7	42.2	36.0	31.6	40.0
4	–	–	–	–	–	–	–	–	–
	0.0	0.0	0.0	0.0	0.0	0.0	0.0	0.0	0.0
5	–	–	–	–	–	–	–	–	–
	0.0	0.0	0.0	0.0	0.0	0.0	0.0	0.0	0.0
6	5	2	10	17	13	11	3	4	4
	10.9	5.3	25.0	15.5	17.6	12.2	21.3	21.1	7.3
7	–	–	–	–	–	–	–	–	–
	0.0	0.0	0.0	0.0	0.0	0.0	0.0	0.0	0.0
8	–	1	–	1	3	2	–	–	1
	0.0	2.6	0.0	0.9	4.1	2.2	0.0	0.0	1.8
9	17	17	10	20	31	31	22	8	21
	37.0	44.7	25.0	18.2	41.9	34.4	36.1	42.1	38.2
10	4	6	2	11	1	5	2	1	1
	8.7	15.8	5.0	10.0	1.4	5.6	3.3	5.3	1.9
total	46	38	40	110	74	90	61	19	55
	100.0	100.0	100.0	100.0	100.0	100.0	100.0	100.0	100.0

Table 12.14. Frequency distribution of sherd numbers and percentages of categories of exterior surface colour on rim sherds in all units. 1 = light grey, 2 = grey, 3 = dark grey-black, 4 = brown-grey / grey-brown, 5 = dark greyish-brown, 6 = light brown/brown, 7 = dark brown / very dark brown, 8 = reddish-grey / dark reddish-grey, 9 = reddish-brown and 10 = red.

Unit	1	2	3	6	7	8	9	11	14
1	11 22.9	– 0.0	5 12.5	12 10.7	61 7.4	9 9.6	12 18.2	3 15.8	3 5.5
2	6 12.5	5 13.2	4 10.0	11 9.8	11 13.6	9 9.6	7 10.6	3 15.8	5 9.1
3	1 2.1	– 0.0	3 7.5	3 2.7	5 6.2	2 2.1	3 7.6	2 10.5	4 7.3
4	– 0.0	– 0.0	3 7.5	7 6.3	4 3.7	7 7.4	1 1.5	– 0.0	– 0.0
5	30 62.6	33 86.8	24 60.0	78 69.6	55 67.9	67 71.3	42 62.1	11 57.9	43 78.2
6	– 0.0	– 0.0	1 2.5	1 0.9	1 1.2	– 0.0	– 0.0	– 0.0	– 0.0
total	48 100.0	38 100.0	40 100.0	112 100.0	81 100.0	94 100.0	66 100.0	19 100.0	55 100.0

Table 12.15. Frequency distributions of categories of core and subsurface colour on rim sherds in all units. 1 = red core and subsurface, 2 = grey to brown core and brown to reddish-brown subsurfaces, 3 = light to dark grey or black core amd red light grey subsurfaces, 4 = light grey core and subsurfaces, 5 = dark grey or black core and subsurfaces and 6 = white core and subsurfaces .

Unit	1	2	3	6	7	8	9	11	14
1	6	13	4	19	10	12	9	4	5
2	2	10	3	14	8	8	6	–	–
3	–	8	–	3	–	–	–	–	1
4	1	2	–	7	2	–	6	–	–
5	–	1	1	–	–	–	–	–	–
total	9	34	8	43	20	20	21	4	6

Table 12.16. Frequency distribution of appendages, potstands, spindle whorls and incense burners in all units. 1 = handle, 2 = lug, 3 = potstand, 4 = spindle whorl and 5 = incense burner.

Unit	1	2	3	6	7	8	9	11	14
1	10	22	13	33	26	28	11	2	15
2	8	6	7	23	15	6	5	–	7
3	6	1	2	10	3	1	1	–	8
4	–	–	2	–	1	–	1	1	–
total	24	29	24	66	45	35	18	3	30

Table 12.17. Frequency distribution of base shapes in all units. 1 = flat, 2 = concave, 3 = convex, 4 = pedestal.

Unit	1	2	3	6	7	8	9	11	14
1	1	3	2	3	1	9	1	–	1
2	1	2	–	1	1	1	1	–	–
3	–	2	–	3	2	–	–	–	–
4	7	4	6	8	10	6	7	1	14
5	3	1	2	2	3	5	–	2	7
total	12	12	10	17	17	21	9	3	22

Table 12.18. Frequency distribution of griddle rim profiles in all units. 1 = straight, 2 = triangular, 3 = overhanging, 4 = rounded, 5 = unthickened.

multi-component character of the site. The various cultural components present at the site are differentially distributed over the whole midden area. In its southeastern part (units 7 and 14) Huecan Saladoid pottery prevails and may be said to occur as a well-defined spatially segregated unit.

3. Radiocarbon dating has provided dates between 2510 ± 40 and 1490 ± 35 BP. They encompass two broad time spans, one ranging from 400/300 to 50 cal BC and a second one ranging from cal AD 255 to 650 (cf. chapter 11, table 11.1). The earliest range of dates derive from the southeastern part of the site and the bottommost levels of its northeastern part.

These observations lead to the conclusion that there are two well-defined cultural components at the Hope Estate site. The Hope Estate 1 component comprising Huecan Saladoid pottery, is most clearly represented by a spatially segregated deposit in the southeastern part of the midden area. This deposit is characterized by a moderately dense refuse deposit consisting of pottery, shell, and some crab remains. In the northeastern part of the midden area the Hope Estate 1 component occurs as a thin and very dispersed artefact deposit. The Hope Estate 2 component comprises Cedrosan Saladoid pottery and is present in the whole northeastern part of the midden area where it overlays the Hope Estate 1 component in units 3-8. The deposit is characterized by a dense crab layer providing all radiocarbon dates from the second time span, i.e., cal AD 255 to 650.

12.4 The Hope Estate 1 component

In order to arrive at an accurate description of the Hope Estate 1 or Huecan Saladoid component at the site it was decided to restrict the analysis to the pottery from units 7, 9 (levels 5-7) and 14. These units yielded Huecan pottery as a relatively separate unit. The amount of Cedrosan intrusion in unit 7 is estimated at 10%, less so in unit 14. Cedrosan pottery is estimated to comprise more than 50% of the potsherds in unit 9, and consequently only levels 5 to 7 are

included in the analysis. Due to the mixture of Huecan and Cedrosan pottery the percentages presented below have to be considered as approximates.

The present sample consists of 9,568 potsherds, weighing in all 60,956 grams. As mentioned above, the mean weight of the sherds in this area is rather low, not exceeding 6.0 grams. Pottery of the Huecan subseries seems to be rather friable, perhaps because of its thinness or otherwise its temper. In many cases wall thickness is less than 7 mm. Four percent of the total amount of pottery in these units, i.e., 389 sherds, show some form of decoration. However, 43 decorated potsherds or 0.2% of this amount seem to belong to the Cedrosan subseries. They consist of white-on-red- and/or polychrome-painted motifs (6.6%), a few incised sherds (3.3%), one red-slipped adorno (0.2%) and one red-and-black painted and incised nubbin (0.2%), typical of the Cedrosan subseries. An incense burner with white and red painted motifs recovered from unit 7, may belong to the Cedrosan subseries as well. As stated above, these sherds occur dispersedly in unit 7 down to a depth of 35 cm, and in unit 14 only in the first 10-20 cm below the present surface. The Huecan pottery from all units (3-14) is taken into consideration for the description of the decorative motifs. Pottery decoration includes predominantly incision, simply modelled nubbins and more complex modelling. Modes of incision consist of linear and curvilinear designs (68.8%), curvilinear incised zones filled with punctations (5.9%) or crosshatching (4.3%) (figs 12.2a-o and 12.5b). They are arranged as symmetrical designs on the vessel walls. One and the same vessel may show one or more forms of incised decoration. Zoned-incised crosshatching also occurs on rim portions only and punctation is to be found without incisions as well. Some of the incised lines and punctations have been filled with a white substance.

Small nubbins (13.9%) embellish curvilinear incised decorations or are attached to the rims of both undecorated and decorated vessels (fig. 12.4a-c). These nubbins commonly have one or more small arches or punctations on top.

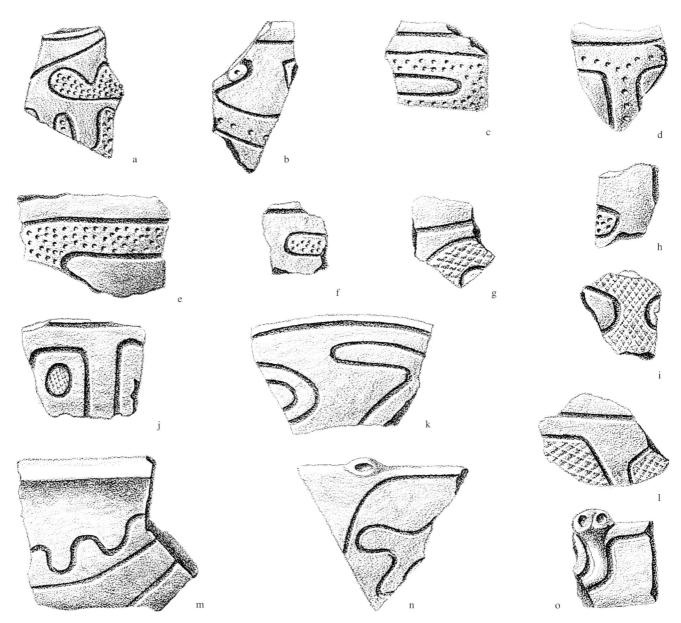

Fig. 12.2. Decorative modes (scale 1:1): a-f. zoned-punctated, g. zoned-incised crosshatching, h. zoned-punctated, i-j. zoned-incised crosshatching, k. curvilinear incisions, l. zoned-incised crosshatching , m-o. curvilinear incisions decorations.

Modelling (4.4%) mainly consists of zoomorphic adornos (figs 12.3a-f, h, 12.4d, e, 12.5a and 12.8b-d) but anthropomorphic modelling has been documented as well (fig. 12.4h). The zoomorphic adornos may be embellished with incisions and punctations. A few examples of zoomorphic head lugs have been found which may belong to the Huecan as well as Cedrosan Saladoid subseries. One example has been found of a finger indented rim (0.3%).

The amount of decorated rim sherds larger than 5 cm is small, i.e., only 25 pieces. Curvilinear incised decoration is applied to the body part of bowls with restricted simple contours and is present also on a small goblet with unrestricted simple contour (fig. 12.6a-c). Curvilinear incised designs and zoned-incised crosshatching are to be found on the interior rim portion of oval dishes with unrestricted simple, composite or inflected contours. Such vessels

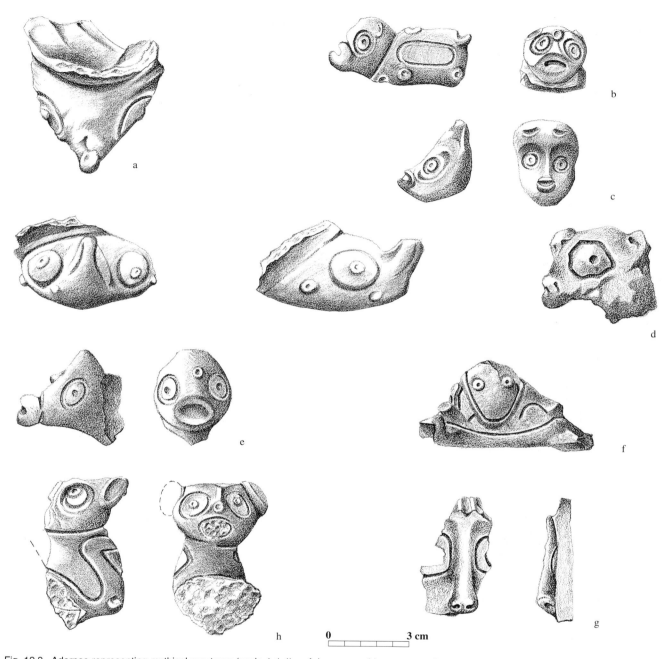

Fig. 12.3. Adornos representing mythical creatures (scale 1:1.4): a-f, h. zoomorphic representation, g. anthropomorphic representation.

sometimes have labial flanges and may bear decorative motifs consisting of curvilinear incised designs filled or not filled with punctations or zoned-incised crosshatching. Zoomorphic head lugs are applied to these vessels in several cases. If so, the opposite side of the bowl represents the tail of the animal and is decorated with curvilinear designs, often similarily filled with punctations. Paired holes are to be found at the 'head' end of the vessel (figs. 12.4d, e and 12.5a).

Single fine-incised lines occur below the rim portion on the interior of bowls with independent restricted composite or inflected contours (fig. 12.4a, c).

161

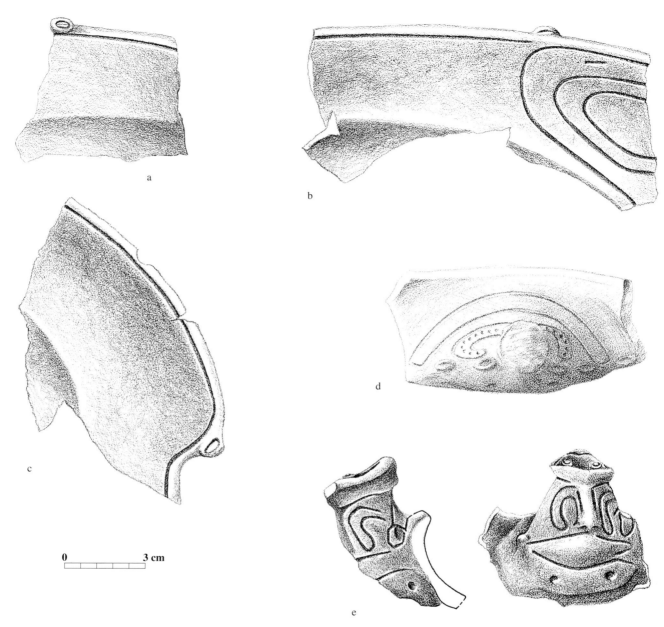

Fig. 12.4. Decorative elements of effigy bowls (scale 1:1.4): a-c. rim sherds with curvilinear incisions and nubbins. d-e. zoomorphic adornos with paired holes on the back side.

Red slip was found on 63 sherds, or 0.6% of the pottery in the units selected. It is found on jars with unrestricted simple contours, dishes with unrestricted inflected contours and a bowl with an independent restricted complex contour. Presumably most of these vessels pertain to the Cedrosan Saladoid subseries. However, red paint or slip was shown by seven sherds belonging to a thin-walled vessel in unit

14-C-3, possibly belonging to the Huecan subseries. The surface of this vessel was left simply smoothed.

Vessel shape was determined of 143 rim sherds from units 7, 9 (levels 5-7) and 14. The shape of 17 rim sherds in this sample could not be determined. Shapes include dishes, some of which are ovoid, bowls and jars with unrestricted simple

Fig. 12.5. Decorative elements of effigy bowls (scale 1: 1,4.): a. zoomorphic adorno with paired holes on the back side, b. sherd with zoned-punctate decoration, c. sherd with curvilinear incised decoration, d. sherd (tail part of an effigy bowl) with zoned-incised crosshatched decoration.

contours (33.8%), bowls with restricted simple contours (20.1%), dishes or bowls with independent restricted, composite or inflected contours (16.1%), occasionally ovoid dishes or bowls with unrestricted, inflected contours (14.5%), dishes with unrestricted, composite contours (12.1%), jars with restricted composite contours (3.2%) and one rim pertaining to a complex vessel shape (0.2%). Individual vessels are represented by 7.7% of their rims, on average.
A few dishes or bowls with unrestricted inflected contours show red slip or white-on-red or polychrome painted motifs. The only complex vessel shape identified is red-slipped as well. These vessels obviously belong to the Cedrosan Saladoid subseries.

Vessel diameters vary between 5 and 50 cm with an average of 25.3 cm while wall thickness varies between 3 and 14 mm with an average of 6.8 mm. The ovoids dishes with zoomorphic representations show very thin walls (between 4 and 5 mm). Bowls with restricted simple contours have an average wall thickness of 5 to 8 mm. Thicker pottery is absent in levels 5 of unit 7, levels 5-6 of unit 9 and levels 3-5 of unit 14.

Rims show predominantly rounded (48.9%) and flattened (32.6%) lips. These forms occur with all vessel shapes. Other shapes such as outwardly thickened lips occur

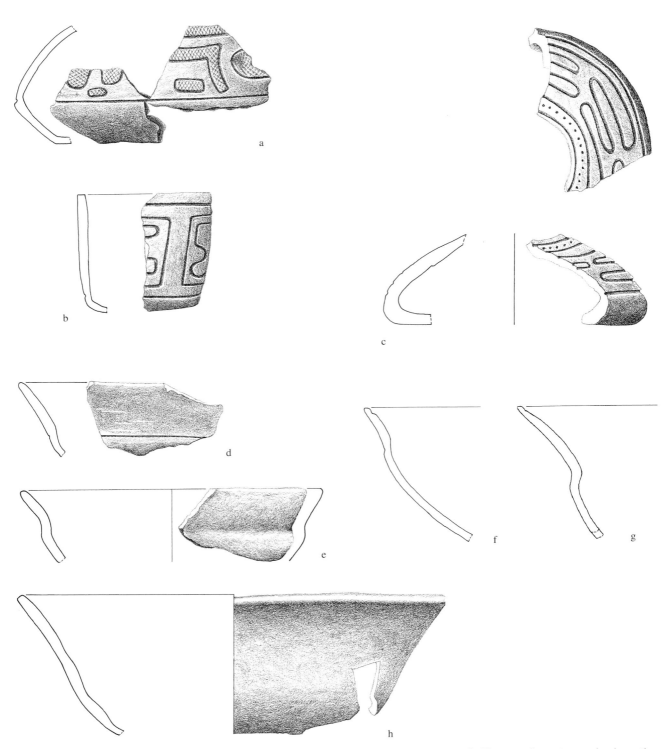

Fig. 12.6. Restricted and unrestricted vessels with composite contours (scale 1:2): a. restricted vessel with composite contour and a decoration of zoned-incised crosshatching and b. unrestricted vessel (goblet) with curvilinear incised decorations, c. restricted vessel with composite contour and curvilinear incion bordered by punctations, d-h. unrestricted vessels.

for 11.8% and are associated with unrestricted vessels with simple, composite or inflected contours, with bowls with restricted simple contours and with bowls with independent restricted inflected contours. Some of these vessels belong to Cedrosan recipients without decoration or showing white-on-red or polychrome painting or red slipped surfaces. Bevelled rims comprise 5.2% and include flanges attached to bowls with unrestricted simple as well as inflected contours and on bowls with independent restricted inflected contours. Inward and double thickened rims occur each for 0.7%. These belong to bowls with unrestricted and restricted simple contours next to bowls with independent restricted inflected contours. These bowls are probably affilated with the Cedrosan subseries.

Surface colours range from light brown to reddish-brown and brown (Munsell colours Hue 7.5 YR 3/2-6/4 and Hue 5YR 4/3-6/4). Surfaces were mostly smoothed or burnished.

Cores show firing conditions of incomplete oxidation; core colours are grey and brown with reddish-brown to brown subsurfaces. Some are incompletely to completely reduced. These sherds have light grey cores with grey to red and reddish brown sub-surfaces or completely dark grey to black cores and subsurfaces respectively.

Appendages in this assemblage consist of 16 handles, nine side lugs and three spout fragments (fig. 12.7a-d). The handles of the Huecan subseries are of crude manufacture and show rounded shapes with circular and oval cross-sections. In level 2 of unit 7 a lug belonging to the Cedrosan subseries was found showing a red-slipped surface and incised decorative motifs filled with black paint.

Base fragments total 228 (2.3%). The shape could be determined of 47 framgents. Flat (53.1%) and concave (34.0%) bases predominate (fig. 12.7e-g). Convex and pedestal bases occur in minor quantities (8.5% and 4.2% respectively; table 12.17). Diameter varies between 4 and 30 cm. The average diameter of these bases is 10.5 cm and the average thickness 7.3 mm. Two fragments of pedestal bases were collected, but they were too small for more detailed analysis.
Potstands are represented by four specimens only. Five fragments of clay discs or spindle whorls were recovered. A white-on-red painted incense burner has been recovered from unit 7. This piece may belong to Cedrosan subseries (fig. 12.8a).

In all 168 griddle sherds have been encountered in the units selected, i.e., 1.7% of the total amount of pottery. Griddle rims are represented by only 27 sherds. Rounded griddle rims are characteristic of this assemblage. They are predominantly rounded with flattened tops (44.0%) and unthickened (32.0%). Only in a few cases (24.0%) other shapes could be documented (fig. 12.7h-j). Diameters vary between 30 and 60 cm with an average of 25.3 mm. Average rim thickness is 16.6 mm and the average thickness of the central part of the artefact is 8.3 mm. All of these griddles have a smoothed bottom.

12.5 The Hope Estate 2 component

The Hope Estate 2 component comprises pottery of the Cedrosan Saladoid subseries. The present sample is not sufficient to distinguish different phases of Cedrosan Saladoid pottery. It is assumed that zoned-incised crosshatched decoration is largely Early Cedrosan Saladoid whereas the Late Cedrosan pottery is decorated especially with white-on-red and polychrome painted decorative motifs and modelled-incised adornos (Rouse 1992).
The pottery from only units 3-6 and 8 has been used in this analysis. Levels 6 and 7 of units 3 and 5 are excluded from the analysis because they contain exclusively Huecan Saladoid pottery. The same is true for levels 5 to 7 of unit 4. Huecan-Cedrosan mixture appears in all levels of units 6 and 8 but Huecan pottery predominates in the lower levels. Levels 5 to 8 of these units are left out of the analysed sample although it should be kept in mind that these levels do not contain only Huecan pottery. Therefore, the percentages provided below are, therefore, to be considered as approximates. The analysed sample consists of 12,928 sherds, weighing in all of 112,178 grams. The average sherd weight of this section is 8.5 grams, the largest sherds in units 4 and 6 weight on 9.4 and 8.9 grams, respectively.

Decorated sherds number 584 in these units selected representing, 4.5%. Seven sherds (1.2%) show zoned-punctated decorative motifs. They may belong amongst others to the Huecan Saladoid subseries. In units 7, 9 (levels 5-7) and 14 this mode is represented by 5.9%. Cedrosan Saladoid decorative modes consist of incision (53.9%), white-on-red, and white-and-red as well as polychrome painting (20.1%), zoned-incised crosshatching (10.7%), nubbins (9.8%), modelling (2.3%), punctation (1.7%), and finger indentation (0.3%).
For the description of the decorative motifs all units are considered. Fine-line incisions and ZIC are to be found on vessel rims (figs. 12.5d, 12.9a and 12.13a, b). Painted motifs occur in white and red-and-white, black-and-red and white-and-orange-and-red. The painted pottery is usually polished. In some cases incision and painting are combined, for example, when incised motifs are filled with black paint. Black paint or smudge occurs on the inner sides of a number of sherds. ZIC is to be found predominantly on the rim portions of vessels.

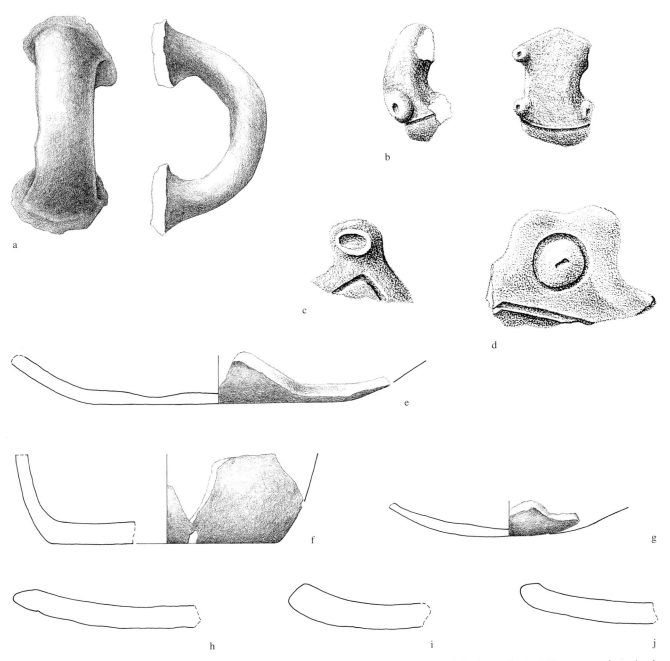

Fig. 12.7. Appendages, base and griddle shapes: a-b. handles (scale 1:1), c-d. lugs (scale 1:1), e-f. flat bases (scale 1:2), g. convex base (scale 1:2), h-j. griddles with rounded rims (scale 1:2).

Nubbins occupy vessel rims. They are often red painted and the incised portion may be filled with black paint. Modelling includes zoomorphic adornos representing turtle, snake and bat heads, as well as geometric and anthropomorphic adornos (fig. 12.10a-g). An example of the latter shows perforated ears and black paint around the eyes (fig. 12.10g). Modelled incised adornos have protruding eyes, which make them different from the Huecan adornos and often carry red or polychrome painting in red, black and white. A few cases of rim points are known (fig. 12.9b-d).

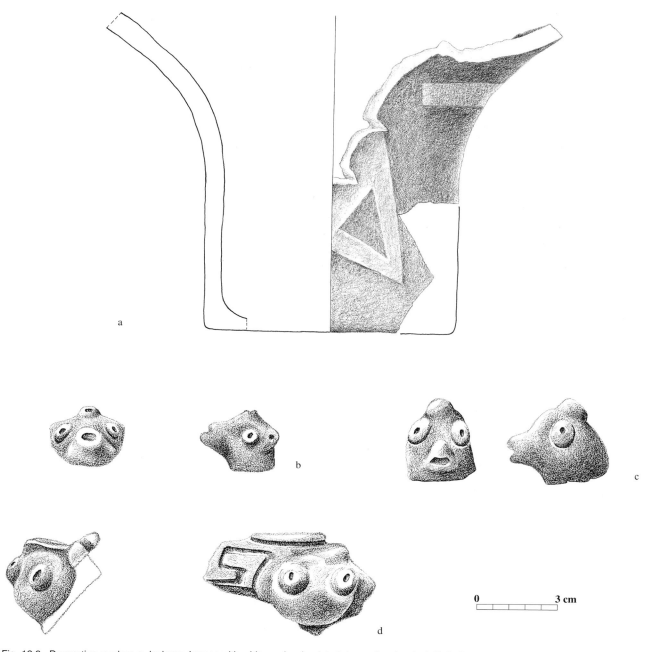

Fig. 12.8. Decorative modes: a. inciense burner with white-and-red painted decoration (scale 1:2), b-d. zoomorphic adornos (scale 1:1.4).

Red slip is present on 609 sherds (4.3%). This number is somewhat higher in unit 8, namely 6.2%. The slip may or may not cover the entire vessel. In the latter instances it has been applied to the interior and/or exterior surfaces as well as the rim. Red slip is found in combination with incision, modelling and nubbins.

Vessel shape could be determined in the case of 478 rim sherds. In all 45 rim sherds could not be classified. Shapes include dishes, bowls and jars with unrestricted simple contours (49.5%), dishes with unrestricted composite contours (13.1%), bowls with unrestricted inflected contours (12.4%), bowls with restricted simple contours (11.7%),

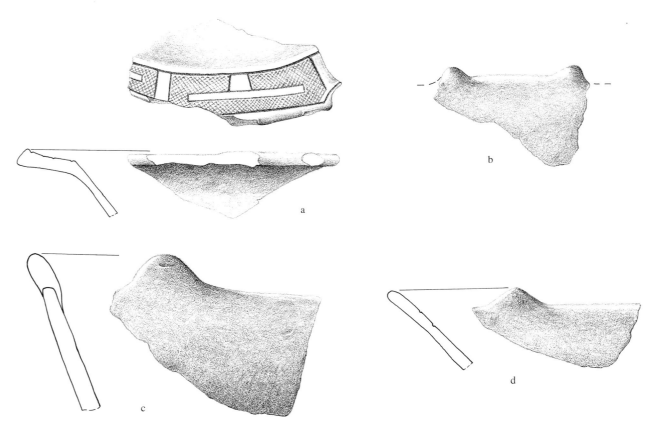

Fig. 12.9. Decorative modes (scale 1:2): a. unrestricted vessel with zoned-incised crosshatched decoration on the rim, b-d. rim points.

bowls with independent restricted composite or inflected contours (9.6%), jars with restricted composite contours (2.3%) and bowls with complex contours (1.3%) (figs 12.9a, 12.11a-g, 12.12a-c, 12.13a-d and 12.14a-c). Inidividual vessels are represented by 6.5% of their rims, on average. Vessel diameters vary between 4 and 54 cm, averaging at 26.7 cm and most vessels have a wall thickness between 3 and 14 mm averaging at 6.8 mm.

Rims are provided with rounded (46.3%) or flattened (25.3%) lips. They are outward thickened (14.4%), bevelled and predominantly flanged (7.6%), inward thickened (4.4%) and double thickened (1.7%). Labial flanges are often associated with bowls with independent restricted composite or inflected contours.

Colours of wall surfaces range from reddish-brown to brown and greyish (Munsell colours Hue 7.5YR 3/2-6/4 and Hue 5YR 4/3-6/4) and red (Hue 2.5YR 4/2 and Hue 10R 4/6-5/8). Surfaces are often highly burnished.
Core colours indicate incomplete oxidation during firing.

Sherds are black and dark-grey in cross-section with reddish-brown to brown subsurfaces. Some show incomplete to complete reduction. These sherds have light-grey cores with grey to red and reddish brown subsurfaces or completely dark-grey to black cores and subsurfaces respectively.

Appendages include 50 handle fragments (rounded and D-shaped) next to 35 side lugs (fig. 12.12a-f). The latter are occasionally perforated. However, a few of these may belong to the Huecan subseries, having become mixed with Cedrosan pottery in the upper levels of units 3-6 and 8. One fragment of a handle is decorated with two snake heads (fig. 12.12e). Ten clay discs or fragments of clay discs were found with a diameter of 8.5 cm and a thickness of 3.1 cm.

Base shapes could be determined for 129 fragments. They are flat (61.3%), concave (27.9%) or convex (8.5%). Three pedestal bases (2.4%) are known. The average diameter of these bases is 9.6 cm and the average thickness 13.0 mm. Some base fragments are decorated with concentric incisions on a plain or red-slipped interior surface.

168

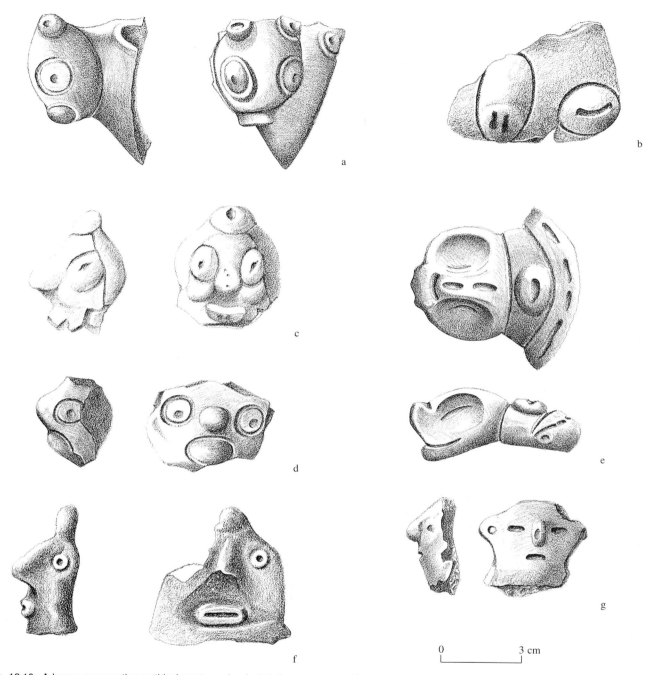

Fig. 12.10. Adornos representing mythical creatures (scale 1:1.4): a-e. zoomorphic representations, f-g. anthropomorphic representations.

Potstands are represented by ten fragments only. One fragment of a potstand has been recovered from unit 6 level 5 and may belong to either one of the two subseries (fig. 12.15h). Two fragments of incense burners have been recovered from units 4 and 5. One specimen is decorated with a white-and-red painted linear design. It was found in unit 7 (fig. 12.8a).

In all 284 griddle sherds weighing 8,300 grams, were collected from the units selected, i.e., 2.1% of the total sample.

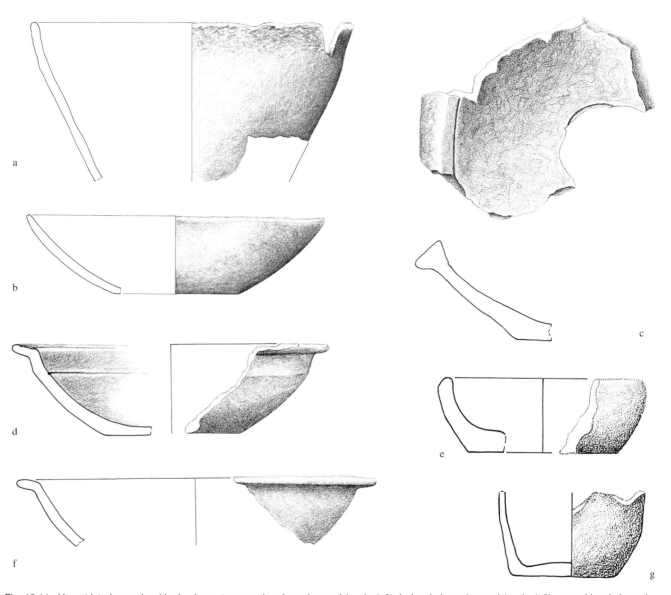

Fig. 12.11. Unrestricted vessels with simple contours: a. jar-shaped vessel (scale 1:3), b. bowl-shaped vessel (scale 1:3), c. oval bowl-shaped vessel (scale 1:2), d. bowl-shaped vessel (scale 1:2), e. miniature vessel (scale !:1), f. bowl-shaped vessel, g. miniature vessel (scale 1:1).

Rims are represented by 63 sherds. Griddle rims are mostly rounded (41.8%), perpendicular and straight (28.2%) or unthickened (14.2%). Triangular (7.9%) and overhanging (7.9%) rims occur but in low quantities. The average diameter is 23.8 cm. Average rim thickness is 14.0 mm and the average thickness of the baking surface is 7.8 mm.

12.5.1 INDIVIDUAL FINDS

Two whole vessels were found associated with the burial of Feature 019 in unit 10. Both represented vessels belonging to the Cedrosan Saladoid subseries. One is a red slipped dish with incised decoration on the interior of the rim, the second one is a bowl with two D-shaped handles (cf. chapter 17, fig. 17.2a, b). A large part of a sizeable, undecorated vessel was found in unit 11.

12.6 Technological analysis

The technological study encompassed research on the manufacturing techniques, a textural analysis of the fabrics (clays and tempers) used for the manufacture of the Huecan pottery

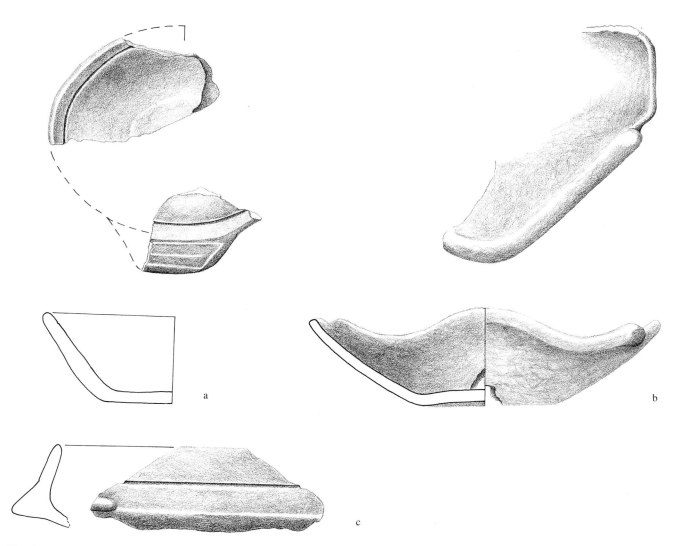

Fig. 12.12. Unrestricted vessels (scale 1:2): a. oval-bowl shaped vessel, b. bowl-shaped vessel with complex shape, c. bowl-shaped vessel.

and the carrying out of tests on two raw clay samples from Hope Estate. This study was made in cooperation with Mr. Loe Jacobs of the Institute of Pottery Technology, Leiden University. A sample of ten sherds including various sherd categories (rim, body, base, decorated, red-slipped, and griddle pieces) was selected for this purpose.

Manufacturing techniques
The following aspects were studied: shaping techniques, surface treatment, decoration techniques and firing.

Shaping techniques
Flattening and coiling are the most commonly used shaping techniques, but occasionally they used in combination with other techniques such as pinching and moulding.

Griddles were made by flattening out a lump of clay between both hands or placed on a more or less flat surface. Manufacture was coarse; the griddles are usually rather thick. The rounded rim was attached as a coil of clay around the circumference and pressed and pinched into shape. In some cases this coil is still visible. The bottom was smoothed and the surface was either smoothed and/or burnished.

Dish-, bowl- and jar-shaped vessels were made partially or completely by coiling. In the case of completely coiled vessels, the base part was often manufactured by pinching or flattening.

The characteristically ovoid dishes with zoomorphic representations were probably predominantly made by pressing

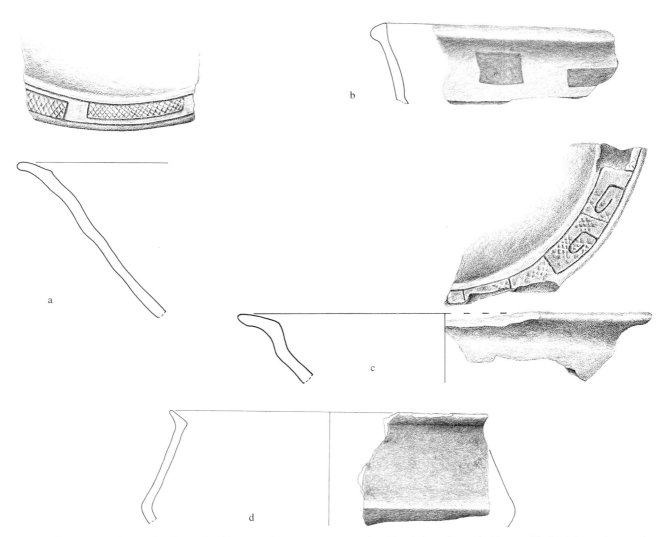

Fig. 12.13. Restricted and unrestricted vessels with composite contour: a. unrestricted bowl-shaped vessel with zoned-incised decorations on the rims (scale 1:2), b. unrestricted vessel with white-on-red painting (scale 1:3), c. unrestricted vessel with zoned-incised decorations on the rim (scale 1:2), d. restricted vessel with composite contour (scale 1:3).

clay into a mould. In those cases a raised edge was made on top of the moulded dish by adding a coil of clay which was modelled into the shape of a rim. The moulding technique does not demand much skill and it provides for a certain standardized vessel shape and size. Moreover, moulding is less time-consuming than coiling, and in the former case even poor clay-sand mixtures can be used for pottery manufacture. The moulds may have been made of pottery as well. In this case dish-shaped vessels may have been used as moulds for the manufacture of other types of dishes, but they are not recognizable as such in the archaeological context. On the other hand, it has been suggested by Stephen Carini (1991, 31) in his study of Huecan and Cedrosan Saladoid

pottery that the wet clay could also have been pressed into *higuera* gourds (*Calabash cresentia*). To make a keeled vessel, two bowls shaped in this manner could have been placed one on top of eachother and then joined at the seams forming the keel.

Surface finish
Smoothing, burnishing and polishing are the commonest finishing techniques that have been observed for the Huecan pottery. They constitute three grades of surface texture produced by closely related techniques. All involve rubbing a tool, a polishing stone, against leather-hard clay to modify the texture and light-reflecting qualities of the surface

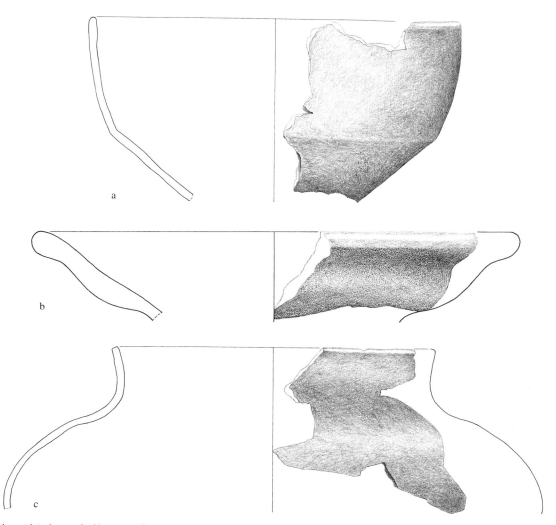

Fig. 12.14. Unrestricted vessel with composite and simple contours, and an independant restricted vessel with composite contour: a. unrestricted vessel with composite contour (scale 1:3), b. unrestricted vessel with simple contour (scale 1:2), c. independant restricted vessel with composite contour (scale 1:3).

(Rye 1981, 89). Its purpose is twofold, aesthetic on the one hand and to affect the permeability and strength of the pottery surface on the other hand (Wallace 1989).

Decoration

Modelling, incising and impressing are the three major techniques which were applied by the Huecan potters. Part of the decorated earthenware shows zoomorphically and anthropomorphically modelled decorative motifs. In these cases, the clay was mostly pre-modelled and appliquéd to the vessel when both were in a plastic state. Modelling was also often combined with incising.

Incising and impressing often occur together on Huecan pottery. Incising was done primarily with a sharp pointed tool when the clay was in a leather-hard condition, producing relatively fine and deep lines. A specific category, is, formed by the zoned-incised crosshatched decoration which was applied when the clay was still rather soft. This is strongly contrasting to the ZIC on Cedrosan pottery, which was applied to a leather-hard to hard clay surface, producing fine, scratched-like incisions. The final appearance of the incised lines also depends on the amount and size of non-plastic materials in the clay. The decorated sherds show mostly very compact textures (cf. section on textural analysis, sherds nos. 1-3).

Impressing such as punctation or arching is often used in combination with incision. Punctation involves the punching depressions into the wet clay, often utilizing a sharp or

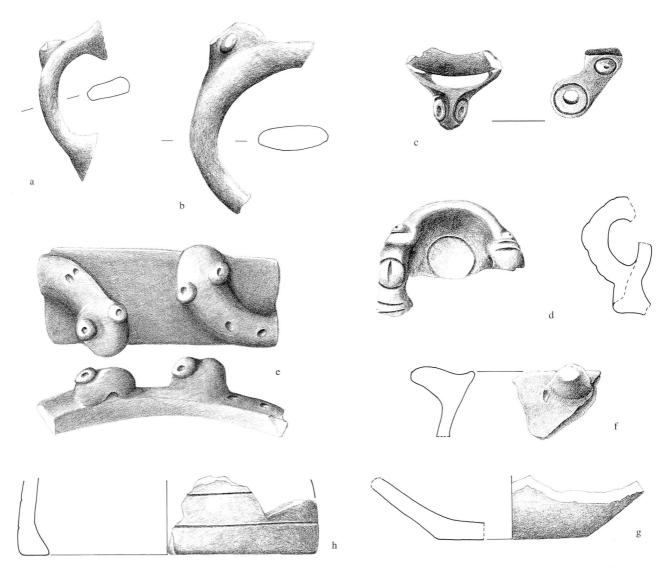

Fig. 12.15. Appendages, base and a potstand (scale 1:2): a-b. handles, c. zoomorphic lug, d. handle decorated with incisions and nubbins, e. handle with a decoration of two snake heads, f. lug, g. flat base , h. part of a potstand.

pointed tool such as a stick, a hollow reed or awl (Rice 1987, 145).

Firing

The pottery was fired under rather low temperatures, i.e., below 800°C. The conditions fluctuated between oxidizing and reducing. In most cases sherd cross-sections show a light grey to grey and brown core and red to reddish-brown and brown subsurfaces.

Both the undecorated and decorated pottery were fired in piles. The surface colour of the pottery, which is reddish-brown or brownish in most cases, could also have been influenced by the timing involved in opening up the pile.

12.6.1 TEXTURAL AND MINERALOGICAL ANALYSIS

An analysis has been carried out to identify the mineralogical and textural composition of the potsherds and to form classes of fabric. By fabric is meant the composition of the fired pottery, i.e., the total appearance of matrix and inclusions. It implies the texture, colour, hardness, type of non-plastics, their shape, size, quality as well as the presence of pores and cracks and their shape.

sherd 1 (14-B-3) decorated rim fragment	
distribution of non-plastics	homogeneous
grain type mono-minerals rock fragments other type	mixed *** clear quartz ** pyroxene ** hematite ** feldspar ** sfalerite ** organic plant material * iron compounds volcanic origin none
prevailing grain size	moderately sorted fine
grain shape	sub-angular to sub-rounded and diverse
prevailing quantity of non-plastic grains	20%
grain colour	mostly light
general texture fabric	compact

Fig. 12.16. Fabric composition of sherd 1.

Macro- and microscopical analysis was performed using magnifications of 10× and 40×. Thin sliced cross-sections, were obtained by cutting the potsherds with a diamond saw and treating them with fine grinding paper in order to obtain a smooth fraction surface. The sherds were refired under oxidizing conditions at a temperature of 750°C for 30 minutes. This removed the organic impurities and improved the visibility of the inclusions, the paste colour and the texture of the fabric in general (Bishop et al. 1982; Jacobs 1983; Hofman 1993). A steel needle was used to test the texture and hardness of the non-plastic grains. This is a particularly accurate way to identify soft minerals such as inclusions of iron oxide.

A set of quantitative and qualitative attribute categories or modes was recorded on the 10 sherds adopting the method used for the Saban material (Hofman 1993, 172, fig. 90). These attributes concern the nature of the inclusions such as type, size and sorting, shape next to relative percentage of the grains. Colours were defined in combination with attributes describing the general texture of the fabric such as density, hardness and porosity.

Results

The sherds are not uniform as to composition. However, there are points of similarity concerning the size and quantities of the grains. This makes comparison of relatively small sherd surfaces difficult.

Because of the occurrence of specific inclusions, mutual relationships are attested to. This also holds true for the more generally occuring non-plastics such as quartz, feldspar and iron-oxide concretions. None of these seemed to have been used as temper materials but occur naturally in the clays. Also, the shell inclusions in sherd no. 9 are probably not added as a form of temper. The occurrence of sphalerite (ZnS) and/or wurtzite in nearly all sherds is noteworthy. Grog has not been identified but the iron-siltstone with

sherd 2 (7-A-3/1) decorated rim fragment	
distribution of non-plastics	homogeneous
grain type mono-minerals	mixed *** clear quartz, feldspar ** pyroxene ** biotite ** iron-siltstone * magnetite * kaolinite * wurtzite * sfalerite volcanic origin
rock fragments other type	none
prevailing grain size	badly sorted fine to medium
grain shape	angular to sub-angular
prevailing quantity of non-plastic grains	25%
grain colour	mixed
general texture fabric	compact

Fig. 12.17. Fabric composition of sherd 2.

inclusions of feldspar in sherd no. 5 looks very similar to grog and could thus very easily be mistaken for it. Sand has possibly been added to the clay as temper in all cases.
The following descriptions of the different fabrics are provided with photomicrographs for reference and illustration of the characteristics of each sherd (figs 12.16-12.25). The quantity of minerals included is indicated by * sporadically **, relatively few, *** dominant.

When analyzing the fabric as a whole, i.e., the texture of the sherd and the total quantity of grain size of the inclusions and their grain size the following relationships can be drawn (table 12.18, fig. 12.26).

12.6.2 TESTS ON RAW CLAY SAMPLES FROM HOPE ESTATE
Two clay samples, collected in the direct environment of the Hope Estate site, have been tested for their properties and suitability as raw materials for pottery manufacture, compar-

ing them with the pre-Columbian sherds.
The first sample, here referred to as H1, is a dark-coloured clay from auger test 5. The second sample, here referred to as H2, is a light-coloured clay from auger test 6.
To measure the drying and firing shrinkage capabilities of both samples testbars were made. The linear drying shrinkage of sample H1 appeared to be 16% and that of sample H2, 11%. These values are rather high, which indicates that both represent good plastic clays, but, on the other hand, as a result of tension cracks may occur during firing. After firing the testbars at a temperature between 700^0C to 900^0C in an oxidizing atmosphere, no noticeable further shrinkage was measured. Obviously, this indicates that in both cases the phase of drying was the most critical one. Apart from this, sample H1 has good firing properties. Firing at 700^0C it resulted in a sherd with good ceramic qualities. The fabric of sample H1 resembles that of the pre-Columbian pottery from Hope Estate. The range of firing colours covers that of the

sherd 3 (7-A-3/2) wall fragment	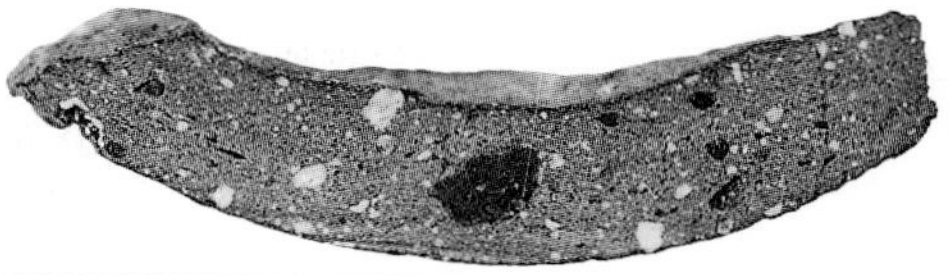
distribution of non-plastics	homogeneous
grain type mono-minerals rock fragments other type	mixed *** quartz conglomerate grains, clear quartz, weathered feldspar ** pyroxene ** iron-siltstone ** magnetite ** iron/manganese nodules ** organic plant material * feldspar with inclusions of iron-oxide volcanic origin none
prevailing grain size	badly sorted medium
grain shape	angular to sub-angular
prevailing quantity of non-plastic grains	15%
grain colour	prevailing light
general texture fabric	compact

Fig. 12.18. Fabric composition of sherd 3.

latter. Its structure, however, is somewhat more compact. This is mainly due to the fact that sample H1 does not contain as many grains as the pre-Columbian fabrics. For an optimal usage of this clay it is necessary to add some sand to it.

In contrast, sample H2 produced a sherd of less ceramic quality. Due to a high amount of salt in the clay, the fabric is pale yellow (Hue 2.5 8/2) in colour. The major reason for the poor quality of this clay is formed by a very low content of fluxes. The result is a sherd with a weak ceramic bound. It is possible, however, to use this clay for manufacturing soft and crumbly pottery of inferior quality.

Fabric composition of sample H1
This contains soft textured white grains with a powdery structure after firing. Smithsonite ($ZnCo_3$), some quartz grains, iron-oxide concretions (sporadically), black coloured

seeds of *Ruppia* (probably *Ruppia maritima*) pointing to a brackish deposit, possibly that of a lagoon and fragmentary particles of calcium carbonate (part of the matrix). The size of these particles seldomly exceeds 2 mm; a size of 1 mm and smaller is dominant. The total quantity is less than 10%.

Fabric composition of sample H2
Just like H1, this sample contains fine particles of calcium carbonate as part of the matrix (positive reaction with HCl). Both the clay and the inclusions are similar to H1. However, H2 has a higher salt content. During firing the combination of salt and calcium causes a bleaching of the colour throughout the fabric. Other grains that were found include e.g., smithsonite, which is transparent and colourless, but on firing, 850^0 C, becomes white while the transparency disappears and the structure becomes soft and powdery. The grain crystals have a rhombohedral shape when broken and show a perfect cleavage. The sample further contains quartz

177

sherd 4 (7-B-3/2) wall fragment	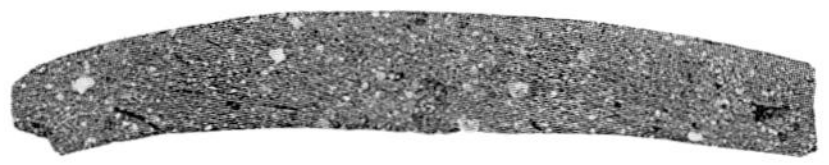
distribution of non-plastics	homogeneous
grain type mono-minerals	mixed *** weathered feldspar ** wurtzite ** sfalerite ** iron-siltstone with inclusions of sfalerite * pyroxene volcanic origin
rock fragments other type	none
prevailing grain size	badly to moderately sorted fine to medium
grain shape	angular to sub-angular
prevailing quantity of non-plastic grains	20%
grain colour	mixed
general texture fabric	compact

Fig. 12.19. Fabric composition of sherd 4.

grains (not dominant), seeds of *Ruppia maritima* (?), and parts of small fish bones.

Properties

To test whether the two clays were suitable for the manufacture of pottery, a few test vessels were made. The following shaping and finishing techniques were tested: mould pressing, coiling, pinching, scraping, smoothing, burnishing and polishing. After these processes the vessels were dried and fired.

Results

Both clays have good plasticity and are suitable for mould pressing. The base parts of the test vessels were made with this technique.

Coils were added on top of the moulded parts. Both clays proved to have good fixing capacities, which is a favourable property when additive techniques such as coiling are applied. The clays were used without changing their composition, i.e., nothing was added or removed. Therefore, the

high percentage of drying shrinkage may eventually have given problems. Since the vessels were dried under normal circumstances in the shade at approximately 200°C, too high physical stress did not occur during the drying process. Moreover, the shapes were made in such a way that sharp corners in the profile were avoided while the walls were thinned by scraping after some pre-drying.

Finally, the surface was smoothed by sweeping it with the fingers and, after a renewed period of drying, it was polished. The surface of sample H2, however, does not allow a good gloss to develop. Moreover, on further drying a scum layer will cover the protruding parts due to the high salt content of the clay.

The clays proved to be suitable for making pottery according to the pinching technique as well. Two small bottle shaped vessels were made, using this technique.

12.7   Synthesis and conclusions

12.7.1   STYLE AND MORPHOLOGY

The ceramic material from the Hope Estate site includes pottery of both the Huecan and Cedrosan Saladoid subseries.

sherd 5 (7-B-3/1) griddle fragment	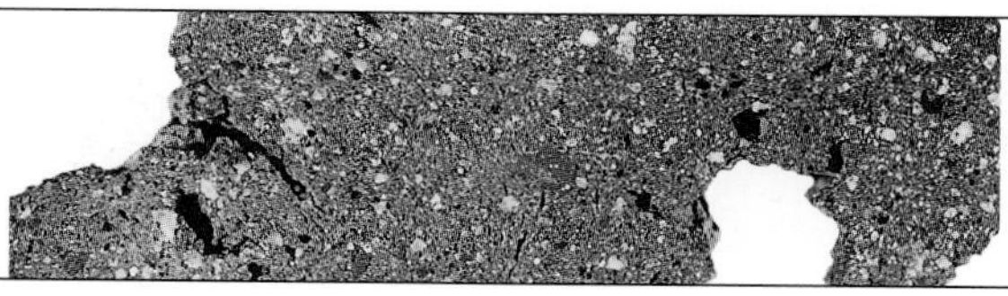
distribution of non-plastics	homogeneous
grain type mono-minerals	mixed *** clear quartz ** feldspar ** pyroxene ** iron-siltstone with inclusions of feldspar ** magnetite ** sandstone volcanic origin
rock fragments other type	none
prevailing grain size	badly sorted medium
grain shape	angular to sub-angular
prevailing quantity of non-plastic grains	25%
grain colour	mixed
general texture fabric	normal and porous

Fig. 12.20. Fabric composition of sherd 5.

On the basis of the pottery analysis, combined with the stratigraphic data and radiocarbon dates two well-defined cultural components can be distinguished at the Hope Estate site. These components are referred to as Hope Estate 1 and Hope Estate 2. Figures 12.27 to 12.30 show the most significant differences between the two cultural components as regards to the ralative quantities of decoration modes, vessel and rim shapes next to and griddle rim profiles.

The pottery of the Hope Estate 1 component belongs to the Huecan Saladoid subseries and is characterized by fairly thin-walled and simple vessel shapes. Characteristic vessel shapes include goblets, dishes, bowls and jars with unrestricted or restricted simple contours, dishes or bowls with unrestricted composite, inflected contours and bowls with independent restricted inflected contours. Vessel shapes are similar although less diverse than the ones reported for the La Hueca site, on Vieques (Chanlatte Baik 1991b, 198, 200-202, figs 1, 3, 4 and 5).

Part of the vessels are decorated with incised motifs on the rim portion or the body. These consist of curvilinear designs filled or not filled with punctations or zoned-incised crosshatching. Some of these incisions are filled with white paint, a feature which has been documented also for La Hueca (e.g., Chanlatte Baik and Narganes Storde 1990, 13; Chanlatte Baik 1991b, 191). Here red paint occasionally served the same purpose. The symmetry shown by the curvilinear designs is noteworthy. In all 4% of the sherds in the Huecan component is decorated. This is slightly higher than the figure obtained at Punta Candelero, i.e., 3.0%. Linear or curvilinear incision, zoned punctation and zoned-incised crosshatching comprise 68.8%, 5.9% and 4.3%, respectively, at Hope Estate. It should be noted that Haviser (1991b, 651) estimated the occurrence of zoned-punctated designs at 7.0%, but denied the existence of zoned-incised crosshatching in the Huecan component of Hope Estate. At Punta Candelero zoned punctation represents 3.0% and zoned-incised crosshatching 57.0% of the sherds, respectively (Rodríguez 1991a, 610). Similar amounts are documented

179

sherd 6 (11-D-3) rim fragment	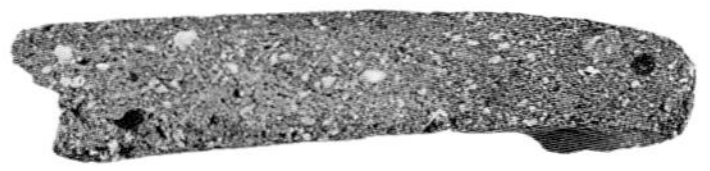
distribution of non-plastics	homogeneous
grain type mono-minerals	mixed *** clear quartz ** feldspar ** iron/manganese nodules ** sandstone ** organic plant material * biotite * wurtzite * sfalerite volcanic origin
rock fragments other type	none
prevailing grain size	badly sorted fine to medium
grain shape	angular to sub-angular
prevailing quantity of non-plastic grains	20-25%
grain colour	mostly light
general texture fabric	open to normal and porous

Fig. 12.21. Fabric composition of sherd 6.

for the La Hueca site (Chanlatte Baik 1991, 190). This is obviously not the case at Hope Estate. Zoned punctation is less common at La Hueca and Punta Candelero than at Hope Estate, but has been documented also for complexes southeast of St. Martin, notably Morel I, Guadeloupe (Clerc 1967, 1970; Hofman et al. this volume), and Folle Anse, Marie Galante (Barbotin 1987).

Other characteristics of the Hope Estate 1 pottery also encountered at La Hueca and Punta Candelero include small nubbins, often appliquéd to the vessel rims or embellishing the curvilinear designs, next to a fair amount of zoomorphical and anthropomorphical adornos (Rodríguez 1991a, 610; Chanlatte Baik 1991b, 190). A typical pottery category is formed by ovoid dishes with inflected contours, representing the body, head and tail of an animal. A large quantity of this type of dishes is known from the La Hueca site where it represents 49.7% of the vessels froms (Chanlatte Baik 1991b, 201, figs 4a and b). This type of dishes is also known from

the site of Morel I, Guadeloupe (Clerc 1968, 48, 59, figs 1-2, 1970, 76, 78, fig. 14; Durand and Petitjean Roget 1991, 58, 67, Pl. I, fig. 4). These dishes have paired perforations at the head/body ends. These may have been used for the inhalation of drugs, the attachment of feathers for additional decorative purposes (Haviser 1991a), for the pouring of liquids at the moment of serving (Barbotin 1987) or, although less likely for suspension. The animals represented on these ceremonial vessels remind of the homeland of this group in the Tropical Lowlands of South America. It is likely that these zoomorphs form part of the Amerindian mythological world and represent creatures incorporated in their myths and belief system. The Saladoid people held to their religious traditions much longer than to other aspects of their culture, such as their subsistence economy which had to be adapted to the island situation and marine environment (cf. also Roe 1989). Griddles associated with the Huecan component have characteristically rounded and unthickened rims, also reported

sherd 7 (7-B-5) rim fragment	
distribution of non-plastics	homogeneous
grain type mono-minerals rock fragments other type	mixed *** weathered feldspar, clear quartz ** pyroxene ** sfalerite ** rock fragments with inclusions of biotite ** iron-siltstone volcanic origin none
prevailing grain size	badly sorted fine to medium
grain shape	angular to sub-angular
prevailing quantity of non-plastic grains	20%
grain colour	mostly light
general texture fabric	compact

Fig. 12.22. Fabric composition of sherd 7.

for the site of Morel I on Guadeloupe (Clerc 1968, 49, 1970, 76).

12.7.2 MANUFACTURE AND FABRIC COMPOSITION

A sample of the Huecan pottery was taken for technological analysis. The manufacturing techniques which could be identified, i.e., coiling, pinching, flattening and moulding, are common for the hand-made ceramics of the region. Moulding seems to have been used for the ovoid dishes with zoomorphic representations. Modelling, incising and impressing form the three major decorative techniques employed by these potters. Occasionally they occur in combination. Zoned-incised crosshatching is somewhat distinct from the other incised decorative designs because it is applied on a dry clay surface. This has also been documented for the zoned-incised crosshatched ware at La Hueca (Chanlatte Baik 1991b, 190).

Only 10 sherds have been analyzed according to fabric. The occurrence of various non-plastics in the clay is particular to the Leeward Islands (cf. also Hofman 1993). The presence of sphalerite and wurtzite in nearly all sherds is noteworthy. Sand temper has been documented for all sherds, but no other temper materials have been definitely identified. Variation in fabric seemed to have been primarily dependent on function (undecorated or decorated wares and use as griddles) and the personal preference of the potter. The analysis of the raw clay samples from Hope Estate showed that sample H1 produced a sherd with good ceramic qualities and that its fabric is very similar to that of the pre-Columbian sherds. Therefore, it cannot be excluded that for the manufacture of their vessels the potters at Hope Estate used clays which were locally available.

12.7.3 THE CULTURAL AFFILIATIONS OF HUECAN SALADOID CERAMICS

The attribution of the pottery from Hope Estate to a La Hueca style and culture, to a separate Huecan subseries of styles and cultures or to a Huecoid series, as well as the relationship between this pottery style and the assumedly subsequent Cedrosan Saladoid subseries has led to much

sherd 8 (14-D-3) decorated wall fragment	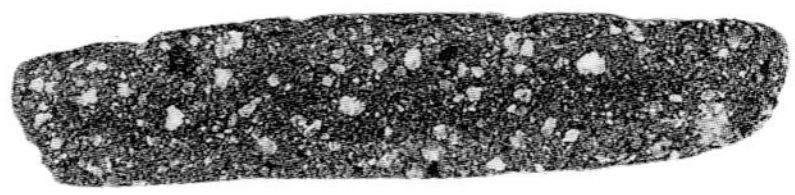
distribution of non-plastics	homogeneous
grain type mono-minerals	mixed *** clear quartz, feldspar ** pyroxene ** magnetite ** biotite ** wurtzite volcanic origin
rock fragments other type	none
prevailing grain size	badly sorted medium
grain shape	angular, broken
prevailing quantity of non-plastic grains	30%
grain colour	mixed/mostly light
general texture fabric	open, porous, crumbly

Fig. 12.23. Fabric composition of sherd 8.

debate in recent years. Much of the discussion has concentrated on the geographical distribution, cultural associations and stratigraphical context of these pottery styles. The lack of Cedrosan white-on-red painted pottery in combination with zoned-incised crosshatching or zoned-punctated decorative motifs in Huecan complexes has led to the suggestion of an earlier or divergent development from the initial Cedrosan Saladoid subseries (Chanlatte Baik 1979, 1981, 1983; Rouse 1986, 1989, 1992). In the latter both elements are found mixed, characterizing the subseries.

The pottery of the Hope Estate 1 component corresponds in style, morphology and technology to that of various assemblages on other islands in the southeast, e.g., the site of Folle Anse on Marie-Galante (Barbotin 1987), the sites of Morel I (Clerc 1964, 1968, 1970; Hofman et al., this volume), Anse St. Marguerite and Anse Patate (Ph. Arnoux, pers. comm., Hofman et al., this volume) on Guadeloupe, the site of Trants on Montserrat (Petersen and Watters 1991, Petersen 1996; Watters and Petersen, this volume), and to the north, the site of La Hueca, on Vieques (Chanlatte Baik 1983, Chanlatte Baik and Narganes 1983, Oliver, this volume) and

the Huecan components of the sites of Punta Candelero, Huamacao (Rodríguez 1991a) and Hacienda Grande (Chanlatte Baik 1995) on the east and north coast of Puerto Rico, respectively. The pottery from all of these sites is distinct from Early Cedrosan Saladoid ceramics both in style and morphology. However, good stratigraphical context and radiocarbon dates are missing from these sites. It is noteworthy that in the complexes to the southeast zoned punctation prevails, whereas those to the north show a prevalence of zoned-incised crosshatching. Incision is sometimes combined with modelling and punctated lines, occasionally filled with white or red paint on the ceramics of the northern complexes.

On the basis of the sample recovered from his test excavations at Hope Estate in 1987-1988, which at that time seemed to lack zoned-incised crosshatching. Haviser (1991a, 655) postulated a separate migration from La Hueca. He put forward the theory that there were two different early pottery styles as the affiliation between La Hueca and Hope Estate had not yet been established beyond doubtt. He believed that the La Hueca pottery represents a style which emerged when

sherd 9 (7-A-B/3) griddle fragment	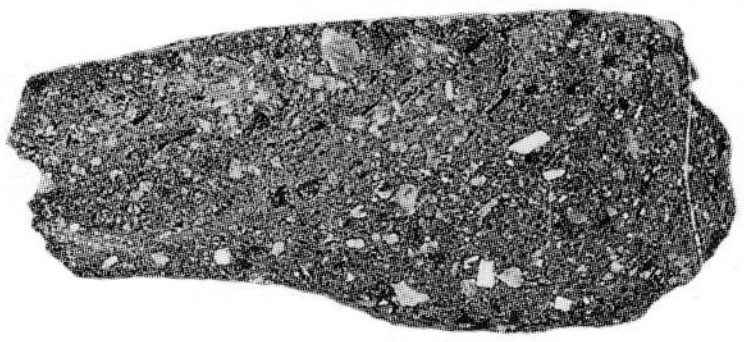
distribution of non-plastics	homogeneous
grain type mono-minerals

rock fragments other type | mixed
*** clear quartz, feldspar
** magnetite
** wurtzite
volcanic origin
none |
prevailing grain size	badly sorted fine to medium
grain shape	angular
prevailing quantity of non-plastic grains	25%
grain colour	mixed/mostly light
general texture fabric	open, porous, light crumbly

Fig. 12.24. Fabric composition of sherd 9.

the 'Early Ceramic-Age people', represented by the Hope Estate assemblage, were mixing with the Saladoid people. However, the present analysis of the pottery sample recovered from the 1993 excavations showed that zoned-incised crosshatching and zoned-punctated decorative motifs co-existed at Hope Estate. Also, an infrared test run by Carini (1991, 117-118) on three decorated sherds (one showing zoned punctations and two pieces showing zoned-incised crosshatching) from Hope Estate proved that they were very closely related in composition.

Rouse called this pottery complex the 'La Hueca style', and has postulated that it formed an early divergence within the Cedrosan Saladoid subseries, parallelling that which led to the Hacienda Grande style of the same subseries (Rouse 1986, 1989, 1992). This divergence would have taken place at different times and at opposite ends of the Cedrosan Saladoid radiation, westward at the Río Guapo on the coast of Venezuela and northward at La Hueca on Vieques. Rouse (1986, 10, 1992, 89) explains this cultural split as a result of the process known as the 'founders' effect according to which the migrants make a selection from the elements of their original culture, in this way dropping particular traits,

in this case painting. The ancestors of the La Hueca culture diverged from the ancestors of the Hacienda Grande culture somewhere along the migration route through the Leeward and the Virgin Islands. The presence of La Hueca style pottery and paraphernalia on the islands of Guadeloupe and St. Martin, for example, may indicate the evidence of a cult and/or elite social class among the people who inhabited these islands. Subsequently, members of this social group would have separated from the rest of the local population and have migrated to eastern Puerto Rico creating the La Hueca complex by developing its distinctive style and culture (Rouse and Alegría 1990, 83-85). Rouse and Alegría (1990, 85) and Rouse (1992, 89-90) suggest that more detailed research at sites such as Hope Estate, situated along the postulated migration route, may help to explain this phenomenon.

Rodríguez (1989) speaks of a new style within the Cedrosan Saladoid subseries, sharing some of its attributes with the Hacienda Grande style, but having some stylistic and technological differences as well. Partially basing himself on data obtained from his lithic analysis he suggests that the La Hueca style may represent a section within the Saladoid

sherd 10 (11-A-3) rim fragment	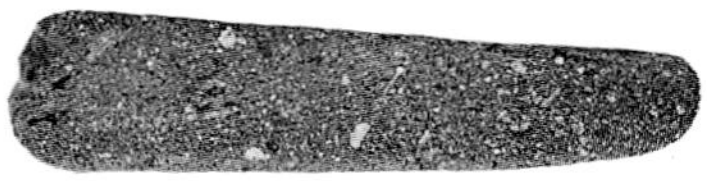 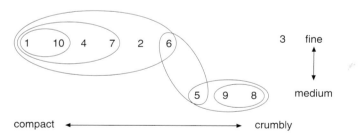
distribution of non-plastics	homogeneous
grain type mono-minerals rock fragments other type	mixed *** weathered feldspar ** sfalerite ** wurtzite ** iron-siltstone * clear quartz volcanic origin none
prevailing grain size	badly sorted fine/some medium
grain shape	sub-angular
prevailing quantity of non-plastic grains	25%
grain colour	mixed
general texture fabric	compact

Fig. 12.25. Fabric composition of sherd 10.

Fig. 12.26. Sherd clusters according to fabric composition.

series specialized in trading of especially exotic materials (Rodríguez 1991b).

These arguments are supported by the compositional analysis of the pottery of the La Hueca and Hacienda Grande complexes which has led to the conclusion that, although both styles are distinct in decorative motifs, the composition of the paste is often identical and that on this basis the La Hueca pottery should indeed be classified as a member of the Saladoid series, rather than as a separate series (Carini 1991, 139).

These views contradict those of Chanlatte Baik who regards this pottery style as a separate 'Huecoid series' preceding the Cedrosan Saladoid subseries in the islands. He postulates an additional migration in order ro explain the presence of La Hueca in the Antilles (Chanlatte Baik 1981, 1983, 1991a). Chanlatte theorizes that a distinctive Huecoid people

184

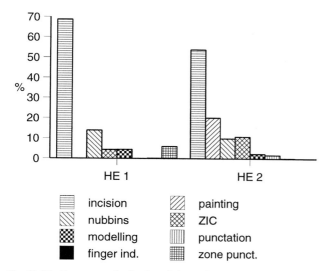

Fig. 12.27. Frequency distribution of decoration modes in the Hope Estate 1 and 2 components.

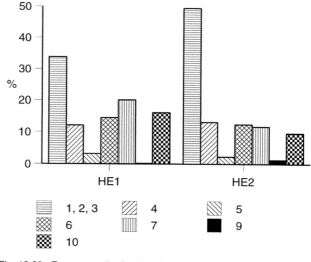

Fig. 12.28. Frequency distribution of vessel shapes in the Hope Estate 1 and 2 components.

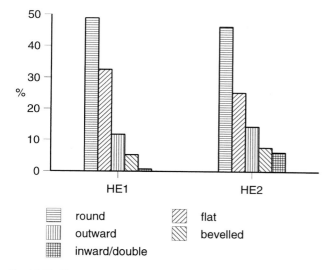

Fig. 12.29. Frequency distribution of rim shapes in the Hope Estate 1 and 2 components.

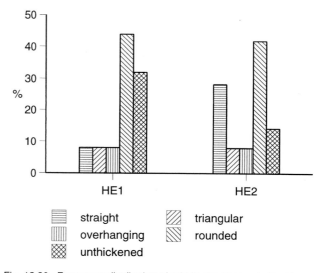

Fig. 12.30. Frequency distribution of griddle rim shapes in the Hope Estate 1 and 2 components.

migrated simultaneously with Cedrosan Saladoid from the mainland, notably from the Río Guapo area on the central Venezuelan coast, directly overseas to Vieques Island, east of Puerto Rico. Pottery from Río Guapo is indeed comparable to the La Hueca style pottery and also lacks the painting. Chanlatte's theory has been challenged by Rouse on the basis that the radiocarbon dates available for the Río Guapo complex (AD 310 and AD 335) are too recent to allow the possibility that Río Guapo is ancestral to La Hueca (Rouse 1992, 88).

The pottery of the Hope Estate 2 component belongs to the Cedrosan Saladoid subseries. This pottery seems to be less friable than Huecan ceramics. In the Cedrosan Saladoid pottery zoned-incised crosshatching is complemented by white-on-red and polychrome painting (white-orange-and-red or white-black-and-red). Other diagnostic decorative features comprise curvilinear and linear incised lines (sometimes used to outline painted designs), simple linear incision (occasionally filled with white paint), modelled-incised

Number	1	10	4	7	2	6	5	9	8	3
Quartz cl.	■	○		■	■	■	■	■	■	■
Quartz Congl. gr.							○			■
Feldspar	●				■	●	●	■	■	○
Weathered feldspar		■	■	■						■
Pyroxene	●		○	●	●		●		●	●
Wurzite		●	●		○	○		●	●	
Sfalerite	●	●	●	●	○	○				
Biotite				●	●	○			●	
Magnetite					○		●	●	●	●
Haematite	●									
Iron comp.	○									
Iron-oxide siltstone		●	●		●		●			
Iron/manganese nodules						●				●
Kaolinite					○					●
Sandstone							●			
Shell								●		
Volcanic rock fragments	●	●	●	●	●	●	●	●	●	●
Nnpl. ± 15%										*
Npl. ± 20%	*		*	*		*				
Npl. ± 25%		*			*	*	*	*		
Npl. ± 30%									*	
Moderately sorted	*		*							
Badly sorted		*	*	*	*	*	*	*	*	*
Angular/sub-angular			*	*	*	*	*			
Angular								*	*	

Table 12.19. Quantitative and qualitative attributes according to type, size and sorting, shape, relative percentage of the grains of each sherd in the sample.

■ = grain type dominantly present.

● = grain type present in relative small quantities.

○ = grain type sporadically present.

* = marked value.

zoomorphic or anthropomorphic adornos applied to tabular lugs and nubbins. Vessels are characterized by a variety of shapes, including bowls with simple composite contours, the so-called inverted bell shape, boat- or kidney-shaped bowls, jars with circular to ovoid shapes, hemispherical bowls, often with D-shaped handles, flanged rim bowls and incense burners. Griddle rims have a variety of shapes, but show an enlargement of the top of the griddle rim in contrast to those from the Hope Estate 1 component which are characterized by rounded and unthickened shapes.

The Hope Estate 2 pottery is similar to the Cedrosan Saladoid pottery of the many other islands of the northern Lesser Antilles, where it is roughly dated between AD 250/400 and AD 600/850. It has been found, e.g., at the sites of Rendez-Vous Bay and Sandy Ground on Anguilla (Douglas 1991), Anse des Pères on St. Martin (Hamburg, this volume), Spring Bay 1 and Kelbey's Ridge 1 on Saba (Hofman 1993), Golden Rock on St. Eustatius (Versteeg and Schinkel 1992), Cayon on St. Kitts (Goodwin 1979) and Indian Creek on Antigua (Rouse 1974, 1976; Faber Morse and Rouse 1995).

12.7.4   CONCLUDING REMARKS

The ceramic material from the Hope Estate site comprises pottery of both the Huecan and the Cedrosan Saladoid subseries. The Huecan Saladoid pottery is characterized by the lack of painting, although red slip was noticed in a few cases, the simplicity of vessel shapes, its relatively thin vessel walls, its bright brown- colour and characteristic designs. The Cedrosan pottery stands out for its bichrome and polychrome painted decorative motifs and the variety of vessel and rim shapes. However, notable similarities between the two Saladoid subseries include the presence of zoned-incised crosshatching on the vessel rim, dishes or bowls representing animal effigies, showing head and tail as well as nubbins embellishing vessel rims.

On the basis of the pottery analysis combined with the stratigraphical data and various considerations of dating, it can be assumed that there are two well-defined segregated components at Hope Estate. These are referred to as the Hope Estate 1 and the Hope Estate 2 components. The Hope Estate 1 component seems to precede the Hope Estate 2 component. Huecan pottery from the Hope Estate 1 component occurs spatially segregated in the southeastern part of the midden area and the lower levels of its northeastern portion. However, elsewhere in the refuse area it occurs mixed with the Cedrosan pottery. This mixture of Huecan and Cedrosan pottery in various parts of the midden can be explained by processes as maintenance and reorganisation of the settlement during the various periods of occupation (cf. also chapter 11).

13 Lithics

Jay B. Haviser

13.1 Introduction

This chapter is concerned with the details of the lithic artefacts recovered from Hope Estate during the 1993 excavation season. These data will be presented as an overall description of the total sample of analysed lithics recovered from the site, including the characteristic raw materials, types of human modification, and vertical provenance. These data will be supplemented by a detailed comparison of the analysed lithics from three excavation units, located in horizontally discrete sections: unit 5, representing the dense northeastern part of the midden area, unit 7, representing the dense but shallow southeastern part of the midden area and unit 11, representing its sparse and shallow southwestern part. The analyses of these lithics from Hope Estate will then be synthesized from a general perspective, using the available local and regional comparative data. It is important to note that this is primary lithic analysis for the large-scale excavations at Hope Estate, and as such it focuses on investigation of the basic lithic raw materials used at the site, supplemented by some general analysis of the lithic modification and lithic tools here. Further identification of the tools is presented by Maaike de Waal in chapter 14. This part of the chapter is meant to present a clear definition of the lithic raw materials from the site as a foundation for the more extensive analyses of lithic modification and exchange networks.

13.2 Previous lithic analysis

As a general reference, some background concerning previous lithic analyses for the Hope Estate site is necessary here. From the initial test excavation in 1987, 702 lithic specimens were recovered and analysed by the author. Of that material, the most common lithic raw material was identified at that time as "grey-green chalky chert", with basalt and chert/flint as the second and third most common materials found at the site, respectively. Stone types, recovered in lesser quantities in 1987, include quartz, haematite, and a material called porphyrite "zemi-stone". Lithic modification and tools noted among the sample from the 1987 excavation include a few polished celts, bifacially chipped axes and choppers, a ground knife, a polished bead, a hammerstone, and polishing stones (Haviser 1988, 48).

From the more substantial 1988 excavation in all 4165 lithic specimens were recovered and analysed by the author, with some assistance provided by L. van der Valk of the Free University (Amsterdam), and B. Fouke of Stony Brook University (New York). Among these 1988 lithic samples, it was again noted that the most common raw material from the site was the "grey-green chalky chert", which through casual identification by B. Fouke, was labelled as a form of radiolarian limestone. It was also noted in 1988 that a large source for this material was present ontop of Hope Hill, directly adjacent to the site. Basalts and cherts were confirmed again as the second and third most common stone materials from Hope Estate. Other lithic raw materials, found in lesser quantities in 1988, include the same as those encountered in 1987, for example quartz, porphyrite and haematite. Still other additional raw materials were noted in 1988, however, such as sandstone, limestone, pumice, calcite, jasper, and amethyst. The conglomerate "zemi-stone" was identified by L. van der Valk as a porphyry rock, probably from a source on St. Martin. The stone tools noted among the specimens from the 1988 excavations were primarily made by bifacial chipping and include axes and choppers, polished celts, ground knives, polished cylindrical beads, hammerstones, and abundant polishing stones. One unique lithic tool type identified from the 1988 excavations is formed by incipient "eared axes", of which several have been chipped from radiolarian limestone, all exhibiting flared proximal corners (Haviser 1991a, 650).

Until the 1993 excavations, the above-mentioned lithic analyses provided the only systematically excavated and analysed lithic samples from the Hope Estate site. The details of the 1993 analysis are presented in the following sections. However, two important new identifications during this analysis should be noted at this stage for the clarification of terms used later in the text. These new identifications relate to the microscopic analysis of radiolarian limestone and porphyrite lithic samples from the site, conducted by M. van Tooren of the Delft University of Technology in The Netherlands. Results of the microscopic analysis showed that the material called "radiolarian limestone" actually represents two lithic types attached to each other, i.e., a core of altered tephrite (volcanic) with limestone (perhaps radiolarian) attached to it. Microscopic analysis of the porphyrite identified this material as a calcirudite (conglomerate), with limestone inclusions; it is of Upper Eocene. For the definition of terms used in this chapter, as well as the subcategories used for the specific identification of lithic modification, the reader is referred to Haviser (1992b).

13.3   Analysed lithic materials

Approximately 200 kilograms of lithic material from Hope Estate were analysed during this study, represented by 12,820 lithic specimens. Of the total number of analysed lithic artefacts, 468 lithic objects exhibit identifiable modifications indicating their use of either tools, ornaments or utilized flakes. Furthermore, an additional

	N	%
chert	1835	14.7
basalt	1578	12.6
tephrite a	3331	26.6
tephrite b	3984	31.8
diorite	760	6.1
limestone	84	0.7
quartz	238	1.9
calcite	373	3.0
sandstone	111	0.9
pumice	34	0.3
haematite	49	0.4
jaspar	66	0.5
calci-rudite	6	0.1
lead-pyrite	7	0.1
amethyst	7	0.1
serpentine	28	0.2
jade/nephrite	5	0.1
carnelian	4	0.1
andesite	16	1.3
other	6	0.1
total	12522	100.0
total weight (g)	190579	100.0

Table 13.1. Total lithic material analysed.

383 lithic specimens showed evidence of modification, could not be identified as belonging to a specific tool or ornament category.

13.3.1   SURFACE COLLECTIONS AND MINIMAL PROVENANCE LITHICS

In all 298 lithic specimens were recovered from locations with poor contextual control, such as surface collections and the excavated units 1 and 2. The latter represent stratigraphic observation units excavated without attention to provenance, where a selective collection strategy was employed. Of these lithic specimens, 34 were identified as having modifications diagnostic of specific tool types or ornaments. Clearly, it can be seen that the ratio of modified specimens to the total sample at 11% is higher for these specimens, than it is for the overall ratios of modified specimens to the total combined lithic sample at 3.5%. This illustrates the selective collection methodology employed in the case of the lithic specimens from locations with poor contextual control. In other words, this portion of the overall sample is biased towards modified specimens. Due to the poor contextual control for these specimens, they are only used as comparative data in the following analyses and have not been incorporated into the statistical calculations.

	N	%
bead/preform	28	6.4
adze	9	2.1
celt	50	11.5
axe	52	12.0
eared-axe	10	2.3
pecking stone	7	1.6
grinding stone	36	8.3
polishing stone	128	29.4
hammerstone	73	16.8
scraper	3	0.7
blade	9	2.1
core	8	1.8
chopper	11	2.5
utilized flake	11	2.5
total	435	100.0

Table 13.2. Total of lithic tools analysed.

	flake	retouch	shatter	raw material	modification
chert	658	515	618	10	25
basalt	852	282	260	79	180
tephrite a	1125	57	299	1511	878
tephite b	1460	1049	906	429	169
diorite	27	–	323	382	19
quartz	1	–	3	233	2
calcite	–	–	–	368	33
limestone	4	–	15	66	–
sandstone	–	–	–	34	3
jaspar	5	4	24	33	1
calci-rudite	1	–	–	5	–
amethyst	–	–	–	2	4
haematite	–	–	–	49	2
lead-pyrite	–	–	–	7	–
serpentine	–	–	–	24	6
jadeite/nephrite	–	–	–	–	5
carnelian	1	–	–	1	2
other	8	–	1	20	–

Table 13.3. Analysed lithic modification types for all lithic materials.

13.4   Analysis of excavated lithic materials

Tables 13.1-13.3 provide a listing of the total amount of analysed lithic material and artefacts recovered from the excavations at Hope Estate. The lithic modification types for all lithic materials are summarized in table 13.3. These lithic specimens were recovered from units 3 to 11. Within the site excavation grid, these units covered significant portions of the northeastern, southeastern, and southwestern sectors of the site. A certain degree of variability in the quantity of recovered lithics is evident within this overall sample due to the use of water screening for units 5 to 10. Thus, these wet-sieved units have produced greater amounts of very small lithic artefacts in contrast to the units which were not water-screened.

As noted above, a total of 12 522 lithic artefacts recovered from controlled excavations were analysed for this study, of which 434 specimens have identifiable modifications for specific (presumed) functions. It can be noted that the vast majority of bulk lithics and specifically modified lithics derive from the surface of the site and downwards to a depth of about 40 cm. The vertical distribution of lithics is not uniform over the site area; for example in the northeastern part of the midden area (unit 5), two separate frequency peaks are noted in levels 2 and 5. The number of lithics in the southwestern part of the midden area (unit 11) is highest in level 3, and the number of lithics in the southeastern part of the midden area (unit 7) is highest in level 2 (fig. 13.1, table 13.4-13.6). This is partly complemented by the fact that the number of identified lithic modification types is very high in level 2 for unit 7, highest in levels 2 and 4 for unit 11, and gradually increases in frequency from level 5 to the surface in unit 5. Within the variety of modification types character-istic of the overall sample, polishing stones, hammerstones and celts are present throughout the vertical distribution of the site, while axes, beads/bead preforms and grinding stones, are concentrated predominantly in the upper levels. Again, however, this vertical distribution of modification types is not paralleled in the horizontal distribution of these objects across the site. For example, unit 7 in the southeastern part of the midden area produced a greater proportion of beads, bead preforms and ornaments than did the other units, while unit 5 in the northeastern part of the midden area produced a far greater proportion of chopping devices, such as adzes and

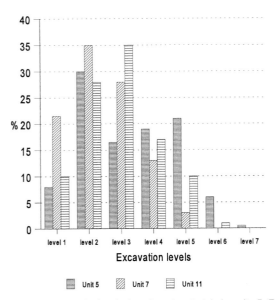

Fig. 13.1. Percentage by level of analyzed materials in units 5, 7 and 11 (unit 5: N=2450; unit 7: N=3284; unit 11: N=800).

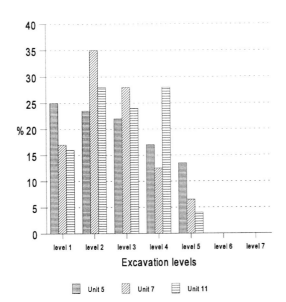

Fig. 13.2. Percentage by level of analyzed tool types in units 5, 7 and 11 (unit 5: N=60; unit 7: N=81; unit 11: N=25).

	1	2	3	4	5	6	7
chert	15	198	79	88	82	12	–
basalt	33	74	30	53	74	21	–
tephrite a	67	114	103	111	102	19	–
tephrite b	44	286	117	172	210	52	3
diorite	24	17	46	19	14	12	3
limestone	3	1	6	3	6	9	1
quartz	3	20	14	4	4	2	1
calcite	–	10	1	2	14	15	–
sandstone	5	7	2	6	1	–	–
pumice	–	–	–	1	–	1	–
haematite	1	–	2	–	–	–	–
jasper	–	2	–	1	1	–	–
calci-rudite	1	–	–	–	–	–	–
lead-pyrite	–	1	1	–	–	–	–
amethyst	–	1	–	–	–	–	–
serpentine	–	2	–	–	–	–	–
jade/nephrite	–	1	–	–	–	–	–
carnelian	–	–	–	–	–	–	–
andesite	–	–	–	–	–	–	–
total	196	734	401	460	508	143	8

Table 13.4. Distribution of lithics in Unit 5.

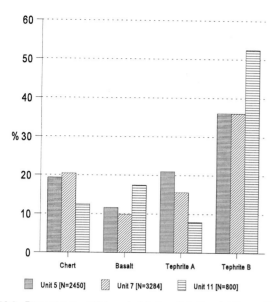

Fig. 13.3. Percentages of lithic materials in unit 5, 7 and 11(note: N represents the total of the unit, not the total of these four lithic materials).

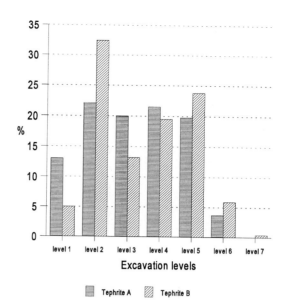

Fig. 13.4. Percentage by level of tephrite in unit 5 (tephrite A: N=516; tephrite B: N=884).

celts.The predominant modification type for all the units (pecking, grinding and polishing stones) is proportionally the most represented in unit 11 in the southwestern sector of the site (fig. 13.2, tables 13.7-13.9).

The general view of the horizontal distribution of the various modified lithics clearly shows that the southeastern part of the midden area, sampled by unit 7, produced the vast majority of beads/bead preforms, axes, and hammerstones, as well as the exclusive evidence of a core among the units used in this comparison. Whereas all of these three units produced polishing stones as the leading modification type, the northeastern part of the midden area, sampled by unit 5, produced the majority of celts, and the southwestern portion of the site, sampled by unit 11, produced the least modified lithics of all. This general versus specific view of the horizontal distribution of lithic tools reflects that there was a focus on ornaments in the southeastern part of the midden area and a distinctive separation in the presence of axes and celts in its southeastern and northeastern portions, respectively. Considering the distribution of the various raw lithic materials, table 13.1 shows that tephrite (A and B), chert/flint and basalt formed the predominant lithic materials used at the site. The tephrites dominate throughout all levels, yet basalts are proportionally more evident in levels 5 to 7, while the cherts are more evident in levels 1 to 4.

In addition, it is important to note that the horizontal distribution of some of these materials over the site area is proportionally variable (fig. 13.3). For the chert material greater proportional evidence is available in the southeastern part of

the midden area within unit 7, levels 1 to 4. The northeastern part of the midden area (unit 5) documents that chert/flint was proportionally dominant in levels 2 to 5. In the southwestern portion of the site (unit 11), chert has its lowest proportional presence but again in levels 2 to 4. With regard to the distribution of basalt, it can be noted that basalt has its greatest proportional presence, in the deepest levels of 4 to 6 in all three units.

For the tephrite distribution first the variability between the two forms of tephrite must be specified. These include tephrite A, which is the limestone portion of this material, and tephrite B, which is the dense, altered volcanic material. It appears that tephrite B was preferred as a usable raw material, with a notable preference in the deeper excavation levels. For example in unit 5, the highest peaks of tephrite B correspond to the two general peaks in the deposit, yet with a preference for tephrite B in its lowermost part and a slight preference for tephrite A in the upper portion (fig. 13.4). In the southwestern sector of the site, a very disproportional preference for tephrite B is represented within unit 11 throughout the excavation; use of tephrite A being restricted in the uppermost levels, with a secondary peak in level 4. Within unit 7 in the southeastern part of the midden area, a proportionally paralleled preference for these two forms of tephrite occurs throughout all of the excavated levels, with a slight preference for tephrite A in levels 2 and 3 (fig. 13.5). Other lithic raw materials included in the overall sample, all iclude lesser quantities. They are nonetheless important in the production of ornaments, notably various local materials

193

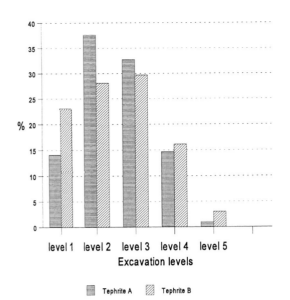

Fig. 13.5. Percentage by level of tephrite in unit 7 (tephrite A: N=511; tephrite B: N=1187).

such as quartz, calcite, haematite, and jasper, as well as exotic (or presumedly exotic) rock materials such as amethyst, carnelian, lead-pyrite, calcirudite, serpentine, and jadeite/nephrite. The most significant information is that the quartz, calcite, amethyst, carnelian, jadeite/nephrite, and serpentine specimens from these excavations were much more common in the southeastern part of the midden area (unit 7), while the calcirudite and lead-pyrite specimens were more better represented in the southwestern portion of the site (unit 11).

The specific characteristics of use shown by the lithic materials seem to be evident (table 13.3). Of the four primary lithic raw materials utilized at the site (tephrite A and B, chert/flint, and basalt), the vast majority of flakes and retouch flakes, indicating lithic reduction at the site, include tephrite B specimens, whereas the vast majority of further modified lithic items belong to the tephrite A category. Basalt follows in the proportional quantity of modified lithic items, with tephrite B ranging third, and chert/flint with the

	1	2	3	4	5
chert	148	239	216	56	11
basalt	70	94	94	48	21
tephrite a	72	192	167	75	5
tephrite b	274	333	353	191	36
diorite	28	19	16	8	12
limestone	3	5	3	1	–
quartz	33	64	17	9	13
calcite	53	155	48	11	5
sandstone	4	3	2	2	–
pumice	1	2	1	2	–
haematite	1	2	–	4	–
jasper	12	25	2	3	–
calci-rudite	–	–	–	–	–
lead-pyrite	1	1	1	1	–
amethyst	–	4	–	–	–
serpentine	–	1	1	1	–
jade/nephrite	–	3	–	–	–
carnelian	–	1	–	–	–
andesite	–	–	1	3	1
total	700	1143	922	415	104

Table 13.5. Distribution of lithics in Unit 7.

194

	1	2	3	4	5	6
chert	9	29	42	17	3	–
basalt	4	39	53	18	25	–
tephrite a	21	22	3	13	4	–
tephrite b	36	114	152	73	43	2
diorite	2	18	11	8	3	2
limestone	–	1	3	–	1	–
quartz	3	1	1	–	–	–
calcite	1	–	2	5	–	–
sandstone	3	–	2	–	–	–
pumice	–	–	–	–	–	–
haematite	–	–	–	–	–	–
jasper	–	1	4	1	–	–
calci-rudite	1	1	1	–	–	–
lead-pyrite	–	–	–	–	–	–
amethyst	–	–	–	1	–	–
serpentine	–	–	–	–	–	–
jade/nephrite	–	–	–	–	–	–
carnelian	–	–	–	–	–	–
andesite	–	–	–	–	–	–
total	80	226	275	136	79	4

Table 13.6. Distribution of lithics in Unit 11.

lowest proportion of further modified lithic items. The proportional evidence for these primary lithic materials indicates that the vast majority of lithics represented by raw material are formed by tephrite A.

The description of the chert/flint material was facilitated by various additional analyses, which were performed exclusively for this material in order to test its physical structure. Thermal alteration was evident on 5.8% of the chert/flint specimens; these items were primarily recovered from the surface downward to level 4. The colour of the chert/flint material ranges from tan (52%), grey (20%), brown (14%), multicoloured but primarily grey/brown (7.6%), other coloured, e.g., white or red (5.8%), and black (0.5%). Both the thermal alteration and colour results for the overall lithic analysis are proportionally similar to the evidence noted in the different units. By observing the stages of cortex removal, it was noted that only 3.8% of the chert specimens were attributable to the primary decortification stage, with 17.2% to the secondary decortification stage, and the major-

ity, 70% to non-decortificated specimens. Of the chert specimens, the majority of the primary decortification specimens came from the surface downward to level 3. However, the horizontal distribution of primary decortification lithics is much better represented among the cherts from the southeastern part of the midden area within unit 7.

For the other lithic materials it can be noted that the majority are represented by raw material specimens, that is, unmodified rocks. Several lithic materials are exclusively represented by either raw material fragments, shatter, and/or exhibit solely grinding modification, with no evidence of chipped reduction at the site. These include quartz, calcite, sandstone, pumice, haematite, lead-pyrite, serpentine, and jadeite/nephrite. Of all these materials, only jasper had retouch flakes evident, while regular flakes were identified for diorite, limestone, jasper, calcirudite, amethyst, carnelian, and andesite.

Modification of these other lithic materials, was in some cases not evident at all, as for the samples of limestone and calcirudite. However, modified calcirudite material was

	1	2	3	4	5	6	7
bead / preform	–	1	2	–	–	–	–
adze	1	–	–	–	–	–	–
celt	3	2	1	1	3	–	–
axe	1	1	1	1	–	–	–
eared-axe	1	–	1	–	–	–	–
pecking stone	–	–	–	–	1	–	–
grinding st.	1	2	–	1	–	–	–
polishing st.	7	5	2	5	1	–	–
hammerstone	14	14	24	13	4	4	–
scraper	–	–	–	–	1	–	–
blade	–	–	2	1	–	–	–
core	–	–	–	–	–	–	–
chopper	–	–	–	–	–	–	–
util. flake	–	2	–	–	–	–	–
total	15	14	13	10	8	–	–

Table 13.7. Distribution of lithic modification types in Unit 5.

found in the surface collections in the form of two ground ornamental "zemi" stones. For the proportion of modified objects among the other, non-primary lithic materials, 2.5% of the diorite specimens appeared to be modified and 0.8% of the quartz, 8.8% of the calcite, 27% of the sandstone, 8.8% of the pumice, 1.5% of the jasper, 57.1% of the amethist, 4% of the haematite, 14% of the lead-pyrite, 21.5% of the serpentine, 100% of the jadeite/nephrite, 50 % of the carnelian, and 4.5% of the other minor materials including andesite.

13.5 Identifiable lithic tool/modification types
The general characteristics of the modified lithics are presented in this section, together with some specific details about individual specimens. The anlysed artefacts include those recovered from the surface and from units 1 and 2.

13.5.1 CHOPPING AND CUTTING INSTRUMENTS
The category of chopping and cutting artefacts consists of adzes, celts, axes, choppers, scrapers, blades, and utilized flakes. These artefacts account for 35.2% of the total number of identifiable lithic tool/modification specimens, with axes predominating.
Of the 66 axes identified in this study, all were bifacially chipped, while 16.6% were characterized by flared proximal corners and consequently have been designated as eared axes.

These eared axes are exclusively made of by tephrite A and average about 6.8 cm in length, 4.9 cm in width and 4.4 cm in thickness. Eared axes were found evenly in all excavation levels, from the surface downward to level 5; and were recovered from the southeastern and northeastern portions of the midden area. The other axes were primarily ovoid to rectangular in shape, with the vast majority of the sample made of tephrite A and a few examples made of tephrite B and basalt. The majority of axes were recovered in the southeastern part of the midden area, with a smaller sample deriving from the northeastern midden area. None were recovered from the southwestern portion of the site. Although they were found in all excavation levels, axes were concentrated from the surface downward to level 4. The axes averaged about 9.1 cm in length, 5.8 cm in width and 4.2 cm in thickness. Celts represent 32.7% of the identified chopping and cutting tools. The celts were primarily produced from tephrite A and to a lesser extent from tephrite B, with a few examples of basalt. The celts are ovoid to petaloid in shape, and although most frequently bifacially chipped, several specimens exhibit complete or partially ground and polished surfaces. The celts average about 6.8 cm in length, 4.9 cm in width and 4.1 cm in thickness. The majority of celts were recovered from the northeastern part of the midden area and to a lesser extent from its southeastern portion; again none were found in the southwestern sector of the site.

	1	2	3	4	5
bead / preform	2	9	2	1	1
adze	–	–	–	–	–
celt	–	1	3	2	–
axe	1	8	3	1	–
eared-axe	–	–	–	–	–
pecking stone	–	1	–	–	–
grinding st.	4	1	–	1	–
polishing st.	4	3	7	2	2
hammerstone	2	4	8	2	1
scraper	–	–	–	–	–
blade	–	–	–	–	–
core	1	–	–	–	–
chopper	–	1	–	1	–
util. flake	–	1	–	–	–
total	14	29	23	10	5

Table 13.8. Distribution of lithic modification types in Unit 7.

	1	2	3	4	5	6
bead / preform	2	–	1	1	–	–
adze	–	–	–	–	–	–
celt	–	–	–	–	–	–
axe	–	–	–	–	–	–
eared-axe	–	–	–	–	–	–
pecking stone	–	–	–	–	–	–
grinding st.	2	–	–	–	–	–
polishing st.	–	5	4	2	1	–
hammerstone	–	1	1	4	–	–
scraper	–	–	–	–	–	–
blade	–	–	–	–	–	–
core	–	–	–	–	–	–
chopper	–	–	–	–	–	–
util. flake	–	1	–	–	–	–
total	4	7	6	7	1	–

Table 13.9. Distribution of lithic modification types in Unit 11.

Choppers represent 6.6% of the identified chopping and cutting artefacts. All of the chopper tools are made of tephrite A and were bifacially chipped, showing heavily battered edges. All of the choppers have a rounded-rectangular shape, measuring an average of about 18 cm in length, 12 cm in width and 7.5 cm in thickness. Choppers were recovered from the southeastern and northeastern portions of the midden area.

Adzes are relatively infrequent in this sample, constituting only 6% of the chopping and cutting tools. All adzes are made of tephrite A show ovoid to rectangular shapes and were manufactured using bifacial chipping. In many cases they have a ground bit bevelled, either intentionally or through use. All of the adzes were recovered from excavation levels 1 to 4 in the northeastern part of the midden area. The adzes average about 7 cm in length, 5 cm in width and 3 cm in thickness.

Scrapers represent 1.8% of this category of artefacts. They are exclusively made of sandstone and siltstone, showing with grinding modification. These few specimens were only found in levels 1, 2, and 5 of the northeastern part of the midden area. Their shape and size vary with the fracturing of the material; they are roughly squared or rectangular flat objects, with at least one edge bifacially ground sharp.

Ten blades have been identified, all made of tephrite A, with the majority found in the northeastern part of the midden area. A few specimens were recovered from the southeastern part of the midden area. In all 70% of the blades were found in excavation levels 3 and 4. The blades average about 5.2 cm in length, 2.5 cm in width and 1.5 cm in thickness. Only 11 utilized flakes were identified, of which nine are chert and two are basalt. They were recovered from excavation levels 1 to 5, occurring in all units at the site. The size and shape of the utilized flakes varies in relationship to the form of the flakes.

13.5.2 PECKING, GRINDING AND POLISHING INSTRUMENTS

For this study, the category of pecking, grinding and polishing artefacts consists of pecking stones, grinding stones, polishing stones, and hammerstones. These items account for 56.6% of the total number of identified lithic tool/modification specimens, with polishing stones predominant.

Polishing stones represent 53.5% of this category of artefacts, albeit the precise identification of most of these stones as being manufactured, rather than naturally altered and then utilized, is not certain. These specimens exhibit totally smoothed surfaces. Less than 25% show actual striations indicative of intentional use. However, due to their presence in this setting, where water-worn stones would not naturally occur, they are at least eoliths. Polishing stones were recovered from the surface downward to level 6 from all units of the site. About 70% of the polishing stones are made of

tephrite B, with the remainder basalt. They average about 3.5 cm in length, 2 cm in width and 2 cm in thickness. Grinding stones represent 15% of this category of artefacts, with the vast majority made of sandstone and a few of basalt. All are fragments of grinding stones, as no complete grinding stone was recovered. One specimen was noted with broad surface grinding on both dorsal and ventral surfaces, but all of the other examples exhibited only dorsal grinding. These were recovered evenly over the area of the site, from the surface downward to level 6, with a greater presence in the upper levels. The size and shape of these specimens vary due to irregular fracturing of the original artefacts. Two fragments of ground haematite were also recovered along with one of ground pumice. These are not grinding stones proper, but, instead, represent stones ground for their usefulness as rasps or to produce red pigment.

Pecking stones are represented by only eight partial specimens, each exhibiting characteristic pecking scars and hertzian cones, localized in the centre of a broad dorsal surface. All of the pecking stones are basalt, with one tephrite B exception, and they have been recovered primarily from the northeastern and southeastern portions of the midden area, from the surface downward to level 6. They average about 15 cm in diameter and about 7 cm in thickness.

Although hammerstones functioned as percussion instruments, they have been included in this category of artefacts. Hammerstones represent 16% of the total number of identified lithic tool/modification specimens, occurring from the surface downward to level 6 in all midden areas of the site. However, they are particularly common in the southeastern part of the midden area. The majority of the hammerstones are made tephrite A, followed closely by a substantial number of basalt specimens, and lesser numbers of tephrite B, chert/flint and jasper pieces. These hammerstones average about 8 cm in length, 6 cm in width and 6 cm in thickness.

13.5.3 UNIQUE OBJECTS

This category of artefacts consists of beads (and bead fragments), bead preforms and other carved or ground/polished objects. These items account for 6.8% of the total number of identified lithic tool/modification specimens, with beads (and bead fragments) predominating.

Beads, bead fragments and bead preforms are represented by four bead preforms, nine bead fragments and nine perforated beads. Two preforms are of diorite, one of carnelian, and one of calcite; three fragments are made of diorite, four fragments of amethyst, one fragment of quartz, and another of calcite. Three of the complete beads are of diorite, two are made of amethyst, two of jadeite/nephrite, two of quartz, one of calcite, and one of carnelian. All of these beads and bead fragments exhibit very fine-polished exterior surfaces with longitudinal perforations, while the preforms are merely roughly ground or finely chipped without perforations. The beads primarily exhibit cylindrical shapes, with some having elongated spherical shapes; they average about 1.5 cm in length, with a 0.8 cm diameter, and a 0.2 cm bore diameter. They have been recovered from the entire area of the site, showing some degree of concentration in the southeastern part of the midden area.

Various other carved and ground/polished objects were recovered. These include five carved and polished, perforated amulets in the form of stylized frogs. These are made of jadeite/nephrite, serpentine and quartz. Two ground, triangular "zemi" stones of calcirudite are also included, along with one ground serpentine disc and one ground, triangular, unidentified object of andesite. These items have not been recovered from a specific areas of the site, yet they seem to be better represented in the southeastern part of the midden area from surface downward to level 6.

13.6   Synthesis and conclusions

A synthesis of the lithic analyses completed thus far is presented below, with only preliminary considerations regarding their correlations within a wider regional framework. A more extensive regional synthesis will be dependent upon further excavations at the site and attendant analyses along with other sites in the region.

Several significant aspects of the manufacture, raw material sources and intra-site distribution of the lithic artefacts at the Hope Estate site have been identified through this analysis. Based on the stages of lithic reduction evident across the various raw materials types, it is quite clear that the primary lithic sources were local to the island. The predominance of tephrite A and B, basalt, diorite, limestone, and other local materials demonstrate this dependence on local materials. This observation is further supported by the fact, that these materials are typically represented by all stages of lithic reduction at the site. The significance of the disproportional relationship between the numerous tephrite A tools, with less evidence of intermediate reduction stages, and the numerous tephrite B specimens reflecting intermediate reduction stages, with less evidence of tools, remains uncertain. A possible suggestion for the latter situation is that the tephrite B tools were transported and discarded elsewhere, while the former situation may be explained by the decomposition of tephrite A, making identification of early reduction stages difficult. The most common non-local lithic material is chert/flint, which exhibits disproportionate quantities of primary, secondary and non-decortification reduction stages. The low percentage of chert/flint primary decortification flakes indicates, that it was collected and initially trimmed at some other location (probably the source). Subsequently, it was transported to Hope Estate and then further reduced to specific tool forms, producing non-decortification debitage.

It is significant to note here, that the primary decortification chert flakes were concentrated in the southeastern part of the midden area, perhaps reflecting use of either a temporally or functionally distinctive character. Whatever the reason, unworked chert/flint is concentrated in this particular portion of the site. A very significant proportion of the exotic materials found at the site are either represented as raw materials or finished objects with little, if any, intermediate stages of reduction. This pertains to 100% of the jadeite/nephrite, 50% of the carnelian, 57% of the amethyst, and 21% of the serpentine pieces, all of which are fully modified items. These data imply that these objects were made elsewhere, and transported as complete forms to the site. With only single flakes of amethyst and carnelian found, these materials may represent minor exceptions to this general situation. Again, the greatest proportion of exotic lithics and ornaments have been recovered from the southeastern part of the midden area, perhaps reflecting some temporal or functional distinctiveness of this area. The somewhat different character of the lithic tools recovered from the southeastern part of the midden area is shown further by its greater proportion of scrapers, hammerstones and axes than characterizing the other midden areas. An apparent concentration of axes in the southeastern part of the midden area and a concentration of celts in the northeastern portion may also relate to temporal and/or functional intra-site distinctions. Temporal distinctiveness is particularly likely given the evidence of two distinctive deposits in the northeastern part of the midden area and the concentration of celts in the upper levels there.

The potential source areas of the relevant local St. Martin lithic raw materials can be identified using the a geological map of the island (fig. 13.6). Volcanic deposits cover much of the higher elevations on St. Martin, with a large outcrop of tephrite A/B material, identical to that found at the site, on the upper elevations of Hope Hill immediately to the east of the site. Diorite and andesite deposits are also represented among these island-wide volcanic deposits interspersed with quartz, jasper, calcite, and possibly pumice and lead-pyrite. Below some of the Eocene deposits shown on the geological map, deposits of the calcirudite conglomerate material may occur, but specific sources have yet to be found. However, the very limited amount of calcirudite material and the presence of only a single reduction flake, combined with the two complete zemi objects, seems to suggest that this material is more likely exotic. Basaltic outcrops on the island are found near the site at Mount France, to the north at Anse Marcel, to the west at Simpson Bay, to the south around Cay Bay and Little Bay, and to the east at Belvedere. Visual observation of the basalt outcrops near the site and those to the north shows that they have the same colour, texture and density as the basalt artefacts from the site. The largest limestone, sandstone and haematite

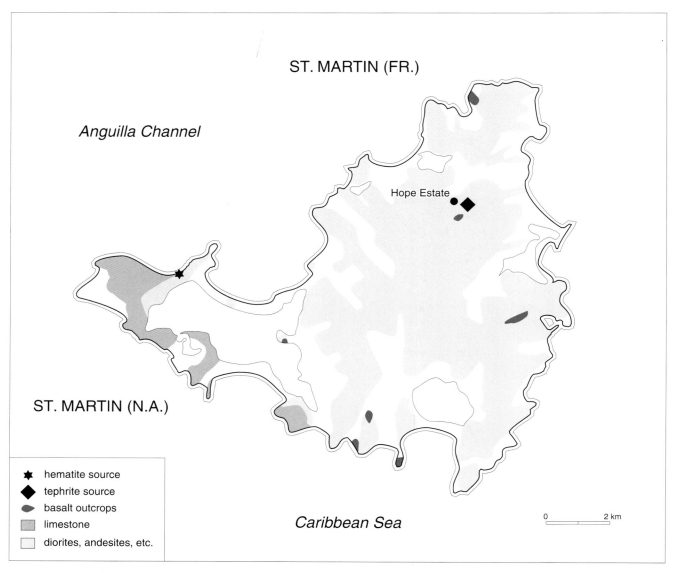

ST. MARTIN (FR.)

Anguilla Channel

Hope Estate

ST. MARTIN (N.A.)

Caribbean Sea

★ hematite source
◆ tephrite source
⬢ basalt outcrops
▨ limestone
☐ diorites, andesites, etc.

0   2 km

Fig. 13.6. Geological map of St. Martin and the potential source areas of lithic raw materials.

source areas on the island are located on the easternmost peninsula of the Lowlands. It is possible that chert outcrops or nodules may occur among these limestone areas, but no local chert sources are known for St. Martin to date. Field inspection of the northeastern area of these limestone deposits at Red Pond on the Lowlands identified a local source of red haematite.

Within the wider Caribbean region, basalt tools, particularly celts, are among the most common lithic objects recovered at prehistoric sites, occurring on almost every island in the region. Thus, identification of basalt is of little help in regional comparisons, unless it is studied at the microscopic level of analysis and island-specific sources can be identified. However, the tephrite identified from St. Martin is a unique and localized lithic source for the Caribbean. Being visually identifiable, artefacts of this material may prove quite useful for future regional studies. Specimens of axes made of tephrite A have already been observed in the archaeological collections from Vieques, Saba, Guadeloupe, Les Saintes while other pieces may be present at Trants on Montserrat (J. Petersen, pers. comm. 1996).

These artefacts considered to be non-local (until new source identifications change this assumption, as may be the case for chert/flint or calcirudite), include chert, calcirudite, jadeite/nephrite, amethyst, serpentine, and carnelian specimens. As noted above, all of these materials, except chert/flint, seem to have been reduced elsewhere and not on the island, or, at least not at the Hope Estate site. The chert/flint sources closest to St. Martin, include Haiti in the Greater Antilles and Antigua in the Lesser Antilles. However, this does not exclude the possibility that chert/flint occurs on other islands, like St. Martin itself, where undiscovered chert sources may occur among the limestone and other deposits. It is worth mentioning that of the wide variety of chert colours reported from Antigua, there is a tan-coloured chert/flint with a dark brown/reddish band just below the cortex (Desmond Nicholson, pers. comm. 1995). Several chert/flint specimens of this same colour have been identified in the Hope Estate sample, suggesting that Antigua was a source, if not the primary source, for the chert/flint material at Hope Estate. Van Tooren identified the presence of discocyclinae and lepidocyclinae fossils of Upper Eocene age in the calcirudite material, which can be considered a packstone. Contrary to what Van Tooren indicates, however, Upper Eocene limestones do occur on St. Martin (as depicted on the geological map of St. Martin by M.J. Goguel); which supports a possible local source for this material. Other potential source areas include Jamaica, Haiti and other islands where Eocene limestones occur.

Van Tooren (appendix in Haviser 1993) notes that jadeite is associated with glaucophane schists which occur on Cuba, Haiti, and the island of Margarita, while nephrite can be found in Jamaica. Both materials are also known from the mainland of South America, notably Brazil. The latter location is consistent with a historical reference by Father Breton in the mid-seventeenth century, that for the Amerindians this material was "one of the most precious jewels received from the men who bring them from the mainland" (Petitjean Roget 1963, 50). An extensive discussion of jadeite/nephrite, and other greenstones has been published by Boomert (1987a). Cody (1991, 593) reports several islands in the Caribbean, where probable jadeite/nephrite prehistoric artefacts have been recovered, including Puerto Rico (Moya 1989), Vieques (Chanlatte Baik 1984), Montserrat (Harrington 1924; Watters and Scaglion 1994), St. Vincent (Bullen and Bullen 1972), St. Kitts (Fewkes 1922), Grenada (Cody 1991), Martinique (Labat 1970), Guadeloupe (Clerc 1970; Hofman et al. this volume), St. Lucia (Haag 1970), St. Croix (Vescelius and Robinson 1979), Trinidad (Fewkes 1922), among others. These finds have been supplemented by others made by the author on Curaçao and Bonaire (Haviser 1991b, 153). The range of evidence for jadeite/nephrite artefacts suggests a South American origin, with a very

widespread distribution over northeastern South America and the Lesser Antilles to Puerto Rico.

Amethyst is known from a smaller number of Caribbean islands. These include St. Martin (Haviser 1991a, 650), Montserrat (Harrington 1924, 124; Watters and Scaglion 1994, 223), Guadeloupe (Hofman et al., this volume), Grenada (Cody 1991, 592), Puerto Rico (Rodriguez 1991a, 611), and Vieques (Chanlatte Baik 1984). The nearest recorded amethyst deposits are in Brazil. However, their growth in mafic lava fissures such as the basalts of Grenada, leaves open the possibility that amethyst may occur naturally on Grenada, as well as on some other islands with similar conditions. Cody (1991) has identified relatively plentiful amethyst from the Pearls site on Grenada, with specimens showing all stages of lithic reduction.

Serpentine is a widespread fibrous mineral in the Caribbean and South America where large outcrops of peridotites occur, which theoretically could include St. Martin. Although probably most often allocated to the general category of "greenstones" in prehistoric collections, serpentine has been rarely specified, except in detailed studies, such as those by Boomert (1987a) for northeastern South America and Wagner and Schubert (1972) for western Venezuela, both regions being source areas for this material. Very few references to the presence of carnelian at prehistoric sites in the Caribbean are available. Carnelian is a red chalcedony, which theoretically can be found where cherts are found, the closest known sources in this case being Haiti and Antigua. The few islands known with sites reported to include carnelian artefacts are Vieques, St. Martin, Montserrat, and Grenada. Furthermore, Watters and Scaglion (1994, 230) indicate that all stages of lithic manufacture for carnelian beads are evident on Montserrat (cf. also Bartone and Crock 1991).

Summarizing, the extensive lithic sample from the excavations at Hope Estate reveals that the inhabitants emphasized immediately available local lithic raw materials, such as altered tephrites and basalts, with sources as close as the adjacent hills. However, they also placed substantial importance on exotic materials, primarily cherts/flints, which were initially reduced at a location other than the site and were brought in as prepared cores. Rare exotics, such as jadeite/nephrite, amethyst, serpentine, carnelian, and calcirudite, seem to have played a key role in the creation of ornaments and sacred objects. These, too, were manufactured elsewhere prior to their importation.

At least two different occupations occur, stratigraphically separated in the northeastern part of the midden area at Hope Estate. The upper deposits in this part of the site produced a concentration of celt tools. Only a single occupation is distinguishable on the basis of the lithics in the remaining part of the Hope Estate site. However, a distinctive horizontal concentration seems to be present in the southeastern part of the midden area on the basis of exotic materials and objects, as well as a concentration of axes. The areal and stratigraphic distinction between axes and celts may be temporally significant. The relative concentration of exotics in the southeastern part of the midden area may be either temporally or functionally significant.

From other studies in the Caribbean, it can be suggested that the inhabitants of the Hope Estate site were one of the very few, early Amerindian populations in the Caribbean, who used exotic lithic materials in substantial numbers. The other comparably early sites in the region include Punta Candelero in Puerto Rico, Sorcé in Vieques, Trants in Montserrat, Morel in Guadeloupe, and Pearls in Grenada. The presence of exotic lithic beads and amulets at these sites, in most cases manufactured elsewhere, may well suggest that these people had extended exchange networks associated with these materials across the region. With the most probable source for several of these exotic materials in South America, such exchange networks, if they existed, may have covered very great distances. It is also possible that the exchange of locally acquired and manufactured lithic items was conducted with equal or greater complexity over shorter distances. The latter suggestion should be an important question to be addressed through future lithic research at the Hope Estate site.

14   Stone tools

Maaike S. de Waal

14.1   Research objectives

At the start of the 1993 excavation campaign the objectives of the lithic tool analysis were defined as follows:

(1) description of the different kinds of stone tools, analysing their function, technology and the raw materials from which they are made;

(2) identification of tools in forms of the different occupation phases at Hope Estate;

(3) classification of the tool categories from the various periods.

As the site appeared to be post-depositionally disturbed, partially by amateur excavations, it became obvious that it would not be easy to assign the stone tools to the site's various habitation periods. The lithic tools themselves were difficult to study due to fragmentation and weathering. Therefore, the objectives of the analysis had to be adjusted. They were limited to a descriptive analysis of the lithic tools, with an emphasis on morphological description. As stone tools have been found in great quantities at Hope Estate, a sample was selected for this purpose. Stone tools from units 3, 4, 7, and 9 were analysed, including a total of 278 stone artefacts. Chert/flint is underrepresented in this sample as not all of this material from these selected units was sent to The Netherlands. The chert/flint flakes were shipped to Curaçao where they have been studied by J. Haviser (cf. chapter 13).

In order to facilitate the systematic description of the lithic tools, a standard form was drawn up. The aim of this form was to record systematically the different categories of lithic tools that are represented in the sample. Seven variables registered, including find number, function, raw material, dimensions (cm), weight (gram), technology of manufacture, and remarks on unusual characteristics. Determination of function and manufacturing technology was made difficult by the above-mentioned fragmentation and weathering of the artefacts. Besides, in most cases the technology of manufacture does not appear to have been very sophisticated. Therefore, it was sometimes difficult to determine whether a lithic specimen represents an implement or not. To simplify this problem, J. Haviser's (1992b, 2) definition of "tool" was employed in this study.

14.2   Categories of stone tools

Seven categories of stone tools have been recognized, i.e., polishing stones, hammerstones, grinding stones, cutting or scraping instruments, drills, axes, and adzes (table 14.1). The categories of axes and adzes are so abundantly represented that a special form was developed to describe these categories in more detail.

14.2.1   POLISHING STONES

Polishing stones are small, smooth pebbles used to smooth and polish pottery surfaces by rubbing them with the stone in order to make the pottery stronger and to give it a brilliant lustre. In all, 79 polishing stones have been identified representing 28.4% of the tool sample. Polishing stones were not worked by man, but were smoothed and polished through use. Therefore, it is often questionable whether these pebbles are tools or not. Although the specimens considered to be polishing stones, were found abundantly at Hope Estate, they do not occur naturally in the site area. The Amerindians must have taken them there from the coast or a nearby streambed where smooth pebbles occur. The use of these stones for polishing pottery is substantiated by the presence of long, parallel striations on some specimens. These may have been caused due to abrasion caused by the pottery surfaces that were being polished (fig. 14.1a). In all 17 polishing stones (21.3%) show this attribute.

Bullen (1973, 114) suggests other functions for pebbles found at archaeological sites. Similar pebbles occurred in great quantities at the Archaic site of Krum Bay, St. Thomas. "They must have been brought there by the Amerindians, but they are far too small to be used as hammerstones. At first, we thought they might be *bola*-stones, but the distribution made clear that this was not the case. They may have been brought to the site by children in imitation of their parents' activities. It is also possible they may have been missiles for slings" (Bullen 1973, 114). The occurrence of polishing use-wear on a considerable number of the Hope Estate pebbles suggests that at least some of them were used as polishing stones. Pebbles of different materials were used as polishing stones. Basalt is the most common material with 53 specimens (67.1%); the remainder are of tephrite, including 26 specimens (32.9%). It is unclear

Unit	3	4	7	9
polishing stones	19	25	13	22
	27.1	24.0	25.0	42.3
hammerstones	4	9	9	3
	5.7	8.7	17.3	5.8
grinding stones	7	6	4	3
	10.0	5.8	7.7	5.8
cut / scrap.stones	6	9	1	-
	8.6	8.7	1.9	-
drills	1	2	-	-
	1.4	1.9	-	-
axes	25	36	16	18
	35.8	34.6	30.8	34.6
adzes	8	17	9	6
	11.4	16.3	17.3	11.5
total	70	104	52	52
	100.0	100.0	100.0	100.0

Table 14.1. Distribution in numbers and percentages of the stone tool categories in Units 3, 4, 7 and 9.

why so many rounded pebbles next to obvious polishing stones were deposited at the site. Most of them are complete and undamaged. Some may have been used only for a short while, leaving them with no obvious wear. It is possible that they were swept onto the midden area, when different activity areas of the site were cleaned.

14.2.2 HAMMERSTONES

Hammerstones are tools that can be used for pounding activities. In all, 25 hammerstones have been identified i.e., 8.9% of the total sample. Hammerstones characteristically exhibit usewear consisting of a concentration of small pits, resulting from hammering activities using one or more sides of the object. Three types of hammering instruments can be distinguished at Hope Estate
The most frequently occurring form is the round ball (fig. 14.1b), of which 13 specimens have been identified. The hammerstones were roughly worked into this form. They became more rounded through use as protruding irregularities would have been broken off in the process. The hammerstones might have been ground even to dull any sharpness on fractured edges, but the weathered state of the pieces prohibits confirmation of this assessment. A second type is formed by four specimens showing a characteristically incomplete, round form (fig. 14.1d). These specimens, were probably manufactured (or produced) in the same way as the round hammerstones, i.e., roughly worked and finished by grinding, with possibility of use modification as well. Finally, one object was apparently selected because it fits

very comfortably in the hand (fig. 14.1c). This tool was at least partially worked into this form by flaking; its surface was intensively smoothed by grinding.
It is quite possible that for single *ad hoc* hammering activities, pieces of rock were used that had not been deliberately shaped into tools. Such specimens are difficult to identify in the archaeological record, as they lack a recognizable form. Besides, weathering may have obscured use-wear. A total of 22 of the recognized hammerstones (88%) are made of tephrite. Three specimens (12%) from units 3 and 7 are of basalt. These materials may have been selected for their toughness and local abundance in the site area. Tephrite also appears to have been easy to flake. Most of the hammerstones found in the refuse do not show any serious damage. Probably, they were not used for long periods of time. Minimal effort was necessary to get or make them and, consequently, they were easily discarded.

14.2.3 GRINDING STONES

Grinding stones can be divided into *metates* and *mados*. *Metates* are stones with flat or concave surfaces that were used as (passive) grinding surfaces or anvils. Specimens chosen for this purpose often seem to have had a naturally rough structure. Grinding was commonly done with the use of an (active) grinding (*mano*). The surface of the metate is smoothed through repeated use, but it can be easily roughened again. An early- historic account reports: "Los indios especialmente muelen en una piedra algo concavada, con otra redonda que en las *manos* traen, a fuerza de brazos,

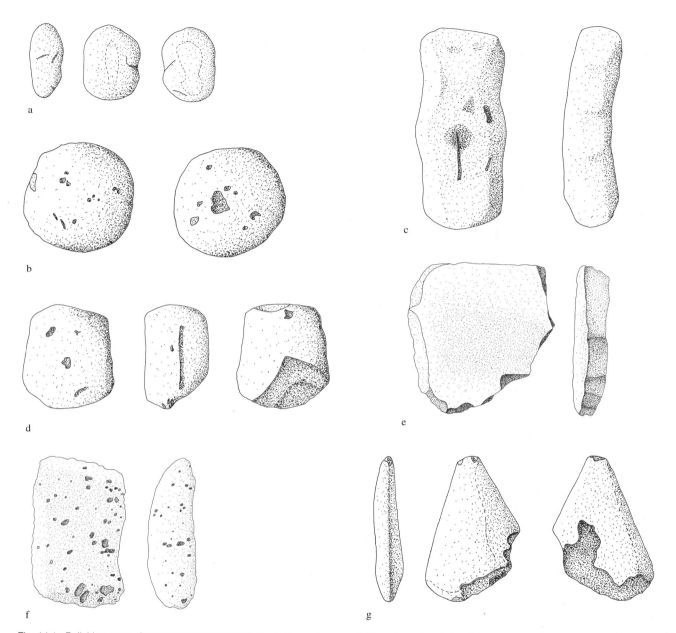

Fig. 14.1. Polishing stone, hammerstones and grinding stones: a. basalt polishing stone showing polishing use wear (scale 1:2), b-c. tephrite hammerstone (scale 1:2), d. tephrite hammerstone with incomplete round form (1:2), e. diorite grinding stone or metate (1:3), f. sandstone grinding stone or manos (1:3), g. pumice grinding stone or manos (scale 1:2).

como suelen los pintores moler las colores" (Oviedo 1979, 94-95). A well-known function of grinding stones is their use in mashing cassava and other vegetable foods. Joyce (1973, 240) states that grinding stones may have been used to prepare fibres and as pigment grinders.

In all 20 grinding implements were identified at Hope Estate (7.2% of the total tool sample), together with 15 *metate* fragments and five *manos*. The *metates* do not show extensive use. They were cut out of sandstone and diorite rocks, selected to provide two grinding surfaces (fig. 14.1e). The grinding ultimately hollowed the used surface. The surfaces of the various examples also reflect to some extent the intensity and/or duration of their use as grinding tools. The Hope Estate grinding stones do not seem to have been

Unit	3	4	7	9
1	1	2	1	1
	3.2	5.0	3.9	4.2
2	1	–	–	–
	3.2	–	–	–
3	1	–	–	–
	3.2	–	–	–
4	–	–	1	–
	–	–	3.9	–
5	1	1	–	2
	3.2	2.5	–	8.3
6	3	3	3	3
	9.7	7.5	11.5	12.5
Prob. 2	6	12	8	3
	19.4	30.0	30.8	12.5
Prob. 4	5	10	4	5
	16.1	25.0	15.4	20.8
Prob. 1 or 3	6	5	5	6
	19.4	12.5	19.1	25.0
Prob. 3 or 4	7	7	4	4
	22.6	17.5	15.4	16.7
total	31	40	26	24
	100.0	100.0	100.0	100.0

Table 14.2. Distribution of axe/adze shapes in Units 3, 4, 7 and 9.

used intensively as the surfaces are not significantly hollowed and worn out. The five *manos* do not exhibit standardized forms (fig. 14.1f, g). They were shaped only roughly to make them fit comfortably in the hand. These specimens are somewhat difficult to recognize as tools, but the varying roughness of their surfaces shows that one or more sides of the artefact was used in grinding. Almost all of the recognized grinding stones show grinding usewear such as striations and smoothed, flattened or concave surfaces.

A total of 11 grinding stones are made of sandstone (55%), five of diorite (25%), two of basalt (10%), one of pumice (5%), and one of tephrite (5%). These materials were selected for their rough surfaces and local occurrence near Hope Estate. Given that the midden area is mainly built from refuse related to food preparation, the relatively small number of grinding stone fragments is surprising. The fact that grinding stones are very durable may explain this: ethnographic examples record that they can be used for more than eighty years, if sharpened every now and then (Prof. dr. L.P. Louwe Kooijmans, pers. comm. 1994). Tools of this kind may have been used again and again and it is not likely that

they would have broken as a result of the grinding activities. In contrast, hammering will readily fracture hammerstones.

14.2.4   CUTTING / SCRAPING TOOLS

The sample of 16 Hope Estate cutting and scraping tools (5.8%) can be divided into three categories: blades, flakes and scrapers. Blades are flakes the length of which is at least twice their width showing generally parallel lateral edges (fig. 14.2a, b). Because of the fact that their length is much larger than their width, it is easy to handle blade tools. It is possible that at least a number of them were hafted, although no evidence of hafting could be found in the present sample.

No usewear was found on the edges of the blades because of weathering. Most likely, they were used for cutting or scraping activities, as in spite of their being corroded they exhibit rather sharp edges. One or two edges of these flakes had been sharpened by removing small flakes and, consequently retouch is visible. Three of these blades, made of tephrite, could be identified.

It is often difficult to distinguish between tools, used flakes and flakes that have not been used, especially in case of relatively durable materials such as chert/flint. Very few of

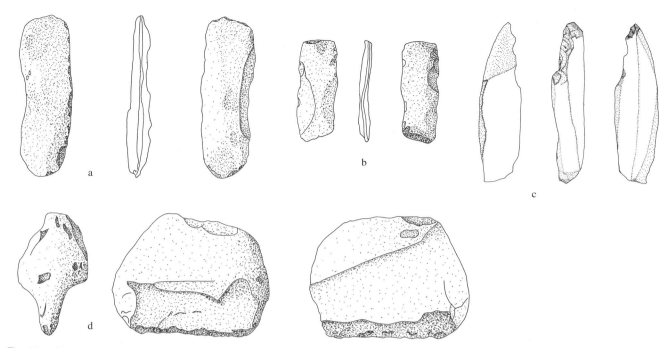

Fig. 14.2. Blades, scraper and drill: a-b. tephrite blades (scale 1:2), c. tephrite scraper (scale 1:2), d. flint drill (scale 1:3).

the flakes and cores were intentionally reworked by secondary retouch into definit recurrent artefact types. Apparently, flakes were used for various tasks in their unmodified state. It is generally thought that all the of chert/flint flakes must have been used because it is a very rare material on the Caribbean islands. Most of the chert/flint found in the West Indies, or at least the northern Lesser Antilles, derives from Long Island near Antigua (Davis 1973, 65-71; Rouse 1992, 65). According to Van der Valk (1987, 1), flint sources occur on St. Martin itself in the Pointe Blanche Formation and, therefore, the material might have been less rare than is commonly believed

Only one scraper was identified in the total tool sample (fig. 14.2d). Its edge is not as sharp as those of the blades. Therefore, it is likely that it was not used for cutting. Its edge is sufficiently sharp to suggest use as a scraper. No usewear was found on it however. It was manufactured using a rounded piece of tephrite. Large flakes struck off both sides created a cutting edge, which was made more regular and durable by the removal of smaller flakes. Cutting tools may have been used for a wide range of activities; e.g., cutting, peeling and grating manioc roots, fish scaling, incising of shells, and cutting (Walker 1985, 239). The seventeenth-century French missionary Breton (1978, 46) described the way the Island Carib grated manioc roots: "Les sauvages se servent de grages qu'ils font avec de petites pierres, qu'ils fichent dans une planche". Ten of

these cutting and scraping tools are made of chert/flint (62.5%), five of tephrite (31.25%) and one of basalt (6.25%). These materials might have been chosen for their nearby availability and for their sharpness when flaked. As they were easy to obtain and shape, they were readily discarded as well. Resharpening by retouch flaking was not necessary as long as the material was widely available and manufacture was rather simple. Most of the cutting and scraping tools were recovered from unit 4; none were found in unit 9.

14.2.5 DRILLS

Three drills were identified in the tool inventory (1.08%), all recovered from units 3 and 4. They all meet the description of drills, provided by Haviser (1992b, 12) (fig. 14.2c). Usewear on drills may be reflected by oblique striations, polish and slight damage to the drill tip. Thusfar no usewear analysis has been carried out for these specimens. The manufacturing technique used to produce the drills is the most elaborate one shown by the Hope Estate lithic sample. They were produced using a flaking technique which was well controlled, i.e., by removing long narrow flakes from a core. A long and thin triangular flake or even a blade was made in this way and subsequently it was worked down by transversal flaking across its long axis. The drills are all of flint. They were probably discarded when they had become dull, broken or exhausted.

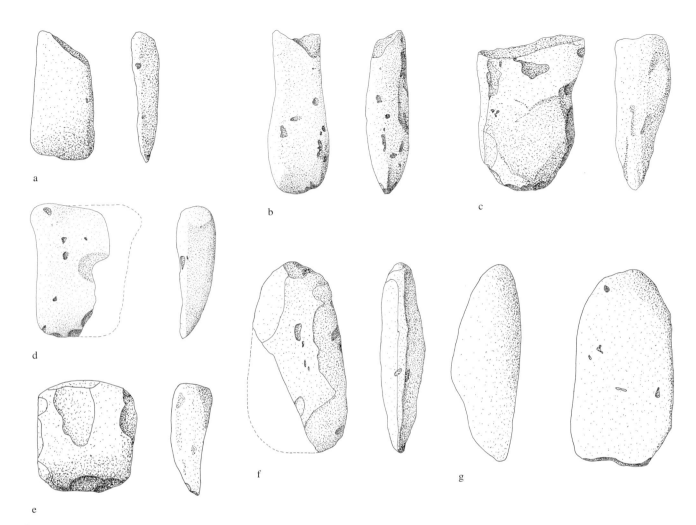

Fig. 14.3. Adzes and axes: a. tephrite adge with square edge and square butt (scale 1:2), b-c. tephrite axes with rounded edges (scale 1:3), d. tephrite eared axe (scale 1:3), e. tephrite axe with a sqare butt (scale 1:2), f. tephrite axe withy a petaloid butt (scale 1:3), g. tephrite axe with a rounded butt (scale 1:2).

Unit	3	4	7	9
1	4 12.9	7 17.5	2 7.7	2 8.3
2	4 12.9	11 27.5	7 26.9	7 29.2
3	15 48.4	16 40.0	13 50.0	13 54.2
4	8 25.8	6 15.0	4 15.4	2 8.3
total	31 100.0	40 100.0	26 100.0	24 100.0

Table 14.3. Distribution of axe/adze finishing stages in Units 3, 4, 7 and 9.

208

Axes and adzes occur in large amounts. All of them are heavily weathered. Almost all of the axes and adzes are oblong in shape, showing two distinct ends. It is possible that some tools had two working ends. No evidence was found for this, since almost all tools are broken at Hope Estate. Different manufacturing techniques are present. Some of the axes/adzes were formed and finished carefully and regularly, whereas other specimens have rough outlines and surfaces The latter may represent different stages in lithic reduction. The functions of these tools are not known exactly and the working ends are not really informative due to weathering. The cutting edges range from not very sharp, via blunt to rounded. In many cases, it was difficult to determine whether the end of a specimen was a butt or a worn-down cutting edge. As the material is very fragmentary, it was impossible distinguish between very rough butt ends and working edges of preforms. Haviser (1992b, 8) defines a preform as "Any piece of lithic material modified to an intended stage of a lithic reduction sequence in a specific assemblage. It must be demonstrable that it is not a finished implement and that it is intended for further modification". To be able to make consistent distinctions, each sharp edge was considered to form a working edge and each blunt or rounded edge a butt end.

The distinction between axes and adzes is based on the cross section: axes have a symmetrical cross section and adzes an asymmetrical one. Haviser (1992b, 12) defines an axe as an implement used for chopping and splitting wood. It is pecked, ground, and/or flaked, and usually it tapers to a point at one end. Use striations may be present on the cutting edge, but due to resharpening and manufacture grinding use striations may not be evident. An adze is defined as an object with an ovoid-triangular outline. The cutting edge is convex, seen from the top and converges with the sides, which taper down to a dull round-pointed poll. Grinding is heavy. The cutting edge of an adze bit shows a skewed or bevelled angle in side view (Haviser 1992b, 11).

A total of 121 of the 135 axes and adzes found have been included in this analysis. The remaining 14 specimens have been deposited in the archaeological museum at St. Martin. The most striking differences among these tools are their morphological distinctions as regards to the forms of the edges and the butt ends. Harris (1983, 258-65) suggests that the various types of Lesser Antillean adzes and axes may reflect different stages of technical and/or stylistic development. His data analysis is based on the selection of 19 butt and 17 blade shapes as primary attributes: "The tentative butt/blade framework seems the result of four major factors: chronology, distribution, culture and function".

14.3   Further analysis of axes and adzes

Eight characteristics of the Hope Estate axes and adzes are described, icluding the shape of the edges, the shape of the butts, general shapes, cross sections, materials used, the dimensions, finishing, secondary use, and morphological groups.

All of the axes and adzes are made of tephrite. The following edge shapes can be distinguished: (1) failing; (2); square (fig. 14.3a); (3) rounded-shaped (fig. 14.3b); (4) petaloid (fig. 14.3c, d); and (5) other, not clear or too fragmentated. The butts are: (1) failing; (2) eared (fig. 14.3e); (3) square (fig. 14.3f); (4) petaloid (fig. 14.3g); (5) rounded-shaped (fig. 14.3h); and (6) other, not clear or too fragmentated. The general shapes of the axes and adzes are (table 14.2): (1) rectangular with square edges and butts; (2) elongated with rounded-shaped edges and butts; (3) elongated with petaloid edges and square butts; (4) elongated with petaloid edges and butts; (5) eared, with eared edges and square butts; and (6) unclassified, not clear or too fragmentated. The axes and adzes are either thick or thin in cross section.

As mentioned above, a difference in shaping and finishing of the tools was noticed. Rough finishing may be a sign of opportunistic, *ad hoc* use of tools, whereas careful finishing suggests be a sign of planned long-term use. The following finishing stages are distinguished: (1) only a rough outline made; (2) the outline of the tool shaped completely, but the surface left unfinished; (3) the tool represents a rather regular specimen showing very few irregularities; and (4) the outline and surface finished completely, ground and/or polished (table 14.3). Secondary use means that when a working end has become blunt and the tool is no longer useful as a chopping implement, it can be still used for other activities, for example, hammering. Joyce (1973, 234) states that "axes are invariably furnished with a curved edge, but that this edge is not always sharp. Some in fact are quite blunt, so they must have fulfilled the function of pounders rather than of axes proper". This also seems to be applicable to some specimens from Hope Estate as well. This secondary use is only visible when it has left use-wear on the former working end. When these traces are not visible and the edge is very blunt and rounded, it has been classified as a probable butt end, indicating that these are probably overly represented in the present sample.

Using the above-mentioned characteristics, 13 groups of stone axes and adzes can be distinguished (table 14.4):

1a.   Adzes with a square edges;
1b.   Axes with square edges;
2.   Axes with rounded shaped edges;

3a. Axes with petaloid edges;
3b. Adzes with petaloid edges;
4.   Eared axes;
5a. Axes with square butts;
5b. Adzes with square butts;
6a. Axes with petaloid butts;
6b. Adzes with petaloid butts;
7a. Axes with rounded shaped butts;
7b. Adzes with rounded shaped butts; and
8.   Unclassified axes/adzes (shape not clear or too much fragmentated)

14.3.1   AXES: TECHNOLOGY AND FUNCTION

In all 95 axes (34.2%) have been identified in the total tool sample.

Technology

Stone axes are manufactured by first chipping them to the approximate size and shape, then pecking in order to reduce the artefacts to nearly final size and shape, and subsequently finishing them by grinding and polishing (Bullen 1973, 110). All of the axes are made of tephrite, which is easy to work and widely available in the site area. Secondary use has been demonstrated in one case.

Function

Undoubtedly, the principal function of axes was the cutting of trees, although other wood-working activities may have been important too. Axes were, important in the construction of houses and in the manufacture of wooden objects such as weapons, canoes, paddles, grater boards (used in the

Unit	3	4	7	9
1a	–	2	–	–
	–	5.0	–	–
1b	1	–	1	1
	3.2	–	3.9	4.2
2	1	–	–	–
	3.2	–	–	–
3a	7	3	3	4
	22.5	7.5	11.5	16.6
3b	1	4	1	1
	3.2	10.0	3.9	4.2
4	1	1	–	2
	3.2	2.5	–	8.3
5a	4	5	3	3
	12.9	12.5	11.5	12.5
5b	2	–	2	3
	6.5	–	7.7	12.5
6a	3	7	4	3
	9.7	17.5	15.4	12.5
6b	2	3	1	1
	6.5	7.5	3.9	4.2
7a	4	8	6	2
	12.9	20.0	23.0	8.3
7b	2	4	2	1
	6.5	10.0	7.7	4.2
8	3	3	3	3
	9.7	7.5	11.5	12.5
total	31	40	26	24
	100.0	100.0	100.0	100.0

Table 14.4. Distribution of the different groups of stone axes and adzes in Units 3, 4, 7 and 9.

processing of manioc roots), figurines and ceremonial objects. Harris (1983, 257) notes that adzes and axes must have been the normal boat-building tools of "coastal" fishermen and travellers. The different forms, dimensions and types of damage shown by axes can provide some ideas of how they were used. For example, for cutting heavy trees to make canoes and houses, which requires lateral action, relatively large, symmetrical axes would have been needed. For the manufacture and finishing of canoes, which demands a somewhat different, vertically directed action, less heavy tools might have been needed, albeit the latter must have been provided with sharp horizontal cutting edges (Barbotin 1973, 143). According to Barbotin (1973, 150), heavy stone axes are seldomly found at settlement sites, but large numbers of axes made out of conch shell (*Strombus gigas*) can be expected. This is not the case at Hope Estate, in spite of its being a habitation site. Large numbers of heavy stone axes have been found at Hope Estate whereas shell axes are less well represented in the available sample.

14.3.2   ADZES: TECHNOLOGY AND FUNCTION
A total number of 40 adzes (14.4%) are represented in the total tool sample.

Technology
The manufacturing technology for adzes is generally the same as that for axes. The tool was first chipped to its approximate size and shape, then pecked to reduce it to its nearly final size and form, and subsequently finished by grinding and polishing. All of the adzes are made of the easily workable and widely available tephrite. One of the adzes shows traces of secondary use.

Function
Adzes, characterised by their asymmetrical cross-section, are described as a form of axe, of which the hafting is not parallel to the edge but perpendicular to it. The distinction between axe and adze is traditionally based on the symmetry or asymmetry of the edge. An adze has a sloping side at the tool edge. Because of this form, an adze offers great precision in wood-working where it can function as a chisel or a gouge. Barbotin (1973, 141) mentions that the splitting and cutting of planks, used to raise the boards of the canoes, would have been done with asymmetric adzes. Another interesting potential function of adzes might have been their use in agricultural work as hoes. However, this function is contradicted by Barbotin (1973, 140), who bases his information on Père Breton (1978). According to Breton, the Island Caribs did not use specially manufactured hoes for cultivating their gardens, but, instead, used a simple, pointed wooden stick. Assuming that this was the case in prehistoric

times as well, there is no reason to believe that axes/adzes were used for agricultural purposes, other than for the clearing of fields (Barbotin 1973, 140).

14.4   Characteristics of Hope Estate axes and adzes
The different morphological groups of axes and adzes are dominated by five categories (table 14.4): (1) axes with rounded-shaped butts (7a; 16.1%); (2) axes with petaloid edges (3a; 14.5%); (3) axes with petaloid butts (6a; 13.8%); (4) axes with square butts (5a; 12.4%); and (5) unclassified axes and unclear or much too fragmentated tools (8; 10.3%). The commonest axe form is the petaloid one. The forms of edges and the butts of axes and adzes are combined in the characteristic shape types (table 14.2). The best represented forms include a probably rounded-shaped edge and a rounded-shaped butt (92; 23.2%), a probably petaloid edge and a petaloid butt (94; 19.3%), a probably square edge and a square butt or a petaloid edge and a square butt (96; 19.0%); and a probably petaloid edge and a square butt or a petaloid edge and a petaloid butt (97; 18.1%). The distribution of the various shapes across the excavation is even, although shape 92 occurs more frequently in units 4 and 7 than it does in units 3 and 9. Cross-section, width, thickness, and weight give information about the artefacts but are insignificant as regards the present typology.

According to Joyce (1973, 233), the surfaces of all Caribbean stone axes and adzes were carefully finished by grinding. However, at Hope Estate, the surfaces of these implements are not very smooth. Unfortunately, due to weathering the original surfaces of the tephrite tools cannot be studied. In most cases it is still possible to determine whether the surfaces was ground or not. Overall, the majority of these tools were not finished very carefully. The most common stage of finishing is stage three (table 14.3): 48.2% of the tools are rather smooth and exhibit very few irregularities.

14.5   Hafting
According to the early historic account of Oviedo, the Taino fixed stone axe blades into wooden shafts for use: "The shaft was cut to the required length and then split at one end; the blade was inserted in the cleft, and a tight 'serving' of cord above and below secured it in its position, and prevented the split from running further down the handle" (Oviedo, cited in Joyce 1973, 234). Rostain (1989, 1), who studied hafted Amazonian axes, stresses that only the stone portions of the generally tools are found: "L'outil démanché n'est rien. Une hache, une herminette sans manche ne peuvent servir selon leur fonction". Rostain's study is interesting in its attempt to better understand axes and adzes in general. Rostain

Unit	3	4	7	9
basalt	12	16	12	19
	17.1	15.4	23.1	36.6
tephrite	48	75	35	31
	68.6	72.1	67.2	59.6
sandstone	3	5	2	1
	4.3	4.8	3.9	1.9
diorite	3	–	2	–
	4.3	–	3.9	–
pumice	–	–	–	1
	–	–	–	1.9
flint	4	8	1	–
	5.7	7.7	1.9	–
total	70	104	52	52
	100.0	100.0	100.0	100.0

Table 14.5. Distribution of lithic marerial in Units 3, 4, 7 and 9.

distinguishes between "direct identification" and "indirect identification". Direct identification of the form of hafting which itself has not been preserved, can be identified from the residues of adhesive materials used to fasten the blade to the shafts. Indirect identification is shown by morphologically primary characteristics, i.e., the shape of the proximal portion or "butt" and the nature of the surface finishing. According to Rostain (1989, 2), a concave section of the proximal portion demonstrates that the blade has been attached only to the shaft, and was not fitted into it. Based on stone tool morphology, Rostain distinguishes between different hafting techniques. Petaloid axes were fastened to wooden shafts with widened tops. The axe blade was inserted into a hole cut out of the thickened part. Eared axes were fastened by tying the 'wings' to the shaft with vegetable fibres. The surface finish occasionally shows the form of hafting of the axe. This applies to secondary characteristics such as damage as well. All of the Hope Estate axes and adzes were examined for primary and secondary characteristics, but unfortunately no such evidence could be found. This was to be expected because of the fragmentary nature of these tools and the weathering of the tephrite tools. Although tools can be different in any geographical area, Rostain's study provides an impression of the original state of the Hope Estate tools.

14.6 Conclusions

The lithic tools recovered from the 1993 excavations at Hope Estate, have been divided into seven categories: polishing stones, hammerstones, grinding stones, cutting/

scraping tools, drills, axes, and adzes. Axes and adzes are abundant and, correspondingly, have been described to some detail.

Units 3 and 4 yielded more lithic tools than units 7 and 9 (table 14.1). In all units the high percentages of polishing stones and axes are striking. Especially in unit 9 the percentage of polishing stones is extremely high (42.3%). Most of the tools were recovered from levels 1, 2, 3 and 4. They are less well represented in level 5 while lithic tools are lacking entirely in levels 6 and 7. Axes occur most frequently in unit 3. Here most of the lithic tools were recovered from level 4. Most of the stone tools of unit 4 were recovered from level 3. The different categories of lithic implements have a rather even distribution across the excavation. However, levels 3-5 yielded the highest amounts of polishing stones next to cutting and scraping tools. Most of the stone tools of unit 7 were found in level 3. Levels 5-7 did not produce any stone tools. Axes occur most frequently in unit 7, polishing stones were especially found in level 3, and hammerstones in level 4. Grinding stones, cutting and scraping stones as well as drills are hardly represented in unit 7. Level 4 of unit 9 produced most of the stone tools. Polishing stones and axes are relatively well represented.

Generally speaking, the analysis of the Hope Estate stone tools has been difficult due to the extensive weathering of some of the lithic raw materials, as well as the fragmentary condition of most specimens. Besides, post-depositional processes and amateur excavations have obliterated the chronology of the site. Therefore, Harris's statement (1983, 258, 265) that "the tentative butt-blade framework seemed the result of four major factors: chronology, distribution, culture and function" cannot be independently assessed here. For instance, it has not been possible to assign the tools to specific periods and, consequently only remarks about their possible functions and manufacturing technology have been made. Emphasis has been given to a morphological description, especially with respect to the axes and adzes. Almost all of them are oblong. It is impossible to say whether the tools had one or two working ends, because almost all of them are broken. The working edges are not really informative. They range from sharp via blunt to rounded. In most cases it is difficult to determine which portion of the tool is the cutting edge and which part represents the tool's end. Consequently, a conservative assessment was necessary: its relatively sharp butt is considered to be the cutting edge. The manufacturing technology of these tools was rather simple. They were chipped to their approximate intended shape and size, subsequently pecked in order to reduce them almost to their final size and shape, and finally finished by grinding and polishing. Rough or incomplete finishing probably results from opportunistic use of materials that were abundantly available in the area of the site. Some of the specimens showing this stage of manufacture may be incomplete cutting or broken preforms. In general, the best represented groups of axes and adzes are those showing petaloid edges, square butts, petaloid butts, rounded-shaped butts, or a combination of these. Tephrite and, to a lesser extent, basalt represent the most frequently used raw materials selected for manufacturing these implements. They occur evenly distributed across all units (table 14.5). Other rock materials have an even distribution across the excavation units as well, with only few differences among the levels.

15 Shell

Richard Jansen

15.1 Introduction

Shellfish was an important part of the diet for the Amerindians at Hope Estate and an important source of material for the manufacture of tools and ornaments. The quantity of shells in the midden at the Hope Estate site is not sufficient to speak of an actual shell midden, but shells constitute an important part of the recovered cultural materials (table 15.1).

15.2 Methods

In excavation units 3 and 4, all sediments were dry sifted through a 10 mm screen. All of the shell material was collected, i.e., shell artefacts as well as the ecofact fragments. From the other units excavated (Units 5-9, 11 and 14) a sample was selected for the study of the shell ecofacts. A 25% sample from all A squares (each unit is divided in four squares: A, B, C and D) was water screened through 10, 4, and 2.7 mm sieves and only from these squares all the shell material was collected. The remaining 75% of the excavation unit was dry sifted through a 10 mm screen and only the artefacts made of shell were collected from the shell material.

The difference between the 10 mm screen and the 2.7 mm screen influences only the smaller species. Some small species were much more abundant in the 2.7 mm screen, but these species form a small part of the total amount of shell material. Fragments in the 2.7 mm screen were often too small to be identified in any case.

15.3 Shell ecofacts

All of the ecofacts were classified according to the different species of shellfish, counted, and weighed by species. Special forms were used for registration of these specimens. The first step was the classification of the material according to shell species. A list of 69 of the most common shellfish species in the Caribbean was used, listing 52 gastropods, 13 bivalves, three *Chiton* species, and one landsnail species (table 15.2).

Cittarium pica (Linné, 1758) outnumbered all the other species in both midden areas and through all levels. Besides *Cittarium pica* a few shells occurred regularly but not in the same quantities as *Cittarium pica*. These species include *Astraea tuber* (Linné, 1758), *Astraea caelata* (Linné, 1758), various *Nerita* species, and *Tectarius muricatus* (Linné, 1758).

Codakia orbicularis (Linné, 1758) and *Chama sarda* (Reeve, 1847) formed the only well represented bivalves species. The shell samples were counted and weighed for each species to get an insight into the food economy. Complete shells and the recognizable individuals were counted in an attempt to calculate MNI's (table 15.3). Shell weights are less useful for this goal (cf. chapters 4 and 9).

	3	4	5	6	8	7	9	14	11	total
A-1	1081,5	1552	784	666,5	487,5	705	1023,1	306,5	86	6692,1
A-2	638,1	1598,5	584,5	832	1600	1159	345,5	784	112	7.653,6
A-3	371,5	954	342,5	702	498	2757,5	865,5	452	122,5	7.065,5
A-4	169,5	717	784	406	1442,5	1549	2769,6	418	146,5	8.402,1
A-5	151,6	446	2087,5	1139	7,5	89	951,5		50	4.922,1
A-6	20,5	22	140,5	2389,5						2.572,5
A-7		2		247						249,0
total	2432,7	5289,5	4725,0	6382,0	4035,5	6259,5	5955,2	1960,5	517,0	37.556,9

Table 15.1. Weight of shell material in grams per layer in all A-squares.

Gastropods individuals were identified by counting the apexes and pelecypods by counting hinges.

15.3.1 CITTARIUM PICA

Cittarium pica, or "West Indian Top Shell", inhabits tide pools and rocky shores, hiding under rocks. The shell is recognizable by its typical pink zig-zag markings. Many complete *Cittarium pica* shells without modifications were recovered from the midden area at Hope Estate (tables 15.4-15.6). These shells are the remains of food processing. However, it is important to note that hermit crabs prefer empty *Cittarium pica* shells and thus transport them sometimes across the area.

Fissurella nodosa	*Thais rustica*	*Fissurella nimbosa*	*Thais deltaoidea*
Acmaea antillarum	*Purpura patula*	*Acmaea pustulata*	*Coralliophyla abbreviata*
Acmaea leucopleura	*Pisania pusio*	*Cittarium pica*	*Pollia aritula*
Tegula excavata	*Colubraria obscura*	*Astraea caleata*	*Latirus angulatus*
Astraea tuber	*Leucozonia nassa*	*Astraea tecta*	*Leucozonia ocellata*
Nerita peloronta	*Oliva reticularis*	*Nerita versicolor*	*Conus mus*
Nerita tessellata	*Bulla striata/umb.*	*Nerita fulgurans*	*Cyphoma gibbosum*
Littorina angustior	*Olivella* sp.	*Nodilittorina tuberculata*	*Columbella mercatoria*
Tectarius muricatus	*Turritella variegata*	*Arca zebra*	*Planaxis nucleus*
Anadara notabilis	*Cerithium litteratum*	*Glycymeris decussata*	*Epitonim lamallosum*
Glycymeris undata	*Hipponix antiquatus*	*Plicatula gibbosa*	*Strombus gigas*
Pecten sp.	*Cypraea cinerea*	*Spondylus americanus*	*Cyprea zebra*
Lucina pensylvanica	*Polonices lacteus*	*Codakia orbicularis*	*Natica canrena*
Chama sarda	*Cassis flammea*	*Pseudochama radians*	*Cypraecassis testiculus*
Pitar albida	*Charonia variegata*	*Mactra fragilus*	*Cymatium nicobaricum*
Cymatium pileare	*Chiton tuberculatis*	*Bursa cubaniana*	*Chiton marmoratus*
Murex donmoorei	*Drymeaus virgulatus*	*Phyllonotus pomum*	*Murex chrysostoma*
Murex bellus			

Table 15.2. List of shell species found at Hope Estate.

	3	4	5	6	8	7	9	14	11	total
A-1	43	58	41	29	28	43	131	6	1	380
A-2	10	30	12	20	32	30	26	21	5	186
A-3	7	32	8	5	3	45	21	10	2	133
A-4	14	19	28	4	28	23	50	8	5	179
A-5	8	6	57	24	1	0	27		2	125
A-6	0	4	5	52						61
A-7			0	5						5
total	82	149	151	139	92	141	250	45	15	1069

Table 15.3. Count of MNI's per layer in all A-squares.

Cittarium pica shells were seldomly used as a material for the manufacturing of tools or ornaments, probably due to the platy structure of the shell.

15.3.2 NERITA SPECIES

Nerites cling to the rocks in the tidal zone. The different species can be distinguished by the number of "teeth" at the

	3	4	5	6	8	7	9	14	11	total
A-1	966	855	570	307	338	222	488	114	68	3928,0
A-2	556	816	184	740	1086	345	191	398	73	4389,0
A-3	301	747	194	531	350	1930	403,5	235	53	4744,5
A-4	83	358	395	115	1350	992	2333	288	69	5983,0
A-5	123	227	1730	878	1	89	757		41	3846,0
A-6	2	0	95	2076						2173,0
A-7			0,5	119						119,5
total	2031,0	3003,0	3168,5	4766,0	3125,0	3578,0	4172,5	1035,0	304,0	25183,0

Table 15.4. Weights of *Cittarium pica* in grams per level.

	3	4	5	6	8	7	9	14	11	total
A-1	4	2	0	0	0	0	0	0	0	6
A-2	3	0	0	0	6	1	0	2	0	12
A-3	0	1	0	2	0	2	1	0	0	6
A-4	2	0	0	0	1	3	3	0	0	9
A-5	0	0	3	1	0	0	1		0	5
A-6	0	0	0	3						3
A-7			0	0						0
total	9	3	3	6	7	6	5	2	0	41

Table 15.5. Count of complete *Cittarium pica* per level.

	3	4	5	6	8	7	9	14	11	total
A-1	17	13	3	8	8	8	7	3	1	68
A-2	5	8	0	12	6	6	5	5	1	48
A-3	3	5	1	1	1	11	3	3	1	29
A-4	1	3	6	1	12	4	22	2	1	52
A-5	2	1	11	3	0	0	12		0	29
A-6	0	0	1	10						11
A-7			0	1						1
total	28	30	22	36	27	29	49	13	4	238

Table 15.6. Count of the MNI's of *Cittarium pica* per level.

mouth of the shells. They are easy to collect, but their small size (a few centimetres at most) makes them an unlikely food source, although, they may have been used to make soup as is still done nowadays. There is also the possibility that they were transported to the site clinging to other shells. The recovery of 91 *Nerita* sp. specimens in 9-A-1 is remarkable,

	3	4	5	6	8	7	9	14	11	total
A-1	7,5	20,5	31	17	19	5	102	0	0	202
A-2	1	9	1	22	13	2	10	1	1	60,0
A-3	1	3	3,5	0	1	0,5	2	0	0	11,0
A-4	0,5	1	0	0	2	0	0	0	1	4,5
A-5	0	0	4,5	1	3	0	0		1	9,5
A-6	0	8,5	0	2						10,5
A-7			0	0						0,0
total	10,0	42	40,0	42,0	38,0	7,5	114,0	1,0	3,0	297,5

Table 15.7. Weights of *Nerita* species in grams per level.

	3	4	5	6	8	7	9	14	11	total
A-1	9	23	21	10	10	5	91	0	0	169
A-2	2	4	2	3	4	2	5	1	0	23
A-3	2	3	2	0	1	1	2	0	0	11
A-4	1	1	0	0	3	0	0	0	0	5
A-5	0	0	5	1	1	0	0		1	8
A-6	0	2	0	2						4
A-7			0	0						0
total	14	33	30	16	19	8	98	1	1	220

Table 15.8. Count of the MNI's of *Nerita* species.

	3	4	5	6	8	7	9	14	11	total
A-1	0	95	126	2	47	225	84	115	11	705
A-2	2	58	52	34	291	278	49	298	0	1062
A-3	32	114	6	113	108	348	192	207	31	1151
A-4	6	141	58	259	17	143	291	75	29	1019
A-5	8	59	201	73	0	0	94		0	435
A-6	8	1	5	51						65
A-7			0	93						93
total	56	468	448	625	463	994	710	695	71	4530

Table 15.9. Weight of *Strombus gigas* in grams per level.

218

given that the quantities in most levels are small (tables 15.7, 15.8).

15.3.3 ASTRAEA SPECIES

The light brown *Astraea* gastropods inhabit the same habitat as *Cittarium pica*. The small quantities found in the midden area may reflect a lesser abundance of this species or a stronger preference for *Cittarium pica*.

15.3.4 STROMBUS GIGAS

Strombus gigas (Linné, 1758) fragments are represented in almost each level at the site but not in quantities large enough that this gastropod can be considered as an important food source (table 15.9). However, it is also possible that the animals were payed out of the shell on the beach, leaving the shells on the spot. Perhaps the shells were too large and too heavy to take all of them to the site. Only the useful part(s) of the shell, mainly the lip, may have been carried inland. This same situation has been suggested for the Golden Rock site on St. Eustatius because of the large quantities of *Strombus gigas* shells at coastal sites (Van der Steen 1992). In both cases the importance of *Strombus gigas* as a food source cannot be determined from the archaeological data.

The *Strombus gigas* shell forms excellent material for the manufacture of tools and ornaments. Parts of *Strombus gigas* shells were obviously carried to the site for manufacturing artefacts and the recovered *Strombus gigas* fragments may represent remnants of the manufacturing processes. The weight table reveals that 53% of the *Strombus gigas* fragments were recovered from the three units in the southeastern part of the site, as opposed to 45% in the five units of the northeastern part.

No complete *Strombus gigas* specimens were recovered, except for three juvenile specimens.

Beds of seagrass in generally shallow water but extending to depths of 60 metres form the habitat of the *Strombus gigas*

lies. Today, it is to be found only far out in the sea as a result of overexploitation. It seems plausible that the Amerindians were able to find *Strombus gigas* shells in shallow waters close to the shore.

15.3.5 REMAINING GASTROPOD SPECIES

The remaining Gastropoda species recovered at Hope Estate are all inhabitants of the rocky tidal zone. The small quantities of these species found point to their incidental collection. Some species were identified just once or twice, while a few were somewhat more common, i.e., *Tectarius muricatus*, *Thais deltaoidea*, and *Oliva reticularis*. All of these are small gastropods, so none of them could have been an important food source.

15.3.6 BIVALVES

Five bivalves species were recovered at the Hope Estate site, all in limited numbers.

Arca zebra (Swainson, 1883) lives attached to rocks under water. A total weight of 244 grams was recovered from all of the subunit A-square samples.

Chama sarda (Reeve, 1847) also lives in rocky areas, close to the shore. The total weight of these in all of the subunit samples was 331 grams, which is relatively high in view of the small size of *Chama sarda*, which suggest that it did not form an important food source.

The weights of *Codakia orbicularis* (Linné, 1758), *Anadara notabilis* (Röding, 1798), and *Mactra fragilus* (Linné, 1758) are so low, that these species were apparently of no importance to the subsistence.

15.3.7 CHITONS

The three *Chiton* species noted on the checklist, all inhabitants of the rocky tidal zone, were rarely recovered from the midden and seem to have been unimportant in the diet.

	3	4	5	6	8	7	9	14	11	total
A-1	11	380	0	229	0,5	0	112	0,5	0	733
A-2	6	568	110	10	0,5	22	0,5	0	0	717
A-3	2	8	35	0	1	13	0,5	0	0	60
A-4	5	2	8	0	0	30	0,5	0	0	46
A-5	1	5	14	0	0	0	0		0	20
A-6	0,5	0	4	1						6
A-7			0,5	0						1
total	26	963	172	240	2	65	114	1	0	1583

Table 15.10. Weight of land snails in grams per level.

15.3.8 LAND SNAILS

Three species of land snails were recovered from the midden area, in some levels in remarkable quantities (table 15.10). These quantities, mainly in the upper levels, indicate that these landsnails were attracted to the midden. Their use as a food supply by the Amerindians seems highly unlikely.

15.4 Subsistence

For all of the subunit samples a proportional distribution was calculated by MNI per level in an attempt to understand better the local food economy (tables 15.11-15.19). However, for the following reasons it is difficult to draw final conclusions as to the contribution of shellfish to subsistence:

1) the problem of determining the portion of shell material, found in the midden area representing remains of shellfish collected for food. For example, 29% of the crab fragments

recovered during the first excavation of 1988 was identified to consist of hermit crabs (Haviser 1988). Thus it is possible that some part of the shell material found its way to the midden as a result of being transported to the site by hermit crabs;
2) the area excavated in 1993 is only a small part of the total excavation area; and
3) the likelihood that *Strombus gigas* is underrepresented in the midden area.

Because of these factors, it is impossible to reconstruct the composition of the exact contribution of the shellfish to the diet.
However, it is possible to calculate the contributions of the various shell species to the overall shellfish diet itself. The proportional distribution of MNI's per level per unit provides a meaningful estimate of the shellfish diet over time.

	A	B	C	D	E	total
level 1	48.8	14.0	20.9	16.3		100.0
level 2	50.0	31.3	12.4		6.3	100.0
level 3	42.8	14.3	28.6	14.3		100.0
level 4	18.7		6.3	56.3	18.7	100.0
level 5	25.0			62.5	12.5	100.0
level 6						
level 7						

Table 15.11. Proportional distribution of the MNI's per level for Unit 3.

	A	B	C	D	E	total
level 1	25.9		39.6	34.5		100.0
level 2	26.7		13.3	46.7	13.3	100.0
level 3	18.7	6.3	9.4	53.1	12.5	100.0
level 4	15.8	21.1	5.3	47.3	10.5	100.0
level 5	16.7			33.3	50.0	100.0
level 6			50.0	25.0	25.0	100.0
level 7						

Table 15.12. Proportional distribution of the MIN's per level for Unit 4.
Legenda for tables 15.12. To 15.19.
A = *Cittarium pica*
B = *Astraea* sp.
C = *Nerita* sp.
D = Gastropoda
E = Bivalves

These MNI counts yield more information than the shell weights because of the difference in average weights of the various shell species.

The vertical distribution shows that shellfish always formed a part of the local subsistence (table 15.1). The choice of species remains consistent through the levels, and conse-quently, the composition of the diet appears not to have changed greatly over time.

The distribution of shell weights is quite variable, each unit has one or more levels with relatively high weights and amounts of shells, but the depths of these levels are so variable that most likely they reflect only situational

	A	B	C	D	E	total
level 1	7.5	2.5	52.5	30.0	7.5	100.0
level 2		8.3	16.7	33.3	41.7	100.0
level 3	12.5	12.5	25.0	50.0		100.0
level 4	20.0	20.0	43.3	16.7		100.0
level 5	24.6	3.5	8.8	63.1		100.0
level 6	20.0	20.0	20.0	40.0		100.0
level 7						

Table 15.13. Proportional disttribution of the MNI's per level for Unit 5.

	A	B	C	D	E	total
layer 1	27.6	3.4	34.5	31.1	3.4	100.0
layer 2	63.2		15.8	21.0		100.0
layer 3	60.0	20.0		20.0		100.0
layer 4	25.0			75.0		100.0
layer 5	16.6	25.0	4.2	54.2		100.0
layer 6	26.5	4.1	4.1	65.3		100.0
layer 7	25.0			75.0		100.0

Table 15.14. Proportional distribution of the MNI's per level for Unit 6.

	A	B	C	D	E	total
layer 1	50.0		31.2	18.8		100.0
layer 2	23.3	6.7	6.7	53.3	10.0	100.0
layer 3	32.5	10.0	2.5	50.0	5.0	100.0
layer 4	30.4	13.1	47.9	8.6		100.0
layer 5						
layer 6						
layer 7						

Table 15.15. Proportional distribution of the MNI's per level for Unit 7.

differences through the midden deposit. Secondly, post-depositional processes are an important factor which may have likely influenced the distribution of the shell materials.

The stratigraphy is too complex to allow really accurate assessment of variations in shellfish use over time. It has been impossible to detect correlations between the alterations in the ceramic and the shellfish distribution throughout the deposit.

Comparing the Hope Estate material with that of the nearby preceramic site of Norman Estate, it is striking that bivalves species are so rarely found at Hope Estate. This seems to

	A	B	C	D	E	total
layer 1	29.6	4.2	36.6	29.6		100.0
layer 2	38.7	6.5	12.9	41.9		100.0
layer 3	33.4		33.3	33.3		100.0
layer 4	52.0	8.0	8.0	28.0	4.0	100.0
layer 5						
layer 6						
layer 7						

Table 15.16. Proportional distribution of the MNI's per level for Unit 8.

	A	B	C	D	E	total
layer 1	5.5	1.6	71.1	20.2	1.6	100.0
layer 2	19.3	15.4	19.2	42.3	3.8	100.0
layer 3	19.1		9.5	47.6	23.8	100.0
layer 4	52.1	8.3		25.0	14.6	100.0
layer 5	46.4	3.6		42.9	7.1	100.0
layer 6						100.0
layer 7						100.0

Table 15.17. Proportional distribution of the MNI's per level for Unit 9.

	A	B	C	D	E	total
layer 1	100.0					100.0
layer 2	20.0			60.0	20.0	100.0
layer 3	50.0			50.0		100.0
layer 4	20.0	60.0		20.0		100.0
layer 5			50.0		50.0	100.0
layer 6						
layer 7						

Table 15.18. Proportional distribution of the MNI's per level for Unit 11.

suggest that between the preceramic and the oldest Ceramic period there was a striking change in this part of the diet.

15.5 Shell artefacts

Shell formed an important raw material for the manufacture of a large number of artefacts at Hope Estate.

Two main categories, or groups of artefacts with a common function, can be distinguished; tools and ornaments. A third category includes specimens which are recognizable as artefacts, but the function of which remains uncertain (table 15.20).

Artefact types can be distinguished on the basis of function. Subtypes have been identified in some cases on the basis of form or the particular shellfish species involved.

Artefacts made of shell are found all across the Caribbean region in all archaeological periods and cultures. Unfortunately, it is difficult to make a typology of shell artefacts, comparable to those of pottery, with time- successive types related to different groups in time and space.

15.5.1 TOOLS

This category consists of artefacts used in daily activities such as house building, agriculture, pottery, and food preparation.

Cypraea zebra scrapers

Nine specimens of this artefact type have been found. They often called "spoons" in the literature. *Cypraea zebra* scrapers are made by cutting the shell along its length axis and removing the inner whorls (fig. 15.1e).

Artefacts of this kind are common in the Caribbean, e.g., on Guadeloupe (Delpuech et al. 1996) and St.Eustatius (Van der Steen 1992, 95). At the Golden Rock site on the latter island in all 81 scrapers or "spoons" made of *Cypraea zebra* (Linné, 1758) were recovered. Traces of use wear suggest that these "spoons" were actually used as scrapers. It has been suggested that they were utilized to scrape some type of soft, probably organic, material, for example, cassava roots (Van der Steen 1992). The scrapers found at Hope

	A	B	C	D	E	total
layer 1	50.0			50.0		100.0
layer 2	41.3		5.8	52.9		100.0
layer 3	25.0	12.5		50.0	12.5	100.0
layer 4	25.0	12.5		62.5		100.0
layer 5						
layer 6						
layer 7						

Table 15.19. Proportional distribution of the MNI's per level for Unit 14.

Category	Type	Subtype
Tools	axes	long axes small triangular axes
	scrapers	*Cypraea zebra* scrapers
	cups	*Cassis* cups
Ornaments	beads	*Oliva* beads *Olivella* beads *Conus* beads *Chama sarda* beads
	Cylindrical beads Pendants	*Oliva* pendants rectangular pendants
	discs	mother-of-pearl
Unidentified	unidentified	*Cyphoma gibbosum* artefacts

Table 15.20. Classification of the shell artefacts from Hope Estate.

Unit	Size	Length	Thickness	Weight
surf.	long	138	18	158
surf.	long	100	14	144
3-B-4	long	–	–	–
4-A-4	long	130	15	155
7-C-3	small	77	11	67
7-D-1	small	65	13	–
7-A-4	small	37	7	–
7-D-4	small	60	10	–
9-D-5	long	119	11	119
10-C-3	long	104	13	135
14-C-2	small	81	11	51

Table 15.21. Short description of the axes. Of 7-A-4 only the upper half is present.

Fig. 15.1. Shell ornaments and artefacts: a. *Oliva* bead (scale 1:1), b. *Olivella* beads (scale 1:1), c. cylindrical beads (scale 1:1), d. *Conus* bead (scale 1:1), e. *Cypraea zebra* scraper (scale 1:1), f-g. rectangular pendants (scale 1:1), h-j. unidentified object (scale 1:1), i-j. unidentified objects (scale 1:2), k. *Strombus gigas* scraper (scale 1:1).

Estate also exhibit traces of use-wear including rounding of the edges.

Axes

These artefacts were made from the lip of a *Strombus gigas* shell. The lip is the thickest portion of the *Strombus gigas* shell. It makes an excellent raw material for all kinds of tools because of the homogeneity of the material. Furthermore, it is easy to collect as well as to shape. This group of artefacts includes 11 specimens (table 15.21). Two represent surface finds and nine were recovered from the midden. Various names can been found in the literature for this artefact type. Names like adzes, celts, chisels and celt-hammers all imply different functions for these artefacts. The name axes has been chosen for the *Strombus gigas* lip artefacts from Hope Estate as this is the most likely use pending on an use-wear investigation. Such an investigation might well separate adzes, celts and chisels.

An axe is a tool for cutting material like wood, and, consequently has a sharp and rounded edge. It is attached to a shaft in such a way that its edge is parallel to the shaft (Van der Steen 1992).

According to size and form the axes of Hope Estate are divided into two subtypes, i.e., long axes and small, triangular axes. Three axes were recovered from the northeastern part of the midden area. Another six axes were recovered from its southeastern part. According to the pottery found, Units 7 and 14 are related to the Huecan Saladoid subseries. Small, triangular axes were recovered from these units (fig. 15.2a-d). These axes are comparable to the La Hueca axes recovered at Vieques (Chanlatte Baik 1984, 38). The larger ones were recovered from the levels related to the Cedrosan Saladoid subseries in the northeastern parts of the midden (fig. 15.2e and f).

15.5.2 CUPS

Two shell "cups" were found at the Hope Estate site. These artefacts are made of a *Cassis* species by cutting out the interior of the shell. The form obtained implies a function as a cup for drinking liquids. One "cup" was recovered from Unit 6, a second one was found at the bottom of a ditch in Unit 12. They are comparable to identical artefacts, the so-called *copas* encountered at Vieques, where they are related to the Huecan (Saladoid) subseries (Chanlatte Baik 1984, 37).

15.5.3 ORNAMENTS

Shell was used as a material for ornaments because of its beauty, colour, and form.

Ethnographic information (Roth 1924) suggests that strings of beads and pendants were used for decoration, representing beauty and wealth for the owner, and the particular rituals.

At the site of Anse á la Gourde, Guadeloupe, for example, more than 1000 beads were found around the pelvis of an inhumated female individual (Delpuech et al. 1996). However, no clear indications have been found suggesting a ritual use for the shell ornaments at Hope Estate. The recovery of 89 beads in one level (level 3 of unit 8) is remarkable, but it is impossible to describe it as a ritual depot, rather than resulting from just the accidental loss of a necklace. This category consists of three ornament types: beads, pendants and discs of which the beads and pendants would have been worn on a string. The (mother-of-pearl) discs may have been worn on a string as well, but the literature suggests, that they were used also as inlays of figurines such as these are known from the Taíno culture (Alegría 1981).

15.5.4 BEADS

A bead is a discoidal or cylindrical object with a central perforation, meant to be threaded on a string (Van der Steen 1992). Four types of beads have been found at the Hope Estate site, all of which are common in the Caribbean region.

Cylindrical beads

Small cylindrical beads form the most common shell artefacts at the Hope Estate site. In all 341 specimens have been recovered (fig. 15.1c). Three forms can be distinguished:
- unperforated cylindrical bead blanks;
- spherical bead blanks; and
- finished beads of which the perforation often shows the form of a "hour glass".

Bead size varies from not more than 1.5 mm in diameter and a few millimetres in thickness to about 5 mm in diameter. Most of the beads have a red or reddish colour which may indicate that they were made of *Chama sarda*. The occurrence of a relatively large number of *Chama sarda* fragments in the midden, possibly representing debris from the fabrication process, supports this hypothesis.

The distribution of the cylindrical beads is striking: 55% were recovered from Units 7, 9, and 14 and 38% were encountered in Units 3, 4, 5, 6, and 8. Considering that the 89 beads found in one level of Unit 8 may from an accidental loss, only 18% of the beads were recovered from the latter group of units.

Oliva reticularis *beads and pendants*

Oliva beads occur in large numbers (fig. 15.1a). *Oliva* beads have been found at various sites all across the Caribbean, e.g., on Union Island (Sutty 1978), in the Virgin Islands (Robinson 1978), on Guadeloupe (Delpuech et al. 1996), Saba (Hoogland 1996), and St. Eustatius (Van der Steen 1992). The olive bead was made by truncating

Fig. 15.2. Shell artefacts of *Strombus gigas* (scale 1:1): a-d. small triangular axes, e-f. large axes, g-h. unidentified objects, possibly drills.

the spires of the apex to some degree. Sometimes the hole was polished. A few of these olive beads exhibit a hole in the apex and one in the body whorl. These modified *Oliva* shells are often referred to in the literature as "pendants" or "tinklers", an artefact made to produce a sound when it is moved.

Robinson (1980) gives two relevant definitions:

– *Oliva* pendant. Olive shell with a single perforation in the body whorl through which a suspension cord can be threaded; and

– *Oliva* bead. Olive shell with a truncated spire forming a hole through which a cord can be threaded over the length of the shell.

Most of the *Oliva* beads in the Hope Estate shell sample have just their spires removed and are provided with a smoothed perforation. One modified *Oliva* shell has only a hole in the body whorl. Following Robinson's definitions, this one would represent a pendant. Four *Oliva* beads show that the apex was removed and simultaneously a hole was made in the body whorl opposite the aperture. As noted above, these artefacts are sometimes called tinklers.

Olivella sp. *beads*
Olivella shells are quite similar to *Oliva* sp., but the former are much smaller (fig. 15.1b). The modification applied is much the same, i.e., the top of the spire was removed and most specimens were left with rough edges.
The 1993 excavation produced 30 *Olivella* beads, scattered over 11 units. During the excavation in 1988, *Olivella* sp. beads represented 50% of the recovered shell artefacts. In all 25 examples were found in one 1 × 1 m unit, which induced Haviser to interpret them as forming a complete necklace (Haviser 1988).

Conus sp. *beads*
Beads of this type are very uncommon at Hope Estate. Only four specimens were found (fig. 15.1.d).

15.5.5   PENDANTS
As noted above, various definitions of pendants have been proposed in the literature:
- a pendant is an object with a hole at its end or edge through which it is threaded on a string, either singly or together with other pendants or beads (Van der Steen 1992, 96); or
- a pendant is a shell with a single perforation in the body whorl through which a cord can be threaded (Robinson 1978, 171).

The definition used here combines the previous ones: a shell pendant is a non-cylindrical object, with one or more perforations through which a cord can be threaded.
Rectangular ornaments with two holes, so-called "plaques", are interpreted here as pendants. Six artefactscan be ascribed to this subtype (fig. 15.1f, g): firstly, three rectangular pendants, "plaques", with oblique sides triangular in cross-section, and two holes. Secondly, a tooth-shaped pendant, thirdly a thin, scratched pendant in the form of a stick, and finally, the upper part of a broken pendant of unknown form.

Mother-of-pearl discs
Fourteen perforated mother-of-pearl fragments have been found in the midden area. Five of them represent very thin, circular discs with a carved pattern on the front and a hole in the middle. Nine other (broken) fragments show different shapes, sometimes being recognizable as artefacts only by their modified holes. The mother-of-pearl discs probable functioned as pendants. Otherwise, the literature suggests additional use as inlays of figurines (Alegría 1981).
Mother-of-pearl is the inner layer of shells. Because of the flatness of the ornaments in question, it is most likely that they were made of oysters.

15.5.6   UNIDENTIFIED ARTEFACTS
This last category includes 31 unidentified artefacts. Human modification of these shells is obvious, but their function(s) is (are) difficult to establish. These artefacts are described according to shell species. Three subtypes of unidentified artefacts are represented by more than one find.

Cyphoma gibbosum *artefacts*
The modification of these shells includes the removal of the reverse side of their body whorls and the subsequent smoothing of the artefacts (fig. 15.1j). No equivalents have been found in shell collections from other sites.

Strombus gigas *artefacts*
This subtype includes five artefacts made of the lip of a *Strombus gigas* conchs not representing axes. Their shape suggest use as scrapers (fig. 15.1k). Artefacts of more or less the same form are known from Barbados (Boomert 1987b), Guadeloupe (Delpuech et al. 1996), and St. Eustatius (Van der Steen 1992). In the latter case they are interpreted as spatulae.

Double-spined Strombus gigas *artefacts*
This subtype includes six specimens, all made of the body whorl of the *Strombus gigas* conch, using its natural shape. Each one is more or less triangular showing two of the conch's spines (fig. 15.1i). References have not been mentioned to this artefact type in the literature, and their function can only be guessed at.

The remaining specimens consists of 13 unique artefacts showing (some) human modification, but providing no further information. Some may represent complete artefacts, others are likely artefact fragments (fig. 15.2g, h). A unique specimen was found in Unit 3-A-1, the shape of which possibly indicates its use as a drill.

15.6   Conclusions
Most of the shellfish species identified represent inhabitants of the tidal zones and rocky shore. Therefore, it is not likely that the Amerindians had to dive for shellfish, but rather they seem to have been satisfied with harvesting in shallow water environments. At the time shellfish populations were relatively untouched, underexploited, and not yet expelled to deeper waters as they are at present. The main conclusion is that most species present in the midden at Hope Estate can be gathered easily. Throughout the habitation of the site species preferences and methods of shellfishing have remained more or less the same.
Cittarium pica was the most important shell species collected for food. The relative abundance of complete *Cittarium pica* shells implies that the entire shell was taken to the

settlement for processing, although they may have been brought in also by hermit crabs which were attracted to the garbage. This and the recovery of complete specimens of smaller shell species support the hypothesis that cooking the animals in their shells in a soup was at least one of the methods of processing.

The shell artefacts recovered at the Hope Estate site distinguish themselves in their amount and diversity. Most artefacts are commonly represented forms in the Caribbean region, except for some unique specimens without reference in the literature.

Based on the study of the ceramics, excavation units 7 and 14 and the lowest levels of units 4 and 5 may be related to the Huecan subseries. The distribution of most shell artefacts is too scattered to draw conclusions regarding cultural affiliations, except for that of the axes.

The other shell artefact types are too small in number and/or too scattered to provide much information. It seems that most of them were in use for a long period of time by the inhabitants of the site, changing little in appearance.

16 Paleoethnobotanical analysis

Lee Newsom and Jantien Molengraaff

16.1 Introduction

Paleoethnobotanical research at the prehistoric Hope Estate site was conducted in conjunction with a multidisciplinary program of archaeological research on the island that was initiated in 1986 (Haviser 1988, 1992a). The plant remains which form the basis of this chapter were recovered in conjunction with two series of field operations at the site. Paleoethnobotanical research was incorporated into the overall research design during the second phase of excavations at Hope Estate. More extensive excavations occurred in January-March 1993. The objectives of the paleoethnobotanical research were centered on two basic themes: to identify and define basic subsistence patterns, including any change that might be detected in the plant-use aspect of subsistence and particularly between differently aged components at the site, and to gather information leading to a more informed understanding of the prehistoric environment when Hope Estate was an active settlement. Related questions involved the interaction of human groups with the natural landscape and the general sustainability of Ceramic Age resource exploitation patterns.

Identified in the course of the excavations at Hope Estate were several distinct deposits of various ages and composition, which together portray different aspects of the settlement pattern. Associated with the Hope Estate 1 or Huecan component at the site is a midden deposit located near the southeastern periphery of the cultural deposits (Haviser 1989). This deposit was originally identified and tested in conjunction with excavation Units XXII T20 and T21 of the 1988 excavations. The deposit subsequently underwent more extensive sampling with the placement of an additional series of 2 × 2 m excavation units during the 1993 work at the site.

Plant remains were recovered and analysed from the Huecan midden area in conjunction with excavation units 7, 9, 14 and XXII T20. Further evidence of a Huecan presence at Hope Estate was verified in deposits located centrally and near the western periphery of the site. The excavation Unit 11, was placed near the western edge of a large central area that appears to have been an occupation surface(s), being largely clear of cultural debris (Hoogland, this volume). This particular excavation unit, which included collection of samples for archaeobotanical analysis, produced a mixture of both Huecan and later Cedrosan Saladoid materials.

A second, relatively extensive midden deposit occurs at the northeastern periphery of the site. This midden is largely contemporaneous with the Cedrosan occupation of Hope Estate judging by the ceramics and associated radiocarbon determinations, but includes also some mixed layers that contain Huecan ceramics (cf. chapter 12). Archaeobotanical samples from a series of excavation units in this northeast midden area are described below. These samples are treated in terms of this analysis as being associated with the Cedrosan occupation at Hope Estate, but the cultural assignment should be viewed with latitude or as being approximate, considering the presence also, however minor, of Huecan materials among these particular midden deposits. Near or at the centre of the site is a large, relatively clear area that has been identified as the primary locus of occupation (cf. chapter 11). This zone of floor deposits and habitation areas was the location of a large macroblock (8 × 13 metres) excavation during the 1993 work, designated unit 12. The macroblock area includes a considerable number of distinctive feature deposits, six of which were sampled and analyzed for archaeobotanical analysis. Five such features are postholes assigned to the Hope Estate 2 or Cedrosan component; the two remaining features, one a large pit and the other of unidentified function, are inferred to be contemporaneous and likewise analyzed as Cedrosan features in the sections below. In the context of investigations that now represent decades of archaeology in the region, Caribbean archaeologists have demonstrated that Native American groups inhabited the Caribbean Islands for several millennia prior to the fateful entry of Europeans into the region. Almost without question, plant foods, medicines, and fuelwood were essential to human survival in the Caribbean, facilitating the successful adaptations of immigrants to the diverse environments of the archipelago. The local vegetation undoubtedly also served as the source of raw materials for building construction, transportation (dugout canoes), weapons, tools, fiber industries, and products such as gums, resins, tannins, dyes, paints, hallucinogens, and fish poisons.

Prior to the 1980s, few primary data had been collected as direct evidence of the plant component of prehistoric economies in the Caribbean.

Much of what was earlier written about prehistoric subsistence and plant use was based on inference and conjecture, derived primarily from ethnohistoric accounts which were, in turn, based upon data acquired from people in various stages of cultural disintegration and change. The extent to which any of the historic observations about plant use and food production can be extended to prehistoric inhabitants of the islands is uncertain.

The previous general reliance in Caribbean archaeology on ethnohistoric information to learn about plant use was due to an overall paucity of archaeobotanical data from the region. Now that these data are being systematically collected from sites such as Hope Estate, we can demonstrate that previous deficiencies in the data base are less a problem of plant preservation, than a reflection of the fact that only recently integrated paleoethnobotanical research has been undertaken in the Caribbean islands. This research has begun to suggest profiles and patterns of plant use on particular islands, as well as on subregional and regional scales (Newsom 1993a; Newsom and Pearsall 1996). The culmination of the data from the series of sites that have undergone paleoethnobotanical investigation is the delineation of a uniquely Caribbean adaptation and pattern of plant use that combined elements shared with mainland areas, for example, manioc cultivation, with native resources and production practices (e.g., *montone* agriculture, terrace systems, etc.) that were developed specifically in response to the Caribbean biological and cultural environment.

The Hope Estate paleoethnobotanical research is an important piece of this emerging profile of Caribbean plant use. The significance and relevance of the Hope Estate archaeobotanical data are placed in perspective with the broader picture of Caribbean adaptations and plant use in the closing sections of this chapter.

This chapter begins with the general bioclimatic setting and an overview of vegetation dynamics on St. Martin, in order to put in better perspective the paleoethnobotanical data presented in later sections.

Following the general floristic summary is a discussion of the field and laboratory procedures used to conduct the research presented here. This is followed by a series of sections outlining the results of analyses, including sample assemblages, summary data, plant identifications, and specific contextual analyses. The discussion and conclusions at the end of the chapter seek to bring all of the data into perspective.

16.2   Floristic background

The extant vegetation on St. Martin is a poor analogue for prehistoric conditions, having been extensively and throughly disturbed by activities associated with European settlement of the island (charcoal production, sugarcane plantations, goat keeping, etc.). At the time of Stoffers'

(1956, 93-101) floristic survey, the vegetation throughout the Dutch portion of the island existed in various stages of secondary and/or fully deflected successions (vegetation so impacted by extended periods of disturbance that the natural vegetation dynamics are permanently altered and succession follows a path apart from natural conditions). The abundant and widespread occurrence of *Acacia* spp. and other thorny plants, while to some extent natural (cf. below), was and is very likely the result of long-term environmental disruption of the island's natural environments. The same conditions and situation ensue for the French portion of the island.

Stoffers (1956, 101) ultimately defined 17 types of vegetation for St. Martin according to three comprehensive bioclimatic classifications: "seasonal formations," including semievergreen, deciduous, and thorn woodlands, among others; "dry evergreen formations," including dry evergreen forest facies, evergreen bushland, and more; and "edaphic communities," including in particular mangrove and strand associations, and manchineel woodland. These three broad vegetation groups follow Beard's (1944, 1949) classification system for the West Indian region.

Beard (1944, 1949), Stoffers (1956), and others have provided very comprehensive and useful syntheses of the regional floristics, including the northern Lesser Antilles in general and St. Martin, in particular.

Nevertheless, considering the unprecedented intensity of disturbance endured by the natural vegetation of this island and others as the result of historic land-use practices, it becomes very difficult to extrapolate to prehistoric conditions based on modern vegetation studies. This being the case, the Holdridge life zone system (Holdridge 1947, 1967) offers the best means by which to attempt to approximate past conditions and vegetation on St. Martin, though still in very generalized terms.

The mean annual biotemperature for St. Martin is approximately 26° Centigrade, while the average total annual rainfall is between approximately 1020 and 1080 millimetres (records spanning 59 years; Stoffers 1956, 78-79).

The combination of these biostatistics, along with the generally low elevations (highest point 400 m) and the position of St. Martin between 18°00' - 18°08' north latitude places the island in the semiarid to sub-humid humidity province of the tropical latitudinal region according to the Holdridge (1947, 1967) system. The dominant vegetation associated with this province and latitude is tropical dry forest.

The vegetation of the neotropical dry forest zone tends to be seasonally semi-deciduous with trees of low to intermediate heights and a double canopy. The upper canopy is relatively low, with trees reaching primarily between 20-25 metres, occasionally to 30 metres tall. The crowns are wide-spreading, often flattopped, and generally not in lateral contact with each other. Trunks tend to be short, stout, and may be strongly buttressed, occasionally armed with conical spines. Leaves tend to be thin and compound in many species, the tree legumes for example, and with very small leaflets. The smaller tree stratum consists of individuals ranging between 10-20 metres tall, mostly with slender crooked or leaning trunks and small, open crowns. Leaves are typically elliptical or rounded, about 4-8 cm long, and evergreen or deciduous. The shrub layer is generally apparent only in cleared areas, often with multiple-stemmed taxa, and likely armed with spines or prickles. Columnar cacti may be present. The ground layer is relatively open; grasses may be abundant in clearings, becoming increasingly common in association with repeated dry-season burnings. Woody vines and epiphytes are common, though the latter tend to be relatively inconspicuous. To come full circle, and to place modern conditions in perspective, the extensive disturbance of St. Martin's natural vegetation has likely resulted in the generally lower tree heights (5-7 metres) recorded by Stoffers (1956); essentially the upper canopy stratum described in the preceding paragraph is missing. There is seemingly also a greater proportion of thorny types, thicker leaves, and grasses. In general, the modern floristic pattern more closely approximates Holdridge's subtropical dry (in this case, degraded) forest zone. Ewel and Whitmore (1973, 10) provide a good summary of this relatively low-stature vegetation: which "… tends to form a complete ground cover and is almost entirely deciduous on moist soils. Palms are usually absent from the canopy, leaves are often small and succulent or coriaceous [leathery in texture; tough], and species with thorns and spines are common. Tree heights usually do not exceed 15 metres and the crowns are typically broad, spreading, and flattened, with sparse foliage. Fire is common on better soils, where the successional vegetation includes many grasses, and large amounts of organic debris accumulate on the soil surface during the dry season… On poorer soils, however, the vegetation is more water-limited and organic debris does not accumulate to the extent that surface fires are possible. Coppicing [the ability to sprout from stumps or stems cut close to the ground surface] is a common means of regeneration of many of the woody species… and successional forests, therefore, often consist of an almost impenetrable maze of tangled, close-growing small stems. Plants here are low in moisture content and the wood of must species is hard and durable."

In terms of the prehistoric landscape and forests on St. Martin, the natural vegetation may be inferred as having existed in dynamic equilibrium, varying under different conditions of rainfall and perhaps also land use approximately between the idealized or projected vegetation of the tropical dry forests outlined using the Holdridge system and

the subtropical dry forms, as outlined by Ewel and Whitmore. The native vegetation that existed prior to European colonization very likely shared characteristics of both forest zones.

16.3 Hope Estate archaeobotany

Well-preserved plant specimens for paleoethnobotanical analysis were collected in conjunction with two separate field seasons at Hope Estate, one in 1988 under the direction of Jay Haviser and Henri Petitjean Roget, and the other in 1993 by Hofman and Hoogland, as mentioned above. The 1988 excavations were of a reconnaissance nature (Haviser 1989), designed to gather basic information leading to a preliminary assessment of the extent, age, and preservation of the cultural deposits. This initial excavation, therefore, did not incorporate special sampling and recovery procedures designed specifically to recover detailed archaeobotanical data. Nevertheless, the project directors recognized during the field work that preserved plant specimens were present and they carefully collected samples of these remains. This first series of archaeobotanical samples from Hope Estate consists of composite assemblages of plant specimens (generally wood remains) deriving from individual midden strata and collected from the general-level excavation screens in 2.8 mm mesh. In 1988-1989 several samples of plant materials from this first field season were summarily examined and two were completely analyzed by Newsom in conjunction with an NSF grant to survey West Indian archaeobotancial remains (Newsom 1993a). This research, conducted at the Florida Museum of Natural History, provided some initial insights into the diversity and extent of plant preservation among the Hope Estate deposits.

Hope Estate archaeobotanical research was formalized during the second field season at the site, with the establishment of systematic recovery and handling procedures designed specifically for archaeobotanical purposes.

Molengraaff oversaw sample collection and processing at the site, carrying out water flotation of some samples, primarily feature fill, using a modified SMAP-type flotation system (Watson 1976) and pumping water from a nearby freshwater pond. Additional samples were collected in the same form as had been done during the earlier excavations, that is, as bulk assemblages of material from the 2.8-mm-mesh-excavation screens, and representative of various individual excavation strata. Archaeobotanical samples were recovered from both major midden deposits and from two locations within the primary habitation zone, including the macroblock unit 12 and the smaller unit 11 near the periphery of this area.

16.3.1 LABORATORY METHODS AND PROCEDURES

The procedures used to process and analyse the screened materials, as well as the light and heavy fractions from the flotation

LOCATION	UNIT	SQUARE/ LEVEL	FEATURE NUMBER	FEATURE DESCRIPTION
Cedrosan deposits:				
NE midden	3	D-3		
NE midden	3	B-7		
NE midden	4	A-4		
NE midden	4	D-4		
NE midden	4	A-6		
NE midden	5	A-2		
NE midden	5	B-2		
NE midden	5	A-3		
NE midden	6	A-2		
NE midden	6	A-4		
NE midden	6	B-5		
NE midden	6	D-5		
NE midden	6	A-6		
NE midden	8	A-2		
NE midden	8	A-3		
NE midden	8	A-4		
NE midden	8	D-4		
NE midden	10	A-2		
NE midden	10	A-3		
NE midden	10	C-3		
NE midden	XVII	A3, level 6		
Macroblock, habitation area	12	south part	64	posthole
Macroblock, habitation area	12	south part	66	posthole
Macroblock, habitation area	12	south part	71	posthole
Macroblock, habitation area	12	south part	74	posthole
Macroblock, habitation area	12	south part	76	unidentified type/function
Macroblock, habitation area	12	south part	88	pit w/ shell, bone, plant, ceramics
HUECAN deposits:				
SE midden	7	A-2		
SE midden	7	A-3		
SE midden	9	A-1		
SE midden	9	C-1		
SE midden	14	A-2		
SE midden	14	A-2	2	soil accumulation layer in midden
SE midden	14	B-2	2	soil accumulation layer in midden
SE midden	14	C-2	2	soil accumulation layer in midden
SE midden	14	D-2	2	soil accumulation layer in midden
SE midden	14	C-3	2	soil accumulation layer in midden
SE midden	14	B-4	2	soil accumulation layer in midden
SE midden	14	D-3	5	yellow soil layer in midden
SE midden	14	C-4	5	yellow soil layer in midden
SE midden	14	B-4	22	dense crab concentration
SE midden	14	A-2	41	dense charcoal, ? hearth
SE midden	14	C-2	41	dense charcoal, ? hearth
SE midden	14	A-2	42	moderately dense crab concentration
SE midden	14	B-2	42	moderately dense crab concentration
SE midden	14	B-3	42	moderately dense crab concentration
SE midden	14	C-3	42	moderately dense crab concentration

LOCATION	UNIT	SQUARE/ LEVEL	FEATURE NUMBER	FEATURE DESCRIPTION
HUECAN deposits:				
SE midden	14	D-2	43	unidentified type/function
SE midden	14	A-3	44	low density crab concentration
SE midden	14	C-2	46	low density crab concentration
SE midden	14	D-2	46	low density crab concentration
SE midden	14	C-3	46	low density crab concentration
SE midden	14	D-3	46	low density crab concentration
SE midden	14	D-2	47	moderately dense crab concentration
SE midden	14	C-3	47	moderately dense crab concentration
SE midden	14	D-3	47	moderately dense crab concentration
SE midden	14	B-3	48	dispersed artefact layer
SE midden	14	B-4	48	dispersed artefact layer
SE midden	14	D-3	49	dense crab concentration
SE midden	XXII	T20, level 3a		
Cedrosan/HUECAN deposits:				
West area	11	A-1		
West area	11	A-2		
West area	11	A-3		
West area	11	A-4		
West area	11	C-4		
West area	11	B-4		
West area	11	D-4		

Table 16.1. Archaeobotanical samples from Hope Estate.

samples were essentially identical, and follow standard archaeobotanical practice. Each sample fraction was weighed, then sieved through graduated mesh sieves with mesh openings of the sizes 4 mm, 2 mm, 1 mm, and 0.42 mm. The individual sample subfractions were subsequently examined under low magnification (10× - 25×) using dissecting microscopes. All identifiable plant remains, including wood greater than 2 mm, were extracted, counted, and weighed.
Seed identifications were made by comparison with modern reference specimens and with the aid of pictorial guides on seed morphology (Delorit 1970; Martin and Barkley 1973). Wood identifications were made on the basis of three-dimensional anatomy, using first a dissecting microscope with enhanced magnification (40× to 125x) to classify specimens by anatomical type. Next individual specimens were further analyzed according to specific anatomical details using a compound microscope and modern reference slides, along with keys to anatomical structure (Record and Hess 1942-1948; Wheeler et al. 1986).
All wood and seed identifications were pursued to the lowest possible taxon. The designation "cf." preceding a given scientific name in the text and tables that follow indicates a very close (or likely), but not definitive match with a particular taxon. Identifications may remain provisional due to an insufficient number of specimens with which to verify important morphological and/or anatomical details and/or problems with preservation (fragmentation, incomplete specimens, burn distortion, etc.).

16.4   Results of analysis

In the sections that follow the plant remains from the various samples and components at Hope Estate are considered and summarized first in broad terms, then by moving progressively into finer scale resolution and with an increasingly refined perspective. To begin, the collective archaeobotanical data are reviewed in general, using summaries and total amounts of material from different contexts. Next the data are considered with an emphasis on broad contrasts between feature deposits, and thus setting the baseline by which to examine possible functional contrasts in plant use. Finally, the data and individual provenances are analyzed with respect to the actual plant identifications, function, and temporal-spatial patterns among the various plant taxa.

UNIT	SQUARE / LEVEL	FEATURE NUMBER	SAMPLE TYPE	SAMPLE VOLUME	WOOD WEIGHT	WOOD DENSITY	SEED TOTAL	SEED DENSITY
3	D-3		screen	–	43.03			
3	B-7		screen	–	9.63			
4	A-4		screen	–	40.92			
4	D-4		screen	–	39.1			
4	A-6		screen	–	2.54			
5	A-2		screen	–	21.22			
5	B-2		screen	–	47.42			
5	A-3		flotation	10	0	0	3	0.3
6	A-2		screen	–	1.89			
6	A-4		screen	–	6.54			
6	B-5		screen	–	2.93			
6	D-5		screen	–	11.67			
6	A-6		screen	–	12.61			
8	A-2		screen	–	15.11			
8	A-3		screen	–	3.13			
8	A-4		screen	–	2.32			
8	D-4		screen	–	13.44			
10	A-2		screen	–	4.8		3	
10	A-3		flotation	10	0.14	0.01	0	0
10	C-3		screen	–	13.18			
XVII	A3, level 6		screen	–	79.98		0	
12	south part	64	flotation	10	0	0	0	0
12	south part	66	flotation	10	0	0	2	0.2
12	south part	71	flotation	10	0	0	0	0
12	south part	74	flotation	10	0	0	1	0.1
12	south part	76	flotation	10	0	0	7	0.7
12	south part	88	flotation	10	4.66	0.46	3	0.3
TOTALS, CEDROSAN:				80	376.26		19	
7	A-2		screen	–	38.16			
7	A-3		flotation	10	0	0	19	1.9
9	A-1		flotation	10	0	0	2	0.2
9	C-1		screen	–	4.58			
14	A-2		flotation	10	0	0	0	0
14	A-2	2	screen	–	4.4			
14	B-2	2	flotation	10	0	0	1	0.1
14	C-2	2	flotation	22	2.13	0.10	2	0.1
14	D-2	2	flotation	10	0	0	1	0.1
14	C-3	2	flotation	10	7.19	0.72	0	0
14	B-4	2	flotation	10	0	0	0	0
14	D-3	5	flotation	10	0	0	1	0.1
14	C-4	5	screen	–	6.52			
14	B-4	22	flotation	8	0	0	0	0
14	A-2	41	flotation	12	3.95	0.33	19	1.6
14	C-2	41	flotation	10	1.95	0.19	10	1.0
14	A-2	42	flotation	7	4.31	0.61	5	0.7
14	B-2	42	flotation	15	20.01	1.33	3	0.2
14	B-3	42	flotation	10	3.64	0.36	0	0
14	C-3	42	flotation	3	0	0	0	0
14	D-2	43	flotation	10	0	0	1	0.1
14	A-3	44	screen	–	0.8			
14	C-2	46	screen	–	3.08			

UNIT	SQUARE / LEVEL	FEATURE NUMBER	SAMPLE TYPE	SAMPLE VOLUME	WOOD WEIGHT	WOOD DENSITY	SEED TOTAL	SEED DENSITY
14	D-2	46	flotation	6	0	0	0	0
14	C-3	46	flotation	10	5.82	0.58	0	0
14	D-3	46	flotation	10	4.52	0.45	0	0
14	D-2	47	flotation	10	0	0	0	0
14	C-3	47	flotation	10	0.08	0.01	0	0
14	D-3	47	flotation	20	6.48	0.32	0	0
14	B-3	48	flotation	12	0		2	0.2
14	B-4	48	flotation	7	0		0	0
14	D-3	49	flotation	10	0		2	0.2
XXII	T20, level 3a		screen	–	4.39		0	
TOTALS, HUECAN:				272	122.01		68	
11	A-1		screen	–	0.74			
11	A-2		screen	–	0.8			
11	A-3		screen	–	0.92			
11	A-4		screen	–	1.04			
11	B-4		flotation	10	1.55	0.15	1	0.1
11	C-4		flotation	10	0	0	0	0
11	D-4		screen	–	2.55			
TOTALS, UNIT 11:				20	7.6		1	
ALL SAMPLES / COMPONENTS:				372	505.87		88	

Table 16.2. Summary of the data for the Hope Estate archaeobotanical samples.

16.4.1   SAMPLE ASSEMBLAGES

All together a total of 67 samples from Hope Estate excavations underwent detailed archaeobotanical analysis. The complete list of samples appears in table 16.1. The full assemblage includes 27 samples from the Hope Estate 2 or Cedrosan Saladoid component which was encountered in the northeastern midden deposit and the macroblock unit 12 occupation surface, 33 samples from the Hope Estate 1 or Huecan component, specifically, the southeastern midden deposit, and an additional 7 samples from Unit 11, which was found to contain a combination of Cedrosan and Huecan materials. The provenance information for each sample appears in table 16.1 according to the respective excavation units and the approximate horizontal (unit quadrants a, b, c, and d) and vertical positions (strata ranging from 1 to 6, cf. Hoogland, this volume). Feature assignments also appear in table 16.1, in the right hand columns.

Individual feature deposits and well-defined living surfaces can be particularly illuminating as to the nature of prehistoric plant use because these deposits often represent specific activity areas and/or isolated dumps of food remains and other refuse. It is sometimes possible to determine the nature or function of individual features/areas along with corresponding patterns within the archaeobotanical taxa. In this way and by careful analysis, specific uses of different plants may be inferred or clarified.

To that end, 17 different features or distinctive areas of the site were sampled separately and analyzed for archaeobotanical data (table 16.1). Among the features examined in conjunction with the Hope Estate 2 or Saladoid component are a series of postholes and a possible posthole (Features 64, 66, 71, 74, and 76), as well as a large pit, Feature 88, that was variously filled with shell, bone, charcoal, and material culture remains. These post and pit features were located in the occupation area of Unit 12.

Eleven features from the southeast midden, specifically, the Huecan deposits, were tested and analyzed for plant remains (table 16.1). These features were all located within excavation Unit 14 and include two distinctive soil accumulation layers (Features 2 and 5), a series of concentrated crab claw deposits and charcoal debris (Features 22, 2, 44, 46, 47, 49), a possible hearth (Feature 41), and a layer of dispersed artefacts (Feature 48). Features will be further discussed below.

16.4.2 SUMMARY DATA

Summary archaeobotanical data for all of the Hope Estate samples, including features as well as general-level deposits, appear in table 16.2. As was aforementioned, the sample assemblage includes two general types of samples that are differentiated according to the means by which the individual samples were processed in the field, that is, by flotation or as a composite collection from the general excavation screens. Thirty one samples derive from the excavation screens, while the balance of 36 samples were recovered as whole samples which subsequently underwent water flotation. The central column in table 16.2 specifies the recovery procedure ("Sample Type") for each of the individual samples.

Flotation samples varied in size, depending on the extent of the individual deposit tested. Thus, flotation sample volumes, shown in the next column of table 16.2, ranged from 3 to 22 litres. Most of the flotation samples were recovered as standard 10-litre samples. A total of 372 litres of sediment (table 16.2, bottom) from various areas of the site underwent flotation, including 80 litres of sample from the Hope Estate 2 or Cedrosan component, 272 litres from the Huecan deposits, and another 20 litres from the Unit 11 area.

The absolute amounts of wood and seed remains recovered from the different deposits tested vary considerably. The right hand columns of table 16.2 report the total quantities of wood remains first by weight and then by density (cf. below), followed by seed data including the actual account for each of the samples, followed again, by density figures. The combined totals for the full sample assemblage appear at the bottom of table 16.2 (505.87 grams wood; 88 seed remains). Subtotals for both categories of plant materials, i.e., wood and seed remains, are provided within table 16.2 for the Cedrosan, Huecan, and mixed-component samples.

The culture-series subtotals reveal some differences between the components examined. These data show that in terms of absolute amounts, greater quantities of wood were recovered in association with the Cedrosan contexts relative to the Huecan contexts (376.26 grams versus ca. 122 grams, table 16.2, subtotals). Conversely, considerably more seed remains (68 as opposed to 19 individual specimens) were recovered from the Huecan relative to the earlier Cedrosan deposits. These are interesting patterns revealed by the plant materials, but they should be considered and interpreted judiciously because the differences among the sample assemblages may be more apparent than real, simply or largely the result of the different sample preparation procedures. To clarify, the flotation samples have a much greater chance to recover small seed remains since the mesh size of the excavation screens very likely produces a bias towards recovery of large-sized materials relative to small seeds and other remains less than 2.8 mm in size. Therefore, flotation-recovered samples (or, alternatively, samples processed

using very fine sieving methods) are the most appropriate by which to assess the differential presence of seed remains. Unfortunately, most of the Cedrosan samples are in fact excavation-screen samples (19 of the 27 samples, or 70%), processed with mesh (2.8 mm) rather coarse for seed recovery. Therefore the amount of seeds recovered with these samples may not be truly representative. The unit 12 post-hole samples (tables 16.1 and 16.2), however, were all processed by flotation and are thus more directly comparable to the Huecan contexts for seed data. The latter, specifically the southeast midden area Units 7, 9, and 14, were primarily flotation samples (nearly 80%; table 16.2). Thus, the seed and wood data from these deposits are very likely more representative or more realistically reflect the different aspects of plant use (fuelwood, plant foods, etc.) to the extent they can be deduced from wood and seed remains. All of this discussion has been simply to point out that the seed data from the Cedrosan contexts, with the exception of the Unit 12 samples (table 16.2), is not directly comparable to the data assembled from the Huecan contexts due to the different recovery methods employed. Therefore, any contrasts and comparisons must be cautiously considered. Likewise, but in mirror image, the greater quantities of wood remains recorded in association with the Cedrosan versus the Huecan contexts may be the result again of sample recovery biases. The excavation-screen samples derive from 2 m square areas versus the smaller areas/volumes sampled by most flotation samples, and so the former necessarily have the potential to include greater quantities of wood remains. This in mind, comparisons between the separate Ceramic Age series may be viewed on the broadest scale only (species presence, etc.) and then still with some care. An additional possible bias with regard to wood remains is discussed below.

Continuing with the general overview of the archaeobotanical samples, for the sake of clarification and in order to focus on specific functional contexts, the archaeobotanical data from table 16.2 relevant to the feature samples are condensed in table 16.3. Most of these contexts were processed by flotation, with the total volumes ranging between 8 and 42 litres of original matrix.

The postholes and Feature 76 (as a possible additional post-hole), all of the Unit 12 macroblock, contained no wood and a paucity of seeds. This suggests that the original posts either rotted in place or were pulled from their original positions; the few seeds that were present may have been situated around the posts and became incorporated in the posthole fill as the posts decayed and/or after their removal. All of the seeds from these contexts belong to a single type (cf. below). The Cedrosan pit feature (Feature 88), in contrast to the contemporaneous posthole contexts, produced 4.66 grams of wood and 3 seeds.

UNIT	SQUARE ./ LEVEL	FEATURE	LAB. PROCESS	TOTAL VOLUME	WOOD WEIGHT	WOOD DENSITY	SEED TOTAL	SEED DENSITY
12	south part	84, posthole	flotation	10	0	0	0	0
12	south part	66, posthole	flotation	10	0	0	2	0.2
12	south part	71, posthole	flotation	10	0	0	0	0
12	south part	74, posthole	flotation	10	0	0	1	0.1
12	south part	76, (uncertain)	flotation	10	0	0	7	0.7
12	south part	88, pit	flotation	10	4.66	0.46	3	0.3
14	level 2	2, soil layer	screen	–	4.4	–	0	–
14	level 2	2, soil layer	flotation	42	2.13	0.05	4	0.1
14	levels 3, 4	2, soil layer	flotation	20	7.19	0.35	0	0
14	level 3	5, yellow soil	flotation	10	0	0	1	0.1
14	level 4	5, yellow soil	screen	–	6.52	–	0	–
14	level 4	22, dense crab	flotation	8	0	0	0	0
14	level 2	41, ? hearth	flotation	22	5.90	0.27	29	1.3
14	level 2	42, ± crab	flotation	22	24.32	1.10	8	0.4
14	level 3	42, ± crab	flotation	13	3.64	0.28	0	0
14	level 2	43, (uncertain)	flotation	10	0	0	1	0.1
14	level 3	44, low crab	screen	–	0.8	–	0	–
14	level 2	46, low crab	screen	–	3.08	–	0	–
14	levels 2,3	46, low crab	flotation	26	10.34	0.40	0	0
14	levels 2,3	47, ± crab	flotation	40	6.56	0.16	0	0
14	levels 3,4	48, artefact layer	flotation	19	0	–	2	0.1
14	level 3	49, dense crab	flotation	10	0	–	2	0.2

Table 16.3. Summary data for the Hope Estate feature contexts.

The wood weight and seed count from the feature convert to density figures of 0.46 grams of wood per litre and 0.3 seeds per litre, respectively (table 16.3). Density data are particularly useful to compare between provenances.

Whereas sample size (volume) partially explains the variability in remains between different contexts, fewer remains being associated with smaller samples and the reverse with regard to larger samples, density data using the standardized measures of wood and seed density (grams per litre and count per litre of sample, respectively) better reveal concentrations and actual differences in sample content. Whether the differences relate to feature function or preservation biases is then the next level of analysis.

Wood and seed density figures, then, are the primary tools used in the sections that follow to compare between the feature deposits from Hope Estate. As such, when comparing down the density columns of table 16.3, it becomes apparent that the relative quantities of plant remains in the pit feature are comparable to some of the other samples. (Note that density data are not appropriate to excavation screen samples and so are not calculated and shown in table 16.3).

Continuing with table 16.3, Features 2 and 5 from the Huecan midden deposits, which are representative of distinctive soil layers, produced wood weights very similar to the Feature 88 pit. Nevertheless, the density data as was just mentioned clarify that the remains in the soil levels were generally more dispersed, but were somewhat concentrated in the deeper levels 3 and 4, where the data more closely approximate Feature 88 (0.35 grams/litre and 0.46 grams/litre, respectively). Seed densities for the soil-layer deposits, however, are somewhat lower than those of the Cedrosan pit feature (ca. 0.1 versus 0.3 seeds/litre).

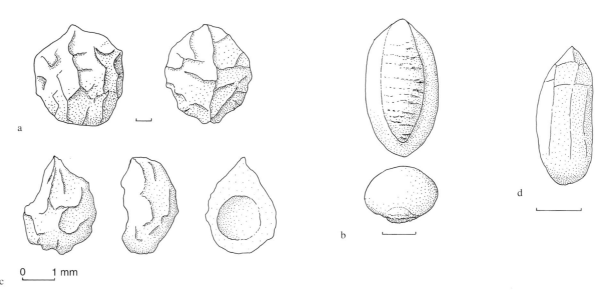

Fig. 16.1. Seed remains from the Hope Estate 1 and 2 components: a. *Celtis* sp., b. Paniceae, c. *Zanthoxylum* sp., d. seednumber 1.

Moving on to the rest of the Unit 14 midden samples (Features 22 through 49 in table 16.3) there are clear contrasts in the summary data between the crab/refuse concentrations, the hearth-like Feature 41, the artefact-layer Feature 48, and Feature 43 (unknown function). The crab/refuse concentrations varied considerably in terms of plant contents: Feature 22 contained no plant remains whatsoever, whereas Feature 42 produced considerable quantities of wood (27.96 grams or 0.80 grams/litre), the most from any deposit analyzed, along with 8 seeds. The sample from the artefact layer, Feature 49, even though nearly 20 litres in volume, produced no wood and only 2 seeds. Finally, the possible hearth, Feature 41, is noteworthy for its exceptional number of seeds (29 specimens, 1.3 seeds/litre) relative to the other contexts analyzed and comparatively moderate quantity of wood. The plant identifications from the feature contexts at Hope Estate are considered in more detail below.

16.4.3   ARCHAEOBOTANICAL IDENTIFICATIONS
The complete list of plant identifications from the Hope Estate excavations appears in table 16.4. At least 12 types of seeds were recovered among the samples, along with 17 distinct wood taxa. The plants identified from seed remains include two taxa, *Celtis* sp. (cockspur)(fig. 16.1.a) and *Mastichodendron foetidissimum* (false mastic), that may have been used for their soft, edible fruits. Two others of the identified seed taxa, panicoid grass (fig. 16.1b) and *Portulaca* sp. (purslane) (table 16.4), may have been important to the prehistoric inhabitants of Hope Estate for their edible grains and/or for the combustible greens, in the case of the latter. Finally, several of the identified taxa

may represent plants that are present among the deposits because of their various potential uses as medicinal plants (cf. Ayensu 1981; Duke 1992; Longuefosse 1995). These plants include a wild member of the bean family (Fabaceae) that compares very strongly with the genus *Crotalaria* sp. (rattlebox), a member of the mallow family (Malvaceae), *Zanthoxylum* sp. (satinwood or wild lime) (fig. 16.1c), Hope Estate seed type 1 (fig. 16.1d), which compares very well with *Verbena* sp. (vervain), and possibly also Hope Estate seed type 2, cf. Anacardiaceae (cashew family, possibly *Comocladia* sp., poison ash, seeds ca. 2 × 2 mm, roughly spherical).

Two additional seed types have been described from the Hope Estate samples. Hope Estate seed type 4 appears to belong to the grass family; this seed type (one specimen) is approximately 3 mm in length by 1.5 mm wide. Hope Estate seed type 5, also recovered as a single specimen, is oblong-cylindric in morphology and about 2 mm long.

Among the wood remains from the Hope Estate samples are at least 17 separate taxa with possible functions or uses ranging from fuelwood to construction elements, including posts, some for medicinal purposes, and more (cf. Record and Hess 1943). Positively identified woods include *Bourreria* sp. (strong bark or strong-back), *Cordia* sp. (Spanish elm), *Guaiacum* sp. (*Lignum vitae*), *Maytenus elliptica* (mayten), *Piscida carthagenesis* (fish poison), and *Zanthoxylum* sp. (wild lime type). Note that the vernacular "*Lignum vitae*" as used here encompasses both species of *Guaiacum* (*G. officinale* and *G. sanctum*) in the Caribbean, the two not being separable to species by wood anatomy alone. An additional wood type was identified as a tree legume belonging to the caesalpiniod anatomical group

238

TAXON	COMMON NAME	POTENTIAL USE*
SEEDS:		
Celtis sp.	cockspur	fresh fruit
Fabaceae, cf. *Crotalaria* sp.	bean family, e.g., rattlebox	medicinal
Malvaceae, *Malva/Sida* sp.	mallow family	medicinal
Mastichodendron foetidissimum	false mastic	fresh fruit
Poaceae, *Panicoid* group	panicoid grass	grain, seed oil
Portulaca sp.	purslane	grain, greens
Zanthoxylum sp.	satinwood, wild lime	medicinal
Hope Estate type 1	cf. *Verbena* sp., vervain	medicinal
Hope Estate type 2	cf. Anacardiaceae, cashew family	medicinal
Hope Estate type 3	small, spherical, rugose	
Hope Estate type 4	cf. Poaceae, grass family	
Hope Estate type 5	oblong, cylindric	
WOOD:		
Bombacaceae, cf. *Ceiba* sp.	cf. Silk cotton	multi-purpose
Bourreria sp.	strong bark, strong-back	fuel
Cordia sp.	Spanish elm	construction
Fabaceae, cf. *Caesalpinia* sp.	bean family, caesalpinoid group	multi-purpose
Guaiacum sp.	*Lignum vitae, guayacan*	fuel, medicine, etc.
Maytenus sp.	mayten	construction
Piscida carthagenesis	fish poison	fuel, medicine, etc.
Sapotaceae	sapodilla family	fuel, construction
Zanthoxylum sp.	wild lime type	medicine, construction
Hope Estate type 2		
Hope Estate type 4	cf. Annonaceae	
Hope Estate type 5		
Hope Estate type 10		
Hope Estate type 11		
Hope Estate type 13		
Hope Estate type 16		
Hope Estate type 19		

Table 16.4. Archaeobotanical identifications from Hope Estate.
* Potential use: based primarily on Ayensu 1981; Duke 1992; Honychurch 1986; Longuefosse 1995; Record and Hess 1943.

(because the legume family is so extensive, individual wood identifications are difficult or impossible to resolve to the levels of genus or species).

And another family-level wood identification is Sapotaceae, the sapodilla or sapote family. The Sapotaceae wood may ultimately be identifiable to genus or anatomical group upon additional analysis.

Eight additional wood taxa from Hope Estate have been classified and described according to anatomical characteristics, but not further identified. Identifications for some of these, for example, wood type 4, which compares strongly with the Annonaceae (the family that includes soursops, guanabana [*Annona* spp.]), but also compares with the spurge (Euphorbiaceae) and sapote families, may be further resolved as more data are collected (with additional excavations and/or more extensive analysis).

Note that original wood types or groups 3, 8, 9, 15, and 17 were canceled as separate or distinct taxa during the course of analysis (that is, they were found to be included variously among the taxa mentioned above, the original apparent differences being resolved and explained by ecological or functional anatomical variation and/or preservation factors [burn distortion, etc.]).

16.4.4   CONTEXTUAL ANALYSES

The distributions and counts of individual seed and wood taxa for each of the Hope Estate samples appear in tables 16.5 and 16.6, respectively. Seed identifications are almost exclusively associated with the flotation samples (cf. tables 16.2 and 16.3). Therefore, table 16.5 includes only flotation samples, with one notation at the bottom of table 16.5 regarding seeds from a single screen sample from the northeast midden Unit 10.

	SQ/ LEVEL	F.	Cocks pur	cf. Rattle box	Mallow fam.	False mastic	Panic. grass	Purs-lane	W. lime	H.E 2	H.E. 1 cf. vervain	H.E. 3*	H.E. 4 cf. grass	H.E. 5	unid. seed	unid. plant	# TAXA
5	A-3		3														1
10	A-3															1	0
12	south	64															0
12	south	66									1				1		1
12	south	71															0
12	south	74									1						1
12	south	76									7					2	1
12	south	88									8						1
7	A-3		19														1
9	A-1		2														1
14	A-2															1	0
14	B-2	2					1									2	1
14	C-2	2									1				1	3	1
14	D-2	2	1													1	1
14	C-3	2															0
14	B-4	2															0
14	D-3	5					1										1
14	B-4	22														1	0
14	A-2	41		3		1	9		2	3			1			3	6
14	C-2	41		2			7		1							5	3
14	A-2	42			1		1		3							1	3
14	B-2	42					2	1								4	2
14	B-3	42														1	0
14	C-3	42															0
14	D-2	43													1		0
14	D-2	46															0
14	C-3	46														1	0
14	D-3	46															0
14	D-2	47															0
14	C-3	47															0
14	D-3	47														1	0
14	B-3	48									1			1			2
14	B-4	48															0
14	D-3	49															0
11	B-4										1					1	1
11	C-4																0
	TOTAL COUNT:		25	5	1	1	21	1	6	3	20	2*	1	1			
	# Contexts present:		4	1	1	1	4	1	2	1	7	–	1	1			

Table 16.5. Counts and distributions of seed remains from flotation samples. *Three seeds were recovered from screen sample 10-A-2, including one specimen of seed type 2 and the only specimens classified as seed type 3.

16.4.5 SEED REMAINS

Beginning with seeds and other non-wood remains, the various taxa are shown across the top of table 16.5, and the individual samples analyzed are listed vertically down the page. At the bottom of table 16.5 the total counts for each seed type is listed, while the column at the right edge of table 16.5 shows the absolute number of taxa recorded for each sample (and collectively, then, for each provenance). As to abundance, cockspur, panicoid grass, and Hope Estate type 1 are the most common seeds types, with totals of 25, 21, and

20 specimens, respectively. Other seed taxa are represented by six or fewer specimens. The number of actual provenances (not total samples, but unique contexts or provenances) in which each of the seed taxa were found to occur, is tabulated below the total counts. Thus, parallelling the frequency data, cockspur, panicoid grass, and seed type 1 are the most common of the seed types, having been recorded from four provenances in the case of the first two, and seven separate contexts for seed type 1. Again, the other seed taxa are much less conspicuous, having been identified from single or only two, in the case of wild lime, contexts.

At this juncture it is useful to point out that cockspur may be disproportionately represented relative to the other seed types because *Celtis* spp. seeds readily mineralize and thus are more prone to long-term preservation in seed banks and archaeological soils (cf. Newsom 1993a). As such, the relative importance of this particular plant food resource cannot be directly assessed against the other seed types and potential foods.

When we examine the individual provenances, it becomes clear that overall seed diversity is quite low, most contexts having two or less seed types present. The northeast midden area (represented by two flotation samples and one screen sample) produced six seeds representative of three taxa: cockspur (3), Hope Estate type 2 (1), and Hope Estate type 3 (2) (table 16.5). Seed diversity is particularly low in conjunction with the occupation surfaces, specifically the unit 12 postholes and pit feature (all Cedrosan) and the unit 11 Cedrosan/Huecan area.

Only one seed type was recovered from these particular provenances, which is Hope Estate type 1, cf. vervain (17 specimens from Unit 12, and one seed from Unit 11). Low diversity might be anticipated for occupation areas swept clean of refuse and other debris. Seed type 1 was also identified from the soil layer designated Feature 2 of unit 14 in the southeastern, Huecan, midden (1 specimen) and in Feature 48 of the same general deposit, again, as a single specimen.

Most of the crab concentrations (Features 22, 42, 46, 47, and 49) were largely devoid of identifiable seed remains. Feature 42, however, a moderate crab concentration, produced 8 seeds including four taxa: mallow family, panic grass, purslane, and wild lime.

Feature 41, the possible hearth, is very distinctive, having produced more seeds and demonstrating greater diversity than any of the other contexts analyzed. Based on two flotation samples (table 16.5), six seed taxa were identified from Feature 41 for a total of 29 individual specimens. Panicoid grass grains are particularly conspicuous (16 specimens). Also recovered in association with this possible hearth or food-preparation context is false mastic, the only provenance from which this plant was identified, wild lime,

cf. rattlebox, Hope Estate type 2 (cf. Anacardiaceae), and the small grass designated Hope Estate type 4 (again, this is the only provenance for this grass). The unique and/or more prominent associations of these plant taxa with the possible hearth Feature 41 is fairly strong contextual information to demonstrate that these plants were in fact used by the prehistoric inhabitants of the site, at least during the Huecan occupation. In contrast, the more broadcast distribution of Hope Estate type 1 and in association with rather homogenous soil layers and general occupation surfaces may be an indication that particular seed type represents nothing more than an intrusive or incidental occurrence at the site (weed seeds that intruded into the site surfaces as part of their natural dispersal in the surrounding area; the carbonisation of type 1 seed specimens may even have occurred in relatively recent times, with the regular burning of the grassy terrain surrounding the site).

Before moving on to discuss the wood data from Hope Estate, two additional non-wood plant specimens from the samples need mention. Among the remains recovered with the Cedrosan midden sample XVII-A3, Level 6 (table 16.2) were two small fragments of parenchymatous tissue. The specimens are too small to have retained vasculature or other anatomical and/or morphological details that would facilitate identification beyond the recognition that they represent soft, starchy plant tissues. It is quite probable that the specimens derive from the subterranean organ(s) of a plant(s), that is, rootstocks or tubers. Thus, the possibility exists that evidence of an additional edible plant resource has been recovered, and which could represent wild and/or cultivated plant foods. The presence in the excavated deposits of artefacts, e.g., ceramic griddle fragments (Haviser 1989; Hofman and Hoogland, this volume), generally associated with edible tubers such as manioc (*Manihot esculenta*) may be interpreted as indirect evidence for some level of reliance on such plants (cf. Newsom 1993a).

16.4.6   WOOD REMAINS

The counts and distributions of Hope Estate wood taxa are recorded in table 16.6. As with table 16.5, the different taxa are listed across the top of the table and the individual samples appear vertically down the left side. The data listed derive from both screen and flotation samples, wood identifications being based on specimens 2-4 mm and larger in transverse section, thus both types of sample are appropriate for analysis andcomparison. Subtotals for the Cedrosan- and Huecan-associated samples follow each sample set and area of the site, and the absolute total counts and relative frequencies of the different woods appear at the bottom of the table. The minimum number of identified specimens (MNI) is shown for each sample in the right column of the table.

UNIT	SQ/L.	F.	SMPL	1 Gua	2	4 Ann	5	6 Sap	7 May	10	11	12 Pisc	13	16	18 Cor	19	20 Bou	21 Cae	22 Zan	23 Cei	MNI
3	D-3		screen	16		11							1			3					48
3	B-7		screen		6		4		13												22
4	A-4		screen	27		4			16												38
4	D-4		screen	32		4	8		7						1						63
4	A-6		screen	6		1	2		16	2											10
5	A-2		screen	15	3	4			1				2								36
5	B-2		screen	55	1				12				1								60
5	A-3		flotat.						2		1										0
6	A-2		screen	2																	2
6	A-4		screen	9																	9
6	B-5		screen	4																	4
6	D-5		screen	8				5													13
6	A-6		screen	13					7												20
8	A-2		screen	12								2									14
8	A-3		screen	5																	5
8	A-4		screen						3						1						4
8	D-4		screen	23					1				1	1							26
10	A-2		screen	9																	9
10	A-3		flotat.	1																	1
10	C-3		screen	8																	8
XVII	A3L6		screen	8								8					4	3	2	1	26
12	south	64	flotat.																		
12	south	66	flotat.																		
12	south	71	flotat.																		
12	south	74	flotat.																		
12	south	76	flotat.																		
12	south	88	flotat.																		
Totals, Cedrosan				253	10	24	19	0	83	2	1	10	5	1	2	3	4	3	2	1	423
7	A-2		sreen	23		3	3		2												31
7	A-3		flotat.																		0
9	A-1		flotat.																		0
9	C-1		screen						1												1
14	A-2		flotat.																		0
14	A-2	2	screen	6																	6
14	B-2	2	flotat.																		0
14	C-2	2	flotat.	3																	3
14	D-2	2	flotat.																		0
14	C-3	2	flotat.	8	1																9
14	B-4	2	flotat.																		0
14	D-3	5	flotat.																		0
14	C-4	5	screen	7	1																7
14	b-4	22	flotat.																		0
14	A-2	41	flotat.	1		1		14													17
14	C-2	41	flotat.	1		1		1	1												4
14	A-2	42	flotat.	4																	4
14	B-2	42	flotat.	28			1														29
14	B-3	42	flotat.	6																	6
14	C-3	42	flotat.																		0
14	D-2	43	flotat.																		0

UNIT	SQ/ L.	F.	SMPL	1 Gua	2	4 Ann	5	6 Sap	7 May	10	11	12 Pisc	13	16	18 Cor	19	20 Bou	21 Cae	22 Zan	23 Cei	MNI
14	A-3	44	screen	1																	1
14	C-2	46	screen	14																	14
14	D-2	46	flotat.																		0
14	C-3	46	flotat.	10					4												14
14	D-3	46	flotat.	9																	9
14	D-2	47	flotat.																		0
14	C-3	47	flotat.	2																	2
14	D-3	47	flotat.	19	2																21
14	B-3	48	flotat.																		0
14	B-3	48	flotat.																		0
14	D-3	49	flotat.																		0
XXII, T20,	v.3a		screen	10																	10
Totals, Huecan				153	4	5	4	15	6	2	0	0	0	0	0	0	0	0	0	0	188
11	A-1		screen	2																	2
11	A-2		screen	2																	3
11	A-3		screen	1							1										1
11	A-4		screen	3																	3
11	B-4		flotat.	4																	4
11	C-4		flotat.																		0
11	D-4		screen	4																	4
Totals, Unit 11				16	0	0	0	0	0	0	1	0	0	0	0	0	0	0	0	0	17
COMBINED SUMMARY				1 Gua	2	4 Ann	5	6 Sap	7 May	10	11	12 Pisc	13	16	18 Cor	19	20 Bou	21 Cae	22 Zan	23 Cei	MNI
Absolute Totals				421	14	29	23	15	89	4	2	10	5	1	2	3	4	3	2	1	628
% of Total Number iden.				67	2	5	4	2	14	>1	>1	1	>1	>1	>1	>1	>1	>1	>1	>1	
Ubiquity				80	12	16	12	4	27	6	4	2	8	2	4	2	2	2	2	2	

Table 16.6. Counts and distributions of wood taxa from flotation and screen samples. Type 1 = *Guaiacum* sp.; Type 4 = Cf. Annonaceae; Type 6 = Sapotaceae; Type 7 = *Maytenus* sp.; Type 12 = *Piscida carth.*; Type 18 = *Cordia* sp.; Type 20 = *Bourreria* sp.; Type 21 = caesalpinoid tree legume; Type 22 = *Zanthoxylum* sp.; Type 23 = cf. *Ceiba* sp.; types 2, 5, 10, 11, 13, 16 and 19 are currently unidentified.

The quantity of wood suitable for identification varied greatly between samples and provenances. Several contexts, for example, the postholes, as mentioned earlier, produced no wood of an identifiable size and/or condition, while others contained considerable quantities of wood charcoal. The samples from the northeast midden Units 3, 4, and 5 contained abundant well-preserved wood remains such that greater than 30-40 specimens (cf. Newsom 1993a) could be identified and/or classified for most provenances (table 16.6, top).

Examining first the individual wood types, *Lignum vitae* (*Guaiacum* sp., or Hope Estate wood type 1) is definitively the most prominent of the wood taxa. This particular wood type dominated both the northeast and southeast midden deposits, and thus both the Cedrosan and Huecan sample assemblages, amounting to 60% of the Cedrosan sample MNI and 81% of the Huecan MNI.

And with the exception of a single specimen of wood type 11, *Lignum vitae* is the only wood type identified among the unit 11 (mixed Cedrosan/Huecan area) samples. Combining the data from the various contexts analyzed, *Lignum vitae* comprised 67% of the full sample assemblage. Not surprisingly, *Lignum vitae* is also the most ubiquitous of the wood types, having been recorded for 80% of the individual provenances (table 16.6, bottom figures for ubiquity, or "percent presence" among the individual sampling contexts).

Of all the other wood taxa from Hope Estate, only mayten (*Maytenus elliptica*, Hope Estate wood 7) approaches the frequencies and ubiquity of *Lignum vitae*. Mayten was identified from 11 Cedrosan samples, including the pit Feature 88, in which it is the exclusive wood type. Mayten was identified from two Huecan contexts (table 16.6). The absolute total for mayten is 89 MNI, comprising 14% of the identified specimens. The ubiquity value for mayten is 27 (27%, or approximately one quarter of the provenances analyzed).

Hope Estate wood type 4, cf. Annonaceae, is next in frequency of occurrence and number identified (29 MNI, 5% frequency; ubiquity = 16, table 16.6). Hope Estate woods 2 and 5 are next in terms of frequency and ubiquity, at 14-15% relative frequency and being documented from 12% of the provenances analyzed (table 16.6, bottom). The remainder of the wood taxa were identified among four or fewer provenances and in relative frequencies of 4% or less of the specimens identified.

Focusing now on the individual excavation units and areas of the site, the Cedrosan midden samples, specifically, the northeast midden area including Units 3 through 10 and unit XVII in table 16.6, show considerable species richness relative to the rest of the samples and areas tested, with 16 individual taxa recognized. The southern portion of this midden in particular (excavation Units 3, 4, and 5, shown at the top of table 16.6) demonstrates comparatively great species diversity, including 10 of the 16 taxa recorded from the northeast midden deposits. Comparing the number of specimens identified between the first units listed (units 3 through 5: 277 MNI) and the rest of the sample assemblage (units 6, 8 and 10: 115 MNI) shows that overall much greater quantities of identifiable wood were recovered from the area of Units 3, 4, and 5. That this particular area of the site produced greater quantities of wood and appears so species rich compared to other areas analyzed, at least the rest of the northeast midden area (Units 6, 8 and 10), is probably accurate since the samples from this entire midden, thus all excavation units, underwent the same handling and recovery procedures (primarily excavation screen samples; table 16.6). It is possible that the observed differences in the amount of wood between the northern and southern sectors of the Cedrosan midden result at least partly from preservation biases (perhaps longer hotter fires in the northern units,

therefore differential destruction of woods resulted in fewer remains and types overall in the northern area). But it is more likely that the differences have something to do with specific activity areas. For example, perhaps food preparation and cooking (?) occurred in proximity of the more southerly midden deposit, this portion of the midden being situated close to the core occupation area (Unit 12 occupation surface), and/or being closer, this portion of the midden tended to collect more refuse and debris from nearby hearth deposits.

Wood data from the Huecan midden are similar to the Cedrosan Saladoid wood assemblage in that *Lignum vitae* and mayten are the two most conspicuous taxa. The numbers of specimens present (188 MNI) and overall diversity of taxa (7 wood types) compares more closely with the northern part of the Cedrosan midden, in which wood remains are less abundant. Beyond these observations it is not possible to compare between the Cedrosan and Huecan midden samples because most of the samples from the southeast (Huecan) midden (excavation Units 7-14) were processed by means of water flotation, as is indicated in table 16.6. Subjecting carbonised wood to water shock can sometimes result in excessive fragmentation and lower frequencies of recovered specimens (cf. Newsom 1993a and 1997 for more detail). Thus the differences in frequencies and types of wood taxa may be at least partially explained by differential sample treatment (flotation versus sieved samples), hence, sampling and handling bias.

Having mentioned this, however, there does seem to be a real difference in terms of species richness between the Cedrosan and slightly later Huecan wood assemblages. The Sapotaceae wood (Hope Estate type 6) was identified exclusively from the Huecan midden, specifically, the possible hearth Feature 41. Conversely, Hope Estate woods 11-23 were documented only from the Cedrosan northeast midden deposits.

16.5   Discussion

Plant remains were recovered from the Hope Estate deposits in conjunction with two excavation seasons at the site. Though the data are limited, the archaeobotanical analyses nevertheless provide basic information to begin to address questions centered on the prehistoric occupation and settlement dynamics. Providing insights into the vegetation during the course of occupation and initiating an understanding of human behaviours related to the plant-use aspect of subsistence are central to this research. That two distinct cultural components, Huecan and Cedrosan, have been verified at the site, along with details of the layout and positioning of the various deposits, are particularly useful to examine plant- and land-use in dynamic perspective.

The current vegetation of St. Martin is, as was indicated earlier, a poor analogue for the floristics associated with the archaeological settlement of the late first millennium BC and early centuries AD. This being the case, the Holdridge life zone system was discussed at the beginning of this chapter to frame a model or approximation of the vegetation that may have characterized the island during the early Ceramic Age when Hope Estate was inhabited. The projected vegetation based on parameters set by the Holdridge system is tropical dry forest, in its various formations.

Eleven plant taxa from among the archaeobotanical samples were identified to genus or species, and at least six other archaeological types were assigned to families and/or possible genera, or tribe, in the case of the Panicoid grass (table 16.2). Viewing these taxa collectively, it is possible to compare the species list to descriptions of major dry forest types. Particularly relevant is Beard's (1949) research describing and categorizing the vegetation of the Windward and Leeward islands.

Under seasonal and evergreen forest formations are listed the major dry forest types for the Lesser Antilles (Beard 1949, 50), including, in order of increasing moisture deficit, (1) evergreen seasonal forest, (2) semi-evergreen seasonal forest, (3) deciduous seasonal forest, (4) dry evergreen forest, (5) evergreen bushland, and (6) littoral woodland. Most of these formations occur in association with a pronounced dry season. Among the plant identifications from Hope Estate are taxa suggestive of the second through fifth of the vegetation types described by Beard. Rainfall patterns would tend to eliminate the first of these forest types for St. Martin, except perhaps during very wet intervals, since evergreen forest occurs in areas with rainfall averages ranging about 2030 mm (to reiterate, St. Martin's rainfall averages between 1025 mm and 1080 mm [around 40 inches]).

Six of the Hope Estate archaeological taxa are prominently associated with semi-evergreen seasonal forest, the second forest type defined by Beard (1949, 77), including *Bourreria succulenta*, (cf.) *Ceiba* sp., *Cordia* spp., *Mastichodendron foetidissimum*, *Zanthoxylum* spp. (formerly *Fagara* spp.), and Sapotaceae (represented by *Mastichodendron* and *Dipholis salicifolia*). This forest formation (Beard 1949, 78-80) tends to occur on hilly land and mostly below about 200 metres (ca. 600 feet) elevation, and where rainfall averages between 1270 mm and 2030 mm (50-80 inches) per annum. The presence of so many taxa among the archaeological remains potentially deriving from semi-evergreen forest may suggest that overall conditions were somewhat wetter at the time Hope Estate was occupied, and/or this vegetation occurred on the windward side of higher terrain (*e.g.,* the island's low mountains, with localized wetter conditions due to orographic effects [Nieuwolt 1977, 64]). Indeed, Stoffers

(1956, 101, 131) identified near Sentry Hill on St. Martin probable remnants of semi-evergreen seasonal forest during his 1952-53 vegetation survey.

At least four of the Hope Estate taxa are also listed for drier forest facies. *Cordia* sp. and *Bourreria* sp., as well as at least one tree legume, are indicated for deciduous seasonal forest (the third of Beard's types mentioned above). Associated rainfall totals for this forest formation lie between 1025 mm and 1538 mm (40-60 inches). *Zanthoxylum* spp. and *Maytenus elliptica*, along with Sapotaceae, and several tree legumes are associated with dry evergreen forest (the fourth type above; rainfall totals about the same as the deciduous seasonal forest). And, again, *Zanthoxylum* sp., a member of the Sapotaceae, *Comocladia ilicifolia* (Anacardiaceae, perhaps Hope Estate seed type 2), as well as *Bourreria succulenta* are associated with evergreen bushland (Beard 1949, 82-84; rainfall between 890-1270 mm [35-50 inches]). Moreover, Beard, citing Stehl (Beard 1949, 82-83), makes the point that *Guaiacum officinale* was very probably once a dominant component of both forms of dry evergreen forest (dry evergreen forest and bushland), prior to heavy extraction pressure that began early in the historic period (cf. Record and Hess [1943, 556] describing intensive exploitation of *Guaiacum* spp. beginning as early as 1508 and in conjunction with harvests for the resin's presumed medicinal value).

The conspicuous presence of *Guaiacum* sp. among the Hope Estate wood samples, together with other taxa associated with the various dry forest types described above, is a strong indication that dry evergreen forests (including dry evergreen forest proper and evergreen bushland) comprised much of the vegetation on the island during the prehistoric occupation. It is likely that moister forest associations, for example, the semi-evergreen and deciduous seasonal forests (types 2 and 3 above), occurred on higher ground and/or in wetter locations. Lower elevation, more exposed terrain was almost certainly vegetated in the drier forest communities. Another relevant consideration is that a more extensive and permanent forest cover, presumably the case at least during the early stages of occupation, would have a positive effect on local moisture conditions, including rainfall patterns, as well as on soils and ground cover.

In addition to insights about the prehistoric environment, the archaeobotanical data from Hope Estate provide some indication of possible subsistence resources and the way the site's inhabitants interacted with the local vegetation. Cockspur, false mastic, and panicoid grass each represent potentially edible plants (table 16.2) and indeed the three have been documented in association with archaeological deposits from around the region. They have been identified from Archaic Age contexts in the Lesser Antilles, including

Twenty Hill on Antigua (cockspur and mastic), Hichmans Shell Midden on Nevis (mastic), and Krum Bay on St. Thomas (mastic and panicoid grass) (Newsom and Pearsall 1996). Cockspur and mastic are ubiquitous in Cedrosan contexts from Pearls, Grenada, and cockspur was among the only seed types (67% ubiquity) recovered from Cedrosan deposits at the Golden Rock site, St. Eustatius (Newsom 1992, 1993a). Purslane, another of the seed types from Hope Estate, has also been documented variously at Archaic and Ceramic Age sites in the Lesser Antilles (Newsom and Pearsall 1996). Since cockspur, mastic, panicoid grass, and perhaps also purslane appear with such regularity in conjunction with archaeological deposits in the Lesser Antilles, it is reasonable to infer that these taxa were important wild plant resources, native tree fruits and small grains or greens, for Archaic and later Ceramic Age human groups. The contextual evidence associating mastic and panicoid grains with the hearth-like feature from Hope Estate is perhaps additional verification of these plants functioning as food items.

Likewise, several plants with potential medicinal value were identified from Hope Estate samples and some in good cultural context, particularly the hearth-like feature (table 16.5). There is nevertheless a strong possibility that the presence of these taxa, cf. *Crotalaria* sp., Malvaceae, wild lime, cf. vervain, perhaps also Anacardiaceae, was simply incidental to the human occupation. Several, like purslane, are widespread weeds of disturbed ground and so could have become incorporated with site deposits when they dispersed naturally. Even so, the plants may still have been recognized and employed by the inhabitants of Hope Estate as useful plants. None of these taxa appear in the samples in quantities particularly suggestive of having been used, but there are no seed remains from Hope Estate that were found to occur in large numbers. Panicoid grass and cockspur are the most abundant of the seed types, with 21 and 25 individual specimens, respectively (table 16.5); the full count for vervain of 20 specimens is very similar.

Evidence of cultivated and/or domesticated plants, long-presumed a hallmark of Ceramic Age occupations of the Caribbean (Rouse 1992) is lacking among the archaeobotanical samples from Hope Estate. Nevertheless, the possible tuber fragments mentioned above from the Cedrosan midden is at least provisional evidence for the presence of edible roots or tubers at the site, and perhaps even cultivated forms. Wood remains from Hope Estate, beyond the general insights about the prehistoric environment, appear to reflect clear patterns of selection and use. The separate taxa are not evenly distributed across the site, either spatially or in terms of absolute numbers, which is a good indication of deliberate and preferential use of certain woods. *Lignum vitae* is conspicuous throughout the deposits tested, and therefore

appears to have been very important as a fuelwood and perhaps for other purposes as well.

It is possible that preservation factors and biases come into play here, because *Lignum vitae*, being an exceptionally dense wood, survives extended periods of burning better than do many other fuelwoods (that is, differential loss and preservation in the context of fuelwood use may account for the proportionately higher relative frequencies and ubiquity of *Lignum vitae*, cf. Newsom 1993a; Record and Hess 1943). Nevertheless, as greater numbers of archaeobotanical sites and samples have come under analysis in the region, definitive patterns are emerging and *Lignum vitae* is a seemingly regular presence in archaeological deposits from the Lesser Antilles. This particular wood has been documented as the most prominent taxon at seven of a total of nine Ceramic Age sites in the Lesser Antilles (including the A-B-C islands) that have been intensively studied, including Wanapa (Bonaire), Tanki Flip (Aruba), Hichmans Site (Nevis), Golden Rock (St. Eustatius), Trants (Montserrat), Santa Barbara (Curaçao), and now also Hope Estate. Such a wide-spread pattern of use suggests more than simple preservation factors to account for the presence of *Lignum vitae*.

Interestingly, *Lignum vitae* has not been documented from Archaic Age sites, though these contexts have been less intensively studied, but likewise, the wood is only recorded for two sites in the Greater Antilles (out of eight total, and including the Virgin Islands): Tutu, St. Thomas and El Bronce, Puerto Rico (Newsom and Pearsall 1996). Thus, intensive reliance on *Lignum vitae* is apparently more strongly associated with the Lesser Antilles in general, and with the Ceramic Age occupations in particular.

Aside from *Lignum vitae*, 16 other woods were discerned among the Hope Estate samples. Fish poison, while only appearing in two samples from the Cedrosan midden at Hope Estate is particularly interesting as another taxon that has been documented from two, perhaps three, additional Cedrosan Saladoid sites in the Lesser Antilles, specifically, Golden Rock, Trants, and tentatively at Hichmans site (Newsom and Pearsall 1996). Fish poison has potential uses not only as fuel, but as a fish stupifier and in medicinal/ritual contexts (cf. Newsom 1992). Mayten and wood taxon 4 are fairly conspicuous among the deposits, while the remainder of the Hope Estate taxa occurred in more restricted distributions. *Maytenus* species are primarily shrubs to medium-sized trees with relatively hard, dense wood (Record and Hess 1943, 122). Their form and density are well suited to fuelwood use (cf. below). The Sapotaceae wood (type 6) from Hope Estate occurred exclusively in association with the possible hearth feature (Feature 41), which is perhaps an indication that this wood was selected for its burning characteristics and/or its interaction with cooked food (smoke imparting distinctive flavour, etc.). Sapotaceae trees/wood are characterized by a milky, sometimes aromatic latex, that has been used for multiple purposes (source of chicle gum, etc. [Record and Hess 1943, 494-507]).

In terms of prehistoric human adaptations, then, the Hope Estate plant remains provide some provisional insights as to plant foods, wood selection, and environment. Clearly the inhabitants of the site focused upon readily available resources from local forests. And by virtue of a generally high resin content, coppicing ability, and/or dense structure, local woods from the dry forests happen also to be superb fuelwoods (Record and Hess 1943; Wartluft and White 1984). That many of the dry forest trees can sustain coppicing was a potentially important factor to the long-term existence of human groups on the island. Coppice growth is an aggressive response to the stress of cutting, after which the tree responds by producing strong, prolific shoot growth. Regeneration is rapid and the trees will continue to respond in this way, as long as cutting is not too frequent or severe. Thus, the forested environment on St. Martin to some extent would have had a natural capability to sustain greater levels of wood extraction (cf. also Newsom 1993b). This natural resiliency of the forests might have indirectly benefitted the human population, translating in cultural terms to a fairly stable wood resource base. That *Lignum vitae*, for one, is so persistently present in the Hope Estate deposits and spanning an occupation of perhaps as long as a millennium, is an indication of such sustainable resource use. If the inhabitants of the site also maintained gardens, including perhaps root crops, there is no indication among the archaeobotanical remains, that the gardening system or other forms of land use over-stressed or adversely impacted natural environments and resources during the span that Hope Estate was occupied.

16.6   Conclusions

This analysis of archaeobotanical remains from the Cedrosan-Huecan settlement at Hope Estate, however limited, has provided insights into plant use and certain human behaviours. The combination of plant taxa identified or tentatively so provides baseline data to suggest that tropical dry forests, particularly dry evergreen formations, were present on the island at the time of the prehistoric occupation.

In terms of subsistence and economic variables, locally available woods were used as fuel and undoubtedly for other purposes. Some of the same trees (e.g., *Lignum vitae*) and other species may have provided useful products such as resins and medicinal materials. Moreover, seed remains from at least four potential plant foods were recovered. Two small unidentified fragments of parenchymatous tissue suggestive of tuber or rootstock are possible evidence for the consumption of imported or native edible roots. No definitive evidence of domesticated crop species was discerned in this analysis, nevertheless the presence of artefacts strongly associated with plant-food processing is at least indirect evidence for reliance on edible rootstocks (*e.g.*, manioc).

17   Human remains

Steffen Baetsen

17.1   Introduction

During the 1993 fieldwork at Hope Estate five human burials were encountered of which three have been excavated.
All of these inhumations were in the northeastern part of the
midden area. No traces of burial pits were observed. Two of
the burials were excavated partially during the 1987 and
1988 campaigns. All of the interments belong to the
Cedrosan Saladoid occupation of the site and were buried in
the upper layers of the refuse deposits. This clearly points to
a reorganization of the settlement layout.

The skeletal material is relatively well preserved, although
fragmented. The physical-anthropological analysis was
performed in the field using special forms designed by Dr
G.J.R. Maat, Department of Anatomy of Leiden University.
Gender and age of the skeletons were determined according
to the methods developed by the Workshop of European
Anthropologists (1980).

17.2   Burials

Feature 011

This burial was partly excavated in 1988. The skeleton was
buried in an extended refuse deposit which yielded no traces
of a burial pit. The skeletal remains are well preserved
although the bones appeared to be fragmented. The skeleton
was bearing east-west, the head facing south. The deceased
was buried in flexed position, lying on its left side. No burial
gifts were encountered. It concerns an adult, probably a
female, aged between 50 and 59 years. The sexual determination is uncertain since several morphological traits of the
cranium and pelvis point to the feminine gender whereas the
mandibula shows clearly male characteristics. The length of
the skeleton could not be calculated as the long bones are
incomplete. The lower extremities, the lumbar vertebrae,
pelvis, femur and tibia of the skeleton were excavated in
1988. According to Jay B. Haviser (pers. comm. 1993),
some lumbar vertebrae were fused, a point that could not be
confirmed. Some vertebrae, however, showed arthritis.

Feature 018

This skeleton was bearing south-north, the head facing east.
It was buried in flexed position on its right side, while both
arms held the left leg (fig. 17.1, 17.2). It concerns an adult,

aged between 35 and 47 years, probably a female. It was not
possible to calculate the length of the skeleton as the long
bones are incomplete. The front teeth show more wear than
the molars, suggesting that the individual chewed with the
front teeth due to a painful abscess at one of the molars. The
associated burial gifts consist of two Late Cedrosan Saladoid
vessels, i.e., a dish and a bowl (figs 17.3a-b), one spoon-like
implement and five complete shells. The spoon-like object
was found to be placed between the arms and the heavily
flexed legs. The shells appeared to be deposited around the
body. The mortuary gifts indicate that the burial can be
dated to a late phase of the Cedrosan Saladoid period. Consequently, it would correspond with the final occupation of
the site. No traces of a burial pit were noticed.

Feature 027

This burial was partly excavated in 1987 as well. The cranium, some vertebrae, the complete left arm and fragments
of the right arm were removed at the time. From the combined data it can be inferred that the individual was buried in

Fig. 17.1. Cedrosan Saladoid burial (F011) in the northeastern part of
the midden.

249

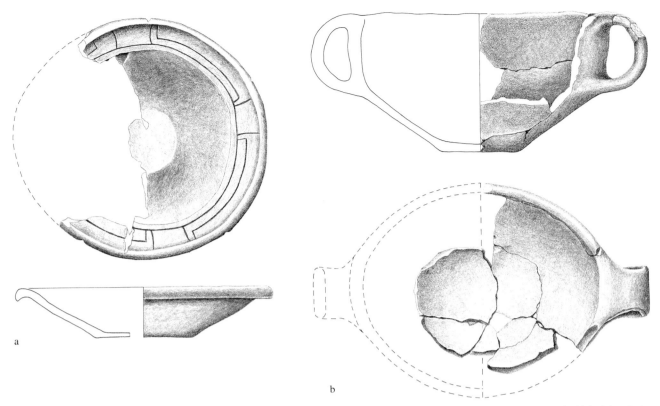

Fig. 17.2. Funerary vessels associated with burial F011: a. dish-shaped unrestricted vessel with a simple contour decorated with incision, b. jar-shaped vessel with an unrestricted composite contour and D-shaped handles.

ventral position with his right arm underneath the abdomen, lying partly below the pelvis. The left arm was extended on top of a rock. The left tibia and foot bones are missing. The right leg was bend around a rock at an angle of about 120 degrees. This position suggests that the individual had fallen or had been thrown on the ground. The skeleton belongs to an adult male, aged between 35 and 44 years. The length of the femur, which was measured in the field, indicated that the individual had a stature of approximately 164 cm. In spite of the unusual practice of interment, the skeleton can possibly be ascribed to the pre-Columbian period. This, at least, is suggested by its location in the midden and the state of preservation of the bones. No burial gifts were found to be associated with the skeleton and no traces of a burial pit were noticed.

17.3   Synthesis

In all five inhumations were encountered all of which were adult individuals. Only three burials were excavated during the 1993 campaign, of which two were partly excavated in 1987 and 1988 by Jay B. Haviser. All are primary burials, one of which was provided with mortuary gifts. No skull

deformations were encountered and only a few pathological changes, i.e., one case of arthritis and some abscesses, were documented.

The five burials belong to a larger cemetery, partly destroyed by road construction works, on the property of Hope Estate. All interments were located in the midden and belong to the latest phase of occupation of the site, i.e., after AD 600. No burials belonging to the earlier occupation of the site have been encountered as yet. The date of around or after AD 600 makes these burials contemporary with those of the Golden Rock site on St. Eustatius where nine burials were found with similar mortuary practices and some of them with burial gifts (Versteeg and Schinkel 1992). The burial practices are less complex than those documented for the post-Saladoid burials of Anse à la Gourde, Guadeloupe (Delpuech et al. 1996, Hoogland et al. 1997, 1998) and Kelbey's Ridge 2, Saba (Hoogland and Hofman 1993; Hoogland 1996). These investigations have shown that both primary and secondary burials with complex burial practices were common in the Leeward Islands during late prehistoric times.

PART FOUR
THE 'LA HUECA PROBLEM'

18 The 'La Hueca Problem' in Puerto Rico and the Caribbean: old problems, new perspectives, possible solutions

José R. Oliver

18.1 Introduction

In the early 1980s, archaeologists were literally stunned by the unexpected uncovering of enormously rich midden deposits that contained not only a heretofore different and early pottery complex, named La Hueca, but also by what is generally regarded as a very rich and diverse quantity micro-lapidary artefacts of gemstone quality (Chanlatte 1979, 1981, 1983; Chanlatte and Narganes 1980, 1983). La Hueca site is located in the small island of Vieques, southeast of the larger island of Puerto Rico. La Hueca remained an atypical, unique site until the discovery in 1986 of yet another La Hueca-related component, this time at Punta Candelero near the coast of Humacao, in southeastern Puerto Rico (Rodríguez 1989, 1991; Rodríguez and Rivera 1991). These two sites have generated one of the most fascinating challenges to Caribbean archaeologists, and are at the core of one of the most heated debates since Rouse (1952, 1964) falsified the 'two migration' hypothesis (i.e., the Crab Culture/Saladoid and Shell Culture/Ostionoid) by demonstrating that the Taínos ('Chicoid') were the end result of a single population movement and subsequent local development. The discovery of La Hueca in 1977 resulted in a profound revision of a previously held model or hypothesis regarding the timing and the nature of the colonization of the Antilles by ceramic-bearing groups coming from South America. This essay is an effort to come to grips with some of these problems and issues. It is also written for the upcoming generation of Caribbean archaeologists "too young to remember".

While new Huecan-related sites between Puerto Rico and Guadeloupe have been excavated since the 1980s, unquestionably, La Hueca and Punta Candelero still hold the keys to most of the answers to the problems. Simply put, this is because they both, but especially La Hueca, stand today as the 'measuring yardstick' against which archaeologists make decisions about the nature and extent to which their site assemblages and reconstructed 'cultures' conform to, or diverge from a 'Huecoid' or 'Huecan' pattern. Therefore, it is fitting to include in this volume a reassessment of what I call the 'La Hueca Problem' from the perspective of the type site in Vieques.

Following the discovery of La Hueca, it was generally thought that more excavations and more absolute dates from potential La Hueca-affiliated sites would finally resolve the Huecoid problems but, alas, this has not been the case, as the thorough analyses of Hope Estate and Trants Estate demonstrate (Hofman, Hoogland, Watters and Petersen, this volume). Why should this be the case is a major objective of this essay.

This paper is certainly not the first, nor will it be the last, attempt to shed light to the 'Huecan problem' (e.g., Siegel 1991). But it will, I hope, bring forth new perspectives since it focuses on a number of crucial details that until now have not been carefully contemplated. Briefly, these details relate to the following: (1) methodology, especially the problem of cross-comparability of analytical units, (2) radiocarbon dates and chronology, and (3) the problem of shifting from observed patterns 'on the ground' to their cultural/behavioral implications and, ultimately, to the identification of the processes (cultural and natural) that conspired to produce the observed patterns (Schiffer 1972, 1984). As Hoogland (this volume) concluded for Hope Estate, our rather *poor* understanding of site formation processes in general and post-depositional processes in particular, has been instrumental in shaping our current views of what I will call the 'La Hueca Problem'. It will be argued that in due course of time archaeologists in the Caribbean have constructed more or less formal 'images' of the Huecoid phenomenon that have become ever more removed from the factual data initially reported for La Hueca-Sorcé and for Punta Candelero sites. That imagery has thus resulted in a series of expectations, when working at other sites in the Antilles, that often depart from what the data from these two key sites allow.

This essay is divided into two parts. Part I presents a synthesis of the state of affairs before the discovery of La Hueca, followed by a discussion of the disagreements that ensued after its discovery. My intention is to recast the debates in terms of the limiting conditions imposed by the available facts. Isolating and identifying precisely what such limitations are will hopefully suggest potential avenues for resolution. Part II endeavors to search for some solutions by rethinking the prevailing approach of characterizing artifact data simply in terms of counts and percentages. To illustrate the methodological points to be made, the microlapidary materials of La Hueca have been selected for detailed re-analysis. The way the microlapidary has been portrayed in publications has had significant impact on how La Hueca is perceived by Caribbean archaeologists. For example, the view of La Hueca as a locus of specialized craftsmen, and as being an 'egalitarian society' because all middens included a 'rich' quantity and/or range of prestige (exotic) microlapidary items, hinges on how the data is qualitatively and quantitatively analyzed. I will also be going back 'to the ground', so-to-speak, by re-examining the stratigraphic evidence available to me and what such associations might imply in terms of microlapidary density distributions and radiocarbon dating. It is my conviction that broad, 'high-level' processes, like migrations, acculturation, and other forms of interaction (convergence, divergence) cannot be adequately addressed until intra-site phenomena have been exhaustively researched.

Luis Chanlatte and Yvonne Narganes graciously allowed to not only use their original laboratory notes, but also provided discussions on a range of issues specific to La Hueca that contributed enormously to a clearer understanding on my part of the site, excavation methodology and interpretations. For all of this I gratefully acknowledge Narganes and Chanlatte their help and valuable insights. Several long discussions were also held with Miguel Rodríguez López regarding Punta Candelero. Rodríguez generously allowed me to copy and examine a detailed distribution map of Punta Candelero's excavation units, including the location of selected microlapidary materials. This essay owes much to their unselfishness and generosity in sharing their research data and views.

18.2   The state of affairs before La Hueca: the Saladoid series

Initially the La Hueca finds, especially the ceramics and microlapidary materials, were regarded as unique and atypical in the Antilles (Chanlatte 1981, Rouse 1985). At first, La Hueca also yielded a few of the earliest radiocarbon dates for a ceramic-bearing site in the region at that time (160 cal BC- AD 130 at 1 sigma), earlier than the ca. AD 1-300 dates then attributed to most initial or early Saladoid styles (e.g., Hacienda Grande style)[1]. The initial, apparent, chronological precedence of La Hueca over dated Saladoid styles everywhere (except Cedros style, Trinidad) raised serious questions about the universally accepted cultural history of the Pre-Columbian Caribbean. It is worthwhile to pause and briefly examine what was the conventional cultural historic reconstruction until the implications of La Hueca first came to wide attention in the 8th International Congress of Caribbean Archaeology, held in St. Kitts in 1979.

Up until then, the conventional cultural historic reconstruction was that the first agriculturist peoples to colonize and conquer the Caribbean correlated with the distribution of a single Saladoid ceramic series (e.g., Rouse 1964; 1985, Rouse and Alegría 1990; see also Siegel 1991, Oliver 1992a). The Saladoid series spread as far north as the south-easternmost tip of Hispaniola within the first century of the Christian Era. The earliest radiocarbon date then belonged to Cedros style in Trinidad (ca. 200 BC) (Rouse and Allaire 1978; Rouse et al. 1985). While in each island the Saladoid pottery showed the expected local variation, all the ceramic styles or complexes were quite closely related and undoubtedly derived from a single ancestral style and homeland (Rouse 1964). The insular Saladoid ceramic styles significantly diverged from the ancestral styles that continued to evolve in the Orinoco Valley. Eventually Rouse (1985) introduced the intermediate 'subseries' in a new hierarchical taxonomy, which grouped the closely related styles of the Orinoco Valley in the Ronquinan Saladoid subseries. The more divergent West Indian-Guyanan-Insular Saladoid styles were regrouped in a new Cedrosan subseries (see also Rouse 1992). No one today disputes that the bearers of the Cedrosan Saladoid ceramics had indeed migrated from the Orinoco and Trinidad-Guyana's toward the West Indies.

By the mid to late 1980s, however, new radiocarbon dates from a number of islands, including Puerto Rico had pushed back the initial Cedrosan Saladoid from ca. AD 1-300 to as early as 500 cal BC and 400 cal BC (Watters 1994; Haviser 1991a, 1997). Likewise, La Hueca-related components at Hope Estate and elsewhere (e.g., El Convento) began to yield early dates between 400 BC and 60 BC (Hoogland, this volume). With the new range of dates, the issue of the chronological priority of Huecan/Huecoid vs. Cedrosan came to a head, since now both Cedrosan Saladoid styles and La Hueca style could be either contemporaneous or earlier at several locations throughout the northeastern Caribbean region.

Before 1980, there was general unanimity and agreement on Rouse's culture historic reconstruction. Saladoid ceramic-bearing groups migrated from the Orinoco (ca. 2100 BC) and once they reached the coast and Trinidad (200 BC) they rapidly branched towards eastern Venezuela and the Antilles, reaching the eastern Puerto Rico and easternmost Hispaniola around AD 1-100 (Rouse and Allaire 1978). Early on, archaeologists had developed an image of a stepping-stone migratory strategy, 'taking possession' of each island and through a process of social segmentation, a splinter group would navigate to the next island and so on. That the Saladoid migration was never such a simple, mechanistic spread has since been fully demonstrated (Watters and Rouse 1989; Keegan 1992, 1997, 17). Rather, islands with higher topographic relief and dependable water sources were generally targeted for initial colonization, whereas low relief limestone islands generally were occupied at a later date. The 'stepping-stone' mode of expansion and the relative speed of migration suggested by the radiocarbon dates available at the time at once 'explained' the emergence of new ceramic styles in each of the islands (founder's effect) and its 'phylogenetic' divergence from a common Saladoid ancestral tradition.

While migration seems to have proceeded relatively rapidly through the Lesser Antilles, once in Puerto Rico the Saladoid expansion was arrested, possibly due to the larger size of this island and probably due to a more substantial Archaic population present in Puerto Rico (as well as Hispaniola). Initially, encounters with the resident Archaic populations (e.g., Coroso, María La Cruz, El Porvenir) were generally interpreted to have resulted in a rapid and thorough acculturation to the Saladoid agro-economic and cultural way of life (cf. Rouse 1964, 508). The image of the Saladoid (and later, Ostionoid) culturally "swamping" Archaic groups, though, began to change in the mid 1970s with the discovery of Archaic sites with non-Saladoid pottery, such as Caimito in Hispaniola and possibly Caimanes-III in Cuba, which indicated more complex forms of interactions. Veloz Maggiolo (1976, 1980; see also 1991), among others, questioned the nature of these interactions.

Closely related early Cedrosan Saladoid styles were to dominate the Caribbean from the Mona Passage to Trinidad and northeastern South America, until about AD 600, when in the Greater Antilles they 'degenerated' into less varied and technologically sophisticated styles (e.g., Cuevas style in Puerto Rico), marking the end of the "inherited" continental ceramic (Saladoid) tradition and the transition to new home-grown ceramic styles, designated in eastern Hispaniola, Puerto Rico, and the Virgin Islands as Ostionan Ostionoid (post AD 600). By the early 1980s, other contemporaneous ceramic styles, Monserrate in Puerto Rico and Magens Bay-I in the Virgin Islands (Elenan Ostionoid), were regarded as sufficiently distinct to constitute a new Elenan Ostionoid subseries (Roe et al. 1985, 1990; Oliver 1990). It is during the early Ostionoid (Period IIIa) that significant changes took place throughout Hispaniola, Puerto Rico, the Virgin Islands; changes that were indicative of the formation of pristine *cacicazgos,* characterized (among other things) by the appearance of stone demarcated precincts (ball courts and plazas) and during Period IIIb by a centralization of political-religious power in larger, first order civic-ceremonial centers, such as Tibes (Curet and Newsom 1997; Curet and Rodríguez 1995; Oliver 1998).

After ca. AD 600, in the Lesser Antilles, the Saladoid series also gave way to new stylistic standards (Allaire 1997), archaeologically recognized as the Troumassoid series, out of which some archaeologists (Rouse 1995) have recently distinguished further divergence: the Marmoran, Troumassean and Suazan subseries. Had we been applying the periodification developed by the 'Berkeley School' and

John H. Rowe for Perú, the Caribbean shifted from an Early Horizon to an Early Intermediate Period of regional development.

As far as ceramic artefacts are concerned, most of the Lesser Antilles would henceforth develop more or less independently from the Greater Antilles. This is not to say that contacts of various sorts did not take place then or later. On the contrary, evidence from Kelbey's Ridge site in Saba is proof of such interaction, if not outright Chican Ostionoid 'colonial' (?) outposts emanating from the Greater Antilles (Hofman 1993; Hoogland 1996; Hoogland and Hofman 1993). Well known is also the XVIth century Spanish reference indicating that Taínos (e.g., historic Chican Ostionoid) fled Puerto Rico and sought and received asylum among Guadeloupe's 'Island Caribs' (Sued Badillo 1995), implying that social networks between the two populations had to be in place well before the Spanish intrusion. Nevertheless south of Guadeloupe, it was abundantly clear that after ca. 600 Leeward islanders were evolving in a different direction than the Greater Antillean groups. The level of sociopolitical integration *(cacicazgos)* that was ultimately achieved in the Greater Antilles (excluding western Cuba) was not attained in the Lesser Antilles. This is, in a nutshell, the conventional view -at least as I see it- on the colonization and conquest of the West Indies by South American agriculturists, *before* the discovery of La Hueca.

The key and most crucial point to remember here is that ALL the ceramic styles (and cultural complexes) present in the Caribbean were entirely derived from a singular ancestral complex that is expressed by the shared (similarity) system of modes and attributes that the higher taxonomic unit, the Cedrosan subseries, encompasses. Caribbean prehistory was portrayed as a classic case of adaptive radiation and continuous phylogenetic branching-off from a singular 'ancestral complex' that had its ultimate (known) origin in the Middle-Lower Orinoco Valley. To be sure, archaeologists endlessly debated over the finer points (e.g., the degree of Barrancoid influence on the Lesser Antillean Saladoid), but the overall model was deeply entrenched and broadly accepted, as can be seen, for example, in Veloz Maggiolo's (1972) earlier work.

The often cited causal factors that 'drove' populations to migrate, diverge and/or merge (including their pottery) were mainly ecological and 'external': (a) population increase (demographics) linked to (b) increased technological efficiency as groups learned to better exploit the insular environments, and (c) intergroup cooperation-competition (e.g., the Barrancoid 'invasion' in the Orinoco 'pushing' the Saladoids). Sociological, political and other 'intra-societal' causal factors were not at the top of the agenda and have only recently been subjected to systematic research. Given the rather straightforward, single origin-radiation model, it is

256

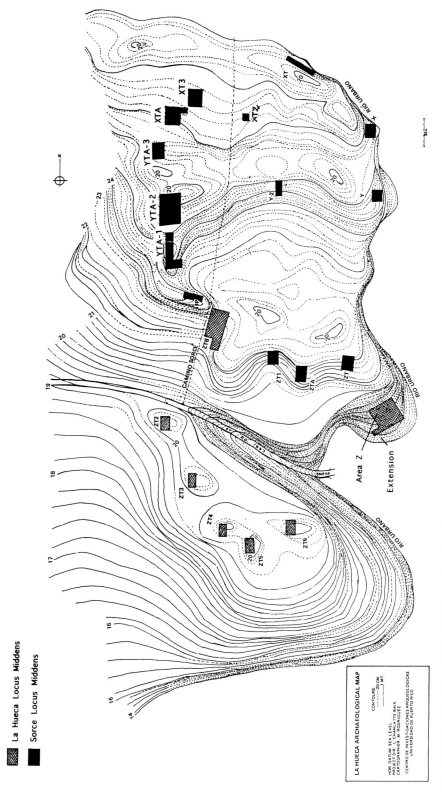

La Hueca Locus Middens

Sorce Locus Middens

Fig. 18.1. Map of La Hueca & Sorcé loci (reproduced from Chanlatte & Narganes 1983).

not surprising that the discovery of an earlier and seemingly non-Saladoid La Hueca style shook us out of complacency and self indulgence. The discovery offered on a silver platter the possibility of two different 'histories' and the impossibility that the two could be equally 'correct'.

18.3   Shifting paradigms:
La Hueca in Historical Context

The discovery of La Hueca in 1977 shook the foundations of the rather comfortable 'monolithic' scheme, above summarized. A new paradigm was emerging, not just because of the Huecan 'anomaly', but also because of novel archaeological theory and methods. The discovery came on the tail-end of the achievements of the processual (New Archaeology) school in the United States, which peaked in 1974. The kinds of questions raised by North American processualists were to be applied, sometimes *confusingly,* to the traditional normative cultural chronology and subsistence ecology concerns in the Caribbean.[2] The same may be said of the *Arqueología Social* as promulgated by Sanoja and Vargas (1974, Vargas 1990), whose tenets were embraced mainly by Spanish-

speaking archaeologists such as Marcio Veloz Maggiolo, Elpidio Ortega and Angel Caba (1981; Veloz 1976, 1980; Veloz et. al. 1976). Although *Arqueología Social* was theoretically grounded in historical materialism and a *sui generis* marxist socio-economic foundation, in practice the explanations about social and economic changes were rooted in the more traditional adaptationist and functional ecological approaches (e.g., Veloz et al. 1976)[3]. Postprocessual critiques are only now beginning to filter into the Caribbean, though it is mainly perceptible in the fields of sociocultural anthropology, ethnohistory and sociology (e.g., Hulme 1993; Whitehead, ed. 1995).

The emphasis on 'confusing' is because often the mid-1970s to early 1980s' literature of the Puerto Rico and Dominican Republic, the necessary distinctions between *archaeological context* and (cultural) *systemic context (sensu* Schiffer 1971, 1984, 27-30) and the behavioral (social) inferences (explanations) about the nature and causes for change (process, dynamics), were not clearly spelled out, in theory or in practice. Changes at the theoretical level, for the most part, did not go hand in hand with concomitant methodological changes in field strategies and research. Artifact and, later, ecofact-oriented relatively small test excavations continued to be the general rule, while the process of site discovery followed no particular controlled sampling strategy. Analyses were still based on simple lists of frequency counts, percentages or nominal units of presence/absence and the ever present Fordian (but, really, 'Meggerian') frequency seriations. Hypotheses were formulated in ways that became difficult to test or falsify. These methodologies limited the

ability to interpret the behavioral, social and processual implications of the archaeological contexts. Indeed, 'contextual archaeological' methods to elicit social-economic relations (as advocated by Veloz Maggiolo, Sanoja and Vargas) so as to firmly establish modes of production vis-a-vis modes of social organization shine by their absence. Of course, through the 1970s, there were a number of significant exceptions, and after the 1980s these became noticeable (e.g., Keegan 1985; Robinson et. al. 1983, 1985; Rodríguez 1985; Sullivan 1981; Watters 1980).

The mid-1970s into the early 1980s was a time for shifting theoretical paradigms. It was also a time when often practical field research strategies and methods lagged behind the demands of theory 'proof'. After the mid-late 1980s, the situation changed considerably for the better, but primarily for those islands with a stronger economies, and backed by exterior or metropolitan capital investment (e.g., Puerto Rico, the Dutch and French islands). Since the mid 1980s, field methodologies have been increasingly synchronized with the research problems at hand (when other than basic cultural chronology). In Puerto Rico, for example, this 'synchronization' was largely achieved not through a home-grown conscious intellectual and academic decision, but in general by the strictures imposed by both State (ICP, 1991) and U.S. Federal Historical Preservation Laws (FHPL, 1993). The 'antiquities laws' essentially forced a new (and some older) generation of archaeologists in Puerto Rico to follow specific sampling methodologies, that were clearly spelled out in the Requests for Proposals (RFP), if they were to successfully bid for the job. Not surprisingly, the RFPs were designed and prepared by archaeologists formed under the processual New Archaeology school. Archaeological research in some of the Lesser Antilles had undergone a similar change as a result of antiquities regulations emanating from government, as is the case in the French West Indies and the *Service Régional de l'Archéologie*. The intervention of the State has been both a blessing and a source of tension between the traditional advocate archaeologists, younger and older university academic and professional (heritage) archaeologists.

It is in this context that La Hueca and Punta Candelero made their mark in the Antilles. The archaeological field research at La Hueca directed by Luis Chanlatte was, and still is, largely unaffected by processualist or historical materialist concerns, remaining within a fundamentally cultural historic framework, both in theory and excavation practice. On the other hand, excavations and research at Punta Candelero were explicitly carried out by Rodríguez within a largely processualist-influenced (indirectly by Gary Vescelius) excavation strategy, which also included the pressures associated with heritage archaeology, since the site was to be impacted by the construction of a tourism hotel resort. While

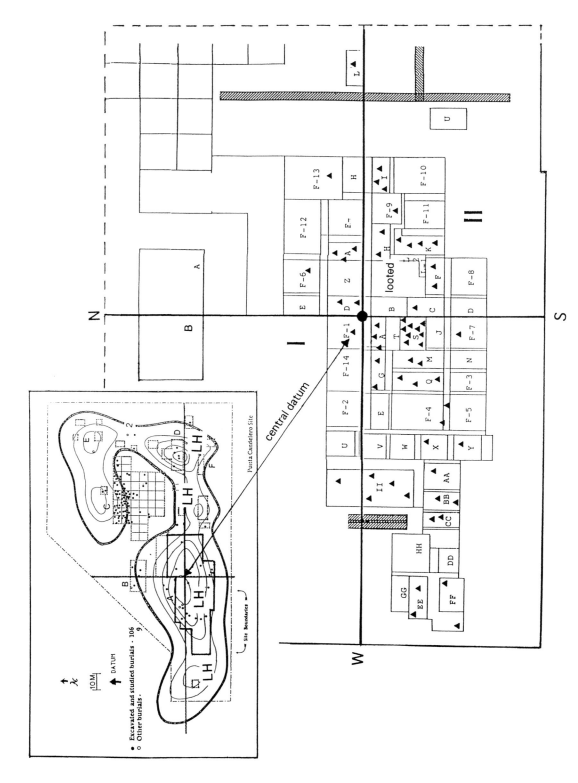

Fig. 18.2. Punta Candelero, Puerto Rico: map and planview. ▲ = *in situ* microlapidary specimen of cache. Inset: map of Punto Candelero site; LH = La Hueca component middens.

258

La Hueca-Sorcé were subjected to a steady but relaxed pace of excavations totaling 20 years (1977-1997), Punta Candelero was to be salvaged in just a couple of seasons at a furious pace of excavations (Rodríguez and Rivera 1991; Rodríguez 1989, 1991a; Crespo 1991).

As Chanlatte (pers. comm. 1997) has insisted, it is true that extensive and broad 'block' excavations have been conducted in Vieques. And I could argue that his method of excavation is consistent with the objectives of normative culture history. But, because excavations in La Hueca and Sorcé were not carried out by *simultaneously* exposing a given stratum or level in all the units within a given block, there can be no claim to a contextual (horizontal) methodology. Rather Chanlatte's strategy was to excavate each 4 m² unit from top to bottom before proceeding to the next, adjoining 4m² unit. Whether joined into a block or isolated, this technique follows the same procedures that had been used since the late 1930s. This approach is bound to create (and has created) all sorts of problems of comparability with sites that have been excavated with horizontal excavation methods.

By way of contrast, Punta Candelero was excavated using a combination of initial square tests and large horizontal excavations (cf. fig. 18.2). But, at Candelero the horizontal block areas were distributed in odd ways and sizes due to the orientation of the coconut palm trees and, further, due to time pressures, some large blocks were treated as a single sample unit (no internal smaller unit subdivisions), although piece-plotting plan views of artifact concentrations and features were made. Rendering the data bases of the two sites in Vieques analytically comparable with Candelero will be a major undertaking. Additionally, as we have seen in this volume (and in Henocq 1995), Hope Estate has been excavated with a range of different approaches, from long trenches to various kinds of block areas (Haviser 1991a; Hope Estate Bulletin, 1994). Hofman's analysis (this volume) already serves as a good example of the difficulties faced, especially in terms of comparing qualitative and quantitative results. In sum, these and other factors, such as the amount of data already processed and published to date, have significantly affected the ways in which the information recovered has been analyzed, interpreted and presented in publications and then compared with other assemblages or sites.

Nevertheless, both La Hueca and Punta Candelero have become a favorite arena for discussing a range of social and anthropological issues, including inter- and intra-group interactions (i.e., behavioral archaeology), modes of social organization, craft specialization, ideology (religion), trade and exchange, to mention just a few. The fact is that neither Candelero nor La Hueca have yet yielded evidence of a single house plan or other types of structures. Without any data about social units (household or other such concepts) most questions about intra-site organization keyed to questions about social stratification, labor or occupational specialization, distribution of material goods/wealth (e.g., gemstones), etc. cannot even be appropriately formulated for testing. The whole discussion (see below) about the multifaceted processes of 'acculturation' or trade/exchange between 'Huecoid' and 'Saladoid' peoples cannot have much hope of resolution when exclusively using a cultural historic, normative methodology and in the absence of any evidence specifying the nature of the social dynamics within a village (and, moreover, to address acculturation or exchange, at least *two* occupational loci are required!). Meanwhile, traditional cultural historic issues (typologies, migrations, etc.) continue to be highlighted above all other issues. The *core* of the current Huecan debate is not an 'old' normative school pitted against the Processualist or '*Arqueología Social*' schools. The main thrust of the arguments have been framed strictly within a culture historic paradigm. Yet, as noted above, many issues that began as a culture historic problem have already taken a direction toward questions that involve the socio-political and economic domains. The "answers" in those domains cannot be gathered using the traditional methods of data recovery. The normative conceptual tools of 'style, 'people', and 'series' should be reevaluated in terms equivalent to 'societies', 'communities', 'households', 'trade partnership relations', etc. In other words, what began as essentially a problem of style and chronology has expanded into a much more diverse range of questions which require different field methods and analytical approaches. La Hueca, which was excavated within a normative culture historic framework, therefore, cannot be now expected to address satisfactorily all of the issues at hand. However, I would contend that comparability can still be significantly improved. Unfortunately this is may be extremely difficult to achieve, because such goal requires all active archaeologists involved to make concessions of their 'favorite' or 'well tested' methods towards some sort of minimal protocol of both excavation strategy and data presentation. I am, however, hopeful that the questions that have arisen on the 'La Hueca Problem' will themselves be a catalyst for the sort of *minimal* standardization that would ensure comparability among sites, components, and various kinds of features and assemblages.

18.4   The comparability of taxonomic units of classification

Chanlatte and Narganes (1990) apply a set of conceptual units that differ from the more widely used system developed originally by Rouse (e.g., 1952, 1986). The two different classificatory approaches are not strictly interchangeable and thus are ripe for creating confusion, particularly since few archaeologists have adopted Chanlatte and Narganes' (1990; Chanlatte 1981) scheme. I am not sure if my Caribbean colleagues have given sufficient thought to Chanlatte and Narganes' classificatory framework and, if they have, it has never been explicitly discussed in terms of the implications for interpretation and comparison. These authors have classified the La Hueca and Sorcé components in terms of periods *(períodos)*, stages *(etapas)*, and phases *(fases)*. The La Hueca components belong to the *Agroalfarero* formative period, in its first stage. This stage is represented (for now) by a single phase, the La Hueca phase (or *Agro-I)*, which includes the assemblages and site components of La Hueca, Punta Candelero and other La Hueca-related assemblages. In practice, a phase also includes individual finds embedded or mixed in Cedrosan deposits thought to have once been an 'homogeneous' Hueca phase component. They often refer to La Hueca and related components (e.g., Punta Candelero) as simply *Agro-I*. It is unclear to me precisely what is the distinction, if any, between Agro-I and the La Hueca phase. They have also, at other times used the term *complejo* (or complex) as synonymous to their phase. The Sorcé components (including the "monserratean") were also classed as belonging to the *Agroalfarero* formative period, in its later second stage of development, represented by what they defined as an Igneri phase (or Agro-II). One of the components is Sorcé.

Thus, in Chanlatte and Narganes' nomenclature, La Hueca is not a style in Rouse's strict sense and usage, but a phase or complex *(fase* or *complejo)* that is representative of the initial formative period whose primary attribute is the dependence on (unspecified) agriculture and a 'tribal organization' (which is inferred, rather than demonstrated). La Hueca, when used by Chanlatte and Narganes (1990) in reference to Vieques, appears to be equivalent to my usage of ceramic component, but it often seems to also encompass what I would regard as a distinct style in Rouse's sense (e.g., when saying that Candelero has La Hueca ceramics). Hence, they bring into play the concept of style (perhaps more as in art history), modified from the original definition provided by Cruxent and Rouse (1958) for Venezuela. For instance, Chanlatte and Narganes classed components such as Tecla, Sorcé, Hacienda Grande and others as belonging to the Agro-II 'period/stage', and all are grouped under an *Igneri phase*. A phase, then, is sometimes a synonymous to a component and at other times a style and yet at others a complex. Obviously, they are not rigid with regard to the taxonomic levels or the degree of exclusivity of their classificatory units; it is also clear that they have not entirely 'divested' themselves of the 'Rousean' classificatory approach, since they just as often group all the *Agro-I* or La Hueca phase ceramic components, styles, or complexes under a broader integrative unit (i.e., Huecoid or, alternatively, Guapoid) that is, apparently, equivalent to

Rouse's series. The latter term is brought up in their various publications when discussing large scale migrations, as Rouse does. Yet, this 'series' is abstracted from a different classificatory approach.

While processual and ecological oriented archaeologists, such as Keegan (e.g., 1985, 1992), would frown and regard these classificatory problems as empty arguments and inconsequential, and argue that what matters is content, I would beg to differ in one respect[4]. I agree that 'content' overrides 'labels'. But still labels do have serious consequences in confounding dialogue among archaeologists. In part, I blame a general *laissez-faire* attitude toward classificatory rigor for adding fuel to the 'La Hueca Problem'. However confusing it might be, the fact is that the data and materials excavated by Chanlatte and Narganes are classified and analytically described using units and assumptions that are not directly equivalent to Rousean units and assumptions.

I will not press the issue further, except to note that it is unhealthy and probably incorrect to assume (as most of us have) that there is an essential or fundamental equivalency between 'Rousean' and 'Chanlattean' units of analysis. A casual inspection of the La Hueca collections at the University of Puerto Rico cannot be a foundation for a systematic equivalency 'test' toward Rousean units, but could only provide some general impressions. The degree of equivalency must be demonstrated rather than assumed. Rouse (1992), myself (1992a, 1998) and many others (e.g., Siegel 1991) have mechanically and rather simplistically equated Rouse's conceptual units with those of Chanlatte and Narganes, and yet only the latter have organized, excavated and analyzed the data according to their own conceptual scheme. Whether we agree or not with their classes, it seems to me dangerous and unproductive to keep translating data from one 'language' to another on the basis of 'sounds' and in the absence of 'meaning'. We will not be able to establish cognates.

Thus, the basic question has yet to be properly addressed: Are the various units comparable, and if so to what degree is there an equivalency? Note that *both* classificatory frameworks have almost precisely the same fundamental objectives: the reconstruction of the history of culturally defined units (e.g., origin, cultural chronology, stylistic convergence or divergence, and borrowing or independent development). But just because the objectives are the same does not imply that the *means* to reach these goals are interchangeable.

One example of the problems entailed by classification procedures can be appreciated in Henocq's edited volume, where Bonnissent (in Henocq 1995, chapter 5, 1-12) provided a "La Hueca" like ceramic trait list of such component at Hope Estate. While this was, indeed, a preliminary report, the seeds for future problems are already in view. The units utilized are not modes in Rouse's strict sense and usage, but in what the analyst arbitrarily chose to be a diagnostic (descriptive) trait or trait combinations. Some measures, such as weight in grams are tabulated, but what for? The reader is left to guess. The degree of clustering is not demonstrated for any of the trait combinations. The collection of loosely associated traits is then elevated to a level comparable to 'style' or 'phase', but it is not clear precisely what are the assumptions behind the formulation of the higher level integrative unit. Nor can these traits be directly compared with those published for La Hueca. In any case, I am not reassured that the basic procedures for identification and segregation are comparable to La Hueca. I may be wrong, but it is my impression that Bonnissent's classification begins with the *a priori* assumption that she *does* have a La Hueca style at Hope Estate (as opposed to a different Huecoid or Huecan style, or even a different ceramic complex/style altogether). If this is the case, the formulation of analytical units is already biased to find what ought to be tested *independently* in the first place.

I am not saying that this or other methods of analysis are "wrong" or "right". I am stating that we should be very weary and careful about what it is that we compare when different assumptions and distinct units of analysis are being used. And the above problem refers only to units of analysis that have been devised to address issues of cultural and stylistic norms of material culture and chronology, which is a separate problem than the inferences to be made of any social dynamic process or behavior attached to patterns of material culture. These too require conceptual categories that are not necessarily equivalent to the 'modes', 'types', and 'styles' or 'phases' discussed earlier.

In the remainder of this paper, it will become obvious that I have not entirely succeeded in avoiding terminological 'equivalencies' between Rouse's and Chanlatte-Narganes' conceptual and analytical units. My own failure or weakness to do so here does not make it right. Nevertheless, this is something that has to be worked-out as a group and not an *ad hoc* exercise by any one individual. Consensus and agreement is critical for a general acceptance and, therefore, for improving our ability to communicate as exactly (i.e., compare) as possible what we mean by this or that label or unit, or by this or the other quantity. Classification *does* matter immensely, and in this I am one hundred percent behind Rouse's so-called 'obsession' with taxonomy. Classification rigor should not be confused with 'obsession'. If properly applied, it would palliate the tendency to hold on to labels as crutches and substitutes for meaningful discourse.

18.5   The La Hueca style: how different is different?

Clearly, the 'La Hueca Problem' with regard to material culture (ceramics, lithics, etc.) boils down to the old problem of 'lumpers' (similarity) and 'splitters' (difference). The central question posed in this section was raised twenty-six years ago by the eminent anthropologist Gregory Baetson (1972) in his collected essays *Steps to an Ecology of Mind,* when he stated that what is significant is the *"differences that make a difference"*. But, just how should one go about determining this? Is it a purely arbitrary matter in the hands of the analyst, or is it inherent in the things that we are looking at (e.g., sites, assemblages, features, potsherds)? Are the 'differences that make a difference' a question of scales (levels of analytical resolution), assumptions about analytical units, kinds of questions *we* are asking? Being explicit about these issues is essentially at the heart of a 'La Hueca Problem' resolution. This aspiration is implicit, and to some degree explicit, in several of the contributions in this volume. Let us examine a selection of the main points of similarity and difference that have arisen between La Hueca or 'Huecan' and Cedrosan Saladoid.

(a)   One site or two sites? What is a site?
The 'site' of Sorcé in Vieques Island was first excavated by Diana López (1975) in the 1970s, and had been known for a long time by that name, well before the discovery of La Hueca[5]. What we know as La Hueca 'site' lies immediately adjacent (to the south) and overlaps with the Sorcé site only in the ZTB and P midden areas (fig. 18.1). From early on, Chanlatte and Narganes (1983) regarded these as separate and distinct sites, with the explicit implication that these were two side-by-side *villages*. Following Rodríguez López (1991), questions remain as to the nature of the relationship of the numerous middens before one can confidently reach a determination. This is one of those questions that needs to be addressed further: Do we mean that a 'site' = a 'village' in terms of a network of kinship and affinal relationships coupled with localized residence, or purely in terms of archaeological patterns (*sensu* Schiffer) of garbage refuse (already an assumption)? In either case the assumption that the spatial segregation of two configurations of garbage middens is synonymous to two villages already implies that we have assumed that 'garbage distribution' equals 'village configuration' and, in turn, that would imply a close kin/affine network that is autonomous or independent from the other kin network. With the data available (i.e., published) from La Hueca-Sorcé, all we can do is to speculate or provide an unproven model based on a loosely defined correlation between archaeological context units (middens) and cultural or social system units (e.g., cultural behavior of garbage disposal at the back of a given house). Moreover a *descriptive* pattern (structure) may be proven to correlate with a given activity (function) but, does it necessarily translate into an explanation of the social dynamics that produced it? The short answer is no. For now, I prefer the more neutral

(and strictly spatial) term *locus* to distinguish the southern semicircle of middens (La Hueca) and the northern group (Sorcé).

Miguel Rodríguez (pers. comm. 1997), who excavated two units (8 m^2) in the YTA midden area (see Chanlatte and Narganes 1983, foto no. 7), found a living or 'occupational floor', including the remains of complete or nearly complete Saladoid vessels left *in situ*. The 'floor' (if that is what it was) would suggest that the location of 'floors' and 'middens' varied through time. If such is the case for Sorcé 'middens(?)' in general, then it cannot be ruled out that such different contexts (discrete living surfaces vs garbage) were also present in the La Hueca locus middens. The presence of a postmold in midden ZTB confirms the suspicion. In sum, the use, function and sociocultural 'behaviors' inferred form the 'middens' cannot not always be assumed to be only 'garbage disposing' acts.

Fact: The La Hueca locus comprises a series of eight middens that contained La Hueca style materials only (fig. 18.1).

Fact: The numerous (ca. 14) Sorcé middens (fig. 18.1) contained at least two components: Hacienda Grande style (to use Rouse's classification), which evolved into what Chanlatte and Narganes have informally designated as a "monserratean". Both components are grouped by Chanlatte and Narganes (1983, 1990) into a single Igneri Phase. (The 'monserratean' materials include ceramic vessels and decorative modes that I would tentatively classify as Cuevas style [terminal Saladoid] and which also include specimens that are transitional to Monserrate style [Elenan Ostionoid] in Rouse's terminology.)

Fact: There are problems with radiocarbon dates in each loci. A comparison of radiocarbon dates between the La Hueca and Sorcé loci indicate a significant temporal overlap.

Fact: At a site-wide scale, the spatial segregation of the Cedrosan-Elenan and La Hueca components is sharp and unambiguous (Chanlatte and Narganes 1980, 1983).

To 'translate' these and other descriptive "facts" into what they might mean in terms of social dynamics and processes is a wholly different undertaking. The 'debate' about the relationship of the La Hueca "site" to Sorcé "site" is, in principle, unanswerable from a culture historic or normative approach alone, since what is required is to determine the potential range of social processes and behaviors that could have lead to such a complete spatial segregation of artefacts between the two loci.

Assuming contemporaneous occupation(s), the question could also be reformulated by asking, how and in what ways did the group of individuals residing in one locus (La Hueca) viewed and related to the others residing in the other locus (Sorcé)? What should we expect to find in terms of patterns of data on-the-ground given a particular instance (say, a moiety as a hypothesis)? Assuming that the occupants

viewed themselves as 'separate', how did one or the other group conceive the boundaries of their respective residential and public spaces, one 'village' or 'two villages'; two neighborhoods, one village? Again, this question must be rephrased in terms of predictive models. Given the two sets of midden configurations in Vieques, could there be other ways of conceptualizing these spaces and spatial boundaries and of recognizing (predicting) those on the ground? Pottery segregation in contemporaneous occupations *is* significant, but it does not automatically translate as separate villages or, for that matter, into moieties. The very fact that the (Huecan) midden configuration at Punta Candelero is linear (fig. 18.2, inset) and is not adjacent to a *simultaneously* occupied Cedrosan Saladoid locus, already suggests more than one pattern of Huecan refuse (if that is what they only are) exist and that contemporaneous adjacency to Cedrosan refuse deposits is not always present.

The one definition that matters, at least in my mind, for determining 'village' space, is a *social* one; it is how and why people interact with each other on a quotidian basis. The questions should be asked in such terms when assessing patterns on-the-ground. Ethnographic analogies can be profitably used, as shown by Heckenberger and Petersen's (1995) study of midden configurations at Trants, one which has remained stable for quite a long time (regardless of artifact changes). These questions may never be fully answered, but to even try we should move from macroconfigurations to assessments of micro-contexts, not to mention a set of conceptual tools distinct from those used purely for formal descriptive analyses of materials, as is the case *thus far* for La Hueca, Sorcé and Punta Candelero. Potsherd disposal is but one small ingredient, and by itself does not constitute 'a context'.

I do not have ready answers to all of these problems, but I do know that we are not going anywhere if the *status quo* is maintained.

(b) Ceramics

The characteristic Saladoid white-on-red (and etc.) painted ceramics and decorated vessel forms are absent in the La Hueca locus. When present, these invariably occur in the top layer of the middens (00-35/40 cm below surface), most probably as a result of either plow disturbance or modern overburden from a nearby road construction, near midden ZTB (Chanlatte and Narganes 1983) (fig. 18.1). The opposite is not quite true (Chanlatte 1983, 76). An undetermined number (but a minority) of La Hueca style 'zic ware' specimens and microlapidary artefacts have been found in the middens of the Sorcé locus. I do not think the evidence is quite there yet to be able to determine precisely by what social and/or natural processes the La Hueca specimens ended up resting in the northern middens, nor do I know in what contexts these minority items were found. Were these specimens, in fact, discarded as refuse in dumps, or where there other contexts as well implying behaviors other than quotidian garbage dumping? Could these all be *only* the result of purposeful prehistoric exchange among contemporaneous groups? And if so, what motivated the exchange? Other possibilities may exist: Were the La Hueca artefacts looted from the La Hueca midden by subsequent occupants of the Sorcé locus and introduced or disposed of in the northern middens? Can we reject that these specimens were replicas (archaisms) of La Hueca, a phenomenon known to occur elsewhere in the New World (e.g., Cupisnique replicas were made during Moche V phase in Northern Coastal Perú [see Shimada 1994]). The possibilities are endless and not all are mutually exclusive. What is certain is that there is not a single 'homogeneous' stratum or deposit (i.e., assemblage or component) comprised of La Hueca ceramics in the Sorcé set of middens (Chanlatte and Narganes, pers. comm. 1997). What are, then, some of the cultural material differences between the Sorcé and the La Hueca loci? The Cedrosan Saladoid ceramics are relatively well known, so I will not detail them here (cf. Chanlatte 1976, 1983; Roe 1989; Rouse 1992;). The ceramics from La Hueca middens exclusively use plastic modification techniques, primarily incision, but also combined with modeling, punctation or other plastic features (Chanlatte 1993; Chanlatte and Narganes 1983, 53-55; Catalogue UPR, 1996). Red or white 'paint' only occurs as mineral pigments filling the fine incisions or engravings. The pigment fill technique is not exclusive of La Hueca. It is also present in other strictly Cedrosan Saladoid components, such as Quebrada Balerio in Paria (Oliver 1980, Plate 7q). Most interestingly, in Saladero (Orinoco) the *design* is present only as red painted zoned hachure designs on a buff surface, a feature often ignored by Caribbean archaeologists. The *design concept* is present, but uses a different technical medium. Why only accept 'similarity' on the basis of technical medium chosen? Does not the potter's conceptual model of 'hachure design' constitute an equally valid argument for 'lumping' Saladero with other Cedrosan styles? Saladero's painted crosshatch could be the origin of the engraved Huecan or Río Guapo 'zic' design, or perhaps both originated from an undetermined third party (my preferred, but unproven, argument). Aesthetically the zoned incised crosshatching designs from the Caribbean are similar to the Amazonian Zoned Hachure specimens found from Marajó Island to the Upper Ucayali and usually associated with early ceramic complexes like Tutishcainyo or Jauarí (Lathrap 1970).

The diagnostic decorated incised type in the La Hueca assemblages is a relatively broad-line-incised design (used as a frame) filled with relatively fine incised crosshatching design (zic). The 'zic' design appears in simple restricted and unrestricted bowls, double-spouted globular vessels probably used for the inhalation of the hallucinogen *cohoba (Anadenanthera peregrina)*, and in effigy vessels. The latter are predominantly zoomorphic 'bat-winged' bowls from circular to pronounced oval horizontal cross-sections (i.e., navicular). The zoned-incised-crosshatch *design* and their associated vessels has led Rouse to the recognition of a singular 'zic ware' type. This category, 'ware,' is not primarily based on paste and temper (as is done in most other instances), but largely in terms of incision *technique,* decorative field, and associated vessel form. In Cedrosan Saladoid styles, like Hacienda Grande, the 'zic ware' crosshatch designs (but not always the broader zoned incision) is always engraved (post fired), whereas in La Hueca I have seen both prefired (on leather-hard dry clay) and postfired engraving techniques.

However, in my limited, impressionistic view, the range of variation of 'zic' designs appears to be qualitatively far greater in the La Hueca assemblages than in the Hacienda Grande style ceramics. Furthermore, I would agree with Chanlatte (pers. comm. 1997) that there is a technical and aesthetic difference between the Cedrosan 'zic ware' and the Huecan 'zic ware'. Illustrations of this contrast can be seen in the Trants Cedrosan 'zic' ceramics (Petersen 1996, fig 14; also Watters 1994, fig. 20) and the 'Huecan' samples (Petersen 1996, fig. 10) from Monserrat. Are we justified in lumping, as Rouse does, both qualitative 'zic' differences into a single 'zic ware' type?

In La Hueca and Punta Candelero, broad-line zonal incision (i.e., the "frames") also occurs without crosshatch fill. Although less frequent than 'zic' designs, La Hueca also exhibits short ungulate incisions in combination with broad-line incision, linear and curvilinear incision combined with punctation, a sort of zoned incised hachure (i.e., a broad crosshatch-like pattern that looks like a chain of diamonds), and others. The latter are a regarded qualitatively as 'a minority' in comparison to the typical 'zic' design, although quantitative data is not yet available to impart more precision to the above observations. In fact, what I have learned is that "almost all" these non 'zic' designs (Narganes, pers. comm. 1997) are present in Midden 'Z' and nowhere else in the La Hueca locus.

Linear incision, which to my eyes are anything but 'linear' (e.g., Petersen 1996, fig. 15), executed before firing on wet clay, is a *technique* common to both Cedrosan and La Hueca ceramics (for discussion see Roe 1989, Rouse and Alegría 1990). The designs and use of space in the vessels seems to be where differences are more prominent, but I have yet to see an adequate qualitative and quantitative (statistical) analysis that would demonstrate clustering or divergence, as the case might be, between assemblages and components. All we have from both La Hueca and Punta Candelero are the quite preliminary qualitative descriptions coupled with a pronounced absence of statistical information by unit and level (or context).

The impossibility to elicit meaningful quantitative ceramic data from specified contexts in either La Hueca or Punta Candelero is, of course, a major stumbling block in addressing 'The La Hueca Problem'. While qualitative analyses are an absolutely necessary first step, quantitative and statistical applications from definable stratigraphic contexts are the only way to achieve precision in comparative analyses, especially when there is strong suspicion that *continuous* rather than discontinuous variation of ceramic modes and types are predominant in the La Hueca and Sorcé loci middens. For example, Chanlatte (1991a, 671) and Narganes (1991, 631) have proposed a two phase occupation, with a long temporal hiatus (abandonment) in between. The first La Hueca locus occupation dates between ca. 100 BC and AD 400/500. In their view, the ceramics of the subsequent reoccupation exhibited only "minor" changes compared to the earlier occupation at the La Hueca locus. Based only on radiocarbon dates (but disassociated from specific contexts within middens), the purported "hiatus" at La Hueca occurred between ca. AD 500 and AD 1000/1300 (cf. table 18.1). Accepting for the moment the validity of a 500 to 800 year hiatus, even if there were no major ceramic changes, at the very least I would expect significant changes in the *frequency* of modes and mode combinations (types), and most probably meaningful but subtle *discontinuous* changes in the *number* of modes and mode combinations, as well as dimensions utilized (or discontinued) in the ceramic complex (see, Lathrap 1962; Spaulding 1960).

Despite La Hueca's ceramic 'distinctiveness', the *earliest* Saladoid sites in Puerto Rico (Hacienda Grande, El Convento, Ensenada Honda) and elsewhere in the Caribbean always included a small minority of La Hueca-like 'zic' ware, as well as microlapidary materials, mainly depicting frogs, but lacking the zoo-iconographic emphases and mineralogical diversity found at La Hueca middens (e.g., Rouse and Alegría 1990). These traits were considered as integral to Hacienda Grande style (Cedrosan Saladoid) by Rouse and others, but are systematically excluded by Chanlatte and Narganes from their classificatory framework. That is, they are excluded as diagnostic of Agro-II/Igneri phase because they are assumed to be borrowed or intruded from Agro-I. Rodríguez López (unpublished data, 1997) has reconstructed the essential vessel set that characterizes the Punta Candelero 'Huecan' component, including both the plain and the decorated vessels. Rodríguez's study indicates that no more than 14 vessel types, excluding the effigy vessels, could be consistently identified. If so, it presents a significant contrast with the more complex and numerous vessel forms typifying the Cedrosan Saladoid vessel set. I do not know how many

vessel form types the average Cedrosan component in Puerto Rico (or elsewhere) has, but I am convinced that it should be at least twice as many, by just looking at those represented in several private collections in Puerto Rico.

On the other hand, as Roe (1989) has stressed, *both* the Cedrosan Saladoid and La Hueca ceramics show overlap in terms of the *undecorated* vessel forms (he and Rouse called 'plain wares'), pertaining to certain simple open bowls, constricted jars with two or three strapped-handles, incense burners *(troumassées)*, and the ubiquitous *burén* clay griddles. It was, therefore, argued that La Hueca differed from Saladoid styles (e.g., Hacienda Grande style) in only *a part* of their total vessel and microlapidary inventory. While some of the ordinary, *undecorated* culinary, liquid storage and an undetermined number of serving vessel forms overlapped with Cedrosan Saladoid ordinary vessels, the *decorated* vessels were different between the two, both in terms of shape and in terms of decorative techniques, designs, and decorative fields.

I could go on and on discussing more groups of attributes that would indicate lumping and others that would indicate splitting. In short, it seems that the whole exercise is a rather arbitrary one, affected by the level of detail we are focusing on. In the end we are still left with the unsolved problem of *lumping* and *splitting* and of *degrees of accepted formal variation* at various levels of analysis – ranging from single attributes to modes, to components, and to styles or ceramic complexes and even subseries. The lack of contexts, beyond the vague 'refuse' midden context, precludes any alternative classification and comparison of ceramics that would include contextual function and meaning in a society or community.

(c) Microlapidary artefacts and materials

In addition to ceramics, the presence of a high number (ca. 2,724) of both local and exotic microlapidary items also imparted a flavor of 'uniqueness' for the La Hueca assemblages. *Tentativelly* (for most require compositional analyses) the materials consist of rock crystal, milky quartz, amethyst, citrine quartz, aventurine quartz (both the green and the brown varieties), translucent 'orange' and 'green' quartzes, agate (unspecified), carnelian (including the brownish sard variety), onyx, common opal, topaz, jade, nephrite, seprentinite, turquoise, malachite, calcite, pyrite, diorite, peridotite, various kinds of chert, and unspeficied metamorphosed 'marbles' (Chanlatte and Narganes 1983; Narganes 1995). The microlithics were found in various stages of reduction. Some fragmented or aborted pieces were modified and re-utilized[6]. Minimally, "nephrite", "jade", aventurine quartz, turquoise, and perhaps carnelian along with some of the serpentinite-like materials, are exotic not only to Vieques-Puerto Rico, but to the West Indies (Oliver and Lathrap 1985; Boomert 1987; Cody 1991, 1993; Rodríguez 1993; Watters 1997b).

The microlapdiary work also included mother-of-pearl and other marine shell materials (e.g., *Oliva sp.*). Bone and 'wood' (what the authors regarded as 'petrified wood') were very rare, but present. As I will discuss in Part II, the maximum diversity of mineral/gem species pertain to La Hueca midden 'Z', just as the widest variability of ceramic incised techniques and designs do. Midden 'Z' is, therefore, the basis for the definition of the La Hueca style, phase, or complex.

At Punta Candelero, a similar range of raw materials, as well as morphological types were also present, but their proportions seem to vary in comparison to La Hueca. One possible material present in Punta Candelero, as yet undetected at La Hueca, is an amber bead.

The sheer quantity and diversity (raw materials *and* forms) of these lapidary items has also heavily contributed the image construction of La Hueca as being 'unique' (different). Other purportedly Cedrosan Saladoid components, such as Prosperity on St. Croix and Trants, on Monserrat have also yielded exotic microlapidary lithic (gemstone) materials, but not in the same quantity and diversity (Robinson and Vescelius 1979; Watters 1994, 1997a, 1997b; Watters and Scaglion 1994). Differences in sampling methods, however, seem to be an important reason for the perceived huge differences in 'richness' for some sites, especially between La Hueca and Cedrosan Saladoid sites. Still, according to Narganes (pers. comm. 1997) the adjacent Sorcé locus, on the whole, has not yielded either the quantity or the diversity of microlapidary observed for the La Hueca locus, and it would further appear that the 'exotic' materials were no longer available.

d) Burial Practices, Middens and the Central Clearing Space

Another important characteristic of La Hueca site, which Chanlatte and Narganes (1990, 15) have often emphasized, is that not a single burial has ever been found in a La Hueca midden context, a fact misrepresented by Rouse and Alegría (1990). At Punta Candelero, all but very few human burials were firmly ascribed to the Cuevas occupation (Crespo 1991) (fig. 18.2, inset). The remaining few individuals could *not* be associated to either occupation (M. Rodríguez, pers. comm. 1997). One crucial point is that at La Hueca only *middens* were excavated, and no tests have been performed in the central open area. If, indeed, the La Hueca occupants buried their dead in a circumscribed burial ground in the central clearing (as the Cedrosan and early Ostionan did), then it is little wonder that 'no burials' were found in midden contexts.[7] 'Not present' is not the same as 'absent'. It cannot be confirmed that this purported difference in mortuary practices between 'Huecans' and 'Cedrosans' (or Agro-II) is not due to excavation sampling strategy — and to the probable partial destruction of the "plaza" by the

paved county road (PR 993). However, a central burial ground unequivocally associated to the La Hueca component was clearly *not* found in Punta Candelero. I am particularly interested in burial data because these may hold important clues to the questions of social organization and the debate of one village and two communities versus two societies and two villages.

By way of contrast, the Sorcé locus middens have yielded an undetermined number human burials (Chanlatte and Narganes 1983, foto 19). The critical mortuary analysis and distribution data within the northern Sorcé locus remain unpublished. Given the sheer size of excavated area (935 m² by 1982) in the La Hueca locus, it is quite probable that human burials were absent from *midden* contexts. It is *not* demonstrated, however, that human burials were also absent from the central clearing or plaza areas of both the Sorcé and the La Hueca loci.

If we now add to the Sorcé map published in 1983 the blocks or trenches excavated on middens since that date (cf. our fig. 18.1; cf. Chanlatte 1991b), it becomes less clear that there was only a single central clearing in this locus. It is feasible now to draw two possible semicircular configurations at Sorcé, a northern and a southern one. Could it be that, given a suspected long occupational history, the axis of the central clearing had shifted north or south? What implications does this have in terms of a centrally localized common burial ground, if it indeed, existed at Sorcé? Assuming contemporaneity, were the deceased of both the La Hueca and Sorcé loci interred in the same common, localized burial ground? How could one be assured that some of those burials in the Sorcé middens were not individuals from the La Hueca locus? Were the La Hueca dead buried outside the confines of either loci? Were they practicing a different burial custom, such as cremation, than those inhabiting the Sorcé locus? There are no answers to these questions. However, mortuary practices can vary to such an extent within a single contemporaneous society, that burial data alone are often insufficient to determine a group's ethnic or cultural identity (cf. Binford 1971, Chapman et al. 1981; Curet and Oliver 1998).

18.6   Competing historical reconstructions: a question of contingency

Given the unresolved 'lumping or splitting' arguments with regards to ceramics, and the blaring poverty of published contextual data, it should not be surprising that all sorts of competing interpretations are possible, and that a reduction (falsification) of alternative interpretive hypotheses has essentially failed. What seems ironic is that the differences between Rouse and Chanlatte are basically predicated upon historical contingency; that is, the order and sequence of reconstructed (or presumed) cultural historic 'events' are ultimately dependent or contingent upon a purely hypothetical origin (or 'starting point'). The origin issue sets their different 'fast-forward' historic-developmental scenarios for arguing the finer points of parallelism, convergence (acculturation), divergence and migrations. The conceptual and theoretical arsenal displayed by the two 'opposing' historical reconstructions come from the same normative culture-history 'factory'. Let us look first at Chanlatte and Narganes' reconstruction of the 'events', keeping in mind the pre-1980 cultural historic model discussed earlier.

Chanlatte and Narganes (1983, 73-76; Chanlatte 1981) proposed a different series to represent a separate and perhaps an earlier, or at least contemporaneous, migration of ceramic-bearing groups from South America, which they designated as Huecoid (or Guapoid) and associated to the Agro-I period/stage. They further proposed that the origin of La Hueca phase could be traced to the little understood Río Guapo, a ceramic style from eastern Venezuela with a single date of ca. AD 320±100. Río Guapo had been tentatively regarded as a Saladoid style in the 1950s; it also shared with La Hueca the anomaly of lacking Saladoid painting and exhibiting an abundance of 'zic' ware (Cruxent and Rouse 1958).[8] The Agro-I, Huecoid population migrated into the Antilles at about the same time or somewhat earlier than the Saladoid. Furthermore, according to Chanlatte's (1981, 1993) scenario, the Huecoid (Agro-I) and the Archaic converged in Vieques and Puerto Rico and through 'strong interaction' (see Rouse 1986 for a definition) resulted in the development of the Agro-III or Ostiones phase, *roughly* comparable to Rouse's early styles of the early Ostionoid series. In addition, upon reaching Vieques, both the Agro-I (La Hueca phase) and Agro-II (Igneri phase) settled side by side, in close physical proximity at La Hueca and Sorcé. This residential adjacency 'explains' the limited one-way 'exchange' of ceramic traits and micro-lapidary items from La Hueca to Sorcé (Why the exchange was not reciprocal, remains to be elucidated). Chanlatte lends as great an involvement of preceramic or Archaic populations as Agro-II or Igneri phase groups in the process of the 'ethnogensis' of Agro-III societies (at least, in their material culture):

…observamos como los *arcaicos* residentes de las islas, reciben a los *agroalfareros-I* quienes vienen desde el Continente [ya] con influencias precerámicas. Con muy poca diferencia de tiempo y por la misma ruta, hacen su entrada los *agroalfareros-II* estableciendo sus asentamientos contigüos a los *agroalfareros-I,* según las evidencias obtenidas en Sorcé, Vieques y en Hacienda Grande, Loíza. […] Los *agroalfareros-I* adoptan técnicas y elementos domésticos de los *arcaicos* y los *agroalfareros II* incorporan rasgos y características de los *agroalfareros-I.* En el transcurso de las interrelaciones y al contacto con los agroalfareros, los arcáicos se vuelven lentamente horticultores y comienzan a desarrollar su propia cerámica [i.e., Agro-III] (Chanlatte 1981, 16-17; emphasis in the original).

Upon reaching Vieques and Puerto Rico the two separate cultural complexes, Agro-I and Agro-II, witnessed a process of asymmetrical convergence that especially involved the resident Archaic groups. La Hueca is seen by Chanlatte as the principal 'receiver' of lithic/shell manufacturing techniques and material goods from the Archaic and at the same time the Agro-I is viewed as the main 'donor' of traits (e.g., 'zic ware') to the Agro-II groups (Chanlatte 1991b). In his view, this intercultural *menage à trois* led to the development of Agro-III (i.e., roughly the Ostionoid in Rouse's terminology).

Chanlatte (1981, 59) argued that very few material and stylistic elements were adopted by the Agro-II (Igneri phase). The presence of a minority of 'zic ware' and of some microlapidary materials found in purportedly 'homogeneous' Saladoid sites was explained by Chanlatte (1981b, 1995) as primarily the result of: (1) Saladoid or Igneri phase potters adopting La Hueca phase 'zic ware' decorative traits and microlapidary materials and (2) that what Rouse, Alegría, and others regarded as a minority Cedrosan Saladoid ware at other sites (e.g., Hacienda Grande, Tecla), is merely the result of inadvertently mixing separate (stratigraphically and/or spatially) and 'pure' La Hueca assemblages with Saladoid ones during excavation (Chanlatte 1995). The 'Huecan' materials are 'intrusive'. In Chanlatte's own words:

…todavía a Rouse y Alegría les confunde la presencia de materiales *huecoides* asociados a las muestras *saladoides tempranas.* Más de una vez hemos explicado que en nuestro concepto tales presencias son intrusivas y se deben a que los saladoides… al entrar a las Antillas, se asientan en las vecindades cercanas de los huecoides y que la existencia de un reducido porcentaje de evidencias asociadas a los materiales saladoides tempranos, sólo testimonian buenas relaciones y posibles prácticas comerciales entre las dos migraciones agroalfareras (Chanlatte 1981b, 59; our underlining).

A problem with the above 'explanation' is that it is only a supposition. On the one hand, 'agro-ceramic migrations' cannot have 'good commercial relationships'; contemporaneous individuals, communities of people do. On the other hand, 'intrusion' assumes that the mere presence of 'zic ware' in Saladoid middens is the result of 'friendly' exchange and that, indeed, it took place between contemporaneous side-by-side villages, when in fact the majority of Cedrosan sites lack such an adjacent Huecan habitation locus. 'Intrusion', as used in the above quote, implies unidirectional (asymmetrical) exchange; it also assumes that other factors for the co-residence of materials (site formation and deformation processes) have been ruled out, when in fact they have yet to be so demonstrated.

Irving Rouse (1985, 1986, 83-85) flatly rejected the 'two migration' hypothesis and questioned the validity of a separate Huecoid (or Guapoid) series in the Caribbean. Instead, he proposed that La Hueca's 'uniqueness' was probably due to a special function of this site (e.g., specialized craftsmen living-workshop site?), but whose cultural material remains were still reasonably well within the range of variation expected of a *Cedrosan* Saladoid series component. This position assumed that the observed difference was at the level of 'wares' and, implicitly, of community, but that examined at the level of ceramic style and, hence, of a 'people' and their (material) 'culture', the differences evaporated. This hierarchical taxonomic differentiation (higher level 'culture-peoples' vs lower level 'wares-communities' or, as in the quote below, 'local families'), is one of the aspects of Rouse's conceptual approach (and technical nomenclature) that Chanlatte and Narganes have had most difficulty in either internalizing or accepting. Durand and Petitjean Roget best summarized Rouse's argument. For Rouse (1990) the La Hueca pottery style:

…n'est qu'une sous-série saladoïde, qu'il nomme 'Huecan-Saladoid' […] Selon l'importance de la répartition de la poterie huecoïde dans les sites où l'on trouve du saladoïde insulaire, explique Rouse, elle indiquerait soit que *"the local families had a free choice between them, as in the case of chinaware and stoneware in our civilization"* où que ces poteries indiqueirant, *"places in which specialized activities took place, in which case we could say Huecan pottery was made and used for particular purpose"* (Durand and Petitjean Roget 1991, 55).

Taking a clue from M. G. Smith's (1965) concept of 'plural societies', Rouse (1990) considered that it was possible and likely to have two side-by-side living communities (e.g., La Hueca-Sorcé, or the Ronquín case of Saladoid and 'fiber wares' [now known as Cedeño] in the Orinoco), each choosing to emphasize different elements of the entire ceramic repertoire and yet share a general (i.e., Saladoid) cultural pattern. This is probably why Rouse was initially very cautious in accepting and proposing a separate stylistic affiliation for La Hueca. We must remember that Rouse uses 'style' in a very specific way, and not at all synonymous with an art historian's definition. This is why he can establish a conceptual correspondence between a given style and a given people that have a given culture. At a lower, more specific level of resolution, communities and familial groups may have exhibited only a part of the total style characterizing a people and a culture. That is also why for Rouse the shared presence of 'zic ware' is the crucial point, and not that one side of the equation lacks paint. He emphasizes 'similarity' simply because it impossible to establish higher levels of taxonomic integration on the basis of what is *not* common or shared! Rouse's (1990; see also 1992) cultural historic reconstruction goes something like this: As the Cedrosan Saladoids

spread through the Antilles northward, they diverged into two separate subseries in the northeastern Caribbean subregion. Rouse also suggested that just as Cedrosan and Huecan styles diverged in the northernmost range of their distribution in the Caribbean, a similar divergence had taken place among the coastal Venezuelan Cedrosan styles, such as between Río Guapo and El Mayal. Once they reached the Virgin Islands Passage area:

…they [Cedrosan Saladoid] diverged, one part settling on Vieques Island and the adjacent shore of the main island [Punta Candelero site], where they became La Hueca people; and the other part proceeding along the north, west and south parts of the main island [Puerto Rico], where we know them as Hacienda Grande people. Our analyses of the Hacienda Grande people's ceramic style and of its culture have supported these conclusions. We have noted a number of stylistic and functional traits that link the Hacienda Grande people with the initial Ceramic-age peoples along the presumed migration route, especially with the La Hueca people… We know of no sharp discontinuities along the route which would negate the hypothesis of radiation and divergence (Rouse and Alegría 1990, 80; our clarification in brackets).

The important difference with Chanlatte's theory, is that at both ends, Rouse considers the Huecan-like styles having historically developed from the same Saladoid ancestry, and yielding similar results.

In the end, Rouse met Chanlatte and Narganes only halfway, by acknowledging that this was not simply a matter of a specialized local community that exhibited a La Hueca ware that was still within the 'cultural' framework of Hacienda Grande style (i.e., a Cedrosan Saladoid member), but rather a broader, distinctive cultural phenomenon. He first accepted La Hueca as a different Cedrosan style and subsequently as a different style in a different Saladoid subseries (i.e., Huecan). These changes of heart were not based on any new data from La Hueca/Sorcé, but as a result of finding an indisputable La Hueca component at Punta Candelero, as well as on other less well known data from sites, such as El Convento in Puerto Rico. The exceptional and unique was no longer.

What are then the points of divergence between Rouse's and Chanlatte and Narganes' interpretation? Chanlatte argues for two unrelated, independent origins in the mainland (Huecoid and Saladoid) that converged in the northeastern Caribbean region. Instead, Rouse assumes no independent origins in the mainland (all derived from a Saladoid background) and suggests not one but two divergences, one in the mainland (Río Guapo vs coastal Saladoid) and another one in the other end of the migratory route (Huecan vs. insular Saladoid). I now wonder what are the odds of two independent divergences (mainland and Vieques) to have yielded precisely the same stylistic results? Presently, however, I am sure that

Rouse would accept that this scenario does not account for the situation in St. Martin. Following his line of reasoning he would have to admit that the purported divergence may have taken place somewhere in the Guadeloupe-St. Martin subregion and maybe earlier than in Vieques, if we accept Haviser's early dates[9]. On the other hand, based on the same evidence, and following Chanlatte and Narganes' reasoning, the data from St Martin would purportedly strengthen their hypothesis of two *independent* separate populations that converged (perhaps earlier in time) further to the south in the Caribbean.

Rouse's earlier interpretation for La Hueca site was that it represented a special function site (a community), where exotic lithic materials were acquired, manufactured and then redistributed onto Saladoid settlements elsewhere. The concept of special function (craftsmen) still would apply to the combined neighboring sites of La Hueca-Punta Candelero. This is a separate issue from the problem of cultural or social ("ethnic") identity; it is about economics and labor organization whose characteristics may or may not be unique to a given society. One must remember that other Cedrosan Saladoid sites, like Prosperity, Pearls or Trants, were also manufacturers and traders of exotic and local but preciously rare gemstone materials. The automatic knee-jerk reaction of assigning any microlapidary 'caches' to a La Hueca origin (e.g., manufacture) by Chanlatte and Narganes is premature. There is ample evidence to refute the thesis that only the Huecan groups had the craftsmanship skills to originate, produce and/or control the distribution of these artefacts. The Hope Estate-I (La Hueca-related) lithic assemblage clearly demonstrates that, at the very least, not all Huecan-related settlements were geared towards the acquisition, manufacture, distribution or even exchange of microlapidary items. In other words, the control of these resources is not exclusive to either Huecan (or Huecoid) or Cedrosan Saladoid groups.

Both sides of the debate have their detractors. For example, Durand and Petitjean Roget (1991, 60), remain unconvinced of Rouse's arguments. These authors noted that La Hueca (Huecoid):

Nous assurons que ce groupe est distinct du Saladoide insulaire, ce qui se montrent les différences entre les formes et l'ornementation des vases, la pratique (qui reste à prouver) de déformations crâniennes qui ne sont pas celles des Saladoïdes et la fabrication d'ammulettes vantour en pierre verte qui n'existent pas dans les cultures, issues de l'évolution du Saladoìde insulaire aux Antilles.

Chanlatte (1983, 1995) furiously contested Rouse's and Alegría's (1990) interpretations of his 'Huecoid' migration hypothesis, while the latter stuck to theirs (e.g., Rouse 1992). Most importantly, all the participants in this debate (e.g., above quote) make use of precisely the same raw data sets. Surely, the very fact that the basic raw data is the same and yet simultaneously yields plausible but different culture historic reconstructions, is an indication that a good deal of the problems rest upon how the raw data (methodology) is analyzed.

Moreover, because of the unyielding intransigence between Rouse and Alegría and Chanlatte and Narganes' theoretical stances, much of the debate has gyrated on constantly reshuffling the 'similarity' vs. 'difference' units of descriptive analysis and their implications for migration and acculturation, rather than focusing on what really mattered: a conscientious presentation and evaluation of *contextual* data. So much of Chanlatte and Narganes publications is dedicated to the defense of their model at the level of model/theory. This is quite an understandable reaction, since from the beginning their postulates have been rejected point blank. As I witnessed in the famous floor debate in the 9th International Congress of Caribbean Archaeology held in Santo Domingo (1981), their initial tentative interpretations were — to put it mildly — publicly rejected by a number of archaeologists. This was not a proud moment for Caribbean archaeology. This is a matter of politics I wish not to expand any further, except to say that whatever the motivations, just or unjust, political or scientific, the end result was anything but constructive for a resolution of the 'La Hueca Problem'.

While Chanlatte and Rouse represent the polar extremes of the intellectual debate, much ambivalence still remains about whether to regard La Hueca as a phenomenon with a separate and distinct origin from the Saladoid, or to whether adopt the hypothesis of a common Saladoid origin and subsequent divergence. The differences may not seem to be as methodologically drastic in retrospect, but they have significant historical implications. They imply two different 'histories' for the same phenomenon. Both allude to the same broad 'processes' of migration, of divergence and convergence, and of interaction and acculturation, but arriving a different reconstructions. It is a typical problem of historical contingency. As paleontologist and natural historian Stephen Jay Gould (1989) effectively explained in the case of 'life's history' (in relation to directed laws of natural evolution or "science" vs. "just history"):

Historical explanations take the form of a narrative: E, the phenomenon to be explained, arose because D came before, preceeded by C, B, and A. If any of these earlier stages had not occurred or had transpired in a different way, then E would not exist (or would exist in a substantially altered form E', requiring a different explanation). Thus E makes sense and can be explained rigurously as the outcome of A through D. But no law of nature enjoined E; any variant E' arising from an altered set of antecedents, would have been equally explicable, though massively different in form and effect... I am not speaking of randomness (for E had to arise as a consequence of A through D), but of the central principle of all history *contingency*. A historical explanation [rests on] an unpredictable sequence of antedated states, where any major change in the step would have altered the result. The final result is, therefore, contingent upon everything that came before the unerasable and determining signature of history (Gould 1989, 283; our clarifications in brackets).

It seems obvious that the evidence for the 'antecedent states' are simply too fragmentary and incomplete to arrive at what Gould (1989) termed *consilience of induction*, or the "jumping together" of many independent lines of *archaeological* evidence that conspire to produce confidence only in one most probable historical explanation (see also Oliver 1992b).

18.7   The 'Huecan-Cedrosan problem' outlined

Confusion over how to deal with the 'La Huecan Problem' without offending or annoying half of one's colleagues has led to bizarre side-stepping by some of us, myself included (Oliver 1992a, 1998). For example, Jay Haviser (1991c, 1997) no longer refers to Huecoid/Agro-I or Huecan Saladoid but instead speaks of a neutered 'Early Ceramic Age' complex, whereas I was content in reciting Rouse's scheme and appending the obligatory cautionary note that "Chanlatte and Narganes present a different view…" as if political correctness would make the problems go away. Nor, I would think, Rouse's 'promotion' of La Hueca into a separate Saladoid subseries does resolve the issue, simply because such promotion still assumes an exclusive Saladoid origin that remains contested by Chanlatte (with just as "powerful" arguments as Rouse's).

It can be concluded that we cannot continue to endlessly argue for or against either historical model and expect a solid, unequivocal resultion. It is necessary to 'come down' from lofty theory posturing, back into the dirt and ask some serious questions about excavation strategies and, equally important, what sort of analytical 'tools' are required for not just intra-site analysis but in particular for inter-site/comparisons. The good news is that through the 1990s, there has been a significant move towards these goals: Hope Estate, Morel, and a number of other sites in the region are being 'prepared' to address these problems. Luck still plays a role: finding the ideally well preserved site, with either horizontal or spatial segregation and minimal post-depositional alteration is simply a matter of luck (and, perhaps, some help from geomorphology). To summarize, the interpretive hypotheses have been stretched beyond what the evidence allows for a comfortable degree of confidence.

Rodríguez López (1991, 613) best summarized the essential, unanswered 'large scale' questions, which I reformulated as follows (adding some of my own):

(1) Does La Hueca represent a ceramic style within the Saladoid series (common origin), yet belonging to a different Huecan Saladoid subseries (phylogenetic divergence)?

(2) Is La Hueca the result of a *separate* but parallel migration to the Saladoid that converged in the northeastern Caribbean sub-area?

(3) Is La Hueca earlier and/or contemporaneous to the rest of the Cedrosan Saladoid components in the Caribbean? What do the stratigraphic evidence, site formation and deformation processes, radiocarbon dates and relative chronology tell us?

(4) If La Hueca components are contemporaneous and adjacent to Cedrosan sites, for how long did they remain so, and why one (usually Huecan) locus is abandoned, whereas the other (Cedrosan) continued? Why segregated but adjoining Huecan-Cedrosan loci occur in only some localities and not others? What does it all mean in terms of social organization and interaction?

(5) Does La Hueca locus in Vieques represent a specialized group (microlapidary traders; a moiety, etc.?) within the context of a Cedrosan Saladoid community or were they historically and culturally independent as well as functionally separate and distinct society?

(6) Is La Hueca problem created by archaeologists' faulty excavation methods and/or assumptions, further compounded by the erroneous *a priori* expectation that 'zic ware' is integral to the Cedrosan Saladoid components and therefore going undetected during analysis?

(7) Finally, what effects did La Hueca had upon the cultural development of later prehistory in the Greater and Lesser Antilles? Was La Hueca *the* ancestral complex that had a direct causal role to play in the genesis of the Ostionoid or Agro-III? If so what was the role of the late Saladoid in relation to the emergence of the early Ostionan and Elenan complexes?

While Rodríguez's questions are right on target, his solution — that the answer lies in finding/excavating more sites — is not likely to entirely resolve these problems. His own excavations at Punta Candelero, and those reported for Hope Estate (this volume; Henocq 1995; Haviser 1991a; Hope Estate Bulletin, 1994), have not settled the problems outlined: Are we to believe that further excavations and more radiocarbon dates will yield the desired answers? The problem is clearly not in "more" but in "how".

I am not saying that new investigations elsewhere are not helpful and necessary. But I am certain so long as La Hueca and Punta Candelero remain the measuring yardstick for all that is "Huecoid" these sites will remain crucial to any satisfactory resolution.

In my view, there are some fundamental observations that can already be made by the Hope Estate study presented in this volume.

(1) There is an horizontal (spatial) separation of an early Huecan-related component at Hope Estate (southeast part) as at La Hueca, but unlike Punta Candelero, a vertical (stratigraphic, temporal) segregation was not confirmed. The lower deposits of the northeast part at Hope Estate proved to contain Huecan-like ceramics (Hope Estate 1) included in what the excavators regard as an Cedrosan Saladoid component (Hope Estate 2) (Hofman, this volume).

(2) The mixture of the two early components is likely to be the result of post-depositional alterations due to both a Saladoid reoccupation and to other natural agencies (Hoogland this volume; cf. Henocq ed. 1995). However, the question of whether La Hueca-related component preceded the Cedrosan component stratigraphically and was subsequently mechanically mixed or whether there was contemporaneity (involving exchange) *and* a mechanical admixture still remain competitive explanations.

(3) The contextual analysis of the absolute dates related to the Hope Estate I component, however, remain problematic (see Hoogland, this volume, for a detailed assessment): the 400 cal BC- 60 cal BC obtained by Haviser were not reconfirmed by the assays obtained by Hofman and Hoogland (but using crab claws for dating rather than charcoal). We are still ignorant of when this Huecan component was abandoned in relation to the (presumably) continued Cedrosan occupation in the northern part. At the moment, it is not possible decide which of the set of dates (400-60 BC or AD 255-650?) actually applies to Hope Estate I. Based on my reassessment of Punta Candelero and La Hueca dates (next section), I am inclined to accept the later range of dates obtained by Hoogland and Hofman.

(4) The lithic analysis (Haviser, this volume) unequivocally indicates that neither Hope Estate I nor Hope Estate II inhabitants were participating in the production or consumption of exotic, gemstone quality, microlapidary work. This is very intriguing, as Haviser noted, because unless the excavations missed spatially resticted caches, it means that they were left outside the pan-Caribbean trade network. Indeed, Cedrosan settlements like Trants in Monserrat were more involved than their contemporaries (Huecan-Agro-I) at Hope Estate!

(5) Given Hofman's (this volume) noted 'differences' in the decorative ceramic modes, Hope Estate I should be regarded as a different style in Rouse's sense. (Could we, perhaps, speak of yet another ware type, 'zip' [zoned incised punctated] for Hope Estate-I?)

The remainder of this paper focuses on La Hueca and the problems of chronology and comparability of typological data with specific reference to microlapidary artefacts as an example. My hope is that in addition to a key contribution of the Hope Estate research — that taphonomy is a the first key for resolving the 'La Hueca Problem' — the ways in which we present and portray data is just as crucial.

18.8   Reviewing contexts: stratigraphy and dates

I have already indicated that the excavation strategy used by Chanlatte and Narganes (1983) was to excavate in units of $4m^2$ from top to bottom before proceeding to the next unit. Initially they established five such units in a cross pattern at the outer edges and center of a suspected midden deposit. Upon confirming the presence of a cultural deposit, they added a number of units adjacent to the positive test unit and proceeded to cover trench or block areas of variable total size. Excavations proceeded initially in 20 cm arbitrary levels, and in later seasons in 10 cm arbitrary levels. Dry-screening was consistently used, and the mesh was a standard 0.33 cm (1/8") except for the units selected for zooarchaeological sampling (1/16"). The latter were based on $1m^2$ samples within the $4m^2$ standard unit. Hereafter, I will use 'excavation' and/or 'unit' to refer to the 2×2 m or $4m^2$ excavation. The excavators were also careful in noting the depth reached by the disturbed plow zone, which averaged around 35 to 40 cm below the surface (hereafter cmBS) in all excavation blocks, except for 'Z' and perhaps part of 'ZTB'. I refer to each excavation area or group of close or adjacent units as a 'block area', followed by the name given to the midden deposit.

The depths of the different levels in different units were measured as follows. Each unit's surface was reset at 00 cm along the higher wall (or its corner?), and each level was begun and stopped at 'X' cmBS. It is for this reason that Narganes (1991) has insisted that listing in her publication the 'depths' radiocarbon samples is 'meaningless', since each depth recorded is relative to that single unit's surface (= 00 cmBS). In a very pronounced sloping surface, as in block 'Z', depths were also calculated on the surface elevation of each unit rather than on an arbitrarily selected high point as an elevation datum (cm below datum). This 'tactic' allowed them to excavate arbitrary levels that approximately followed the slope of the terrain. I would assume that eventually all of these depths below the individual unit's surface can be tied to an elevation datum, say to the wall or corner of the unit at the top of the slope, in order to accurately render all of the levels' depths across a block, trench or even site. For the moment, these data (along with the stratigraphy) have not been published. Thus, the ordering of the radiocarbon assays (or any assemblage) across a block/midden or the entire locus by depths based on cm below surface (cmBS) is meaningless, except for that one unit in particular, keeping in mind that it covers an area of $4m^2$ and 0.8 or 0.4 m^3 within which a charcoal sample or aggregate sample collected 'in level' could have come from (due to arbitrary 20 or 10 cm level excavation).

Chanlatte and Narganes' choice of a minimal $4m^2$ sampling size already indicates that, in the absence of piece-plotted plan views, the level of resolution for spatial-quantitative analyses will *never* be more precise than a $2 \times 2m^2$ area. That also means that any comparison with La Hueca assemblages *ipso facto* requires a conversion factor (e.g., to items per m^2 or m^3) something I have rarely seen in the published literature. (For a practical example, see Merher's [1995] treatment of Late Woodland-Mississippian garbage pits.) One of the most baffling problems in reassessing La Hueca refers to the radiocarbon dates, recently summarized by Narganes (1991). As shown in table 18.1, the La Hueca dates range from a minimum of 160 cal BC to a maximum of AD 1440 (at 2 sigma) for the entire locus. In other words, it was "occupied" through all the periods of the Ceramic Age! The Sorcé locus *charcoal* dates range from a minimum of 90 cal BC to cal AD 770 (at 2 sigma), except for two assays (table 18.3). The range of dates for Sorcé is non-controversial given its ceramic stylistic range (Hacienda Grande to Monserrate in Rouse's terminology) and in comparison to dates reported for Puerto Rico and the Virgin Islands. The dates for Punta Candelero are also as problematic as those of La Hueca locus (cf. tables 18.2, 18.4).

The 34 dates from La Hueca can be grouped into two sets, an early and a late one (table 18.1). A "hiatus" in this array seems to occur between approximately cal AD 400/500 and cal AD 1200. Chanlatte and Narganes (pers. comm. 1997) indicated that both sets of dates, without exception, are associated with a La Hueca style or complex ceramic assemblage. I have a hard time accepting all these dates as being unequivocally associated with an *unchanged* or essentially *static* style or complex. But I fully agree with their assertion that many of us, myself included (Oliver 1998), have dismissed the *late dates* without any basis on which to do so. Since Punta Candelero also has the same problem with dates, there is really no means to assess and compare with La Hueca. And now the dates for Hope Estate-I barely overlap the *early* group dates of La Hueca; they are much earlier. While the late dates from La Hueca simply do not fit our expectations, it does not amount to a justification for *selectively* rejecting the "inconvenient" dates. Ultimately, the array of dates must first make sense within a site (and its individual units) before meaningful comparisons and inferences can be made.

One problem that requires further attention is that Chanlatte and Narganes have not yet indicated if the samples submitted to Teledyne Isotopes were (a) an aggregate of charcoal bits from a given arbitrary level, (b) a single specimen from a level, (c) a single specimen from a discrete feature, and/or (d) an aggregate of charcoal bits from a discrete feature. As is known, an aggregate of charcoal bits has unwanted averaging effects, as each charcoal bit *may* have a significantly different date by itself. If such data are known to them, my first step would be to eliminate all of the aggregate charcoal samples from any further consideration. Another problem

relates to marine shell dates. In their case their samples are all from *Strombus sp.*, which eases somewhat problems of comparison and assessment (Chanlatte and Narganes 1983, 33). The problem with marine carbonates is that "whereas the effects of (δ ^{13}C) fractionation can be accurately quantified, *the marine [reservoir] effect cannot* (Bowman 1990, 25; my emphasis). Experiments on known age shells have shown that"apparent ages differing by *a few centuries* can be obtained for localities in close proximity"(ibid.). Bowman (1990, 24-6) cites other uncertainties inherent to marine carbonates that are not encountered with wood charcoal. Hence, the marine dates are difficult to assess in calendar terms; they should not be even"converted"to calendric values.

Despite all of these issues, however, some interesting observations can still be made, even in the absence of precise contextual or stratigraphic data. The observations I offer here were only possible thanks to Chanlatte and Narganes. They allowed me to present the radiocarbon dates and their unit provenience (tables 18.1, 18.3). I respected their condition of not tabulating here the specific depths of the specific samples, since they plan to do so in a future publication. As a compromise, I have provided the maximum and minimum depth range (in cmBS) of the set of assays reported for each block area (cf. figs 18.3-18.4), or discuss their relationship to the plow zone layer or some other published stratigraphic information. In the following pages I discuss the data from excavations up to the 1982 field season.

18.8.1   BLOCK 'ZT2'

Midden 'ZT2' consists of 12 adjoining excavation units, plus three other isolated units. In total, 64 m^2 were excavated up to 1982. The units were placed to the edge of the midden. The highest surface point of the midden is judged to be about 20.60 m above mean sea level (mASL), while its lowest surface point is around 20.20 mASL (based on the map in fig. 18.1). In other words, there is a ca. 40 cm difference between the top of the mound and the lowest surface point at the peripheral edge of the mound. Two strata were recognized: a 00-35 cmBS plow zone (i.e., Ap Horizon), followed by a 20-25 cm thick stratum reaching an *average* depth of 60 cmBS. The lower stratum was described as 'homogeneous' in terms of cultural material content.

Six charcoals, calibrated at 1 and 2 sigma (Method A), and a shell sample have been dated. The excavators specifically noted that *"they were obtained from a layer that included part of the plow zone"*. In their own words:

La profundidad máxima alcanzada fue de 0.60 centímetros [sic; 0.60 metros], constituyendo un sólo estrato cultural homogéneo… Los primeros treinticinco [35] centímetros están revueltos por el arado [i.e., Ap Horizon]. Recogimos cinco muestras de carbón vegetal para fines cronológicos. Las enviamos al laboratorio de

Teledyne Isotopes, *con nuestras reservas de confiabilidad, por haberlas obtenido de niveles que comprendían parte del estrato removido por el arado* [ref. to samples I-12742, I-12,743, I-12744, I-12745, I-12743] (Chanlatte y Narganes 1983, 23; our emphasis and clarifications in brackets).

I am surprised at just how the description of a thick plow zone has, over time, slipped away from any recent discussions regarding La Hueca chronology.
The calibrated range of these dates seems to confirm their caution and reservation. Three charcoal dates calibrated between cal AD 240 and cal AD 650 while two other dates

calibrated between cal AD 900 and cal AD 1290 (at 2 sigma). Since I do not know if these samples represent aggregates of charcoal bits from a level, or single charcoals, it is difficult to properly assess them. All of the *charcoal* dates merit caution; they came from within a plow zone or from the next lower arbitrary level which still encompassed part of the plow zone.
The uncalibrated shell dated to 1810 ± 80 BP. However, without knowing the marine reservoir effect, it cannot either be taken at face value. Because the shell was obtained from the Ap stratum, the question of a lateral displacement (due to disc/blade plowing) and intrusion into the midden remains a

Sample No.	Block/Unit depth**	Radiocarbon years b.p.	Uncal. bc/ad (@1 sigma)	RANGE of CALIBRATED BC-AD* (method A: 1 sigma)	(method A: 2 sigma)
I-11,142	Block 'Z': Z-20	405±75	a.d. 1470-1620	[wood date- not calibrated]	
I-10,549	Block 'Z': Z-9	1525±85	a.d. 340-510	[shell date- marine correction unknown]	
I-10,553	Block 'Z': Z-9	1565±80	a.d. 305-465	[shell date- marine correction unknown]	
I-11,321	Block 'Z': Z-V	1845±80	a.d. 25-185	cal. A.D. 80 - 320	cal. A.D. 1 - 400
I-11,320	Block 'Z': Z-W	1770±80	a.d. 100-260	cal. A.D. 130 - 390	cal. A.D. 70 - 430
I-11,141	Block 'Z': Z-16	1705±80	a.d. 165-325	cal. A.D. 240 - 420	cal. A.D. 130 - 540
I-11,322	Block 'Z': Z-X	1945±80	75 b.c.- a.d. 90	cal. 40 B.C. - A.D. 130	cal. B.C. 160 - A.D. 320
I-10,980	Block 'Z': Z-11	1735±85	a.d. 130-300	cal. A.D. 180 - 420	cal. A.D. 80 - 540
I-10,979	Block 'Z': Z-8	1820±85	a.d. 45-215	cal. A.D. 80 - 340	cal. A.D. 30 - 420
I-11,140	Block 'Z': Z-15	1730±80	a.d. 135-295	cal. A.D. 240 - 418	cal. A.D. 90 - 540
I-11,139	Block 'Z': Z-15	1800±80	a.d. 70-230	cal. A.D. 130 - 380	cal. A.D. 30 - 420
I-15,185	New Extension 'Z': C-12	540±80	a.d. 1330-1490	cal. A.D. 1330 - 1440	cal. A.D. 1290 - 1490
I-15,186	New Extension 'Z': C-10	520±80	a.d. 1360-1510	cal. A.D. 1330 - 1440	cal. A.D. 1290 - 1620
I-15.187	New Extension 'Z': B-9	690±80	a.d. 1180-1340	cal. A.D. 1260 - 1390	cal. A.D. 1210 - 1420
I-15,188	New Extension 'Z': A-9	700±80	a.d. 1170-1330	cal. A.D. 1260 - 1390	cal. A.D. 1210 - 1410
I-11,189	New Extension 'Z': B-9	790±85	a.d. 1075-1245	cal. A.D. 1160 - 1290	cal. A.D. 1030 - 1390
I-15,238	New Extension 'Z': B-10	570±80	a.d. 1300-1460	cal. A.D. 1300 - 1430	cal. A.D. 1280 - 1470
I-15,239	New Extension 'Z': B-10	660±80	a.d. 1210-1370	cal. A.D. 1280 - 1400	cal. A.D. 1220 - 1430
I-15,240	New Extension 'Z': B-10	630±80	a.d. 1240-1400	cal. A.D. 1290 - 1410	cal. A.D. 1260 - 1440
I-12,856	Block Z-T-B: C-8	1810±80	a.d. 60-220	cal. A.D. 90 - 340	cal. A.D. 30 - 420
I-12,859	Block Z-T-B: C-4	1880±80	10 b.c.-a.d. 150	cal. A.D. 30 - 240	cal. 40 B.C. - A.D. 380
I-12,858	Block Z-T-B: B-3	1820±80	a.d. 50-210	cal. A.D. 90 - 340	cal. A.D. 30 - 420
I-15,241	Block Z-T-B: I-7	1880±80	10 b.c.-a.d. 150	[shell date- marine correction unknown]	
I-12,860	Block Z-T-B: C-1	1780±80	a.d. 90-250	cal. A.D. 130 - 380	cal. A.D. 70 - 430
I-12,745	Block Z-T-2: L-9	1560±80	a.d. 310-470	cal. A.D. 420 - 600	cal. A.D. 260 - 650
I-12,743	Block Z-T-2: L-8	950±80	a.d. 920-1080	cal. A.D. 1000 - 1210	cal. A.D. 900 - 1260
I-13,426	Block Z-T-2: K-7	1810±80	a.d. 60-220	[shell date- marine correction unknown]	
I-12,744	Block Z-T-2: K-9	1640±80	a.d. 230-390	cal. A.D. 260 - 540	cal. A.D. 240 - 620
I-12,746	Block Z-T-2: LL-9	1600±80	a.d. 270-430	cal. A.D. 390 - 560	cal. A.D. 260 - 640
I-12,742	Block Z-T-2: K-7	900±80	a.d. 970-1130	cal. A.D. 1030 - 1260	cal. A.D. 990 - 1290
I-13,427	Block Z-T-3: H-4	1840±80	a.d. 30-190	[shell date- marine correction unknown]	
I-13,428	Block Z-T-4: E-5	1930±80	60 b.c.- a.d. 100	[shell date- marine correction unknown]	
I-15,242	Block Z-T-5: H-10	1230±80	a.d. 640 -800	[shell date- marine correction unknown]	
I-13,429	Block Z-T-6: G-5	1640±80	a.d. 230-390	[shell date- marine correction unknown]	

Fig. 18.1. Map of La Hueca & Sorcé loci (reproduced from Chanlatte & Narganes 1883).

possibility. Unworked shells also have other problems. For example, they could already be ancient materials by the time they were collected (intentionally or not) and redeposited or discarded in a refuse midden, or vice versa, discarded by later peoples (Sorcé?) and intruded into the midden by plowing or other means. Even accepting its contemporane-

Sample No.	Unit depth (cm)	Radiocarbon years b.p.	Uncal. bc/ad (@1 sigma)	RANGE of CALIBRATED BC-AD*	
				(method A: 1 sigma)	(method A: 2 sigma)
I-14,979	Test C (80-90 cm)	2120±80	250-90 b.c.	[Shell date- marine reservoir unknown]	
I-14,978	Test A (60-70 cm)	2020±80	150 b.c.-a.d. 10	cal. 160 B.C. - A.D.70	cal. 340 B.C. - A.D. 220
I-15,408	Unit J (60-70 cm)	1310±80	a.d. 560-720	cal. A.D. 650 - 800	cal. A.D. 600 - 940
I-15,410	Unit F4 (40-50 cm)	1260±80	a.d. 610-770	cal. A.D. 670 - 880	cal. A.D. 640 - 980
I-15,409	Unit L (40-50 cm)	1230±80	a.d. 640-800	cal. A.D. 690 - 940	cal. A.D. 650 -990
I-15,431	Unit C (80-90 cm)	1220±80	a.d. 650-810	[Shell date- marine correction unknown]	
I-15,432	Unit I (70-80 cm)	1000±110	a.d. 840-1060	cal. A.D. 900 - 1180	cal. A.D. 780 - 1280
I-15,429	Unit L2 (80-90 cm)	860±90	a.d. 1010-1170	[Shell date- marine correction unknown]	
I-15,407	Unit F (60-70 cm)	690±80	a.d. 1180-1340	cal. A.D. 1260 - 1390	cal. A.D. 1210 - 1420

Fig. 18.2. Excavation Blocks, La Hueca component, Punta Candelero site. Inset: map of Punta Candelero site (courtesy of Rodríguez López).

Sample No.	Block/Area depth**	Radiocarbon years b.p.	Uncal. bc/ad (@1 sigma)	RANGE of CALIBRATED BC-AD*	
				(method A: 1 sigma)	(method A: 2 sigma)
I-13,425	Block Area Z-T-A	2110±80	240-80 b.c.	cal. 350 B.C.-A.D. 1	cal. 360 B.C. - A.D. 70
I-14,814	Block Area Z-T-A	1240±80	a.d. 630-790	[shell date- marine correction unknown]	
I-14,815	Block Area Z-T	1380±80	a.d. 490-650	[shell date- marine correction unknown]	
I-14,816	Block Area Z-T	1350±80	a.d. 520-680	[shell date- marine correction unknown]	
I-12,857	Block Area Z-T-B	1580±80	a.d. 290-450	cal. A.D. 410-600	cal. A.D. 260-650
I-10,550	Block Area 'X'	1505±85	a.d. 360-530	cal. A.D. 430-640	cal. A.D. 390-690
I-10,548	Block Area 'X'	1440±85	a.d. 425-595	cal. A.D. 540-660	cal. A.D. 430-770
I-11,319	Block Area YTA-1	1915±80	45 b.c.-a.d.115	cal. A.D. 1-220	cal. 90 B.C. - A.D. 320
I-11,685	Block YTA-1: L-36	1740±75	a.d. 135-285	cal. A.D. 240-410	cal. A.D. 90-530
I-11,317	Block YTA-1: L-5	1615±75	a.d. 260-410	cal. A.D. 360-540	cal. A.D. 260-640
I-11,316	Block YTA-1: G-5	1555±75	a.d. 320-470	cal. A.D. 420-600	cal. A.D. 340-650
I-11.318	Block Area YTA-1	1490±75	a.d. 385-535	cal. A.D. 430-650	cal. A.D. 420--690
I-11,926	Block Area YTA-2	1720±80	a.d. 150-310	cal. A.D. 240-420	cal. A.D. 130-540
I-11,925	Block Area YTA-2	1665±80	a.d 205-365	cal. A.D. 260-530	cal. A.D. 180-600
I-11,686	Block Area YTA-2	1575±80	a.d. 300-450	cal. A.D. 420-600	cal. A.D. 260-640
I-11,927	Block Area YTA-2	1565±80	a.d. 305-465	cal. A.D. 420-600	cal. A.D. 260-650
I-11,687	Block YTA-2: I-22	1565±75	a.d. 310-460	cal. A.D. 420-600	cal. A.D. 260-650
I-10,547	Block Area YTA-3	1575±85	a.d. 290-480	cal. A.D. 410-600	cal. A.D. 260-650
I-10,551	Block Area YTA-3	1210±85	a.d. 625-795	[shell date- marine correction unknown]	
I-10,552	Block Area YTA-3	1230±80	a.d. 640-800	[shell date- marine correction unknown]	
I-14,850	Block Area X-T-3	1340±80	a.d. 530-690	[shell date- marine correction unknown]	
I-14,847	Block Area X-T-3	1220±80	a.d. 640-800	[shell date- marine correction unknown]	
I-14,848	Block Area X-T-3	1190±80	a.d. 680-840	[shell date- marine correction unknown]	
I-14,813	Block Area X-T-3	1180±80	a.d. 690-850	cal. A.D. 770-980	cal. A.D. 670-1020
I-14,846	Block Area X-T-3	1150±80	a.d. 720-880	[shell date- marine correction unknown]	
I-14,845	Block Area X-T-3	1080±80	a.d. 790-950	[shell date- marine correction unknown]	

Fig. 18.3. Excavation unit map blocks ZTB, La Hueca locus.

ous deposition with the rest of the refuse, the inability to calibrate these radiocarbon years to calendric dates makes it, for now, difficult to assess and compare with the calibrated charcoal dates. And still another possibility is that often abandoned middens make for excellent garden plots *(conucos),* as is often the case among modern South American Indians. Hence, we cannot reject the possibility that these superficial, mixed samples were not intruded as a result cultivation activities by later groups, that need not to have resided nearby or be related to La Hueca or even Sorcé occupants.

Given the stated *average* depth of 60 cm BS for the 'ZT2' excavations, only the lowest level (40-60 cmBS) would most likely retain stratigraphic integrity. Sharp stratigraphic breaks were not in evidence at 'ZT2'. If there were any, the plow had disturbed them. When Chanlatte and Narganes (1983, 23) speak of 'homogeneity' they primarily refer to cultural stratigraphy and to the levels below the plowzone. Homogeneity, however, is not always equivalent to stratigraphic integrity.

Again, what truly surprised me is just how easily we seem to have forgotten the context in which these dates were found, including the warnings that were originally provided by Chanlatte and Narganes about their reliability. Even Narganes (1991) herself, had gradually come to accept them as reliable, while others, like myself, had quite arbitrarily rejected some and accepted other dates to suit our preferred models. To some extent, Narganes (1991) was correct in insisting that we had been very arbitrary in our judgment for selection, but she erred in assuming them to be dating the layers of 'events' in which they were embedded. I prefer now the view that none of the dates within an Ap stratum or a mixed Ap and subsoil (probably the local A horizon) inspire much confidence, until proven otherwise.

18.8.2   BLOCK 'ZT3'

The next midden, in block ZT3 (fig. 18.2, table 18.1), showed more or less the same two strata as 'ZT2': a 35/40 cm thick superficial plow zone followed by a 20-30 cm thick 'homogeneous' stratum. The average depth of the deposit was also about 60 cmBS (ibid. 1983, 24; pers. comm. 1997). A total of 14 units were placed adjacent to each other, near the center of the midden, with an isolated unit to the southeast (total area = 60 m²). A single *Strombus* shell assay dated to approximately 1840 ± 80 BP (table 18.1). The shell also comes from within the plow zone and, therefore, does not inspire much confidence either. Nevertheless this shell also yielded a 'reading' in radiocarbon years consistent with the shell date from 'ZT2'. One might tentatively and cautiously suggest that the two shell assays, from 'ZT2' and 'ZT3' represent a time that dates the upper, later portions of the midden deposits. But again, the local marine reservoir may have an effect on the apparent age of the shell, measured in terms of "a few centuries" (Bowman 1990, 25).

18.8.3   BLOCK 'ZT4'

Block 'ZT4' consists of 11 adjacent units and six other units (68 m² area) placed at various points around the block area. This midden is located near, or crossed by, the pathway leading to Sr. Román's home. Again the excavators mention the presence of a ca. 35 cm thick plow zone. The maximum depth of the deposit reached on the average 40-50 cmBS, with only a "few" units reaching 60 cmBS (ibid. 1983, 25; pers. comm. 1997). Except for the few 60 cmBS units, the remainder were essentially disturbed by plowing, with only 5-15 cm of potentially undisturbed deposits left for securing datable samples. The only sample dated came from a *Strombus* shell (1930 ± 80 BP) recovered from a level that most likely overlapped or was entirely within the plow zone (table 18.1), so that here too the date will have to remain suspect. In comparison with the previous two shell dates, this one is nearly 100 radiocarbon years earlier. Assuming that the samples were not dragged by plowing from elsewhere, could this mean that a longer time span is involved in the deposition of ecofacts on the upper 1/2 or 2/3 of the 'ZT2'-3' than the 'ZT4' middens? It is just as likely that the discrepancy among shell dates is due to the marine reservoir effect.

Sample No.	Block/Unit depth (cm)	Radiocarbon years b.p.	Uncal. bc/ad (@1 sigma)	RANGE of CALIBRATED BC-AD*	
				(method A: 1 sigma)	(method A: 2 sigma)
I-15,679	Postmold E-4	1230±80	a.d. 640-800	cal. A.D. 690-940	cal. A.D. 650-990
I-15,678	Postmold E-1	1170±80	a.d. 700-860	cal. A.D. 780-980	cal. A.D. 690-1020
I-15,430	Unit C4 (60-70 cm)	850±80	a.d. 1030-1190	[Shell date- marine correction unknown]	

Fig. 18.4. Excavation unit map blocks Z, La Hueca locus.

18.8.4 BLOCK 'ZT5'

Block 'ZT5' consists of a 4 x 16 m trench and four additional 2 × 2 m units. Chanlatte and Narganes (1983, 26) noted that they were only able to excavate peripheral edges of the mounded midden (to 1982), hence only reaching an average depth of 40 cmBS. This means that only 5 to perhaps 10 cm of undisturbed (unplowed) deposit was available. This midden also yielded a single *Strombus* shell assay (1230 ± 80 BP). The date comes from near the base of the 35-40 cm plow zone, or perhaps just below it. The shell assay shows about 700 radiocarbon years difference (more recent) when compared to the other shell dates discussed above. Is, therefore, the top mixed strata of the deposit that much later in time than the other middens discussed thus far? It do not think that we have yet sufficient contextual data to evaluate this. I have already commented on my misgivings about shell dates, so this one will also merit a low degree of confidence.

18.8.5 BLOCK 'ZT6'

Block 'ZT6' consists of 28 contiguous units in a block area, totaling 112 m². An additional 28 units excavated by 1982 turned out to be culturally sterile. Here too a 35 cm or so thick plow zone was detected. The average depth reached was 60 cmBS (ibid., 28). And, again, the scarcity of charcoal forced the excavators to submit a single *Strombus* shell sample dated to 1640 ± 80 BP (table 18.1). Once again, it came from an arbitrary level overlapping the plow zone.

18.8.6 CONCLUSIONS ON THE SHALLOW SOUTHERN 'ZT' UNITS

To summarize, I fully agree with Chanlatte and Narganes' (1983, 23, 33) *original* caution in accepting the charcoal and shell dates from the ZT2 to ZT6 blocks. But I disagree with Narganes' (1991) more recent appraisal; just because we now have *more* assays encompassing a large temporal span it does not mean that the entire range of dates suddenly become acceptable. The fact that we are getting early to late dates does not imply that they provide a "globalized" time range for the middens in question.

Given that all the samples came from within, or uncomfortably close to, the Ap horizon (plowzone) the possibility that post-occupation charcoals from buried O and A horizons were vertically displaced and mixed together through plowing cannot be firmly rejected. Problems could further be compounded *if* several 'in-level' or feature charcoal samples were combined for aggregate dating. There is also the problem of lateral dragging and vertical displacement by the plow. What evidence is there that could refute once and for all the possibility that charcoals were dragged from all over the place as a result of disc plowing? Without a better

understanding of *local* marine reservoir effects, the shell dates are not helpful. They have a relatively broad temporal range from 1930 BP to 1230 BP. This range may or may not be significant given that experimentaly known same-age shells can yield discrepancies of a few centuries. As Bowman (1990, 25) noted, "for an archaeologist requiring a date for a shell midden a possible systematic deviation of this magnitude might render the results useless".

18.8.7 BLOCK 'ZTB'

Block ZTB is one of the two most complex in La Hueca. The excavation consisted of 83 3/4 units covering 335 m² of area (fig. 18.3). It is also the largest area (to 1982) excavated in contiguous units, and has reached average depths of about 130 cmBS. The complexity, however, is in the stratigraphy.

The excavators noted:

The best evidence for… cultural superposition and contamination we obtained from [unit] B-1, where all the layers, from the surface, presented a cultural mixture in proportions of fifty percent… This mixture stops at eighty centimetres of depth [80 cmBS], where a nearly sterile stratum with little archaeological evidence [materials] begins. From one metre twenty centimetres [120 cmBS], approximately, we again encountered pure Agro-I samples [La Hueca component] (Chanlatte and Narganes 1983, 32; our translation and clarifications in brackets).

La mejor evidencia de… superposición y contaminación cultural la obtuvimos en [la unidad] B-1, donde todas las capas, desde la superficie, presentaron mezcla cultural en proporción de cincuenta porciento… Esta mezcla se detiene a los ochenta centímetros de profundidad, dando comienzo a un estrato casi estéril con pocas evidencias arqueológicas. A partir de un metro veinte centímetros, aproximadamente, volvimos a encontrar puras las muestras AGRO-I (Chanlatte and Narganes 1983, 32).

Several units in the northwestern area of the block yielded a top layer of mixed Agro-I (La Hueca) and Agro-II (Igneri phase or Cedrosan) materials that could be directly attributed to overburden that was dumped over the Huecan deposit from the Sorcé road to the west and from the nearby northwestern (Agro-II/Saladoid) midden 'P'. However, the cited 50:50 mixture of La Hueca and Saladoid materials must have involved something other than simply dumping Saladoid materials (taken from midden 'P') on top of a La Hueca midden. Could plowing also account for the subsequent mixing in approximately equal proportions? Only in part, since the mixture seems to have continued from 35/40 to about 80 cmBS on these northern and western units (Chanlatte and Narganes 1983, 33). A 25-30 cm diametre plow disc would have disturbed to a depth of around 40 cmBS. Here we seem to have a situation that seems to be similar to the lowest levels of the northern part of Hope Estate. Could it also signal an overlying of Saladoid deposits

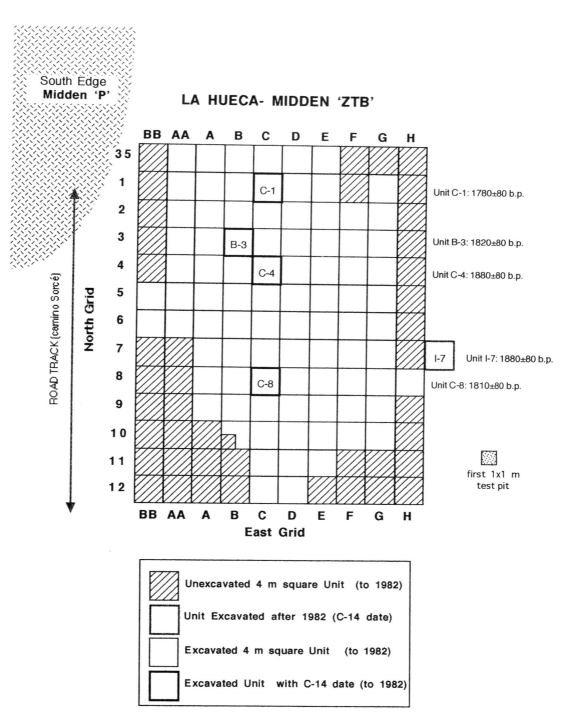

Fig.18.3. Excavation unit map block ZTB, La Hueca locus. Plowzone reported for the southern half of the block. The north and northwestern units show the following: 0-35 cm BS road + midden P overburden; 35-80 cm BS of mixed La Hueca and 'Agro-II' components; 80-120 a low artefacts density layer; 120-130+ cm BS a dense La Hueca basal component. The C-14 dates range in depth between 80 cm and 120 cm below surface at unit. Two postmolds were reported at the base of the central part o the block (Chanlatte and Narganes 1983; pers. comm 1997).

over the Huecan, but which were "mixed" as a result of (still) prehistoric post-depositional activities? More likely, this lower mixed layer could in fact be a plowzone (Ap2 horizon) buried by the recent road overburden (Ap1 horizon). This is also one of the few block areas that have yielded postmolds at the base, which also suggest that it had been the locus of a (house?) structure, at some point in its history (Chanlatte and Narganes 1983, foto 4, 8).

Between 80 cmBS and 120 cmBS (in and around unit B-3) they detected a layer with a very low artifact content, followed by a dense refuse midden deposit containing only La Hueca artefacts. Chanlatte and Narganes, however, did not mention whether the low density stratum (at 80-120 cmBS), identified in the northwest area of the block also extended to the south and east. Since the reported maximum depth averaged 130 cmBS, it means that a ca. 10 cm thick basal deposit with only La Hueca materials was present in the vicinity of unit B-3.

At the same time, all the southern units, approximately from North Grid 8 to 12 (in fig. 18.3), from top to bottom, yielded La Hueca artefacts (ibid., 29), except in the plow zone, where the excavators reported finding intrusive Cedrosan Saladoid/Agro-II ceramics (e.g., in unit D-8). Here, in the southern block section, they reported finding a "hard layer" typical of the plow zone in the area. The average maximum depth of 80 cmBS contrasts with the 120+ cmBS of the north-northwestern units in this block. The difference in total thickness, however, may be related not only to the natural gradient, but also to the added height resulting from the road and/or overburden from the nearby midden 'P'.

Without the benefit of wall profiles, it is difficult to reconstruct the depositional and post-depositional history of this large block area. The 80 to 120 cmBS stratum with low density of midden refuse (Hueca complex) in and around unit B-1 (fig. 18.3) is particularly intriguing, because it signals a different function or functions for this sector other than midden accumulation or simply being "nearly sterile". The presence of two postmolds already sends alarm bells of the complexity of the depositional history of this block, and the potential problems of prehistoric postdepositional processes.

Until details of the stratigraphy are published, I would tentatively conclude that: (1) between 00-35/40 cmBS (Ap1 horizon) the 50:50 proportion of artefact mixtures is most likely the result of plowing and road overburden; (2) at 35/40-80 cmBS the 50:50 mixture may possibly be a buried plowzone (Ap2) layer or a prehistoric disturbance, a situation similar to Hope Estate's northern part lower strata (Hoogland, this volume); (3) the low density (Huecan) refuse layer between 80-120 cmBS indicates a change in the depositional nature of this locus that may

be cultural (change in use/function), natural (slope wash?) or both; and, (4) that there was certainly a lower "pure" La Hueca stratum (120+ cmBS) resting on the sterile 'alluvial loam (?)'. In summary, I concur with Chanlatte and Narganes, except for the significance of the low density ("nearly sterile") layer. I will return to the latter shortly.

All the radiocarbon assays from ZTB were said to be collected from *hearths* or were clearly well below the plow-zone/overburden and the mixed 40-80 cmBS layer, and quite *probably* from below the low artifact density stratum. The latter is a supposition since I do not known the extent of this layer, nor its thickness throughout ZTB. Nevertheless, I found the ZTB charcoal assays to be the most reliable for dating the La Hueca component in Vieques. Among other things, here five dates were *"directly obtained from hearth areas"*. The excavators were very specific about this:

The maximum depth was of 1.30 metres, comprised of a single cultural stratum, slightly contaminated to the northwest due to its proximity [to midden 'P']. *We selected five charcoal samples for dating. The samples were obtained directly from hearth areas....* (Chanlatte and Narganes 1983, 31; our translation; emphasis and clarifications ours).

La profundidad máxima fue 1.30 metros, constituyendo un sólo estrato cultural, ligeramente contaminado hacia el noroeste debido a la cercanía [of midden 'P']. Seleccionamos cinco muestras de carbón vegetal para fines de cronología. Las muestras fueron *obtenidas directamente de áreas de fogones...* (Chanlatte and Narganes 1983, 31; emphasis and clarifications ours).

Three of the charcoal dates consistently calibrated between AD 30 and AD 430, while another was somewhat earlier at, 40 cal BC and cal AD 380, but well within the 2 sigma range (table 18.1). Taking all four dates in consideration, I have no trouble accepting that the hearth areas each dated anywhere between 40 BC and AD 430 with a 95% degree of confidence. We don't even need to consider the uncalibrated *Strombus* shell assay (1880 ± 80 BP) to increase confidence, even though it *appears* to be within an acceptable 2 sigma range of the charcoal dates (yet subject to marine reservoir effect).

One of the dates mentioned above, calibrated to cal AD 30-420 (at 2 sigma), comes from unit C-3, adjacent to the northwestern unit B-1 above detailed (fig. 18.3), so that the stratigraphic description provided would apply. It was collected either at the base of the mixed layer or at the top of the underlying nearly sterile layer. If this date comes from the nearly sterile layer, then it would be a foregone conclusion that the accumulation of this layer was very rapid and not much time elapsed between the basal Huecan deposit and the low density layer above it. The assay falls well

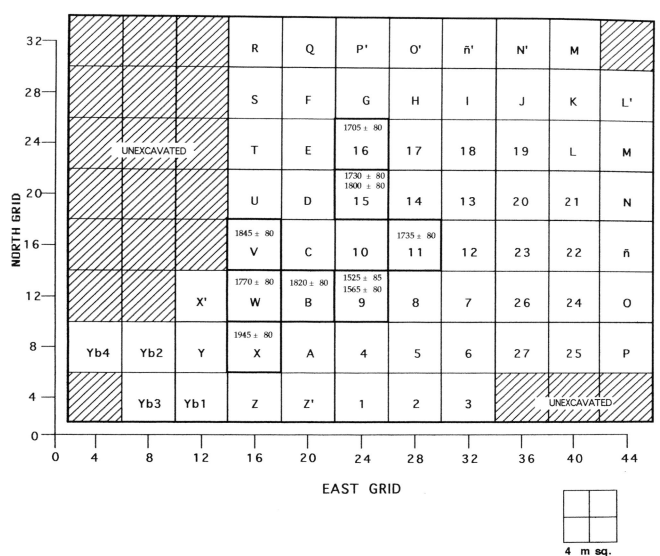

LA HUECA LOCUS: BLOCK/MIDDEN 'Z'
Designation of Excavation Units & Location of C-14 Dates

4 m sq.

TOTAL EXCAVATIONS TO 1982

264 square meters

66 Units (ea. 4 m sq.)

Fig. 18.4. Excavation unit map block Z, La Hueca locus. All dates above given in uncalibrated radiocarbon years BP (see table 18.1). Extension of excavation area toward Urbano Creek added after the 1982 excavation season. Eight C-14 dates ranging between cal AD 1290 and 1440.

within the 2 sigma range of the other three lowermost charcoal dates. If so, it provides a strong argument against a long "hiatus" and subsequent reoccupation hypothesis proposed by Chanlatte (1991) and Narganes (1991), at least for this block area. The stratum, we must remember was not sterile but *nearly* so.

In conclusion, the most probable date range for the ZTB's lower deposit (probably including the low density layer) in association with exclusive La Hueca materials is 40 cal BC – cal AD 430 at 2 sigma (table 18.1). This date range encompasses Cedrosan Saladoid dates obtained for Sorcé and many other Hacienda Grande style sites in Puerto Rico and the Virgins Islands. The case for contemporaneity is quite strong here.

I would, however, caution against extrapolating the ZTB date ranges to the rest of the La Hueca midden deposits; they may or may have not been in use during that time range. However, with the reliable charcoal dates of ZTB, I am somewhat more encouraged to cautiously accept the charcoal dates from ZT2 calibrated between AD 240 and AD 640, and favoring the lower (earlier) 2 sigma. The other blocks were only shell-dated, and thus a conclusive assessment cannot be made yet.

18.8.8   BLOCK 'Z'

Finally we have reached the second largest excavated deposit of La Hueca locus (figs 18.1 and 18.4). It is also the midden with the largest amount and the richest diversity of artefacts. As Chanlatte told me recently, the La Hueca complex is practically defined in terms of what has been recovered from this block. At least, in terms artefacts, this midden is where the widest range of decorative ceramic designs and techniques as well as types of microlapidary were found. By contrast, barely a single tray of *decorated* ceramics was available for each of the other excavations (save for ZTB). This qualitative 'richness', and sheer numerical profusion, may be deceiving since midden 'Z' also contained the second largest number of units excavated and the largest volume excavated. Up to the 1982, the sampled area at block 'Z' consisted of 66 units (264 m²) and reached depths below surface of over 260 cmBS and as much as 350 cmBS in the central portion of the block (fig. 18.4; Chanlatte 1991a, 671; Chanlatte and Narganes 1981, 504). A quick comparison with 'ZT2' sample (64 m² x ca. 0.60 cmBS or 38.40m³) shows a drastic difference with the average volume sampled in block 'Z' (264 m² x ca. 2.5 mBS or 660m³). Block 'Z' has a volumetric size that is *approximately* 17 times greater than, for example, block 'ZT2'. Yet, in terms of volume sampled, block 'Z' (660m³) compares more closely with block 'ZTB' (ca. 435m³). Comparisons of absolute counts between different blocks will be a distortion of this sampling reality[10]. Any comparative assessment would have to entail

probabilistic statements that would have to be addressed by means of appropriate statistical applications, such as testing whether greater typological diversity and more quantity is (or not) directly proportional to volume sampled. This is why, I think, qualitative (presence/absence) or simple numerical trait lists commonly published (and *not* just by Chanlatte and Narganes), seem so inadequate. Some of these issues will be briefly investigated in the next and last section dealing with the microlapidary artefacts.

The stratigraphy in block 'Z', in my view, is far more complex than Chanlatte and Narganes initially indicated in their publications. Chanlatte (1991, 671) noted the following, well after the 1982 season considered in this study:

Deposit 'Z'... *also* [in reference to 'ZTB'] presented evidence of two Huecoid occupations separated by *a layer of sterile sand at one metre of depth [below the surface]*. The maximum depth reached for this deposit was three metres and fifty centimetres. No significant changes were observed in the cultural remains, only that in the upper stratum the [cultural material] samples were less numerous. The chronology obtained in the 'Z' [deposit] ranged from AD 5 to AD 1430 (Chanlatte 1991a, 671; our emphasis and translation; clarifications in brackets)

To begin with, I think that I have presented above a forceful argument against a long chronological "hiatus" being represented in block 'ZTB' by the low density stratum. This was not described in their original report (1983) as a "sterile" layer, but as having a "low density" of artefacts (and ecofacts, I presume). The range of dates they provide, however, is not what it seems by reading the above quote. It seems to suggest that these dates are stratigraphically arrayed from bottom (early) to top (late) following the expected principle of stratigraphic accumulation. As it will be shown, this is not such a simple matter. But before doing so, it is necessary to discuss the regime of deposition for the 'Z' locus.

The stratigraphy is not as straightforward as Chanlatte indicated. This "hunch" is due to reasonable assumptions relative to the topographical features in and around block 'Z'. Due to its location, no sugar cane would have been cultivated in this place. Indeed, an Ap horizon has not been detected and therefore is not a factor for assessing radiocarbon dates and the deposit's cultural integrity. The problems lie in other characteristics of the midden.

As they acknowledged, midden 'Z' is unique in that it is located on a rather steep slope that, prior to excavation, seemed somewhat more gentler. The difference in elevation is about 4 metres from the 19.00-18.60 mASL elevation contour at the top of the slope to about 15.00 mASL near the edge of the Urbano Creek, covered by a distance of about 47-50 metres (calculations based on the map in fig. 18.1). Thus there is a drop of about 12.5 cm for every metre downslope, at surface level. The block, as of 1982, seems to be placed near the top of the slope and runs 32 metres downslope. The sharp south-trending slope is also dissected (as briefly judged from several color slides shown to me by Narganes in 1997) by what *may* have been deeper drainages so that an east-west cross-section of the block would provide an undulating basal surface, perhaps a U shaped "channel". I would not be surprised that 'pockets' would also develop within the south-trending slope/drainage area. Given such relief and slope gradient, the probabilities for the natural displacement of the *light fraction* materials — artefacts, ecofacts and others — is quite high. Rainfall, and even mud slides (e.g., as in Paso del Indio site, Puerto Rico) would and should be present, especially in a region prone to tropical storms and hurricanes. Like Narganes (pers. comm. 1997), I am tempted to correlate the sterile sandy layer (at ca. 100 cmBS) with one such rapid and intense tropical storm event. But whether this 'event' resulted in the hypothesized long-term abandonment of block 'Z' is not so easily deduced from the data available to me. (I would keep this sterile layer as a distinct and separate feature than the low density layer of block 'ZTB'.) It would very important to know how thick was this layer, and if it was a continuous or discontinuous one throughout the entire excavation, including the extension to block 'Z' excavated after 1982.

What really worries me is not the intense and rapid storm events, but those quotidian erosional/depositional processes that have continual, long term effects on the primary cultural deposits. Even a most careful and detailed excavation might not be able to visually isolate among quotidian displacement events when these are of small duration, of relatively low intensity, and repeated over and over (low energy slope wash). Only the very rapid, high energy events would leave more easily visible (to the naked eye) signatures, such as perhaps was the sandy layer reported for this block. Without microscopic analyses of sediments (i.e., particle size analyses), and other pedological and geomorphological studies (i.e., soil profile development), it is almost certain that a macroscopic, unaided viewing of soils during the excavation would not allow an unequivocal discrimination of such cumulative 'small' events.

Gravity and low energy erosion displacing the light fraction cultural refuse over longer distances downslope along with the less frequent (but probably seasonal, cyclical) high energy events displacing the heavier fraction over shorter distances would be expected in this midden area. The light fraction would include the very small bits of microlapidary materials, bivalves, mother-of-pearl and, of course, charcoals and other macrobotanical (floating) elements. At the other end of the spectrum, the heavy fraction will include artefacts such as coral graters, lithic celts and manos and the larger sherd fragments. Other features, like bones, ash and charcoals ("food dumps") would be severely affected by both

low and high energy erosional events. I would expect that there would be a tendency for the light fraction to travel much farther downslope than the heavier fraction, and also that pockets or deeper crevices of the drainages would act as natural "collectors" of the finer as well as heavier materials. These would show up in distribution plots as "hot spots" of high density of materials, and would give the effect of an uneven, distribution of materials in the block. The resulting "deposits" should not be taken as an indication of special "activity" areas, but rather the result of cumulative post-depositional, erosion factors.

Given these factors, one would expect that patterns of archaeological deposition in block 'Z' are a palimpsest reflecting these climatic and topographic factors of "distortion", rather than reflecting the behavioral patterns conditioned by culture and habits of refuse-dumping. In consequence, this block is where radiocarbon assaying *and* their associations with material culture would be most difficult to correlate with any specific context or 'event'. I would not expect anything in this block to be a primary, undisturbed deposition. I would expect that cases to contrary would be very exceptional and rare (and I would assume highly localized in space).

While I will stick to the above assumptions as valid (until evidence to the contrary is presented) there are two interesting factors to be kept in mind. Unquestionably all of the artifact materials collected within this slope are exclusively La Hueca in style above *and* below the sterile sandy lens or layer of discontinuity. And while I am weary of any dates being associated with any specific contexts (which have yet to be described in detail) they may be, in the last analysis, still related to the block area *as a whole*. But each individual date cannot be "plugged" to any specific event or moment, since there is every probability that there are no primary units of deposition that have remained unaffected by (at least) these two natural forces: gravity (slope) and rain (wash).

We are then faced with an interesting situation: if all human activities range between a certain time span, most of the datable organic matter would likely date within that time span of intense refuse dumping (since houses or living surfaces are very unlikely in this zone). Occasional charcoal bits and other organic materials of colonial to modern origin could also end up washed down the drainage, but ought to have generally remained in the upper portions of block's strata, perhaps still mixed with Huecan materials (unless a particularly violent storm gouged a drainage and became subsequently filled or a deep vertical gully developed, both of which should be detectable in the stratigraphy). Whereas, the initial (Huecan/ Agro-I) refuse dumping (and charcoals) would have to be more limited to the lower strata, overall. But toward the base of the slope and the Urbano Creek, the processes of erosion (displacement) and accumulation would be considerably different than in the upper slope. One would expect that an alluvial fan would develop in this portion of the block 'Z' area, and probably encompasses the area or extension excavated after 1982.

To test whether the predictions of this model are valid, a geomorphologic and geochronologic study of slope drainage patterns could be conducted as a control, preferably a trench dissecting the naturally formed landscape adjacent or near the 'Z' area.

Keeping the above model in mind, I turn now to the assessment of the radiocarbon dates from Block 'Z' (fig. 18.4, table 18.1). First I will discuss the dates from the block area excavated up to 1982, which is in the upper portion of the slope. The dates come from a wide range of depths, 20 cmBS to 260 cmBS. Here, re-calculating depths below surface to an elevation datum or horizon is important for obvious reasons. The majority of the assays come from below 150 cmBS and were obtained from the center units where the deposit(s) was/were thick and deep and, of course, below the sandy layer (if indeed it straddled the dated units)[11] I have reasons to believe that the deepest midden deposits were in units Z-13 through Z-18; that this was an area along the slope that coincided with a natural south-rending 'U' shaped drainage, while units to the east and west of Z-13 to Z-18, the basal, sterile (buried) surface was reached at a higher elevation.

Seven of the 11 charcoal dates in this block calibrated between a minimum of AD 1 and a maximum of AD 540 (at 2 sigma); encompassing what Rouse (1992) estimated to be the duration of the Cedrosan Saladoid styles in Puerto Rico (i.e., Hacienda Grande and Cuevas). An eigth date, 160 cal BC - cal AD 130, falls within the upper 2 sigma range. While no particular date at any particular depth can be specifically associated to a ceramic or lithic assemblage (given the depositional model above discussed), it is reasonable to suggest that these charcoals probably relate to various times at which this refuse midden was actively used (and altered by slope wash, etc.). Since all the cultural materials are exclusively La Hueca in style, then all seven dates would have to relate to La Hueca phase or style. The dates articulate well with those obtained for the 'ZTB' block area (cal AD 30-430). It would seem then that a 160 BC to AD 540 time range is indicated for these two deposits. That includes the low density stratum to basal layer of 'ZTB' and for the lowest (below sterile layer) strata of block 'Z'. The two *Strombus* shell dates from block 'Z', both from unit Z-9, although uncorrected, also *seem* to fall within 2 sigma of the charcoal dates.

The safe conclusion, given the slope wash model, is that all of the lower, basal depositions in midden 'Z' pertain to a period *or* periods between 160 cal BC and cal AD 540.

Now, it is theoretically possible that if some of these samples indeed dated to after AD 300 and others earlier (if such precision in calibration were possible), then the later dates could be the result of displacement (slope wash) of light organic matter from activities associated with the Sorcé locus activities.

The only discordant assay in block 'Z' came from a wood trunk or post dated to ca. AD 1470-1629 (uncalibrated). It came from the top of unit Z-20, to the western side of the block area. Thanks to a color slide view provided by Chanlatte and Narganes, I am confident that this post is an intrusive element and, by its date, quite probably an early colonial period discarded fence or house post (not an *in situ* feature). It was most likely thrown and subsequently displaced down slope and is unrelated to earlier refuse dumping and depositions.

The real surprise for me was to discover that ALL the very late radiocarbon assays were found in an extension to the Block 'Z' area (effected after the 1982 season), further down slope and to the south-southwest of the block area illustrated in figure 18.4. This excavation sector is closer to Urbano Creek, and it is the zone I would predict that alluvial fan redepositions should be found. And here is where I am hesitant to accept Chanlatte's two occupation theory. First, the array of dates discussed above belong to the *higher* slope area of the block 'Z' excavation and, furthermore, they are all from below the 100 cmBS sand layer. It is also evident that Chanlatte and Narganes imply that the so-called hiatus of ca. 700 years is represented by the sterile sandy layer. Unfortunately, there seem to be no dates available either for the sandy layer or the topmost stratum/strata in that or any other part of block 'Z' block. This means that we cannot confirm if the late dates in the new block 'Z' extension are consistent with the 'upper' strata of the upslope portion of the block 'Z' area.

All the late dates come from the new excavations downslope, and all the dates are consistently calibrated to about AD 1200/1300 and AD 1400/1490 (at 2 sigma). The dates here were obtained between 60 to 120 cmBS but, as noted, they cannot be tied to the stratigraphy and dates further upslope until Chanlatte and Narganes are ready to divulge this information. Nor do I know if any of the dates collected up to 100 cmBS deep are, indeed, linked to, or fall above or below, the sterile sandy layer, or even if the sandy layer extends that far downslope (or indeed, if the sterile sandy layer is only limited to the lower part of the slope! [but see previous footnote 11]).

The sharp *spatial* segregation of these two sets dates is to me the most intriguing and fascinating problem of La Hueca. It is this late set of dates that everyone but Chanlatte and Narganes have systematically ignored. Upon further questioning, both Chanlatte and Narganes indicated to me that, like the earlier block 'Z' excavations, the extension of block 'Z' was also characterized by exclusively La Hueca style materials. They further indicated that the stylistic differences between the two areas of Block 'Z' were "minor" or "small". Furthermore, as Chanlatte (1991, 671) noted *"no se observaron cambios significativos culturales"* above or below the sandy discontinuity.

Essentially, we are left with four alternatives: (1) that some "single event" natural agent conspired to contaminate the charcoals from the downslope extension of block 'Z' and, thus only the early (upslope) dates should be accepted; (2) that the early dates in the upslope block 'Z' are somehow unacceptable and that only the late dates are acceptable; (3) that both sets of dates are acceptable and that they reflect two different La Hueca occupation periods, and (4) that none of the block 'Z' dates are reliable. All alternatives are problematic. I am inclined to accept the first hypothesis, and perhaps blame the proximity of the Urbano Creek for contamination. However, if contamination took place (modern carbon exchange from water or river flooding), how come all dated to the same range? Could it be that the contamination was a single flooding event, a change of river course? Or could it be due to a single, high energy depositional event in the form of an alluvial fan? The latter is not probable because if materials were displaced in a downslope, they would include early as well as late dated charcoals.

I find the second option as highly improbable given the confidence I placed on the 'ZTB' charcoal dates. As for the third option, I would contemplate this possibility if and *only* if (a) there is no evidence indicating post-depositional disturbances, and (b) the materials and artefacts in the extension units indicate sufficient variation and change (at least in frequency of modes or a shift in central value of modes) from those in the upslope block units (and/or those above the sandy layer). I simply have a very hard time accepting a nearly 700 years hiatus without any material change, or only a "minor" or "insignificant" change. Or else, we must be facing the most conservative and traditional people on the face of the Earth since Olduvai Gorge. The fourth alternative is, to say the least, most unpleasant and, in my view, highly unlikely. Some samples *must* be related to the time or times when the midden was actively used.

There is only one argument left against the late set of dates. That 'zic ware' traits are shared with (or as argued by Chanlatte, adopted by) Cedrosan Saladoid components; not one Cedrosan Saladoid component dates beyond AD 600/650 or so, the latest (cf. Oliver 1995). This assertion excludes a consideration of the Sorcé locus dates (table 18.3), but I am ready to defend this assertion if need be. However, I generally dislike negative evidence. The real proof is held in the geomorphological and sedimentary evidence contained in the lower portion of the block 'Z'.

Should we contemplate the possibility of abandonment and reoccupation, then we also should be able to find evidence of where these La Hueca people resettled between ca. AD 500 and AD 1200. I can already anticipate that someone will say: Punta Candelero!

18.9   Punta Candelero's radiocarbon dates

Punta Candelero's (fig. 18.2) radiocarbon dates also presented interpretive problems of their own. Nine assays were obtained for the La Hueca component (table 18.2) and three assays were obtained for the Cuevas component. Excluding the marine shell specimens, the dates firmly associated with the local La Hueca component are equally baffling, especially since all come from 40 cmBS or greater depths. Shell specimens (n=3), at any rate, also show an apparently similar temporal spread as the charcoal assays do (Rodríguez 1991, 627). Assay I-14987 (340 cal BC - cal AD 220 at 2 sigma) encompasses the 2 sigma range of the earliest assay from Block 'Z' at La Hueca. The remaining eight dates presumably associated with La Hueca component, however, range between cal AD 600 (minimum) and cal AD 1420 (maximum at 2 sigma). Indeed, this suite of dates encompass (and extend beyond) to the approximate period of the hypothesized abandonment of Midden 'Z' activities in La Hueca (cal AD 500 and AD 1200) (Narganes 1991). Meanwhile at Punta Candelero, if there was a hiatus at all, it would have been between roughly AD 70 and AD 650, a period that is associated with the more reliable dates for La Hueca (e.g., those from midden ZTB and the pre-1982 block Z area excavated).

Given the above, one might again invoke the reoccupation hypothesis that Narganes (1991) proposed for La Hueca in Vieques (based on Midden 'Z' data). On principle, just as I argued for La Hueca, if the late dates for the Huecan component at Candelero indeed reflect the resettling of a group from La Hueca, Vieques (producing an occupation hiatus there), then I would expect that the ceramic and other artifact assemblages in Punta Candelero would represent an intermediate developmental stage between the materials recovered in the upslope portion of La Hueca's block 'Z' and the downslope extension of that block. I have a hunch that the Punta Candelero materials, in terms of style and typological features, will not show a stylistically intermediate developmental position.

At Punta Candelero the only two charcoal assays (from postmolds) firmly associated with the Cuevas (terminal Saladoid) component dated to cal AD 650-990 (at 2 sigma) and cal AD 690-1020 (at 2 sigma) (table 18.4). A marine shell date (850 ± 80 BP) from a Cuevas context also appears to fall (very roughly) within the same 2 sigma range as the charcoal dates. The upper sigma probability range would appear to be too late in terms of what one might expect from the terminal dates of Cuevas components (AD 600/700) elsewhere in Puerto Rico and the Virgin Islands.

Rodríguez López (1991) provided a candid and explicit commentary on these "confusing" (his words) sets of dates. The two earliest dates (I-14,979 and I-14978), acceptable for Rodríguez, were obtained prior to the clearing of the vegetation from the site. The rest were obtained after the excavation area was cleared of vegetation and had been exposed to the elements during a whole season. It seems that in a sandy matrix, denuded from vegetation, the potential for infiltration and contamination cannot be underestimated. Similar problems have been reported for the sandy deposits at the Ronquín site (Saladoid) in the Middle Orinoco (Roosevelt 1980). Thus, on the basis of the possibility of infiltration (downward migration) or rain water contamination of charcoals, Rodríguez is cautiously inclined to reject the late dates. However, the problematic Huecan dates were obtained from the middens that were stratigraphically overlaid by Cuevas deposits, which may as well be yet another source of contamination. While Rodríguez thought that even the Cuevas-related charcoal dates were "too late", the 2 sigma calibration reduces the calendric range to a tolerable Cuevas chronological margin, to ca. AD 650 and AD 690 (cf. tables 18.2 and 18.3). The lower 2 sigma is comparable to the late Cuevas lowest deposit dated to cal AD 650 for Lower Camp site in Culebra Island (Oliver 1992a, 1995).

Unlike the La Hueca locus, in Punta Candelero there is an clear, incontrovertible *vertical* stratigraphic (and hence chronological) priority of the Huecan deposits over the overlying Cuevas deposits. On stratigraphic grounds, the La Hueca component *precedes* the Cuevas (Saladoid) component. I am much more prone to give a greater reliance to the stratigraphic position and relative chronology, than to the contradictory sets of radiocarbon dates. My impression, again, is that in the sandy matrix, site formation and post-depositional factors at Punta Candelero have greatly affected the distribution of the light fraction materials.

To summarize, I am confident that La Hueca middens (ZTB, Z and probably ZT2) date between 160 cal BC and cal AD 530. There was no occupational "hiatus" in the low density stratum in the ZTB block, and that this change in midden function was not much later than the early (lower Huecan deposit) occupation. In the upslope portion of block 'Z'', the sterile lens or layer and the upper strata were not dated, so there is really no means to determine how much later the midden remained in use. Although I am suspicious of the very late dates found exclusively downslope in the block 'Z' (extension), I do not have yet the means to reject them off hand. They do date "something". I provided several alternative explanations and have favored the possibility of post-depositional factors (river contamination, alluvial fan redeposition) only as possibilities, but as yet I have no "hard"

proof. Perhaps in a future publication, Chanlatte and Narganes will be able to discuss the details of the stratigraphic data and test whether my model of slopewash and redeposition applies or not.

18.10 Reassessment of the microlapidary lithic materials from La Hueca

This final section will be devoted to the analysis of the microlapidary artefacts and materials from the La Hueca locus. It will be brief and to the point. The analysis focuses on the problem of comparability. I will focus in particular on what is it meant when one says that La Hueca has a rich and diverse assemblage of microlapidary in comparison to other Huecan or Saladoid sites. This assertion relates to the statements that La Hueca is both an egalitarian community and a residential locus of specialist lapidary craftsmen. On the one hand, this perception is predicated upon the richness and diversity of microlapidary and, on the other hand, the qualitative assessment that all middens (i.e., everyone in this locus) had equal access to manufacturing, using and trading these exotic body decorations. This view also gave rise to the hypothesis that La Hueca (along with Punta Candelero) was a special manufacturing center controlling the circulation of these goods. Control of manufacture and circulation is implied given the assertion that the neighbors inhabiting the Sorcé locus had only a small proportion of these microlapidary items.

One major problem in assessing these statements lies in the ways in which the La Hueca data has been tabulated and then compared to other sites. At Punta Candelero "thousands" of microlapidary artefacts have been recovered, although Rodríguez (1991; pers. comm. 1997) estimates that only about 33% (= 572 complete microlapidary artefacts) of the excavated units have been analyzed to date. If so, and all things being equal, this would indicate that Punta Candelero could have at least 3 times more (= 1,760 +) complete microlapidary artefacts. That figure would be a *very crude* estimate for 'richness' relative to the ca. 2,724 complete microlapidary artefacts from La Hueca or to the 494 microlapidary lithics said to come from Trants site in Monserrat (Watter and Scaglion 1994). Is La Hueca 'richer' than Punta Candelero or Trants? Yes and not necessarily. Yes in absolute terms, but not necessarily in relative terms. For example, to 1990, only a total of 14.25 m² were excavated at Trants, in contrast to 935 m² total excavation in La Hueca and ca. 1,325 m² for Punta Candelero. Obviously, even at the level of 'site', a more appropriate comparison would entail, at the very least, the relation "number of specimens per area sampled". Using the above grossly estimated figures would indicate that on the average 1.33+ specimens/m² were present in Candelero, versus 2.91/m² at La Hueca. (And it does not take into account

LA HUECA, BLOCK 'Z' MICROLAPIDARY LITHICS & SHELL*

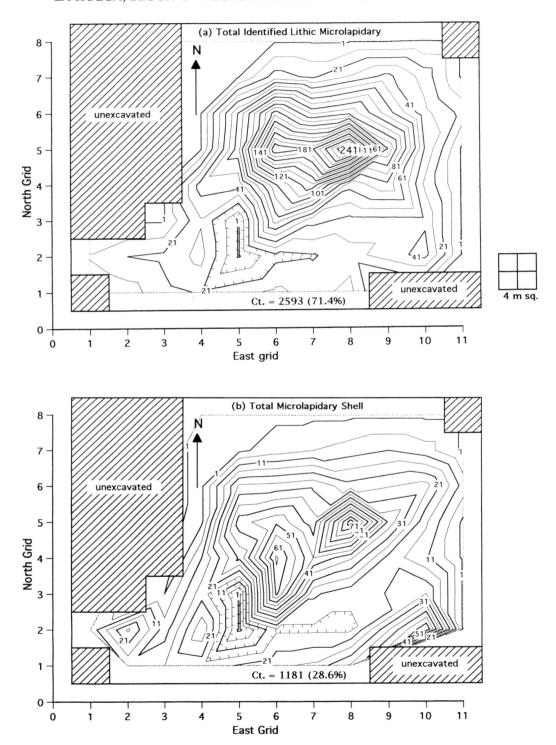

Fig. 18.5. La Hueca, Block 'Z': distribution of all microlapidary lithics and shell (*bone + wood microlapidary, total Ct. = 7 (0,001%).

284

differences in screen-size!) I do not know the total number of microlapidary specimens excavated in Trants, but a whole site to whole site comparison should be expressed as counts/m^2. Thus if, for the sake of argument, Trants yielded 50 specimens in 14.25m^2, then the figure would be 3.51/m^2. In other words, Trants would be, on the average, 'richer' than either La Hueca or Punta Candelero. A very different image of richness would begin to emerge with all the attending interpretive consequences. To date, I have not yet seen any such comparisons evaluated in such manner. I would also make the same argument for expressing MNI figures in terms of MNI/m^2 or m^3 for different zooarchaeological specimens, ceramic modes or types, etc.

This same approach can be applied to ever more discrete comparative units: between blocks, units, components, strata or levels, and features or discrete contexts within strata. A more precise index of comparison, of course, would have to be in terms of volume (count or items per cm^3 or m^3), since, for example, the Punta Candelero Huecan stratum (or strata) may theoretically be much "thinner" than at La Hueca. The more discrete the unit area or volume of comparison is the more precise will be the figure. At a whole site level of comparison La Hueca is 'richer' (e.g., 2.91/m^2) than Punta Candelero (e.g., 1.33/m^2) by a factor of nearly 3, but this expression *assumes* an even, regular distribution across all excavated units and levels. For certain general descriptive statements, this level of resolution is sufficiently adequate; but as soon as the level of resolution is increased, such 'regularity' will most likely vanish. Instead of assuming regularity (via averages) one could apply an expectation of random distribution (using random tables), and measure these against the actual distribution using, for example, a four-cell χ^2 Test (or some other similar statistic). If the χ^2 Test demonstrates a non-random distribution, and a high tendency to aggregate or cluster, then we know that the assumption of regularity is invalid. Even so, clustering only means that, and the cause for aggregation could still be cultural or natural, or a combination of both.

The important point here is that these quantitative and statistical considerations are not commonplace in the published comparative assessments of La Hueca and other Huecan sites. That being the case, distortions of the value or significance of the compared units (whether fauna, ceramic attributes, shell or lithic tool types) would seem most likely. One problem has been the diverse ways in which the data are represented. For example, Miguel Rodríguez (1991) presented a preliminary count of microlapidary in terms of two basic morphological types, beads and pendants, and by the type of lithic raw material. Whereas, Narganes (1995) presented hers in terms of counts of 17 morphological types and a qualitative assessment of the range of raw materials present in each formal type. The quantitative aspects of

'richness' cannot be easily compared since neither provides a useful statement of sample size or volume. Of course, neither of these papers were intended to compare their data sets, but a number of us, in publications or in conversations during conferences, do make constant comparisons. These are the sort of papers that form the basis for such formal and informal comparisons and, hence, add to the construction of an imprecise or even inacurrate sense of richness or poverty for the La Hueca microlapidary complex. I will not dwell on this obvious point any further, and move on to first describe the nature of the microlapidary sample under consideration and then provide results and some conclusions of this study. I will limit the study to two levels of resolution: a comparison of microlapidary materials between whole blocks and a distribution analysis within block Z.

18.10.1   THE MICROLAPIDARY SAMPLE FROM LA HUECA
The data base used here comes from two separate table lists (List 1 and 2) prepared by Narganes and published in Chanlatte and Narganes' (1983) appendices as percentage histograms. For various reasons, the two lists do not come out to the same totals as they should. In other words each list is based on a different sample size. Additionally, the published data included an number of errors that can be ascribed to the press editors in Santo Domingo. The first raw data table of summary counts and the histogram percents (Chanlatte and Narganes 1983, 61-64; 95-99) match precisely the counts checked against the original laboratory notes ("List 1"). This table and the histograms tabulate the frequency of specimens on the basis of formal types (i.e., amulet beads, biomorphic beads, etc.) and classes of material (lithic, bone, wood, shell). The second list was not published in table form, but only as histograms (Chanlatte and Narganes 1983, 100-ff.). The published histograms (in simple percents), when evaluated against the total number of specimens provided in pages 61-64 of their publcation, simply do not add up (both sets should have ended of with the same total count and percent). I will not go into the details of why, except to say that the discrepancy is the result of each table or list being based on a different total specimen universe. (Narganes and I are presently working together to reconcile the discrepancy between list 1 and list 2).

Given these problems, I have recalculated both lists using the original laboratory lists and not the published ones. In this process, I have respected their classifications (i.e., they were not altered) of formal types, raw material identification, and stage of manufacture. The resulting amended lists (three sets of tables, over 20 pages long) are too long to reproduce here in detail, but have been made available to Chanlatte and Narganes[12].

In the first set, fourteen tables and seven histograms summarizing the microlapidary lithic data for each block as a whole

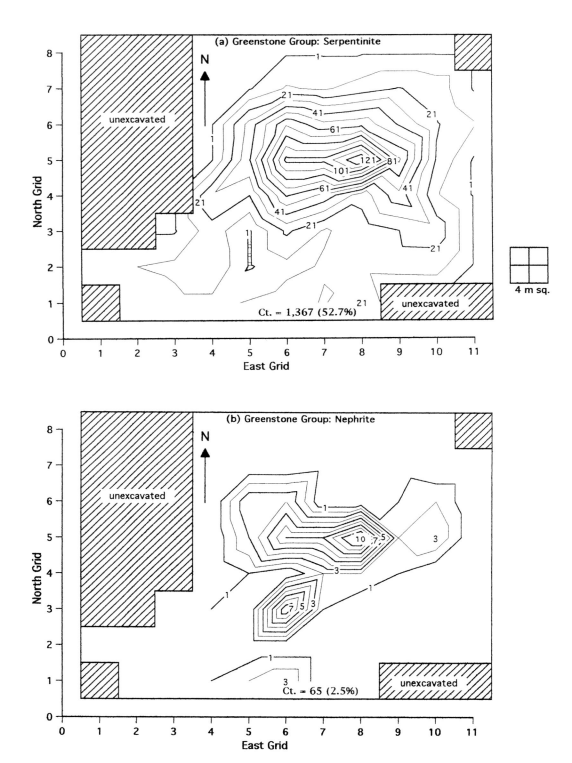

Fig. 18.6. La Hueca, block 'Z': distribution of microlapidary lithics of greenstone group.

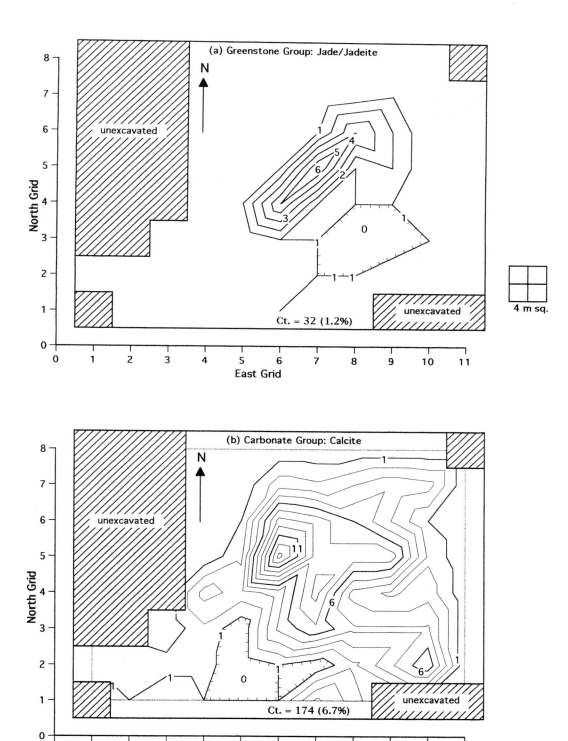

Fig. 18.7. La Hueca, block 'Z': distribution of microlapidary lithics of greenstone and carbonate group.

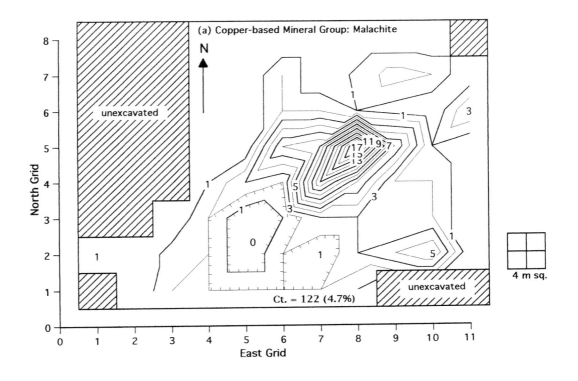

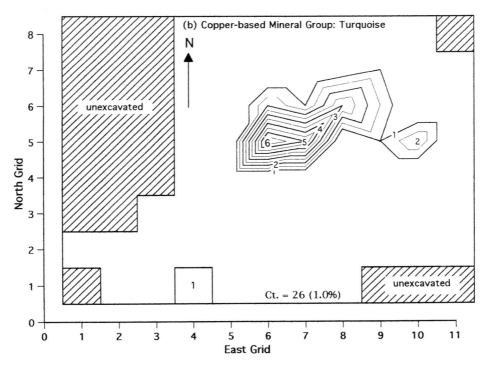

Fig.18.8. La Hueca, block 'Z': distribution of microlapidary lithics of copper-based mineral group.

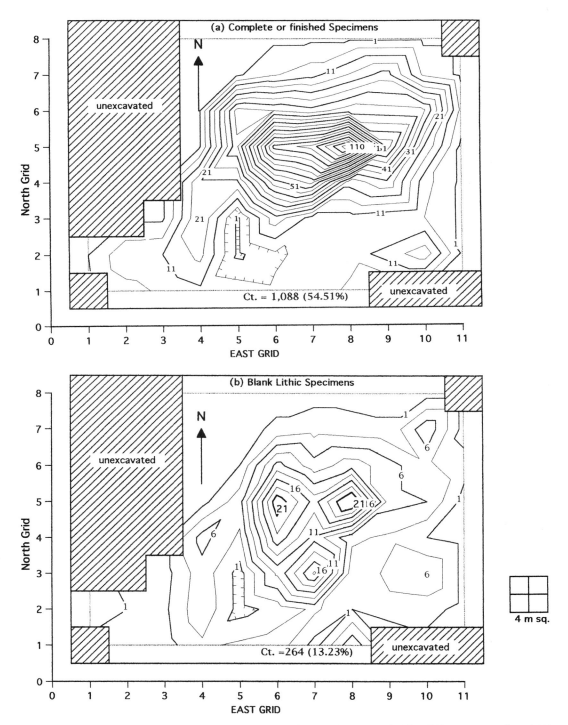

Fig. 18.9. La Hueca, block 'Z': distribution/density by manufacture stages. Sample size of microlapidary lithics/gemstone Ct. = 1,996.

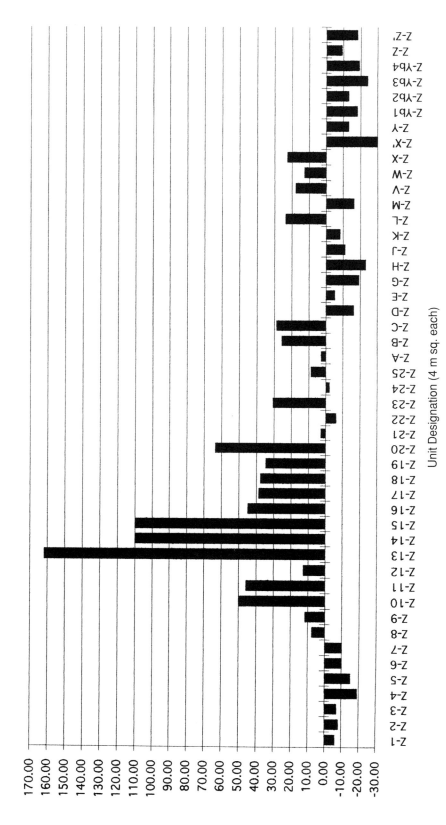

Fig. 18.10. La Hueca, block 'Z': micro-lithics above/below mean. Mean block 'Z' = 30.24 items/unit (= 0.00).

290

were produced (see footnote 8). The specimens were organized in terms of the morphological types and raw material types (by mineral species). Two tables for each block were prepared; one presented the numerical counts and totals, while the other presented an average frequency per 4m^2 unit. The latter data were then plotted as histograms or bargraphs. These data presented an average because they assumed a regular or even distribution throughout the excavations. But at the same time, they allowed to make accurate statements about frequencies between blocks, regardless of how small or large the excavated area is. In figure 18.11, I chose to only plot in bargraphs the microlithic materials by mineral species per each block as a whole, but the resulting tables can also provide the data for plotting by morphological types and by both morphological types and raw materials. Other calculations, such as diversity of raw materials are also possible. However, due to available publication space, these results could not be fully presented here.

A second set of tables were prepared presenting summary counts (Ct.) of all the microlapidary materials per each individual unit (of 4m^2) within block 'Z' (up to 1982) and the counts of microlapidary lithic by major morphological types for each individual unit. These figures were cross-checked and based on Narganes' laboratory "List 1". The tables generated also include other details, such as specific morphological sub-type counts, the raw material type, and the stage of manufacture of the specimens. Here, I elected only to show two density contour distribution maps for the complete and incomplete specimens in Block 'Z' (fig. 18.9a and 18.9b), as well as others showing the distribution of individual mineral species (figs 18.5-18.8). Still other tables in this set provided the number of specimens (by formal type and by manufacture stage) above or below the expected mean for the whole block 'Z'. For example, complete (finished) microlithic specimens were found to be on the average 16.48 per unit (of 4m^2). In order to assess how much each excavated unit actually conformed to this mean or average (a prediction), the mean 16.48/4m^2 was added (+) or subtracted (-) from the actual count of specimens obtained for each excavated 4m^2 unit. Thus, in Z-4 there were -11.48 (less) specimens than the expected mean (16.48/4m^2) whereas unit Z-13 yielded +93.52 (more) specimens than would have been expected if the distribution were to be even and regular (as is assumed in the average 16.48/4m^2). This provided an index of deviation from the average as well as a means to assess clustering/dispersion that is not detected when one compares at the level of, say blocks. For this paper I elected to present the total count of all microlapidary lithic specimens (regardless of material and form types) above (+) or below (-) the mean in figure 18.10, where Ct. = 1996 specimens is divided by 66 units (ea. 4m^2) yielding (=) 30.2 average of *identified* specimens per 4m^2. The

distribution results in the histogram will be discussed shortly.

All of the above alluded tables provided the basis for various elemental calculations. But from here on, one can also move to all sorts of other statistical exercises that, for example, test random vs. non-random distributions, for nearest neighbor analyses and the like. I have not done so here because in the absence of volume or density and distribution by depth (stratigraphic units) it would yield unreliable results. But perhaps more important, sophisticated statistics should be used only when they are necessary. The next and last section will show conclusively that the distribution with block 'Z' is not regular and does not even come close to the expected average or mean distribution. It will show a that there are one or more loci of high concentration or clustering.

Alegría in a personal comment to Miguel Rodríguez once quipped something to the effect that several hundred of the beads found closely packed in Punta Candelero could just represent a single necklace! The comment is quite significant, statistically speaking, because then our image of richness — regardless of all of the above — would be somewhat warped. One possible way to come around this problem would be to do some experiments. For example, a strand of 'toad' beads could be made, threading the larger-sized specimens toward the "chest area" and decreasing in size toward the back of the necklace. One might make two or three different sized necklaces (or even bracelets), some with separators and/or pendants. One could then use the results as approximate unit-measures for the category "experimental neckalce". Each necklace would have 'x' number of beads of a particular size and formal type. The counts of indiviual beads by size categories would constitute a unit necklace. Thus, for each block and sample of beads (preferrably from the same stratigraphic context) one could calculate the MNI of necklace units, just as zooarchaeologists do with their specimens. It is conceivable that the 3,000+ specimens could amount to just a few "complete" necklaces or bracelet units for a given slice of time. Now that would certainly place the concept of 'wealth' and 'richness' in a completely different light!

18.10.2   INTER-BLOCK / MIDDEN COMPARATIVE ANALYSIS

The data obtained from the first set of tables suggest the following observations (fig. 18.11).

(1) The total average count (Ct.) per unit (4m^2) varies significantly from block to block area, as follows: 'ZT2'= 5.9 specimens/unit; 'ZT3' = 2.4/unit; 'ZT6'= 1.96/unit; 'ZT4' = 1.63/unit; and 'ZT5' = 0.63/unit. The largest sampled areas, belonging to 'ZTB '(335 m^2) and 'Z' (264 m^2), the average density of microlapidary items per unit were significantly higher than in all other La Hueca locus middens ('ZTB' = 4.51/unit and 'Z' = 46.0/unit).

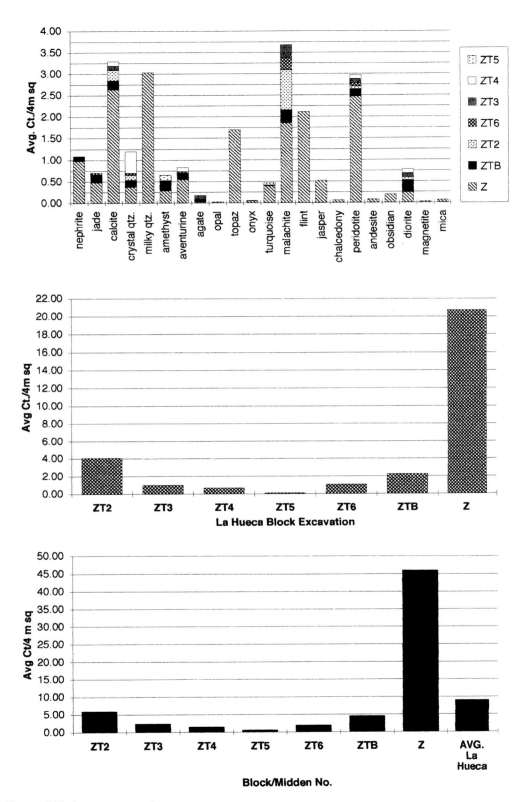

Fig. 18.11. La Hueca, all blocks: average counts.

292

There is no doubt then that midden 'Z' exceeds in richness the next richest of middens ('ZTB' and 'ZT2') by a factor of × 9. The average for the entire La Hueca locus is 9.0/unit (including unidentified).

(2) The average density (Ct/unit) indices at the level of block area can also be assessed in terms of the different proportions (of different raw materials and type of adornos). In terms of raw material, regardless of block area, serpentinite ("soft greenstones") dominate as the choice material (#1 in ordinal rank), but exhibiting a different average frequency per block. The blocks with most mineralogical diversity (excludes non-identified) are as follows: 'Z', Ct = 23; 'ZTB', Ct. = 13; 'ZT2', 'ZT4' and 'ZT6', Ct. = 6 ea.; and 'ZT5' Ct. = 2 (fig. 18.11).

The low diversity in ZT5 is probably due to the impact this midden had due to the road, forcing Chanlatte and Narganes to excavate toward the edges (and 3 of the 5 specimens could not identified as to raw material). Otherwise, all the middens on the southern part of the La Hueca locus show a limited range of raw materials and low average densities of specimens. It would be interesting to compare these indices (Ct./4m^2 and diversity) with the indices of the purportedly 'poorer' middens of the Sorcé locus: How far above or below the mean must yet be determined. This is, in a real sense, a test for the assertion that 'any La Hueca midden is richer than any other Sorcé (or Hacienda Grande) midden'. There are a few other things I wish to call attention to. Let us assume that each of the 'ZT-' middens is the refuse of a nearby habitation structure. Given that, let us examine the statement, *"egalitarianism is indicated because all middens showed more or less equal representation of exotic or rare materials"*. Aventurine is certainly an exotic material, and found in 'ZT4' at the rate of 0.10/unit (3.7% of all microlithics) and in 'ZT6' at the rate of 0.04/unit (1.8%), whereas in block 'ZTB' the rate was 0.14/unit (3.01%). Only 'ZTB' included aventurine beads, in addition to the amulet-beads ('frog/toad') present as well in the other two blocks. It is very rare and only present in three of the six 'ZT-' middens. Amethyst, another rare gemstone also of the quartz group, is present in 'ZT5' (0.13/unit; 19.8% of all microlithics) and in 'ZTB' (0.23/unit; 5.20% of all microlithics), yet absent in the other 'ZT-' middens. The picture that begins to emerge is that some (aventurine) of the exotic or truly rare materials are restricted to some middens, while others (amethyst) are restricted to other middens. Yet, all do have one or another rare or exotic material included in the sample. Jade and/or jade-like specimens were found in 'ZT6' (= 0.04/unit; 1.8% of all microlapidary) and 'ZTB' (= 0.18/unit; 0.11%), so again the alluded pattern is repeated. Another constant is that 'ZTB' is always involved, regardless which raw mineral is being evaluated (it has the widest diversity). It is also the only 'ZT-' block to contain possible nephrite specimens (but needs to be confirmed) at a rate of 0.11/unit (2.54% of all microlapidary specimens). Another interesting bit of information refers to crystal quartz, since this particular material holds such a widespread shamanistic symbolism through lowland South America. While by no means geologically rare or exotic in the Caribbean or even, perhaps, Vieques Island, this gemstone was very rare in terms of Ct/4m^2 unit: 'ZT2'' = 0.1/unit, 'ZT4' = 0.5/unit, 'ZT6' = 0.04/unit, and 'ZTB' = 0.15/unit; blocks 'ZT3' and 'ZT5' lacked crystal quartz.

The above statement on egalitarianism should be qualified. Exotic and rare materials are present in all six of the 'ZT-' units, but the *particular* gemstone species differ among the groups of middens. That would signal access and/or disposal of exotic or rare materials by all, but not to the specific kinds of gemstones. The one confirmed exception is "nephrite" group, which occurs in small amounts only in 'ZTB'. The conclusion is that the individuals who resided near midden 'ZTB' and discarded materials there did control and have access to more diverse materials than the others. Now if all had access to some range of materials, but those near the 'ZTB' block had access to a wider range and even a monopoly on the nephrite group (assuming that it is correctly identified) it may mean that some members of the local lineages (or whatever) residing in or near 'ZTB' were 'richer' and in control of a wider range of gemstone wealth, whereas the others ('ZT2' to 'ZT6') while having access to exotic and rare materials exhibited lower degree of wealth. The users of the 'ZTB' midden apparently had exclusive use or 'rights' (to discard) the "nephrite" materials. One might speculate that this would be possible in societies where there are ranked lineages, but not necessarily stratified. Of course, because we are ignorant of the distributions and calculations by stratigraphic level (component) and have been forced to lump (in the case of 'ZTB') ca. 120cm worth of microlapidary artefacts/unworked raw materials, the above comments must be regarded with due caution. Another factor that needs to be considered along with the above is the evidence for unworked, partially worked, and re-used rare or exotic lithics, which would provide a better index of "wealth and control", of who makes it, who gets it and/or keeps the finished product.

18.10.3   INTRA-BLOCK 'Z' MICROLAPIDARY ANALYSIS

At least 23 different types of gemstones and raw lithic materials were detected by Narganes (1983), although since 1982 further identifications have been been made (Narganes 1995).

The location of block 'Z' indicates that it was most probably a refuse dump. Whether it was a communal dump used by all members of the community or whether only *some* households were the habitual users of the refuse dump remains to be determined. This is an important observation, because one will certainly arrive at different conclusions, depending on which possibility one assumes to be "true". By far block 'Z' (fig. 18.11) surpasses all other block areas in terms of average count, which is at 46/4m^2 unit or an average of 11.5/m^2. It also has the widest lithological diversity (=23) of all blocks[13]. This high mineral diversity (x 3) may be due to (1) its *unrestricted* use as a communal dump, or (2) that this refuse area was *habitually restricted* to a/some household group(s), in which case the the highest degree of 'gemstone' wealth/prestige and control of the rare and exotic materials was also restricted. This wealth is also paralleled by the wider range of decorated ceramic modes and types in the La Hueca locus. For now there is no basis to support either interpretation.

Thus far, I have been proposing some inferences and comparative statements at a gross level of whole block excavation areas. The basis for assessing 'richness' (and possible wealth and/or prestige differences) between block areas of different sizes required the conversion of absolute counts to average counts per unit of 4m^2 (which can easily be converted to Ct./m^2) so that the distortions of sample size could be held constant. At this level of resolution the necessary assumption of regular (average) distribution per unit had to be made for obvious reasons, but also because I do not have the data of counts for each individual excavation unit to elaborate upon.

As a test for the assumption of "regular" distribution in space, I have obtained the specific counts of microlapidary materials for each unit within block 'Z'.

The results are quite interesting. The total counts of microlapidary *lithic* materials (excludes shell, bone and wood) show an uneven, irregular distribution when observed in a bargraph format. Unit Z-13, -14 and -15 are well above all others in terms of total count. I suspect, that these are also the units with the thickest deposit strata, a factor I could not control since I do not have the depths of each unit and thicknesses of the individual strata. In figure 18.10, the same data is provided in terms of an "expected" mean for Block 'Z'. The expected average of microlithics per each unit in Block 'Z' is 30.24 specimens. In the bargraph (fig. 18.10) the mean is set at 0.00, and each unit will show 'x' number of microlithic specimens above (positive) or below (negative) the expected mean. (The bargraph excluded the units that did not yield any specimens, which would record as -30.24; that is, each unit had 30.24 items below the expected mean.) Again, there is a clustering tendency of high concentrations in units Z-13 through Z-20, Z-10-11, and Z-23, well above an expected regular density distribution (i.e., 30 items or more).

The above bargraphs are useful but difficult to visualize in the context of a block area. I have taken the counts of microlapidary materials for each unit and plotted them on a contour map that reflects artifact density within the block. The visual impact is easier to assess. There are but two caveats. First, the resulting density distribution map is calculated as follows: the software package, Delta Graph ©, takes the count value for each 4m^2 and places it at the "geographic" center of the unit. Then it calculates the contour densities by simultaneously considering the values placed at the centers of each adjoining square unit, so that the total effect appears to be a smoother distribution than in reality. The reality is that in absence of piece-plotting, the smallest possible unit is not a center point, but a 4m^2 area. Still, the overall distribution shows quite nicely the peaks and valleys of microlapidary distribution. The second limitation is that this contour model is only bidimensional; it collapses the vertical dimension (depth) into a single plane. The contours *only* reflect areas of higher to lower concentrations of materials. Nevertheless, these plots (figs 18.5 to 18.9) provide useful visual trends of distribution. In order to be able use the software, I had to convert each square unit designation given by Chanlatte into a northing and easting, and the values (counts) are automatically located at the intersection of the X and Y axes (i.e., center of the 4m^2 unit).

I will comment briefly on the result and trends of microlapidary distribution. At this juncture I would like to remind the reader of the model I presented earlier of the depositional and post-depositional factors that were likely involved in the formation of this deposit, along a relatively steep gradient — in particular my comments about the drainages and the displacement of light fraction artefacts, as well as the "hot spots" or areas in the drainage/slope that functioned as "collectors".

Figures 18.5a and 18.5b plot the total distribution of identified lithic (71% of all microlapidary) and shell (28.6%) microlapidary materials in block 'Z'. The microlithic distribution concentrates in the central portion of block 'Z' between North-5/East 6-8 axes. The frequency drops gradually away from this core area, with two minor increases in North 2/East 4 and North 2/East 10. Given the sloping terrain and the deeper depth reached in excavation in the central units, this pattern is not surprising. The microlapidary shell, most of which are small, and light fraction (mother of pearl), clearly show a downslope trend, far more pronounced than the microlithics. Both seem to stop their downward "slippage" in the North 2-3 and east 4-5 grid area, probably representing a higher, sterile base surface. I would conclude that this distribution is largely governed by (a) the slope gradient and slope wash, and (b) by the probable presence of a U-shaped drainage basin, or perhaps a pocket, at the center of the block, where the materials first began to accumulate and where the deposit is "thickest". Toward the edges of the U-shaped drainage or pocket, frequencies decrease, as the sterile basal surface slope rides higher. The lighter fraction (most of the shell) show a more pronounced northeast to southwest scatter trend, reinforcing my tentative interpretation.

Figure 18.6a shows the distribution of serpentinite, and because it is the most abundant of all lithic materials (52.7% of al microliths), its distribution parallels the distribution of all microlithics. Nephrite (tentatively identified as such), on the other hand, is quite rare and spatially restricted to two high points, with again showing a northeast to southwest distribution trend, somewhat like the shell materials, but less spread out (fig. 18. 6b). Jade/jade-like shows an even more restricted distribution and again the same trend (fig. 18.7a). The group designated as 'calcite' or 'crystallized calcite' (some may be quartzes) shows a peak in the same central portion, but the spread extends to the southeast corner (distribution figure not shown here). Aventurine (fig. 18. 7b), however has a different pattern: it does have its high peak in North-5/East-8 grid, and a second equally high peak in the southeast corner of the block in a somewhat similar manner than calcite. Crystal quartz (distribution not shown) departs from all other tendencies, by being concentrated further south and east of the block but, like aventurine, with discontinuous scatters around the high density area. The copper-based minerals, malachite and turquoise are shown in figures 18.8a and 18.8b. Malachite, which has known sources in Puerto Rico, does have a wide distribution and tends to be concentrated in the central portion of the block. Turquoise, which has no known sources in the Caribbean, is equally found in the central portion of the block, but it is much rarer and spatially restricted.

All of these data, point to the slope-wash effects hypothesized earlier, and also seem to suggest that the initial dumping and lowest point of the drainage has a general northeast to southwest trend, which would be consistent with the highest numbers concentrated along such axis. In other words, the U-shaped drainage would be where refuse began to accumulate first and, thus, would have resulted in the "thickest" deposit of the block area.

Finally a brief comment on manufacturing stages. Complete or finished microlapidary specimens (fig. 18.9a) practically duplicates the same pattern of distribution of all microlapidary lithic specimens (all stages of manufacture) (fig. 18.5a). About 13% of all the microlithics were regarded as blanks and their distribution again is largely concentrated in the central portion of the block area (not shown here). Microlithic fragments (17.3%) and incomplete or partly worked specimens (15%; cf. fig. 18.9b) also peak in the central portion of block 'Z'.

The distribution analysis within block 'Z' suggests a pattern that is consistent with an initial dumping phase from upslope toward a possible U-shaped drainage that carried materials in a northwest to southwest direction downslope. It also does not contradict the notion that as the drainage filled-up with refuse, materials began to spread east and west as well as continuing the downslope trajectory. At this level of resolution (intra-block, individual units), it is clear that the distribution is irregular, that not all areas in the block had an equal chance to be the recipient of specific microlapidary types; but I strongly suspect that the pattern is linked primarily to the forces of gradient and slope wash, and in later phases to the filling and outflowing of materials from the former deeper drainages. There is only one way to test this: to plot these distributions by strata and/or depth, possibly using AutoCad © or Surfer © programs that allow for three-dimensional modeling. One factor that will be very relevant to these distribution models and could not be accounted for due to lack of information is the sterile lens reported for block 'Z'. The entire distribution patterns could substantially change above and below this stratum. Finally, it would have been much more productive to have had the possibility to compare block 'Z' with the distribution plots of the other middens that were not located on a steep slope, like for example 'ZT3' or 'ZTB'.

18.11   Conclusions

It is customary to end a study such as this with a concluding synthesis. Yet, the whole point of this essay was precisely to demonstrate the reasons why sweeping conclusions cannot be reached if one adheres to the principles of scientific proof, in Karl Popper's sense, or of historical contingency proof as discussed by Stephen Jay Gould (1989). To force a "choice" between Rouse's cultural historic interpretations and those of Chanlatte on the basis of the available evidence would violate 'Popperian' standards. Instead, I will provide some concluding observations that reflect the themes discussed in this paper.

(1) **Distinctiveness of Material Culture**. Regardless of how (historical development) it happened, once in the northeastern Caribbean region, there is little question in my mind that La Hueca and Hueca-related components were already distinct from the Cedrosan Saladoid in terms of their *portable* material culture (e.g., pottery, tools, microlapidary). The same, however, cannot be said about their social organization and other features of lifestyle; too little data exist to enable anyone to extend this distinctiveness to other aspects of culture. At the very least, historical relatedness can be argued for three distinct *ceramic complexes:* La Hueca, Hope Estate, and Punta Candelero. The site of Morel I (Guadeloupe) does have a significant amount of Huecan-like ceramics, but there is no clear vertical segregation from Cedrosan materials. Others, like Anse Patate in Guadeloupe and Folle Anse in Marie-Galante have not yielded the necessary data for a proper evaluation. Whether all this warrants a separate Huecoid 'series' nomenclature or a Huecan Saladoid cannot yet

be resolved. A separate Huecoid classification advocated by Chanlatte and others is predicated upon the assumption that these ceramic complexes had an origin independent from the Saladoid. Conversely, their classification as Huecan Saladoid ceramic complexes, as Rouse and other suggested, do imply a common origin in the Saladoid series. Neither classification can be said to be fully supported by empirical evidence.

(2) **Chronology**. I have presented a detailed discussion on my assessment of La Hueca. It ranges from as early as ca. 160 BC to about AD 550, thus overlapping entirely with the range of dates determined for both early (Hacienda Grande) and late (Cuevas) Saladoid. They were, in Vieques-Puerto Rico, contemporaneous. Later radiocarbon dates remain, at the moment, under suspicion, but must not be rejected off-hand. At Punta Candelero, the dates are problematic for the early occupation, but the deposit underlies a Cuevas occupation that seems to be a terminal Cuevas (ca. AD 700). This would suggest that Punta Candelero was solely occupied by La Hueca ceramic bearing groups at *any* time *prior* to approximately AD 700, the latest known dates for Cuevas style survival in *all* Puerto Rico and adjacent islands. Thus, while the site itself was a La Hueca-like settlement, it was apparently contemporaneous to other Cuevas sites in Puerto Rico as well as Culebra Island. The dates from Hope Estate-I are ambivalent: Haviser's dates based on charcoal indicate an earlier date ranging between 400-60 BC whereas the crab-claw carbon dates reported by Hoogland (this volume) indicate a later date range between AD 255-650. The latter range also encompasses the early set of La Hueca dates. I am still very skeptical of marine carbonate dates; crab-claws also suffer from the same unkown marine reservoir effect as *Strombus* shells. I would cautiously consider the charcoal dates of Hope Estate-I complex as reflecting an initial La Hueca-related occupation. The dates from these three sites, accepting the 400-60 BC date for Hope estate I, suggest a spread from south to north; the ceramic differences between the northern group (Punta Candelero-LaHueca) and the southern Hope Estate-I (the 'zip' rather than 'zic' emphasis) may well be the result of diachronic developmental changes. However, Haviser's early dates remains to be fully explained.

(3) **Methodological Problems**. I have pointed out in some detail that two of the problems that need to be sorted out are (1) the limited use/availability of *contextual* archaeological data and (2) low degree of *comparability* of analytical units. We must move away from simple percent or counts of trait lists without any reference to sampling size (screens) and area (excavated units in m² or m³) towards more precise and quantitative approaches. Concepts such as 'richness/poverty' and 'diversity-homogeneity' are only meaningful if they are backed by valid statistics and when they are based on *comparable* samples. Likewise, decisions on similarity-difference,

which are used to make inferences about the history of the bearers of ceramic styles must be based on comparable analytical units. I have suggested that questions regarding such things as diffusion, borrowing, transmission of heritage and tradition, independent development, and other such phenomena must be rephrased in terms of understanding the *social action* or dynamics that *could* have produced the observed results. We cannot do this by strictly limiting ourselves to descriptive or morphological analyses of artefacts and features; the normative tools of classification as used by Rouse and others, cannot be expected to tell us about the details of social action that lead to explanations of the above noted questions. It is worth emphasizing the methodological point that many problems against a satisfactory resolution originate in (a) the loose correlation between what Schiffer called *archaeological context* (e.g., patterns on the ground) and *systemic context* (i.e., the social/cultural behaviors producing patterns) and (b) the fact that we still are trying to come to grips with *post-depositional processes*. The latter are precisely the reasons why we often elicit 'behaviors' that may well be incorrect because the depositional (archaeological) context is not primary. Indeed, as Hoogland argued for Hope Estate, post-depositional processes should henceforth be our foremost concern during fieldwork.

18.11.1   CLOSING REMARKS

In this extended and detailed essay I have endeavored to provide a thorough and detailed reassessment of the La Hueca. The degree of detail reached here was necessary because I feel that far too many reviews on the 'La Hueca Problem' have been so synoptic and synthetic that crucial and highly significant observations have, of necessity, been overlooked, ignored or simply forgotten. I am also responding to a surprisingly large number of my Caribbean colleagues who have been pressuring and/or asking to, in a sense, define my position with regards to La Hueca. Any critical evaluation is bound to displease some and please others. Whichever the reaction might be, the research for this essay was carried out without any preconceived or favorite theories, methods or hypotheses. Much to my own chagrin, I discovered just how much unintentional prejudices or misconceptions I had, finding that I was the first in line among those that should have known better. I still believe that both Rouse et al. as well as Chanlatte, Narganes et al. have a strong case for their respective historical reconstructions, just as I am convinced that both cannot be right at the same time. Because both historical reconstructions remain in contention, I have instead focused in the only area that can help us reject and/or modify either model, or come up with yet other possibilities: the question of methodological assumptions which in turn affect field excavation strategies and analyses, and the limits of what can be or not be said with confidence.

I made it a special point to emphasize the problem of comparability of analytical and interpretive units, and hope that the microlapidary study did at least point some ways in which to make it happen. It is likely that others thought of these already, but never got around to put it in print. In fact, raising the issue of comparability was Rodríguez's idea. I wish to conclude by noting that this study was only possible thanks to the unselfishness of Luis Chanlatte, Yvonne Narganes, and Miguel Rodríguez, all of whom are ultimately the first-hand experts on the La Hueca phenomenon, and also because of the many long hours of discussion I had with Ben at Yale. This fact alone allowed me to gain an appreciation of their respective views. I will not, however, pretend that I have at all times understood their writings and oral comments. All errors or misunderstandings are my own responsibility.

notes

1 The notation of radiocarbon dates is according to the conventions published in Radiocarbon.

2 This brief synopsis cannot cover all the details and nuances of a history of archaeological theory and practice in the Caribbean. Exceptions to the above generalizations should be expected.

3 For another critical evaluation see Moscoso (1986).

4 I am referring to a friendly, informal discussion Bill Keegan and I held in St. Croix in 1993. To be fair, Keegan was actually being critical to the blind application of classificatory labels, as a sort of 'filing system'. He felt then that the 'Roussean' units were not indispensable for addressing the questions we ask about past societies. But, I do recall he was specific in his insistence that we could do away with them and still do our job effectively. Here we agreed to disagree.

5 Diana López, having just returned from Mexico, applied the type-variety classification method to the Sorcé materials. It was because of the unfamiliarity of Puerto Rican archaeologists with the methods and assumptions behind the type-variety that her thesis, unfortunately, has received undeserved little attention.

6 When I use "jade" and "nephrite" I am referring to jade-like, nephrite-like and other unspecified greenstone materials.

7 In figure 18.1, at the center of the La Hueca ring of middens there is a "channel-like" feature (and depression) that is a road and not a "river". Contour lines around the road are probably the result of road construction.

8 Strictly speaking, Río Guapo is a non-issue. The site has succumbed to fluvial erosion and thus it is no longer available for further hypothesis testing. A single date, as Chanlatte noted, cannot be used as a weapon of proof or falsification. However, Cruxent (pers. comm.) has long insisted that fluvial water level changes are the main culprit for the eroded state of the sherds and, thus, the lack of paint. Furthermore, the excavation tests were too small for anyone to be reasonably comfortable with the assertion, "paint is absent". Once again, 'not present' is not the same as 'absent'.

9 Haviser's (1991a) excavation was the only one at Hope Estate to obtain charcoal dates ranging between 400 BC and 60 BC. As Hoogland pointed out (this volume), the new dates obtained near Haviser's tests suggest a later time frame, cal AD 255-650, that significantly overlap those from La Hueca site, as evaluated in Part II of this essay.

10 The volumes provided here are, in fact, not accurate because I am using the calculated *average* depths published by Chanlatte and Narganes (1983). I only include these rough calculations to illustrate the point that there are huge differences in sample size between middens. It is not just a question of area (number of units), but of volume as well. The simplistic comparison of number of items (counts or percents) from one block to another block without it being tied to a conversion factor, such as items per volume unit, renders the comparison meaningless, except, perhaps, at the level of 'whole site'. The concepts of 'richness' and 'diversity' have to be reevaluated in terms of the implications of sample size, not to mention the methods of recovery (i.e., wet or dry screen, screen mesh sizes, etc.). At Candelero, for example, screens of 1/16" were the standard; *double* the rentention size of La Hueca.

11 After this essay was completed, Narganes (pers. comm. 1998) informed that the sterile (sand) layer indeed was detected throughout all the excavation units in Block Z. This would strenghten the hypothesis of a generalized rather than localized event, very likely linked to weather (rainstorm?). I do not know if this layer extended all the way downslope into the Block Z extension, but it is likely.

12 I am at present working-out the possibility of making the full set of tables and figures available through a Web Page (within the Institute of Archaeology web site).

13 These figures depend on whether one follows the original list 1 or list 2.

19   Is La Hueca style pottery present at Trants?

David R. Watters and James B. Petersen

The answers to the seemingly straightforward question posed in the title are the subject of this brief contribution. The answers, however, are decidedly less direct, precise, or exact. They are fraught with issues related to theoretical, methodological, and analytical concerns, and they abound in problems associated with a lack of consistent terminology.

Is pottery attributable to the La Hueca style present at the prehistoric site of Trants (MS-G1) on Montserrat? Without doubt, certain ceramic artefacts recovered at Trants can be generally attributed to the La Hueca style (figs 19.1a-d) (cf. Chanlatte Baik 1984, plates 6-13). La Hueca style pottery is characterized by various attributes, some of which include typical curvilinear incision and zoned-incised-cross-hatched (ZIC) decoration (the latter sometimes infilled with yellow, red or other pigment), along with a combination of zoomorphic (e.g., dog) and anthropomorphic adornos produced by modeling, incision and/or punctation. Other La Hueca style attributes include node or "nubbin" attachments and various vessel forms, often open, such as bowls with and without pedestals, and occasional D-shaped handles, among others (Chanlatte Baik 1984, 26-33). Zoned punctations, sometimes arranged similar to ZIC decoration, are also characteristic of La Hueca style pottery, as seen as Hope Estate. All of these attributes are represented to one degree or another at the Trants site. So the simple answer is "yes, Trants has La Hueca style pottery."

Does that mean that Trants has Huecan Saladoid pottery? If one agrees with the notion that the Saladoid ceramic series in the Antilles has two separate and distinguishable subseries, the Huecan and the Cedrosan, and one further agrees that Trants has yielded pottery attributable to both subseries, then the answer is "yes, Trants has Huecan Saladoid pottery." Trants also has Cedrosan Saladoid pottery (figs 19.1e-h) (cf. Rouse 1992, 74-90).

Does that mean that Trants has Huecoid pottery? If one does not agree with the notion that the Saladoid ceramic series in the Antilles can be segregated into two subseries, and one instead accepts Huecoid as a separate ceramic series in its own right (cf. Chanlatte Baik 1984; Rouse 1992), then the answer is "yes, Trants has Huecoid pottery." Trants also has Saladoid pottery.

Thus, regardless of whether one considers Trants pottery from the level of style (La Hueca), subseries (Huecan Saladoid), or series (Huecoid), some pertinent ceramic artefacts assuredly have been recovered at Trants. Just as assuredly, ceramics from the Cedrosan Saladoid subseries or the Saladoid series have been recovered at Trants and, in fact, they are the dominant ceramics (Petersen 1996; Petersen and Watters 1991; Watters 1994).

If Trants yielded such a diversity of ceramics, then why have the authors consistently referred to it as a Saladoid site, and why have they labelled its white-on-red (WOR) and ZIC pottery as Cedrosan Saladoid? The primary reasons are threefold. Trants has: (1) no spatially distinct sectors across the site correlating with differentially distributed WOR or ZIC ceramics; and (2) no vertically distinct segments in the excavation units correlating with a stratigraphic differentiation between WOR and ZIC, although WOR pottery seems to have increased over time; but Trants does have (3) WOR and ZIC ceramics with predominantly Cedrosan Saladoid attributes. Notably, although different in some aspects of morphology and decoration, various attributes of ceramic paste, manufacture, surface finish and even decoration (e.g., incision) are common between the WOR and ZIC pottery from Trants.

These commonalities have led us to postulate a close relationship between these outwardly distinctive ceramics at Trants, presumably reflecting a common ware. Such a close relationship between WOR and ZIC ceramics has been suggested previously on the basis of compositional analysis of these and other pottery forms from elsewhere in the region (Carini 1991). What has been consistently observed at Trants, through three separate field seasons, is a shared spatial distribution for distinctive but interrelated WOR and ZIC sherds, in all areas of the site so far examined, and their stratigraphic co-occurrence in undisturbed context in the intact deposits found beneath the 25 cm plowzone (Petersen and Watters 1995, 136-138).

The spatial differentiation observed at various sites by other archaeologists, such as at La Hueca and Sorcé by Chanlatte Baik, at Punta Candelero by Rodríguez, and to a lesser degree at Hope Estate by Hofman and Hoogland, does not have a counterpart at the Trants site. Trants also does not

Fig. 19.1. Ceramic artefacts from Trants: a. rim sherd showing linear and curvilinear incisions containing zoned-incised-crosshatched (ZIC) elements (scale 1:2), b. zoomorphic (dog) adorno (scale 1:1), c. rim sherd showing linear and curvilinear incisions containing ZIC elements (scale 1:2), d. bowl rim sherd showing linear incisions containing ZIC elements along with node attachments. ZIC elements are infilled with red pigment (scale 1:1), e. rim sherd showing white-on-red (WOR) elements (scale 1:2), f. spout rim sherd showing polychrome (red, black, white) and modeled decoration (scale 1:2), g. zoomorphic (possibly bat) adorno (scale 1:1), h. zoomorphic (turtle) adorno (scale 1:1).

reveal a counterpart of the somewhat stratigraphically differentiated ceramics at Hope Estate, regarded as two separate components (Hope Estate 1 and Hope Estate 2) by Hofman (this volume).

Thus, selected individual artefacts at Trants certainly fall within the La Hueca style and, by extension, might be argued to represent the Huecan Saladoid ceramic subseries. In this sense, Trants does have La Hueca style pottery. However, the Huecan Saladoid attribution becomes more problematical when one begins to refer to it as a "component."

Component, sensu stricto, means something is a constituent part of something else. Component implies the constituent part is able to be distinguished or differentiated; constituent means that part is essential or integral. Herein lies the crux of the major issues for Trants. La Hueca style ceramics at Trants are able to be distinguished, to a degree, from other ceramics based on certain attributes identified in La Hueca style pottery at other sites. The amalgamation of these La Hueca style ceramics allows one to propose a Huecan Saladoid component exists within the Trants ceramic assemblage. But, in view of its sparse representation within the larger ceramic assemblage, La Hueca style pottery may not be a constituent part of that assemblage, in the sense that it is an essential or integral part.

La Hueca style ceramics are not able to be segregated with respect to their distribution within the Trants site because they do not cluster in any site dimension. Their distribution, like the distributions of painted ceramics and other ceramic forms, is dispersed. Thus, La Hueca style ceramics do not constitute a separate component of the Trants site itself, either in a spatial (areal) dimension, or stratigraphically. Then, to return to the original question, it can be stated that La Hueca style pottery exists at Trants. La Hueca style pottery makes up a portion of the ceramic assemblage and can be said to constitute a Huecan Saladoid component of the assemblage. There is, however, no Huecan Saladoid component of the Trants site, by which we mean there is no separate, distinguishable stratigraphic level or stratum and no separate, distinguishable spatial sector of the site that consists exclusively (or even primarily) of La Hueca style pottery. The predominant pottery at Trants is Cedrosan Saladoid and, based on that observation, we have continued to refer to Trants as a Saladoid site. Trants certainly is not a Huecoid site nor does it have a separate, distinguishable Huecoid component. We look forward to further publication of the detailed results of our ongoing Trants analyses, along with other regional samples, to further assess the interrelationships between La Hueca style and Cedrosan Saladoid ceramics, as has been undertaken at Hope Estate by Hofman and Hoogland.

20 The presence of a Huecan assemblage on Guadeloupe: the case of Morel I

Corinne L. Hofman, Menno L.P. Hoogland and André Delpuech

20.1 Introduction

The site of Morel is situated on Grande-Terre, in the eastern part of Guadeloupe. The geological basis of the Grande-Terre is an uplifted limestone formation of marine origin. The site of Morel is situated on the Atlantic coast of Grande-Terre ca. 1 km east of the present town of Le Moule (fig. 20.1). It is one of the most mentioned sites in the archaeological literature on Guadeloupe and the ceramic chronology of this island is based on stratigraphic data from Morel (Rouse 1986, 1992).

The site is known since the 19th century, but it was Edgar Clerc who actually conducted archaeological research on the site during the late fifties, sixties and early seventies. Clerc discerned four different components, which he labelled Morel I to IV. Morel I, being the oldest of the four components, is one of the most southern assemblages that produced Huecan Saladoid material on the Lesser Antilles to date. During the early nineties an international team composed by the Service Archéologique of the Direction Régionale des Affaires Culturelles of Guadeloupe (DRAC) and the Faculty of Archaeology of Leiden University (UL) conducted salvage excavations at Morel. New data were collected as to the presence of a pre-Cedrosan Saladoid occupation at the site before the time of Christ. More evidence of these early horticulturalists occupying the Guadeloupean archipelago has been found further to the west at the sites of Anse St. Marguerite and Anse Patate and to the southeast, on the island of Marie-Galante, at the site of Folle Anse.

20.2 Previous research

The site of Morel is situated on a low, elongated coastal terrace some one to four metres asl. Towards the south, at a distance of 70-180 m, the terrace is bordered by the plateau of Grande-Terre. As discussed below the coastal landscape has been severely altered by natural processes and human interference. Nowadays the beach is eroded and the dune deposits, some 2-3 m in thickness have disappeared. In its present state the site extends some 300 m along the shore line and has a width of only 10 to 30 m.

During the late fifties and early sixties, when Clerc excavated at Morel, the dune was still intact and the site extended more towards the sea. Clerc excavated a large number of 2 × 2 m testpits in the dunes. He distinguished four components at the site, Morel I to IV, extending from east to west and superposing each other in some areas over a thickness of approximately 2 m. When he determined the horizontal stratigraphy of the site, Clerc divided the site into sectors by placing steel bars along the beach of which some are still present in the present-day lagoon. The vertical and horizontal distribution of the four Morel components are shown in figure 20.2.

In his publications Clerc (1964, 1968, 1970) described the stratigraphic layers as follows:

- Morel I: 15 cm above mean sea level, layer of 10 - 15 cm light sand and sparsely distributed artefacts.
- Morel II: 0,5 m - 1 m above mean sea level, layer of 30 to 60 cm containing artefacts.
- Morel III: 1 - 2.10 m disperse layer of artefacts.
- Morel IV: 2.10 - 2.30 m above mean sea level (depth to surface of 20 to 40 cm), layer of 30 to 40 cm.

Ripley and Adelaide Bullen excavated some test units at Morel in 1965 and confirmed the stratigraphic data (Bullen and Bullen 1973). They applied the ceramic typology they had used for other islands to the four assemblages. They attributed terms as Insular and Modified Saladoid to the Morel I and II assemblages, Terminal Saladoid and Caliviny to the Morel III assemblage and Suazey to the Morel IV assemblage.

In 1981 Henri Petitjean Roget, applying the Bullen's ceramic typology, placed the four Morel assemblages into the cultural chronology of Guadeloupe (table 20.1).

It is also from that period on that Morel I to IV showed up in the chronological charts developed by Rouse (1986, 1992).

In 1984, Pierre Bodu, a french archaeologist, then a civil servant in Guadeloupe, excavated at Morel and mentioned a large number of Morel I and II ceramics in context (Bodu n.d. a and b).

Recently sand pillage, looting and natural erosion have largely contributed to the near complete destruction of the

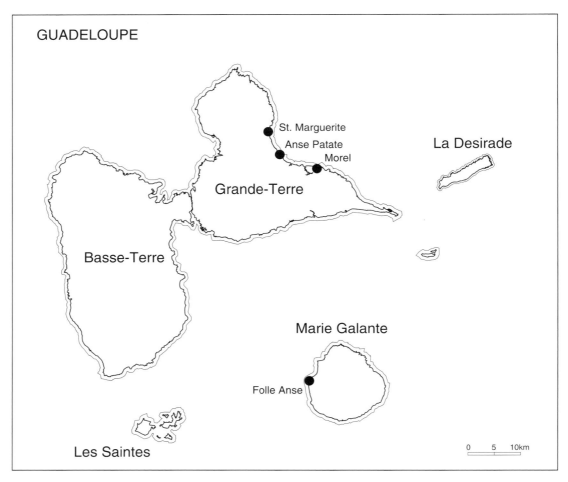

Fig. 20.1. The island of Guadeloupe with the location of the sites with a Huecan Saladoid component.

site. In the last few years some spectacular finds amongst which a burial with a collier of semi-precious gemstones (Durand and Petitjean Roget 1991) and two small wooden amulets representing a dog and a jaguar (Petitjean Roget 1995) were recovered from the beach after heavy hurricanes.

20.3 The 1993 and 1995 excavations

20.3.1 THE SITE OF MOREL I

In 1993 a DRAC/UL team made a reconnaissance of the site to verify its state of conservation, its extension and the occurrence of archaeological material in situ. Nine trenches have been made perpendicular to the beach along a distance of 300 m (fig. 20.3). The distribution of the archaeological deposits encountered in the trenches differed from the stratigraphic layers described by Clerc. It appeared that archaeological material only occurred in very low densities in sandy deposits. Furthermore a number of features were documented, mostly pits, postholes and a few caches.

In the central part of the site most deposits could be attributed to the Morel II component and the upper deposit to the Morel III component. This is confirmed by radiocarbon dates. A wood sample of one of the postholes in trench 5 produced a radiocarbon date of 1720±35 BP (cal AD 250-410) and a shell sample from the upper layer provided a date of 1635±30 BP (cal AD 705-795). The eastern trenches 7, 10 and 11 produced some material of the Morel III component. The Morel IV component was not recognized in either of the trenches. Few artefacts of the Morel I component were recovered from the western trenches.

Besides the distribution pattern of archaeological deposits, the trenches provided important information on the geomorphology of the site. Clayish deposits rich in organic material were encountered in trenches 6 and 8. The deposits extended over a width of some 6 to 8 m and were about 1 m in thickness. They represent a channel running parallel to the coast

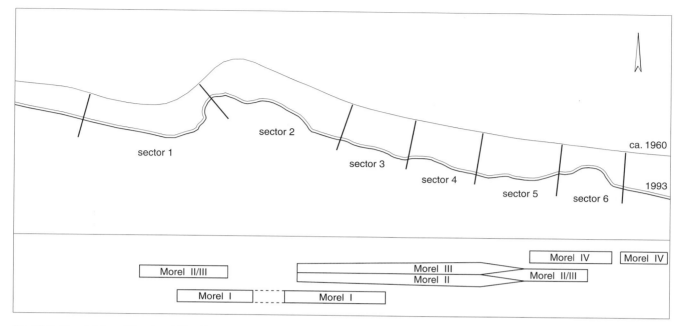

Fig. 20.2. The division of the site of Morel in 6 sectors and the schematic stratigraphy according to E. Clerc.

assemblage	date in AD (not calibrated)	attribution
Morel I	AD 220 ± 100 (Y-1137) AD 245 ± 100 (Y-1138)	Insular Saladoid AD 0 -350
Morel II	AD 550 ± 80 (Y-1245) AD 570 ± 100 (Y-1136)	Modified Saladoid AD 300 - 750
Morel III	not dated	Terminal Saladoid AD 600 - 750
Morel IV	AD 850 ± 80 (Y-1246)	Suazey AD 800 - 1500

Table 20.1. Chronology of the Morel site with radiocarbon dates (Y = Yale) (after Petitjean Roget 1981).

at a distance of 25 to 35m of the present shoreline. In section the channel had a flat bottom and quite steep sides. East of trench 6 the clayish deposits in the channel fill changed in nature and in trench 4 and 5 a clayish deposit was encountered in the section of this trench. This deposit might represent a kind of shallow depression or fresh water lake which collected the water from the upper terrace.
A radiocarbon date on a wood sample from the channel fill produced a date of 1910±30 BP (GrN-20166), calibrated this is between cal AD 60 and 210.

In 1995 a salvage excavation was planned after hurricane Luis. The hurricane had uncovered an archaeological deposit in the western part of the site, then severely threatened by further destruction. Focus was laid on the area where besides a number of burials, an occupation layer had been uncovered by high seas and storms.
A surface area of 600 m^2 has been excavated (fig. 20.3). The archaeological deposits were embedded in a dark brown layer, partly indured revealing archaeological remains belonging to both the Huecan and Cedrosan subseries. The channel fill identified during the 1993 campaign in the most western trenches were present in units 21 and 32. The date of the channel deposits could be more precisely determined by two radiocarbon samples from 1 × 1 m test unit 32. The date for the lower deposits could be confirmed by a radiocarbon date

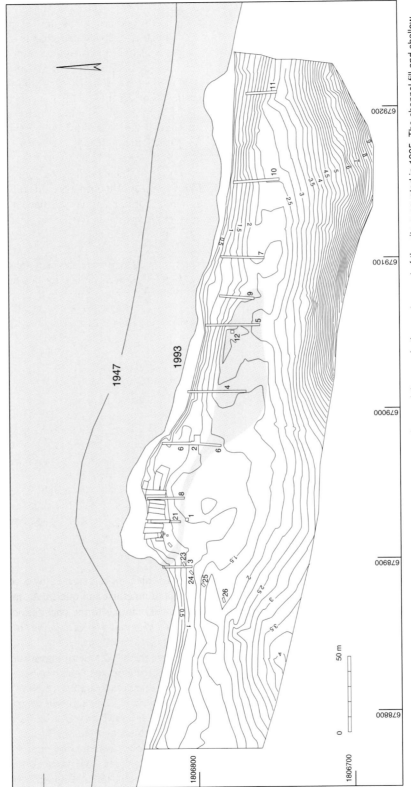

Fig. 20.3. Map of the site of Morel; location of the trenches of the 1993 excavations and the area in the western part of the site excavated in 1995. The channel fill and shallow clayish depression are indicated in grey. The reconstructed shoreline of 1947 shows the impact of the coastal erosion.

on a shell sample (*Cittarium pica*) from the lowest layers of the channel near the habitation area. It produced a date of 2370 ± 30 BP (GrN-22329), this is between 100 cal BC and cal AD 50.

The upper layer of the same 1 × 1 m test unit consisted of a refuse layer and it provided a sample of exoskeletal remains of land crabs which produced a radiocarbon date of 1510 ± 30 BP (cal AD 835-980). This means that by that time the channel was filled at this spot. The outlet of the channel to the sea is situated just west of the excavated area and probably also delimited the site at the southwest side.

The study of aerial photographs made in 1947 and 1993 revealed more data on the transformation of the coast east of Le Moule. The aerial photograph of 1993 was overlaid by the one of 1947 and it appeared that some 50 m of land had disappeared due to coastal erosion in the mean time. Figure 20.3 shows the reconstructed shoreline of 1947.
Further geological research will be executed in 1999 to determine the precise nature of the channel fill, the deposits in the depression and the coastal transformations.

The Morel I component seems to be concentrated in the western part of the site. However, it has severely suffered from erosion and very little of it remains. Presently the archaeological deposits lay on the beachrock, which probably was formed after the Amerindian occupation because artefacts and burials were concretized in it. Morel I ceramics and semi-precious stones were recovered in the channel deposits which were overlain by the Morel II component somewhat more to the east. A number of human burials, several dog burials and one burial of an agouti were uncovered in this area. Some of these were completely and other partly taken into the beachrock. All burials seem to belong to the Morel II assemblage. This was confirmed by radiocarbon dating on two of the human burials producing dates of 1700 ± 100 BP (cal AD 120-590) and 1770 ± 100 BP (cal AD 60 and 530). The first of these two skeletons had an amulet in green stone representing a frog on the front of the neck (fig. 20.6.a).
In this same area, Durand had found a burial during the late eighties. This burial had a collier with quartz and amethist beads and greenstone amulets (Durand and Petit-jean Roget 1991). Petitjean Roget interpreted it as a 'Hue-coid' artefact. A radiocarbon date on a bone sample of the mandibula of this skeleton, done in 1993, produced a date of 2420 ± 120 BP (Grn-20875) which gives an very early calibrated date between the range of 800 and 340 cal BC, or 320 and 200 cal BC. On the basis of this early date the burial might well be attributed to the Morel I assemblage described by Clerc.

Clerc (1964) described the most important characteristics of Morel I assemblage as follows: extreme fine ceramics, the presence of bowls with two holes, zoned-punctate decorations, the thickness of the rim is similar to the thickness of the wall, vessels are all unrestricted, they have outflaring walls-inverted bell-shaped profiles (figs 20.4 and 20.5). In the same layers he found pottery with linear incisions filled with a thick white paint or in some cases red paint. This pottery is associated with shell tools with parallel edges.

In contrast, Clerc describes the Morel II assemblage as follows: most of the rims are thickened; often they have a triangular form, many vessels have a D-shaped handle a lug or a simple button, almost all vessels have a red, white-on-red or polychrome paint.

The ceramic analysis of the material recovered from the 1993 and 1995 excavations reveals that only five percent of the decorated pottery found in the western part of the site show Huecan characteristics. Decorative modes consist of zoned-punctation, zoned-incised crosshatching and modelled zoomorphic adornos (fig. 20. 6).
The recovered vessels have unrestricted and restricted shapes with simple contours and thin walls ranging from 4 to 6 mm. Vessel diameters vary between 18 and 40 cm. Some vessels have inflected contours with diameters between 18 and 28 cm. These are the characteristic vessels with paired holes on the back of a zoomorphic adorno (fig. 20.6. b-d). One vessel has an independant restricted shape with a composite contour. This vessel has a diameter of 23 cm. All vessels have rounded and flattened rims.
Surface colours range from light brown to brown and reddish-brown and have smoothed or burnished surfaces. Firing colours indicate a firing under incomplete or relatively well-oxidizing conditions.
Griddles are flat with rounded rims.

Morel I lithics are represented by a collection of beads and amulets of amethist and quartz. A small frog amulet of quartz, very similar to the ones found at Hope Estate, La Hueca and Punta Candelero is part of the collection.

20.4 Related assemblages in the Guadeloupean archipelago

The site of Anse St. Marguerite or Gros Cap is situated on the north coast of Grande-Terre. The site extends to about 1 km along the shoreline.
Philippe Arnoux, a local amateur archaeologist, executed some test units and collected material at this site during the seventies (Arnoux 1976). He identified at least two occupation

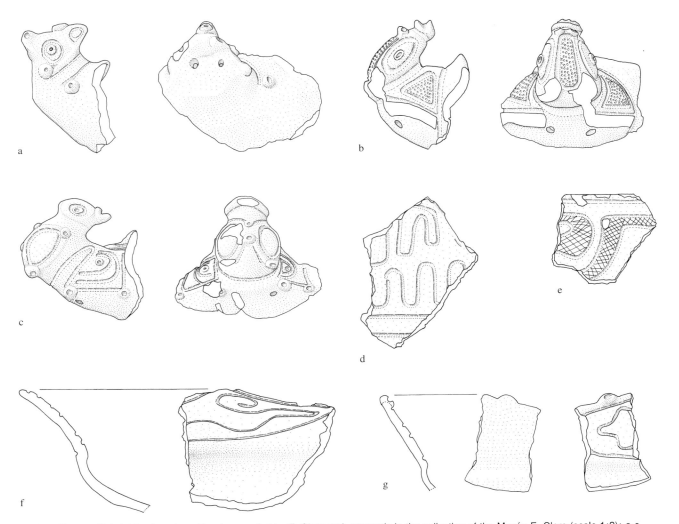

Fig. 20.4. Huecan Saladoid pottery from Morel excavated by E. Clerc and presently in the collection of the Musée E. Clerc (scale 1:2): a-c. zoomorphic adornos, d. sherd with curvilinear incisions, e. rim sherd with ZIC, f-g. rim sherds of effigy bowls.

phases, one Saladoid and one Suazoid. The Amerindian deposits are overlaid by a colonial cemetery.

Arnoux describes the stratigraphy of the site showing a variation in archaeological deposits from the coast to the more inland location. In the test units situated more to the coast a depth of 2 m was attained. The general stratigraphy of the coastal part of the site is as follows:

level 1:   layer of approx. 80 cm to 1 m of grey-black sand
level 2:   layer of approx. 40 to 50 cm of white ashy sand
level 3:   layer of approx. 1 to 1.20 m of white sterile sand

The distribution of artefacts is almost limited to the first layer which contains an abundancy of ceramics with interior or exterior decorations, white paint on a red slip, many shells and faunal remains. The second layer is sterile. In the third layer only some complete shells were recovered.

Further landinward, approximately 500 m from the first test unit, three test units were made and revealed a somewhat different stratigraphy:

level 1:   layer 1 of approx. 20 to 25 cm of brownish sandy earth, layer 2 of approx. 20 to 25 cm of sandy earth mixed with grayish sand.
level 2:   layer 3 of approx. 40 to 50 cm of blackish-grey ashy sand.
level 3:   layer 4 of approx. 30 cm of yellow sand, layer 5 of approx. 20 cm of yellow clayish sand.

The distribution of artefacts is particularly restricted to the first (layers 1 and 2) and third (layers 4 and 5) levels. In the first level mainly thick red-slipped ceramics, legged griddles, lots of shells (mainly *Cittarium pica*), corals and fish bones were found. In the second level (layer 3) only a few shell fragments were present and in layers 4 and 5 lots of very small fragments of *Cittarium pica*. It was also in this layer that Arnoux had recovered some dispersed artefacts amongst which ceramics belonging to the Huecan and Cedrosan Saladoid subseries (fig. 20.7.a, b).

Excavations at the site in 1997 by a team of DRAC/UL confirmed the stratigraphy. At a depth of 1.20 m a dispersed layer of small shell fragments, mainly *Cittarium Pica*, has been recognized.

20.4.2   The site of Anse Patate

The site of Anse Patate is located to the east of Anse Marguerite on the north coast of Grande-Terre. Small test units (0.80 × 1 m) made by Arnoux in 1980 revealed a topsoil of 15 cm of black soil mixed with sand and treeroots. This layer is followed at 40 cm by a layer containing ceramics (post-Saladoid), shells and faunal remains mixed with many rocks. This layer has a thickness to 70-80 cm. From 80 cm on a layer of grayish sand with many ceramics of large sizes (Saladoid), shells and many faunal remains has been recognized. A number of hearths have been identified. At the bottom of this layer Huecan ceramics have been recovered. The Huecan ceramics are characterized by curvilinear-incised designs, zoned-punctate decorations and modelled-incised adornos with paired holes on the back side similar to the ones from Morel (fig. 20.7.c).
From 1.00 m on a sterile layer of yellowish red underlayed the Amerindian deposits.

20.4.3   THE SITE OF FOLLE ANSE

The site of Folle Anse is located on the southeast coast of Marie-Galante. The island of Marie-Galante is situated approximately 30 km to the southeast of Basse-Terre. The island pertains to the outer arc of the Lesser Antilles and is composed of a tertiary calcareous material on a volcanic base. The site of Folle Anse is located on a sandy strip of land approximately 2 m asl. At the west it is bordered by the Caribbean Sea and in the east by marshlands.
It was Père Barbotin who excavated five units of approximately 30 m² in total at the site of Folle Anse during the sixties (Barbotin 1970). Later it was a local inhabitant of Marie-Galante, Mr. Grandguillotte (pers. comm.) who also made a few excavation units at the site.

Barbotin (1970) described the stratigraphy of the site as follows:

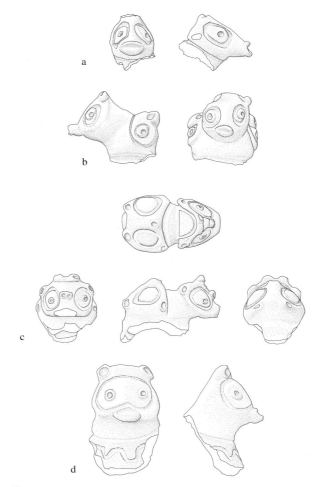

Fig. 20.5. Huecan Saladoid pottery from Morel in the collection of Y. Delaplace (scale 1:2): a-d. zoomorphic adornos.

– Level 1:   surface - 10 cm, layer of 10-15 cm containing many ceramics.
– Level 2:   10-20 cm, layer with painted or incised ceramics.
– Level 3:   20-40 cm, layer of approx. 10 cm of sand, rather ashy with many shells and faunal remains,
40-60 cm, sterile layer.
– Level 4:   60-90 cm, layer of white beach sand with traces of another occupation.

In one of his later publications Barbotin (1987) describes that at a depth of about 1.40 m he identified an occupation layer with a very disperse layer of artefacts. He describes a very particular set of artefacts including pottery of high qualtiy with zoomorphic adornos having paired holes on the

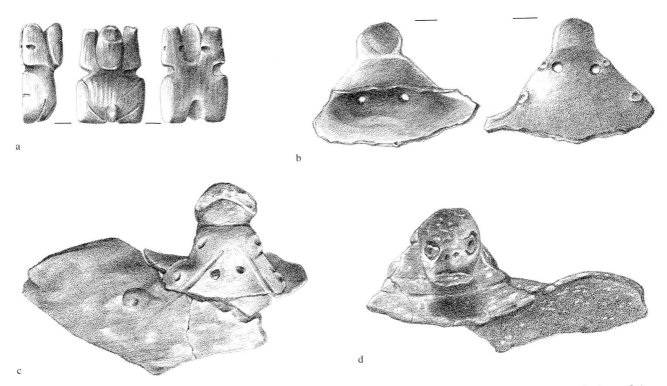

Fig. 20.6. Cedrosan Saladoid stonework and Huecan Saladoid pottery from Morel excavated in 1993 and 1995: a. greenstone Cedrosan Saladoid amulet (scale 1:1), b-d. Huecan Saladoid zoomorphic adornos, parts of effigy bowls.

back side, curvilinear incisions filled with punctations, white painted decorations on plain surfaces and shell tools with parallel edges (fig. 20.8).

On the basis of distribution and characteristics of the artefacts Barbotin distinguished several occupation phases at Folle Anse and compared them to the Morel site. Level 4 can be compared to the Morel I assemblage, Level 3 to the Morel II assemblage and Level 1 to the Morel IV assemblage. For Level 2 Barbotin could not find an affiliation with Morel III.

20.5 Interpretations and conclusions

Although the Morel I deposits as identified and described by Clerc were not found at that point anywhere in the 1993 and 1995 trenches and units, some ceramic sherds clearly belonging to the Huecan Saladoid subseries were individualized in the most northwestern trenches. It is hypothesized that the original Huecan deposits had been completely destroyed by erosion and that part of its material washed ashore after severe storms and hurricanes. Only a marginal portion of the entire site seemed relatively well preserved. It comprises the refuse deposits in the channel and the lowest layers in the middle trenches with a clear stratigraphic segregation. The stratigraphy in this area shows a rapid accumulation of sand

with a diffuse distribution of artefacts over a relative shallow depth. Morel IV, which was identified by Clerc in the eastern part of the site, was not found. This part of the occupation of Morel has probably been completely destroyed by either natural erosion or human interference.

It has been demonstrated that the present topography does not correspond to the one during the Amerindian occupation. Progressive retreat of the coastline must have occurred and this process was probably accellerated by sand winning in the dunes for construction works. The study of aereal photographs shows that since 1947 the beach has retreated approximately 50 m. From the fieldnotes of Clerc, it can be concluded that at least a layer of sand of one or two metres in thickness has dissapeared in the dune area. Also, these changes might be related to a relative transgression of the sea level and/or tectonic movement, which could lead to the sinking of this part of the Atlantic coast of Grande-Terre. The geomorphological data revealed that the Huecan Saladoid settlement was situated on the end of a spit of land, bordered by the sea in the north, by the outlet of the channel in the east and by a channel and shallow depression filled with fresh water in the south (fig. 20.3). On the basis of this information and stratigraphic evidence it has been suggested

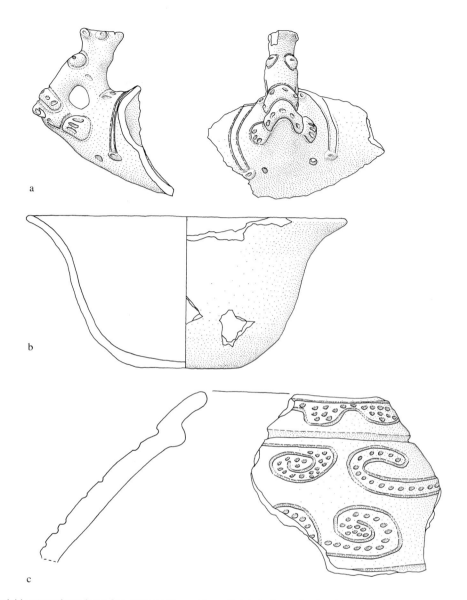

Fig. 20.7. Huecan Saladoid pottery from Anse Ste. Marguerite and Anse Patate in the collection Arnoux: a. zoomorphic adorno from Anse Ste. Marguerite (scale 1:2), b. unrestricted vessel with a complex contour from Anse Ste. Marguerite (scale 1:2), c. restricted vessel decorated with curvilinear incisions and punctations from Anse Patate (scale 1:1).

that during the Morel I occupation, the site could have been located in a saline or mangrove-like environment. A similar situation can be found today in the area of the Salines of the Pointe des Chateaux at the far east end of Grande Terre. The complex geological context at Morel with its marine transformation processes, the presence of both Huecan and Cedrosan material, the diversity of radiocarbon dates incite a prudent evaluation of the stratigraphic homogeneity of the deposits excavated during the 1995 campaign.

Morel I ceramics represent the characteristics of the Huecan Saladoid subseries as defined for sites as La Hueca and Hope Estate. The assemblage consists of vessels with paired holes, curvilinear decorative motifs filled with punctations or zic and modelled adornos. Vessels have thin walls and the variety of shapes is limited. Griddles have rounded rims. Amongst this material there are also ceramics painted in white-on-red, vessel shapes and adornos clearly affiliated to the Cedrosan Saladoid subseries. These two well-distinct

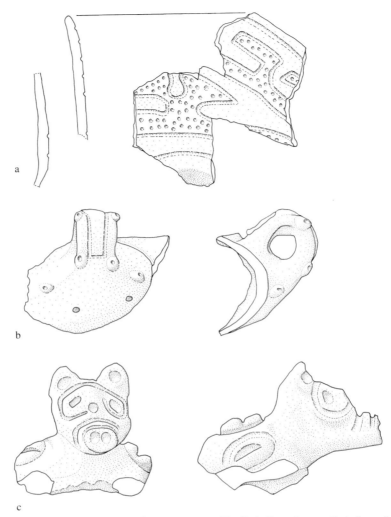

Fig. 20.8. Huecan Saladoid pottery from Folle Anse, Marie-Galante excavated by Barbotin and presently in the collection of the Musée E. Clerc (scale 1:2): a. tail part of an effigy bowl, b. restricted vessel with handle, decorated with incision and nubbins, c. zoomorphic adorno.

ceramic styles are stratigraphically not well segregated in the excavation units of 1995.

Radiocarbon dates recently obtained for Morel I, produced dates between 300 BC-AD 300. The earliest dates situated around 300 BC are earlier than the ones obtained by Clerc but contemporeneous with the earliest dates obtained for Hope Estate, St. Martin.

The distribution of sites that produced ceramics belonging to the Huecan Saladoid subseries is restricted to the north coast of Grande-Terre, Guadeloupe and the southeastern coast of the island of Marie-Galante. Until now four sites have been inventorized to have produced Huecan Saladoid ceramics in the Guadeloupean archipelago. Large quantities of material have come to the surface due to natural and human impact. Progressive retreat of the coastline and sand pillage have, in the past decades, largely destroyed the sites, a phenomenon that threathens the entire coastal area of Guadeloupe. The perpetual coastal erosion and the exposure of archaeological materials has made the beaches of Guadeloupe 'supermarkets' for private collectors. Archaeological research on these sites has become difficult and the interpretation rather ambiguous.

21   Synthesis and evaluation

Corinne L. Hofman and Menno L.P. Hoogland

21.1   Introduction

Prospective investigations and test excavations were conducted at three pre-Columbian sites on the island of St. Martin in the beginning of 1993. Systematic research on site level provided insights in the spatial distribution of arte- and ecofacts as well as in the processes of site formation and post-depositional disturbance. A detailed analysis of the various categories of material finds next to a description of the material culture in general yielded information on the exploitation of the natural resources and the provenience of raw materials on the island. The present volume presents the results obtained from the sites of Norman Estate, Hope Estate and Anse des Pères, dated from the end of the third millenium BC upto the ninth century AD. As such, these sites cover an important part of the pre-Columbian settlement history of St. Martin, i.e., that from the preceramic to the end of the Saladoid period. The research at Hope Estate gave a new impetus to the discussion on the so-called 'La Hueca problem'. Contributions from various scholars on Huecan sites of neighbouring islands, i.e., La Hueca, Vieques, Trants, Montserrat and Morel, Guadeloupe, have brought this discussion in a broader regional perspective.

21.2   Norman Estate

The site of Norman Estate (NE1 and NE3) is situated in the northeastern part of St. Martin. Activity area NE 1 is located on a plateau in the middle of a valley approximately 8 m above MSL and 1,5 km from the north and east coasts of the island. Prospective investigations of the area and auger tests indicated the presence of a second activity area, referred to as NE3. Six test units made in the NE1 and NE3 sites clearly showed that both are characterized by a continuous preceramic occupation. NE1 consists essentially of shells and faunal remains. In contrast, NE3 yielded little food debris, but an abundance of lithic materials. NE1 has been interpreted as a refuse deposit, while NE3 might have been a campsite. Four radiocarbon measurements have been obtained from NE 1 to date. These dates range from 2400 to 1900 cal BC and consequently belong to the earliest dates known from the northern Lesser Antilles.

Amongst the lithic material, a distinction should be made between flint cores and flakes, reduced with an expedient

flake technology. Moreover, unworked water-worn pebbles have been recovered as well as volcanic hypabyssal and limestone flakes, which cannot be associated with a specific reduction technology to date. No cores or core tools have been recovered. The absence of cores indicate that the lithic collection is incomplete. The lithic materials recovered from NE1 and NE3 suggest that similar technologies were used for the production of lithic tools in both areas. With the exception of flint, most material used is probably available locally. The fact that the lithic assemblage of Norman Estate is incomplete, limits comparison with those of contemporary sites in the region. The lithic inventories and technologies of the various contemporary sites in the Leeward Islands show differences with Norman Estate which seem to form the result of environmental restrictions rather than cultural habits.

Arca zebra is the most common shell species. Codakia orbicularis, Anadara notabilis and Chama sarda are other species which are represented in relatively substantial numbers. These shells were collected in a coastal environment. Only a few artefacts, all made of Strombus gigas, have been recovered. A marine orientation for the exploitation of the subsistence resources (shells as well as vertebrates) is a recurrent phenomenon of the preceramic sites in the northern Lesser Antilles. A strong dependence on a single shellfish species, such as is observed at Norman Estate, has been reported also for sites on Antigua (Jolly Beach and South Pier), St. Kitts (Sugar Factory Pier) and St. Thomas (Krum Bay). The shell artefacts are difficult to compare, mainly due to the small samples recovered from these sites and the small scale of excavated areas. The vertebrate remains from Norman Estate very much resemble those from Krum Bay, Jolly Beach and Hichman's Shell Heap on Nevis. Faunal remains consist mainly of fishbones. Reef fish species, most of which inhabit shallow coral reefs, predominante. A preference for Scaridae can be noticed. Haemulidae, Acanthuridae and Lutjanidae are other important species. No significant difference has been observed between the faunal composition of the NE1 and NE3 sites. This may indicate a cultural affinity between the two sites. The site of Norman Estate is the first preceramic site that has been recovered on St. Martin. The nature of the deposit and the composition of the artefact assemblage shows clear resemblances to that of contemporary sites on other islands of the northern Lesser Antilles. The site of Norman Estate can consequently be atributed to the Ortoiroid series.

21.3   Anse des Pères

The site of Anse des Pères is situated in the northwestern part of St. Martin. The area of the site has been determined through a program of systematic testing. These tests yielded substantial information on the concentration of archaeological materials at this site. The total area is 15000 m² of which 3000 m² is a dense midden. Six randomly chosen units of 1 m² were excavated in the two densest parts of this midden. The fill of the units was water-screened utilizing sieves with 10, 6 and 2,7 mm mesh. Three radiocarbon samples provided dates between cal AD 730 and 959, which places the site in the Late Cedrosan Saladoid period.

The pottery material illustrates the attribution of the site to the Late Cedrosan Saladoid subseries, by the presence of a large number of diagnostic traits of the ceramics of this phase. Open vessel shapes with rounded rims are predominant. Diagnostic decorations include incisions, white-on-red and polychrome painting, zoned-incised crosshatching and modelling. The ceramics from Anse des Pères do not exhibit Barrancoid influences as is the case with the Late Cedrosan pottery of the more southern islands of the Antilles. A number of complete vessels were found pointing to the undisturbed character of the site.

With respect to the lithic material, two technologies could be identified. One unstandardized technology aimed at the production of flakes to be used as tools was found to be associated with flint and quartz, another technology related to the production of core tools, mainly in the form of axes, appeared to be related to the use of cherty carbonate and volcanic rocks. A third group of artefacts consists of water-worn pebbles. All raw materials, except flint, are locally available on the island. The lithic assemblage resembles that of the other Saladoid sites in the region.

Shells, obtained by sieving with 10 mm mesh, are abundantly present at the site. Cittarium pica is the most common shell species which was collected for subsistence purposes. Other species include Arca zebra and Astraea tuber. The shell artefacts recovered comprise a number of beads made of Oliva sp. and Olivella sp. as well as some amulets. One of the units yielded a vessel made of a Charonia variegata gastropod. The entire shell assemblage, is similar to that of Golden Rock, St. Eustatius. This confirms the chronological position of the Anse des Pères site.

The faunal remains encountered at Anse des Pères include bones of mammals, birds, reptiles and fish. The most frequent species are the rice rats (Oryzomyni), fish (Haemulidae, Carangidae), pigeons (Columbidae), water turtles, and land crabs. A relatively high percentage of vertebrates and land crabs is noticeable. This relates Anse des Pères to other Late Saladoid sites in the region. One artefact of worked turtle bone, which appeared to be identical to a specimen from Golden Rock, St. Eustatius, has been recovered. Its function is unknown.

The site of Anse des Pères is clearly related to the late stage of the Cedrosan Saladoid. The material shows many resemblances with that encountered at the contemporaneous sites of the northern Lesser Antilles, such as Golden Rock, St. Eustatius, Sugar Factory Pier, St. Kitts and Indian Creek, Antigua. However, the outcome of the radiocarbon samples confirms a continuation of the Cedrosan occupation on the northern Lesser Antilles onto the 10th century AD. The small size of these islands can be one of the reasons for the longstanding continuation of the Saladoid tradition. Further, from a geographical perspective, the northern Lesser Antilles lie in the periphery of the Greater Antilles to the northwest and the southern Lesser Antilles to the southeast. This position might provide an explanation for the fact that the smaller islands of the northern Lesser Antilles formed an enclave for Saladoid groups amidst a changing social-political landscape.

21.4   Hope Estate

The site of Hope Estate is situated in the northeastern part of the island just as Norman Estate. The site occupies a plateau with an elevation of 80 m asl and has a surface area of approximately 1 ha. It is bounded by the Mont Caréta (401 m) to the southwest, by the Montagne France (360 m) to the south and by Hope Hill (292 m) to the east. From 1987 onwards, test excavations have been conducted at the site of Hope Estate by, amongst others Jay B. Haviser. These yielded some very early radiocarbon measurements from the site, i.e., about 500 cal BC, and the presence of Huecan Saladoid pottery.

In all, 144 m² have been excavated in 1993. A unit of 13 × 8 m was excavated to test the presence of features, while nine units of 2 × 2 m were dug to obtain a sample of the cultural materials present. These excavations confirmed that Hope Estate represents a multicomponent site with dates running from 400/300 cal BC to cal AD 650. However, the correlation between both data sets in combination with the pottery analysis makes the interpretation of the site's occupation rather complex. Particularly, the occurrence of Huecan Saladoid pottery and charcoal yielding early radiocarbon dates in the Cedrosan Saladoid deposits at the site points to the significance of the processes of formation and post-depositional disturbance. The stratigraphy and radiocarbon dates suggest that the settlement at Hope Estate site can be divided chronologically into several occupation phases.

The ceramic material from the Hope Estate site includes a Hope Estate 1 or Huecan Saladoid component and a Hope

Estate 2 or Cedrosan Saladoid component. The major differences between the Hope Estate 1 and 2 pottery assemblages is that the former lacks painting, although a red slip has been noticed in a few cases, shows simple vessel shapes and overall thinner vessel walls, has a bright brown colour and is decorated in some way. The Cedrosan pottery stands out for its bichrome and polychrome painted decorative motifs and the variety of its vessel and rim shapes. However, similarities between the two styles are noticed by the presence of zoned-incised crosshatched (ZIC) decorations placed on vessel rims or filling curvilinear incised lines and nubbins added to vessel rims. Effigy dishes or bowls with two holes representing zoomorphically modelled adornos with heads and tails, are typically Huecan.

Several significant aspects of the manufacture, raw material sources and intra-site distribution of the lithic artefacts at the Hope Estate site could be identified. Based on the stages of lithic reduction of the various raw materials, it can be concluded that the primary sources of stone materials were local. They show a predominance of tephrite A and B, next to basalt, diorite and limestone. Chert is the largest non-local lithic material. It exhibits disproportionate quantities of primary, secondary, and non-decortification reduction stages. These Huecan and Cedrosan Amerindians extremely valued exotic stone materials. Cherts were brought in as prepared cores. Rare exotics, such as jadeite/nephrite, amethyst, serpentine, carnelian, and calci-rudite, played a key role in the assemblage of ornamental or sacred objects. They too, were manufactured away from the site prior to importation. The presence of beads and amulets made of exotic stone materials, predominantly manufactured elsewhere, suggests that the Huecan/Cedrosan Amerindians at Hope Estate obtained them through some form of extended exchange network. As the most probable sources of several of these exotic materials are to be found on the mainland of South America, such exchange networks, if they existed, may have covered great distances.

The manufacturing technology of the tools is rather simple. The best represented groups of axes and adzes include axes with petaloid edges, axes with square butts, axes with petaloid butts, and axes with rounded-shaped butts. These tools are mainly made of first tephrite and than basalt. The Hope Estate stone tool inventory does not deviate from that common in Caribbean prehistory. The West Indian lithic assemblages are characterized by materials that are abundantly available locally and are worked by a simple manufacturing technology.

Most of the shell species identified at the site include mollusks at home in the tidal zone and rocky environment. Therefore, it is not likely that the Amerindians dived to obtain shellfish; they seem to have been content with shallow-water harvesting. The shell populations encountered by the first settlers were certainly unexploited and not yet expelled to deeper waters. Therefore, it can be concluded that most shell species present in the midden area were easy to find and to gather, at a location which could be reached easily, and that throughout the habitation of the Hope Estate site species preference and shellfishing methods did not change. Cittarium pica formed the most important shellfish species collected. The relative abundance of complete Cittarium pica gastropods implies that the shells were cooked (of course, it is possible that complete Cittarium pica shells were deposited in the midden by hermit crabs attracted by the garbage). The additional recovery of complete specimens of smaller shell species confirms the hypothesis that cooking of the shells was one of the methods of food preparation. The shell artefacts recovered at the Hope Estate site can be distinguished according to amount and diversity. Most artefacts are commonly found in the Caribbean area. It seems that most shell implements were in use for a long period of time by both the Hope Estate 1 and 2 cultures.

Paleoethnobotanical analysis provided insights into plant use and certain human behaviors. These data suggest that tropical dry forests, particularly dry evergreen formations, were present on the island during pre-Columbian times. Locally available woods were used as fuel and some species may have provided resins and medicinal materials. No conclusive evidence has been found for the consumption of imported or native edible roots, but the presence of artefacts strongly associated with plant-food processing may be considered to form indirect evidence for the reliance on edible rootcrops, e.g., manioc.

Hope Estate is certainly one of the most important pre-Columbian sites on the Lesser Antilles, mainly due to the fact that it revealed relatively large quantities of Huecan pottery and artefacts as a spatially and chronologically segregated component. The nature of the relationships with sites producing Huecan ceramics on neighbouring islands should be assessed carefully in order to establish the position of Hope Estate within the Huecan distribution area. Northwest of St. Martin the sites of La Hueca, Vieques and Punta Candelero, Puerto Rico, revealed spatially segregated Huecan deposits next to middens yielding Early and Late Cedrosan materials. The richness of both pottery and lithic assemblages in some parts of the La Hueca site gives it a unique character. On the other hand, the sites of Trants, Montserrat and Morel, Guadeloupe situated to the southeast of St. Martin, provided Huecan materials in a less clear stratigraphic context. In both cases, Huecan and Early Cedrosan Saladoid pottery were found associated in a single component. However, it should be noted that the archaeological record is incomplete since only midden deposits have been documented at these sites. Structural features and burials associated with the Huecan occupation have not been found as yet. The coexistence and contemporaneity of both pottery styles at Trants, Morel and other Guadeloupean sites may well lead to the rejection of chronological arguments to explain the difference between the Huecan and Cedrosan subseries. Instead, it would be more appropriate to postulate for a social explanation. The Hope Estate site would then have functioned in a social network relating the Lesser Antilles and the eastern Greater Antilles.

References

Alegría, R.E. 1981. El uso de la terminología ethno-historica para designar las culturas aborigenes de las Antillas. *Cuadernos Prehispánicos* 9, 5-32.

Allaire, L. 1983. Changements lithiques dans l'archéologie de la Martinique. *Proceedings of the Tenth International Congress for the study of the Pre-Columbian Cultures of the Lesser Antilles*, 299-310. Centre de Recherche Caraïbes, Université de Montréal, Montréal.

Allaire, L. 1997. The Lesser Antilles before Columbus. In: S. Wilson (ed.), *Indigenous People of the Caribbean*, 20-28. University Press of Florida, Gainesville.

Andreieff, P., D. Westercamp, F. Garrabé, J.R. Bonneton & J. Dagain 1988. Stratigraphie de l'île de Saint-Martin (Petites Antilles septentrionales), *Géologie de la France*, 2/3, 71-88.

Armstrong, D.V. 1980. Shellfish gatherers of St. Kitts: a study of Archaic subsistence and settlement patterns. *Proceedings of the Eighth International Congress for the Study of the Pre-Columbian Cultures of the Lesser Antilles*, 152-167. Arizona State University, Anthropological Research Papers No. 22. Tempe, Arizona.

Arnoux, Ph. 1976. Anse Marguerite "Dit Gros Cap", Guadeloupe. Proceedings of the Sixth *International Congress for the Study of the Pre-Columbian Cultures of the Lesser Antilles*, 21-27, Pointe à Pitre, Guadeloupe

Arnoux, Ph. n.d.. Carnet de Fouille.

Ayensu, E.S. 1981. *Medicinal Plants of the West Indies*. Reference Publications, Inc., Algonac, Michigan.

Baetson, G. 1972. *Steps to an Ecology of Mind*. Ballantine Books, New York.

Barbotin, M. 1970. Les sites archéologiques de Marie-Galante (Guadeloupe). *Proceedings of the Third International Congress for the Study of the Pre-Columbian Cultures of the Lesser Antilles*, 27-44. Florida State Museum, Gainesville.

Barbotin, M. 1973. Tentative d'explication de la forme et du volume des haches précolombiennes de Marie-Galante et de quelques autres pierres. *Proceedings of the Fourth International Congress for the Study of pre-Columbian Cultures of the Lesser Antilles*, 140-150. Florida State Museum, Gainesville.

Barbotin, M. 1987. *Archéologie Antillaise. Arawaks et Caraïbes*. Parc Naturel de Guadeloupe, Guadeloupe.

Barret, J.B. & C. Léton 1989. *Rapport sur l'étude de la stratigraphie du site de Hope Estate, St. Martin FWI*. CERA, Martinique.

Bartone, R.N. & J.G. Crock 1991. Flaked stone industry at the early Saladoid Trants site, Montserrat, West Indies. *Proceedings of the Fourteenth International Congress for Caribbean Archaeology*, 124-146. Barbados.

Bartone, R.N. & J.G. Crock 1998. Archaeology of Trants, Montserrat. Part 4. Flaked stone and stone bead industries. *Annals of the Carnegie Museum*, vol. 67, no. 3, 197-224.

Beard, J.S. 1944. Climax vegetation in Tropical America. *Ecology* 25, 127-158.

Beard, J.S. 1949. *The Natural Vegetation of the Windward and Leeward Islands*. Oxford Forestry Memoirs, number 21. Clarendon Press, Oxford.

Beuker, J.R. 1983. *Vakmanschap in vuursteen*. Museumfonds publicatie nr.8, Assen.

Binford, L.R. 1971. Mortuary Practices: Their Study and Their Potential. Approaches to the Social Dimensions of Mortuary Practices, edited by J. A. Brown, 6-29. Memoirs No. 25, Society for American Archaeology. *American Antiquity* 36 (3, Part 2).

Bishop, R.L., R.L. Rands & G.R. Holley 1982. Ceramic compositional analysis in archaeological perspective. In: M.B. Shiffer (ed.), *Advances in archaeological method and theory* 5, 275-330. Academic Press, New York.

Bodu, P. 1984. Le site de Morel. Rapport de fouille pour le Ministère de la Culture. Direction des Antiquités, Guadeloupe.

Bond, J. 1993. *Birds of the West Indies*. 5th ed. Houghton Mifflin, Boston.

Boomert, A. 1987a. Gifts of the Amazon: 'Green Stone' pendants and beads as items of ceremonial exchange in Amazonia and the Caribbean. *Antropológica* 67, 33-54, Caracas.

Boomert, A. 1987b. Notes on Barbados Prehistory. *Journal of the Barbados Museum and Historical Society* 37, 8-43.

Bouts, W. & T. Pot 1989. Computerised recordings and analysis of excavated human dental remains. In: C.
A. Roberts, F. Lee & J. Bintliff (eds), *Burial Archaeology: current research, methods and developments*, 113-128. BAR International Series 211, Oxford.

Bowman, S. 1990. *Radiocarbon Dating*. British Museum Press, London.

Breton, R. 1978. *Relations de l'île de Guadeloupe,* Tome 1, 45-75, Société d'Histoire de la Guadeloupe, Guadeloupe.

Brothwell, D. R. 1981. *Digging up bones*. Oxford University Press, Oxford.

Bullbrook, J.A. & I. Rouse 1953. *On the excavation of a shell mound at Palo Seco, Trinidad, British West Indies*. Yale University Publications in Anthropology no. 50, New Haven.

Bullen, R.P. 1973. Krum Bay, a pre-ceramic workshop on St. Thomas. *Proceedings of the Fourth International Congress for the Study of the Pre-Columbian Cultures of the Lesser Antilles,* 110-114. Florida State Museum, Gainesville.

Bullen, R.P. & A.K. Bullen 1966. Three Indian sites on St. Martin. *Nieuwe West-Indische Gids* vol. 45, 2/3, 137-147.

Bullen, R.P. & A.K. Bullen 1972. Archaeological Investigations on St. Vincent and the Grenadines, West Indies. William C. Bryant Foundation, *American Studies* 8, Orlando.

Bullen, R.P. & A.K. Bullen 1973. Stratigraphic tests at two sites on Guadeloupe. *Proceedings of the Fourth International Congress for the Study of the Pre-Columbian Cultures of the Lesser Antilles,* 192-196. Florida State Museum, Gainesville.

Bush, P.R. & G. de G. Sieveking 1986. Geochemistry and the provenance of flint axes. In: G. de G. Sieveking & M.B. Hart (eds), *The scientific study of flint and chert*. Proceedings of the Fourth International Flint Symposium (Brighton polytechnics 10-15 april 1983*)*, 133-140. University Press, Cambridge.

Carbone, V.A. 1980. Puerto Rico Prehistory: an outline, Appendix A. In: *A Cultural Resources Reconnaissance of Five Projects in Puerto Rico*. Report on file, U.S. Army Corps of Engineers, Mobile District, Mobile, Alabama.

Carini, S.P. 1991. *Compositional Analysis of West Indian Saladoid Ceramics and their Relevance to Puerto Rican Prehistory*. Unpublished Ph.D. dissertation, University of Connecticut. University Microfilms, Ann Arbor.

Catalogue U.P.R. (several authors) 1996. *Culturas indígenas de Puerto Rico. Colecciones arqueológicas*. Museo de Historia, Antropología y Arte de la Universidad de Puerto Rico. Río Piedras.

Chace, F.A., Jr. & H.H. Hobbs, Jr. 1969. The freshwater and terrestrial decapod crustaceans of the West Indies with special reference to Dominica. *U.S. National Museum Bulletin* 292, 45-48.

Chanlatte Baik, L.A. 1976. *Investigaciones arqueológicas en Guayanilla, Puerto Rico, Parte I (Tecla)*. Museo del Hombre Dominicano, Fundación García Arévalo, Inc., Santo Domingo.

Chanlatte Baik, L.A. 1979. Excavaciónes arqueólogicas en Vieques. Revista del Museo de Antropología. *Historia y Arte de la Universidad de Puerto Rico 1* (1), 55-59.

Chanlatte Baik, L.A. 1981. *La Hueca y Sorcé (Vieques, Puerto Rico). Primeras migraciónes agroalfareras Antillanas: nuevo esquema para los procesos culturales de la arqueología Antillana,* Santo Domingo.

Chanlatte Baik, L.A. 1983. Sorcé-Vieques: Climax cultural del Igneri y su participacion en los procesos socioculturales antillanos. *Proceedings of the Ninth International Congress for the Study of the Pre-Columbian Cultures of the Lesser Antilles,* 73-96. Centre de Recherches Caraïbes, Université de Montréal, Montréal.

Chanlatte Baik, L.A. 1984. *Catalogo Arqueología de Vieques*. Universidad de Puerto Rico, Recinto de Rio Piedras.

Chanlatte Baik, L.A. 1985. Asentamiento Agro-I, complejo cultural La Hueca, Vieques, Puerto Rico. *Proceedings of the Tenth International Congress for the Study of Pre-Columbian Cultures of the Lesser Antilles,* 225-250. Centre de Recherches Caraïbes, Universitè de Montréal, Montréal.

Chanlatte Baik, L.A. 1991a. Doble Estratigrafía Agro-II (Saladoide). *Proceedings of the Thirteenth International Congress for Caribbean Archaeology,* 667-681. Reports of the Archaeological-Anthropological Institute of the Netherlands Antilles, No. 9. Willemstad, Curaçao.

Chanlatte Baik, L.A. 1991b. El Inciso Entrecruzado y las Primeras Migraciones Agroalfareras Antillanas. *Proceedings of the Fourteenth Congress for Caribbean Archaeology,* 187-203. Barbados.

Chanlatte Baik, L.A. 1995. Presencia Huecoide en Hacienda Grande, Loiza. *Proceedings of the Fifteenth Congress for Caribbean Archaeology,* 501-510. San Juan, Puerto Rico..

Chanlatte Baik, L.A. & Y. M. Narganes Storde 1980. La Hueca, Vieques: nuevo complejo cultural agroalfarero en la arqueología antillana. *Proceedings of the Eigth International Congress for the Study of the Pre-Columbian Cultures of the Lesser Antilles,* 501-523. Tempe, Arizona.

Chanlatte Baik, L.A. & I.M. Narganes Storde 1983. *Vieques, Puerto Rico: asiento de una nueva cultura aborigen Antillana*. Impresora Corporan, Santo Domingo.

Chanlatte Baik, L.A. & I.M. Narganes Storde 1990. *La Nueva Arqueológia de Puerto Rico (su proyeccíon en Las Antillas)*. Santo Domingo, República Dominicana.

Chapman, R., & K.I. Kinnes & K. (eds). 1981. *The Archaeology of Death*. University of Cambridge Press. Cambridge.

Chappell, S. 1987. *Stone age morphology and distribution in Neolithic Britain*. BAR International Series 177, Oxford.

Christman, R.A. 1953. Geology of St. Bartholome, St. Maarten and Anguilla. *Bulletin of the Geological Society of America* 64, 65-96.

Clerc, E. 1964. Le peuplement précolombien des Antilles et ses vestiges en Guadeloupe. *Bulletin de la Société d'Histoire de la Guadeloupe, no. 2*. Guadeloupe.

Clerc, E. 1968. Sites Précolombiens de la côte nord-est de la Grande-Terre de Guadeloupe. *Proceedings of the Second International Congress for the Study of the Pre-Columbian Cultures of the Lesser Antilles*, pp. 47-60. Florida State Museum, Gainesville.

Clerc, E. 1970. Recherches Archéologiques en Guadeloupe. L'Archéologie Précolombienne aux Antilles Françaises, no. 36-37, *Parallèles*, 3 et 4ème trimèstre, 68-97.

Clerc, E. N.d. Carnet de fouille.

Cochran, W.G. 1963. *Sampling Techniques*. Willey and Sons, New York.

Cody, A.K. 1991. From the Site of Pearls, Grenada: Exotic Lithics and Radiocarbon Dates. *Proceedings of the Thirteenth International Congress for Caribbean Archaeology*, 589-604.. Reports of the Archaeological Anthropological Institute of the Netherlands Antilles, No. 9. Willemstad, Curaçao.

Cody, A.K. 1993. Distribution of Exotic Stone Artifacts through the Lesser Antilles: Their Implications for Prehistoric Interaction and Exchange. *Proceedings of the Fourteenth International Congress for Carribean Archaeology*, 306-314. Barbados.

Collins, M.B. 1975. Lithic technology as a means of processual inference. In: E. Swanson (ed.), *Lithic Technology*, 15-34. Mouton Publishers, The Hague.

Crespo, E. 1991. Informe preliminar sobre los enterramientos humanos en el yacimiento de Punta Candelero, Puerto Rico. *Proceedings of the Thirteenth International Congress for Caribbean Archaeology*, 840-853. Curaçao. Reports of the Archaeological-Anthropological Institute of the Netherlands Antilles, No. 9. Willemstad, Curaçao.

Crock, J.G., J.B. Petersen & N. Douglas 1995. Preceramic Anguilla: a view from the Whitehead's Bluff site. *Proceedings of the Fifteenth International Congress for Caribbean Archaeology*, 283-292. San Juan, Puerto Rico.

Cruxent, J.M. & I. Rouse 1958. *An Archeological Chronology of Venezuela*, vol. 1. Social Science Monographs, no. 6. Pan American Union, Washington, D.C.

Curet, L.A. & L.A. Newsom 1997. *The Archaeological Project of the Ceremonial Center of Tibes: a progress Report*. Paper presented at the Society for American Archaeology, Nashville, Tennessee.

Curet, L.A. & J.R. Oliver 1998. Mortuary Practices, Social Development, and Ideology in Precolumbian Puerto Rico. *Latin American Antiquity*. Vol 9 (3), 217-319.

Curet, L.A. & L.A. Rodríguez Gracía 1995. Informe preliminar del proyecto arqueológico de Tibes. *Proceedings of the Sixteenth International Congress of Caribbean Archaeology*, Part 1, 113-126. Basse-Terre, Guadeloupe.

Davis, D.D. 1973. Some notes concerning the Archaic occupation of Antigua. *Proceedings of the Fifth International Congress for the Study of pre-Columbian Cultures of the Lesser Antilles*, 65-71. Florida State Museum, Gainesville.

Davis, D.D. 1982. Archaic settlement and resource exploitation in the Lesser Antilles: preliminary information of Antigua. *Caribbean Journal of Science* 17(1-4), 107-122.

Davis, D.D. 1993. Archaic blade production on Antigua, West Indies. *American Antiquity* 58, 688-697.

DeBoer, W.R. & D.W. Lathrap 1979. The making and breaking of Shipibo-Conibo ceramics. In: C. Kramer (ed.), *Ethno-Archaeology: the implications of ethnology for archaeology*, 102-138. Columbia University Press, New York.

deFrance, S.D. 1988. *Zooarchaeological Investigations of Subsistence Strategies at the Maisabel Site, Puerto Rico*. Unpublished Master's thesis, Department of Anthropology, University of Florida, Gainesville.

deFrance, S.D. 1989. Saladoid and Ostionoid subsistence adaptations: zooarchaeological data from a coastal occupation on Puerto Rico. In: P.E. Siegel (ed.), *Early Ceramic Population Lifeways and Adaptive Strategies in the Caribbean*, 57-77. BAR International Series 506, Oxford.

Delorit, R.J. 1970. *Illustrated Taxonomy Manual of Weed Seeds*. Agronomy Publications, River Falls, Wisconsin.

Delpuech, A., C.L. Hofman & M.L.P. Hoogland 1996. *Le site de l'Anse à la Gourde, Guadeloupe*. Rapport de fouille programmée. Service archéologie, Guadeloupe/Faculty of Archaeology, Leiden University.

de Oviedo, G.F. 1979. *Sumario de la natural historia de las Indias*. ed. Miranda, J., Mexico [first edited in 1534].

de Waal, M.S. 1996. *The Petite Riviere excavations, La Desirade, French West Indies. Fieldwork report and subsistence studies for a pre-Columbian site with Late Saladoid components*. Unpulbished MS thesis, Leiden University, Leiden.

Douglas, N. 1991. Recent Amerindian finds on Anguilla. *Proceedings of the Thirteenth International Congress for Caribbean Archaeology*, 576-588. Reports of the Archaeological-Anthropological Institute of the Netherlands Antilles, No. 9. Willemstad, Curaçao.

Drewett, P.L. (ed.) 1991. *Prehistoric Barbados*. Institute of Archaeology, University College, London/Barbados Museum and Historical Society.

Driskell, B.N. 1986. *The chipped stone tool production/use cycle. Its potential in activity analysis of disturbed sites*. BAR International Series 305, Oxford.

Drooger, C.W. 1951. Foraminifera from the tertiary of Anguilla, St. Martin and Tintamarre. *Proceedings of the Koninklijke Nederlandse Akademie voor Wetenschappen*, Series B 54, 54-65.

Duke, J.A. 1992. *Handbook of Edible Weeds*. CRC Press, Boca Raton.

Dunham, A. 1962. Classification of Carbonate rocks according to depositional texture. In: W.E. Ham (ed.), *Classification of Carbonate Rocks*. American Association of Petroleum Geologists Memoir no.1, 108-121.

Durand, J-F. & H. Petitjean Roget 1991. A propos d'un collier funéraire à Morel, Guadeloupe: les Huecoïdes sont-ils un mythe. *Proceedings of the Twelfth Congress for Caribbean Archaeology*, 51-72. A.I.A.C., Martinique.

Ewel, J.J. & J.L. Whitmore 1973. The Ecological Life Zones of Puerto Rico and the U.S. Virgin Islands. Institite of Tropical Forestry, Rio Piedras, U.S.D.A. Forest Service Research Paper ITF-18.

Faber Morse B. & I. Rouse 1995. The Indian Creek period: A late Saladoid manifestation on the island of Antigua. *Proceedings of the Sixteenth Congress for Caribbean Archaeology,* Part 2, 312-321. Basse Terre, Guadeloupe.

Faber Morse, B. & I. Rouse. in press. *ZIC ware finds from the Indian Creek site, Antigua.* Paper presented at the Seventeenth Congress for Caribbean Archaeology. July 1997. Nassau, Bahamas.

Fandrich, J.E. 1990. Subsistence at Pearls, Grenada, W.I. (200 A.D.). In: W.F. Keegan & A. Cody (eds), *Progress report on the Archaeological Excavation at the Site of Pearls, Grenada, August 1989.* Miscellaneous Project Report Number 44. Florida Museum of Natural History, Department of Anthropology, Gainesville.

Fewkes, J.W. 1922. *A Prehistoric Island Culture Area of America.* Thirty-Fourth Annual Report of the Bureau of American Ethnology, 1912-1913, Washington D.C.

Flannery, K.V. (ed.) 1976. *The early Mesoamerican village.* Academic Press, New York.

Flügel, E. 1987. *Mikrofazielle Untersuchungsmethoden von Kalken.* Springer-Verlag, Berlin.

FHPL (various authors) 1993. *Federal Historic Preservation Laws.* U.S. Department of Interior-National Park Service Cultural Resource Program. Washington, D.C.

Garrison, R.E. 1974. Radiolarian cherts, pelagic limestones and igneous rocks in eugeosynclinal assemblages. In: K.J. Hsü & H.C. Jenkyns (eds), *Pelagic sediments: on land and under the sea*, 301-326. Special Publications of the International Association of Sedimentologists no.1.

Goodwin, R.C. 1978. The Lesser Antilles Archaic: new data from St.Kitts. *Journal of the Virgin Islands Archaeological Society* No 5, 6-16.

Goodwin, R.C. 1979. *The Prehistoric Cultural Ecology of St. Kitts, West Indies: A Case Study in Island Archaeology.* Unpublished Ph.D. dissertation, Arizona State University. University Microfilms, Ann Arbor.

Goodwin, R.C. 1980. Demographic Change and the Crab-Shell Dichotomy. *Proceedings of the Eighth International Congress for the Study of the Pre-Columbian Cultures of the Lesser Antilles*, 45-68. Arizona State University, Anthropological Research Papers No. 22. Tempe, Arizona.

Gould, S.J. 1989. *Wonderful Life.* W. W. Norton and Company, New York.

Grunau, H.R. 1963. Radiolarian cherts and associated rocks in space and time. *Ecologae Geologica Helvetia* 58:157-208.

Haag, W.G. 1970. Stone Artifacts in the Lesser Antilles. *Proceedings of the Third International Congress for the Study of Pre-Columbian Cultures of the Lesser Antilles*, 129-138. Florida State Museum, Gainesville.

Hamburg, T.D. 1994. *Cedrosan Saladoid Pottery at Friars Bay St. Martin (FWI).* Unpublished Master's thesis, Leiden University, Leiden.

Harrington, M.R. 1924. A West Indian Gem Center. *Indian Notes* 1 (4): 184-189, Museum of the American Indian, Heye Foundation, New York.

Harris, P.O.B. 1983. Antillean Axes/Adzes: Persistance of an Archaic tradition. *Proceedings of the Ninth International Congress for the Study of the pre-Columbian Cultures of the Lesser Antilles*, 257-290. Centre de Recherches Caraïbes, Université de Montréal.

Haviser, J.B. 1987. *An Archaeological Excavation at the Cupecoy Bay site (SM-001), St. Maarten, Netherlands Antilles.* Reports of the Institute of Archaeology and Anthropology of the Netherlands Antilles, Curaçao.

Haviser, J.B. 1988. *An Archaeological Survey of St. Martin/ St. Maarten.* Reports of the Archaeological-Anthropological Institute of the Netherlands Antilles, No. 7, Curaçao.

Haviser, J.B. 1991a. Preliminary Results from Test Excavations at the Hope Estate Site, St. Martin. *Proceedings of the Thirteenth International Congress for Caribbean Archaeology*, 647-666. Willemstad, Curaçao. Reports of the Archaeological-Anthropological Institute of the Netherlands Antilles, No. 9.

Haviser, J.B. 1991b. The First Bonaireans. Reports of the Archaeological-Anthropological Institute of the Netherlands Antilles, No. 10. Curaçao.

Haviser, J.B. 1991c. Development of a Prehistoric Interaction Sphere in the Northern Lesser Antilles. *Nieuwe West-Indische Gids* 65(3-4):129-151.

Haviser, J.B. 1992a. A Post-Saladoid Interaction Sphere at Anguilla-St. Martin, in the Northern Lesser Antilles. Paper presented at the 57th Annual Meeting of the Society for American Archaeology, Pittsburgh, Pennsylvania, USA, April 1992.

Haviser, J.B. 1992b. Terms used in the Hope Estate Lithic Analysis Form. *Reports of the Archaeological-Anthropological Institute of the Netherlands Antilles,* 1-16, Curaçao.

Haviser, J.B. 1992c. Prehistoric archaeological research on St. Martin/St. Maarten, by the Archaeological and Anthropological Institute of the Netherlands Antilles (AAINA). *Bulletin Annuel, Association Archéologique Hope Estate* no. 1, 4-7.

Haviser, J.B. 1993. 1993 Lithic Analysis, Hope Estate. *Reports of the Archaeological-Anthropological Institute of the Netherlands Antilles,* Curaçao.

Haviser, J.B. 1997. Settlement Strategies in Early Ceramic Age. In: S. Wilson (ed.), Indigenous People of the Caribbean, 57-69. University Press of Florida, Gainesville.

Heckenberger, M. & J. Petersen 1995. Concentric Circular Village Patterns in the Caribbean: Comparisons from Amazonia. *Proceedings of the Sixteenth International Congress of Caribbean Archaeology,* Part 2, 379-390. Basse-Terre, Guadeloupe.

Henocq, Ch. 1992. The different Amerindian peoples of St. Martin. *Bulletin Annuel, Association Archéologique Hope Estate* no. 1, 16-23.

Henocq, Ch. 1994. St. Martin, a cross-roads of civilizations since 4000 years. *Bulletin Annuel, Association Archéologique Hope Estate* no. 3, 16-21.

Henocq, Ch. (ed.) 1995. *Rapport de Fouille Programmée. Saint Martin, Hope Estate: Occupations Pré- Saladoïdes et Saladoïdes.* Technical Report presented to the Ministère de la Culture et de la Francophonie- Direction Régionale des Affaires Culturelles de la Guadeloupe. Association Archéologique Hope Estate.

Hofman, C.L. 1993. *In Search of the Native Population of Pre-Columbian Saba (400 - 1450 A.D.). Part one: Pottery styles and their interpretations,* Unpublished Ph.D. dissertation, Leiden University, Leiden.

Hofman, C.L. 1995. Three late prehistoric sites in the periphery of Guadeloupe: Grande Anse, Les Saintes and Morne Cybele 1 and 2, La Desirade. *Proceedings of the Sixteenth International Congress for Caribbean Archaeology,* Part 2, 156-167. Basse-Terre, Guadeloupe

Hofman, C.L. 1997. Le site the Grande Anse, Terre-de-Bas, Les Saintes. Rapport de fouille programmé pour le Ministère de la Culture. DRAC/Faculty of Archaeology. Basse-Terre/Leiden.

Hofman, C.L. & M.L.P. Hoogland 1992. *Classification of Six post-Saladoid Assemblages from Saba, N.A. (850-1450 A.D.).* Paper presented at the 57th Annual Meeting of the Society for American Archaeology, Pittsburgh, April 8-12, 1992.

Hofman, C.L. & M.L.P. Hoogland (eds) 1993. *Hope Estate Excavations 1993,* Fieldwork report. Leiden University, Leiden.

Holdridge, L.R. 1947. Determination of world plant formations from simple climatic data. *Science* 105 (2727), 367-368.

Holdridge, L.R. 1967. *Life Zone Ecology.* Tropical Science Center, San José, Costa Rica.

Holdridge, L.R., C.R. Grenke, W.H. Hatheway, T. Liang & J.A. Tosi, Jr. 1992. *Forest Environments in Tropical Life Zones: a Pilot Study.* Pergamon Press, Oxford.

Honeychurch, P.N. 1986. *Caribbean Wild Plants and their Uses.* Macmillan Publishers, Ltd., London.

Hoogland, M.L.P. 1996. *In Search of the Native Population of Pre-Columbian Saba (400-1450 A.D.). Part Two. Settlements in their natural and social environment.* Unpublished Ph.D. dissertation, Leiden University, Leiden.

Hoogland, M.L.P., T. Romon & P. Brasselet 1997. *Rites funéraires amérindiens dans l'archipel Circum- Caraïbe.* Rapport de Recherche pour le Ministère de la Culture. DRAC/Faculty of Archaeology. Basse- Terre/Leiden.

Hoogland, M.L.P., T. Romon & P. Brasselet *1998 Rites funéraires amérindiens dans l'archipel Circum-Caraïbe.* Rapport de Recherche pour le Ministère de la Culture. DRAC/Faculty of Archaeology. Basse-Terre/Leiden.

Hoogland M.L.P. & C.L. Hofman 1993. Kelbey's Ridge 2, A 14th century Taino settlement on Saba, Netherlands Antilles. *Analecta Praehistorica Leidensia* 26, 163-181. Leiden.

Hope Estate Bulletin (various authors) 1994. *Bulletin* No. 3. Association Archéologique Hope Estate., St. Martin.

Hulme, P. 1991. *Recopilación de las leyes para la protección del patrimonio arqueológico nacional.* Instituto de Cultural Puertorriqueña. San Juan, Puerto Rico.

Hulme, P. 1993. Making Sense of the Native Caribbean. *Nieuwe West-Indische Gids,* 67(3-4), 189-220.

Humfrey, M. 1975. *Sea Shells of the West Indies: A Guide to the Marine Molluscs of the Caribbean.* Taplinger publishing company, New York.

Hutcheson H. & P. Callow 1986. Cores. In: P. Callow & J.M. Cronford (eds), *La cotte de St. Brélade, Jersey excavations by C.B.N. Mc Burney/G. Brochet et al. 1961-1978,* 240-243. Geo, Norwich.

Jacobs, L. 1983. A summary of the research methods. *Newsletter, Dept. of Pottery Technology I,* 34-36, Leiden.

Jones, A.R. 1985. Dietary Change and Human Population at Indian Creek, Antigua. *American Antiquity* 50 (3), 518-536.

Joyce, Th.A. 1973. *Central American and West Indian Archaeology being an introduction to the archaeology of the states of Nicaragua, Costa Rica, Panama and the West Indies.* Reprinted. Books for Libraries Press, Freeport, New York. [Originally published in 1916].

Keegan, W.F. 1985. *Dynamic Horticulturalists: Population Expansion in the Prehistoric Bahamas.* Unpublished Ph.D. dissertation, University of California, Los Angeles. University Microfilms, Ann Arbor.

Keegan, W.F. 1986. The Ecology of Lucayan Arawak Fishing Practices. *American Antiquity* 51 (4), 816-825.

Keegan, W.F. 1989. Transition from a Terrestrial to a Maritime Economy: A New View of the Crab/Shell Dichotomy. In: P.E. Siegel (ed.), *Early Ceramic Population Lifeways and Adaptive Strategies in the Caribbean,* 119-128. BAR International Series 506. Oxford.

Keegan, W.F. 1992. *The People Who Discovered Columbus: The Prehistory of the Bahamas.* Gainesville: University Press of Florida.

Keegan, W.F. 1997. *Bahamian Archaeology: Life in the Bahamas, Turks and Caicos, Before Columbus.* Media Publishers. Nassau.

Kloos, P. 1975. *Galibi, een Karaïbendorp in Suriname*, Eldorado, Paramaribo.

Knippenberg, S. 1995. Provenance of flint and chert in the Leeward region, West Indies. *Proceedings of the Sixteenth International Congress for Caribbean Archaeology*, Part 2, 261-271. Basse Terre, Guadeloupe.

Knippenberg S., M. Nokkert, A. Brokke & T. Hamburg 1995. A late Saladoid occupation at Anse des Pères, St. Martin. *Proceedings of the Sixteenth Congress for Caribbean Archaeology*, Part 1, 352-372. Basse-Terre, Guadeloupe.

Kozák, V., D. Baxter, L. Williamson & R.L. Carneiro 1979. The Héta Indians: fish in a dry ground. *Anthropological Papers of the American Museum of Natural History* 55 (part 6), 349-434.

Kozlowski, J.K. 1974. *Preceramic cultures in the Caribbean.* Panstwowe Wydawnictwo Naukowe Warszawa, Kraków.

Labat, Père J.B. 1970. *The Memoirs of Père Labat, 1693-1705.* Translated and Abridged by John Eaden. Frank Cass and Co., London.

Lathrap, D.W. 1962. *Yarinacocha. Stratigraphic Excavations in the Peruvian Montaña.* Unpublished Ph.D. dissertation, Harvard University, Cambridge, Massachusetts.
Lathrap, D.W. 1970. *The Upper Amazon.* Ancient Peoples and Places, vol. 70. Thames & Hudson, London.

Lippold, L.K. 1991. Animal Resource Utilization by Saladoid Peoples at Pearls, Grenada, West Indies. *Proceedings of the Thirteenth International Congress for Caribbean Archaeology*, 264-268. Reports of the Archaeological-Anthropological Institute of the Netherlands Antilles, No. 9. Willemstad, Curaçao.

Longuefosse, J.-L. 1995. *100 Plantes Médicinales de la Caraïbe.* Gondwana Editions, Trinité, Martinique.

López Sotomayor, D. 1975. *Vieques: Un Momento de su Historia.* Tésis de Maestría, Universidad Autónoma Nacional de México, Mexico, D.F.

Lundberg, E.R. 1989. *Preceramic procurement patterns at Krum-Bay, Virgin Islands.* Unpublished Ph.D. dissertation, University of Illinois, Urbana. University Microfilms, Ann Arbor.

Lundberg, E.R. 1991. Interrelationships among preceramic complexes of Puerto Rico and the Virgin Islands. *Proceedings of the Thirteenth Congress for Caribbean Archaeology*, 73-85. Reports of the Archaeological-Anthropological Institute of the Netherlands Antilles, No. 9. Willemstad, Curaçao.

Martin, A.C. & W.D. Barkley 1973. *Seed Identification Manual.* The University of California Press, Berkeley.

Martin-Kaye, P.H.A. 1959. *Reports on the geology of the Leeward and the British Virgin Islands.* Voice Publishing Co., Ltd., St. Lucia, W.I.

Mehrer, M.W. 1995. *Cahokia's Countryside: Household Archaeology, Settlement Patterns and Social Power.* Northern Illinois University Press. DeKalb, Illinois.

Miron, E. 1992. *Axes and adzes from Canaan.* Prähistorische Bronzefunde Abteilung IX, Band 19.

Morales, A. & K. Rosenlund 1979. *Fish Bone Measurements. An attempt to standardize the measuring of fish bones from archaeological sites.* Steenstrupia, Copenhagen.

Morgan, G.S. & Ch. A. Woods 1986. Extinction and the Zoogeography of West Indian Land Mammals. *Biological Journal of the Linnean Society* 28, 167-203.

Morison, S.E. 1963. *Journals and other documents on the life and voyages of Christopher Columbus.*
Heritage Press, New York.

Moscoso, F. 1986. *Tribu y clases en el Caribe antigüo.* Universidad Central del Este, Vol. 63. San Pedro de Macorís, Dominican Republic.

Moya, J.C. 1989. *Analisis Preliminar de las Fuentes de Procedencia de las Piezas Líthicas de Punta Candelero, Humacao.* Informe sometido al Universidad del Turabo, Puerto Rico.

Munsell Soil Color Chart 1976. *Munsell Color Chart.* Kollmorgen Corporation, Baltimore.

Murray, P. 1980. Discard location: the ethnographical data. *American Antiquity* 45, 490-502.
National Academy of Sciences.

Murray, P. 1983. *Firewood Crops: Shrub and Tree Species for Energy Production, Volume 2.* National Academy Press.

Nagelkerken, W.P. 1981. *Distribution and Ecology of the Groupers (Serranidae) and Snappers (Lutjanidae) of the Netherlands Antilles.* Publications of the Foundation for Scientific Research in Surinam and the Netherlands Antilles 107, Utrecht.

Narganes Storde, Y.M. 1982. *Vertebrate Faunal remains from Sorcé, Vieques, Puerto Rico.* Unpublished Master's Thesis. University of Georgia, Athens.

Narganes Storde, Y.M. 1991. Secuencia chronológica de dos sitios arqueológicos de Puerto Rico (Sorcé, Vieques y Tecla, Guayanilla). *Proceedings of the Thirteenth International Congress for Caribbean Archaeology*, 628-646, Reports of the Archaeological-Anthropological Institute of the Netherlands Antilles, No. 9, Willemstad, Curaçao.

Narganes Storde, Y.M. 1995. *La lapidaria Agro 2 de Sorcé e Tecla, Puerto Rico.* Paper presented at the Sixteenth International Congress for Caribbean Archaeology, Part 2, 17-26. Basse Terre, Guadeloupe.

Newsom, L.A. 1992. Wood exploitation at Golden Rock (GR-1). In: A.H. Versteeg & K. Schinkel (eds), *The Archaeology of St. Eustatius: the Golden Rock Site*, 213-227. St. Eustatius Historical Foundation No.2, St. Eustatius and the Foundation for Scientific Research in the Caribbean Region No. 131. Amsterdam.

Newsom, L.A. 1993a. Native West Indian Plant Use. Ph.D. dissertation, Department of Anthropology, University of Florida University Microfilms, Ann Arbor, Michigan.

Newsom, L.A. 1993b. Plants and people: cultural, biological, and ecological responses to wood exploitation. In: C.M. Scarry (ed.), *Foraging and Farming in the Eastern Woodlands,* 115-137. University Press of Florida, Gainesville.

Newsom, L.A. 1997. Archaeobotanical research at Shell Ridge Midden, Palmer Site (8SO2), Sarasota County, Florida. *Florida Anthropologist.*

Newsom, L.A. & D.M. Pearsall 1996. Temporal and spatial trends indicated by a survey of archaeological data from the Caribbean islands. In: P. Minnis (ed.), *People and Plants in Ancient North America.* Smithsonian Institution Press.

Nieuwolt, S. 1977. *Tropical Climatology.* John Wiley and Sons, London. Washington,

Nodine, B.K. 1990. *Aceramic populations in the Lesser Antilles: evidence from Antigua, West Indies.* Paper presented at the Society for American Archaeology, Las Vegas.

Nokkert, M. 1995. *Prehistoric Resource Exploitation on St. Martin: faunal remains from the pre-Ceramic Norman Estate and the Saladoid Anse des Pères sites.* Unpublished Master's thesis. Leiden University, Leiden.

Ohnuna, K. & C. Bergman 1982. Experimental studies in the determination of flaking mode. *Bulletin of the Institute of Archaeology* 19, 161-170.

Oliver, J.R. 1980. *Excavaciones arqueológicas en la Quebrada de Balerio, Golfo de Paria, Estado Sucre, Venezuela.* Cuadernos Falconianos, Ediciones U.N.E.F.M., Coro, Venezuela.

Oliver, J.R. 1990. Ceramic Analysis of L-22 and L-23 Sites. *Excavation and Analysis Results of Archaeological Investigations at Medianía Alta (L-22) and Vieques (L-23), Loíza, Puerto Rico.* Final report submitted to PRASA. Grossman and Associates, New York.

Oliver, J.R. 1992a. *Results of the Archaeological Testing and Data Recovery Investigations at the Lower Camp Site, Culebra Island, Puerto Rico.* Final Report Submitted to the U. S. Department of the Interior, National Park Service, Atlanta. Garrow and Associates, Inc., Memphis.

Oliver, J.R. 1992b. Donald W. Lathrap: Approaches and Contributions in New World Archaeology. *Journal of the Steward Anthropological Society.* Vol. 20(1-2), 283-345. University of Illinois [reprinted from Antropológica, Caracas, Venezuela 1991].

Oliver, J.R. 1995. The Archaeology of Lower Camp: Understanding Variability in Peripheral Zones. *Proceedings of the Fifteenth International Congress for Caribbean Archaeology,* 485-500. ICP-IACA, San Juan, Puerto Rico.

Oliver, J.R. 1998. *El centro ceremonial de Caguana, Puerto Rico: Simbolismo iconográfico, cosmovisión y el poderío caciquil taíno de Borinquen.* BAR International Series 727, Oxford.

Oliver, J.R. & D.W. Lathrap 1985. *The Exotic Lapidary Art of La Hueca: Possible Quarry Sources and Pan- Caribbean Trade Network.* Unpublished Ms. filed at Ancient Technologies and Archaeological Materials Laboratory (ATAM), University of Illinois at Urbana-Champaign.

O'Miller, T. 1979. Stonework of the Xêtá Indians Of Brasil. In: B. Hayden (ed.), *Lithic use-wear analysis,* 401-407 Academic Press.

Ortega, E. & M. Veloz Maggiolo 1973. El precerámico de Santo Domingo, nuevos lugares, y su posible relación con otros puntos del área antillana. *Papeles Ocasionales No. 1.* Museo del Hombre Dominicano. Santo Domingo, Republica Dominicana.

Ortega, E., M. Veloz Maggiolo & P. Pina Peña 1976. El Caimito: un antiguo complejo ceramista de las Antillas Mayores. *Proceedings of the Sixth International Congress for the Study of Precolumbian Cultures of the Lesser Antilles,* 276-282. Gainesville.

Palm, J.PH. de (ed.), 1985. Encyclopedie van de Nederlandse Antillen. SENA, Willemstad, Curaçao.

Pantel, A.G. 1991. How sophisticated was "the primitive"? Preceramic source materials, lithic reduction processes, cultural contexts and archaeological inferences. *Proceedings of the Fourteenth International Congress for Caribbean Archaeology,* 157-169. Barbados.

Parry, W.J. & R.L. Kelly 1987. Expedient core technology and sedentism. In: J.K. Johnson & C.A. Morrow (eds), *The organisation of core technology,* 285-304. Westview Press, Boulder.

Petersen, J.B. 1996. Archaeology of Trants, Monserrat, Part 3 Chronological and Settlement Data. *Annals of Carnegie Museum,* 65(4), 323-361. Pittsburgh.

Petersen, J.B. & D.R. Watters 1991. Archaeological Testing at the Early Saladoid Trants site, Montserrat, West Indies. *Proceedings of the Fourteenth International Congress for Caribbean Archaeology,* 286-305. Barbados.

Petersen, J.B. & D.R. Watters 1995. A Preliminary Analysis of Amerindian Ceramics from the Trants Site, Montserrat. *Proceedings of the Fifteenth International Congress for Caribbean Archaeology,* 131-140. San Juan, Puerto Rico.

Petitjean Roget, J. 1963. The Caribs as seen through the Dictionary of Reverend Father Breton. *Proceedings of the First International Congress for the Study of Pre-Columbian Cultures in the Lesser Antilles,* 43-68. Florida State Museum, Gainesville.

Petitjean Roget, J. 1968. Etude d'un horizon Arawak et Proto-Arawak à la Martinique à partir du niveau II du Diamant. *Proceedings of the Second International Congress for the Study of Pre-Columbian Cultures in the Lesser Antilles,* 61-68. Florida State Museum, Gainesville.

Pregill, G.K., D.W. Steadman & D.R. Watters. 1994. *Late Quaternary Vertebrate Faunas of the Lesser Antilles: Historical Components of Caribbean Biogeography.* Bulletin of Carnegie Museum of Natural History, nr. 30. Pittsburgh.

Quitmeyer, J.E. 1985. Zooarchaeological methods for the analysis of shell middens at King's Bay. In: W.H. Adams (ed.), *Aboriginal subsistence and settlement of the King's Bay locality. Volume 2: Zooarchaeology,* 49- 58. Department of Anthropology Report of Investigations 2, University of Florida, Gainesville.

Randall, John E. 1968. *Caribbean Reef Fishes*. T.F.H. Publication, Neptune Beach New Jersey.

Record, S.J. & R.W. Hess 1942-1948. *Timbers of the New World*. Yale University Press, New Haven.
1942-1948 Keys to American Woods. In *Tropical Woods* 72, 19-29 (1942), 73, 23-42 (1943), 75, 8-26 (1943), 76, 32-47 (1944), 85, 1-19 (1946), 94, 29-52 (1948).

Reitz, E.J. 1989. Appendix B: Vertebrate Fauna from Krum Bay, St Thomas, Virgin Islands. In: E.R. Lundberg, *Preceramic Procurement Patterns at Krum Bay, Virgin Islands,* 274-289. Unpublished Ph.D. dissertation, University of Illinois, Urbana.

Reitz, E.J. 1994. Archaeology of Trants, Montserrat, Part 2 Vertebrate Fauna. *Annals of Carnegie Museum*, 63(4), 297-317.

Reitz E.J. & J.A. Dukes 1995. Use of Vertebrate Resources at Trants, a Saladoid site on Montserrat. *Proceedings of the Fifteenth International Congress for Caribbean Archaeology*, 201-208. San Juan, Puerto Rico.

Rice, P.M. 1987. *Pottery Analysis, a sourcebook*. University of Chicago Press, Chicago and London.

Robinson, L.S. 1978. Modified Oliva shells from the Virgin Islands, a morphological study. *Proceedings of the Seventh International Congress for the Study of the pre-Columbian Cultures of the Lesser Antilles*, 169-187. Centre de Recherche Caraïbes, Université de Montréal, Montréal.

Robinson, L.S. 1980. The crab motif in aboriginal West Indian shellwork, *Proceedings of the Eigth International Congress for the Study of the Pre-Columbian Cultures of the Lesser Antilles,* 187-194. Arizona State University, Anthropological Papers no. 22. Tempe, Arizona.

Robinson, L., E. Lundberg & J. B. Walker 1983. *Archaeological Data Recovery at El Bronce, Puerto Rico, Final Report, Phase 1.* Archaeological Services, Inc., Puerto Rico.

Robinson, L., E. Lundberg & J. B. Walker 1985. *Archaeological Data Recovery at El Bronce, Puerto Rico, Final Report, Phase 2.* Archaeological Services, Inc., Puerto Rico.

Robinson L. & G.S. Vescelius 1979. *Exotic Items in Archaeological Collections from St. Croix: Prehistoric Imports and Their Implications*. Paper presented at the Eigth International Congress for the Study of the Pre- Columbian Cultures of the Lesser Antilles, St. Kitts and Nevis.

Rodríguez López, M. 1985. *Cultural Resources Survey at Camp Santiago, Salinas, Puerto Rico.* Publicación de la Universidad del Turabo, Puerto Rico.

Rodríguez López, M. 1989. The zoned incised crosshatch (ZIC) ware of early Precolumbian ceramic age sites in Puerto Rico and Vieques. In: P.E. Siegel (ed.), *Early Ceramic Population and Lifeways and Adaptive Strategies in the Caribbean,* 249-266. BAR International Series 506, Oxford.

Rodríguez López, M. 1991a. Arqueología de Punta Candelero, Puerto Rico. *Proceedings of Thirteenth International Congress for Caribbean Archaeology*, 605-627. Reports of the Archaeological-Anthropological Institute of the Netherlands Antilles, No. 9. Willemstad, Curaçao.

Rodríguez López, M. 1991b. Early trade Networks in the Caribbean. *Proceedings of the Fourteenth Congress for Caribbean Archaeology*, 306-314. Barbados.

Rodríguez López, M. & V. Rivera 1991. Puerto Rico and the Caribbean Pre-Saladoid "Crosshatch Connection." *Proceedings of the Twelfth Congress of the International Association for Caribbean Archaeology,* Cayenne, French Guyana.

Roe, P. 1989. A Grammatical analysis of Cedrosan Saladoid Vessel form categories and surface decoration: aesthetic and technical styles in early Antillean ceramics. In: P.E. Siegel (ed.), *Early Ceramic Population and Lifeways and Adaptive Strategies in the Caribbean*, 267-282. BAR International Series 506, Oxford.

Roe, P.G., A. Gus Pantel & M.B. Hamilton 1985. *Monserrate Restudied: A Preliminary Report on the Excavation and Mapping, Lithic Artifacts, and Human Osteological Collections From the 1978 CEAPRC Field Season*. Paper presented at the XIth International Congress of Caribbean Archaeology, San Juan, Puerto Rico.

Roe, G.R., A.G. Pantel & M.B. Hamilton 1990. Monserrate restudied: the 1978 Centro field season at Luquillo Beach: Excavation overview, lithics and physical anthropological remains. *Proceedings of the Eleventh Congress for Caribbean Archaeology*, 338-365. San Juan, Puerto Rico.

Roosevelt, A. C. 1980. *Parmana: Prehistoric Maize and Manioc Subsistence along the Amazon and Orinoco*. Academic Press, New York.

Rösing, F.W. 1977. Methoden und Aussagemöglichkeiten der antropologischen Leichenbrandbearbeitung. *Archäeologie und Naturwissenshaft*, 1, 53-80.

Rostain, S. 1989. Approche pour une compréhension de l'émmanchement des haches d'Amazonie. *Proceedings of the Thirteenth International Congress for Caribbean Archaeology*, 1-11. Reports of the Archaeological Anthropological Institute of the Netherlands Antilles, No. 9. Willemstad, Curaçao.

Rostain, S. 1994. *L'occupation Amérindienne ancienne du littoral de Guyane*. Unpublished Ph.D. dissertation, Université de Paris I, Paris.

Roth, W.R. 1924. *An introductory study of the arts, crafts and customs of the Guiana Indians*. 38th Annual Report of the Bureau of American Ethnology. Smithsonian Institution, Washington, D.C.

Rouse, I. 1964. Prehistory of the West Indies. *Science* 144 (3618), 499-513.

Rouse, I. 1974. The Indian Creek excavations. *Proceedings of the Fifth International Congress for the Study of Pre-Columbian Cultures of the Lesser Antilles,* 166-176. Florida State Museum, Gainesville.

Rouse, I. 1976. The Saladoid sequence on Antigua and its aftermath. *Proceedings of the Sixth International Congress for the Study of Pre-Columbian Cultures of the Lesser Antilles*, 35-41, Florida State Museum, Gainesville.

Rouse, I. 1977. Pattern and process in West Indian archaeology. *World Archaeology,* vol. 9 (1), 1-11.

Rouse, I. 1983. Diffusion and Interaction in the Orinoco Valley and on the Coast. *Proceedings of the Ninth International Congress for the Study of Pre-Columbian Cultures of the Lesser Antilles*, 1-11. Centre de Recherches Caraïbes, University of Montreal, Montréal.

Rouse, I. 1985. Arawakan Phylogeny, Caribbean Chronology, and Their Implications for the Study of Population Movement. *Antropológica* (63-64), 9-22.

Rouse, I. 1986. *Migrations in Prehistory. Inferring Population Movement from Cultural Remains.* Yale University Press, New Haven.

Rouse, I. 1989. Peoples and Cultures of the Saladoid Frontier in the Greater Antilles. In: P.E. Siegel (ed.), *Early Ceramic Population and Lifeways and Adaptive Strategies in the Caribbean*, 383-403. BAR International Series 506, Oxford.

Rouse, I. 1990. Social, Linguistic, and Stylistic Plurality in the West Indies. *Proceedings of the Eleventh Congress of the International Association for Caribbean Archaeology,* 56-63. San Juan, Puerto Rico.

Rouse, I. 1992. *The Tainos. Rise and Decline of the People who Greeted Columbus.* Yale University Press, New Haven.

Rouse, I. 1995. Letter to the participants in the workshop held at Yale [University] during July, 1994 with copies to other interested persons. Unpublished document.

Rouse, I. & R.E. Alegría 1990. *Excavations at María de la Cruz Cave and Hacienda Grande Village site, Loiza, Puerto Rico.* Yale University Publications in Anthropology, No. 80, New Haven.

Rouse, I. & L. Allaire. 1978. Caribbean. In: R. E. Taylor & C. W. Meighan (eds), *Chronologies in New World Archaeology*, Academic Press, New York.

Rouse, I., L. Allaire & A. Boomert 1985. *Eastern Venezuela, the Guianas, and the West Indies.* MS prepared for an unpublished volume, "Chronologies in South American Archaeology", comp. Clement W. Meighan. Department of Anthropology, Yale University, New Haven.

Rye, O.S. 1981. *Pottery Technology: Principles and Reconstruction.* Manuals on Archaeology 4, Taraxacum, Washington.

Sanoja Obediente, M. & I. Vargas 1974. *Antiguas formaciones y modos de producción venezolanos.* Monte Avila editores. Caracas, Venezuela.

Schiffer, M.B. 1972. Archaeological Context and Systemic Context. *American Antiquity,* 37 (2), 156-165.

Schiffer, M.B. 1976. *Behavioural Archaeology.* Academic Press, New York.

Schiffer, M.B. 1984. *Behavioral Archaeology.* Academic Press, San Francisco.

Schiffer, M.B. 1987. *Formational processes of the archaeological record.* University of New Mexico Press, Albuquerque.

Schinkel, K. 1992. The Golden Rock features. In: A.H. Versteeg & K. Schinkel (eds), *The Archaeology of St. Eustatius, The Golden Rock Site.* Publication of the St. Eustatius Historical Foundation, no 2. Publication of the Foundation for Scientific Research in the Caribbean Region, no 131, Amsterdam.

Schlanger, N. 1992. *Techno- en typologische analyse van Midden-Paleolithische vuursteen complexen.* Typescript, Leiden University, Leiden.

Seiler-Baldinger, A. 1987. *Indianer im Tiefland Südamerikas.* Museum für Völkerkunde, Basel.

Shepard, A.O. 1963. *Ceramics for the Archaeologist.* Fourth printing, Carnegie Institution of Washington, Washington D.C.

Shimada, I. 1994. *Pampa Grande and the Mochica Culture.* University of Texas Press, Austin, Texas.

Siegel, P.E. 1989. Site structure, demography and social complexity in the early ceramic age of the Caribbean. In: P.E. Siegel (ed.), *Early ceramic lifeways and adaptive strategies in the Caribbean*, 193-247. BAR International Series 506, Oxford.

Siegel, P.E. 1991. Migration Research in Saladoid Archaeology: A Review. *The Florida Anthropologist*, 44 (1), 79-91.

Siegel, P.E. 1992. *Ideology, power and social complexity in prehistoric Puerto Rico,* 2 vols. Unpublished Ph.D. dissertation, State University of New York, Binghamton. University Microfilms, Ann Arbor, Michigan.

Smith, M.G. 1965. *The Plural Society in the British West Indies.* University of California Press, Berkeley, California.

Solomiac, H. 1974. Livret-Guide d'Excursions dans les Antilles Françaises. *VIIème conférence géologique des Caraïbes*, 98-108, Orléans.

Spaulding, A.C. 1960. The Dimensions of Archaeology. In: G.E. Dole & R. L. Carneiro (eds), *Essays in the Science of Culture in Honor of Leslie A. White*, 437-456. Thomas Y. Crowell Company, New York.

Steadman, D.W., D.R. Watters, E.J. Reitz & G.K. Pregill 1984. Vertebrates from archaeological sites on Montserrat, West Indies. *Annals of Carnegie Museum* 53, 1-29.

Steenvoorden, R.I. 1987. *Het aardewerk van Golden Rock, St. Eustatius, Ned. Antillen.* Unpublished Master's thesis, Leiden University, Leiden.

Steininger, F.F. 1986. First Results of Researches on Nutrition Strategies at the Arawak Settlement at Pointe de Caille, NNW Vieux Fort, St. Lucia, West Indies. Grabungen und Forschungen auf St. Lucia, 1984. *Mitteilungen der Prähistorischen Kommission der Österreichischen Akademie der Wissenschaften*, Band 23, 37-50 +

69-75. Verlag der Österreichischen Akademie der Wissenschaften, Wien.

Stoffers, A.L. 1956. *Studies on the Flora of Curaçao and other Caribbean Islands, Volume 1, the Vegetation of the Netherlands Antilles.* Uitgaven "Natuurwetenschappelijke Studiekring voor Suriname en de Nederlandse Antillen", Utrecht, Number 15, Martinus Nijhoff, The Hague.

Stokes, A.V. 1993. Appendix 1: Analysis of the Vertebrate Fauna from the Pearls Site (GREN-A-1): Prehistoric Subsistence on the Coast of Grenada (A.D. 200). In: W.F. Keegan (comp.) *Archaeology at Pearls, Grenada: The 1990 Field Season*, Miscellaneous Project Report Number 47, Department of Anthropology, Florida Museum of Natural History, University of Florida, Gainesville.

Stuiver M. & T.F. Braziunas 1993. Modelling atmospheric ^{14}C influences and ^{14}C ages of marine samples to 10,000 BC. *Radiocarbon*, vol. 35 (1), 137-189.

Stuiver M. & P.J. Reimer 1993. Extended ^{14}C Data Base and Revised CAL 3.0. ^{14}C Age Calibration program. *Radiocarbon*, vol. 35 (1), 215-230.

Sued Badillo, J. 1995. The Island Caribs: New Approaches to the Question of Ethnicity in the Early Colonial Caribbean. In: N. Whitehead (ed.), *Wolves from the Sea*, 62-89. KITLV Press, Leiden.

Sullivan, S. 1981. *Prehistoric Patterns of Exploitation and Colonization in the Turks and Caicos Islands.* Unpublished Ph.D. thesis. Department of Anthropology, University of Illinois, Urbana, Illinois. University Microfilms International, Ann Arbor.

Sullivan, A.P. & K.C. Rozen 1985. Debitage analysis and archaeological interpretation. *American Antiquity* 50, 755-779.

Sutty, L.A. 1978. A study of shells and shell objects from six precolumbian sites in the Grenadines of St. Vincent and Grenada. *Proceedings of the Seventh International Congress for the Study of the pre-Columbian Cultures of the Lesser Antilles*, 195-209. Centre de Recherche Caraïbes, Université de Montréal.

Sypkens Smit M.P. & A.H. Versteeg 1988. An archaeological reconnaissance of St. Martin. *Studies in honour of Dr. Pieter Wagenaar Hummelinck.* Foundation for Scientific Resarch in Surinam and the Netherlands Antilles, no. 123. Amsterdam.

Van der Klift, H.M. 1985. Animal and Plant Remains from the Golden Rock Site on St. Eustatius. In Versteeg, A.H., H.M. van der Klift, G.J.R. Maat, H.J.M. Meuffels, R.R. van Zweden & W. Roeleveld, *Archaeological Investigations on St. Eustatius (Neth. Antilles)*, 12-23. Interim Report, Leiden University, Leiden.

Van der Klift, H.M. 1992. Faunal remains of the Golden Rock site. In: A.H. Versteeg & K. Schinkel (eds), *The Archaeology of St. Eustatius: the Golden Rock Site*, 74-83. Publication of the St. Eustatius Historical Foundation, no. 2, Publication of the Foundation for Scientific Research in the Caribbean Region, No. 131.

Van der Steen, E.J. 1992. Shell Artefacts of Golden Rock. In: A.H. Versteeg & K. Schinkel (eds), *The Archaeology of St. Eustatius, The Golden Rock Site.* Publication of the St. Eustatius Historical Foundation, no 2. Publication of the Foundation for Scientific Research in the Caribbean Region, no 131, Amsterdam.

Van der Valk, L. 1987. *Identification of two rock samples from an Indian site on Great Key, Sint Maarten, Netherlands Antilles.* Report. Amsterdam.

Vargas Arenas, I. 1990. *Arqueología, Ciencia y Sociedad.* Editorial Abre Brecha, Caracas, Venezuela.

Veloz Maggiolo, M. 1972. *Arqueología prehistórica de Santo Domingo.* MacGraw-Hill Far Eastern Publishers, Ltd. Singapore.

Veloz Maggiolo, M. 1976. *Medioambiente y adaptacíon humana en la prehistoría de Santo Domingo*, Vol. 1. Editorial de la Universidad Autónoma de Santo Domingo, Santo Domingo.

Veloz Maggiolo, M. 1980. *Las sociedades arcaicas de Santo Domingo.* Museo del Hombre Dominicano- Fundación García Arévalo, Inc., Santo Domingo.

Veloz Maggiolo, M. 1991. *Panorama histórico del Caribe precolombino.* Edícion Banco Central de la República Dominicana, Santo Domingo.

Veloz Maggiolo M. & E. Ortega 1973. *El precerámico de Santo Domingo. Nuevos lugares y su posible relacíon con otros puntos del area Antilliana.* Museo del Hombre Dominicano, papeles Ocasionales no.1.

Veloz Maggiolo, M., E. Ortega & A. Caba 1981. *Los modos de vida meillacoides y sus posibles orígenes.* Museo del Hombre Dominicano. Santo Domingo.

Veloz Maggiolo, M., I. Vargas, M. Sanoja & F. Luna Calderón 1976. *Arqueología de Yuma (Dominican Republic).* Taller, Santo Domingo.

Verpoorte, A. 1993. *Stenen op een eiland: veldverkenning van de vuursteenvoorkomens en werkplaatsen van Long Island, Antigua, West Indies.* Unpublished Master's thesis, Leiden University, Leiden.

Versteeg, A.H. & K. Schinkel (eds)1992. *The Archaeology of St. Eustatius: The Golden Rock Site.* Publication of the St. Eustatius Historical Foundation 2/Publication of the Foundation for Scientific Research in the Caribbean Region, no. 131, Amsterdam.

Vescelius, G. & L. Robinson 1979. *Exotic items in Archaeological Collections from St. Croix: Prehistoric Imports and their Implications.* Paper presented to the Eighth International Congress for the Study of Pre-Columbian Cultures of the Lesser Antilles, St. Kitts and Nevis.

Vidal, N. 1992. *Les fouilles archéologiques du site précolombien de la plage de Dizac, le Diamant.* Unpublished Master's thesis. Université de Paris, Paris.

Wagner, E. & C. Schubert 1972. Pre-Hispanic Workshops of Serpentine Artifacts, Venezuelan Andes and Possible Raw Material Source. *Science* 175:888-890.

Walker, J. 1980. Analysis and replication of lithic artifacts from the Sugar Factory Pier site, St. Kitts. *Proceedings of the Eighth International Congress for the Study of Pre-Columbian Cultures of the Lesser Antilles*, 69-79. Arizona State University Anthropological Research Papers No. 22, Tempe, Arizona.

Walker, J. 1981. Use-wear analysis of Caribbean flaked stone tools. *Proceedings of the Ninth International Congress for the Study of Pre-Columbian Cultures of the Lesser Antilles*, 239-248. Centre de Recherches Caraïbes, Université de Montréal, Montréal.

Walker, J. 1985. A preliminary report on the lithic and osteological remains from the 1980, 1981, 1982 field seasons at Hacienda Grande. *Proceedings of the Tenth International Congress for the Study of Pre-Columbian Cultures of the Lesser Antilles*, 181-224. Centre de Recherche Caraïbes, Université de Montréal, Montréal.

Wallace, D. 1989. Functional factors of mica and ceramic burnishing. In: G. Bronitsky (ed.), *Pottery Technology Ideas and Approaches*, 33-39. Westview Press, Boulder/San Francisco/London.

Warmke, G.L. & Abbot, R.T. 1961. *Caribbean seashells*. Livingstone Publ. Company., Narbeth, Pennsylvania.

Wartluft, J.L. & S. White 1984. *Comparing Simple Charcoal Production Technologies for the Caribbean: Montserrat Fuelwood/Charcoal/Cookstove Project*. Volunteers in Technical Assistance, Arlington, Virginia.

Waselkov, G.A. 1982. *Shellfish Gathering and Shell Midden Archaeology*. Unpublished Ph.D. dissertation, The University of North Carolina at Chapel Hill. University Microfilms international, Ann Arbor, Michigan.

Watson, P.J. 1976. In pursuit of prehistoric subsistence: a comparative account of some contemporary flotation techniques. *Midcontinental Journal of Archaeology* 1,77-100.

Watters, D.R. 1980. *Transect surveying and Prehistoric site locations on Barbuda and Montserrat, Leeward Islands, West Indies*. Unpublished Ph.D. dissertation, University of Pittsburgh.

Watters, D.R. 1994. Archaeology of Trants, Monserrat. *Annals of Carnegie Museum* 63 (3), 215-237.

Watters, D.R. 1997a. Stone Beads in Prehistoric Caribbean. *Bead Study Trust Newsletter*, 29, 7-8.

Watters D.R. 1997b. Maritime Trade in Prehistoric Eastern Caribbean. In: S. Wilson (ed.), *Indigenous People of the Caribbean*, 88-89 University Press of Florida, Gainesville.

Watters, D.R., E.J. Reitz, D. W. Steadman and G. K. Pregill 1984. Vertebrates from Archaeological sites on Barbuda, West Indies. *Annals of Carnegie Museum* 53, 383-412.

Watters, D.R. & I.B. Rouse 1989. Environmental diversity and maritime adaptations in the Caribbean area. In: P.E. Siegel (ed.), *Early Ceramic Lifeways and Adaptive Strategies in the Caribbean*, 129-141. BAR International Series 506, Oxford.

Watters, D.R. & R. Scaglion 1994. Beads and Pendants from Trants, Montserrat: Implications for the prehistoric lapidary industry of the Caribbean. *Annals of Carnegie Museum*, Vol. 63, No. 3, 215-237.

Westermann, J.H. 1953. *Nature Preservation in the Caribbean. A Review of Literature on the Destruction and Preservation of the Flora and Fauna in the Caribbean Area*. Foundation for Scientific Research in Surinam and the Netherlands Antilles, 9. Utrecht.

Watermann, J.H. 1957. *De geologische geschiedenis der drie Bovenwindse eilanden St.Martin, Saba en St.Eustatius*. Uitgaven van de "Natuurwetenschappelijke Werkgroep Nederlandse Antillen" no.7, Curaçao.

Weyl, R. 1966. *Geologie der Antillen*. Beitrage zur Regionalen Geologie der Erde, Band 4. Gebrüder Borntraeger, Berlin-Nikolassee.

Wheeler, E.A., R.G. Pearson, C.A. LaPasha, T. Zack & W. Hatley 1986. *Computer-Aided Wood Identification*. The North Carolina Agricultural Research Service, Bulletin 474. North Carolina State University, Raleigh.

Wilson, S.N. 1989. The prehistoric settlement pattern of Nevis, West Indies. *Journal of Field Archaeology* 16(4), 427-440.

Wilson, S.N. 1993. The archaeological Settlement Survey of Nevis: 1984-1988. *Proceedings of the Thirteenth International Congress for Caribbean Archaeology*, 269-279. Reports of the Archaeological-Anthropological Institute of the Netherlands Antilles, No. 9. Willemstad, Curaçao.

Wing, E.S. 1969. Vertebrate Remains excavated from San Salvador Island, Bahamas. *Caribbean Journal of Science* 9 (102), 25-29.

Wing, E.S. 1989. Human exploitation of animal resources in the Caribbean. In: C.A. Woods (ed.), *Biogeography of the West Indies: Past, Present and Future*, 137-152 Sandhill Crane Press, Gainesville, Florida.

Wing, E.S. 1990. Animal Remains from the Hacienda Grande Site, Puerto Rico. Appendix to: Rouse, I. & R. Alegría, *Excavations at María de la Cruz cave and Hacienda Grande, Village site Loiza, Puerto Rico*. Yale University Publications in Anthroplogy, no. 80. New Haven.

Wing E.S. 1991a. Animal Exploitation in Prehistoric Barbados. *Proceedings of the Fourteenth Congress of the International Association for Caribbean Archaeology*, 360-367. Barbados.

Wing E.S. 1991b. Economy and Subsistence I - Faunal remains. In: P.L. Drewett (ed.), *Prehistoric Barbados*, 134-152. Archetype Publications, London.

Wing, E.S. 1992. *Vertebrate Remains Excavated from the Sites of Spring Bay and Kelbey's Ridge, Saba, Netherlands Antilles*. Ms. on file Environmental Archaeology, Florida Museum of Natural History, Gainesville.

Wing, E.S. 1993. The Realm between wild and domestic. In: A.S. Clason, E. Payne & H.P. Uerpmann (eds), *Skeletons in Her Cupboard: Festschrift for Juliet Clutton-Brock*, 243-250. Oxbow Monograph, 34, Oxford.

Wing, E.S. 1995a. Rice Rats and Saladoid People as Seen at Hope Estate. *Proceedings of the Fifteenth International Congress for the Study of Pre-Columbian Cultures of the Lesser Antilles*, 219-232. San Juan, Puerto Rico.

Wing E.S. 1995b. Land Crab Remains in Caribbean Sites. *Proceedings of the Sixteenth International Congress for Caribbean Archaeology*, Part 1, 105-112. Basse Terre, Guadeloupe.

Wing, E.S. 1996. *Vertebrate Remains Excavated from the Sites of Spring Bay and Kelbey's Ridge, Saba, Netherlands Antilles*. Appendix 2 in M.L.P. Hoogland 1996. *In search of the Native Population of pre-Columbian Saba. Part Two. Settlements in their natural and social environment.* Unpublished Ph.D. dissertation. Leiden University, Leiden.

Wing, E.S. & A.B. Brown 1979. *Paleonutrition: Method and Theory in Prehistoric Foodways.* Academic Press, New York.

Wing, E.S., Ch. A. Hoffman & C.E. Ray 1968. Vertebrate Remains from Indian Sites on Antigua, West Indies. *Caribbean Journal of Science* 8 (3 and 4), 123-139.

Wing, E.S. & E.J. Reitz 1982. Prehistoric Fishing Economies of the Caribbean. *Journal of New World Archaeology*, 5 (2), 13-32.

Wing, E.S. & S. Scudder 1980 Use of animals by the prehistoric inhabitants of St. Kitts, West Indies. *Proceedings of the Eighth International Congress for the Study of the Pre-Columbian Cultures of the Lesser Antilles*, 237-245. Arizona State University Anthropological Research Papers No. 22.

Whitehead, N. (ed.) 1995. *Wolves from the Sea.* KITLV Press, Leiden, The Netherlands.

Workshop of European Anthropologists 1980. Recommendations for age and sex determinations of skeletons. *Journal of Human Evolution* 9, 517-549.

Colophon:

Graphic design:	H.A. de Lorm
Copy editing:	C.L. Hofman and M.L.P. Hoogland
Photography:	J. Pauptit
Drawings:	A.E.A. van Driel, I. Perrera, M.L.P. Hoogland, M. Van den Bel, M. de Waal, S. Knippenberg, Renzo Duin, Rineke van Muysenberg and Dennis Nieweg
Picture editing:	P. Deunhouwer, P. De Jong, J. Oliver and Michiel Kappers
Printing:	Orientaliste, Leuven, Belgium